INTERLOCKING CONSTITUTIONS

The existence of interactions between different but overlapping legal systems has always presented challenges to black letter law. This is particularly true of the relationship between international law and domestic law and the relationship between federal law and the laws of individual federation members. Moreover some organizations have created their own supranational constitutional systems: the United Nations Charter is the best known, and is often referred to as the 'World Constitution', but the European Court of Justice in Luxembourg views the European Treaties as a 'Constitutional Charter' for Europe, while the European Court of Human Rights has defined the European Convention on Human Rights as a constitutional instrument of 'European public order'.

It is in the dynamic relationship between domestic constitutional laws, EU law, the ECHR and the UN Charter that the most persistent difficulties arise. In this context 'interordinal instability' not only provokes strong academic interest, but also affects what has been called 'governance' or 'global government' and undermines both legal certainty and individual fundamental rights. Different solutions – constitutionalist and pluralist – have been explored, but none of them has received global acceptance. In this book Luis I Gordillo analyses the interordinal instabilities which arise at the European level, focusing on three main strands of case law and their implications: *Solange*, *Bosphorus* and *Kadi*. To solve the difficulties caused by this instability Gordillo proposes a form of soft constitutionalism, which he calls 'interordinal constitutionalism', as a means to bring order and stability to global legal governance.

The original Spanish thesis on which this book is based was awarded the Nicolás Pérez Serrano Prize by the Centro de Estudios Políticos y Constitucionales, for the best dissertation in constitutional law 2009–2010

Volume 8 in the series Hart Monographs in Transnational and International Law

Hart Monographs in Transnational and International Law

Series Editor: Craig Scott, Professor of Law, Osgoode Hall Law School of York University, Toronto

The objective of this series is to publish high-quality scholarship in public international law and private international law, as well as work that adopts 'transnational law' as its thematic, theoretical or doctrinal focus. The series strives to be a leading venue for work of the following sort:

* critical reappraisals of foundational concepts and core doctrinal principles of both public and private international law, and their operation in practice, including insights drawn from general legal theory;
* analysis and development of conceptions of 'transnational law', including in relation to the role of unofficial law and informal processes in transnational regulation and in relation to theories and studies of 'governance' in transnational spheres; and
* empirical studies of the emergence, evolution and transformation of international and/or transnational legal orders, including accounts and explanations of how law is constructed within different communities of interpretation and practice.

The series will also be home to monographs that explore the interactions between the ever-integrating fields of public and private international law. Of special interest are explorations of the extent to which these interactions are structured by higher-order principles and policies, on the one hand, and by politics and the exercise of various forms of power, on the other hand.

The series is open to work not only by law scholars but also by scholars from cognate disciplines.

Recent titles in this series

Volume 4 Between Governing and Governance: On the Emergence, Function and Form of Europe's Post-National Constellation
Poul Kjaer

Volume 5 Rough Consensus and Running Code: A Theory of Transnational Private Law
Gralf-Peter Calliess and Peer Zumbansen

Volume 6 The Payment Order of Antiquity and the Middle Ages: A Legal History
Benjamin Geva

Volume 7 The Concept of Unity in Public International Law
Mario Prost

Interlocking Constitutions

Towards an Interordinal Theory of National, European and UN Law

Luis I Gordillo

•HART•
PUBLISHING

OXFORD AND PORTLAND OREGON
2012

Published in the United Kingdom by Hart Publishing Ltd
16C Worcester Place, Oxford, OX1 2JW
Telephone: +44 (0)1865 517530
Fax: +44 (0)1865 510710
E-mail: mail@hartpub.co.uk
Website: http://www.hartpub.co.uk

Published in North America (US and Canada) by
Hart Publishing
c/o International Specialized Book Services
920 NE 58th Avenue, Suite 300
Portland, OR 97213-3786
USA
Tel: +1 503 287 3093 or toll-free: (1) 800 944 6190
Fax: +1 503 280 8832
E-mail: orders@isbs.com
Website: http://www.isbs.com

British Library Cataloguing in Publication Data
Data Available

ISBN: 978-1-84946-221-1

Typeset by Hope Services, Abingdon
Printed and bound in Great Britain by
TJ International Ltd, Padstow, Cornwall

To my parents, Luis and Virtudes

Foreword

The best indicator of the quality of a work is the difficulty in writing its foreword. I had already read the book which I am now attempting to prologue in its original version, which Luis I Gordillo presented as a doctoral thesis at the University of Deusto, and in its preparatory version, as I was the director of the dissertation. But now, when I read the final version of the book, I find it difficult to write a foreword for it, whatever the content of a foreword should be. If the purpose of a foreword is to serve as an introduction for a book, it is important to mention that the introduction to this book that is to be found in the 'Introduction' section is clear enough; its object and methodology are perfectly defined in those pages and adding anything else would just cause confusion. However, if the content of the foreword is understandable in the sense of its gloss, there is not much left to do. The work approaches its objective with such rigour and so exhaustively that it would be superfluous or reiterative to make any comment. But, even at risk of falling into the aforementioned traps, I would like to emphasize some of the merits of this work.

First of all, it is important to highlight the relevance of the subject at the present time. As mentioned in the Introduction, the book, as with any other scientific work, starts with a pretty obvious assertion: the complexity of the interordinal relations that increasing and ongoing internationalization cause, in the broad sense, to political, social, cultural and economic relations, and as a consequence, to legal relations. Nowadays, the law is often a kind of 'magma' where any legal actor has to distinguish its elements in order to organize the relationship between them. Luis I Gordillo's work states it and he has delved into the hard field of rules and methods that allows legal actors to organize this 'relationship between elements'. He has made this analysis of the reality in which the phenomenon is produced with technical accuracy, criticizing the failures of the precarious system in which the actual legal systems fall and making proposals for rationalization. In order to accomplish this task, the author avoids artificially easy and false stereotypes and besides performing a critical analysis, he carries out a deeper analysis which confronts the problems that national legal systems, individually considered, create.

One of the keys to the actual process, born in fact some years ago, which drives the jurist to give answers to the problems related to globalization (in very different fields) and integration, is based in the basic platform from which we are to focus. It is still the platform of state law because the state is still the basic political structure – and hence the legal one – that takes part within the continental and worldwide net. Actually, if one can find legal problems raised in one national legal structure that could be similar to those brought up in another state, the answers possess peculiarities because state legal systems are non-unique. When we thought that the relationship between international law and municipal law was more or less pacific, new relationships with different parameters would appear . . . the increasing international cooperation both worldwide and, especially, within the process of the supranational integration which the former European Communities, now the European Union, brought to life, set out new problems which the states should resolve but at the same time are willing to keep themselves as a political sovereign structure. We are witnessing a tension between the Sovereign National State and the International and supranational organization in its legal dimension. It is enough to revisit the specialized bibliography of the last few decades to understand what the latter meant for the recent past and present meaning of the national legal systems. To cite some examples: the attempt to address European integration through constitutional standards and procedures, the decisions of the Constitutional Courts with regard to the challenges of this integration process, the need to adapt the mechanisms of the common law to continental structures (the Council of Europe and the European Union), or the simple position of the judicial bodies when they are required to apply the new international and EU law are a demonstration of a widespread legal phenomenon. But there is a new complication: How to organize the relations of legal orders when it is no longer a question of applicability of municipal, European or international law, but a question of how to interlock the different dimensions of those legal orders? Are we considering these problems from the state platform or are we capable of having another point of view?

I must stress that it is a new challenge that has been studied in European legal science in the last few decades, but Luis I Gordillo faced this subject with technical rigour and without evading any of the problems, including the more recent ones. Moreover, in dealing with this subject he also avoids the more common academic 'fault', that of using a strictly national perspective and a single-disciplinary perspective, by approaching the issue using a comparative and multidisciplinary methodology, which without doubt enriches the final outcome, because the problem is multi-disciplinary and not only national, both from an academic and a dogmatic point of view.

For me it has been a pleasure to supervise this work at the doctoral stage, a work from which I have learned a lot . . . and is there any better indicator of the quality of a work than to have learned from it? Maybe this statement could be taken as partial because I was the supervisor of the dissertation, but it has been recognized twice, first by the jury which evaluated the doctoral thesis, integrated by a multi-disciplinary panel of some of the most highly specialized experts in the field – Ignacio Mª Bebide-Ezpeleta (University of Deusto), Laurence Burgorgue-Larsen (University of Paris-Sorbonne), José Luis Cascajo-Castro (University of Salamanca), Javier Díez-Hochleitner (University Autónoma of Madrid), Luis López-Guerra (Carlos III University and European Court of Human Rights) – who gave the thesis the maximum grade of Cum Laude unanimously, and then by the jury which awarded him the Nicolás Pérez-Serrano Prize of the Center for Political and Constitutional Studies for the best doctoral thesis of the year 2009–2010, made up of Clara Mapelli-Marchena (Center for Political and Constitutional Studies), Javier Pérez-Royo (University of Seville), Rosa Ripollés-Serrano (Cortes Generales-National Parliament) and Juan Antonio Xiol-Ríos (Supreme Court).

Now, it is up to the specialized reader to judge the work, which certainly would enrich him or her not only with information, but by provoking doubts and showing new problems within a rich and changing subject, as the author emphasizes.

Pablo Pérez Tremps
Professor of Law, Carlos III University (Madrid)
Judge of the Spanish Constitutional Court

Contents

Abbreviations

ECJ	European Court of Justice
ECtHR	European Court of Human Rights
ECHR	European Convention of Human Rights
CFI	Court of First Instance (latter General Court)
TFEU	Treaty on the Functioning of the European Union
TEU	Treaty on the European Union
TEU-L	Treaty on the European Union (as amended by the Lisbon Treaty)
TEC	Treaty on the European Community
EC	European Community
EU	European Union
CFSP	Common Foreign and Security Policy
ICJ	International Court of Justice
WTO	World Trade Organization
ILC	International Law Commission
UN	United Nations
UNSC	United Nations Security Council
UNMIK	United Nations Interim Administration Mission in Kosovo
MOU	Memorandum of Understanding
GATT	The General Agreement on Tariffs and Trade
EAW	European Arrest Warrant
KFOR	Kosovo Force
TCN	Troop Contributing Nation
COMKFOR	Commander of KFOR

Table of Cases

ECtHR

ECJ

Court of First Instance /General Court

Permanent Court of International Justice

International Court of Justice (ICJ)

Spanish Constitutional Court

German Constitutional Court

Italian Constitutional Court

Polish Constitutional Court

French Constitutional Council

US Supreme Court

International Criminal Tribunal for the former Yugoslavia (ICTY)

UK Supreme Court (and the House of Lords)

Other Courts

Introduction

1. BACKGROUND

1. The existence of interactions between different legal orders, albeit overlapping, has always aroused the interest of the doctrine whether the relationship is between international law and the domestic law of the states or between federal law and the members of the federation.[1] According to Mirkine-Guetzévitch, historically, the existing doctrines on interordinal relations between international law and national law could be classified as 'parallelism' (recognition of the coexistence of two separate independent legal orders), 'internationalism' (recognition of the primacy of international law) or 'constitutional nationalism' (recognition of the primacy of national law).[2] However, the classification finally imposed on the doctrine is the one opposing *dualism* to *monism*. Thus, 'parallelism' would be equivalent to *dualism* while 'internationalism' and 'constitutional nationalism' would be equivalent to the *monistic* conception.[3] Despite the irreconcilable differences that these different conceptions had, the need to make the system viable and the very existence of the international society led from existing conflicts into pragmatic solutions.[4] Likewise, in the national field, discussions about the primacy of federal law in connection with the constitutions of the Federated States were intense, especially during the early years of American federalism.[5]

[1] See the classic work of A La Pérgola, *Costituzione e adattamento dell'ordinamento interno al diritto internazionale* (Giuffrè, Milano, 1961), and the Spanish version (translated by Professor Cascajo and Professor Rodriguez-Zapata) A La Pérgola, *Constitución del Estado y normas internacionales* (UNAM, México, 1985).

[2] See B Mirkine-Guetzévitch, 'Droit international et droit constitutionnel' (1931) 38(1931-IV) *Recueil des Cours de l'Académie de Droit International de La Haye* 307.

[3] An historical analysis maybe found at B Mirkine-Guetzévitch, *Derecho constitucional internacional* (L Legaz y Lecambra (tr)) (Revista de Derecho Privado, Madrid, 1936), especially at 29–61.

[4] See L Legaz y Lacambra, 'La primacía del Derecho de gentes sobre el Derecho interno como problema jurídico y político' (1977) 152 *Revista de Política Internacional* 7 and M Virally, 'Sur un pont aux ânes : les rapports entre droit international et droits internes' in H Roling *et al* (eds), *Mélanges offerts à Henri Rolin. Problèmes de droit des gens* (Pedone, Paris, 1964) 488 at 488–505.

[5] On the American case, see AC McLaughlin, *A Constitutional History of the United States* (Appleton-Century-Crofts, New York, 1935); JC Calhoun and RM Lence, *Union and Liberty: The Political Philosophy of John C Calhoun* (Liberty Fund, Indianapolis, 1992); JP Feldman, *La bataille américaine du fédéralisme: John C Calhoun et l'annulation (1828–1833)* (PUF, Paris, 2004); N Pérez Serrano, *La noble obra política de un gran Juez (Juan Marshall)* (Real Academia de Ciencias Morales y Políticas, Madrid, 1955). On the German case, see E Von Puttkamer, *Föderative Elemente im deutschen Staatsrecht seit 1648* (Musterschmidt, Göttingen, 1955); K Loewenstein, 'The Government and Politics of Germany' in JT Shotwell (ed), *Governments of Continental Europe* (Macmillan, New York, 1940) 279; L Michael, 'El Estado federal experimental' (2006) 6 *Revista de Derecho Constitucional Europeo* 11. The application of the American experience to the EU has

2. But the problems at the time of the discussions between supporters of monism or dualism regarding international law or primacy or faculty not to apply a federal law contrary to the Constitution of the federate State in the discussion of federalism would be simple compared with the current situation. Indeed, in those cases the difficulties focused on the problem of coordination between 'only' two legal systems (international and internal order) or perhaps three in the case of the United States (if we add the relationship between Federated States law and international law). Since the end of the Second World War there have been many new and parallel systems. The United Nations Organization (UN) and its specialized agencies or, more recently, the World Trade Organization (WTO) structure international society from a political and economic view. In Europe, the system of protection of human rights established by the Council of Europe and that developed within the European Union (EU) are the most troubled systems in this sense, despite being two different systems, as shown by recent decisions of its major interpreters. But these are only some examples and the list is by no means exhaustive. The picture is enhanced as international organizations emerge whose bodies approve actions that must be executed. The coordination between general international law and specific or regional 'suborders' is by no means a new phenomenon, but issues relating to the relationship between general law and special rules, or even among their own special rules, are gaining in importance. Thus, in relation to the WTO, many questions have been raised regarding the relationship between international trade law and international environmental law or international labour law.[6] Moreover, the emergence of specialized international criminal courts makes one wonder about its relations with the International Court of Justice.[7] In this context, once feasible solutions, developed in the field of interpretation of treaties or relations between successive treaties, are now, at least, incomplete.

3. Typically, the relationships between different orders have not been subject to regulation through specific provisions contained in the founding treaties of the legal systems in question. It is true that Article 103 of the UN Charter proclaims

been largely theorized: see JHH Weiler, *The Constitution of Europe. 'Do the New Clothes Have an Emperor?' and Other Essays on European Integration* (Cambridge University Press, Cambridge, 1999) 10–101; and JP Jacqué, 'Back to Philadelphia' (2002) 463 *Revue du Marché Commun et de l'Union Européenne* 661.

[6] The scholarship on this issue is huge. See N Perdikis and R Read (eds), *The WTO and the Regulation of International Trade. Recent Trade Disputes between the European Union and the United States* (Edward Elgar, Northampton, 2005); PT Stoll and F Schorkop, *WTO. World Economic Order, World Trade Law* (Max Planck Institute for International and Comparative Law, Martinus Nijhoff, The Hague, 2006) 243–80; MJ Trebilcock and R Howse, *The Regulation of International Trade* 2nd edn (Routledge, London, 1999) 395–440 (on international trade law and environmental law) and 441–563 (on international labour law); E McKendrick, H Kronke and R Goode, *Transnational Commercial Law: Text, Cases, and Materials* (Oxford University Press, Oxford, 2007) 89–106 and 129–30.

[7] See HAM Hebel, JG Lammers and J Schukking (eds), *Reflections on the International Criminal Court. Essays in Honour of Adriaan Bos* (Cambridge University Press, Cambridge, 1999), especially 'Part II. The International Criminal Court in Perspective'.

the primacy of the obligations derived from it over any other international obligation agreed by the Member States of this organization. Within the European Union, Article 307 TEC (Article 351 TFEU) voices a provisional coexistence between community obligations and those from previous agreements concluded by Member States and third parties. But the original EU Treaties did not contain any indication of their relations with the European Convention on Human Rights (ECHR). In that context, it was difficult to apply systematically the classical solutions on the relationship between successive treaties without questioning the uniformity of the rules applied to the internal market. Similarly, the fact that the founding states (except France) did not apply a Community rule deemed contrary to the ECHR, while France, which was not a member in the initial period, could execute it without a word of complaint, would have threatened the unity of the market that was being built. This kind of question is the inevitable consequence of the current 'fragmentation' of international law in orders and different and uncoordinated sub-systems.[8]

Thus, the potential for conflict multiplies exponentially as each of these systems is constantly evolving through the decisions of its major interpreters or supervisory bodies.[9] The consequence of this changing or evolving nature and of the different orders that must coexist is an increase in the chances of clash or conflict as if they were shifting tectonic plates drifting over the Earth's mantle. With this background, even if the different systems strive to make the measures adopted within it compatible with other orders or, at least, with their essential values, the risk of conflict does not disappear at all, since what today might be acceptable to another, tomorrow might not be the case, given the constant development they undergo.

4. This situation creates an apparent complexity in the management of interterritorial relationships, a complexity that also affects, in a significant manner, legal security. For individuals (either an individual or a legal person, from a foundation to the largest corporation) perhaps the most important thing is to live under a firm order making predictable the legal consequences of their actions. Because talking about 'fragmentation of international law', 'legal pluralism' or orders that organize their coexistence through 'counterlimits' or 'contrapunctual law' principles or, more generally, the so-called 'global governance' that some call 'governance' (to give some examples that we shall discuss in this book) is undoubtedly of great interest to the doctrine, and tries to understand some realities and influence them, there is no doubt that these ideas have inspired the solutions that supranational courts have given in the litigation that

[8] On the so-called 'fragmentation of international law', see I Buffard *et al*, *International law between universalism and fragmentation: Festschrift in honour of Gerhard Hafner* (Martinus Nijhoff, Leiden, 2008).

[9] The ECtHR has developed an evolutive interpretation of the ECHR, that is, as a 'living instrument to be interpreted in light of present-day conditions'. See *Loizidou v Turkey* App No 15318/89 (ECtHR, 23 March 1995, Series A vol 310) para 71.

has arisen. But it raises some doubts about the fact that these doctrinal models or theoretical constructions may provide confidence (in terms of legal certainty) to multinational companies and investment funds that operate in a context that could be described as transnational.[10]

Even if the various jurisdictions involved, either national or supranational, develop through constructive dialogue laudable and complex efforts to at least keep coexistence in a complex scenario in which the inherent contradictions among orders come to light, the presumed victim who claims a violation of their fundamental rights (recognized in some of the applying overlapping orders) will hardly be in a position to wait for such 'cross-jurisdictional' dialogue, or for the complex doctrinal constructions to tell him which court he should go to in order to file the complaint or what are the regulations applicable to his case. The uncertainty about the applicable law or litigation expenses will constitute, without any doubt, an obstacle that few would try to overcome in order to assert their rights. But we must clear up any lingering doubts as to the addressee of the potential criticisms. Criticism shall not be directed at the doctrine (which has made strenuous efforts to shed some light) or at the courts (operating at the limit of their powers and possibilities), but at their political power, unable to provide a solution to the deep-seated problem or, perhaps satisfied with the status quo or, even worse, simply passive.[11]

5. In fact, a construction based on the principle of hierarchy (which later became 'constitutionalist') would not make it possible, in the current situation, to report the real situation or to give answers to the specific problems that arise, unless an approach of rather simplistic and questionable value is carried out. Furthermore, if the construction based on Kelsen's pyramid has a clear utility in the context of internormative relations within any legal order, it is less effective at coordinating complex interordinal relationships where, in addition, each order would consider that its rules prevail over the other. On the other hand, a vision founded on the idea of a 'mesh' or 'net' (which in this book we shall call 'pluralism') would be conceptually more accurate, but it would not be at all clear that it would be capable of giving a practical answer to the existing difficulties.[12] Certainly in the (few) cases in which the founders of the orders had organized the interordinal relations of that legal system and other existing systems or in those situations where the rules of the relevant orders were fully

[10] See C Scott, '"Transnational law" as proto-concept: Three conceptions' (2009) 10(6–7) *German Law Journal* 859; and P Zumbansen, 'Transnational law' in J Smits (ed), *Encyclopedia of Comparative Law* (Edward Elgar, Northampton, 2006) 738.

[11] See JP Jacqué, 'Droit constitutionnel national, Droit communautaire, CEDH, Charte des Nations Unies. L'instabilité des rapports de système entre ordres juridiques' (2007) 60 *Revue Française de Droit Constitutionnel* 3 at 5.

[12] See F Ost and M Van de Kerchove, *De la pyramide au réseau? Pour une théorie dialectique du droit* (Publications des facultés universitaires Saint-Louis, Bruxelles, 2002) 545–79 and R Bustos Gisbert, *La Constitución Red: Un estudio sobre supraestatalidad y Constitución* (IVAP, Oñate, 2005).

compatible among them. However, the usual assumption happens to be one in which information is missing on the coordination of the interordinal relations and/or the rules arising from the legal systems in disputes are incompatible, in which case the judge (or the equivalent authority) would have to rely on the general rules on successive treaties or in the classic conceptions of relations between national and international law.

6. Certainly, the application of the rules governing the relationships between successive treaties is, at least, delicate in cases of orders deriving from international agreements whose members maintain close ties at various levels, as if they were Russian dolls.[13] Thus, all members of the EU are members of the Council of Europe, whose members are all part of the UN. The treaties supporting each legal order establish mandatory rules that cannot be exempted through an agreement between several of its members. Indeed, in most cases, these orders are comprehensive or complete systems, in the sense that the relationships established between the parties cannot be decomposed into a set of bilateral relations. Moreover, the provisions of the Vienna Convention on the Law of Treaties (in particular Article 30 on successive treaties and Article 41 dealing with the *inter partes* agreements within a multilateral treaty) do not always offer appropriate solutions, especially in cases where there are powers or transfer of powers from the Member States to an organization they belong to, as in the case of the EU. To make it more complex, the application of rules on the successive treaties is difficult when not all states have become party to the same treaties at the same time. Thus, Germany became a UN member in 1973 and France did not ratify the ECHR until 1974. By that time, the European Economic Community, whose founding treaty entered into force in 1958, already had a past and the ECJ had already proved its importance.

Besides, we should note the intention of some organizations to establish their own constitutional order. Thus, if the United Nations Charter is sometimes introduced as the 'Global Constitution', the Court of Justice in Luxembourg considers the Treaties as a 'Constitutional Charter' and, on the other hand, the European Court of Human Rights (ECtHR) has defined the ECHR as the constitutional instrument of a 'European public order'. In this context, recourse to the rules governing the relations between these orders that consider themselves as constitutional orders through general rules of treaty law seems, at best, insufficient. Moreover, regarding the application of the rules on relations between national and international law, the primacy and direct effect of EC/EU rules guaranteed by the Luxembourg judges would deviate from the traditional views on the subject.

7. In this kind of 'legal globalization' where different orders established by founding texts that share all or a group of members of other systems and each

[13] This ingenious comparison appears in JP Jacqué (2007) (n 11) at 6.

seems to move at its own pace, the interest in analysing the rules and internal procedures would give in to the challenge of understanding and, if possible, resolve any possible conflicts that may arise between them. Thus, the judges have emerged as the guarantors (sometimes vigilantes) that the obvious contradictions have not triggered irreconcilable conflicts. A series of unilateral declarations, doing their best to ensure that their content was nonetheless tolerated by the interpreters of the other legal systems, has set minimum standard rules that essentially all have accepted. But, given that each judge decides on the basis of the legal instrument used for their competence, in a kind of *Kompetenz-Kompetenz* judicial loop, the absence of final or all-encompassing solutions is not surprising. Thanks are due to these courts for being able to measure time and not having provoked irreconcilable differences that could have led to unsolvable crisis. The differences among major interpreters have become 'theories' and 'obiter dicta' and, through a rich dialogue fed by jurisprudential conceptions, they have been able to find concrete solutions to specific problems as they arose without compromising individual projects converging. The livelihood of the entire system owes much to the tolerance and the mutual opening of the national and supranational jurisdictions. In this sense, the most important difficulties when coordinating the interordinal relationships have mainly arisen around national constitutional law, the law of the EU (before the EC), the ECHR and the UN Charter.

2. METHODOLOGY AND STRUCTURE

8. The difficulties deriving from the instability of interordinal relationships, far from being a theoretical problem or one of little visible impact, and aside from meaning a breach in legal security (a prerequisite for the very existence of a rule of law), it has implications for the individual and, specifically, on his or her rights and obligations.[14]

Thus, we can cite the case of a small Turkish charter flight company, from which the Irish Government seized one of their two aircraft when it was refuelling at the airport in Dublin. Ireland justified the seizure under an EC regulation that implemented the sanctions imposed by the Security Council of the United Nations to the Republics of Serbia and Montenegro. The Turkish company countered the embargo, arguing essentially that the regulation was not applicable (because it had deposited the income earned from the rental of the aircraft, owned by the former Yugoslavian public airline, in blocked accounts) and, subsidiarily, that the seizure of the aircraft was against its fundamental right to

[14] See, for instance, the issues about the implementation in Spain of the European Arrest Warrant in Spanish Constitutional Court, Judgment No 199/2009. In a dissenting Opinion, Justice Pablo Pérez Tremps defended the need for a preliminary ruling procedure before the ECJ to solve the underlying legal issue. The Spanish Constitutional Court finally referred to the ECJ for such a procedure in June 2011 (Case No 6922-2008).

property, as recognized by the ECHR. The case was sent before the Irish courts and the ECJ, and ended up in the ECtHR. Deep down, in this case two things were illustrated. The first referred to the old controversy of whether the EC/EU was bound by the ECHR, even though it had never been ratified. Ultimately, there was the question whether the decisions of the ECtHR, in the end, could overrule or at least compel ECJ case law, at least in terms of fundamental rights. Also indirectly it raised the issue, although the ECtHR did not take it into consideration, about the control of the sanctions activity of the UN Security Council and its adjustment to fundamental rights, as they were protected, inter alia, by the ECHR.

Another interesting case is that of a Saudi resident and a Sweden-based foundation. Following their inclusion on the so-called blacklists of one of the sanctions committees of the United Nations, all their funds in the EU were frozen by virtue of a regulation that implemented those sanctions at the EC/EU level (*Kadi and Al Barakaat* case). Both parties concerned appealed to national authorities and, subsequently, to the EC/EU courts alleging, among other grounds, an attempt against their fundamental rights. Specifically, they alleged a violation of the right to be heard, the violation of the right to respect for property and the principle of proportionality and, thirdly, the violation of the right to effective judicial protection. EC/EU courts were faced with the uncomfortable situation of either complying with international law and applying the sanctions (denying an effective remedy to those concerned) or to protecting the victims and ignoring the UN sanctions (so the Union would incur an infringement that it has always criticized when incurred by other actors). The Court of First Instance chose, basically, the first option and the ECJ, in essence, the second one.

9. In these and other cases discussed in this book it is clear that there is a problem of constitutional significance. The instability of interordinal relations, apart from an indubitable academic interest and besides affecting 'governance' or 'global governance', ends up having an impact on legal security (in terms of predictability) and on the fundamental rights of individuals, and compromises the very existence of a rule of law. So, first, the messy interordinal overlap prevents individuals from having a clear idea regarding their particular 'charter of rights and obligations', that is, what fundamental rights are recognized and what obligations they have. Secondly, the very existence of different levels of protection of fundamental rights according to the applicable legal order does not seem a priori objectionable. Now the problem arises when the minimum rights considered by some orders as indispensable are not respected – this is where the application of an EC/EU regulation (being a direct development of a UN sanction) does not comply with one or more of the fundamental rights recognized as such in the national Constitution. This would be the case, for example, of the right to a fair trial (also called due process guarantees), a right that states traditionally recognize as absolute in their Constitutions, which is included in the ECHR and has also been established as fundamental in the EU legal order but, on the other hand, those sanctioned by the UN Security Council do not have.

10. The solutions to this situation range from the establishment of a comprehensive legal system integrated by the other subsystems, based on the principle of hierarchy and in the most strict version of which the UN Charter appears at the top of the Kelsen pyramid (called 'constitutionalist'), to concepts called 'pluralistic' which, in essence, try to extend the concept of freedom typical of the Anglo-Saxon systems to the interordinal relationships. That is, each legal order (in its interpreter, eg, the Constitutional Court) shall act and develop freely as long as it does not harm others. Following the 'pluralistic' theories, in order to avoid potential conflicts, legal orders should (on behalf of their freedom) assume the essential principles of the others so as to operate a kind of synchronization that avoids contradictions between them.

However, all these proposals have their problems and none of them has been accepted by the major interpreters of the legal orders at stake. The solution proposed here will bring some order to the European scope, which is the ideal legal laboratory for studying this issue since it is the focal point of the more developed supranational orders of constitutional nature, and will consist of the adoption of an interordinal constitutionalist model, based on the 'soft constitutionalist' approaches. But also, as we shall conclude, in order to make this model successful it will ultimately require the intervention of political power.

11. To sum up, the thesis supported here is that the solution to the interordinal instability and management of real conflicts that such instability (due to the messy overlapping of different legal systems) produces in the European scope is to embrace interordinal constitutionalism, that is, to adopt a soft 'constitutionalist' approach to managing the situation and face the challenges issued from the so-called fragmentation of the international law – that is, a model that assumes the existence of an international or global community of some kind, in which the principles underlying the different orders are universalized and, finally, in which there are common rules or principles to redirect conflicts that may occur, while the whole system slowly navigates to a kind of synchronization of the standards of protection of fundamental rights.

12. To verify this hypothesis, and given the breadth and complexity of the object of analysis, first, this book has been limited to the European context, an 'ideal laboratory', as stated above, in which to test a demonstration of the postulates hereby enunciated. That is, as seen in the examples described above (for example, the aircraft seized or the freezing of funds by UN mandate), this situation of instability and overlapping orders becomes particularly intense in Europe, where, besides the national orders, different legal systems of a constitutional nature such as EC/EU law, the ECHR or the UN Charter converge. Thus, this book has focused on this particularly dense point of convergence of legal systems, the European arena.

Secondly, to address the many complex issues that arise and justify the hypothesis put forward, the author has followed a method of work by segmenting or compartmentalizing the study of the interordinal relationships, following an order directly proportional to the level of attention that such problems have attracted in the doctrine and jurisprudence to date. Therefore, first the relationship between the Constitution and EC/EU law is discussed, then all the ins and outs of the EU law/ECHR binomial, and ending up with an analysis of the UN Charter, EU law and ECHR triad.

In Part IV the hypothesis supported is put to the test. That is, the soft constitutionalist model advocated is compared with other models and possibilities of coordinating interordinal relationships, analysing the impact that the adoption of a model and others has as well as their real viability, that is, to what extent the courts operating in the European context, especially the ECJ, are willing to embrace this interordinal constitutionalism.

Finally, the conclusions, far from representing a summary of what has already been stated or what the reader has been able to observe through the text, try to go further. That is, the conclusions resulting directly from the research upon which this book is based are set forth, but with an attempt to extend and generalize the results. Thus, the internalization of basic principles of coexistence together with an intervention of political power will make the model hereby described to be used in the European context ultimately successful and may, therefore, be exported to other areas.

13. From the formal viewpoint, this book is structured into four distinct parts.

In Part I, we recognize the principles on which the national constitutional jurisprudence and the ECJ have built the interordinal relations of the legal orders of which they are the ultimate guardians. Then, we consider the attempts to reconcile the positions adopted until reaching the last codification attempts of these coexistence principles that appear in the failed Constitutional Treaty and, more recently, in the successfully ratified Treaty of Lisbon.

Part II focuses on analysing the relationship between the EU legal order and the ECHR, particularly in light of the leading developments in case law and the dialogue established between the ECtHR and the ECJ. Given the specialization of the ECtHR, the topic of this dialogue has been fundamental rights, whose protection systems established at different overlapping levels (national, EU and Council of Europe) has been the leitmotif of the Praetorian evolution. Therefore, first, the role of fundamental rights in the European Union is analysed. Then, an approach to the relationships between the EU legal order and the ECHR is carried out from the point of view of EC/EU law, reviewing the substance of the doctrine that so far had ruled on the issue. Next, we study the relations between the two systems, in this case, from the standpoint of the European Convention, with particular reference to recent developments in case law. Finally, we review the current situation and possible developments of the issue in light of the responses and the silences of the courts in Luxembourg and Strasbourg.

In Part III we analyse the relationships and interactions established between the law of the United Nations Organization, particularly as regards the sanctions adopted by the Security Council, and EC/EU law. We begin with a chapter devoted to the Security Council, its forms of action and the difficulties of demanding accountability of international organizations. Then, we pay particular attention to the relationship between the Security Council resolutions and the ECHR, especially the possibility that the UN could be bound by the ECHR in the light of the recent case law of the ECtHR on the matter.

Finally, in Part IV we discuss the various possibilities for coordinating the relationships among the orders of a constitutional nature, especially from the standpoint of the European Union order, taking into account the consequences derived from the option for either approach.

The concluding section has been drafted in the form of statements or theses as clearly and concisely as possible to develop the scope of such claims without repeating or summarizing what was already said in the main section of the book.

14. As to the scientific method used by the author, this book follows a methodology of empirical, comparative, inductive-deductive and historical research. First, a method of empirical analysis has been followed in the sense that the source of information and answers to the problems set forth at the beginning of the investigation is experience. Thus, particularly, I have resorted to selected case law of the different national and supranational courts that have ruled on the subject of study and also the most representative doctrine that has ruled on the matter. Secondly, I have used a comparative approach by contrasting the answers and solutions that doctrine and jurisprudence have contributed to analogous or similar difficulties within the different legal orders the object of attention. Thirdly, the method is also, simultaneously, inductive and deductive. It is inductive as is necessary through the systematic classification of the conclusions reached as a result of the analysis of doctrine and jurisprudence to establish the principles governing interordinal relations. The deduction would not oppose the aforementioned, but the deductive process would be closely linked to the inductive one. Thus, induction aims to provide data or conclusions about some realities, but to relate those data, to build categories and establish comprehensive argument schemes as final conclusions, I resort to the deductive system. Besides, in a complementary manner, when it comes to showing the evolution of a certain doctrinal and jurisprudential construction, I have turned to the historical method of analysis.

15. Finally, we should make a brief but not irrelevant reflection of a rather subjective nature. The object of study, the interordinal relations among orders of constitutional nature or what could also be described as 'pseudo-constitutional' orders, is particularly complex, comprehensive and seems to be immersed in an unstable evolutionary process that has not yet come to an end (and perhaps never will). As the final draft progressed, new issues and possibilities for development appeared, under penalty of perpetuating this book, so they have been postponed for further investigation. What the author wants to make clear is that he is fully aware of the complexity of the topic chosen and the ambitious nature of the project. But it is not meant to be a perfect work (in the sense of finished or completed). Instead the author's intention is much more modest: to be the start of a much broader research, which the author hopes to pursue in the coming years.

I

National Constitutional Law and EC/EU Law

1. The question of the relationship between national law and EC (now EU) law is one of the classic themes of legal doctrine and has been extensively studied.[1] Through different ways, with different justifications according to the states, and with more or less legal certainty, the primacy of EC/EU law over preceding and subsequent national law has finally been imposed.[2] Moreover, the argument that leads the national judge to recognize the primacy of EC/EU law is nothing extraordinary, since its origin is found in national constitutional law itself, whether it is a traditional clause that establishes the supremacy of international treaties or a more specific clause regarding the membership of the state concerned to a supranational organization. In all cases, primacy finds its support and justification in the Constitution itself, even at the expense of a broad interpretation of it. By contrast, a conflict between EC/EU law and national constitutional law would be channelled differently given the differing views of the EU and the national judge.[3]

2. In this first part we will discuss the principles on which the national Constitutional Courts and the ECJ have built relationships between the orders of which they are the ultimate guardians. Next, we shall consider the attempts to reconcile the positions they have all taken until reaching the last attempts to codify these coexistence principles in the failed Constitutional Treaty and, more recently, in the Treaty of Lisbon.

[1] As is well known, with the entry into force of the Lisbon Treaty on 1 December 2009, the EC disappears and the EU assumes the only legal personality. Thus all the references made to the (European) Community and Community law shall be understood as also applicable to the new EU and part of the *acquis* of the EU law, except where otherwise stated.

[2] See JV Louis and T Ronse, *L'ordre juridique de l'Union européenne* (Bruylant, Bruxelles, 2005) 371–85; M Claes, *The National Courts' mandate in the European Constitution* (Hart, Oxford, 2006) 149–65; and P Craig and G De Búrca, *EU Law: Text, Cases and Materials* 4th edn (Oxford University Press, London, 2008) 353–74.

[3] See P Pérez Tremps, *Constitución Española y Comunidad Europea* (Civitas, Madrid, 1994); A López Castillo, *Constitución e integración: el fundamento constitucional de la integración supranacional europea en España y en la RFA* (CEC, Madrid, 1996), JM Jover Gómez-Ferrer, *Constitución y Derecho comunitario* (Universidad Carlos III-Boletín Oficial del Estado, Madrid, 2004); DR Phelan, *Revolt or Revolution: The Constitutional Boundaries of the European Community* (Sweet & Maxwell, Dublin, 1997); M Claes, *The National Courts' mandate in the European Constitution* (Hart, Oxford, 2006); or 'Constitución europea y constituciones nacionales' in M Cartabia *et al* (eds) (Tirant, Valencia, 2005).

1

Different Legal Orders and Different Legal Pyramids

1. A judge acts within the scope of a legal order whose norms are binding and must govern their legal arguments. Such an order could not recognize the primacy of the rules issued by another legal system unless the system itself gives permission to do so. Thus, while the guardian of the Law's Empire, its legitimacy is based on its own constitutional order. Certainly, in this sense, it would have discretion and nothing would prevent it from getting inspiration from concepts drawn from other legal orders as long as they are compatible with the structure and principles of their own system. But in any case, a judge must apply these concepts as elements of the legal order of which he is the guardian and not as a rule issued by a foreign legal order. That is, the interaction, which has been called 'cross-fertilization' and is even to a certain degree a harmonization of concepts, in no way suppresses the barriers between different orders or their autonomy.[1]

1. PRIMACY ACCORDING TO THE ECJ

2. The assertion of the primacy of EC/EU law by the Court of Justice should not be a surprise. Article 220 TEU (now Article 19 TEU-L) states that the Court of Justice and the Court of First Instance (now the General Court) shall ensure respect for the law in the interpretation and application of the present Treaty.

On the other hand, Article 249 TEU (now Article 288 TFEU) provides that Regulations shall have a general scope and be binding in their entirety and directly applicable in all Member States. It helped the ECJ to justify, in its famous decision *Costa v ENEL*, the primacy of Community law.[2]

[1] On the concept of cross-fertilization, see GH Fox and BR Roth, *Democratic Governance and International Law* (Cambridge University Press, Cambridge 2000) 204–7; W Van Gerven, 'Harmonization of Private Law: do we need it?' (2004) 41(2) *Common Market Law Review* 505; M Claes, *The National Courts' Mandate in the European Constitution* (Hart, Oxford, 2006) 258–60.

[2] Case 6/64 *Flaminio Costa v ENEL* [1964] ECR-1141. On this leading case, see B De Witte, 'Direct Effect, Supremacy, and the Nature of the Legal Order' in P Craig and G de Búrca (eds), *The Evolution of EU Law* (Oxford University Press, Oxford, 1999) 177.

However, this does not in itself determine the realization of the particular nature of the EC/EU. Even in the field of general international law, an international judge could not recognize a principle other than the primacy of international law over national law, because otherwise it would deny the value of international law itself and the principle of *pacta sunt servanda* that the judge would be responsible for enforcing.[3]

3. Primacy is not a specific feature of the EC/EU legal order. On the contrary, what is original is the way in which relations are coordinated between that order and the national one. In classic international law, the configuration of these relations corresponds to national law while in this case it is a question governed by EC/EU law itself. Thus, in the case of relations between different state orders, international law recognizes the ability of states to determine modalities of implementation of international standards with the only condition being to ensure their effective implementation. In case of breach, the offending state must repair the damage, in which case the penalty may, if necessary, be enforced through reciprocity. However, EC/EU law is not applied only to relations among Member States, but also to relations between Member States and individuals and to relations among individuals.[4]

Thus, direct effect would complete the primacy, and therefore the classic mechanisms of international law would not meet the objectives of the Treaty, since through bilateralization of relations that would be established, and the application of the classic reciprocity principle would affect both the unit of the national market and the rights derived to individuals of the Treaty. We should not forget what the ECJ pointed out long ago:

> direct applicability in such circumstances means that rules of Community law must be fully and uniformly applied in all the member States from the date of their entry into force and for so long as they continue in force;
>
> these provisions are therefore a direct source of rights and duties for all those affected thereby, whether member States or individuals, who are parties to legal relationships under Community law; . . .
>
> furthermore, in accordance with the principle of the precedence of Community law, the relationship between provisions of the treaty and directly applicable measures of the institutions on the one hand and the national law of the member states on the other is such that those provisions and measures not only by their entry into force render automatically inapplicable any conflicting provision of current national law

[3] See JV Louis and T Ronse, *L'ordre juridique de l'Union européenne* (Bruylant, Bruxelles, 2005) 246–67; K Lenaerts, P Van Nuffel and R Bray, *Constitutional Law of the European Union* 2nd edn (Thompson, London. 2005) 665–703; and KJ Alter, *Establishing the supremacy of European Law: the Making of an International Rule of Law in Europe* (Oxford University Press, Oxford, 2002) 182–232.

[4] The ECJ is reluctant to accept the effectiveness of WTO rules within the EC/EU legal order. See P Craig and G de Búrca, *EU Law: Text, Cases and Materials* 4th edn (Oxford University Press, London, 2008) 206–13; and K Lenaerts, P Van Nuffel and R Bray, *Constitutional Law of the European Union* 2nd edn (Thompson, London, 2005) 744–8.

> but – in so far as they are an integral part of, and take precedence in, the legal order applicable in the territory of each of the member states – also preclude the valid adoption of new national legislative measures to the extent to which they would be incompatible with community provisions.[5]

Therefore, that is why in order to ensure the primacy and uniform application of EC/EU law, the EC Treaty established a system of centralized control, maintained by the subsequent reforms.

4. Even if a system such as the one described is not common in the international arena, nor is it very innovative given that the ECJ has no power to override national legislation contrary to the treaties. That is, the classical principle *Bundesrecht bricht Landesrecht* would not apply in this area. However, the Court of Justice has been able, through skilful use of the procedures made available by the EC/EU Treaties, to reach an equivalent result. It is true that an action for omission would respond to traditional principles of international law to the extent that the confirmation of omission occurs after a proper process that affects the organs of the state concerned and ends with a declarative sentence. The execution of the decision for an omission would also correspond to the national authorities; otherwise, it would entail the imposition of economic sanctions on the state concerned and, where appropriate, the payment of appropriate compensation to individuals. But the classic layout of international law would subsist in any case since the national legal order would continue to be intangible and the only possibility of intervention would be indirect, through the obligation to satisfy certain compensations.[6]

The innovation took place, however, through the creation of the preliminary ruling. In fact, this process of interpretation allows the Court to intervene preventively when the case is still pending at the national level. The presumptive infringement of EC/EU law would not be final yet, since the national judge is able to enforce the ECJ ruling by means of its own judgment. The task of ensuring primacy in this case would be entrusted to the national judge, who would become the ordinary judge of EC/EU law. In fact, according to the ECJ the Member States are obliged, under the principle of loyal cooperation established in Article 10 TEU (now Article 4 TEU-L), to repeal the national law incompatible with EC/EU law and, meanwhile, to avoid its enforcement.[7] This obligation not only concerns the central (or federal) institutions but also the relevant

[5] Case 106/77 *Amministrazione delle finanze dello Stato v Simmenthal* [1978] ECR-629 paras 14, 15 and 17. See A Barav, 'Les effets du droit communautaire directement applicable' (1978) 14 *Cahiers de Droit Européen* 265 ; and D Carreau, 'Droit communautaire et droits nationaux: concurrence ou primauté? La contribution de l'arrêt Simmenthal' (1978) 14 *Revue Trimestrielle de Droit Européen* 381.

[6] See P Craig and G De Búrca (2008) (n 4) 428–58.

[7] Case 104/86, *Commission v Italy* [1988] ECR-1799 paras 11–12; V Constantinesco and D Simon 'Chronique de jurisprudence de la Cour de justice des Communautés européennes. Institutions et ordre juridique communautaire' (1989) *Journal du droit international* 395.

authorities at the local or regional level.[8] This obligation is especially qualified in the case of national judges. Indeed, as stated by the Luxembourg Court in the *Simmenthal* case:

> [A] national court which is called upon, within the limits of its jurisdiction, to apply provisions of Community law is under a duty to give full effect to those provisions, if necessary refusing of its own motion to apply any conflicting provision of national legislation, even if adopted subsequently, and it is not necessary for the court to request or await the prior setting aside of such provision by legislative or other constitutional means.[9]

This solution allows potential conflicts to be eliminated as these would not face a 'foreign' judge in relation to national authorities; instead, the issue would ultimately be solved by national courts. However, it would still be necessary for the national authorities to accept this task in its entirety and avoid the application of national measures contrary to EC/EU law. To do this, they would have to find in their respective national orders a legal title enabling them to carry out this task, whether it is a constitutional authorization provided for ratification of EU treaties or, in specific cases such as the United Kingdom, a general legislative authorization.[10]

5. The difficulty lies in the fact that, to the extent that the empowerment of the national judge is derived from the Constitution, it would be difficult to allow him to disregard the application of a constitutional rule contrary to EC/EU law. Now, for the Court of Justice primacy can only be absolute and, in this sense, national constitutional law would not enjoy a special immunity. The opposite would permit Member States to avoid their obligations through a revision of the Constitution or through a reinterpretation of it.[11]

Similarly, very old ECJ case law affirms the primacy of EC/EU law over the national law of Member States, regardless of their nature. In this sense, primacy would be imposed even before the alleged violations of fundamental rights, as provided in the Constitution of a Member State or of the principles of a national constitutional structure because otherwise it might affect the validity of an EC/EU act or to its effects on the territory of that state, which the ECJ is

[8] Case 103/88, *Fratelli Costanzo v Comune di Milano* [1989] ECR-1839 para 31. See L Ortúzar Andechaga, 'Efecto directo de las directivas respecto de la Administracion. (Sentencia de 22 de junio de 1989, asunto 103/88, Constanzo)' (1990) 13 *Revista de Estudios e Investigación de las Comunidades Europeas* 29.

[9] Case 106/77, *Simmenthal* (n 5) para 24.

[10] See M Claes, 'Constitucionalizando Europa desde su fuente: las 'cláusulas europeas' en las Constituciones nacionales: evolución y tipología' in M Cartabia and others (eds), *Constitución europea y constituciones nacionales* (Tirant, Valencia, 2005) 123 at 123–90; K Lenaerts, P Van Nuffel and R Bray (2005) (n 4) 678–700. For the specific case of the UK, see P Kinder-Gest. 'Primauté du droit communautaire et droit anglais ou comment concilier l'inconciliable?' (1991) 4 *Revue des affaires européennes* 19.

[11] See JP Jacqué, 'Droit constitutionnel national, Droit communautaire, CEDH, Charte des Nations Unies. L'instabilité des rapports de système entre ordres juridiques' (2007) 60 *Revue Française de Droit Constitutionnel* 3 at 10 (note 15).

not willing to allow.[12] This doctrine, which settled the *Handelsgesellschaft* case, was never rebutted by the ECJ. Therefore, this way, the mission assigned to the Court of Justice by the treaties consists in the obligation of making EC/EU law prevail over national rules, whether they are of a constitutional nature or not.

2. THE PRIMACY OF EC/EU LAW AGAINST THE 'COUNTER-LIMITS' IMPOSED BY NATIONAL CONSTITUTIONAL COURTS

6. This view of the primacy of EC/EU law, eminently based on previous court resolutions, could hardly be accepted like that by the national judge to whom the Constitution is the supreme and fundamental law within his legal order.[13] In fact, since the 1970s the constitutional courts of Member States have been developing a jurisprudence according to which they accept the primacy of EC/EU law on the national level, but they only accept it as long as this supranational law does not affect certain values and principles established by national constitutional law, in which case the national constitutional courts would reserve the possibility of controlling the constitutionality of EC/EU legal acts.[14] These values and principles of a constitutional nature are what the Italian doctrine has called *controlimiti* and are, in fact, a limit to European integration in general and a limit to the primacy of EC/EU law in particular, given that they tend to preserve the supremacy of certain constitutional rules regarding the protection of fundamental rights and the constitutional structure of the state.[15] All this is on the understanding that the primacy rule would only be applied in the case of competences transferred to the EC/EU. That is, an EC/EU act adopted *ultra vires* could not prevail over a rule of national law, whether constitutional in nature or not. In this case, the question of jurisdiction should be resolved by the EC/EU courts, although some say that the ECJ decision should somehow be brought before the national constitutional judge.[16]

[12] Case 11/70, *Internationale Handelsgesellschaft mbH v Einfuhr- und Vorratsstelle für Getreide und Futtermittel* [1970] ECR-1125 para 3.

[13] See V Constantinesco, 'La primauté du droit communautaire, mythe ou réalité?' in LJ Constantinesco and others (eds), *Rechtsvergleichung, Europarecht und Staatenintegration: Gedächtnisschrift für Léontin-Jean Constantinesco* (Carl Heymans, Köln, 1983) 109 at 114.

[14] For an overview on the constitutional jurisdiction within Europe on EC/EU law primacy, see P Pérez Tremps, 'La jurisdicción constitucional y la integración europea' (2009) 29 *Revista Española de Derecho Europeo* 19 at 26–40.

[15] On the *controlimiti* (counter-limits), see M Cartabia, *Principi inviolabili e integrazione europea* (Giuffrè, Milano, 1995); A Celotto, 'Derecho UE y derecho nacional: primauté vs contralímites' in M Cartabia and others (eds), *Constitución europea y constituciones nacionales* (Tirant, Valencia, 2005) 287; A Ruggeri '"Tradizioni costituzionali comuni" e "controlimiti", tra teoria delle fonti e teoria dell'interpretazione' (2003) 1 *Diritto Pubblico Comparato ed Europeo* 102; and A Ruggeri, 'Trattato costituzionale, europeizzazione dei "controlimiti" e tecniche di risoluzione delle antinomie tra diritto comunitario e diritto interno (profili problematici)' in S Staiano (ed), *Giurisprudenza costituzionale e principi fondamentali: alla ricerca del nucleo duro delle costituzioni: atti del convegno annuale del Gruppo di Pisa, Capri, 3-4 giugno 2005* (G Giappichelli, Torino, 2006) 827.

[16] See JP Jacqué (2007) (n 11) at 13.

2.1. Germany and the Protection of Fundamental Rights

7. Although the first case law was Italian, the doctrine often quotes as a precursor to the jurisprudence of European integration and its limits the famous decision of the German Federal Constitutional Court in the *Internationale Handelsgesellschaft* case, better known as *Solange I*, on 29 May 1974.[17] For the purposes of this work, in this famous resolution, the highest court in Karlsruhe declared:

> Article 24 of the Basic Law refers to the transfer of sovereign rights to interstate institutions. This can not be interpreted literally. Article 24 of the Basic Law, like any other constitutional rule of similar fundamental nature, must be understood and interpreted within the context of the Constitution in its entirety. This implies that it does not open the way to change the basic structure of the Constitution on which lies its identity without changing the Constitution . . . But Article 24 . . . makes it impossible for a reform of the Treaty to undermine the identity of the current Constitution of the Federal Republic of Germany by an invasion of its constituent structures.[18]
>
> The section on fundamental rights of the Basic Law is an essence of indispensable character of the current Constitution of the Federal Republic of Germany and belongs to the constitutional structure of the Basic Law.[19]
>
> As long as a sufficient development of the integration process of the Community has not been reached so that Community law can also have a catalogue of fundamental rights approved by a parliament and in force adjusted to the catalogue of fundamental rights contained in the Basic Law, it is appropriate and permissible for a court of the Federal Republic of Germany to go to the Federal Constitutional Court through the 'control standards' procedure.[20]

That is, it clearly stated the absolute prevalence of the fundamental rights established in the Basic Law, as long as the European Community had not produced a catalogue of fundamental rights, being able, as a last resort, to become its guarantor.

8. On the other hand, the *Solange II* opinion, handed down 12 years later, still considered fundamental rights as unrenounceable, but accepted that the Court of Justice of the European Communities dispensed an equal protection in this matter. Therefore as long as the level of protection of fundamental rights was equivalent to that guaranteed by the Constitutional German Court, the highest court in Karlsruhe would refrain from exercising its jurisdiction in the application of this particular supranational law.[21]

[17] Case *Solange I* 2 BvL 52/71 BVerfGE 37 271 (German Constitutional Court, 29 May 1974). On this leading decision, see U Scheuner, 'Fundamental Rights in European Community Law and in National Constitutional Law' (1975) 12 *Common Market Law Review* 171.

[18] Case *Solange I* (n 17) para 279.

[19] Case *Solange I* (n 17) para 280.

[20] Case *Solange I* (n 17) para 285.

[21] See case *Solange II* 2 BvR 197/83 BVerfGE 73 339 (German Constitutional Court, 22 October 1986). On this leading decision, see JM Baño León, 'Los derechos fundamentales en la Comunidad

While the European Communities, specially the case law of the Court of Justice of the European Communities in general, guarantee effective protection of fundamental rights against the sovereign power of the Communities, that has to be considered essentially equivalent to the unconditional protection of fundamental rights provided by the Basic Law, provided that it generally ensures the essential content of fundamental rights, the BVerfGE shall not exercise hereafter its jurisdiction in the application of derived Community law which is alleged as the basis of conduct by courts or authorities in the field of sovereignty of the Federal Republic of Germany, and therefore shall not review the said derived Law in light of the fundamental rights of the Basic Law; therefore, the appropriate referral under paragraph 1 of Article 100 of the BL is inadmissible.[22]

9. Later, in the opinion on the *Maastricht* case, it was claimed that the German Constitutional Court would ensure effective protection of fundamental rights against governmental authority of the Communities and that such protection should be observed in the essentials, since the protection of fundamental rights that the Basic Law requires guarantees in general the content of fundamental rights. That assurance function on the applicability of Community law shall be carried out within the framework of a 'cooperative relationship' with the Court of Justice of the European Communities, which shall ensure the protection of fundamental rights in individual cases for the whole territory of the EU, so the German Constitutional Court seemed to be the guarantor of a general and peremptory standard of fundamental rights.[23]

10. A few years there was a decision on the banana market regulation (*Bananenmarktordnung* or *Bananenstreit*), in which the German Highest Court declared the case law that had been established in the *Maastricht* case to be applicable and confirmed its validity under the new conditions provided in Article 23.1 of the Basic Law, which sets the scope, limits and conditions for exercising the power of integration.[24] This provision states the following:

Europea y la competencia del juez nacional' (1987) 54 *Revista Española de Derecho Administrativo* 277 and GC Rodríguez Iglesias and U Wölker, 'Derecho Comunitario, derechos fundamentales y control de constitucionalidad: la decisión del Tribunal Constitucional Federal Alemán de 22 de octubre de 1986' (1987) 14(3) *Revista de Instituciones Europeas* 667.

[22] See *Solange II* BVerfGE 73, 339 (387) (n 21).

[23] Case *Maastricht* 2 BvR 2134/92 and 2 BvR 2159/92, BverfGE 89, 155 (German Constitutional Court, 12 October 1993). See M Herdegen. 'Maastricht and the German Constitutional Court: Constitutional restraints for "an ever closer Union"' (1994) 31(2) *Common Market Law Review* 235; U Everling. 'The Maastricht Judgment of the German Federal Constitutional Court and its Significance for the Development of the European Union' (1994) 14 *Yearbook of European Law* 1; K Hailbronner, 'The European Union from the Perspective of the German Constitutional Court' (1995) 37 *German Yearbook of International Law* 93. This decision implies a major change in the case law established in *Eurocontrol I* 2 BvR 1107/77 and 195/79 BverfGE 58, 1 (German Constitutional Court, 23 June 1981).

[24] Case *Bananenmarktordnung* (or *Bananenstreit* or simply *Bananas*) 2 BvL 1/97 BVerfGE 102, 147 (German Constitutional Court, 7 June 2000). See S Griller, 'Primacy of Community Law: A Hidden Agenda of the Charter of Fundamental Rights' in D Melissas and I Pernice (eds), *Perspectives of the Nice Treaty and the Intergovernmental Conference in 2004* (Nomos, Baden-Baden, 2002) 47. This

With a view to establishing a united Europe, the Federal Republic of Germany shall participate in the development of the European Union that is committed to democratic, social, and federal principles, to the rule of law, and to the principle of subsidiarity, and that guarantees a level of protection of basic rights essentially comparable to that afforded by this Basic Law. To this end the Federation may transfer sovereign powers by a law with the consent of the Bundesrat.

Thus, and as announced in the *Maastricht* case, it is the German Constitutional Court that has to ensure, in cooperation with the ECJ, that the effective protection of fundamental rights for German residents shall be 'substantially similar' to the protection required by the Basic Law.[25] Thus, the German Constitutional Court shall only exercise its jurisdiction in this area if the ECJ moves away from the standard of protection that the German Highest Court identified in its *Solange II* opinion.[26] This does not mean, as stated by the Constitutional Court in Karlsruhe, that it requires exactly the same level of protection of the fundamental rights affected by community legislation that the German Basic Law grants in its field. The constitutional requirements, however, shall be satisfied if the protection granted by the ECJ is 'substantially similar' to that recognized by the Basic Law as long as it safeguards their 'essential content'.[27]

11. That is, upon the decision in the *Bananenmarktordnung* case (sometimes called *Solange III*), the German Constitutional Court accepted, in principle, its inability to decide on the protection of fundamental rights in Community acts, given that the jurisdiction of the Luxembourg Court can always be activated through the prejudicial question of Article 234 TEU (now Article 267 TFEU).[28] Thus, it admits that the German model of protection is not the only possible reference to meet the demand of respect for fundamental rights established by Article 1 of the Basic Law. Nevertheless, it requires that national control can only be operated in cases of continuing and systematic violations of rights, showing the surpassing inadequacy of EC/EU guardianship requests. Indeed,

decision has also been called *Solange III*: see I Pernice, 'Les bananes et les droits fondamentaux: la Cour constitutionnelle allemande fait le point' (2001) 37(3–4) *Cahiers de Droit Européen* 427; W Zimmer, 'De nouvelles bases pour la coopération entre la Cour Constitutionnelle Fédérale et la Cour de Justice de Luxembourg? (à propos de BverfGE, 7 juin 2000, *Solange III*)' (2001) Mai, *Europe* 3; A López Castillo, 'Un nuevo paso en la andadura iuscomunitaria del Tribunal Constitucional Federal de Alemania. El Auto (Sala Segunda) de 7 de junio de 2000' (2001) 61 *Revista Española de Derecho Constitucional* 349 ; J Callewaert, 'Les droits fondamentaux entre cours nationales et européennes' (2001) 48 *Revue Trimestrielle des Droits de l'Homme* 1183.

[25] The decision establishes that the level of protection has to be '*Wesentlichen gleich*'. See Case *Bananenmarktordnung* (2000) (n 24) para 163.

[26] *Ibid*, BverfGE 102, 147 (163). See also the standard established in *Solange II* BVerfGE 73, 339 (n 21) paras 378–81.

[27] Case *Bananenmarktordnung* (2000) (n 24) para 164 and Case *Solange II* (1986) (n 21) paras 340 and 387.

[28] See W Zimmer, 'De nouvelles bases pour la coopération entre la Cour Constitutionnelle Fédérale et la Cour de Justice de Luxembourg? (à propos de BverfGE, 7 juin 2000, *Solange III*)' (2001) Mai, *Europe* 3.

this decision has been read by the doctrine as a 'peace treaty' of the German Constitutional Court with the ECJ, leading back the hypothesis of conflict to an extreme laboratory hypothesis.[29]

Finally, the recent decision by the highest court in Karlsruhe on the compatibility of the Lisbon Treaty with the Basic Law confirms the constitutionality of the Treaty and maintains the previous case law concerning the European Union. However, the Court emphasized the need to strengthen mechanisms of participation of the federal Parliament in the EC/EU legislative process.[30]

2.2. Italy and the *Controlimiti*

12. Regarding Italy, the opening of the Italian order to EC/EU law was made through Article 11 of the 1947 Constitution, which provides that:

> Italy rejects war as an instrument of aggression against the freedom of other countries and as a means of solving international disputes therefore agrees, on equal footing with other States, the limitations of sovereignty necessary for an order that ensures peace and justice among nationals, and shall promote and encourage international organizations in this path.

Initially, the Italian Constitutional Court ruled that a national law contrary to Community law was also unconstitutional, so that ordinary judges could not decide to declare the nullity or non-application of a national law when it came into conflict with Community law; instead it should bring the matter before the Constitutional Court by means of a 'question of constitutional legitimacy'.[31]

13. Soon after, the ECJ established in the *Simmenthal* decision that, under the principle of primacy, the national judge has jurisdiction to declare unenforceable those laws contrary to the EC legal order.[32] The strong statement by the

[29] On the Peace Treaty, see C Grewe. 'Le "traité de paix" avec la Cour de Luxembourg: l'arrêt de la Cour constitutionnelle allemande du 7 juin 2000 relatif au règlement du marché de la banane' (2001) 37(1) *Revue Trimestrielle de Droit Européen* 1. Scholarship seems to agree on the theoreticals of the problem, due to the entry into force of Nice and its declaration of fundamental rights. See I Pernice, 'Les bananes et les droits fondamentaux: la Cour constitutionnelle allemande fait le point' (2001) 37(3–4) *Cahiers de Droit Européen* 427 at 440.

[30] See *Vertrag von Lissabon* (Lisbon Treaty) BVerfG 2 BvE 2/08 (German Constitutional Court, 30 June 2009). See C Tomuschat, 'The Ruling of the German Constitutional Court on the Treaty of Lisbon' (2009) 10(8) *German Law Journal* 1259; D Doukas, 'The verdict of the German Federal Constitutional Court on the Lisbon Treaty: Not guilty, but don't do it again!' (2009) 34(6) *European Law Review* 866; and A López Castillo and AJ Menéndez, 'Sentencia Lisboa del Tribunal Constitucional Federal Alemán' (2011) .

[31] See Case *Frontini* Decision No 183/1973 (Italian Constitutional Court, 18 December 1973), Case *Industrie Chimiche Italia Centrale* Decision No 232/1975 (Italian Constitutional Court, 22 October 1975) and Case *Società UNIL-IT/Società Ariete* Decision No 163/1977 (Italian Constitutional Court, 22 December 1977). On the 'appeal for constitutional legitimacy' within Italian legal order (*questione di legittimità costituzionale*), see G De Vergottini, *Diritto costituzionale* 6th edn (CEDAM, Padova, 2008) 653–69.

[32] Case 106/77 *Simmenthal* (n 5) para 10.

ECJ made the Italian Constitutional Court change its stance and the *Granital* opinion. After recognizing the separation between EC and national law, it assumed that it had no jurisdiction to judge the adequacy of internal rules regarding Community law and recognized the jurisdiction of ordinary judges to disapply those national rules that violate the content of EC provisions.[33]

14. However, the Constitutional Court continued to consider that there are at least two situations in which it does have jurisdiction.

First, since the *Frontini* (1973) decision, the Court has held that is competent to decide on those cases in which a Community legal act does not conform to the fundamental principles of the Italian constitutional order or to the human rights considered inviolable. Indeed, this judgment states that:

> [B]ased on Article 11 of the Constitution some limitations of sovereignty have been passed only to achieve the goals set out therein; and should, therefore, be excluded that these limitations . . . may in any case grant the organs of the EEC an unacceptable power to violate the fundamental principles of our constitutional order, or the inalienable rights of individuals.[34]

To support this possible intervention, the Court relies on the justification offered in Articles 2 and 3 of the Italian Constitution, which provide for the recognition and guarantee of individual rights by the Republic, and the equal rights of all before the law. Indeed, since the *Fragd* case, the Italian Constitutional Court recognizes that the EC/EU legal order foresees a 'broad and effective' guardianship system of fundamental rights, and besides, derived from the common principles of the Member States' orders, they are an integral and essential part of EC/EU law. Therefore, in this context it would be rare that a violation of fundamental rights in which the EC/EU could not provide for a remedy may happen. However, if such a situation should occur, the Constitutional Court reaffirms its authority in order to verify, through the control of constitutionality of the implementing law, if a treaty provision, as interpreted and applied by the institutions and EC/EU bodies, is or is not contrary to the Italian constitutional order and whether it does or does not injure the inalienable rights of the individuals.[35]

Secondly, the Constitutional Court promptly restores its once-denied power to control the adjustment to EC/EU law of national law rules when they may

[33] Case *Granital* Decision No 170/1984 (Italian Constitutional Court, 5 June 1984). For a comment, see A Barav, 'Cour Constitutionnelle italienne et droit communautaire: le fantôme de Simmenthal' (1985) 21(2) *Revue Trimestrielle de Droit Européen* 313; G Gaja, 'New Developments in a Continuing Story: the Relationship Between EEC Law and Italian Law' (1990) 27(1) *Common Market Law Review* 83 and P Pérez Tremps, 'Justicia comunitaria, justicia constitucional y tribunales ordinarios frente al Derecho Comunitario (Comentario a la Sentencia de la Corte Constitucional italiana número 170/1984, de 8 de junio)' (1985) 13 *Revista Española de Derecho Constitucional* 157.

[34] Case *Frontini* (1973) (n 31) para 9.

[35] Case *Fragd* Decision No 232/1989 (Italian Constitutional Court 13–21 April 1989).

involve non-compliance with certain obligations imposed by an EC/EU rule and derived from the state's membership of the EU.[36]

15. In summary, the Italian Constitutional Court establishes as the limits of the primacy of EC/EU law the general principles of its constitutional order and the inalienable rights of the individual (*Granital* and *Fragd* cases).[37] The doctrine has identified them with the name of *controlimiti* (see above), which refer to fundamental principles that 'guide and unify' the order by determining its features and, as such, would be inviolable and could not be affected by the performance of foreign orders and/or external courts.[38] Recently, the Italian Highest Court has progressed in the matter by recognizing itself as competent to activate the preliminary ruling proceeding before the ECJ.[39] The doctrine has interpreted this move as the strengthening of the acceptance of the supremacy of EC/EU law by the Court, the only exception being the 'counter-limits' of which the Constitutional Court would be the ultimate guardian.[40]

2.3. Poland and its Reluctance to give up its Recently Recovered Sovereignty

16. The case law of the Polish Constitutional Court could also be seen as representative of the reticence and reserve that the national constitutional courts still show in relation to the absolute supremacy of EC/EU law. Thus, the Polish Court of High Instance would be very sensitive to the preservation of its newly recovered sovereignty, but also appears receptive to the constitutional case law of the early Member States. Therefore, regarding the relations between EC/EU law and the Constitution it has taken a position that reflects, at least from a theoretical point of view, that of many national jurisdictions, although in practice they have been showing a respectful attitude towards EC/EU legislation.[41]

[36] See case *Umbrian Vineyards* Decision No 384/1994 (Italian Constitutional Court 7–10 November 1994), where the Court declared a regional law unconstitutional for being contrary to Regulation CEE/822/1987 and therefore to Articles 11 and 117 of the Italian Constitution. See A *Sáiz Arnáiz, 'El Derecho Comunitario, ¿parámetro de la constitucionalidad de las leyes internas?* (a propósito de la sentencia nº 384 de 1994, de la Corte Costituzionale italiana)› (1995) 22(2) *Revista de Instituciones Europeas* 571 at 585–91.

[37] See A La Pérgola and P Del Duca, 'Community Law, International Law and the Italian Constitution' (1985) 79(3) *American Journal of International Law* 598.

[38] See case *Fragd* (1989) (n 35). On the 'counter-limits' doctrine, see M Cartabia, *Principi inviolabili e integrazione europea* (Giuffrè, Milano, 1995) 133; and P Pérez Tremps, 'La jurisdicción constitucional y la integración europea' (2009) 29 *Revista Española de Derecho Europeo* 19 at 38–40.

[39] See Decisions Nos 348 and 349/2007 (Italian Constitutional Court, 22 October 2007) and Decisions Nos 102 and 103/2008 (Italian Constitutional Court, 12 February 2008). See also the answer of the ECJ in Case C-169/08 *Presidente del Consiglio dei Ministri y Regione Sardegna* [2009] ECR I-10821.

[40] See LS Rossi, 'Corte costituzionale (Italian Constitutional Court): Decisions 348 and 349/2007 of 22 October 2007, and 102 and 103/2008, of 12 February 2008' (2009) 46(1) *Common Market Law Review* 319 especially at 330–1.

[41] Case *European Arrest Warrant* P 1/05 (Polish Constitutional Court 27 April 2005). There exists an English translation of the legal reasoning at <http://www.trybunal.gov.pl/eng/summaries/summaries_assets/documents/P_1_05_full_GB.pdf>. See A Nußberger, 'Poland: The Constitutional

17. Thus, in its opinion of 11 May 2005 concerning the entry of Poland into the European Union, the Polish Constitutional Court found that the accession was based on Article 90.1 of the Constitution which authorized the transfer, through a treaty, of the powers of state organs in relation to certain matters to an international organization or to international bodies.[42] By virtue of this authorization, two independent legal orders would coexist within the Polish territory subject, to two different jurisdictions regarding their control of conformity. But this autonomy would not imply *per se* an absence of relationships and interactions or exclude the existence of conflicts between the rules issued by each of the orders. So, in case of antinomies, the solution could come from the primacy afforded to international law and, in particular, to EC/EU law by the Constitution. However, since it would be based on the Constitution itself, this primacy could not take part in a possible conflict between a constitutional and an EC/EU rule. The primacy of EC/EU law would not, therefore, imply a supremacy over the Constitution. The Polish Constitutional Court recognized, therefore, the existence of an obligation to interpret national law in conformity and in a favourable manner with EC/EU law, but this obligation had its limits in the case of a specific provision of the Constitution:

> The principle of interpreting domestic law in a manner 'sympathetic to European law', as formulated within the Constitutional Tribunal's jurisprudence, has its limits. In no event may it lead to results contradicting the explicit wording of constitutional norms or being irreconcilable with the minimum guarantee functions realised by the Constitution. In particular, the norms of the Constitution within the field of individual rights and freedoms indicate a minimum and unsurpassable threshold which may not be lowered or questioned as a result of the introduction of Community provisions.[43]

18. For this reason, in the case of the European Arrest Warrant (EAW), the Polish Constitutional Court annulled the national law transposing the framework Decision on the EAW, given that the national implementation measure considered the surrender of Polish nationals, which in the opinion of the Polish Court was contrary to the constitutional ban on extraditing nationals.[44]

Tribunal on the implementation of the European Arrest Warrant' (2008) 6(1) *International Journal of Constitutional Law* 162 and K Kowalik-Bánczyk, 'Should We Polish It Up? The Polish Constitutional Tribunal and the Idea of Supremacy of EU Law' (2005) 6(10) *German Law Journal* 1356.

[42] Case *Accession Treaty* Decision No K 18/04 (Polish Constitutional Court, 11 May 2005) paras 5–7. There exists an English translation that reproduces the legal reasoning of this decision at <http://www.trybunal.gov.pl/eng/summaries/documents/K_18_04_GB.pdf>. See A Lazowski. 'Accession Treaty – Polish Constitutional Tribunal' (2007) 3(1) *European Constitutional Law Review* 148 at 158–61.

[43] Case *Accession Treaty* Decision No K 18/04 (n 42) para 14.

[44] But the Court postponed the effects for up to 18 months (the maximum allowed) in order to amend the Constitution and avoid any non-fulfilment of EC/EU obligations. See Case *European Arrest Warrant* P 1/05 (n 41). On the Constitutional issues which arose with the implementation of the European Arrest Warrant see LI Gordillo, 'El juez nacional y el juez europeo ante la Euro-orden'

19. So, in case of conflict with a specific provision, the Constitution would avoid the application of EC/EU law. Therefore, in this situation, the constituent power should amend the Fundamental law, or the political power to negotiate the withdrawal of the Union. However, there are those who criticize the 'minimalist' position adopted by this Court, and state that, despite the orthodoxy of its legal argument, it would have a development similar to the one experienced by its Italian and German counterparts.[45]

2.4. France: From Preserving its Sovereignty to the Absence of Explicit Contradictions

20. Although using different arguments, the recent decisions adopted by French and Spanish constitutional courts clearly illustrate the present attitude of the jurisdictions that have gradually deepened their reflections on the relationship between EC/EU law and national law. In the case of France, the thread of the evolution of case law of the French Constitutional Council on this issue has been the concept of sovereignty. However, this case law has moved in two different ways. Indeed, initially, the French Constitutional Council made a distinction between a 'limitation of sovereignty' and a 'transfer of sovereignty'.[46] Thus, while the limitations would be (with certain conditions) accepted, the transfers would be completely rejected. According to the French *Conseil* 'subject to reciprocity, France agrees to limitations of sovereignty necessary for the organization and preservation of peace'. However, 'no provision of a constitutional nature authorizes transfers of all or part of national sovereignty regardless of the international organization'.[47]

21. However, the Constitutional Council finally left that dispute, widely criticized and difficult to concretize. Instead, it turned to the new category of 'essential conditions pertaining to the exercise of national sovereignty' to establish the ultimate limits of integration and relations between national and Community order. The concept of 'essential conditions of the exercise of national sovereignty' had already appeared in Decision 70-39 DC (*Traités des Communautés européennes* case), which stated in its last paragraph that the rule under control 'can not involve, either for its nature, or its significance, an attack on the essential conditions of the exercise of national sovereignty'.[48] In

in M Revenga Sánchez (ed), *El poder judicial: VI Congreso de la Asociación de Constitucionalistas de España* (Tirant, Valencia, 2009) 755.

[45] See JP Jacqué (2007) (n 11) at 12.

[46] Case *Elections to the European Parliament* Decision No 76-71 DC (French Constitutional Council, 30 December 1976). See R Kovar and D Simon, 'A propos de la Décision du Conseil constitutionnel français du 30 décembre 1976 relative à l'élection de l'assemblée parlementaire européenne au suffrage universel direct' (1977) 13(4) *Revue Trimestrielle de Droit Européen* 665.

[47] Case *Elections to the European Parliament* (1976) (n 46) para 2.

[48] Case *EC Economic regime* Decision No 70-39 DC (French Constitutional Council, 19 June 1970).

this case, the Prime Minister appealed to the Constitutional Council in order to examine the compatibility with the Constitution of a decision (in fact it was an agreement subject to approval) of the Council of Ministers of the European Communities on the financing by their own resources and of a treaty that increased the budgetary powers of the European Parliament. Decision 70-39 DC recognized, finally, the compatibility of both texts. Since then, the Council, by an implicit reference to the preamble of the Constitution of 1946 by which France agrees to the limitations of sovereignty necessary for the organization and preservation of peace, admitted the transfer of powers to the EC/EU that do not affect the essential conditions of the exercise of national sovereignty.[49]

22. After these initial decisions, the concept of sovereignty was put on ice until the decision issued on the occasion of the possible unconstitutionality of Additional Protocol No 6 of the European Convention on Human Rights, which eliminated the death penalty in peacetime.[50] In this decision, not only were all kinds of damage to essential conditions of the exercise of national sovereignty excluded in this specific case, but also it concretized which those conditions are in principle. Therefore, paragraph 2 stated that the text under control was not inconsistent with the state's duty to ensure respect for the institutions of the republic, continuity of life of the nation, and a guarantee of the rights and freedoms of citizens.[51] From this decision on, the Constitutional Council appealed to the concept of essential conditions of the exercise of national sovereignty as part of the constitutional framework of international action by public authorities.[52]

[49] C Emeri and JC Gautron. 'La réforme du régime financier des Communautés et la décision du Conseil constitutionnel français du 21 juin 1970' (1971) 1 *Revue du droit public et de la science politique* 157.

[50] Case *Abolition of the death penalty* Decision No 85-188 DC (French Constitutional Council, 22 May 1985).

[51] Para 2 states literally: '*Considérant que cet engagement international n'est pas incompatible avec le devoir pour l'Etat d'assurer le respect des institutions de la République, la continuité de la vie de la nation et la garantie des droits et libertés des citoyens . . .*'. See L Favoreu, 'La décision du conseil constitutionnel du 22 Mai 1985 rélative au Protocole no. 6 additionnel à la Convention européenne des droits de l'homme' (1986) 31 *Annuaire Français de Droit International* 868; N Lenoir, 'Les rapports entre le droit constitutionnel français et le droit international à travers le filtre de l'article 54 de la Constitution de 1958' in PM Dupuy (ed), *Droit international et droit interne dans la jurisprudence comparée du Conseil constitutionnel et du Conseil d'État* (Panthéon-Assas, Paris, 2001) 11 at 21–4.

[52] Case *Schengen* Decision No 91-294 DC (French Constitutional Council, 25 July 1991); Case *Maastricht I* Decision No 92-308 DC (French Constitutional Council, 9 April 1992); Case *Maastricht II* Decision No 92-312 DC (French Constitutional Council, 2 September 1992). On the *Schengen* case, see P Gaïa, 'Commentaire de la décision du Conseil constitutionnel no 91-294 du 25 juillet 1991: loi autorisant l'approbation de la Convention d'application de l'Accord de Schengen, du 14 juin 1985' (1992) 17(1) *Revue de la recherche juridique* 25. On the *Maastricht* decisions, see L Favoreu and L Philip, 'Maastricht I, II, III' in L Favoreu *et al* (ed), *Les grandes décisions du Conseil Constitutionnel* 12th edn (Dalloz, Paris, 2003) 778 especially at 798 and 800–1, where the limits imposed by the national sovereignty are analysed.

23. This case law from the highest French court raised several questions. Thus, on one hand, it is difficult to determine the nature and scope of this constitutional limit. The essential conditions of the exercise of national sovereignty represent a limit other than their own mandates and constitutional requirements.[53] That is, this formulation implies, as already anticipated in Decision 85-188 DC, that the nonconformity of a treaty with the Constitution may come from either a clause directly contrary to principles or rules of constitutional value, or, more unclearly, from an impairment of the essential conditions of the exercise of national sovereignty.[54] Thus, the 'essential conditions' would become a principle that goes beyond the actual wording of the French Constitution, and therefore, the principle that goes beyond the actual wording of the Fundamental Law leaves a very wide margin of interpretation to the Constitutional Council, without the aforementioned body having contributed much to determine the elements or content of this concept.[55]

24. For nearly a decade there were no major developments in the case law of the *Conseil* on the relationship between the Constitution and EC/EU law, until Decision 2004-496 DC, in which the Constitutional Council confirmed the jurisdictional immunity of secondary EC/EU law.[56] In this case, the authors of the appeal claimed the unconstitutionality of the law implementing an EC/EU directive. For the Council, the obligation to comply with EC/EU law is derived from Article 88-1 of the French Constitution regarding the participation of France in the Community and the Union:

[53] So it is stated at para 14 of the Case *Maastricht I* (1992) (n 52) when the *Conseil* established that 'should an international agreement entered into to this end involve a clause conflicting with the Constitution or jeopardising the essential conditions for the exercise of national sovereignty, authorisation to ratify would require prior revision of the Constitution'.

[54] See B Genevois, 'Le Conseil constitutionnel et le droit communautaire dérivé' (2004) 2004(4) *Revue Française de Droit Administratif* 651 at 384 and *ibid*, 'Le Traité sur l'Union Européenne et la Constitution révisée, à propos de la décision du Conseil constitutionnel n° 92-312 DC du 2 septembre 1992' (1992) 8(6) 937.

[55] P Pérez Tremps, *Constitución Española y Comunidad Europea* (Civitas, Madrid, 1994) 99–100 and L Favoreu, 'Le contrôle de constitutionnalité du Traité de Maastricht et le développement du droit constitutionnel international' XCVII(1–2) *Revue Générale de Droit International Public* 39.

[56] Case *Law on confidence in the digital economy* Decision No 2004-496 DC (French Constitutional Council, 10 June 2004). See E Sales, 'La transposition des directives communautaires: une exigence de valeur constitutionnelle sous réserve de constitutionnalité' (2005) 41(3) *Revue Trimestrielle de Droit Européen* 597; Dutheil de la Rochère, J, ‹Conseil constitutionnel (French Constitutional Court), Decision No 2004-496 of 10 June 2004, Loi pour la confiance dans l›économie numérique (e-commerce)› (2005) 42(3) *Common Market Law Review* 859, X Magnon, 'Le chemin communautaire du Conseil constitutionnel : entre ombre et lumière, principe et conséquence de la spécificité constitutionnelle du droit communautaire (Commentaire du volet communautaire des décisions du Conseil constitutionnel n° 2004-496 DC du 10 juin 2004, Loi pour la confiance dans l'économie numérique, et n° 2004-497 DC du 1er juillet 2004, Loi relative aux communications électroniques et aux services de communication audiovisuelle)' (2004) 8–9 *Europe* 6. See also the Case *Constitutional Treaty* Decision No 2004-505 DC (French Constitutional Council, 19 November 2004), where the *Conseil* maintains the position stated in *Digital Economy*.

> The Republic shall participate in the European Union constituted by States which have freely chosen to exercise some of their powers in common by virtue of the Treaty on European Union and of the Treaty on the Functioning of the European Union, as they result from the treaty signed in Lisbon on 13 December, 2007.[57]

Thus, under this constitutional provision, lawmakers must respect EC/EU law when implementing an EC/EU directive. Therefore, it is not (or shouldn't be) for the Council to rule on the constitutionality of the law implementing the Directive. Only the EC/EU Court could determine whether the policy in question complies with the limits of EC/EU competence and fundamental rights. The French constitutional judge could only intervene in two situations. First, within the scope of its discretion, the national lawmaker can go beyond what is imposed by the directive. To the extent that it exercises a power that is not subject to Community law, the control on constitutionality shall be exercised normally. Second, the *Conseil* would retain the power to intervene in the hypothesis of a contradiction between the directive and a specific constitutional provision. In fact, the scope of authorization derived from Article 88-1 must be interpreted in the light of other provisions of the Constitution. If these provisions have not been modified, it is because they must still be applied. Certainly, the assumptions of this particular type of antinomy should be, at best, limited. Some have referred to possible conflicts derived from the principle of secularism or the principle of equality, but taking into account the competences of the Union, it seems unlikely to get to a situation like this.[58]

25. The evolution of the formulation of this limit in the Decision on the law regarding copyright and related rights is particularly interesting.[59] Indeed, the Constitutional Council abandoned the reference to 'specific provisions' in order to replace it with the 'rule or principle inherent to the constitutional identity of France'.[60]

In doing so, the *Conseil* would place itself closer to the Italian and Spanish constitutional courts, but, above all, this case law shows the influence of the wording of Article I-5 of the failed Constitutional Treaty, whose wording has

[57] This rule is amended with each modification of the EU Treaties.

[58] On the implications of the Case *Law on confidence in the digital economy* (2004) (n 56) see JP Camby, 'Le droit communautaire est-il soluble dans la Constitution?' (2004) 4 *Revue du droit public et de la science politique en France et à l'étranger* 878 ; A Levade, 'Le Conseil constitutionnel aux prises avec le droit communautaire dérivé', *ibid*, 889; and J Roux, 'Le Conseil constitutionnel, le droit communautaire dérivé et la Constitution', *ibid*, 912.

[59] Case *Law on Copyright and Related Rights in the Information Society* Decision No 2006-540 DC (French Constitutional Council 27 July 2006). For a comment, see F Chaltiel, 'Nouvelle précision sur les rapports entre le droit constitutionnel et le droit communautaire : La décision du Conseil constitutionnel du 27 juillet 2006 sur la loi relative aux droits d'auteurs' (2006) 68 *Revue Française de Droit Constitutionnel* 837.

[60] Case *Law on Copyright* (2006) (n 59) para 19, which in its original version states '*la transposition d'une directive ne saurait aller à l'encontre d'une règle ou d'un principe inhérent à l'identité constitutionnelle de la France, sauf à ce que le constituant y ait consenti*'.

been recovered almost entirely by the Treaty of Lisbon.[61] Thus, the new Article 4 of the Treaty on European Union (TEU-L) provides:

> The Union shall respect the equality of Member States before the Treaties as well as their national identities, inherent in their fundamental structures, political and constitutional, inclusive of regional and local self-government. It shall respect their essential State functions, including ensuring the territorial integrity of the State, maintaining law and order and safeguarding national security. In particular, national security remains the sole responsibility of each Member State.

In any case, we must remember that, ultimately, the primacy of EU law that the Constitutional Council recognizes will be based in the French Constitution itself rather than in a rule or principle from the EC/EU legal order.[62]

26. The interordinal relation rules between French constitutional law and EC/EU law have not experienced major changes in recent years. We had to wait until the very interesting (at least for EU lawyers) judicial dialogue established among the French ordinary courts, the Conseil and the ECJ on the *Melki/Abdeli* cases dealing with the EC/EU compatibility of the new procedure for control of constitutionality (QPC, *Question Prioritaire de Constitutionnalité*) issued from the last reform on the Fundamental Law in 2008.[63]

Briefly, the new *QPC* (priority preliminary ruling on the issue of constitutionality) allows any person involved in legal proceedings before a court to argue that a statutory provision infringes rights and freedoms guaranteed by the French Constitution. But unlike other systems, where the individual may directly (or by means of a lower court) lodge a similar appeal before the Constitutional Court, in France, the application is referred by the *Conseil d'Etat* or the *Cour de cassation* to the Constitutional Council, which could eventually repeal the

[61] The *Treaty establishing a Constitution for Europe* was signed in Rome on 29 October 2004 (OJ C 310/01, 16 December 2004). On the other hand, see the *Treaty of Lisbon amending the Treaty on European Union and the Treaty establishing the European Community*, signed at Lisbon, 13 December 2007 (OJ C 306/01, 17 December 2007) and *the Consolidated versions of the Treaty on European Union and the Treaty on the Functioning of the European Union* (OJ C 83/01, 30 March 2010).

[62] See F Picod, 'Le contrôle de constitutionnalité des actes de droit dérivé de l'Union européenne' (2005) 18 *Les Cahiers du Conseil Constitutionnel* 144 ; J Roux, 'Le Conseil constitutionnel, le droit communautaire derive et la Constitution' (2004) 4 *Revue du droit public et de la science politique en France et à l'étranger* 912, B Genevois, 'Le Conseil constitutionnel et le droit communautaire dérivé' (2004) 2004(4) *Revue Française de Droit Administratif* 651 ; C Charpy, 'The Status of (Secondary) Community Law in the French Internal Order. The Recent Case-Law of the Conseil Constitutionnel and the Conseil d'Etat' (2007) 3(3) *European Constitutional Law Review* 436.

[63] See the Cases *Aziz Melki* and *Sélim Abdeli* Decisions Nos 10-40001 and 10-40002 (French Cour de cassation, 16 April 2010); Case *Act pertaining to the Opening up to Competition and the Regulation of Online Betting and Gambling* Decision No 2010605 DC (French Constitutional Council, 12 May 2010); Case *Rujovic* Decision No 312305 (French *Conseil d'État*, 14 May 2010); and Joined Cases C188/10 and C189/10 *Melki and Abdeli* [2010] unpublished, para 52. For a brief explanation of the *QPC*, the rules regulating the procedure and plenty of doctrinal references, visit the site of the Conseil at <http://www.conseil-constitutionnel.fr/conseil-constitutionnel/francais/la-question-prioritaire-de-constitutionnalite/la-question-prioritaire-de-constitutionnalite-qpc.47106.html>.

challenged statutory provision. So the main difference with other constitutional systems is that in France, the highest ordinary courts (*Conseil d'Etat* or the *Cour de cassation*) act as a filter, selecting which cases will be ultimately be decided by the Constitutional Council.[64]

Basically, and for the purposes of this work, the problem that arose in *Melki* was the compatibility between the national QPC (where the Constitutional Council ultimately decides) and the preliminary ruling before the EU judicial power (where the ECJ has the last word). As is well known, the Supreme ordinary courts (the *Conseil d'État* and the *Cour de cassation*) may refer to the ECJ and to the *Conseil* the relevant preliminary ruling. But what if there exists a kind of hybrid case, where one may doubt the compatibililty of a national law with both the national Constitution and EU law at the same time. A few problems may arise at this moment. To sum up, basically, if the *Cour de cassation* (for instance) decides to refer the case to the ECJ for a preliminary ruling and this Court gives a final decision disregarding the possible unconstitutionalty of the national provision (where it has no competence to decide), the Constitutional Council would have lost the opportunity to decide and if it does in the future in a similar case, it could imply a kind of reversal of the ECJ decision. Conversely, if the *Conseil d'État* decides to refer the case to the Constitutional Council, this organ may also become judge of the validity of the national implementing measure under EU Law, disregarding the ultimate competence of the ECJ to control the validity of these acts. All of this taking into account that the Constitutional Council refuses to refer cases to the ECJ for preliminary ruling, given also its peremptory deadlines to solve the applications it receives.[65]

The final answer on the EU compatibility of the QPC resulted from a complex dialogue between the *Conseil d'État*, the *Cour de cassation*, the Constitutional Council and the ECJ. The decision on the *Meldi/Abdeli* cases took into account the previous decisions of the national courts dealing with this compatitiblity[66] and in this sense established two main principles. On the one hand, and in order to ensure the primacy of EU law,

[64] On the French Priority Preliminary ruling on Constitutionality (*QPC*), see D Rousseau, *La question prioritaire de constitutionnalité* (Lextenso éditions, Paris, 2010); and X Magnon *et al*, *QPC – La question prioritaire de constitutionnalité. Pratique et contentieux* (Litec, Paris, 2011).

[65] For all the possibilities and complications derived from the relationship between the EU preliminary ruling and the French *QPC* as well as critical views of the *Melki/Abdeli* case, see X Magnon, 'La QPC face au droit de l'Union : la brute, les bons et le truand' (2010) 84(4) *Revue Française de Droit Constitutionnel* 761; D Sarmiento, 'L'arrêt Melki : esquisse d'un dialogue des juges constitutionnels et européens sur toile de fond française' (2010) 46(3) *Revue Trimestrielle de Droit Européen* 588; A Pliakos, 'Le contrôle de constitutionnalité et le droit de l'Union européenne: la réaffirmation du principe de primauté' (2010) 46(3–5) *Cahiers de Droit Européen* 487; D Simon and A Rigaux, 'La priorité de la question prioritaire de constitutionnalité : harmonie(s) et dissonances(s) des monologues juridictionnels croisés' (2010) 29 *Cahiers du Conseil Constitutionnel* 63; and R Mehdi, 'French supreme courts and European Union law: Between historical compromise and accepted loyalty' (2011) 48(2) *Common Market Law Review* 439.

[66] Case *Regulation of Online Betting and Gambling* (2010) (n 63) and Case *Rujovic* (2010) (n 63).

> the functioning of that system of cooperation requires the national court to be free to refer to the Court of Justice for a preliminary ruling any question that it considers necessary, at whatever stage of the proceedings it considers appropriate, even at the end of an interlocutory procedure for the review of constitutionality.[67]

On the other hand, the ECJ added that in so far as

> national law lays down an obligation to initiate an interlocutory procedure for the review of constitutionality, which would prevent the national court from immediately disapplying a national legislative provision which it considers to be contrary to EU law, the functioning of the system established by Article 267 TFEU nevertheless requires that that court be free, first, to adopt any measure necessary to ensure the provisional judicial protection of the rights conferred under the European Union's legal order and, second, to disapply, at the end of such an interlocutory procedure, that national legislative provision if that court holds it to be contrary to EU law.[68]

That is to say, the *QPC* is compatible with EU law as long as it does not prevent the referral to the ECJ by the ordinary Court both before the submission of the case and after the decision of the Constitutional Court. The ECJ adopts the view of the Conseil d'État and not that of the Constitutional Council, which only considered a simultaneous referral. However, this jurisprudence compromises the priority of the *QPC*. Having two different procedural remedies (one issued from the alleged violation of EU law and the other from the possible breach of a constitutional rule) the ordinary Court has to be able (in the case of doubt about the interpretation or the validity of an EU legal act) to refer a preliminary ruling to the ECJ before issuing a *QPC* for the Constitutional Council. So, the *QPC* is compatible with EU law as long as it does not have priority if the ordinary judge decides to refer the case to the ECJ for a preliminary ruling.[69]

2.5. Spain: The Advantages of Being Last

27. The Spanish Constitutional Court's position in Declaration No 1/2004 of 13 December, which analyses and determines the compatibility of the national Constitution with the aborted Constitutional Treaty, shows signs of an opening by the Spanish Constitutional Court which, in addition, took advantage of other courts' dogmatic constructions, especially the Italian and German courts, that have been developing for decades.[70]

[67] Joined Cases C188/10 and C189/10 *Melki* [2010] (n 63) para 52.

[68] Joined Cases C188/10 and C189/10 *Melki* [2010] (n 63) para 53.

[69] See X Magnon, 'La QPC face au droit de l'Union : la brute, les bons et le truand' (2010) 84(4) *Revue Française de Droit Constitutionnel* 761 at 786.

[70] See Case *European Constitution* Declaration No 1/2004 (Spanish Constitutional Court, 13 December 2004). The literature on this leading decision is huge. Among others, see JL Cascajo Castro, 'Integración europea y constituciones nacionales' (2005) 1 *Revista d'estudis autonòmics i federals* 61; Del Valle Gálvez, JA, 'Constitution espagnole et Traité constitutionnel européen – La Déclaration du Tribunal Constitucional du 13 décembre 2004' (2005) 41(5–6) Cahiers de Droit Européen 705; B Mathieu, ‹Constitution européenne et constitutions nationales : l›habile

After having given some signs that their understanding of EC/EU law was changing (for example, Judgment No 58/2004), regarding Declaration No 1/2004 the Constitutional Court carried out a desired jurisprudential shift giving a new scope to Article 93 of the Spanish Constitution, which is the constitutional provision that establishes and allows European integration.[71]

28. In its legal reasoning, the Constitutional Court began by recalling that Article 93 [Spanish Constitution] was conceived in view of 'our integration into the European Communities'.[72] Then, as detailed below, it precludes its consid-

convergence des juges constitutionnels français et espagnol. À propos des décisions n° 2004-505 DC du Conseil constitutionnel français et 1/2004 DTC du Tribunal constitutionnel espagnol› 18 *Cahiers du Conseil Constitutionnel* 141; L Burgorgue-Larsen, 'La déclaration du 13 décembre 2004 (DTC n° /2004): "Un Solange II à l'espagnole"' (2005) *ibid* 154; A López Castillo, A Sáiz Arnáiz and V Ferreres Comella, *Constitución Española y Constitución Europea. Análisis de la Declaración del Tribunal Constitucional (DTC 1/2004, de 13 de diciembre)* (CEPC, Madrid, 2005); I Gómez Fernández, 'La Constitución Española "frente" al Tratado por el que se establece una Constitución para Europa: entre la necesidad y la conveniencia de una reforma constitucional' (2005) 14 *Revista Española de Derecho Europeo* 297; Martín y Pérez de Nanclares, J, 'La declaración 1/2004 del Tribunal Constitucional: un giro jurisprudencial en la concepción del artículo 93 de la Constitución española' (2005) 6 *Revista General de Derecho Europeo*; P Cruz Villalón, 'El Tratado según la constitución: tres planteamientos' in M Carrillo López and H López Bofill (eds), *La Constitución Europea : actas del III Congreso Nacional de Constitucionalistas de España* (Tirant, Valencia, 2006) 21; JM Areilza Carvajal, 'La inserción de España en la nueva Unión Europea: la relación entre la Constitución española y el Tratado constitucional. Comentario a la DTC 1/2004, de 13 de diciembre de 2004' (2005) 73 *Revista Española de Derecho Constitucional* 365; R Alonso García, 'Constitución Española y Constitución Europea: Guión para una colisión virtual y otros matices sobre el principio de primacía' *ibid* 339; R Alonso García, 'The Spanish Constitution and the European Constitution: the script for a virtual collision and other observations on the principle of primacy' (2005) 6(6) *German Law Journal* 1001; A López Castillo, 'La Unión Europea "en constitución" y la Constitución estatal en espera de reformas: a propósito de la DTC 1/2004, de 13 de diciembre de 2004' (2005) 15 *Teoría y realidad constitucional* 427; A López Castillo, 'La Unión Europea en "constitución" y la Constitución estatal en (espera) de reformas: A propósito de la DTC1/2004 de 13 de diciembre' in A López Castillo, A Sáiz Arnáiz and V Ferreres Comella (eds), *Constitución Española y Constitución Europea. Análisis de la Declaración del Tribunal Constitucional (DTC 1/2004, de 13 de diciembre)* (CEPC, Madrid, 2005) 13; C Plaza, 'The Constitution for Europe and the Spanish Constitutional Court' (2006) 12(3) *European Public Law* 253; A Rodríguez, '¿Quién debe ser el defensor de la Constitución española? comentario a la DTC 1/2004, de 13 de diciembre' (2005) 5 *Revista de Derecho Constitucional Europeo* 327; and P Pérez Tremps and A Sáiz Arnaiz, 'Spain's Ratification of the Treaty Establishing a Constitution for Europe: Prior Constitutional Review, Referendum and Parliamentary Approval' in A Albi and J Ziller (eds), *The European Constitution and national constitutions: ratification and beyond* (Kluwer, Alphen aan den Rijn, 2007) 45.

[71] On Judgment No 58/2004 (Spanish Constitutional Court, 19 April 2004), see JI Ugartemendia Eceizabarrena, 'El "recurso" a la prejudicial (234 TCE) como "cuestión" de amparo. A propósito de la' (2004) 11 *Revista Española de Derecho Europeo* 441; and A Mangas Martín, *La Constitución Europea* (Iustel, Madrid, 2005) 167, where the author celebrates the change in the interpretation of Art 93 of the Spanish Constitution (the 'Spanish European clause').

[72] This very same article has been used (after being dismissed to articulate the accession of Spain into NATO) for the ratification of the Treaty on the International Criminal Court; see the Organic Law 6/2000 (4 October 2000). Some scholars have argued this very exceptional use of Art 93 to exclude it from being the 'Spanish European clause'. See A Sáiz Arnáiz, 'De primacía, supremacía y derechos fundamentales en la Europea integrada: la Declaración del Tribunal Constitucional de 13 de diciembre de 2004 y el Tratado por el que se establece una Constitución para Europa' in A López Castillo, A Sáiz Arnáiz and V Ferreres Comella (eds), *Constitución Española y Constitución*

eration as the mere provision of 'organic-procedural nature' according to Judgment No 28/1991 and states that integration goes beyond this mere procedure, since it means 'the integration into a different supranational entity' that creates a specific legal order guided by its principles (Declaration No 1/2004, para 2).[73] Then, the Court recalls, as it already did in Declaration No 1/1992, paragraph 4 (although with no relevance), that the 'complexity' involved in Article 93 'is not insignificant', but it is necessary to 'keep deepening to respond to the request' made by the Government. Article 93 [Spanish Constitution] is now qualified by the Constitutional Court as the ultimate foundation of Spain's incorporation to the European integration process and its entailment to EC/EU law, in addition to being 'a provision of "organic-procedural nature" (Judgment No 28/1991, paragraph 4 and Declaration No 1/1992, paragraph 4)'.[74]

The Constitutional Court was preparing itself to make its very own 'Copernican revolution' stating that 'this was the only dimension considered in the above statement only to determine, in response to the question raised then, whether Article 93 [Spanish Constitution] was the appropriate mechanism to put forth an exception on the limit established by Article 13.2 [Spanish Constitution]'.[75] That is, in the case of Declaration No 1/1992, whether in a contradiction between former Article 8 B TEC and Article 13.2 of the Constitution, Article 93 incorporated or not 'a review channel equivalent to the constitutional amendments procedures contained in Part X EC'.[76] In short, the Constitutional Court justifies its prior understanding of Article 93 in accordance with the needs of the moment and assumes that Declaration No 1/2004 'operates in a very different context', because now there is not 'a contradiction

Europea. Análisis de la Declaración del Tribunal Constitucional (DTC 1/2004, de 13 de diciembre) (CEPC, Madrid, 2005) 51 at 55. In favour of this 'European clause', see I Gómez Fernández, 'La Constitución Española "frente" al Tratado por el que se establece una Constitución para Europa: entre la necesidad y la conveniencia de una reforma constitucional' (2005) 14 *Revista Española de Derecho Europeo* 297 at 298.

[73] On the characterization of Art 93 as being of 'organic-procedural nature', see Judgment No 28/1991 (Spanish Constitutional Court, 14 February 1991) para 4(4) and the subsequent *Maastricht* Decision No 1/1992 (Spanish Constitutional Court, 1 July 1992) para 4, largely criticized by the Spanish scholarship. See A Mangas Martín, 'La Constitución y la ley ante el Derecho comunitario (Comentario a la sentencia del Tribunal Constitucional español 28/1991, de 14 de febrero, sobre la Ley Orgánica del Régimen Electoral General y el Acta relativa a las elecciones al Parlamento Europeo)' (1987) 14(2) *Revista de Instituciones Europeas* 587; A Mangas Martín, 'La Declaración del Tribunal Constitucional sobre el artículo 13.2 de la Constitución: una reforma constitucional innecesaria o insuficiente' (1992) 44(2) *Revista Española de Derecho Internacional* 381; DJ Liñán Nogueras and A Mangas Martín, *Instituciones y Derecho de la Unión Europea* 4th edn (Tecnos, Madrid, 2004) 512.

[74] See Case *European Constitution* (2004) (n 70) para 2; P Pérez Tremps, *Constitución Española y Comunidad Europea* (Civitas, Madrid 1994) 36–7 and A Jimenez-Blanco Carrillo de Albornoz, 'Notas a la Sentencia 64/1991, de 22 de marzo (Asunto APESCO)' (1994) 118 *Noticias de la Unión Europea* 63 at 63–4.

[75] The expression 'Copernican revolution' has been used by J Martín y Pérez de Nanclares, 'La declaración 1/2004 del Tribunal Constitucional: un giro jurisprudencial en la concepción del artículo 93 de la Constitución española' (2005) 6 *Revista General de Derecho Europeo* at 7.

[76] Case *European Constitution* (2004) (n 70) para 2.

with the text' of a constitutional rule.[77] Article 93 shall, therefore, be from now on the 'ultimate basis' of integration that, besides, 'acts as a hinge by which the Constitution itself gives entry into our constitutional system to other legal orders through the transfer of the exercise of powers' (paragraph 2).[78] That is how the Court 'confers Article 93 [Spanish Constitution] a substantive or material dimension that can not be ignored' (Declaration No 1/2004 paragraph 2). Thus, the new structure of Article 93 would be completed, to whose 'organic-procedural' nature should be now add (not replace) a new substantive scope clearly of much greater significance than the previous one.

29. The 'accepted order' which is EC/EU law shall be in conformity with the 'basic principles and values' of the Spanish Constitution.[79] That is, the 'inevitable limits to the sovereign powers of the state' that cause the transfer of the exercise of powers and the consequent integration of European order into the national one can only be acceptable to the extent that the supranational organization and its law are 'consistent with fundamental principles of social and democratic state of law established by the national Constitution'. The Constitutional Court, thus, recognizes that the substantive nature of Article 93 implies the existence of material limits to integration. Indeed, those limits would not be 'expressly contained' in the aforementioned article, 'but they are implicitly derived from the Constitution and the essential meaning of the provision itself' (Declaration No 1/2004, paragraph 2):

> Those material limits, not expressly contained in the constitutional provision, but that are implicitly derived from the Constitution and the essential meaning of the provision itself, are the respect for state sovereignty, our basic constitutional structures and value systems and fundamental principles established in our Constitution, where fundamental rights acquire their own substantivity (Article 10.1 [Spanish Constitution]).[80]

Nevertheless, as established by the Court:

> In the inconceivable case that in the subsequent circumstances that European Union law were irreconcilable with the Spanish Constitution, without the hypothetical excesses of European law on the European Constitution would be remedied by the

[77] See on this point A Sáiz Arnáiz, 'De primacía, supremacía y derechos fundamentales en la Europea integrada: la Declaración del Tribunal Constitucional de 13 de diciembre de 2004 y el Tratado por el que se establece una Constitución para Europa' in A López Castillo, A Sáiz Arnáiz and V Ferreres Comella (eds), *Constitución Española y Constitución Europea. Análisis de la Declaración del Tribunal Constitucional (DTC 1/2004, de 13 de diciembre)* (CEPC, Madrid, 2005) 51 at 56.

[78] See I Gómez Fernández, 'La Constitución Española "frente" al Tratado por el que se establece una Constitución para Europa: entre la necesidad y la conveniencia de una reforma constitucional' (2005) 14 *Revista Española de Derecho Europeo* 297 at 298.

[79] The need for respecting the 'principles and basic values' of the Constitution is repeated in paras 2 and 3 of Case *European Constitution* (2004) (n 70).

[80] Those limits are 'respected' as the Spanish Constitutional Court argues (Case *European Constitution* (2004) (n 70) para 2).

ordinary channels provided by it, as a last resort the preservation of the sovereignty of the Spanish people and the supremacy of the Constitution could lead this Court to address the issues that may arise, that from the current perspective are deemed non-existent, through the constitutional procedures required, all besides that the safeguard of that sovereignty is always ultimately guaranteed by the [possible withdrawal of the Union], a true counterpoint . . . [of the primacy principle of EC/EU law].

30. That is to say, although the Spanish Constitution is silent about the existence of some specific *controlimiti* (unlike the German case), the Spanish Constitutional Court itself has specified them in respect of state sovereignty (a concept difficult to define), basic constitutional structures and the system of fundamental values and principles established in the Constitution. In fact, it seems that the Spanish Highest interpreter has rescued the classical principles that private law includes in the concept of 'public order' and under which it precludes the application of foreign law contrary to the fundamental principles of the legal order of the country whose courts are aware of the matter.[81] These fundamental principles would refer to those that guarantee the legal cohesion of society of the state concerned and among which private law include rules of a constitutional nature derived from the national Constitution itself, EC/EU law, general international law but also from ordinary law. The difficulty, then, is the same as in the case of public law; public order is a concept that encompasses a set of principles that will be specified by the courts on a case-by-case basis.[82]

31. Returning to the above-mentioned limitations set as *controlimiti* by the Spanish Constitutional Court, the primacy of EC/EU law would not affect the supremacy of the Constitution, since the primacy of EC/EU law would be based on constitutional supremacy. Similarly, within the competences transferred to the EU, the Constitution would prevent the application of national law contrary to an EC/EU act regulating this particular area.[83] In this sense, the primacy principle would be closer to a specific nature of competence principle that would allow us to choose, between two equally valid rules within their respective jurisdictions, the applicable law whether we are or not under the scope of the powers of the European Union.[84]

[81] See AL Calvo Caravaca and J Carrascosa González, *Derecho Internacional Privado* (Comares, Granada, 2008) 348–70; and A Bucher, 'L'Ordre public et le But social des Lois en Droit international privé' (1994) 239 (1993-II) *Recueil des Cours de l'Académie de Droit International de La Haye* 9.

[82] AL Calvo Caravaca and J Carrascosa González, *Derecho Internacional Privado* (Comares, Granada, 2008) 357–60.

[83] See Del Valle Gálvez, JA, 'Constitution espagnole et Traité constitutionnel européen – La Déclaration du Tribunal Constitucional du 13 décembre 2004' (2005) 41(5–6) *Cahiers de Droit Européen* 705.

[84] JP Jacqué, 'Droit constitutionnel national, Droit communautaire, CEDH, Charte des Nations Unies. L'instabilité des rapports de système entre ordres juridiques' (2007) 60 *Revue Française de Droit Constitutionnel* 3 at 15, who revisits arguments already developed in JP Jacqué, 'A propos de la guerre des juges: accords et désaccords entre le juge français et la Cour de justice des Communautés

However, there are some who have lately been supporting a sort of decentralization of the control of legality of EC/EU acts. Indeed, as pointed out by Professor Pérez Tremps, some are in favour of extending the constitutional internal control mechanisms to the EC/EU validity judgement of the internal rules that develop or implement EC/EU law.[85] Thus, equating the violation by the internal regulation implementing an EC/EU legal act to a violation of the Constitution, the Constitutional Court could intervene and expel from the Spanish legal order the relevant internatal act dissenting with the EC/EU legal order.[86] The question is far from being peaceful and only the Italian Constitutional Court has accepted so far – really cautiously – this possibility in the case of a regional law on planting vineyards.[87] But maybe the Spanish Constitutional Court is moving in this direction. In a recent and historical shift from its previous case law, it has decided to refer to the ECJ a preliminary ruling dealing with the implementation of the EAW.[88]

32. Whatever the degree of openness of the constitutional judges of the Member States in relation to EC/EU law, the foundation of their respective case law is the same. The primacy of EC/EU law finds its origin and legitimacy in the national Constitution itself. Therefore, that primacy could not go against, at least, certain rules contained in the National Fundamental Text. The differences between some jurisdictions and others lay in the protected constitutional rules, from all the express provisions to certain structural principles including fundamental rights.[89]

européennes› (1981) 1981(4) *Revue administrative de l'Est de la France* 5 at 29.

[85] P Pérez Tremps, 'La jurisdicción constitucional y la integración europea' (2009) 29 *Revista Española de Derecho Europeo* 19 at 44–5.

[86] This is the current opinion of the Spanish Council of State (the supreme consultative body of the Government). See Consejo de Estado, *Informe del Consejo de Estado sobre la inserción del Derecho europeo en el ordenamiento español*, E 1/2007 (14 February 2008) available at <http://www.consejo-estado.es/pdf/Europa.pdf> at 360–3. An analysis of this report may be found in MP Andrés Sáez de Santamaría, *El informe del Consejo de Estado sobre la inserción del Derecho europeo en el ordenamiento español: texto del informe, estudios y ponencias* (Consejo de Estado, CEPC, 2008).

[87] Case *Umbrian Vineyards* Decision No 384/1994 (Italian Constitutional Court 7–10 November 1994) (n 34). See A Sáiz Arnáiz, 'El Derecho Comunitario, ¿parámetro de la constitucionalidad de las leyes internas? (a propósito de la sentencia nº 384 de 1994, de la Corte Costituzionale italiana)' (1995) 22(2) *Revista de Instituciones Europeas* 571 at 585–91; R Alonso García, 'Los tribunales constitucionales y el control del Derecho interno conectado con el comunitario' (2005) 2 Foro: *Revista de ciencias jurídicas y sociales* 153; I Gómez Fernández, *Conflicto y Cooperación entre la Constitución y el Derecho Internacional* (Tirant, Valencia, 2005) 397.

[88] See pending Case No 6922-2008 (Spanish Constitutional Court, 9 June 2011).

[89] On this point, see P Pérez Tremps, 'La jurisdicción constitucional y la integración europea' (2009) 29 *Revista Española de Derecho Europeo* 19 at 26–40.

2

The Attempted Reconciliation

1. The study of the case law of the ECJ and of the national jurisdictions reveals the existence of theoretical and antagonists' estimates in relation to the source of the primacy and the regulatory status of national constitutional law. In all Member States there are, to continue with the expression that has become so popular, 'counterlimits'.[1] Although we can say that this concept (or the idea it represents) is commonly shared, the differences come to light when specifying the scope of these limits. However, this issue, although very important from a conceptual standpoint and despite formal and substantive problems, such as the procedural means to enforce its limits or exact coverage, it would be 'hardly conceivable', given the extension of the powers of the EU, for it to take place between this supranational law and the constitutional provisions relating to the institutional structure of Member States.[2] However, the most troubling problem would concern a possible conflict with fundamental rights in a broad sense, that is, including guarantees issued from citizenship.

The different conceptions of primacy according to the ECJ and national courts could have led to serious conflicts. However, until now there have been only a few alerts in the form of positioning by the main actors and the consequences of this construction have never been enforced, which shows their basically symbolic-constitutional nature, although there are important voices claiming its application.[3] This coexistence among the different legal orders is possible through mutual restraint by the parties involved, the national and EU judges. In this regard, as noted by former Advocate General, now judge of the

[1] Among the latest states to access the EU, Estonia, for instance, has included the so-called 'counter-limits' within its Constitution. See the *Law amending the Estonian Constitution*, Official Journal RT I 64 429 (10 October 2003); F De Montalvo Jääskeläinen, 'Constitución de Estonia' (2005) 65 *Revista de las Cortes Generales* 219.

[2] The expression 'hardly conceivable' was used by the Spanish Constitutional Court in its Decision No 1/2004 para 4.

[3] P Pérez Tremps, 'La jurisdicción constitucional y la integración europea' (2009) 29 *Revista Española de Derecho Europeo* 19 at 39. Among those who claim the need for the use of these safeguard clauses one can find the former president of the German Constitutional Court. See R Herzog and L Gerken, *Stop the European Court of Justice* (Centrum für Europäische Politik, 2008); R Herzog and L Gerken. 'The Spirit of the Time: Revise the European Constitution to Protect National Parliamentary Democracy' (2007) 3(2) *European Constitutional Law Review* 209; and the reply of K Hänsch, 'The Spirit of the Time: A Reply to Roman Herzog and Lüder Gerken', *ibid*, 219.

ECJ, Antonio Tizzano:

> [E]very system tends to search for points of convergence – and sometimes even of compromise – among the various jurisdictional authorities . . . It is indeed true that . . . [the ECJ and the national constitutional court] are bound by a principle of identity as well as by an intrinsic coherence of their own; but it is also true that so far, all have shown great sensitivity with overall system requirements and their harmony.[4]

However, without underestimating the essential role played by judges through that kind of dialogue or attitude of mutual deference they practise (and which we will discuss in more detail below), the absence of major conflicts is also due to other factors.[5]

1. THE CONCILIATORY ATTITUDE OF THE EU AND NATIONAL AUTHORITIES

1.1. The Prior Control of Constitutionality

2. At the national level, prevention of conflicts is derived, first, from the precautions adopted before the ratification of the successive reforms of the EU treaties. Verification by the constitutional judge, in those states that have this possibility, compatibility between the national Constitution and the treaties, as well as possible constitutional amendments removing any incompatibilities, allow the avoidance *ab initio* of the causes of conflict. On the other hand, the EC/EU lawmaker is receptive to the possible exceptions of unconstitutionality that Member States shall submit during the legislative process. Thus, even when it could hide behind the primacy of EC/EU law and ignore the arguments submitted by the states, the final result shows that, by contrast, it adopts a conciliatory attitude and echoes the concerns of the state. Certainly, this remedy of aprioristic nature is not an absolute guarantee, since the interpretation of constitutional provisions may evolve. All this without the special ability of lawyers to discover conflicts and antinomies where at first glance there are none.[6]

[4] See A Tizzano, 'La protection des droits fondamentaux en Europe : la Cour de justice et les juridictions constitutionnelles nationales' (2006) 1 *Revue du Droit de l'Union Européenne* 9 at 9.

[5] See AM Slaughter, A Stone Sweet and JHH Weiler, *The European Courts and National Courts. Doctrine and Jurisprudence. Legal change in its social context* (Hart, Oxford, 1998), especially A Stone Sweet, 'Constitutional Dialogues in the European Community' in AM Slaughter, A Stone Sweet and JHH Weiler (eds), *The European Courts and National Courts. Doctrine and Jurisprudence. Legal change in its social context* (Hart, Oxford, 1998) 305; and M Cartabia, 'Europe and Rights: Taking Dialogue Seriously' (2009) 5(1) *European Constitutional Law Review* 5.

[6] See the opinion of the then Director of the Legal Service of the Council in a doctrinal paper, JP Jacqué, 'Droit constitutionnel national, Droit communautaire, CEDH, Charte des Nations Unies. L'instabilité des rapports de système entre ordres juridiques' (2007) 60 *Revue Française de Droit Constitutionnel* 3 at 16.

1.2. The Community of Values between the Union and the Member States

3. The second element of conciliation that shall be appointed refers to the fact that, after long evolution, nowadays it is possible to say that there is a community of values established between the Member States and the EU, limiting the chances for conflict.[7] One could say that this process began with the first case law of the German Constitutional Court, followed by the protection of fundamental rights through case law developed by the ECJ (see below), which then ended up being inserted into the text of treaties (Articles 6 TEU and TEU-L), up to the Charter of Fundamental Rights of the European Union. Indeed, the Charter states the following in its preamble:

> The peoples of Europe, in creating an ever closer union among them, are resolved to share a peaceful future based on common values.
>
> . . .
>
> The Union contributes to the preservation and to the development of these common values while respecting the diversity of the cultures and traditions of the peoples of Europe.[8]

Indeed, although until the entry into force of the Lisbon Treaty the Charter did not have the same value as the treaties, that did not mean that it has not deployed any legal effects.[9]

In this regard, Article 6.1 TEU established:

> The Union is founded on the principles of liberty, democracy, respect for human rights and fundamental freedoms and the rule of law, principles which are common to the Member States.

On the other hand, the new Article 2 of the Treaty on European Union as amended by Lisbon (TEU-L), taking up some of the content of Article 6.1 TEU, provides:

> The Union is founded on the values of respect for human dignity, freedom, democracy, equality, the rule of law and respect for human rights, including the rights of persons belonging to minorities. These values are common to the Member States in a society in which pluralism, non-discrimination, tolerance, justice, solidarity and equality between women and men prevail.

[7] See P Magnette, *Le régime politique de l'Union européenne* (Presses de sciences-politiques, Paris, 2003) at 234 and JP Jacqué, 'Les principes constitutionnels fondamentaux dans le Projet de Traité établissant la Constitution Européenne› in LS Rossi (ed), *Vers une nouvelle architecture de l'Union européenne: le projet de Traité Constitution* (Bruylant, Bruxelles, 2004) 47.

[8] The Charter of Fundamental rights has been solemnly proclaimed first on 7 December 2000 and second on 12 December 2007 (OJ C83/389, 30 March 2010).

[9] S Peers and A Ward (eds) *The European Union Charter of Fundamental Rights. Politics, Law and Policy* (Hart, Oxford, 2004). On the legal value of the Charter (before and after the Lisbon Treaty), see below.

4. Not long ago, as previously mentioned, the German Constitutional Court in its decision in the *Bananenmarktordnung* (or *Bananas*) case widely assumed the existence of these shared common values and limited considerably the chances of an appeal before that institution based on the breach of fundamental rights guarantees by an EC provision.[10] It is true that the evolution of EC/EU law, started in this field by the ECJ, was not innocent. By assuming the concerns regarding fundamental rights aired by, among others, the German Constitutional Court, the Court wanted to gain legitimacy and authority to preserve the primacy of EC law and its uniform application. This attitude of the Luxembourg Court has most recently been demonstrated by its decision in the *Kadi and Al Barakaat* case of 2008, delivered after the clarion call given by the European Court of Human Rights in its opinion on the *Bosphorus* case of 2005.[11]

1.3. The Attitude of Deference and Reconciliation Adopted by the Courts

5. Thirdly, mutual restraint of the EC/EU and national courts has played an essential role. Indeed, if national judges have established 'counterlimits' to primacy, so far they have not been invoked, apart from a few caveats concerning demarcation of territory.[12] Thus, constitutional courts in Europe have taken a position on the primacy of EC/EU law that could be synthesized in the generally accepted rule as a starting principle, the existence of some limits, ways of collaboration to enable coexistence and, finally, the last clause being reserved for the highest interpreters of the national Constitution.[13]

Thus, in principle, as a general rule, the primacy of EC/EU law in the national sphere is accepted. However, this is not an unconditional approval, but is subject to certain limitations derived from the national Constitution. The Constitution, referring to the terminology used by the Spanish Constitutional Court, would enjoy ultimate supremacy, that is, EC/EU law could not modify it. However, EC/EU law is often the instigator of certain national constitutional reforms, promoted by national authorities, on the evidence of blatant contradictions, to reconcile the constitutional legitimacy to the achievement of European integration. In any case, there would always be certain constitutional principles and values (which French doctrine calls 'hard core' or *noyeau dur*)

[10] See the Case *Bananenmarktordnung* (2000) 2 BvL 1/97 BVerfGE 102 147 (German Constitutional Court, 7 June 2000) paras 161–64 and the comments of I Pernice, 'Les bananes et les droits fondamentaux : la Cour constitutionnelle allemande fait le point' (2001) 37(3–4) *Cahiers de Droit Européen* 427; and J Callewaert, 'Les droits fondamentaux entre cours nationales et européennes' (2001) 48 *Revue Trimestrielle des Droits de l'Homme* 1183.

[11] Case *Bosphorus Hava Yolları Turizm ve Ticaret Anonim irketi v Ireland* App No 45036/98 (ECtHR, 30 June 2005, 2005-VI) and Joined Cases C-402/05 P and C-415/05 P *Kadi* and *Al Barakaat International Foundation v Council* [2008] ECR I-6351. These two leading decisions and their implications will be largely analysed below.

[12] See the *Solange* saga at the German Constitutional Court.

[13] See P Pérez Tremps, 'La jurisdicción constitucional y la integración europea' (2009) 29 *Revista Española de Derecho Europeo* 19 at 27–28.

which would be irrevocable, meaning that no case could be affected by EC/EU law. From these assumptions, there are basically two ways of collaboration. The first, the prime example of which has been the *Solange* case law of the *Bundesverfassungsgericht*, assumes the principle that there is an equivalent level of protection of these principles and basic values shared by both EC/EU and national orders. Secondly, the integration process leads national legal order, including the Constitution, to be interpreted in accordance with EC/EU law. But finally, in case of conflict, that is, if the EU law violates these principles and basic constitutional values, the constitutional jurisdiction reserves itself the right to intervene by controlling the constitutionality of EC/EU provisions.[14]

6. On the other hand, the ECJ has adopted a constructive attitude. Thus, in the *Kreil* case, in which the heart of the matter was a German constitutional provision prohibiting women from working in armed military units, the Luxembourg Court showed a cautious attitude.[15] Indeed, it recalled the principle of non-discrimination in access to work, but was careful to highlight the potential conflict between EC law and the national Constitution (an argument which, however, the German Government used), and brought the issue back towards the relationship between Community law and national ordinary law, avoiding an insistence on the possible antinomy of constitutional origin. On the other hand, the German authorities got the message implicit in the opinion and adapted their constitutional order, modifying the relevant provision of the Basic Law.[16] But what is important to stress is that the ECJ used all the resources available to avoid potential conflicts.

7. In the *Schmidberger* case, the ECJ had to rule on a national decision that authorized a demonstration whose implementation seriously affected the free movement of goods on a national highway.[17] The case concerned, therefore, a

[14] *Ibid* at 27–28, where Professor Pérez Tremps states the fundamental principles on which national Constitutional Courts base their position vis-à-vis EU law. Those principles are developed at 28–40. See also M Kumm. 'The Jurisprudence of Constitutional Conflict: Constitutional Supremacy in Europe before and after the Constitutional Treaty' (2005) 11(3) *European Law Journal* 262 at 282–304.

[15] Case C-285/98 *Tanja Kreil v Germany* [2000] ECR I-69. On this case, see HW Laubinger and U Repkewitz, 'Freiwilliger Waffendienst von Frauen in der Bundeswehr' (2000) 91 *Verwaltungsarchiv* 297; JA Kämmerer, 'Gleichberechtigung am Gewehr' (2000) 2000(1) *Europarecht* 102; J Langer, 'Case C-273/97, *Angela Maria Sirdar v The Army Board, Secretary of State for Defence*. Case C-285/98, *Tanja Kreil v Germany*' (2000) 37(6) *Common Market Law Review* 1433; and J Gerkrath, 'Le principe de l'égalité de traitement et l'accès des femmes aux emplois dans les unités armées dans la Bundeswehr' (2000) Décembre, *Europe* 5.

[16] MA Martín Vida, 'La reforma del artículo 12a de la Ley Fundamental de Bonn a raíz de la Sentencia "Kreil" del Tribunal de Justicia' (2004) 1 *Revista de Derecho Constitucional Europeo* 357.

[17] Case C-112/00 *Schmidberger v Austria* [2003] ECR I-5659 paras 79–80. See A Rigaux and D Simon, 'Entraves résultant d'actes de particuliers' (2003) Août–Septembre, *Europe* 15; C Brown, 'Case C-112/00, *Eugen Schmidberger, Internationale Transporte und Planzuge v Austria*' (2003) 40(6) *Common Market Law Review* 1499; L González Vaqué, 'El difícil equilibrio entre la libre circulación de mercancías y los derechos fundamentales en materia de libertad de expresión y de reunión: la sentencia "Schmidberger"' (2003) 227 *Gaceta Jurídica de la Unión Europea y de la*

conflict between freedom of movement, guaranteed by the EC Treaty, and the rights to freedom of expression and freedom of peaceful assembly guaranteed by the Austrian Constitution, but also by EC/EU law, particularly through the ECHR interpretation of these rights according to the Court of Strasbourg, which were to be taken into account by the ECJ case law. However, EC/EU law required respect for fundamental rights as guaranteed by Article 6 TEU, both to the EU authorities and to Member States when implementing EC/EU law. Indeed, Article 6.2 TEU stated:

> The Union shall respect fundamental rights, as guaranteed by the European Convention for the Protection of Human Rights and Fundamental Freedoms signed in Rome on 4 November 1950 and as they result from the constitutional traditions common to the Member States, as general principles of Community law.[18]

On the other hand, Article 6.3 TEU-L provides:

> Fundamental rights, as guaranteed by the European Convention for the Protection of Human Rights and Fundamental Freedoms and as they result from the constitutional traditions common to the Member States, shall constitute general principles of the Union's law.

In this case, the fact that fundamental rights concerned were also recognized by EC/EU law and the national Constitution made the solution of the dispute easier because Austria would have done nothing but to apply some rights – freedom of expression and assembly – guaranteed by EC/EU law in relation to the implementation of a freedom also guaranteed under the EC Treaty, which in this case was the free movement of goods. This conflict between one of the four EC fundamental freedoms and fundamental rights was solved by pondering the interests at stake and taking into account the wide margin of appreciation of national authorities. So, in this particular situation the restriction of intra-community exchanges was not proportionate regarding the legitimate objective of protecting fundamental rights.

8. However, the ECJ went further in the *Omega* case, in which the respect for human dignity was compromised in a Member State in which that principle has a special constitutional protection.[19] Indeed, paragraph 1 of Article 1 of the German Basic Law is very clear when it establishes that 'human dignity shall be

Competencia 61; F Ronkes Agerbeek, 'Freedom of expression in the Brenner corridor: the *Schmidberger* case' (2004) 29(2) *European Law Review* 255; and A Alemanno, 'À la recherche d'un juste équilibre entre libertés fondamentales et droits fondamentaux dans le cadre du marché intérieur' (2004) 2004(4) *Revue du Droit de l'Union Européenne* 709.

[18] The issue of fundamental rights and EU will be developed below.

[19] Case C-36/02 *Omega Spielhallen- und Automatenaufstellungs- GmbH v Oberbürgermeisterin der Bundesstadt Bonn* [2004] ECR I-9609. See *ibid* and T Ackermann, 'Case C-36/02, *Omega Spielhallen- und Automatenaufstellungs - GmbH v Oberburgermeisterin der Bundesstadt Bonn*' (2005) 42(4) *Common Market Law Review* 1107, M Bulterman and HR Kranenborg, 'What if rules on free movement and human rights collide? About laser games and human dignity: the Omega case' (2006) 31(1) *European Law Review* 93.

inviolable. To respect and protect it shall be the duty of all state authority.' Moreover, this principle is protected by the intangibility clause of Article 79 of the fundamental text which prohibits any constitutional amendment that could affect it.[20] The Federal Republic considered that the organization of laser tag games in which participants shoot each other was a threat to public order and undermined a fundamental value established in the Constitution, such as human dignity. However, respect for human dignity is a principle which was protected by EC/EU law, although the broad concept of dignity that the German law had was not shared by other Member States who, moreover, saw no problem in the practice of such games.[21] Thus, the ECJ had to determine whether a restriction on freedom to provide services based on a purely national conception of a fundamental right guaranteed by EC/EU law was admissible. The ECJ admitted that the concept of public order could vary from one state to another and that Member States enjoy in this regard a discretion that is, in turn, subject to a proportionality control. Thus, in the words of the Luxembourg Court:

> It is not indispensable in that respect for the restrictive measure issued by the authorities of a Member State to correspond to a conception shared by all Member States as regards the precise way in which the fundamental right or legitimate interest in question is to be protected. . . .
>
> On the contrary, as is apparent from well-established case-law subsequent to Schindler, the need for, and proportionality of, the provisions adopted are not excluded merely because one Member State has chosen a system of protection different from that adopted by another State.[22]

Thus, national interpretations of fundamental rights would be equally protected and respected by EC/EU law, although the ECJ also reserves the right to control the proportionality of the measures.

[20] Article 79.3 of the German Constitution says: 'Amendments to this Basic Law affecting the division of the Federation into Länder, their participation on principle in the legislative process, or the principles laid down in Articles 1 and 20 shall be inadmissible'. Note that the human dignity principle is included in Art 1. On the constitutional concept of dignity, see P Häberle, *El Estado constitucional* (H Fix-Fierro (tr)) (UNAM, México, 2001) 169–78, where the author identifies human dignity with the very essence of democracy; and E Benda, 'Dignidad humana y derechos de la personalidad' in A López Pina (tr), C Hesse and others (eds), *Manual de Derecho Constitucional* 2nd edn (Marcial Pons-IVAP, Madrid, 2001) 117 at 124–6.

[21] On the protection of human dignity by EC/EU law, see Case C-377/98 *Netherlands v Parliament and Council* [2001] ECR I-7079. For a comment, see C Maubernard, 'Le "droit fondamental à la dignité humaine" en droit communautaire : la brevetabilité du vivant à l'épreuve de la jurisprudence de la Cour dejustice des Communautés européennes' (2003) 14(54) *Revue Trimestrielle des Droits de l'Homme* 483 and TM Spranger, 'Case C-377/98, *Kingdom of the Netherlands v European Parliament and Council of the European Union*, Judgment of the Full Court of 9 October 2001, [2001] ECR I-7079' (2002) 39(5) *Common Market Law Review* 1147.

[22] Case C-36/02 *Omega* (n 19) paras 37–38. At para 41, the ECJ concluded that 'Community law does not preclude an economic activity consisting of the commercial exploitation of games simulating acts of homicide from being made subject to a national prohibition measure adopted on grounds of protecting public policy by reason of the fact that that activity is an affront to human dignity'.

2. THE CODIFICATION OF THE INTERORDINAL RELATIONS PRINCIPLES

9. Despite the best efforts of the national constitutional courts and the ECJ, these complicated solutions do not always offer the certainty and legal security sought by the defendant and there comes a time when it is necessary that the relations between different systems are subject to some form of positive regulation by the constituent power. On this issue, the so-called European Constitution, or rather, the Constitutional Treaty, included a number of useful clarifications. After its failure, some of these innovations were undertaken by the Lisbon Treaty, which entered into force, after a long dénouement, in December 2009.

2.1. The Constitutional Treaty or the So-called European Constitution

10. Regarding the relationship between Community and national order, the Constitutional Treaty tried to reconcile the EU's and the national approach recognizing, on the one hand, the primacy of EU law (Article I-6) but on the other, assuming a number of limitations inspired by the 'counterlimits' which, after decades of jurisprudential developments, established the national constitutional jurisdictions (Article I-5).

2.1.1. The Principle of Primacy in the Constitutional Treaty

11. Article I-6 of the European Constitutional Treaty, entitled 'Union law', provided:

> The Constitution and law adopted by the institutions of the Union in exercising competences conferred on it shall have primacy over the law of the Member States.[23]

At the insistence of the British Government, the Intergovernmental Conference that drafted the Treaty included a Declaration (No 1) regarding the said provision stating the following:

> The Conference notes that Article I-6 reflects existing case-law of the Court of Justice of the European Communities and of the Court of First Instance.

This statement of Declaration No 1 throws almost more shadows than light on the question. The simple referral to the CFI/ECJ case law does not explain what constitutes such case law. Moreover, insofar as Article I-6 established the primacy of the whole Union law, it necessarily adds a dimension to the primacy established in the case law that has always been, strictly speaking, limited to Community law, without being clear about to what extent the clause also affects non-EU pillars, which would have ceased to exist upon the entry into force of

[23] OJ C 310/12, 16 December 2004.

the Constitution.[24] In this sense, one might then ask two questions. First, the meaning of the codification of the primacy of EU law, and second, whether this meant some kind of breakthrough or innovation with respect to the status quo.[25]

2.1.1.1. The Implications of the Codification of the Principle of Primacy

12. A fundamental principle of international law states that in the relations between nations which are contracting parties to a treaty, the provisions of national law cannot override those set in the Treaty.[26] However, it does not seem that the Convention wanted to codify the general principle of international law. Rather, the Convention which drafted the Constitutional Treaty wanted to codify the internal supremacy that the ECJ drew up for the first time in its famous opinion of the *Costa v ENEL* case.[27] Thus, primary law (the Treaties) would prevail over the national law of states not only in international relations between states (which would be the consequence of the principle *pacta sunt servanda*), but also and especially in the internal relationships regarding the legal orders of each Member State, either the relationship between the state concerned and individuals (national or foreign) or in horizontal relationships between individuals. First, the primacy rule of EC law would be aimed at the legislative and executive bodies of the Member States, but let us not forget that this doctrine was mainly developed in the case of the definition of the role of the domestic judge. Similarly, there is little doubt that Article I-6, although not expressly referring to national courts, was primarily directed at them.[28]

13. Thus, this mandate addressed to national judges consisted of the obligation to disapply any domestic rule incompatible with any EU rule to be applied in a specific case submitted to the judge. The classic formulation of this rule appears in the *Simmenthal* case, in which the ECJ ruled that the national judge in charge of enforcing the provisions of EC/EU law is obliged to ensure the full effectiveness of those rules although in order to do so he had to disapply any

[24] See Editorial. 'The CFSP under the EU Constitutional Treaty – Issues of depillarization' (2005) 42(2), *ibid*, 325; PJ Kuijper, 'The evolution of the Third Pillar from Maastricht to the European Constitution: Institutional aspects' (2004) 41, *ibid*, 609; and H Su, 'Can Constitution-Building Advance European Integration? A Three-Pillared Institutionalist Analysis' (2004) 26(4) *Journal of European Integration* 353.

[25] Scholars have argued that the codification of this principle implied a qualitative change in its legal configuration. See T Öhlinger, 'Die Ratifikation des Verfassungsvertrages in Österreich – Anmerkungen zum konstitutionellen Gehalt des Verfassungsvertrages' in W Hummer and W Obwexer (eds), *Der Vertrag über eine Verfassung für Europa* (Nomos, Baden-Baden, 2007) 343.

[26] Case *Interpretation of the Convention Between Greece and Bulgaria Respecting Reciprocal Emigration, Signed at Neuilly-Sur-Seine on November 27th, 1919 (The Greco-Bulgarian "Communities")* Advisory Opinion No 17 (Permanent Court of International Justice 31 July 1930, Series B 17 1930, 3–46) at 32.

[27] Case 6/64 *Costa v ENEL* [1964] ECR-1141.

[28] B De Witte, 'Article I-6 – Le droit de l'Union' in L Burgorgue-Larsen, A Levade and F Picod (eds), *Traité établissant une Constitution pour l'Europe: commentaire article par article* (Bruylant, Bruxelles, 2007) 107 at 111.

conflicting provision of national law, even if they are subsequent.[29] But, as the aforementioned decision provides, this obligation would be limited to cases where national judges are responsible for implementing EC/EU law. Therefore, it can be deduced that there is a need for the national judge to apply EC/EU law in order to disregard incompatible national law.

14. In any case, the most controversial aspect of the ECJ's case law is that, according to this body, EC/EU law prevails over any provision of national law, whatever its nature or its position in the national legal hierarchy. Which means that from this perspective, the primacy of EC/EU law over national law would also be applied to the domestic constitutional provisions.[30] In this regard, the Permanent Court of International Justice already said long ago that 'a State cannot rely, as against another State, on the provisions of the latter's Constitution'.[31] Thus, in the case of the EU, the obligation to grant primacy to EC/EU law over national law would only have two valued exceptions. The first would be in those cases where the relevant EC/EU rule was incompatible with an international treaty concluded by the Member State concerned before its accession to the EU, a situation in which, moreover, the national government would be required to eliminate this pre-existing obligation.[32] The second exception would take place in the event that the EC/EU rule were, as such, contrary to a rule of international law that would be binding for the EC/EU and that would have direct effect.[33]

2.1.1.2. The Codification Effects of Primacy in the Intergovernmental Pillars

15. Article I-6 of the Constitutional Treaty did not strictly speaking reflect the case law of the Court rather than Community law, that is, the first pillar. However, the article referred to the EU law that, after the entry into force of the Constitutional Treaty, it could have incorporated Community law itself, but also the law of the intergovernmental pillars, namely, the rules of the EU Treaty and the acts of derived law regarding the second and third pillars of the Union. Since the distinction between Community law and Union law (both understood in the strict sense) would have disappeared with the entry into force of the Constitutional Treaty (as has happened with Lisbon), which merged and codified existing treaties into one, it seems clear that Article I-6 referred to the entire

[29] Case 106/77 *Simmenthal* [1978] ECR-629 para 24.

[30] Case 11/70 *Internationale Handelsgesellschaft mbH v Einfuhr- und Vorratsstelle für Getreide und Futtermittel* [1970] ECR-1125 para 3.

[31] Case *Treatment of Polish Nationals and Other Persons of Polish Origin or Speech in the Danzig Territory* Advisory Opinion No 23 (Permanent Court of International Justice 4 February 1932, Series A/B 44 1933, 3–46) 24.

[32] This rule, established by Art 307 TEC, was maintained in Art III-435 of the Constitutional Treaty. With the entry into force of the Lisbon Treaty its content is effective by means of its integration into Art 351 TFEU.

[33] On this specific question in particular and about the relationship between EU law and international law, see below.

and merged Law. This went beyond the ECJ's jurisprudence given that it did not have the opportunity to declare on the internal primacy of EU law, and some even deny that the doctrine of primacy could be applied to the Law of intergovernmental pillars which, according to their elaboration, would be closer to traditional international law.[34] However, in general terms, it is broadly accepted that international law allows national legal orders the freedom to recognize or not the internal direct effect to the conventional rules and, therefore, primacy, regardless of any possible international responsibility that may be incurred by the state.[35] On this issue, we should remember that when the ECJ established its doctrine on primacy in the *Costa v ENEL* case, it placed special emphasis on the particular nature of the Treaty on the European Economic Community in respect of any other international treaty. If the supranational nature of this treaty was an important reason to impose on national judges the duty to recognize its primacy in their respective domestic law, one could, at least, doubt that the ECJ reached the same conclusion in the case of the EU Treaty and the law derived from the second and third pillars.

16. However, it could also be argued that the decisive factor in establishing the primacy principle was the procedure of the preliminary ruling itself. Thus, while the Court acts within this preliminary ruling procedure, where a national court with a pending case participates, the expected outcome is that the ECJ will impose a precise obligation upon the national judge. In this logic, if the ECJ had to rule, in the course of a preliminary ruling, on what to do with the national provision inconsistent with a provision of EU law (in the strict sense), almost certainly it would proclaim the primacy of the relevant rule pertaining to the intergovernmental pillars. It could, therefore, be concluded that the primacy of EU law in its entirety was present, at least in essence, in the existing case law before Lisbon and that the ECJ has not had occasion to state it explicitly due to the particulars of the second and third pillars.[36] If this were the case, Article I-6 of the failed Constitutional Treaty would have reflected latent ECJ case law and the Declaration would thus be compatible with the text of that provision. Nevertheless, although this situation was more likely in the scope of

[34] Within the third pillar a kind of 'indirect (direct) effect' was theorized. See M Fletcher. 'Extending "indirect effect" to the third pillar: the significance of Pupino?' (2005) 30(6) *European Law Review* 862, D Sarmiento, 'Un paso más en la constitucionalización del Tercer Pilar de la Unión Europea. La Sentencia María Pupino y el efecto directo de las Decisiones marco' (2005) 10 *Revista Electrónica de Estudios Internacionales* 1. Others just think that the ECJ would automatically extend the classic principles of the first pillar to the policies once covered by the third pillar. See S Peers, 'Salvation outside the Church: Judicial protection in the third Pillar after the Pupino and Segi judgments' (2007) 44(4) *Common Market Law Review* 883 at 926–8 and PJ Kuijper, 'The evolution of the Third Pillar from Maastricht to the European Constitution: Institutional aspects' (2004) 41(2) *Common Market Law Review* 609 at 610–13.

[35] On this issue, see below.

[36] This opinion is sustained in B De Witte, 'Article I-6 – Le droit de l'Union' in L Burgorgue-Larsen, A Levade and F Picod (eds), *Traité établissant une Constitution pour l'Europe : commentaire article par article* (Bruylant, Bruxelles, 2007) 107 at 113.

the third pillar, in the case of the second pillar (the Common Foreign and Security Policy), in principle, their rules would not have been invoked before national courts and therefore would not benefit from the primacy.[37]

2.1.2. *The Limitations of the Principle of Primacy*

17. In the federal systems, the primacy of federal law is guaranteed by the fact that its application is mostly controlled by the federal courts. In the case of the EU this is not so, and for primacy to be indeed a reality it must be admitted and accepted by national courts, which are responsible for applying EC/EU law in the domestic sphere. In this sense, as self-imposed limitations, the Constitutional Treaty included the aforementioned Article I-5. In this provision, described by some people as 'rhetorical' and whose main mission was to prevent an 'against-states' drift of further dynamics of EU institutions, three dimensions can be identified: the equality of Member States, respect for their fundamental structural identity and respect for their essential functions.[38]

18. Regarding the first idea, the equality of Member States before the Constitution is a principle that was introduced at the request of Portugal, supported by all countries of medium and small size. This principle would be more of a statement or political commitment than a true vocation to deploy immediate legal effects, at least in the strict sense. We all know the difference between states when it comes to integrating the various institutions that have always existed and that would not have changed with the Constitutional Treaty (Malta does not elect the same number of MEPs as Germany). Certainly, according to the Constitutional Treaty, there was equality between Member States in decision-making procedures, at least in two cases – those cases requiring unanimity or when an initiative is open to accession by any Member State. However, the Constitutional Treaty greatly increased the number of situations in which the Council, for example, voted by an absolute majority to respect the status quo in Nice.[39]

19. On the other hand, the former requirement to respect the national identity of Member States was clarified twice in the Constitutional Treaty and it seemed that a structural design had to be inferred. It was, above all, about the identity 'inherent in their fundamental political and constitutional structures' of the Member States. Many members of the Convention which drafted the Constitutional Treaty also wanted that respect for regional and local identities to remain at the same level as national identities. Hence the addition of this provision regarding the

[37] As will be seen below, the ECJ established its competence to control the *ultra vires* of second pillar acts. See Case C-355/04 P *Segi v Council* [2007] ECR I-1657 and Case C-354/04 P *Gestoras Pro Amnistía v Council* [2007] ECR I-1579 at para 54 of both decisions.

[38] See M Blanquet, 'Article I-5 – Relations entre l'Union et les Etats membres' in L Burgorgue-Larsen, A Levade and F Picod (eds), *Traité établissant une Constitution pour l'Europe : commentaire article par article* (Bruylant, Bruxelles, 2007) 96 at 102–5.

[39] *Ibid* at 103.

local level, which would not, however, be the establishment of a specific type of local identity or protection outside their state structure, since the text refers only to local and regional autonomy as a single dimension, since protection of fundamental structures refers to national identity.[40]

20. Finally, respect for the 'essential State functions' is a more classic clause. Thus, Article I-5 belongs to the category of derogations traditionally registered in the treaties on which the Union is founded (public policy, public security . . .). Anyway, two features should be stressed. On the one hand, the essential functions mentioned in the precept (territorial integrity, maintenance of public order and safeguarding of national security) refer to a sovereigntist, liberal and minimal concept of the state. On the other hand, however, Article I-5 was not exhaustive, by providing '(. . .) including (. . .)'. This would allow identification of the essential state functions with a wide discretion and be open to the evolution of conceptions, maybe also leading to identification of new essential functions, as the ECJ did. Thus, for instance, the Luxembourg Court in the *Cali* case identified a general interest objective among the essential functions of the state on environment protection. Thus, specifically, the ECJ established:

> The anti-pollution surveillance . . . is a task in the public interest which forms part of the essential functions of the State as regards protection of the environment in maritime areas.[41]

2.1.3. The Acceptance of the Primacy Principle of the Constitutional Treaty by the Constitutional Jurisdictions

21. As seen above, the text of Article I-6 referred to national law without distinction between the Constitution and other domestic legal sources. Declaration No 1 would reinforce this interpretation since the ECJ has consistently argued that primacy is equally applied in relation to national Constitutions. Thus, one might think that the ratification of Article I-6 involved a full acceptance of the position of the ECJ by Member States and the obligation to eliminate the constitutional provisions that might be contrary to this principle.

22. However, this was not the case with the Spanish Constitutional Court or the French Constitutional Council when they analysed the primacy principle established in Article I-6 under the prior control of constitutionality of the Constitutional Treaty. Both jurisdictions agreed that the ratification of Article I-6 did not require the previous revision of their Constitutions, to the extent that it did not change the nature of the relationship between EC/EU law and national constitutional law. Both Madrid and Paris felt that the primacy of

[40] See the *Final report of Working Group V*, "Complementary Competencies" (European Convention, CONV 375/1/02 REV 1, 4 November 2002).

[41] Case C-343/95 *Diego Calì & Figli Srl v Servizi ecologici porto di Genova SpA (SEPG)* [1997] ECR I-01547 para 22.

Article I-6 did not affect the ultimate supremacy of the national Constitution (a term used by the Spanish Constitutional Court) on any other source of law in domestic legal order. Thus, to deny EU law the top of the pyramid's internal regulations, despite the sharp wording of Article I-6, both the Spanish Constitutional Court and the Constitutional Council set forth Article I-5, paragraph 1 which, as seen above, forced the EU to respect the equality of states, their national identity as well as their essential functions.[42]

So, on the one hand, the French Constitutional Council established, with the usual terseness found in its judgments:

> pursuant to Article I-5, the Union shall respect the national identities of Member States 'inherent in their fundamental structures, political and constitutional'; pursuant to Article I-6 'The Constitution and law adopted by the institutions of the Union in exercising competences conferred on it shall have primacy over the law of the Member States'; a declaration annexed to the Treaty shows that this Article does not confer on the principle of primacy any greater scope that than which it previously had.[43]

On the other hand, much more eloquently, the Spanish Constitutional Court established that to correctly interpret the primacy set forth in the Constitutional Treaty, 'Article I-5.1 is explicit enough', which along with I-2, the Charter of Fundamental Rights, Article II-113 and other provisions:

> establish the guarantee of the existence of states and their basic structures, as well as their values, principles and fundamental rights, that in no case could reach beyond recognition after the phenomenon of transfer of the exercise of powers to the supranational organization, a guarantee whose absence or lack of an explicit proclamation justified in earlier stages reticence opposed to the primacy of Community law against the different Constitutions by popular decisions of constitutional courts of some States, in what has been called within the doctrine the dialogue between constitutional courts and the Court of Justice of the European Communities. In other words, the limits to which related the reticence of such constitutional jurisdictions now appear unequivocally proclaimed by the Treaty submitted to our consideration, in order to place its provisions to the requirements of the Constitutions of the Member States.

[42] See A López Castillo, 'La Unión Europea en "constitución" y la Constitución estatal en (espera) de reformas: A propósito de la DTC1/2004 de 13 de diciembre' in A López Castillo, A Sáiz Arnáiz and V Ferreres Comella (eds), *Constitución Española y Constitución Europea. Análisis de la Declaración del Tribunal Constitucional (DTC 1/2004, de 13 de diciembre)* (CEPC, Madrid, 2005) 13 at 26–39.

[43] Case *Constitutional Treaty* Decision No 2004-505 DC (French Constitutional Council, 19 November 2004) paras 9–13 and especially 12. See D Chamussy, 'Le Conseil constitutionnel face à la primauté du droit communautaire. Cons. const. 19 novembre 2004, Traité établissant une constitution pour l'Europe' (2005) 61(4) *Actualité Juridique – Droit Administratif* 219, B Genevois, 'Le Conseil constitutionnel et la primauté du droit communautaire' (2005) 2005(2) *Revue Française de Droit Administratif* 239 and E Bruce. 'La primauté du droit communautaire. Retour sur la portée de l'article 88-1 de la Constitution dans la jurisprudence récente du Conseil constitutionnel' (2005) 192 *Les Petites Affiches* 3.

> Thus, the primacy proclaimed in the Treaty establishing a Constitution for Europe operates according to an Order built on common values of the integrated State Constitutions in the Union and their constitutional traditions.
>
> On the basis of those guarantees it should be also stressed that the primacy established for the Treaty and its derived law established in the disputed Article I-6 is specifically contracted to the exercise of the powers conferred on the European Union. It is not, therefore, a primacy of general scope, but only referred to the powers of the Union.[44]

23. Thus, both constitutional courts saw in this provision the recognition, by the Constitutional Treaty itself, of a limitation to primacy just where the national constitutions, or at least their 'fundamental structures', were concerned by the implementation of an EU legal act. The combined interpretation of Articles I-5 and I-6 of the Constitutional Treaty allowed the two national jurisdictions to state, each in its own way, that Article I-6 was fully consistent with the existing constitutional order.[45] This conclusion was quite handy, but also extremely comfortable on the part of both highest interpreters, as it avoided a constitutional amendment, a possibility that in the case of Spain is always surrounded by controversy, since it is not at all certain that the ECJ had accepted that paragraph 1 of Article I-5 added an intrinsic limit to the principle of primacy. It is more likely that it had agreed to annul an EC/EU act precisely alleging that it did not respect the fundamental constitutional structures of the states, but this did not mean enabling the national judge to activate a kind of EU law constitutional control, in this sense based on Article I-5 of the Constitutional Treaty.[46]

2.2. The Lisbon Treaty

24. The Lisbon Treaty, unlike the Constitutional Treaty, abolishes the explicit clause of the primacy of EU law. Instead, it includes a Declaration (No 17) 'concerning primacy'. According to this Declaration:

> The Conference recalls that, in accordance with well settled case law of the Court of Justice of the European Union, the Treaties and the law adopted by the Union on the basis of the Treaties have primacy over the law of Member States, under the conditions laid down by the said case law.
>
> The Conference has also decided to attach as an Annex to this Final Act the Opinion of the Council Legal Service on the primacy of EC law as set out in 11197/07 (JUR 260):

[44] Case *European Constitution* (2004) Declaration No 1/2004 (Spanish Constitutional Court, 13 December 2004) para 3.

[45] The case *European Constitution* (2004) (n 45) had strong dissenting opinions of three members of the Court (Mr Javier Delgado Barrio, Mr Roberto García-Calvo y Montiel and Mr Ramón Rodríguez Arribas). On the other hand, as is well known, the *Conseil* adopts its decision unanimously without any dissenting opinions.

[46] Of the same opinion is B De Witte, 'Article I-6 – Le droit de l'Union' in L Burgorgue-Larsen, A Levade and F Picod (eds), *Traité établissant une Constitution pour l'Europe: commentaire article par article* (Bruylant, Bruxelles, 2007) 107 at 116.

> '*Opinion of the Council Legal Service of 22 June 2007*
>
> *It results from the case-law of the Court of Justice that primacy of EC law is a cornerstone principle of Community law. According to the Court, this principle is inherent to the specific nature of the European Community. At the time of the first judgment of this established case law (Costa/ENEL, 15 July 1964, Case 6/641 (. . .)) there was no mention of primacy in the treaty. It is still the case today. The fact that the principle of primacy will not be included in the future treaty shall not in any way change the existence of the principle and the existing case-law of the Court of Justice.*'

25. The obvious question to be asked is whether this difference between the Constitutional Treaty and the Lisbon Treaty is significant, that is, if it changes the effects of the primacy principle as analysed above. First, one might point out that the supremacy clause would have made explicit the prior case law without altering it significantly. That is, the national law of Member States contrary to EU law would be disapplied, allowing the direct applicability of the latter. In essence, this would have meant a prolongation of the current situation. No reservations would have eliminated from the constitutional courts of some Member States that declare themselves empowered to ultimately ensure a certain standard of protection of fundamental rights or the protection of certain national constitutional structures. It could have been argued that primacy was only recognized on the condition that the Union exercised the powers expressly conferred, which could be controlled by national courts.[47] Secondly, it should be stressed that the Constitutional Treaty, as seen above, could have granted primacy on which it was no longer the law of the 'third pillar' but also in relation to the framework decisions of the Common Foreign and Security Policy (CFSP) including international treaties agreed within the CFSP framework.[48] This possibility seems complicated under the Lisbon Treaty, which states that the CFSP shall be governed by specific rules and procedures.[49] In this sense, the Lisbon Treaty, unlike the Constitutional Treaty, would preserve the intergovernmental nature of the CFSP. Thus, despite some differences, especially concerning the intergovernmental pillars already seen above, the Constitutional Treaty did not change the substance of the primacy rule.[50]

[47] See S Griller, 'Is this a Constitution? Remarks on a Contested Concept' in S Griller and J Ziller (eds), *The Lisbon Treaty: EU Constitutionalism Without a Constitutional Treaty?* (Springer, Vienna, 2008) 21 at 47–8.

[48] See B De Witte, 'Article I-6 – Le droit de l'Union' in L Burgorgue-Larsen, A Levade and F Picod (eds), *Traité établissant une Constitution pour l'Europe : commentaire article par article* (Bruylant, Bruxelles, 2007) 107 at 112–14; and M Dougan, 'The Treaty of Lisbon 2007: Winning minds, not hearts' (2008) 45(3) *Common Market Law Review* 617 at 621–6.

[49] See Art 24(1.1) TEU-L.

[50] S Griller, 'Is this a Constitution? Remarks on a Contested Concept' in S Griller and J Ziller (eds), *The Lisbon Treaty: EU Constitutionalism Without a Constitutional Treaty?* (Springer, Vienna, 2008) 21 at 48–9.

26. Thus, if one accepts that the Constitutional Treaty would not have changed the conception of the primacy principle and would hardly have affected its expansion, it is difficult to argue that the Lisbon Treaty itself would have done it, given its silence on the matter.[51]

Likewise, we must bear in mind that the content of Article I-5 of the Constitutional Treaty is contained in the new Article 4 of the TEU in its wording by the Treaty of Lisbon (TEU-L) on the preservation of national identity, the fundamental constitutional structures and essential state functions.[52] Moreover, to this article, which specified the self-imposed limits by the new Union arising from the eventual entry into force of Lisbon, we should take into account the addition of a paragraph according to which all powers not conferred upon the Union in the Treaties belong to the Member States. This addition might seem superfluous, since the new Article 5 TEU-L includes the text of former Article I-11 of the Constitutional Treaty regarding the fundamental principles under which the European Union shall exercise its powers, but will undoubtedly contribute to strengthen, at least from the standpoint of the gestures, the limitations and concessions that the Union has set.[53]

27. In conclusion, the solutions that have been developed, both those incorporated in the treaties and those provided by the national constitutional jurisdictions, do not question the essential elements of any of the orders at stake; instead they are arrangements and pragmatic agreements (some explicit, some implicit) in order to keep progressing with integration. These agreements would mean an acceptance on the part of the supreme guardians of the respective orders of the other's existence, or better of their right to exist but also the existence of instruments of pressure to hold back any desire to invade occupied fields.[54] Thus, from the EU side, the question of primacy, even if founded on the national Constitution by a national judge, in addition to the political cost that would entail, would trigger a process for non-compliance with any possible economic sanctions. On the other hand, from the national side, any attack on the Constitution could lead to questioning the primacy of EC/EU law and, for the same reason, the unity of the internal market. However, despite the feeling that

[51] See J Ziller, *Il nouvo Trattato europeo* (Il Mulino, Bologna, 2007) 139.

[52] In that sense, Art 4 TEU-L would go beyond the TEU after Nice, where it is only possible to find Art 6.3 stating that 'The Union shall respect the national identities of its Member States'.

[53] And analysis of these principles may be found in JC Gautron, 'Article I-11 – Principes fondamentaux' in L Burgorgue-Larsen, A Levade and F Picod (eds), *Traité établissant une Constitution pour l'Europe : commentaire article par article* (Bruylant, Bruxelles, 2007) 181.

[54] Scholars have written largely on this issue. There are those who defend an approach based on legal pluralism and those who stand for a constitutionalist vision of the global legal order. These approaches will be developed below. Nonetheless, an illustrative work explaining the main visions and principles of this very interesting debate is available in M Poiares Maduro, 'Contrapunctual Law: Europe's Constitutional Pluralism in Action' in N Walker (ed), *Sovereignty in transition* (Oxford, Hart, 2003 (reprinted 2006)) 501 where the author proposes four principles to articulate the very coexistence among legal orders: pluralism, vertical coherence and horizontal consistency, universality and institutional preference.

the principles of a sort of Cold War between the courts is being re-started, where if one presses the attack button the other will respond with the same forcefulness, assuring mutual destruction, the truth is that both sides have managed to overcome with good sense, elegance and cleverness the problems that have been brought up, ensuring a relatively peaceful coexistence, seeking pragmatic solutions to specific problems and showing, most of the time, that they coped with the needs of the European project better than the political authorities, who are more vulnerable to short-sighted calculations.[55]

[55] See M Kumm, 'The Jurisprudence of Constitutional Conflict: Constitutional Supremacy in Europe before and after the Constitutional Treaty' (2005) 11(3) *European Law Journal* 262 and P Pérez Tremps, 'La jurisdicción constitucional y la integración europea' (2009) 29 *Revista Española de Derecho Europeo* 19 at 26–40.

II

European Union Law and the European Convention on Human Rights

PRELIMINARY ARGUMENTS

1. The interordinal relations between EC/EU law and the ECHR has been an object of study for a long time, although a reliable conclusion has never been reached. Nonetheless, after recent case-law development (case of *Senator Lines*, judgments in *Matthews* and *Bosphorus*, among others) it is possible to bring forward a theory, at least a provisional one, about this matter and point out its possible evolution, while we wait for the long-expected accession of the EU to the ECHR.

2. Therefore, the objective of the following chapters would be to analyse the interordinal relations between the EC/EU legal order and the ECHR, especially in the light of new case-law developments and the open dialogue between the ECtHR and the ECJ. Given the specialization of the ECtHR, the guiding principles of this dialogue have been the fundamental rights, whose protection systems established in different overlapped levels (national, EU and that of the Council of Europe) have been the vector of the praetorian evolution. Because of that, in the first place, an analysis of the fundamental rights in the EU will be carried out. Secondly, an approach to the relationship between the EU legal order and the ECHR from the point of view of EC/EU law, reviewing the essential part of the doctrine that up to the present moment had made comments on this matter. Thirdly, a study of the relationship between both systems, in this case, from the ECHR point of view, with special mention of the latest case-law developments. And last, an assessment of the current situation and the possible evolution of the matter, bearing in mind the answers and silence from the Luxembourg and Strasbourg jurisdictions.

3

The Fundamental Rights and the Union

1. A COMMUNITY/UNION BASED ON THE RULE OF LAW

1. For the ECJ, the Treaty establishing the European Coal and Steel Community, the Treaty establishing the European Atomic Energy Community, the Treaty establishing the European Economic Community (after some amends, the European Community), to which could be added the subsequent Treaty on the European Union, represented the Constitution of the EC/EU. After the Lisbon Treaty, the same can be applicable to the current treaties: TEU-L, TFEU, the Charter and the still-existing Treaty establishing the European Atomic Energy Community. This statement does not mean that this 'Constitution' is equivalent to that of one of the Member States, but that the Court considers these treaties as the 'internal Constitution' of the EC/EU.[1] Namely, the Court does not pretend to establish, by means of case law, a European state to replace the Member States, but only to stress that treaties establish rules of a constitutional nature as they organize the division of duties among the institutions, define their greater or lesser extent and establish a series of guarantees for their addressees.[2] In this regard, and avoiding terminological discussions referring to the term 'Constitution', we shall highlight the characteristics that, according to the Court, define the Community (now the Union) established by the treaties.

2. One could say that the origin of the existence of a Community/Union based on the rule of law was first stated in the judgment in *Les Verts v Parliament*. In this judgment the Court stated the following:

[1] Opinion 1/76 *Draft Agreement establishing a European laying-up fund for inland waterway vessels* [1977] ECR 741 paras 5 and 12. On this opinion, see M Hardy, 'Opinion 1/76 of the Court of Justice: The Rhine Case and the Treaty-making Powers of the Community' (1977) 14 *Common Market Law Review* 561 and TC Hartley, 'International Competence of the Community' (1977) 2 *European Law Review* 275.

[2] On the concept of 'Constitution' applied to the Treaties, see JL Cascajo Castro, 'Constitución y Derecho constitucional en la Unión Europea' (2005) 15 *Teoría y realidad constitucional* 89; JL Cascajo Castro, 'Notas para un breve ensayo sobre "Constitución e interpretación constitucional"' (2003) 51(1) *Estudios de Deusto* 81; LI Gordillo, 'Constitución, constitucionalización y constitucionalismo de la Unión' (2005) 53(2) *Estudios de Deusto* 253 and references quoted there.

> it must first be emphasized in this regard that the European Economic Community is a Community based on the rule of law, inasmuch as neither its Member States nor its institutions can avoid a review of the question whether the measures adopted by them are in conformity with the basic constitutional charter, the Treaty.[3]

Regarding this decision, the Court did not issue a birth certificate to a Community based on the rule of law, but only stated its existence, because at least implicitly, the Court had already mentioned this matter in its well-known judgment *Van Gend en Loos*, highlighting the particular nature of the Treaty which established the European Economic Community.[4] Some years later, in its decision on the European Economic Area, it described the EEC Treaty as the constitutional charter of a Community based on the rule of law.[5]

Therefore, from the description of the European Community as a Community based on the rule of law, the Court established a full system of resources and thus admitted the passive legitimation of the European Parliament, in other words, the possibility that its acts will be examined before the Court, even when the Treaty remains silent. In its definition of a Community based on the rule of law, the Court emphasized two elements of the rule of law: the submission of the public authorities to the existing law and the existence of a judicial review process in order to guarantee respect for those rules.[6] This definition would not be complete, since nothing would prevent the author of a given act to act in an arbitrary way, even if the author is respecting the rules of the Treaty. A Community/Union based on the rule of law would mean, then, a Community/ Union fully submitted to the lawmaker's will but which, even respecting the treaties, could behave according to its own will. The notion thus includes among its principles respect for fundamental rights.

[3] Case 294/83 *Les Verts v Parliament* [1986] ECR 1339 para 23. The literature about this leading decision is huge. As a sample, see JP Jacqué, 'Recours en annulation, campagne d'information pour l'élection du Parlement européen' (1986) 22(3) *Revue Trimestrielle de Droit Européen* 500 and R Kovar, 'Cour de Justice, 23 avril 1986, affaire C-294/83, Parti écologiste "Les Verts" contre Parlement européen' (1987) 23(3–4) *Cahiers de Droit Européen* 314.

[4] Case 26/62 *Van Gend en Loos v Nederlandse Administratie der Belastingen* [1963] ECR 1. For a first comment, see SA Riesenfeld and RM Buxbaum, 'NV Algemene Transport- En Expeditie Onderneming van Gend & Loos c. Administration Fiscale Neerlandaise: A Pioneering Decision of the Court of Justice of the European Communities' (1964) 58(1) *American Journal of International Law* 152. More recently, B de Witte, 'Direct Effect, Supremacy, and the Nature of the Legal Order' in P Craig and G de Búrca (eds), *The Evolution of EU Law* (Oxford University Press, Oxford, 1999) 177.

[5] Opinion 1/91 *Draft agreement between the Community, on the one hand, and the countries of the European Free Trade Association, on the other, relating to the creation of the European Economic Area* [1991] ECR I-06079 para 21. See D Simon and A Rigaux, 'L'avis de la Cour de justice sur le projet d'accord CEE/AELE portant création de l'Espace économique européen (EEE)' (1992) Février, *Europe* 1; and N Burrows, 'The Risks of Widening without Deepening' (1992) 17(4) *European Law Review* 352.

[6] Many books and papers have been drafted on the rule of law. Among others, see E Díaz, *Estado de Derecho y sociedad democrática* 1st edn, 1966 (Taurus, Madrid, 1998) 44–55; 'Revisión de Elías Díaz. Sus libros y sus críticos' in LL Hierro, FJ Laporta and A Ruiz Miguel (eds) (CEPC, Madrid, 2007) 47–68. For a comparative perspective, see L Heuschling, État *de droit, Rechtsstaat, Rule of Law* (Dalloz, Paris, 2002).

3. Thus shaped, the Community/Union based on the rule of law is not only a community of rules, but a Community/Union in which judicial review is guaranteed by the respect by the authorities of the norms of the rule of law. This idea goes beyond the material rules of the treaties and includes fundamental rights. But the very existence of a Community/Union of law does not imply either that the power of appreciation of the EU institutions shall be in the judge's hands, since this would affect the institutional balance and could turn the Community/Union into a Community of judges.[7] In fact, the judge's role is to guarantee that the discretionary power of the institutions shall not turn into an arbitrary power.

4. On the other hand, the TEC had (and now the TFEU has) undoubtedly an economic vocation. Its application implies the adoption of measures which are difficult for the EC/EU judge to control. Namely, the judge should carry out a review of the the expediency of the measures, which is usually the responsibility of the EU institutions, and which would put the judge in the position of the lawmaker. The ECJ has always been very careful not to exceed this limit when exercising the legality control of EC/EU acts. Thus, as was established in the case *Consten Grundig*:

> the exercise of the Commission's powers necessarily implies complex evaluations on economic matters. A judicial review of these evaluations must take account of their nature by confining itself to an examination of the relevance of the facts and of the legal consequences which the Commission deduces therefrom. This review must in the first place be carried out in respect of the reasons given for the decisions which must set out the facts and considerations on which the said evaluations are based.[8]

Nevertheless, even in this case, the respect for the rule of law would be guaranteed by the appeal to the manifest error theory, as well as by the use of principles such as legal certainty, proportionality or legitimate expectation that would restrict the discretionary power agreed with the institutions. However, there are well founded opinions that say that the system of resources established by the Treaties is incomplete due to the lack of an action for annulment submitted by individuals against acts of a general nature, in the case of the ancient community pillar, and the lack of a complete system of resources in order to guarantee the legality of the institutions' acts, in the old intergovernmental pillars.[9]

[7] See JP Jacqué, 'The principle of institutional balance' (2004) 41(2) *Common Market Law Review* 383.

[8] Joined Cases 56 and 58/64 *Consten SàRL and Grundig Verkaufs GmbH v Commission* [1966] ECR 299. On these cases, see B Baardman. 'Cour de Justice, 13 juillet 1966, affaires jointes 56 et 58–64, Consten S.à.R.L. et Grundig-Verkaufs-GmbH contre Commission' (1966) 2 *Cahiers de Droit Européen* 669; and G Schrans, 'L'application du droit communautaire des ententes économiques par la Cour de justice des Communautés européennes (affaire Grundig-Consten)' (1967) 20 *Revue Critique de Jurisprudence Belge* 180.

[9] On the case of the so-called first pillar, see the largely criticized Case C-50/00 P *Unión de Pequeños Agricultores v Council* [2002] ECR I-6677. This case has been studied in depth by scholars. As an example, see P Gilliaux, 'L'arrêt Unión de Pequeños Agricultores: entre subsidiairité

5. The importance the Court attaches to the existence of a Community/Union based on the rule of law is shown in the case *Les Verts (Green Party)*, where the Community judge used his power of interpretation to complete the Treaty and, therefore, allow the plaintiffs to challenge an act of the European Parliament which, if followed by a literal interpretation of the Treaty, would escape from its control. This attitude of the Court is also proved by the case law in the field of non-compliance, while the ECJ holds that the non-compliance confirmation involves the full ban on national authorities applying a national provision which has been declared incompatible with the Treaty.[10] On the other hand, although the Treaties do not allow the Court to revoke a national measure contrary to EC/EU law, it has developed its case law in such a way as guarantees, thanks to the participation of the national judge, respect for EC/EU legality.

6. The Treaty of Amsterdam already confirmed the importance of respecting the rule of law, comparing it to the level of primary law. Indeed, Article 6.1 TEU established that the Union was founded on the principles of liberty, democracy, respect for human rights and fundamental freedoms and the rule of law, principles which are common to the Member States.[11]

The new Article 2 TEU-L maintains:

> The Union is founded on the values of respect for human dignity, freedom, democracy, equality, the rule of law and respect for human rights, including the rights of persons belonging to minorities. These values are common to the Member States in a society in which pluralism, non-discrimination, tolerance, justice, solidarity and equality between women and men prevail.[12]

The Court review is based on the new Article 19 TFEU (formerly Article 220 TEC), according to which:

> The Court of Justice of the European Union . . . shall ensure that in the interpretation and application of the Treaties the law is observed.

juridicitonnelle et effectivité' (2003) 39(1–2) *Cahiers de Droit Européen* 177, D Hanf, 'Talking with the "pouvoir constituant" in Times of Constitutional Reform: The European Court of Justice on Private Applicants' Access to Justice' (2003) 10 *Maastricht Journal of European and Comparative Law* 265 and JA Usher, 'Direct and individual concern – an effective remedy or a conventional solution?' (2003) 28(5) *European Law Review* 575. The absence of a complete system of appeals within the intergovernmental pillars has been recognized by the ECJ in its case law on the *Pupino*, *Segi* and *OMPI-PMOI* saga (below). See R Alonso García, *Sistema Jurídico de la Unión Europea* 1st edn (Thompson-Civitas, Madrid, 2007) 264–6.

[10] Case 48/71 *Commission v Italy* [1972] ECR 529. See MF Gayet and D Simon, 'Constatation de manquement et effet direct du droit communautaire' (1973) 9 *Cahiers de Droit Européen* 301 and JA Winter, 'Case 48/71, Second Art Treasures Case. Commission of the EC v Italian Republic' (1973) 10(3) *Common Market Law Review* 318 and 327.

[11] OJ C 325/1 (24 December 2002).

[12] OJ C 306/11, 17 December 2007.

2. RESPECT FOR FUNDAMENTAL RIGHTS

7. Fundamental rights are one of the classics of EC/EU law. The Treaties do not contain specific provisions for the protection of fundamental rights.[13] This situation has generated plenty of doctrinal contributions on the question of to what extent the EC/EU is bound to respect fundamental rights and even what would it be.[14] Despite the initial silence of the Treaties, fundamental rights have entered the scene with the help of the Court of Justice. Subsequently, this case law was confirmed by consecutive amendments to the Treaties. The drafting of the Charter of Fundamental Rights, proclaimed twice so far, and the problem concerning the accession of the EC/EU to the European Convention on Human Rights have been studied widely by the European doctrine. The new Lisbon Treaty, which grants the Charter the same legal status as the Treaties, although removing it from the text that the Constitutional Treaty had unified, and which expects the incorporation of the Union into the Convention, portends new developments in relations between the system emanating from the European Convention and that from the Union.

[13] Until Art F TEU (7 February 1992) there was no explicit mention of fundamental rights (OJ C 191, 29 July 1992).

[14] The literature is huge. See P Pescatore, 'The context and significance of fundamental rights in the law of the European Communities' (1981) 2(3–4) *Human Rights Law Journal* 295; A Bleckmann, 'Die Grundrechte im Europäischen Gemeinschaftsrecht, ein Beitrag zu den Methoden des EG-Rechts' (1981) *Europäische Grundrechte Zeitschrift* 257; J Schwarze, 'The Administrative Law of the Community and the Protection of Human Rights' (1986) 23(2) *Common Market Law Review* 401; MA Dauses, 'The protection of fundamental rights in the Community legal order' (1985) 10(6) *European Law Review* 398; HG Schermers, 'The European Communities Bound by Fundamental Human Rights' (1990) 27(2) *Common Market Law Review* 249, M Zuleeg, 'Der Schutz der Menschenrechte im Gemeinschaftsrecht' (1992) *Die* Öffentliche *Verwaltung* 937; A O'Neill and J Coppel, 'The European Court of Justice: taking rights seriously?' (1992) 29(4) *Common Market Law Review* 669; JHH Weiler and N Lockhart, '"Taking Rights Seriously" seriously: the European Court and its Fundamental Rights Jurisprudence – Part I' (1995) 32(1) *ibid* 51; JHH Weiler and N Lockhart, '"Taking Rights Seriously" seriously: the European Court and its Fundamental Rights Jurisprudence – Part II' (2) 579; P Alston and J Weiler, 'An "Ever Closer Union" in Need of a Human Rights Policy' (1998) 9(4) *European Journal of International Law* 658; GC Rodríguez Iglesias, 'The Protection of Fundamental Rights in the Case Law of the Court of Justice of the European Communities' (1995) 1(2) *Columbia Journal of European Law* 169; K Lenaerts, 'Le respect des Droits fondamentaux en tant que principe constitucionnel de l'Union Européenne' in M Dony, A De Walsche and M Waelbroeck (eds), *Mélanges en hommage à Michel Waelbroeck* (Bruylant, Bruxelles, 1999) 423; D Waelbroeck, 'Fundamental rights in the European Union – possible developments in the years to come' in A Dashwood *et al* (ed), *The Developing role of the European Court of Justice* (European Policy Forum and Frankfurter Institut, London and Frankfurt am Main, 1995) 17; K Lenaerts, 'Fundamental Rights in the European Union' (2000) 25(6) *European Law Review* 575; A Von Bogdandy, 'The European Union as a Human Rights organization? Human Rights and the core of the European Union' (2000) 37(6) *Common Market Law Review* 1307; AG Chueca Sancho, *Los derechos fundamentales en la Unión Europea* 2nd edn (Bosch, Barcelona, 1999), J Corcuera Atienza *et al*, *La protección de los derechos fundamentales en la Unión Europea* (Dykinson, Madrid, 2002); FJ Matía Portilla *et al* (eds), *La protección de los derechos fundamentales en la Unión Europea* (Civitas, Madrid, 2002); L López Guerra, 'Hacia un concepto europeo de derechos fundamentales' (2003) 65(2) *Revista Vasca de Administración Pública* 191; and L Aguiar de Luque, 'Los derechos fundamentales en el proceso de integración europea' (2003) 18 *Cuadernos de Derecho Público* 173.

8. Some authors analyse the evolution of European integration, taking into account the increasingly important role given to fundamental rights in the process of creating an ever closer Union among the peoples of Europe.[15] Although the founding Treaties completely obviated the question of fundamental rights, these have become increasingly important since the late 1960s.[16] Since then, the issue has evolved as it gave increased recognition to these rights and, above all, increased effectiveness from the Court of Justice. Right before the Treaty of Lisbon entered into force, the fundamental rights were recognized as the Union's founding principles, which must be respected by their institutions and, moreover, are part of the general principles of Community/Union law, whose effectiveness is ensured by the Court of Justice.[17] Once the Lisbon Treaty had entered into force, the Charter of Fundamental Rights was fully binding and the Union could accede to the European Convention on Human Rights.

2.1. The Initial Silence of the Treaties

9. The European Treaties did not originally contain any general provision on fundamental rights, even if one accepts that certain principles such as non-discrimination or the freedom to provide services may, in certain cases, be coincidental with some human rights provisions.[18] An explanation of this silence is simple. Given the economic nature of the Treaties, the authors did not think there could be a risk of collision between EU law and human rights. When drafting the Treaties, the conception of the majority regarding the nature of human rights included within this category civil and political rights, thus making it difficult to conceive possible interferences between regulations of an economic nature and fundamental rights.

10. Experience has shown, however, how that assessment was wrong, because it ignored the fact that fundamental rights act as a limit for the activity of every public authority (whether it is local, regional, national or supranational) and may even be applied to the relations among individuals.[19] Thus, in the debate in

[15] A Clapham, A Cassese and JHH Weiler, *European Union – The Human Rights Challenge Vol III, Human Rights and the European Community: The Substantive Law* (Nomos, Baden-Baden, 1991).

[16] The ECJ passed lightly over this issue in Case 29/69 *Stauder v Stadt Ulm* [1969] ECR 419.

[17] For a very accurate account on the evolution of fundamental rights within the EU, see HG Schermers and D Waelbroeck, *Judicial Protection in the European Union* 6th edn (Kluwer, The Hague, 2001).

[18] JP Jacqué, *Droit institutionnel de l'Union Européenne* 4th edn (Dalloz, Paris, 2006) 51–2; and HG Schermers and D Waelbroeck, *Judicial Protection in the European Union* 6th edn (Kluwer, The Hague, 2001).

[19] On the possibility of application of fundamental rights in private relations, see the German doctrine on the so-called *Drittwirkung der Grundrechte* or, simply, *Drittwirkung*. W Leisner, *Grundrechte und Privatrecht* (CH Beck, München, 1960); W Rüfner, 'Drittwirkung der Grundrechte – Versuch einer Bilanz' in P Selmer and I Von Münch (eds), *Gedächtnisschrift für Wolfgang Martens* (De Gruyter, Berlin, 1987) 215; C Starck, 'Derechos fundamentales y Derecho Privado' (2002) 66 *Revista Española de Derecho Constitucional* 65; M Venegas Grau, *Derechos fundamentales y derecho privado: los derechos fundamentales en las relaciones entre particulares y el principio de autonomía privada*

Ireland on the ratification of the Single European Act, the argument according to which EU integration could affect the absolute right to life from the very moment of conception as recognized by the Irish Constitution was initially dismissed (Article 40.3(3)). Subsequently, the Court had to decide a question on the compatibility with EC law of a measure banning Irish dissemination of information within the country about the conditions under which clinics from other Member States legally practised abortion.[20] In this controversial case, the Court held that the issue was affected by the rules on freedom to provide services and therefore fell within the remit of the EU. This case shows that it is not possible to exclude a priori any interference between the activity of the Union and matters relating to fundamental rights. The risk of collision has been magnified since the entry into force of the TEU in the field of police and judicial cooperation in criminal matters (Title VI TEU) and after the communitarization (ie transfer to the first pillar) that operated the Treaty of Amsterdam from Title VI, in particular those relating to visas, asylum, immigration and judicial cooperation in civil matters.[21]

2.2. The Case Law Momentum

11. Given the silence of the Treaties, the matter was soon brought before the Court of Justice. In its first decisions, the Court refused to consider the line of argument from the appellants, that is to say, that certain EC acts were void because they violated the fundamental rights protected by national Constitutions.[22]

12. This case law highlighted a number of problems. First, it meant that the creation of the Communities brought with it a deficit in the protection of fundamental rights. That is, it was clear that the powers exercised by the states were subject to the respect for fundamental rights established in national Constitutions. However, transferring such powers to a supranational level (the EC/EU) would then imply that the exercise of them should no longer be subject to the limits set out by the fundamental rights established in national Constitutions. A positive answer would have implied that the creation of the EC

(Universidad Carlos III, Madrid, 2004). Dealing with the application of fundamental rights within the ECHR system, see FG Jacobs, RC White and C Ovey, *Jacobs and White: the European Convention on Human Rights* (Oxford University Press, Oxford, 2006) 51–2; and A Clapham, *Human Rights in Private Sphere* (Clarendon Press, Oxford, 1993).

[20] Case C-159/90 *The Society for the Protection of Unborn Children Ireland Ltd v Stephen Grogan and others* [1991] ECR I-4685. See B Wilkinson, 'Abortion, the Irish Constitution and the EEC' (1992) Spring, *Public Law* 20; and DR Phelan, 'Right to Life of The Unborn v Promotion of Trade in Services: The European Court of Justice and the Normative Shaping of the European Union' (1992) 55(5) *Modern Law Review* 670.

[21] JP Jacqué, *Droit institutionnel de l'Union Européenne* 4th edn (Dalloz, Paris, 2006) 54.

[22] Case 1/58 *Friedrich Stork & Cie v ECSC High Authority* [1959] ECR 17, Joined Cases 36, 37, 38/59 and 40/59 *Präsident Ruhrkohlen-Verkaufsgesellschaft and others v ECSC High Authority* [1960] ECR 423, all of them commented in LJ Brinkhorst and HG Schermers, *Judicial remedies in the European Communities: a case book* 2nd edn (Kluwer, Deventer, 1977) 181–91.

involved a reduction in the protection of individual rights. In addition, it would be necessary to explain why some powers whose exercise was limited by the European Convention on Human Rights in five of the six Member States (France did not ratify it until 1974) would escape all control after an eventual transfer to the EC. Likewise, the reason why individuals who had a direct appeal before the Strasbourg authorities (the Commission and, where appropriate, the Court) would lose this right after a possible transfer of powers should be justified.[23]

13. So it was only a question of time before the first dispute arose among the various courts responsible for the protection of fundamental rights. Thus, according to this, individuals began to lodge applications before the national courts and even the Court of Justice and arguing that certain EC acts were void since they violated fundamental rights protected by the relevant national Constitution. Since the ECJ did not exercise proper control over the compliance of fundamental rights by the EC acts, some national courts that saw a potential threat against rights protected by their respective Constitutions finally started to declare themselves competent to review EC acts in light of the constitutional fundamental rights, which entailed, at the very best, a threat to the uniform application of EC law.[24] Then an interesting process began, which some have described as a 'dialogue', in which the highest courts involved were taking their stance and setting the conditions for accepting the approach of their counterparts.[25]

2.3. Dialogue between the ECJ and the National Constitutional Courts

2.3.1. First Stage: The Establishment of the Red Lines

14. As mentioned above, the Italian *Corte costituzionale* was the first to issue a statement on the constitutional limits of the integration process. In its famous judgment of the case *Frontini* (1973) it established the theory of the *controlimiti*, according to which the limitation of sovereignty resulting from the European integration process could not, under any circumstances, lead to award the EC institutions an 'unacceptable power to violate the fundamental principles of our constitutional order or the inalienable rights of the human being'.[26]

[23] JP Jacqué, *Droit institutionnel de l'Union Européenne* 4th edn (Dalloz, Paris, 2006) 53.

[24] See Case *Solange I* 2 BvL 52/71 BVerfGE 37 271 (German Constitutional Court, 29 May 1974).

[25] An assessment of the so-called dialogue between national courts and the ECJ may be found in AM Slaughter, A Stone Sweet and JHH Weiler, *The European Courts & National Courts. Doctrine and Jurisprudence. Legal change in its social context* (Hart, Oxford, 1998), especially in A Stone Sweet, 'Constitucional Dialogues in the European Community', *ibid*, 305.

[26] Case *Frontini* Decision No 183/1973 (Italian Constitutional Court, 18 December 1973), where the Italian Constitutional Court stated '*deve quindi escludersi che siffatte limitazioni, concretamente puntualizzate nel Trattato di Roma – sottoscritto da Paesi i cui ordinamenti si ispirano ai principi dello Stato di diritto e garantiscono le libertà essenziali dei cittadini –, possano comunque comportare per gli organi della C.E.E. un inammissibile potere di violare i principi fondamentali del nostro ordinamento costituzionale, o i diritti inalienabili della persona umana*'.

This doctrine was later reasserted in the *Granital* (1984) and *Fragd* (1989) cases.[27]

15. In turn, the German Constitutional Court said in its very famous decision of 1974 (*Solange I*) that '[a]s long as the integration process has not progressed so far that Community law receives a catalogue of fundamental rights decided on by a parliament and of settled validity, which is adequate in comparison with the catalogue of fundamental rights contained in the Basic Law, a reference by a court of the Federal Republic of Germany to the Federal Constitutional Court in judicial review proceeding . . .' if it is not entirely convinced by the response that the Luxembourg Court has given regarding the compatibility between the EC rule in question and the fundamental rights recognized by the German legal order.[28] However, in case of an infringement of a fundamental right, the Constitutional Court did not declare itself competent to invalidate a Community rule, but to declare unconstitutional any act of the German public authorities tending to implement this EC act.[29]

16. Moreover, the ECJ began to pay greater attention to fundamental rights. In 1969 (*Stauder* case), the Court recognized, at least implicitly, in an *obiter dictum* that the individual's fundamental rights were part of the general principles of Community law.[30] A year later in the *Internationale Handelsgesellschaft* case, in which the appellant had alleged an infringement of the fundamental rights from a Community act, the Court in Luxembourg, even though denying that such infringement had occurred, expressly admitted that 'respect for fundamental rights forms an integral part of the general principles of law protected by the Court of Justice' and in order to define these rights had to guided by the 'constitutional traditions common to the Member States'.[31] A few years later (case of *Nold*, 1974), the Court confirmed its jurisprudence by referring to national instruments which the Member States had joined or were involved in drafting – in particular, those referred to the European Convention.[32]

Shortly after (case of *Wachauf*, 1989), the Court reordered all previous findings on fundamental rights and specified definitively a jurisprudence that has remained up to the present day, by virtue of which 'fundamental rights form an integral part of the general principles of the law, the observance of which is

[27] See Case *Granital* Decision No 170/1984 (Italian Constitutional Court, 5 June 1984) 4, where the court revisits the *Frontini* doctrine, and the Case *Fragd* (Italian Constitutional Court, Decision No 232/1989) para 3.

[28] See the Case *Solange I* (German Constitutional Court, 1974) (n 24).

[29] R Alonso García (2007) (n 9) 259.

[30] The French version of the decision stated: '*la disposition litigieuse ne revele aucun element susceptible de mettre en cause les droits fondamentaux de la personne compris dans les principes généraux du droit communautaire*', Case 29/69 *Stauder* (n 16). See CD Ehlermann, 'Anmerkung zu EuGH, Urteil v. 12.11.1969, Rs. 29/69' (1970) *Europarecht* 41.

[31] Case 11/70, *Internationale Handelsgesellschaft mbH v Einfuhr- und Vorratsstelle für Getreide und Futtermittel* [1970] ECR-1125 para 4.

[32] Case 4/73 *Nold, Kohlen- und Baustoffgroßhandlung v Commission* [1974] ECR 491.

ensured by the Court. In safeguarding those rights, the Court has to look to the constitutional traditions common to the Member States, so that measures which are incompatible with the fundamental rights recognized by the constitutions of those states may not find acceptance in the Community. International treaties concerning the protection of human rights on which the Member States have collaborated or to which they have acceded can also supply guidelines to which regard should be had in the context of Community law'.[33]

2.3.2. Second Stage: The Rapprochement of Positions

17. Thus, following the evolution of the jurisprudence of the Court of Justice, the German Constitutional Court changed its doctrine on the relationship between EC law and the German Constitution. So, after an initial shift in the case of *Eurocontrol* (1981), the Court of Karlsruhe radically altered its jurisprudence in the famous judgment *Solange II* (1986).[34] In the latter case, reversing the terms used in *Solange I* the Constitutional Court of Germany decided that 'the European Communities . . . shall provide effective protection of fundamental rights against the public power of the Communities, that shall be considered equivalent, on the essentials, to the protection of the fundamental rights offered unconditionally by the Basic Law . . . hereafter, the BVerfGE shall not exercise its unlimited jurisdiction regarding the application of the secondary Community law . . . and, therefore, will not review such secondary law in the light of the fundamental rights of the Basic Law'.[35] This new doctrine of 'equal protection', which was put back into question in the case of *Maastricht* (1993), would be definitely confirmed in the decision of the Highest interpreter of the German Basic Law regarding the *Bananas* case (2000).[36] Thus, the Constitutional Court of Germany has granted almost full immunity to EC/EU law, subject to an unlikely deterioration in the general level of protection of rights within the EC/EU, leaving the control of the adjustment of the EC/EU acts to the fundamental rights in the hands of the Luxembourg Court.[37]

18. On the other hand, the French Constitutional Council also assumed, in its own way, this doctrine of 'equal protection' with the only limit that of entering into clear conflict with the constitutional text. After a series of Decisions which defined the relationship between EC/EU law and French Constitutional law dur-

[33] Case 5/88 *Hubert Wachauf v Bundesamt für Ernährung und Forstwirtschaft* [1989] ECR 2609. For a comment, see L Costato, 'Potere d'iniziativa dell'affittuario e destino delle quote latte a fine rapporto' (1989) II *Rivista di diritto agrario* 265.

[34] See Case *Eurocontrol I* 2 BvR 1107/77 and 195/79 BverfGE 58, 1 (German Constitutional Court, 23 June 1981) and Case *Solange II* 2 BvR 197/83 BVerfGE 73 339 (German Constitutional Court, 22 October 1986) para 339.

[35] Case *Solange II* (n 34) para 387.

[36] See Case *Maastricht* 2 BvR 2134/92 and 2 BvR 2159/92, BverfGE 89, 155 (German Constitutional Court, 1994) and Case *Bananenmarktordnung* 2 BvL 1/97 BVerfGE 102, 147 (German Constitutional Court, 7 June 2000).

[37] JP Jacqué, *Droit institutionnel de l'Union Européenne* 4th edn (Dalloz, Paris, 2006) 57.

ing an intensive year, 2004, the *Conseil* ruled in the case of the law on bioethics that the transposition into domestic law of an EC directive arises from a constitutional requirement that could only be opposed by the existence of an express provision contrary to the Constitution.[38] So, as the Constitutional Council services have interpreted, only in case of conflict with an express provision contrary to the French Constitution would the obligation of transposition be unconstitutional, although it would exist as an EC/EU obligation.[39]

19. On a different matter, the European Court of Human Rights also ratified these views relating to the equal protection doctrine. Without prejudice to a further visit to this issue below, the position of the Court in Strasbourg can be summarized as follows. At first (case of *M & Co*, 1990), the ECtHR recognized that it would be difficult to accept that the transfer of powers to the European Communities would get them out of respecting the fundamental rights which, instead, the national authorities were constitutionally bound to comply with by exercising their powers.[40] In the case *Bosphorus* (2005), to which we will return later, the Court in Strasbourg has recognized the importance of international cooperation through organizations like the European Union.[41] Given the direct applicability of EC/EU law, whose authorities act as a true public power, there may be infringements of the citizens' fundamental rights recognized in the ECHR, which are under the jurisdiction of the Member States by the European authorities. In order to reconcile respect for the Convention with the importance given to the EC/EU, the ECtHR uses a formula similar to that already used in the Constitutional Court of Germany in its judgment *Solange II*. Thus, the Strasbourg Court provided a presumption of conformity of EC/EU law regarding the ECHR, a presumption which may be rebutted by showing that EC/EU law does not provide a protection equivalent to that afforded by the Convention. By 'equivalent to' the Court means a protection 'comparable to', but not 'identical to', as regards both the substantive guarantees offered and the mechanisms controlling their observance.[42]

[38] Case *Law on bioethics* Decision No 2004-498 DC (French Constitutional Council, 29 July 2004) para 4.

[39] See the document *La jurisprudence constitutionnelle française relative au droit communautaire à la veille de l'examen par le Conseil constitutionnel du traité établissant une Constitution pour l'Europe*, 8 November 2004 drafted by the Legal Services of the Constitutional Council, available at <http://www.conseil-constitutionnel.fr/decision/2004/2004505/note.pdf>. The quote is at 57. It should be noted that the concept of Constitution within French law is wider, since it includes the so-called *bloc de constitutionnalité*. See L Favoreu and P Gaia, *Droit constitutionnel* 10th edn (Dalloz, Paris, 2007) 117–32 and L Favoreu, 'El bloque de la constitucionalidad' (1990) 5 *Revista del Centro de Estudios Constitucionales* 45.

[40] Case *M & Co v Germany* App No 13258/87 (Commission Decision, 9 February 1990, 64 DR 138).

[41] Case *Bosphorus Hava Yolları Turizm ve Ticaret Anonim irketi v Ireland* App No 45036/98 (ECtHR, 30 June 2005, 2005-VI).

[42] Case *Bosphorus* (ECtHR, 2005) (n 41) para 155.

3. THE LEGAL STATUS OF FUNDAMENTAL RIGHTS

20. Having thus stated the question, at present, the difficulty lies in specifying 20hat rights will be considered fundamental by the Court of Justice and what will be its content.[43] Therefore, it is necessary to analyse the ECJ case law in this field to specify what rights are protected (and to what extent) and, until the existence of the Charter as a conventional instrument, what makes the ECJ decide to protect certain rights and not others.

In this regard, a first question that must be borne in mind is that when the Court examines whether a particular provision of EC/EU law is in compliance with fundamental rights or not, it is always from the point of view of EC/EU law, and not from the national Constitution's perspective.[44] That is to say, the Court does not use as reference standards (to use a French expression commonly accepted by the doctrine) a particular provision of a certain national Constitution, but, in the absence of a positive EC/EU rule, it will use the so-called general principles of EC/EU law that are, of course, integrated by the constitutional traditions common to the Member States. In this sense, and setting aside the Charter for the moment, as qualified sources in which are shown (if not all, at least part of) the common constitutional traditions are the international treaties on human rights that the states have signed or in which they have directly participated in the drafting.[45] Here, the European Convention on Human Rights becomes very important, because even if at first the Court avoided referring to it directly, today it doesn't blush when it comes to quoting it as a document which contains the fundamental rights fruit of the common constitutional traditions whose respect the ECJ has to guarantee. However, the Luxembourg Court tries not to be expressly and irrevocably constrained (although there is a gradual change in attitude) by the jurisprudence of the Strasbourg Court and, thus, set itself up as highest interpreter of fundamental rights (including those contained in the ECHR) within the EC/EU.

3.1. The General Principles of Law

21. Since initially the EC legal order lacked of a Bill of Rights or something similar, when the Court was obliged to recognize the existence of certain funda-

[43] As will be analysed further, after the Lisbon Treaty, the Charter of Fundamental Rights has the same legal value as the Treaties, except for the exceptions awarded to Poland, the UK and, ultimately, the Czech Republic.

[44] Joined Cases 41, 121 and 796/79 *Vittorio Testa, Salvino Maggio and Carmine Vitale v Bundesanstalt für Arbeit* [1980] ECR 1979 para 18, where it assures that 'as the Court has repeatedly emphasized, the question of a possible infringement of fundamental rights by a measure of the Community institutions can only be judged in the light of Community law itself, since fundamental rights form an integral part of the general principles of the law, the observance of which it ensures'.

[45] Case 4/73 *Nold* [1974] (n 32) para 13.

mental rights, it determined that they were obligations as being part of the general principles of law. This was quite understandable. To accept the direct link from the catalogues of rights of the national Constitutions would have called into question the principle of primacy of EC law. Moreover, given the lack of homogeneity among the different catalogues (and the different value assigned to each fundamental right), the ECJ would have needed to opt for one or the other statement, with all the problems of legal and political systems that would involve. Not to mention the loss of legal certainty that this situation would entail.[46]

22. The European Community Treaty (TEC) did not contain express reference to general principles of EC law, except for Article 288 (Article 340 TFEU) which based the extra contractual liability of the Community on the general principles common to the Member States.[47] The Court's jurisprudence has upgraded the general principles to the level of source of law. The Court has justified the use of this source starting from the primary law. Indeed, Article 220 TEC (Article 19 TEU-L) assigns to the Court of Justice and the CFI (now the General Court) the task of ensuring the respect for the law in the interpretation and application of the Treaties.[48] The recognition of 'the law' (in general) as a source of EC/EU law has enabled the Court to rely on the general principles of law when interpreting and applying EC/EU law.[49]

23. The question that arises then is what the source of those principles is, or, in other words, from where does the EC/EU judge deduce the general principles of law. In the case *Handelsgesellschaft*, the Court of Justice already declared the autonomy of the general principles of EC law although, at the same time, it recognized that the protection of fundamental rights was inspired by the constitutional traditions common to the Member States.[50] Nevertheless, the 'discovery' of the general principles within the EC/EU order has its own characteristics which are derived from the specific nature of the EC/EU legal system. In fact, the identification of some principles, which subsequently will be consecrated as

[46] See HG Schermers and D Waelbroeck, *Judicial Protection in the European Union* 6th edn (Kluwer, The Hague, 2001) 28–132, T Tridimas, *The General Principles of EU Law* 2nd edn (Oxford University Press, Oxford, 2006), JV Louis and T Ronse, *L'ordre juridique de l'Union européenne* (Bruylant, Bruxelles, 2005) 235–43, K Lenaerts, 'Interlocking Legal Orders in the European Union and Comparative Law' (2003) 52(4) *International and Comparative Law Quarterly* 873 and X Groussot, *General Principles of Community Law* (Europa Law, Groningen, 2006).

[47] Even today, references to the general principles of law are rare and always in a way to award the ECJ a huge margin of appreciation.

[48] See the wording of the new Art 19 TEU-L.

[49] Joined Cases C-46/93 and C-48/93 *Brasserie du Pêcheur v Germany* and *The Queen v Secretary of State for Transport ex parte Factortame* [1996] ECR I-1029 paras 24–30. For a comment, see N Emiliou, 'State Liability under Community Law: Shedding more light on the Francovich Principle?' (1996) 21(5) *European Law Review* 399 and P Oliver, 'Case C-46/93 and C-48/93, Brasserie du Pêcheur v Germany, and The Queen v Secretary of State for Transport ex parte Factortame, *et al*' (1997) 34(3) *Common Market Law Review* 635 at 635–58.

[50] Case 11/70 *Internationale Handelsgesellschaft* (n 31) paras 3–4.

general to EC/EU law, is made according to both an eclectic and pragmatic reasoning. Thus, in the first place, we will resort to the principles of international law, of the Member States' national law, and also to a series of principles deduced from the EC/EU legal order itself. Moreover, some principles are backed by the Charter of Fundamental Rights.[51] Then, before attributing to these principles the quality of general principles of the law it is necessary to verify that they are compatible with the characteristics of the EC/EU legal order. This would lead to a selective acceptance materialized in a filter operation intended to prevent the cohesion of the EC/EU legal system from being affected.[52]

24. The doctrine has classified the general principles of the Community law in three categories: fundamental rights, principles derived from the rule of law and structural principles. The first category, highlighted here, refers to the fundamental rights and civil liberties that, in general terms, are guaranteed both by the national constitutional and international instruments protecting human rights, among which we shall highlight the European Convention on Human Rights. This does not prevent these fundamental rights from being also subject to regulation by EC/EU law.[53] These rights are not understood as absolute prerogatives, but as the social function of property and protected activities, that is to say, under the cover of certain limits justified by general interest objectives of the EC/EU, as long as the essential content of those rights is not affected.[54] Among the fundamental rights established by the Court we may find protection of private and family life, protection of the home, and protection of correspondence and religious freedom, to which we shall add those rights closely related to economic freedom, such as property rights, free exercise of economic activities, professional privilege (secrecy) and freedom of association, etc.[55] With regard to social rights, even though there is a movement which is strongly proposing its protection, the recognition of fundamental social rights is still at a primitive stage of protection.[56] Likewise, there is a doctrinal and jurisprudential

[51] Case T-54/99 *max.mobil v Commission* ECR II-313, on the right to an effective remedy. This decision (recognizing fundamental rights relying on the Charter) was subsequently revoked by the ECJ. The question at stake seemed to be, on the other hand, the legal value of the Charter and its possible direct applicability. See Case C-141/02 P *Commission v max-mobil* [2005] ECR I-1283. For a comment, see F Castillo de la Torre, 'Case C-141/02 P, Commission v T-Mobile Austria GmbH, formerly max.mobil, judgment of the Court of Justice (Grand Chamber) of 22 February 2005' (2005) 42(6) *Common Market Law Review* at 1751.

[52] D Simon, *Le système juridique communautaire* 3rd edn (PUF, Paris, 2001) 358–9.

[53] See, for instance, Art 2 of Council Regulation 2679/98/EC of 7 December 1998 on the functioning of the internal market in relation to the free movement of goods among the Member States (OJ L 337, 12 December 1998) stating that 'This Regulation may not be interpreted as affecting in any way the exercise of fundamental rights as recognised in Member States, including the right or freedom to strike'.

[54] Case 4/73 *Nold* (n 32) para 14.

[55] A list of the fundamental rights recognized by the ECJ in its case law may be found below.

[56] See T Kingreen, 'Basic Rights of Equality and Social Rights' in E Ehlers (ed), *European Fundamental Rights and Freedoms* (De Gruyter Recht, Berlin, 2007) 466.

trend which advocates that the protection of fundamental rights should be introduced into the logic of European Union citizenship.[57]

The second category consists of the principles derived from the rule of law. Indeed, the Court of Justice has recognized in its jurisprudence that the principles inherent in the rule of law are applicable to the EC/EU.[58] Among them, we shall highlight the principle of legal certainty, effective judicial protection and the right to a trial with all guarantees and a number of principles linked to good governance.[59]

The third category, the structural principles, unlike the first two, do not directly aim to guarantee the protection of citizens, even though they may have that effect indirectly. These are principles derived from the economic and political structure of the EC/EU, which provides a criterion to establish a subclassification. Thus, regarding the constitutional principles, we may mention all those principles regulating the separation of powers, such as the principle of institutional balance, pre-emption, subsidiarity, proportionality, loyal cooperation or equality and solidarity among the Member States. We may also mention in this subcategory the principles that guarantee the common and general application of the EC/EU legal order, such as the principles of primacy and direct effect, or, even though such general principles have not yet been defined, good administrative practices or good financial management. The doctrine has also pointed out the gradual establishment of the principle prohibiting the abuse of the law.[60] With regard to the economic principles, we shall mainly mention the principles of free movement and non-discrimination, complemented by the principles of free competition and unity of the single internal market.[61] We should bear in mind that this is not a closed list: it is being defined and clarified through successive court cases and is fully linked to the permanent process of evolution and integration of the EU.

[57] Case C-85/96 *Martínez Sala v Freistaat Bayern* [1998] ECR I-2691 and Case C-168/91 *Christos Konstantinidis v Stadt Altensteig* [1993] ECR I-1191, Opinion of AG Jacobs. A study on this question may be found in S Kadelbach, 'Union Citizenship' in A Von Bogdandy and J Bast (eds), *Principles of European Constitutional Law* (Hart, Oxford, 2006) 453. As is well known, Union citizenship was an initiative of the Spanish Government. See the letter of the President of the Spanish Government to the then President of the Council (the *taoiseach*) published at (1990) 3 *Revista de Instituciones Europeas* 780–1 and the official proposal of the Spanish Government, F Laursen and S Vanhoonacker, *The Intergovernmental Conference on Political Union – Institutional Reforms, New Policies and International Identity of the European Community* (EIPA-IEAP, Martinus Nijhoff, Maastricht, 1992) 325. See E Pérez Vera, 'Citoyenneté de l'Union européenne, nationalité et condition des étrangers' (1996) 261 *Recueil des Cours de l'Académie de Droit International de La Haye* 243.

[58] J Rideau, *De la Communauté de droit à l'Union de droit: continuités et avatars européens* (LGDJ, Paris, 2000), 'Une communauté de droit: Festschrift für Gil Carlos Rodríguez Iglesias' in N Colneric and others (eds) (BWV Berliner Wissenschafts, Berlin, 2003).

[59] D Simon, *Le système juridique communautaire* 3rd edn (PUF, Paris, 2001) 366–7.

[60] *Ibid* at 368.

[61] D Ehlers and U Becker, *European fundamental rights and freedoms* (Walter de Gruyter, Berlin, 2007) 175–370.

25. The general principles of law are part of EC/EU law and, therefore, its violation constitutes a breach of this Treaty or of any other rule relating to their application within the meaning and scope of the provisions of Article 230 TEC (Article 263 TFEU).[62] In fact, as one author has noted, they would constitute a kind of 'super-legality' to the extent that the general principles impose on the institutions the elaboration and implementation of secondary law.[63] Occasionally, the Court has even applied a general principle which was in contradiction with the wording of the Treaty.[64] Moreover, the Court considers that the general principles also impose on the Member States when they act within the scope of EC/EU law.[65] In other words, is it not the Court of Justice's duty to guarantee the respect of the general principles regarding Member State proceedings that are enshrined within the scope of the powers reserved (*Cinéthèque* case, 1985) or outside the scope of EC/EU law.[66] On the contrary, the measures taken in application of EC/EU law are meant to respect the general principles of law, and national jurisdictions are required to take on the consequences of this subordination of national law to EC/EU law. Therefore, the jurisprudential construction of the general principles of law, which was necessary to develop in order to take into account the protection requirements of fundamental rights imposed by the national Constitutions, has had a wider effect and a larger scope. In fact, the cohesion that in terms of dogma the general principles have given to the EC/EU legal system has contributed, likewise, to reinforcing the rule of law within the domestic legal systems of the Member States.[67]

3.2. The Progressive Integration of Human Rights within the Treaties

26. As mentioned above, the consecration of fundamental rights in EC/EU law, being considered as general principles, was made by the Court of Justice.

[62] Case 112/77 *Töpfer v Commission* [1978] ECR 1019. See JA Usher, 'Article 173 EEC: Breach of a General Principle as a Ground for Annulment' (1978) 3 *European Law Review* 383.

[63] D Simon, *Le système juridique communautaire* 3rd edn (PUF, Paris, 2001) 369.

[64] Case C-70/88 *European Parliament v Council of the EC* [1991] ECR I-4529, where the application of the principle of democracy was discussed as well as the institutional balance. For a comment see JP Jacqué, 'La légitimation active du Parlement européen ou il n'était pas nécessaire d'espérer pour entreprendre' (1990) 26(4) *Revue Trimestrielle de Droit Européen* 620; K Bradley, 'Sense and Sensibility: Parliament v Council Continued' (1991) 16(3) *European Law Review* 245; and K Lenaerts, P Van Nuffel and R Bray, *Constitutional Law of the European Union* 2nd edn (Thompson, London, 2005) 712.

[65] See, for instance, Case 5/88 *Hubert Wachauf* [1989] (n 33), Case C-260/89 *Elliniki Radiophonia Tiléorassi AE (ERT) et al v Dimotiki Etairia Pliroforissis et al* [1991] ECR I-2925, Case C-159/90 *Grogan* [1991] (n 20) and Case C-396/98 *Grundstückgemeinschaft Schloßstraße GbR v Finanzamt Paderborn* [2000] ECR I-4279.

[66] Joined Cases 60 and 61/84 *Cinéthèque SA et autres v Fédération nationale des cinémas français* [1985] ECR 2605. See JHH Weiler, 'The European Court at a Crossroads: Community Human Rights and Member State Action' in F Capotorti *et al* (ed), *Du droit international au droit de l'intégration – Liber amicorum Pierre Pescatore* (Nomos Verlag, Baden-Baden, 1987) 821.

[67] L Dubois, *Droit Communautaire et protection des droits fondamentaux dans les* États *membres* (Economica, Paris, 1995).

Nevertheless, the Member States and the institutions are also taking steps in that direction. A Joint Declaration of the European Parliament and the Commission of 1977 already showed the importance that these two institutions gave to the question.[68] Likewise, in the preamble of the Single European Act, the Member States were 'determined to work together to promote democracy on the basis of the fundamental rights recognized in the constitutions and laws of the Member States, in the Convention for the Protection of Human Rights and Fundamental Freedoms and the European Social Charter, notably freedom, equality and social justice'.[69]

27. The European Union Treaty was a turning point regarding this subject. In fact, Article F.2 (subsequently Articles 6.2 TEU and 6 TEU-L) revisited the Court's case law so that respect for fundamental rights is one of the general principles of the law. Moreover, it reproduced the reference to the European Convention on Human Rights and to the constitutional traditions common to the Member States as a source of fundamental rights. But Article F was initially located in a part of the Treaty that was out of the Court's control. On the other hand, Article K.2, placed in Title VI (relating to cooperation in the field of justice and home affairs), imposed likewise, in that context, respect for the European Convention on Human Rights and for the Geneva Convention on refugees. Moreover, in the scope of the Union's External Action, Article 130 U of the TEC (Article 177 TEC after Nice and Article 208 TFEU) made respect for human rights and fundamental freedoms one of the objectives of EC/EU policy on development cooperation.[70]

28. This consolidation of the body of case law was really important, but progress did not stop there. During the negotiations of the Amsterdam Treaty, the question regarding fundamental rights could not be ignored after the Justice Court's ruling regarding the accession of the Community to the ECHR.[71] But it was impossible to reach an agreement on the accession because the Amsterdam Treaty introduced modifications of major importance. First of all, it explicitly imposed on the candidate States respect for the principles mentioned in Article 6.1 of the TEU (which are now in Article 2 TEU-L) among which we may find respect for human rights and the rule of law. Then, it established a suspension procedure of the right to vote and of the rights derived from the Treaty regarding a 'serious and persistent' violation of the principles set out in Article 6 TEU (Article 2 TEU-L) by a Member State. Meanwhile, the Treaty of Nice introduced a procedure, which Lisbon has kept, allowing in the case of 'a clear risk

[68] Joint Declaration by the European Parliament, the Council and the Commission, OJ C 103/1 (27 April 1977).

[69] See Preamble (recital 3) of the Single European Act (OJ L 169, 29 June 1987).

[70] JP Jacqué, *Droit institutionnel de l'Union Européenne* in 4th edn (Dalloz, Paris, 2006) 59.

[71] Opinion 2/94, *Accession by the Community to the ECHR* [1996] ECR I-1759. This question will be revisited below.

of a serious violation by a Member State' recommendations to be made to the latter, before confirming the 'serious and persistent breach' which requires the suspension of rights (Article 7 TEU-L).[72]

Moreover, it should be noted that Amsterdam extended the Court's scope to include also Article 6.2 TEU (the content now appears in Article 6 TEU-L), which requires institutions to respect fundamental rights, both at the EC level and in the context of Title VI. Unlike what was considered at the time, especially by the Court of Justice, the Treaty of Amsterdam did not implement a specific resource on fundamental rights, but it legitimized the invocation of the violation of fundamental rights under existing resources.[73] But these are not the only contributions to the reform of Amsterdam. Indeed, the Treaty allows the Community to take appropriate action to fight discrimination based on sex, racial or ethnic origin, religion or belief, disability, age or sexual orientation (Articles 13 TEC, 19 TFEU) and to promote equality between men and women (Articles 141 TEC, 157 TFEU). Article 136 TEC (Article 151 TFEU) on social policy contains a reference to fundamental social rights, such as those contained in the European Social Charter and the Community Charter of Fundamental Social Rights of Workers.[74] The Amsterdam Treaty established an additional way of protecting the rights of individuals regarding the processing of personal data by the Community (Articles 286 TEC, 16 TFEU). It also establishes the principle of access for citizens to documents of the Parliament, the Commission and the Council (Articles 255 TEC, 15 TFEU). Therefore, the Treaty of Amsterdam sets the pace of an important era not only because it established the jurisprudential *acquis* in the field, but because it develops in certain specific areas, as we have seen, the protection of fundamental rights.

3.3. The Scope of the Obligation to Respect Fundamental Rights

29. The control that the Court of Justice exercises in the field of protection of fundamental rights is exercised over the EC/EU acts and this control is also extended over the acts of Member States if they implement the EU legislation.[75] The consolidated case law stresses that when the Member States act according to the dispositions of EC/EU law, they must respect the same principles to which the EC/EU is subject. Thus, the unity of EC/EU law is preserved by including the national implementing measures.

[72] See Art 7.1 TEU. The consolidated version of the TEU (prior to Lisbon) may be consulted at OJ C 321 E 1 (29 December 2006).

[73] Art 46 TEU, after Nice. This disposition has been abrogated by the Lisbon Treaty (Arts 82–89 TFEU). JP Jacqué (2006) (n 70) at 60.

[74] European Social Charter CETS No 035 signed at Turin (18 October 1961) entered into force on 26 February 1965. The Charter of Fundamental Social Rights was adopted the Heads of State or Government of 11 Member States at the Strasbourg Summit on 9 December 1989. The Charter was not signed by the United Kingdom until 1998 (after Tony Blair became Prime Minister).

[75] Case 5/88 *Wachauf* (n 33) para 19 and Case C-292/97 *Kjell Karlsson and others* [2000] ECR I-2737 paras 45 and 58.

30. A sensitive issue that has long remained unanswered is that there was a chance to control, through the obligation to respect fundamental rights, not only the positive national measures of enforcement or implementation of EC/EU law, but also those that restricted the exercise of the freedoms guaranteed by the Treaty. In the *Rutili* case, the Court considered that a national measure restricting freedom of movement for reasons of public order should be considered in the light of the principles and limits established in the European Convention on Human Rights.[76] Specifically, the Court ordered that 'these limitations placed on the powers of member states in respect of control of aliens are a specific manifestation of the more general principle, enshrined in Articles 8, 9, 10 and 11 of the ECHR . . . which provide, in identical terms, that no restrictions in the interests of national security or public safety shall be placed on the rights secured by the above-quoted articles other than such as are necessary for the protection of those interests "in a democratic society"'.[77] However, in the *Cinétèque* case, which was to analyse the compatibility of a measure prohibiting the circulation of new films on videocassettes in relation to freedom of expression, the Court considered that its job was not to guarantee the respect for fundamental rights in a sector that was beyond the scope of EC law itself, and which belonged exclusively to the assessment of the national judge.[78]

31. The criteria applied by the Court when establishing its competence to assess the compatibility of the action of a Member State with fundamental rights lies in knowing whether or not it is a question that falls within the specific field of EC/EU law. The Court recognizes no attribution to verify the conformity of the national action with fundamental rights as a general rule and only exercises its control in areas that are in the field of EC/EU law.[79] On the other hand, it is clear that within the scope of EC/EU law, the Court ensures observance of fundamental rights by the Member States and institutions. One might wonder if the Treaty of Amsterdam did not introduce a constraint at this point since the drafting of Article 46(d) TEU circumscribed the competence of the Court regarding fundamental rights to the action of the institutions. It does not seem that the Court has interpreted this provision to the effect of excluding the national implementing and execution measures of the treaty and the EC/EU acts especially after the repeal of Article 46 TEU by Lisbon.[80]

[76] Case 36/75 *Roland Rutili v Ministre de l'intérieur* [1975] ECR 1219.

[77] Case 36/75 *Rutili* [1975] (n 76) para 32.

[78] Joined Cases 60 and 61/84 *Cinéthèque* [1985] (n 66), Case C-260/89 *ERT* [1991] (n 65). See PJ Slot, 'Case C-202/88, France v Commission (Telecom); Case C-41/90, Hofner and Elser v Macroton GmbH; Case C-260/89, Elliniki Radiophonia Tileorassi (ERT) v Dimotiki' (1991) 28(4) *Common Market Law Review* 964; D Chalmers, 'Competition and Industrial Property. Television and the European Court of Justice, Libertarianism Run Rife' (1992) 17(3) *European Law Review* 248 and SM Taylor, 'Article 90 and Telecommunications Monopolies' (1994) 15(6) *European Competition Law Review* 322.

[79] Case C-299/95 *Friedrich Kremzow v Republik Österreich* [1997] ECR I-2629. See D Simon, 'Kremzow contre l'Autriche' (1997) Juillet, *Europe* 10.

[80] JP Jacqué (2006) (n 70) 62.

3.4. The Competence of the EC/EU Regarding Fundamental Rights

32. If, as the Court confirmed in its Opinion 2/94, the EC/EU must respect fundamental rights, it would be worth considering whether the EC/EU had competence to legislate in this area. This issue has a different extent and consequences depending on whether the action of the EC/EU was internal or external.

33. At the domestic level, and except for some specific provisions of the treaties, especially the Treaty of Amsterdam (gender equality, transparency, data protection, etc.), there was no specific attribution of jurisdiction in the matter. Some have argued that the protection of fundamental rights was a horizontal objective of the treaties and that, consequently, the EC/EU would be authorized to legislate in this area acting under Article 308 TEC (Article 352 TFEU).[81] This argument encounters various obstacles. First, the protection of fundamental rights is not an objective of the EC/EU, but rather an obligation to which it is subjected. The fact that the EC/EU must respect human rights does not mean that it has jurisdiction to adopt specific rules in this area. Indeed, the role of the EC/EU is to ensure that when adopting a legal act it does not affect human rights. Thus, the EC/EU does not have the competence to adopt legislation on inviolability of the home, but when defining the powers of the Commission's investigations on possible violations of European competition law it should ensure that this right is being respected.[82] Similarly, the EC/EU cannot adopt a law on religious freedom, but when it comes to regulating the slaughter of animals, for example, it has to ensure that there is no breach of that freedom and therefore it has added specific rules for cases of ritual slaughter.[83] Certainly, there are some limit cases where it is necessary to adopt certain specific legislation in order to allow the accomplishment of the internal market. Thus, to promote the free flow of data, for example, it was necessary to harmonize the

[81] JP Jacqué, 'Droits fondamentaux et compétences internes de la Communauté européenne' in G Cohen-Jonathan (ed), *Libertés, justice, tolérance. Mélanges en hommage au Doyen Gérard Cohen-Jonathan* (Bruylant, Bruxelles, 2004) 1007.

[82] See Joined Cases 46/87 and 227/88 *Hoechst AG v Commission* [1989] ECR 2859 para 18, which recognizes the right to respect for the home, and Case 85/87 *Dow Benelux v Commission* [1989] ECR 3137 paras 28–29. For two interesting comments, see RK Lauwaars, 'Joined Cases 46/87 and 227/88, Hoechst AG v Commission; Case 85/87, Dow Benelux NV v Commission' (1990) 27(2) *Common Market Law Review* 355; and J Shaw, 'Recent Developments in the Field of Competition Procedure' (1990) 15(4) *European Law Review* 326. Subsequently, the ECJ extended the protection afforded to a private home to business premises and offices of companies. See Case C-94/00 *Roquette Frères* [2002] ECR I-9011 para 25. For a comment, see M Lienemeyer and D Waelbroeck, 'Case C-94/00, Roquette Frères SA v Directeur Général de la Concurrence, de la Consommation et de la Répression des Fraudes. Judgment of the Court of Justice (Full Court) of 22 October 2002' (2003) 40(6) *Common Market Law Review* 1481. See also de opinion of AG Mischo in a doctrinal paper: J Mischo, 'Hoechst, Colas, Roquette: illustration d'une convergence' in N Colneric, JP Puissochet and DV Ruiz-Jarabo y Colomer (eds), *Une communauté de droit: Festschrift für Gil Carlos Rodríguez Iglesias* (Berliner Wissenshafts, Berlin, 2003) 137.

[83] Council Directive 93/119/EC on the protection of animals at the time of slaughter or killing, OJ L 340/21 (31 December 1993).

national legislations on data protection.[84] However, these hypotheses arise due to the need to remove obstacles to free movement and have nothing to do with any supposed horizontal objective of the EC/EU on human rights.[85] Moreover, when the competition or goal that has been assigned to the EC/EU is horizontal, the treaties have mentioned it (for example, equality between men and women in Article 3.2 TEU (Article 8 TFEU) or the environmental protection of Article 6 TEU (Article 11 TFEU). However, there is no prevision of this kind in regard to fundamental rights. It is difficult to find convincing arguments in favour of a thesis that argues for a general EC/EU competence in order to adopt measures regarding fundamental rights. Taking into account the jurisprudence of the Court of Justice, it resolved some time ago in its Opinion 2/94 that the only possible legal basis to act in this field would be Article 308 TEC (Article 352 TFEU), but it then pointed out the impossibility of using this way to increase the EU's powers. The implications of the Opinion were not entirely clear in the eyes of the doctrine. Some interpreted it that the Court only said that Article 308 TEC (Article 352 TFEU) was an insufficient legal basis for justifying accession to the ECHR.[86] Others felt that it excluded any possibility of the EC/EU legislating in the field of fundamental rights.[87] The Court's final position seems to be closer to this second interpretation. Thus, in a later case, it would indicate that the obligation to respect fundamental rights could not lead to expanding the application scope of the treaties' provisions beyond the EC/EU powers, even through Article 308 TEC (Article 352 TFEU).[88] The final *conventionalization* of the Charter (that is, its transformation into primary law) seems to have confirmed this argument, since the Charter has been finally approved by the Member States as a Treaty, but not by the EU itself.

34. As regards EC/EU external action, the situation was clearer. By virtue of its obligation to respect fundamental rights, the EC/EU may add in the international agreements to conclude with third parties clauses requiring the parties

[84] Directive 2002/58/EC of the European Parliament and of the Council on privacy and electronic communications, OJ L 201/37 (31 July 2002).

[85] JP Jacqué, 'Droits fondamentaux et compétences internes de la Communauté européenne' in G Cohen-Jonathan (ed), *Libertés, justice, tolérance. Mélanges en hommage au Doyen Gérard Cohen-Jonathan* (Bruylant, Bruxelles, 2004) 1007.

[86] O de Schutter and Y Lejeune, 'L'adhésion de la Communauté à la Convention européenne des droits de l'homme' (1996) 32(5–6) Cahiers de droit européen 555 and P Wachsmann, 'L'avis 2/94 de la Cour de justice relatif à l'adhésion de la Communauté européenne à la Convention de sauvegarde des droits de l'homme et des libertés fondamentales' (1996) 32(3) *Revue Trimestrielle de Droit Européen* 467.

[87] JM Areilza Carvajal, 'El Dictamen 2/1994 del Tribunal de Justicia o cómo no abordar el espinoso asunto de las competencias comunitarias' (1996) 47 *Revista española de derecho constitucional* 333 at 343–5.

[88] Case C-249/96 *Lisa Jacqueline Grant v South-West Trains Ltd* [1998] ECR I-621. For a comment, see T Connor, 'Community Discrimination Law: No Right to Equal Treatment in Employment in Respect of Same Sex Partner' (1998) 23(4) *European Law Review* 378 and N Bamforth, 'Sexual Orientation Discrimination after Grant v South-West Trains' (2000) 63(5) *Modern Law Review* 694.

to respect fundamental rights. In addition, according to a well-established practice of the institutions, respect for those clauses is an essential element of the agreements which allows, through appeal to the international law of treaties, the suspension or termination of any agreement to be encouraged when the clauses regarding human rights are violated. In addition, the EC/EU in the field of development cooperation policy can pursue a specific objective related to respect for human rights and fundamental freedoms (Articles 177 TEC, 208 TFEU). However, the question is to what extent this goal ensures performance of specific actions in the field of human rights. The answer is not entirely clear. In a case in 1996, the Court considered that an agreement concluded in the field of development cooperation could pursue an aim related to human rights, but found that the agreement in question did not therefore establish a specific cooperation in this field, which seemed to leave the door open.[89]

4. SOURCES OF RIGHTS PROTECTED AT EU LEVEL

35. It has already been stated that fundamental rights integrate the general principles of law ensured by the Court of Justice. But it has not yet been established what sources or which exercise determine what rights will be finally protected within the EC/EU and to what extent. Since the *Handelsgesellschaft* case (1970), the Court has continued to declare the autonomy of the general principles of law on the one hand, while on the other, it recognizes that the source of these general principles is not completely independent of legal cultures and traditions of the Member States.[90] In the *Nold* case (1974), the Luxembourg Court would state that there were two sources of inspiration qualified to identify fundamental rights at EU level: the common constitutional traditions and the international treaties on human rights.[91]

4.1. International Treaties

36. The source that best reflects fundamental rights and civil liberties that are generally recognized in Europe is the ECHR.[92] Since 1974 all Member States of the Communities (and nowadays of the EU) have ratified this Convention and, consequently, one could easily deduce that the EC/EU is subject to the principles

[89] Case C-268/94 *Portugal v Council* [1996] ECR I-6177. See S Peers, 'Case C-268/94, Portugal v. Council' (1998) 35(2) *Common Market Law Review* 539 and N Burrows. 'Development Cooperation Defined' (1997) 22(6) *European Law Review* 594.

[90] Case 11/70 *Internationale Handelsgesellschaft* [1970] (n 31) paras 3–4.

[91] Case 4/73 *Nold* [1974] (n 32) para 13.

[92] See the Convention for the Protection of Human Rights and Fundamental Freedoms CETS No 5, signed at Rome on 4 November 11 1950, entered into force on 3 September 1953. It has been amended lately by the Protocol No 14, which amended the control system of the Convention. The entry into force of this last Protocol was blocked by Russia till 2010.

expressed in the said international instrument.[93] Before 3 May 1974 it could be argued that the Convention, as such, could not be applied in the EC legal order at all because France had not ratified it.[94] However, even then, given that France had accepted most of the rights and freedoms listed in the Convention through national legislation, fundamental rights could be regarded as general principles common to the Member States. This was what the Court did in the case of *Nold*, one of the basic decisions in this matter, issued just a couple of weeks after the French ratification. In this case, the Court did not mention the Convention specifically, but considered that:

> Fundamental rights form an integral part of the general principles of law, the observance of which it ensures.
>
> In safeguarding these rights, the Court is bound to draw inspiration from constitutional traditions common to the member States, and it cannot therefore uphold measures which are incompatible with fundamental rights recognized and protected by the constitutions of those States.
>
> Similarly, international treaties for the protection of human rights on which the member states have collaborated or of which they are signatories, can supply guidelines which should be followed within the framework of Community law.[95]

The interesting part of this ruling is that the Court makes an explicit reference to the Constitutions of the Member States and international treaties concerning the protection of fundamental rights. From then on, both sources would be taken into consideration by the Court.

37. After the *Nold* case the Court referred several times to the ECHR. In the *Hauer* case, for example, it interpreted Article 1 of the Additional Protocol to the Convention (right to property), in the *Rutili* case Protocol No 4 (freedom of movement), in the *Van Landewijck* case Article 6 (right to a fair trial) and in the *VBVB and VBBB* cases Article 10 of the Convention (freedom of expression).[96]

[93] HG Schermers and D Waelbroeck, *Judicial Protection in the European Union* 6th edn (Kluwer, The Hague, 2001) 40.

[94] *Décret* No 74-360 of 3 May 1974 (*Journal Officiel de la République Française*, 4 May 1974).

[95] Case 4/73 *Nold* [1974] (n 32) para 13.

[96] Case 44/79 *Hauer v Land Rheinland-Pfalz* [1979] ECR 3727 paras 17–19. On this leading case, see C Colinet, 'La protection du droit de propriété dans la Communauté européenne au travers de l'arrêt "Hauer" de la Cour de justice des Communautés européennes, du 13/12/1979' in R Bieber and others (eds), *Das Europa der zweiten Generation – Gedächtnisschrift für Christoph Sasse* (Nomos, Baden-Baden, 1981) 739. See also Case C-293/97 *The Queen v Minister of Agriculture, Fisheries and Food, ex parte Standley* [1999] ECR I-2603 para 54; Case 36/75 *Rutili v Ministre de l'Intérieur* [1975] (n 76) para 32 (see C Tomuschat. 'La libre circulation et le statut politique des ressortissants communautaires. Cour de justice des Communautés européennes, 28.10.1975, affaire 36/75 (Rutili)' (1976) 12 *Cahiers de Droit Européen* 58); Joined Cases 209–215 and 218/78 *Van Landewyck v Commission (FEDETAB)* [1980] ECR 3125 paras 79–81 (see T Van Rijn, 'Joined Cases 209 to 215, 218/78, Heinz van Landewijck Sárl a.o. v Commission of the European Communities (FEDETAB)' (1982) 19(3) *Common Market Law Review* 351; Joined Cases 43 and 63/82 *VBVB and VBBB v Commission* [1984] ECR 19 paras 13–34 (see SB Hornsby, 'Public and private resale price maintenance systems in the publishing sector: the need for equal treatment in European Law' (1985) 10(6) *European Law Review* 381).

In the *Kirk* case the Court ruled that the principle established in Article 7 of the Convention (no punishment without law) is part of the general principles of law, compliance with which is ensured by the Court itself, and in the *Akzo* case it applied Article 8 of the Convention (respect for private and family life).[97] In the *Hoechst* case, the Court accepted the fundamental right to inviolability of domicile, but expressly restricted it to the homes of individuals. Indeed, following the analysis of Article 8.1 ECHR, it at first determined that this right did not extend to the business premises of companies.[98] However, after the Strasbourg Court had ruled (in the *Chappell, Niemitz, Funke* and *Colas Est* cases),[99] in the *Roquette* case the Court, after taking note of these cases, finally extended the protection afforded by Article 8 of the Convention to business premises.[100] In fact, it seems that from the *Roquette* case on, there has been a radical change in the value that the Court grants to the ECHR. Indeed, the argument of the ECJ in *Hoechst* was based on the assumption that the Strasbourg Court had not ruled on the issue, nor was there a relevant right registered as a principle common to the laws of the Member States.[101] In other words, the Court seemed to admit in *Hoechst* that if there had existed jurisprudence from Strasbourg on the

[97] Case 63/83 *Regina v Kent Kirk* [1984] ECR 2689 para 22 (see N Foster, 'General Issues in the Kent Kirk Case' 10(5) *European Law Review* 276). See also Joined Cases C-74/95 and C-129/95 *Procura della Repubblica presso la Pretura circondariale di Torino et Pretura circondariale di Torino* [1996] ECR I-6609 para 25; Case 5/85 *AKZO Chemie v Commission (Akzo II)* [1986] ECR 2585 paras 25–27 (see J Shaw, 'The AKZO Saga Continues' (1987) 12(4) *European Law Review* 199).

[98] Joined Cases 46/87 and 227/88 *Hoechst* [1989] (n 82) paras 17–18 and Case 85/87 *Dow* [1989] (n 82) paras 28–29. The literature on this issue is huge. For an overview, see RK Lauwaars, 'Joined Cases 46/87 and 227/88, Hoechst AG v Commission; Case 85/87, Dow Benelux NV v Commission' (1990) 27(2) *Common Market Law Review* 355; and J Shaw, 'Recent Developments in the Field of Competition Procedure' (1990) 15(4) *European Law Review* 326.

[99] The case law on *Chappell*, though previous to *Hoechst*, was not taken into account by the ECJ in this particular case. See Case *Chappell v the UK* App No 10461/83 (ECtHR, 30 March 1989, Series A 152); Case *Niemietz v Germany* App No 18131/91 (ECtHR 16 December 1992, Series A 251); Case *Funke v France* App No 10828/84 (ECtHR 25 February 1993, Series A 256); Case *Sociétés Colas Est et al v France* App No 37971/97 (ECtHR 16 April 2002, ECHR 2002-III). The case law established in *Colas Est* has been strongly reassured by the ECtHR in Case *Van Rossem v Belgium* App No 41872/98 (ECtHR 9 December 2004). See L Burgorgue-Larsen, 'La protection du domicile des personnes morales : (arrêt "Stés Colas Est et autres" du 16 avril 2002)' in P Tavernier (ed), *La France et la Cour européenne des droits de l'homme : la jurisprudence en 2002 : présentation, commentaires et débats* (Bruylant, Bruxelles, 2003) 178 and J Andriantsimbazovina *et al*, *Les grands arrêts de la Cour européenne des droits de l'homme* 4th edn (PUF, Paris, 2007) 476–9.

[100] Case C-94/00 *Roquette Frères* [2002] (n 82) para 25. See M Lienemeyer and D Waelbroeck, 'Case C-94/00, Roquette Frères SA v Directeur Général de la Concurrence, de la Consommation et de la Répression des Fraudes. Judgment of the Court of Justice (Full Court) of 22 October 2002' (2003) 40(6) *Common Market Law Review* 1481 1482–1485 and J Mischo (2003) (n 82) 137 at 137–45.

[101] This would be the conclusion after reading Joined Cases 46/87 and 227/88 *Hoechst* [1989] (n 82) paras 17–18. But it should not necessarily be like that since the ECtHR had already made a decision on the issue in *Chappell* [1989] (n 99) (30 March 1989), just a few months before the ECJ made its judgment on Joined Cases 46/87 and 227/88 *Hoechst* [1989] (n 82) (21 September 1989). In fact, some scholars affirm that the ECJ decision was simply contrary to ECtHR case law. See J Andriantsimbazovina *et al*, *Les grands arrêts de la Cour européenne des droits de l'homme* 4th edn (PUF, Paris, 2007) 478.

subject it would have followed it.[102] This initial bias that seemed like a gracious concession of the Court became a sort of obligation in *Roquette*. Thus, the ECJ established in this latter case that '[f]or the purposes of determining the scope of that principle in relation to the protection of business premises, *regard must be had* to the case-law of the European Court of Human Rights subsequent to the judgment in *Hoechst*'.[103] The term '*regard must be had*' is stronger than previous references made by the ECJ to a mere source from which it should 'draw inspiration'.[104] Likewise, the direct allusion to the 'European Court of Human Rights' suggests that Luxembourg would be preparing to accept the ECtHR as an authority in the field of fundamental rights.

38. As foreseen, among the international instruments of protection of fundamental rights, the ECHR stood fast in a prominent place. Not that the Court refused to consider other treaties, but the ECHR with its established judicial system (the direct action of individuals) has been developing a European case law on fundamental rights becoming the most advanced international instrument in this matter. Therefore, is not surprising that when Member States, during a meeting in Maastricht, integrated the case law of the Court of Justice in Article 6.2 TEU (Article 6 TEU-L), it only made reference to the common constitutional traditions and to the ECHR. However, the Court has also referred to other international instruments and treaties in its jurisprudence. Thus, in the *Defrenne* case, the ECJ rejected a sex discrimination claim based on a specific interpretation of the European Social Charter and Convention No 111 of the International Labour Organization.[105] In other cases, the Court has referred to the International Covenant on Civil and Political Rights.[106] Besides, more recently, in the case of the European Parliament appeal against the family reunification Directive, the Court, confirming the legality of the rule, used not only the ECHR and the International Covenant on Civil and Political Rights but also the International Convention on the Rights of the Child, as well as the European

[102] Case 374/87 *Orkem v Commission* [1989] ECR 3283 para 30 referring equally to Art 6 ECHR. See M Lienemeyer and D Waelbroeck, 'Case C-94/00, Roquette Frères SA v Directeur Général de la Concurrence, de la Consommation et de la Répression des Fraudes. Judgment of the Court of Justice (Full Court) of 22 October 2002' (2003) 40(6) *Common Market Law Review* 1481 at 1483.

[103] Case C-94/00 *Roquette Frères* [2002] (n 82) para 29. The English version uses quite a strong wording: 'regard must be had'. On the other hand, the French version uses a softer one: '*il convient de tenir compte*'.

[104] The obligation of the Court in order to merely 'draw inspiration' is stated in Case 4/73 *Nold* [1974] (n 32) para 13, Case C-260/89 *ERT* [1991] (n 65) para 41 and Case C-274/99 P *Connolly v Commission* [2001] ECR I-1611 para 39.

[105] Case 149/77 *Defrenne v Sabena* [1978] ECR 1365 para 28. See L Imbrechts, 'L'égalité de rémunération entre hommes et femmes' (1986) 22(2) *Revue Trimestrielle de Droit Européen* 231.

[106] Case 374/87 *Orkem* [1989] paras 18 and 31 (see J Shaw, 'Recent Developments in the Field of Competition Procedure' (1990) 15(4) *European Law Review* 326); Joined Cases 297/88 and C-197/89 *Dzodzi v Belgium* [1990] ECR I-3763 para 68 (see M Bravo-Ferrer Delgado and N La Casta Muñoa, 'Joined Cases C-297/88 and C-197/89, Massam Dzodzi v Belgian State; Case C-231/89, Krystyna Gmurzynska-Bscher v Oberfinanzdirektion Köln' (1992) 29(1) *Common Market Law Review* 152) and Case C-249/96 *Lisa Jacqueline Grant v South-West Trains Ltd* [1998] (n 88) paras 43–44.

Social Charter of 18 October 1961, the revised European Social Charter of 3 May 1987 and the European Convention on the Legal Status of Migrant Workers of 24 November 1977.[107] Therefore, in principle, all these international instruments are relevant to the Court of Justice in order to establish the fundamental rights.

39. A question that arises is whether the international agreements on fundamental rights to which the Member States are signatories must represent a minimum standard (ground) beyond which the Court would have discretion to increase the scope of protection or if, conversely, they are the only possible common standard between Member States and, therefore, an impassable maximum protection (shelter).[108] Regarding the ECHR, it seems to be a minimum rather than a maximum, and while the level of protection of rights does not fall below the level of protection of the Convention, EC/EU law can develop a protection of a higher degree.[109] This point of view is the one that prevailed in the drafting of the Charter of Fundamental Rights of the European Union (Article 52.3).[110]

In relation to other international agreements signed within the Council of Europe, the situation is more controversial. Thus, in the case of the Convention on Action against Trafficking in Human Beings, the EU pushed for the introduction of a clause whereby the EU Member States, in their mutual relations, shall apply the Union's own rules instead of the provisions of the Convention:

> [Article 40.3.] Parties which are members of the European Union shall, in their mutual relations, apply Community and European Union rules in so far as there are Community or European Union rules governing the particular subject concerned and applicable to the specific case, without prejudice to the object and purpose of the present Convention and without prejudice to its full application with other Parties.[111]

This practice has been criticized, not only for preventing the application of international standards on human rights protection within the EU, but also for implicitly allowing the application of standards of protection of fundamental rights below the level awarded within the Council of Europe.[112] On the other hand, the *EU Network of Independent Experts on Fundamental Rights* has insisted since its inception in 2002 to equate the protection of fundamental

[107] Case C-540/03 *Parliament v Council* [2006] ECR I-5769. See B Masson, 'L'harmonisation des conditions du regroupement familial : la Cour fait la leçon sur le titre IV CE (CJCE, 27 juin 2006, Parlement européen c/Conseil de l'Union européenne)' (2006) 42(4) *Revue Trimestrielle de Droit Européen* 673.

[108] See P Craig and G de Búrca, *EU Law. Text, Cases and Materials* 4th edn (Oxford University Press, London, 2008) 385–6.

[109] Case 137/84 *Ministère public v Robert Heinrich Maria Mutsch* [1985] ECR 2681, Opinion of AG Lenz.

[110] This aspect has not changed after the last proclamation of the Charter at Strasbourg (12 December 2007).

[111] Council of Europe Convention on Action against Trafficking in Human Beings, CETS No 197 (Warsaw, 16 May 2005).

[112] P Craig and G de Búrca (2008) (n 108) at 386.

rights within the European Union to international standards to save Member States from having to choose between their loyalty to the law of the EU, other agreements or international engagements.[113]

4.2. Common Constitutional Traditions

40. Despite the prominence acquired by this expression, not only in the Court of Justice (*Handelgesellschaft* case, 1970), but also in the text of treaties (Articles 6.2 TEU, 6 TEU-L), the ECJ has referred only very few times to the constitutional traditions common to the Member States, choosing instead to base its arguments on the ECHR or other international treaties. Thus, while the Advocate General has occasionally analysed common constitutional provisions, the Court, meanwhile, has rarely mentioned some specific national provision.[114] The reason seems logical. It is much more difficult for the Court to recognize a common subjective right if it does not explicitly appear in the constitutional texts of all Member States, while an instrument such as the ECHR shall more accurately reflect the values, principles and rights shared by its signatories. Furthermore, the reluctance of the Court may also be related to the fear of compromising the primacy of EC/EU law. Indeed, quoting a provision of the Constitution of one or more Member States might suggest that the Court subdues the validity of EU law to its conformity with national Constitutions, a possibility that was bluntly dismissed in its famous ruling in the case *Costa v ENEL*, and that has constantly been evoked.[115] Thus, as stated in the case *Hauer*, 'the introduction of special criteria for assessment stemming from the legislation or constitutional law of a particular Member State would, by damaging the substantive unity and efficacy of Community law, lead inevitably to the destruction of the unity of the common market and the jeopardizing of the cohesion of the Community'.[116] Thus, it is quite usual that, together with the 'common constitutional traditions' the Court mentions some international convention (the ECHR is commonly quoted) implicitly or explicitly stating that these traditions are reflected in it.[117]

41. Moreover, in some rare cases, the Court of First Instance, even rejecting the claims of the appellants, has left open the possibility that the 'common parlia-

[113] See the *Report on the situation of fundamental rights in the European Union and its Member States in 2002 by the EU network of independent experts in fundamental Rights* (Brussels, 31 March 2003) 21–4 where it denounces the inconsistency of the situation where states have to comply with contradictory obligations.

[114] Case 17/74 *Transocean Marine Paint Association v Commission* [1974] ECR 1063 para 15. On this case, see JA Usher, 'The influence of national concepts on decisions of the European Court – a Case Study: The Transocean Case' (1976) 1 *European Law Review* 359.

[115] Case 6/64 *Costa v ENEL* [1964] ECR-1141. See B De Witte (1999) (n 4) 177.

[116] Case 44/79 *Hauer* (n 96) para 14 quoting Case 11/70 *Internationale Handelsgesellschaft* [1970] (n 31).

[117] Case 44/79 *Hauer* (n 96) paras 14–20.

mentary traditions' also constitute a source of inspiration to specify general principles of Community law.[118]

42. In the case of the common constitutional traditions as a source of inspiration for fundamental rights, a question also arises regarding the level of protection, that is to say, whether there is a standard maximum or minimum. If the Court adopted the rule of 'lowest common denominator' or common minimum standard of protection, there would run the risk of granting protection only to those rights recognized by all Member States (or most of them), ignoring some fundamental rights, even in the EC/EU law framework. Moreover, the position of the 'maximum standard' could lead to a totally different situation; a right recognized in only one of the States could be enforced by the Court to the rest of the Member States, through the general principles of law.[119] EC/EU case law seems to have discarded this second possibility. Thus, in a case in which the right to remain silent in antitrust proceedings was analysed, the CFI ruled that '[i]n the field of competition law, the national laws of the Member States do not, in general, recognise a right not to incriminate oneself. It is, therefore, immaterial to the result of the present case whether or not, as the applicant claims, there is such a principle in German law.'[120] In other cases, the Advocate General has taken the position that a general principle can be extracted from the legal systems of various states even if its legal nature or extent varies from one state to another.[121] Thus, in general, it can be concluded that the Court of Justice would be prepared to recognize that a particular right is integrated into the general principles if several Member States, although not necessarily all of them, expressly grant this right.[122]

43. In another vein, even if there is a general consensus among Member States about the existence of a particular right, it would easily appear a dispute over its scope, that is, on how that right should be interpreted and integrated into the general principles of EC/EU law. A very revealing example of this is the case of the inviolability of the home. To what extent is this right absolute? Is a judicial authorization required or is the administrative authorization sufficient in order

[118] Joined Cases T-222/99, T-327/99 and T-329/99 *Martínez and others v Parliament* [2001] ECR II-2823. See E Gianfrancesco, 'I limiti alla costituzione di gruppi politici all'interno del Parlamento europeo' (2002) *I Diritto pubblico comparato ed europeo* 278.

[119] LFM Besselink, 'Entrapped by the maximum standard: On Fundamental Rights, Pluralism and Subsidiarity in the European Union' (1998) 35(3) *Common Market Law Review* 629.

[120] Case T-112/98 *Mannesmannröhren-Werke v Commission* [2001] ECR II-729 para 84. See PR Willis, '"You have the right to remain silent . . .", or do you? The privilege against self-incrimination following Mannesmannröhren-Werke and others' (2001) 22(8) *European Competition Law Review* 313.

[121] Case 155/79 *AM & S Europe Ltd v Commission* [1982] ECR 1575, Opinion of AG Warner. See IS Forrester, 'Legal Professional Privilege: Limitations on the Commission's Powers of Inspection following the AM & S Judgment' (1983) 20(1) *Common Market Law Review* 75; and GT Pagone, 'Legal Professional Privilege in the European Communities: The AM & S Case and Australian Law' (1984) 33(3) *International & Comparative Law Quarterly* 663.

[122] P Craig and G de Búrca (2008) (n 108) 389.

to make searches in cases of alleged violations of competition law? Is it only applied to natural persons or also to legal persons?[123] That is, although the idea of 'common constitutional traditions' as a basis of the general principles of law is very suggestive, it is difficult to just forget the fact that usually the differences between legal systems of Member States are large. Moreover, even if the Court accepted the argument in a case of one of the parties under which a particular right should be recognized as part of EC/EU law, the manner in which the Court would actually make this recognition and the scope it would give to it could not be the expected one.[124] Let us not forget that the Court upholds one principle above all: the autonomy of EC/EU law.

4.3. The Charter of Fundamental Rights

4.3.1. Introduction

44. The idea that the EC/EU is to have its own Bill of Rights is not new. The European Commission had already noted this possibility in an internal document in 1979.[125] However, the debate regarding accession to the ECHR eclipsed that option, which nonetheless reappeared strongly in the periods in which accession seemed more distant. Thus, the European Council finally decided, in Cologne in 1999, to draft a Charter that allows the citizens of the Union to be shown the importance of fundamental rights and their scope. This 'Charter', drafted in less than a year by an ad hoc body (called 'the Convention'), began as an interinstitutional agreement 'solemnly proclaimed' by the presidents of the European Parliament, the European Commission and the Council of the Union on 7 December 2000 at Nice. The discussion about the value of the Charter was overlapped by the intense media discussion surrounding the drafting of the Constitutional Treaty. The 'Constitution for Europe' would be a breakthrough, inter alia, for fundamental rights within the Union in general and the legal status of the Charter in particular. Indeed, the Constitutional Treaty recognized under Article I-9.1 'rights, freedoms and principles set forth in the Charter of Fundamental Rights', which included in its provisions a kind of dogma section and which ordered the EU to accede to the ECHR (Article I-9.2).[126]

[123] See Lienemeyer, M and Waelbroeck, D, 'Case C-94/00, *Roquette Frères SA v Directeur Général de la Concurrence, de la Consommation et de la Répression des Fraudes*. Judgment of the Court of Justice (Full Court) of 22 October 2002' (2003) 40(6) *Common Market Law Review* 1481 and the references quoted there.

[124] For example, so was the disappointment of the claimants in Case 44/79 *Hauer* [1979] (n 96) and Case 11/70 *Internationale Handelsgesellschaft* [1970] (n 31).

[125] See the memorandum of the Commission *Accession of the Communities to the European Convention on Human Rights* COM (79) 210 final *Bull EC* (Supplement 2/79, 2 May 1979, 12).

[126] Sudre, F, 'Article I-9' in Burgorgue-Larsen, L, Levade, A and Picod, F (eds), *Traité établissant une Constitution pour l'Europe: commentaire article par article* (Bruylant, Bruxelles, 2007) 141

45. The aim of this work is not to analyse the content of the Charter or the problems that the wording could give rise to.[127] Nevertheless, it seems relevant to refer to the life it had before its elevation to convention status through Lisbon. The draft was put forward by the so-called Committee of Wise Men, who analysed the situation in Austria after the arrival of the coalition government, of which Haider's FPÖ is part.[128] The Charter has also become a qualified factor in the interpretation of EC/EU law. The first to put it forward in a process were the Advocates General, followed by the Court of First Instance.[129] On the other hand, the Court of Justice did not incorporate it until 2006. Probably this delay was due to the fact that the Luxembourg Court was waiting for the ratification of the 'Constitution for Europe', which incorporated the Charter in its text and granted the Charter the rank of a Treaty.[130] Therefore, when the Court realised that the 'Constitution' would not be ratified, at least in the near future, it dusted down the text of the Charter and introduced it into its legal reasonings as an interpretive element. In its decision on the Directive on family reunification, the ECJ established that:

> While the Charter is not a legally binding instrument, the Community legislature did, however, acknowledge its importance by stating, in the second recital in the preamble to the Directive, that the Directive observes the principles recognised not only by Article 8 of the ECHR but also in the Charter. Furthermore, the principal aim of the Charter, as is apparent from its preamble, is to reaffirm 'rights as they result, in particular, from the constitutional traditions and international obligations common to the Member States, the Treaty on European Union, the Community Treaties, the [ECHR], the Social Charters adopted by the Community and by the Council of Europe and the case-law of the Court . . . and of the European Court of Human Rights'.[131]

This is the only way to understand that even the Strasbourg Court mentioned the Charter before its Luxembourg counterpart.[132] Even national courts referred to the Charter to strengthen the legitimacy of their foundations.[133]

[127] It has been discussed whether Art 53 of the Charter would entail any attack on EU law supremacy. See O de Schutter, 'Promoting and Protecting Fundamental Rights in the European Union: The relations between the European Convention of Human Rights, the European Charter and the EU member states' constitutions. Briefing Paper' European Parliament, Directorate General Internal Policies of the Union (Brussels, 2007). Another debate is the one about the differences (if any) between rights and principles.

[128] The report, drafted by Martti Ahtisaari, Jochen Frowein and Marcelino Oreja, was adopted in Paris on 8 September 2000. A copy of the report is kept at the Max Planck Institute for Comparative Public Law and International Law in Heidelberg (Germany). An electronic copy is available at <http://www.mpil.de/shared/data/pdf/report.pdf >.

[129] Case C-173/99 *Broadcasting, Entertainment, Cinematographic and Theatre Union (BECTU)* [2001] ECR I-4881, Opinion of AG A Tizzano, para 26. See Case T-54/99 *max.mobil* [2002] (n 51) and the appeal in Case C-141/02 P *max.mobil* [2005] (n 51).

[130] See A Hinarejos Parga, 'Recent Human Rights Developments in the EU Courts: The Charter of Fundamental Rights, the European Arrest Warrant and Terror Lists' (2007) 7(4) *Human Rights Law Review* 793.

[131] Case C-540/03 *Parliament v Council* [2006] (n 107) para 38.

[132] Case *Christine Goodwin v the UK* App No 28957/95 (ECtHR, 11 July 2002, 2002-VI) on transsexual marriage, paras 58 and 100.

[133] See Judgment No 292/2000 (Spanish Constitutional Court, 30 November 2000) on personal data, para 8, quoting the Charter even before its proclamation.

4.3.2. The Charter's Legal Status

46. Although, until the entry into force of the Lisbon Treaty, its direct applicability as primary law was dismissed, we must not underestimate the importance that the Charter had until the last amendment of the Treaties even though it was denied convention status at first. That is, as the doctrine says, 'the absence of binding force [as such] does not imply, *per se*, the absence of legal effects'.[134]

47. The Charter is a document of unquestionable hermeneutic importance where, in essence, the constitutional traditions common to the Member States are brought together. Even before the entry into force of the Lisbon Treaty, it has been producing legal effects from three points of view. First, as an inter-institutional agreement, the EU institutions are obliged to respect it and to ensure that their acts will not undermine the fundamental rights proclaimed therein.[135] Second, as mentioned above, the Court of Justice may apply the Charter on a case-by-case basis, recognizing the binding nature of one or more of its precepts as general principles of law. Finally, some national constitutional provisions shall give legal effect to its provisions.[136]

48. For instance, regarding Spain, Article 10.2 of the Constitution grants, at least, an interpretation value to Treaties and international agreements related to human rights when implementing, at the domestic level, the fundamental rights recognized by the Constitution. That is to say, 'the principles relating to the fundamental rights and liberties recognised by the Constitution shall be interpreted in conformity with those international treaties'.[137] On the other hand, the Organic Law 1/2008, dated 30 July 2008, ratifying the Lisbon Treaty has

[134] R Alonso García (2007) (n 9) 256.

[135] See *Texte en application de la Charte des Droits Fondamentaux de l'Union Européenne – Communication de M. le President et de M. Vitorino* SEC(2001)380/3 (Brussels, 13 March 2001) and *Communication from the Commission – Compliance with the Charter of Fundamental Rights in Commission legislative proposals – Methodology for systematic and rigorous monitoring* COM(2005) 172 final (Brussels, 27 April 2005). The European Union Agency for Fundamental Rights (FRA) advises EU institutions on human rights compliance when adopting legal acts. See Art 4(2) of Council Regulation (EC) No 168/2007 establishing a European Union Agency for Fundamental Rights, OJ L 53/1 (22 February 2007).

[136] See FJ Matía Portilla, 'La eficacia de la Carta de Niza' in FJ Matía Portilla (ed), *La protección de los Derechos fundamentales en la Unión Europea* (Civitas, Madrid 2002) 123 and L Aguiar de Luque, 'La Carta europea de derechos y las constituciones nacionales' in A Pizzorusso (ed), *Riflessi della Carta europea dei diritti sulla giustizia e la giurisprudenza costituzionale: Italia e Spagna a confronto. Dottorato di ricerca in 'giustizia costituzionale e diritti fondamentali': giornata italo-spagnola di giustizia costituzionale* (Giuffrè, Milano, 2003) 23.

[137] See A Sáiz Arnáiz, *La apertura constitucional al Derecho internacional y europeo de los derechos humanos. El artículo 10.2 de la Constitución española* (CGPJ, Madrid, 1999) 205–77; A Queralt Jiménez, 'Los usos del canon europeo en la jurisprudencia del Tribunal Constitucional: una muestra del proceso de armonización europea en materia de derechos fundamentales' (2007) 20 *Teoría y Realidad Constitucional* 435; and A Queralt Jiménez, *La interpretacion de los derechos: del Tribunal de Estrasburgo al Tribunal Constitucional* (CEPC, Madrid, 2008).

placed the Charter in an unusual legal position. That is, before the entry into force of the Lisbon Treaty (which gives the Charter the status of an international treaty), it seems that Spanish law had already incorporated the content of the Charter, according to Article 2 of the Organic Law:

> Article 2. Charter of Fundamental Rights of the European Union.
>
> According to the provisions of the second paragraph of Article 10 of the Spanish Constitution and paragraph 8 of Article 1 of the Lisbon Treaty, the rules relating to fundamental rights and freedoms that the Constitution recognizes shall be also interpreted in accordance with the provisions of the Charter of Fundamental Rights, published in the 'Official Journal of the European Union' of 14 December 2007, whose full text reads as follows . . .[138]

49. In another vein, some institutions and bodies of the European Union have used the Charter provisions since its first proclamation. The Commission, through an internal decision in March 2001, decided that, henceforth, it would carry out a preliminary compatibility analysis with the Charter regarding the legislative proposals that could have an impact on fundamental rights. This has resulted in the introduction of 'recitals' in the Commission's legislative proposals on which it is mentioned that a prior compatibility test has been carried out with the fundamental right that could be affected. Four years later, the Commission published a communication which reported on the impact of the Charter in its legislative proposals.[139] Likewise, it commissioned an external report on the impact of this new legislative policy on the protection of fundamental rights.[140]

50. The European Ombudsman also makes repeated reference to various provisions of the Charter in his annual reports, the right to good administration and the right of access to the Ombudsman (Articles 41–43). Thus, for example, in its annual report of 8 April 2002 it condemned the actions of some institutions who failed to observe many of the rights established in the Charter, particularly in relation to their own selection and regulation systems of their personnel, and stated that:

> There have been many claims presented that the Charter should be included in the Treaty, or in a possible Constitution of the European Union. To me, the most urgent task is for the institutions to show that they respect the promises which they made to European citizens in proclaiming the Charter. There is no point in giving legal status to a text if it is not intended to be followed in practice. I therefore do hope that, in the

[138] Organic Law 1/2008 authorizing the ratification of the Lisbon Treaty, BOE 184 (31 July 2008).

[139] See *Compliance with the Charter of Fundamental Rights in Commission legislative proposals* COM(2005) 172 final (n 135) and H Toner, 'Impact assessments and fundamental rights protection in EU law' (2006) 31(3) *European Law Review* 316.

[140] See the Final Report on the *Preparatory study for impact assessment and ex ante evaluation of Fundamental Rights Agency* (European policy evaluation consortium, February 2005) at <http://ec.europa.eu/justice_home/doc_centre/rights/doc/study_epec_fund_rights_agency_en.pdf>.

coming year, the institutions will prove in practice that they respect the Charter of Fundamental Rights. This would be good news for the citizens and would surely enhance the relations between them and the institutions.[141]

In a more recent speech, the holder of the post at the time, Nikiforos Diamandouros, said that the debate that started following the failure to ratify the Constitutional Treaty on the legal status of the Charter has not been a change in the attitude of the EC/EU body.

For the European Ombudsman, the principal yardstick to measure compliance with human rights is the Charter of Fundamental Rights of the European Union.[142]

51. Although the Court of First Instance and the Advocates General quickly added the Charter in their arguments, we had to wait several years before the Court of Justice did the same.[143] As mentioned before, this delay could be due to the fact that the Court was waiting for the Charter to change into binding law through an appropriate constitutional mechanism. Thus, only when it became clear that this was not going to happen (at least, not in the near future) did the ECJ decide to incorporate it in its jurisprudence.[144] Thus, after years of silence, the Court of Justice finally followed the practice of the Advocates General, who had already mentioned it, and of the Court of First Instance, and referred to the Charter as the instrument that reaffirms the general principles of law common to the Member States.[145]

In a later case, citing the Court of First Instance, the ECJ confirmed this point by referring expressly to Article 47:

The right to an effective remedy for everyone whose rights and freedoms guaranteed by the law of the Union are violated has, moreover, been reaffirmed by Article 47 of the Charter of fundamental rights of the European Union, proclaimed on 7 December 2000 in Nice (OJ 2000 C 364, p 1). Although this document does not have legally

[141] J Söderman, 'The European Ombudsman. Annual Report 2011' Office for official publications (Luxembourg) at 12.

[142] The speech was given at the Foro de Nueva Economía (Madrid, 28 April 2006), text available at <http://www.ombudsman.europa.eu/speeches/en/2006-04-28.htm>.

[143] Case C-173/99 *BECTU* [2001] (n 129), Opinion of AG A. Tizzano; Joined Cases C-20/00 and C-64/00 *Booker Aquaculture Ltd et al v The Scottish Ministres* [2003] ECR I-7411, Opinion of AG J Mischo (20 September 2001), para 125; Joined Cases C-122/99 P and C-125/99 P D and Sweden v Council [2001] ECR I-4319, Opinion of AG J Mischo (22 February 2001), para 97; Case C-459/99 *Mouvemente contre le racisme v Belgium* [2002] ECR I-6591, Opinion of AG C Stix-Hackl (13 September 2001), para 64; Case 60/00 *Mary Carpenter v Secretary of State for Home Department* [2002] ECR I-6279, Opinion of AG C Stix-Hackl (13 September 2001); Case C-270/99 P *Z v Parliament* [2001] ECR I-9197, Opinion of AG F Jacobs (22 March 2001), para 40; Case C-377/98, *Netherlands v Parliament and Council* [2001] ECR I-7079, Opinion of AG F Jacobs (14 June 2001), paras 197 and 210. At the then CFI, see Case T-54/99 *max.mobil* [2002] (n 51) or Case T-242/02 *The Sunrider Corp v OAMI* [2005] ECR II-2793 para 51 where the then CFI accepted the definition of the Charter to set up the boundaries of a right.

[144] A Hinarejos Parga (2007) (n 30) at 794–5.

[145] Case C-540/03 *Parliament v Council* [2006] (n 107) para 38.

binding force, it does show the importance of the rights it sets out in the Community legal order.[146]

The inclusion of the Charter on the reasoning of the Court as a qualified source of general principles of law would confirm that this document has definitively entered the constitutional practice of the European Union, even before the entry into force of the Lisbon Treaty.[147]

4.3.3. The Charter after the Treaty of Lisbon

52. The Lisbon Treaty, unlike the 'Constitution for Europe', has not incorporated the Charter in its articles but, nevertheless, has awarded it the same legal value as the Treaties themselves. This amputation of the Constitutional Treaty shows, without a doubt, the refusal of certain states to every vestige of a 'formal constitutionalization' or *statalization* of the Union.[148] However, having ratified the Treaty of Lisbon, the new Article 6 of the Treaty on European Union (TEU-L) returns to the text of Article I-9 of the Constitutional Treaty, making a reference to the Charter, in its final version of 2007, and awarding it 'the same legal value as the Treaties'.[149] Article 6.1 TEU-L provides that '[t]he provisions of the Charter shall not extend in any way the competences of the Union as defined in the Treaties'. This statement has been reinforced by Declaration No 1, which says that '[t]he Charter does not extend the field of application of Union law beyond the powers of the Union or establish any new power or task for the Union, or modify powers and tasks as defined by the Treaties'.

53. In addition to this Declaration, the United Kingdom and Poland negotiated a protocol specifically aimed at clarifying the implementation of the Charter in certain aspects, a protocol that also applied to the Czech Republic as a condition for ratifying the Lisbon Treaty.[150] On the one hand, it makes clear that the

[146] Case C-131/03 P *Reynolds Tobacco and others v Commission* [2006] ECR I-7795 para 30.

[147] P Craig and G de Búrca (2008) (n 108) at 418.

[148] A Berramdane, 'Le traité de Lisbonne et le retour des États' (2008) 9–10 La Semaine Juridique 23 at 26. Some scholars argue that even after Lisbon the EU has a real Constitution. See, for instance, S Griller, 'Is this a Constitution? Remarks on a Contested Concept' in S Griller and J Ziller (eds), *The Lisbon Treaty: EU Constitutionalism Without a Constitutional Treaty?* (Springer, Vienna 2008) 21 at 50.

[149] The TEU-L refers to the proclamation of the Charter in Strasbourg on 12 December 2007.

[150] See Protocol No. 30 on the application of the Charter to the UK and Poland (OJ C 306/156, 17 December 2007). The Czech President, Václav Klaus, accepted ratification of the Lisbon Treaty at the European Council held in Brussels on 29–30 October 2009. In exchange, Protocol No 30 would also be applicable to the Czech Republic. See Annex I (Protocol on the Application of the Charter of Fundamental Rights of the European Union to the Czech Republic) to the Presidency Conclusions CONCL 3 15265/09 (Brussels, 30 October 2009) available at <http://www.se2009.eu/polopoly_fs/1.21646!menu/standard/file/ER%20conclusions.pdf>. The ratification of the Lisbon Treaty was finally possible after the dismissal of the case on the possible unconstitutionality of the Treaty brought up by 17 Czech Senators before the Constitutional Court. On 3 November 2009, the Czech Constitutional Court affirmed the compatibility between the Lisbon Treaty and the Czech Constitution. See the document of the Swedish Presidency at < http://www.se2009.eu/en/meetings_news/2009/11/3/after_the_czech_verdict_only_signature_left>.

Charter does not broaden the jurisdiction of the EU Courts or the national courts of those countries to question the internal regulations of both states (Article 1.1 of the Protocol). Moreover, it is expressly understood that the title IV of the Charter (entitled 'Solidarity' and related to social rights) does not establish any new right that could be held before the national courts of both countries (Article 1.2). In fact, it is more a statement than a protocol. Given that the Charter sees itself as a text that does nothing but reaffirm a number of rights that other texts, both of international and constitutional nature, have previously proclaimed, the EU courts could remain so 'creative' as they have been until now in the area of fundamental rights. The same could happen to the domestic courts, which, according to the last paragraph of the protocol, are still bound by all other obligations of Poland and the United Kingdom (and finally also the Czech Republic), among which are obviously those resulting from considering, as sources of EU law (Articles 6.3 TEU, 4.2 TEU-L), all international and domestic constitutional texts leading to 'find' the rights that the Charter reaffirms. In this sense, it would be a reiteration of what was already established in the horizontal clauses of the Charter. It would be different if we conclude that the Charter goes beyond the mere recognition of the existing rights, which cannot be discarded and will depend on the interpretation given by the Court of Justice. Anyway, the lack of clarity regarding the scope of the said protocol is pitiful.

54. From the political viewpoint, and without taking into account the Polish (nor the Czech) case, the insistence of the United Kingdom is rather strange, since two years earlier it had signed the Constitutional Treaty, which included the Charter without reserve. The doctrine suggests that perhaps the British Government would be ready to simplify the process of ratification of the Lisbon Treaty and, thus, meant that this is very different from the 'Constitution for Europe', so a referendum would not be necessary for Britain to give its consent to the new text. In fact, this time the ratification was carried out by the British Parliament. Moreover, from the legal standpoint, the effect of this Protocol is to be relativized. Indeed, this addition does not affect the EC/EU *acquis* on the subject. Thus, the plaintiffs could base their arguments, not only on the Charter, but also on the fundamental rights jurisprudence developed by the Court of Justice.[151]

[151] P Craig. 'The Lisbon Treaty, Process, Architecture and Substance' (2008) 33(2) *European Law Review* 137 at 163. On the legal value of the Charter after Lisbon, see JR Canedo Arrillaga and LI Gordillo Pérez, 'Los derechos fundamentales en la Unión Europea a la espera de Lisboa' (2008) 39 *Cuadernos Europeos de Deusto* 27 at 47–58 and A Alì, 'La tutela dei diritti fondamentali della persona umana nell'Unione europea' in P de Cesari (ed), *Trattato di diritto privato dell'Unione europea, II. Persona e famiglia* (Giappichelli, Torino, 2008) 47 at 55–64.

5. THE RIGHTS RECOGNIZED BY EC/EU CASE LAW

55. As seen above, the Court of Justice, the jealous guardian of the autonomy of EC/EU law, turns to the category of general principles of law in order to acknowledge case by case the fundamental rights as deemed appropriate within the EC/EU. It is not, therefore, possible to establish a definitive Bill of Rights, but it is interesting to outline the rights that EC/EU law has recognized. Thus, the Court of Justice and the Court of First Instance have set the following fundamental rights:

- the principle of equal treatment, which involves treating people who are in the same situation in the same way. This implies the prohibition of any sort of discrimination, especially on the grounds of nationality (Articles 12 TEC, 18 TFEU) or between men and women (Articles 3.2 TEC, 8 TFEU and Articles 140 TEC, 156 TFEU). Many provisions of the treaties refer to the obligation to treat all participants in the market the same way, such as Article 34.2 TEU (Article 40 TFEU). The ECJ has declared that the prohibition of discrimination is a specific realization of the general principle of equality, which is one of the fundamental principles of law and requires that similar situations are not treated differently unless the difference is objectively justified.[152] Recently, the ECJ has taken a further step in its case law in favour of equal treatment and non-discrimination on grounds of sex and has established that Member States are obliged to treat in the same way a heterosexual marriage to life partners of the same sex if, under national law, in relation to the specific legal status (for example, right to a widow's pension), registered partners and married couples are in a comparable situation;[153]
- the right to a fair trial (Article 6 ECHR),[154] including the right to effective judicial control (that is, the right to a legal remedy, Article 13 ECHR),[155] the

[152] Joined Cases 117/76 and 16/77 *Albert Ruckdeschel and Hansa-Lagerhaus Ströh v Hauptzollamt Hamburg-St. Annen; Diamalt AG v Hauptzollamt Itzehoe* (*Ruckdeschel*) [1977] ECR 1753 para 7. See also Case C-280/93 *Germany v Council* [1994] ECR I-04973 para 68.

[153] Case C-267/06 *Tadao Maruko v Versorgungsanstalt der deutschen Bühnen* [2008] ECR I-1757 para 72. In this case, the ECJ did not rely upon the ECHR but on a Council Directive itself (see Council Directive 2000/78/EC establishing a general framework for equal treatment in employment and occupation, OJ L 303/16, 2 December 2000). See C Tobler and K Waaldijk, 'Case C-267/06, Tadao Maruko v Versorgungsanstalt der deutschen Bühnen, Judgment of the Grand Chamber of the Court of Justice of 1 April 2008' (2009) 46(2) *Common Market Law Review* 723 at 729 and 741–6.

[154] Case 98/79 *Josette Pecastaing v Belgium* [1980] ECR 691 paras 21–22 and Joined Cases C-174/98 P and C-189/98 P *Netherlands and Van der Wal v Commission* [2000] ECR I-1 paras 17–18.

[155] Case 222/84 *Marguerite Johnston v Chief Constable of the Royal Ulster Constabulary* [1986] ECR 1651 para 18. The most representative cases dealing with this right may be Case C-50/00 P *Unión de Pequeños Agricultores* [2002] (n 9) paras 32–45 and Case C-263/02 P *Commission v Jégo-Quéré* [2004] ECR I-3425 paras 29–50.

right to trial without undue delay,[156] the right to adversarial proceedings,[157] the presumption of innocence,[158] the right to be defended[159] and call witnesses;[160]
- the principle of non-retroactivity of criminal provisions (Article 7 ECHR);[161]
- the retroactive imposition of a lighter penalty (Article 15 of International Covenant on Civil and Political Rights);[162]
- the principle of *non bis in idem* (Article 4 of the seventh protocol of the ECHR);[163]
- human dignity;[164]
- respect for private life,[165] family life,[166] to home and correspondence (Article 8 ECHR),[167] in particular, respect for personal physical integrity,[168] the right to keep one's own personal health status secret,[169] medical confidentiality,[170] and the right to inviolability of the domicile;[171]
- freedom to manifest one's religion (Article 9 ECHR);[172]

[156] Case C-185/95 P *Baustahlgewebe v Commission* [1998] ECR I-8417 paras 20–22 and 26–48.

[157] Case C-17/98 *Emesa Sugar (Free Zone)* [2000] ECR I-665 paras 10–18. The Court established that the fact that one of the parties cannot send comments in response to the Opinion of the AG is not against the right to a fair trial (see below).

[158] Case C-199/92 P *Hüls v Commission* [1999] ECR I-4287 paras 149–50.

[159] Case C-7/98 *Dieter Krombach and André Bamberski* [2000] ECR I-1935 paras 35–46.

[160] Case T-9/99 *HFB Holding für Fernwärmetechnik Beteiligungsgesellschaft mbH & Co KG and others v Commission* [2002] ECR II-1487 paras 389–92. This decision was appealed (C-202/02) and subsequently dismissed by the ECJ in Joined Cases C-189/02 P, C-202/02 P, C-205/02 P to C-208/02 P and C-213/02 P *Dansk Rørindustri and others v Commission* [2005] ECR I-5425.

[161] On the prohibition of imposing retroactive sanctions, see Case 63/83, *Regina v Kent Kirk* [1984] (n 97) para 22. On the non-retroactivity of criminal provisions, see Case T-23/99 *LR AF 1998 v Commission* [2002] ECR II-1705 paras 218–38. This decision was appealed (C-206/02) and subsequently dismissed by the ECJ in Joined Cases C-189/02 P, C-202/02 P, C-205/02 P to C-208/02 P and C-213/02 P *Dansk Rørindustri* [2005] (n 160).

[162] Case T-48/96 *Acme Industry & Co Ltd v Council* [1999] ECR II-3089 para 30.

[163] Joined Cases C-238/99 P, C-244/99 P, C-245/99 P, C-247/99 P, C-250/99 P to C-252/99 P and C-254/99 P *Limburgse Vinyl Maatschappij and others v Commission* [2002] ECR I-8375 paras 59–63. See AL Calvo Caravaca and MP Canedo Arrillaga, 'Non bis in idem en Derecho antitrust' (2006) 54(1) *Estudios de Deusto* 11.

[164] Case C-337/98 *Commission v France* [2000] ECR I-8377 paras 70–77.

[165] Case 165/82 *Commission v UK* [1983] ECR 3431 para 13, although this decision did not mention the ECHR. On personal data protection, see Case C-369/98 *TR & P Fisher* [2000] ECR I-6751 paras 32–38.

[166] Case 249/86 *Commission v Germany* [1989] ECR 1263 para 10. On family reunification, see Case C-60/00 *Mary Carpenter* [2002] (n 143) paras 40–46 and Case C-109/01 *Hacene Akrich* [2003] ECR I-9607 paras 58–60.

[167] Dealing with the Commission powers to implement searches within antitrust law, see Case 136/79 *National Panasonic v Commission* [1980] ECR 2033 paras 19–20 and Case 5/85 *AKZO Chemie* [1986] (n 97) paras 25–27.

[168] Case T-121/89 *X v Commission* [1992] ECR II-2195 paras 53–59, appealed and subsequently revoked by Case C-404/92 P *X v Commission* [1994] ECR I-4737 paras 17–24, where it was established that the Commission violated Art 8 ECHR when carrying out substitutive tests on AIDS to a candidate who had already refused to have a regular test.

[169] Case T-176/94 *K v Commission* [1995] ECR I-A-00203, II-00621 para 31.

[170] Case C-62/90 *Commission v Germany* [1992] ECR I-2575 para 23.

[171] Joined Cases 46/87 and 227/88 *Hoechst* [1989] (n 82) paras 17–18 and the change from its previous case law in Case C-94/00 *Roquette Frères* [2002] (n 82) paras 22–99.

[172] Case 130/75 *Prais v Council* [1975] ECR 1589 paras 6–19.

– freedom of expression (Article 10 ECHR);[173]
– freedom of association (Article 11 ECHR)[174] and the right of peaceful assembly,[175] in particular the right to join a union and take part in their activities;[176]
– property rights or ownership rights as protected by the constitutional law of the Member States[177] and by Article 1 of Protocol No 1 of the ECHR;[178]
– freedom to undertake an economic activity (corporate or professional);[179] and
– the right of everyone who is lawfully within the territory of a state to move freely within it (Article 2 of Protocol No 4 of the ECHR).[180]

56. From the prior case law we may outline that these fundamental rights are, of course, absolute, but must be understood in the light of its social function. The EU may subject the enjoyment of fundamental rights to certain restrictions, provided that such restrictions actually correspond to the objectives of general interest pursued by the EU and do not constitute a disproportionate and intolerable interference which infringes the essence of the right guaranteed.[181] These limitations must also keep adequate proportionality in relation to the public interest pursued.[182]

As one may easily see, to establish a proper balance between the interests that underlie the fundamental rights to be protected is always a complex issue and subject to criticism.[183] However, the ECHR provides that certain fundamental rights

[173] See, for instance, Joined Cases 43/82 and 63/82 *VBVB and VBBB* [1984] (n 96) para 34 and Case C-112/00 *Schmidberger v Austria* [2003] ECR I-5659 paras 79–80.

[174] Case C-415/93 *Union royale belge des sociétés de football association and others v Bosman and others* (*Bosman*) [1995] ECR I-4921 para 79, Joined Cases T-222/99, T-327/99 and T-329/99 *Martínez and others* [2001] (n 118) paras 230–235 (appealed and confirmed by the ECJ in Case C-488/01 P *Martínez v Parliament* [2003] ECR I-13355).

[175] Case C-235/92 P *Montecatini v Commission* [1999] ECR I-4539 para §137 and Case C-112/00 *Schmidberger* (n 173) paras 79–80.

[176] Case 36/75 *Rutili v Ministre de l'Intérieur* [1975] (n 76) paras 31–32 (where the Court mentions Arts 8, 9, 10 and 11 ECHR). On the particular case of the freedom of association of Community officers interpreted under the «general principles of labour law' (without mentioning the ECHR) see Case 175/73 *Union Syndicale and others v Council* [1974] ECR 917 paras 14–15.

[177] Case 4/73 *Nold* [1974] (n 32) para 14.

[178] Case 44/79 *Hauer* [1979] (n 96) paras 17–30 and Joined Cases C-20/00 and C-64/00 *Booker Aquaculture e Hydro Seafood* [2003] ECR I-7411 para 67.

[179] Case 230/78 *Eridania* [1979] ECR 2749 paras 20–22. This fundamental right has been brought up before the Court, generally together with the right to property (in which case the Court has considered them jointly, as in Case 4/73 *Nold* [1974] (n 32)) or sometimes with the right to undertake an economic activity (Case 44/79 *Hauer* [1979] (n 96)).

[180] Case 36/75 *Rutili* [1975] (n 76) para 32.

[181] Case 265/87 *Schräder v Hauptzollamt Gronau* [1989] ECR 2237 para 15.

[182] On the principle of proportionality see K Lenaerts, P Van Nuffel and R Bray, *Constitutional Law of the European Union* 2nd edn (Thompson, London, 2005) 109–15.

[183] See Case C-280/93 *Germany v Council* [1994] (n 152) and the critics of the equilibrium interest case law in U Everling, 'Will Europe Slip on Bananas? The Bananas Judgment of the Court of Justice and National Courts' (1996) 33(3) *Common Market Law Review* 401 at 416–19.

> shall not be subject to more restrictions than the ones prescribed by law and are necessary in a democratic society for public safety, protection of public order, health, morals or the protection of rights and freedoms of others.[184]

The ECJ has taken into account this fact in its many decisions on fundamental rights.[185] Besides, it is also an extremely casuistic jurisprudence, and there are times when the ECJ, balancing the proportionality of the measures, directly analyses the discretion of the authority concerned.[186] Nevertheless, some other times, the proportionality of the actions are left to the consideration of what the relevant national law sets.[187]

On the other hand, and with an eye on the subsequent ratification of the Lisbon Treaty, Article 52.1 of the Charter of Fundamental Rights already stated that:

> Any limitation on the exercise of the rights and freedoms recognised by this Charter must be provided for by law and respect the essence of those rights and freedoms. Subject to the principle of proportionality, limitations may be made only if they are necessary and genuinely meet objectives of general interest recognised by the Union or the need to protect the rights and freedoms of others.[188]

[184] That is the almost identical wording of Arts 8(2), 9(2), 10(2) and 11(2) ECHR providing respectively for the right to respect for private and family life, freedom of thought, conscience and religion, freedom of expression, freedom of assembly and association. In this context regard must be had to the margin of appreciation test that implements the ECtHR.

[185] Case 36/75 *Rutili* [1975] (n 76) para 32 and Case 136/79 *National Panasonic* [1980] (n 167) para 19.

[186] Case C-71/02 *Herbert Karner* [2004] ECR I-3025 paras 50–51.

[187] Case C-368/95 *Vereinigte Familiapress Zeitungsverlags- und vertriebs GmbH v Bauer Verlag* [1997] ECR I-3689 paras 26–33.

[188] About those and other possible restrictions to the rights recognized in the Charter, see D Triantafyllou, 'The European Charter of fundamental rights and the "rule of law": restricting fundamental rights by reference' (2002) 39(1) *Common Market Law Review* 53 and A Mangas Martín, 'Artículo 52. Alcance e interpretación de los derechos y principios' in A Mangas Martín (ed), *Carta de los Derechos Fundamentales de la Unión Europea* (Fundación BBVA, Bilbao, 2008) 826 at 832–7.

4

The European Convention on Human Rights According to the European Court of Justice

1. TWO DIFFERENT LEGAL ORDERS

1. The European Convention on Human Rights (ECHR) and the EU Treaties are different international legal instruments. Indeed, at first, the six Member States of the communities were not all part of the Convention, since France did not ratify it until 1974. That is, in the beginning, legally speaking, there was complete separation between the two instruments.

2. The first change came when the Court of Justice in Luxembourg modified its jurisprudence on fundamental rights and decided to take them into consideration as general principles of law.[1] It was, therefore, necessary to identify those rights that would become general principles. In the same decision, the Court appointed as a source of fundamental rights the common constitutional traditions and international treaties which the Member States would have signed or ratified.[2] This solution had its logic and ultimately served to protect Member States from incurring international responsibility. In fact, while the Community's powers were still exercised by states, the powers of the latter were limited by the rights guaranteed by those international treaties. To prevent the transfer of powers to the Community from implying a waiver of this warranty, it was essential for this function to be ensured at the EC level.[3]

[1] Case 4/73 *Nold, Kohlen- und Baustoffgroßhandlung v Commission* [1974] ECR 491 para 13. See TC Hartley, 'Fundamental Rights in Community Law' (1975) *European Law Review* 54.

[2] Case 4/73 *Nold* [1974] (n 1) para 13. The French version of this decision refers to 'instruments internationaux . . . auxquels les états membres ont cooperé ou adheré'. The English version also refers to 'international treaties . . . in which the Member States have cooperated or to which they have adhered'. It does make sense that the Court used this wording, since France only ratified the ECHR a few months before the decision was made public. See MM Mendelson, ‹The European Court of Justice and human rights› (1981) 1 *Yearbook of European Law* 125.

[3] JP Jacqué, 'Droit constitutionnel national, Droit communautaire, CEDH, Charte des Nations Unies. L'instabilité des rapports de système entre ordres juridiques' (2007) 60 *Revue Française de Droit Constitutionnel* 3 at 22.

3. The risks of mutual ignorance between the two dispositions were quickly discovered by the legal practitioners at that time. The Member States of the Communities which were, at the same time, members of the Convention (since 1974, all of them) were in an international position that could be judged as fragile to say the least. The Constitution of the European Coal and Steel Community did not foresee that their actions would undermine the fundamental rights of citizens, regardless of the legal instrument of protection used (national Constitution or international treaty). However, the development of the Communities and the intelligence of some lawyers and legal practitioners meant that, in quite a short period of time, one could argue that there was a conflict between an act of Community institutions and a fundamental right protected by the national Constitution or, where appropriate, by the ECHR. The first case, a conflict between the national Constitution and EC/EU law, has already been analysed. The second assumption is more complex because, first, it involves at least three actors: the EC/EU institution concerned (subject to EC/EU law); the European Court of Human Rights (ECtHR), and until the entry into force of Protocol No 11 in 1998, also the European Commission of Human Rights (subject to the ECHR); and the Member State concerned (under its own Constitution, EC/EU law and the ECHR).

The European Commission of Human Rights, which previously shared duties with the ECtHR, soon stated that the transfer of competences from the Member States of the Convention to other international organizations was not banned. However, it was to be borne in mind that the transfer could not exclude the responsibility of the state concerned regarding the powers transferred.[4] Thus, if condemned by the ECtHR, a state would be responsible for an act of an EC/EU institution which, in principle, would not have to respond to nor be brought before the ECtHR, since it was not a member of the Convention.

2. THE THESIS OF FUNCTIONAL SUCCESSION

4. To establish a kind of consistency of the legal orders and between legal and reciprocal obligations of the Member States of the Convention and the EC/EU, one member of the Court of Justice, in an academic paper, proposed a solution based on the German *Hypothekentheorie*: the Community shall be obliged by virtue of succession by the obligations derived from the Convention.[5]

[4] See App No 235/56 (Commission Decision, 10 June 1958, 2 DR 257) and Case *M & Co v Germany* App No 13258/87 (Commission Decision, 9 February 1990, 64 DR 138).

[5] The thesis of the functional succession was suggested by Judge Pescatore in a doctrinal paper. See P Pescatore, 'External relations in the case-law of the Court of Justice of the European Communities' (1979) 16(4) *Common Market Law Review* 615 and more explicitly P Pescatore, 'La Cour de Justice des Communautés Européennes et la Convention Européenne des Droits de l'Homme' in GJ Wiarda, F Matscher and H Petzold (eds), *Protecting human rights, the European dimension: studies in honour of / Protection des droits de l'homme, la dimension européenne. Mélanges en l'honneur de Gérard J Wiarda* 2nd edn (C Heymanns, Cologne, 1990) 441. Later,

5. The European Community was created by states which were already bound by the ECHR in the exercise of their powers. Through the Treaties establishing the Communities, these states have pooled some of their more important public powers, especially in law making and economic and social management, conferring their exercise to common institutions. According to this theory, with this transfer, the states were unable, and, besides, did not want to exclude the exercise of such powers from the limits and controls derived from the ECHR.

6. The ECHR is the expression of a form of common political and legal culture among the founding states of the EC/EU. Indeed it expresses a social way of life that includes values such as democracy, human rights and fundamental freedoms and the rule of law. The EC/EU, as an institution common to all states which are part of the Convention, shall obviously be placed in the same political and legal movement. The EC/EU shall be bound to comply with the Convention as well as the states that have created it, becoming, therefore, Member States. From this we shall point out, *inter alia*, that under the Convention, the Court is in exactly the same situation as the courts of the Member States of the Convention. Regarding the Convention and its organs, the Court would be 'domestic jurisdiction'. Supporters of this theory argue that the ECJ, with its references to the Convention, apart from using it as arguments of authority or as a tool of great hermeneutical value to specify its own general principles, is directly applying the ECHR. Thus, they have concluded that if the Court has applied the Convention it is because it is an obligation and not by a gracious act of goodwill.

7. The aforementioned would be, therefore, nothing but a manifestation of the substitution effect that the Court of Justice has already recognized in other customs and trade agreements, particularly the General Agreement on Tariffs and Trade (GATT). Thus, in the *International Fruit* case of 1972, the ECJ stated:

> The Community has assumed the functions inherent in the tariff and trade policy . . .
>
> By conferring those powers on the Community, the member states showed their wish to bind it by the obligations entered into under the General Agreement.
>
> . . .
>
> It therefore appears that, in so far as under the EEC Treaty the Community has assumed the powers previously exercised by member states in the area governed by the

following basically the same arguments, P Pescatore, 'La coopération entre la Cour communautaire, les juridictions nationales et la Cour européenne des droits de l'Homme dans la protection des droits fondamentaux – Enquête sur un problème virtuel' (2003) 466 *Revue du Marché Commun et de L'Union Européenne* 151. German scholarship gathers a similar conclusion applying to this issue the well known *Theorie der Hypothek*. See A Bleckmann, *Die Bindung der Europäischen Gemeinschaft an die Europäische Menschenrechtskonvention* (C Heymanns, Köln, 1986) 113–16 and R Uerpmann-Wittzack, 'The Constitutional Role of Multilateral Treaty Systems' in A Von Bogdandy and J Bast (eds), *Principles of European Constitutional Law* (Hart, Oxford, 2006) 145 at 167–70.

> General Agreement, the provisions of that agreement have the effect of binding the Community.[6]

8. This would, in fact, be a concretion of the effect of succession recognized by international law, except that, in this case, we are not talking about an assumption of territorial nor general succession, but a limited functional succession. The exercise of the functions transferred to the EC/EU has taken place, due to the use of an expression in the *Hypothekentheorie* '*cum onere et emolumento*' that is, the EC/EU would not have acquired their duties and responsibilities free from servitude, but, equally to Member States that are at the origin of this transfer, it shall exercise its powers in compliance with the obligations under the ECHR, and shall respect the values self-contained in the constitutional traditions common to the Member States.[7] With this interpretation that supporters of the thesis about the functional succession propose, the creation of the EC/EU would not, therefore, have caused any breach or disruption in regard to international law or to the ideas that have shaped the modern constitutional state theory.

9. In support of this argument, those who advocate this view put forward Article 307 TEC (Article 351 TFEU). This provision would represent the translation in EC/EU law of the principle of relative effect of treaties and of its binding force (*pacta sunt servanda*), as provided in Article 26 of the Vienna Convention on the Law of Treaties:

> Every treaty in force is binding upon the parties to it and must be performed by them in good faith.[8]

On the other hand, the first paragraph of Article 307 TEC (Article 351 TFEU) provided the following:

> The rights and obligations arising from agreements concluded before 1 January 1958 or, for acceding States, before the date of their accession, between one or more Member States on the one hand, and one or more third countries on the other, shall not be affected by the provisions of the Treaties.

[6] Joined Cases 21/72 to 24/72 *International Fruit Company and others v Produktschap voor Groenten en Fruit* [1972] ECR 1219, especially paras 14, 15 and 18. In this case, scholars are not reluctant to recognize that there has taken place an 'implicit accession' of the EC/EU (*ibid* at 167–70), a 'functional succession' [*Funktionsnachfolge*] (W Schroeder and M Selmayr, 'Die EG, das GATT und die Vollzugslehre' (1998) 7 *Juristenzeitung* 344) or a 'legal functional sucesión' [*funktionelle Rechtsnachfolge*] (C Tomuschat, 'Artikel 281' in H Von der Groeben and J Schwarze (eds), *Vertrag über die Europäische Union und Vertrag zur Gründung der Europäischen Gemeinschaft. Kommentar* 6th edn (Nomos, Baden-Baden, 2004) paras 53–70). In any case, the practical effect would have been the same: the EC/EU would be bound by the GATT Agreements.

[7] P Pescatore, 'La Cour de Justice des Communautés Européennes et la Convention Européenne des Droits de l'Homme' in GJ Wiarda, F Matscher and H Petzold (eds), *Protecting human rights, the European dimension: studies in honour of / Protection des droits de l'homme, la dimension européenne. Mélanges en l'honneur de Gérard J. Wiarda* 2nd edn (C Heymanns, Cologne, 1990) 441 at 450–1.

[8] The Vienna Convention on the Law of Treaties (Vienna, 23 May 1969, 1155 *UN Treaty Series* 331) entered into force on 27 January 1980.

Thus, since the vast majority of Member States of the EC/EU had ratified the European Convention before the entry into force between them of the Rome Treaty and that by virtue of Article 210 EEC Treaty (subsequently Article 281 TEC) the Community would have legal personality (after Lisbon, the EU will succeed the Communities and will have personality, Article 47 TFEU), some found in this provision an implicit assertion of the binding nature of the ECHR in Community law. On the occasion of the judgment of the case *Attorney General v Juan C Burgoa*, the ECJ rejected this interpretation by clarifying the scope of Article 307.1 (Article 351 TFEU).[9] First of all, the Court recognized, despite his silence on the matter, that this provision meant the obligation of the institutions of the EC not to impede the implementation of the agreements of the Member States derived from a prior agreement.[10] Nevertheless, the Court continued as follows:

> . . . that duty of the Community institutions is directed only to permitting the member state concerned to perform its obligations under the prior agreement and does not bind the Community as regards the non-member country in question.[11]

This article, therefore, is not intended to impose new obligations on the EC/EU in international law, and even less intended to confer coercive character directly to the ECHR. At most, this provision would mean that the EC/EU has the obligation to respect the rules of the ECHR in order not to undermine or impede its implementation by Member States, which are bound by this international instrument for the protection of human rights.[12]

10. Moreover, the strict conditions under which, one could certainly argue, the Court of Justice accepted in 1972 the functional succession of the Community in the obligations of Member States in the application of the GATT agreements, would be subsequently synthesized by the Advocate General, Mr Capotorti, in his conclusions about the case *Procureur général v Arbelaiz-Emazabel*.[13] In fact, to support the thesis of succession would require 1) that all Member States of the EC/EU were already parties to the international agreement at the time of the conclusion of the Treaty of Rome; 2) that Member States were willing to make this subrogation and trying to achieve the objectives of the agreement; 3) that the EC/EU had exercised its powers in the field of that international agreement; and 4) that third Member States of the international

[9] Case 812/79 *Attorney General v Juan C Burgoa* [1980] ECR 2787. See RR Churchill and NG Foster, 'European Community Law and Prior Treaty Obligations of Member States: The Spanish Fishermen's Cases' (1987) 36(3) *International and Comparative Law Quarterly* 504.

[10] Case 812/79 *Burgoa* [1980] (n 9) para 9.

[11] Case 812/79 *Burgoa* [1980] (n 9) para 9.

[12] See O de Schutter and O l'Hoest, 'La Cour européenne des droits de l'homme juge du droit communautaire : Gibraltar, l'Union européenne, et la Convention européenne des droits de l'homme' (2000) 36(1–2) *Cahiers de Droit Européen* 141 at 177.

[13] Case 181/80 *Procureur général près la Cour d'Appel de Pau and others v José Arbelaiz-Emazabel* [1981] ECR 2961.

agreement had recognized the replacement of the EC/EU and their Member States.[14]

Thus, although the first condition could be mitigated or put forth (do not forget that France did not ratify the ECHR until 1974) in the event of an exclusive competence of the EC/EU, the rest of the conditions would remain difficult to accomplish in the case of the ECHR.[15] Even today, when it seems there is no longer any state against, it would be difficult to see when and how the EC/EU would have exercised its jurisdiction in the area of the ECHR.[16]

11. Thus, although the effect of 'replacement' or 'succession' was soon embraced by the Court of Justice to justify the implicit commitment of the EC to commercial and customs treaties, it is however not enough to justify a potential functional succession in the case of the ECHR.[17] In fact, it should be pointed out that the ECJ accepted the theory of functional succession in respect of the GATT Agreement and the Convention on the Northeast Atlantic Fisheries, but not on the Treaty on the World Trade Organization, but the question soon became irrelevant given the formal accession of the Community to the WTO in 1994.[18] Moreover, in a context in which either the European Commission or the ECJ or the ECtHR have supported the validity of this thesis, the doctrine is mainly pronounced by the rejection of this possibility.[19]

[14] See N Karamaoun, 'Le contrôle effectué par le juge de Strasbourg sur le droit communautaire: d'un paradoxe à l'autre' in P Leuprecht and others (eds), *Les Juridictions internationales: complémentarité ou concurrence?* (Bruylant, Bruxelles, 2005) 75 at 80–2.

[15] One of the scholars strongly opposing this theory points out that the Court could have excluded this theory taking into account that not all the members of the then EC were at the same time full members of the ECHR. See JP Jacqué (2007) (n 3) at 21.

[16] Nonetheless, the Commission advocated differently in its memorandum on the *Senator Lines* case before the ECtHR. See N Karamaoun, 'Le contrôle effectué par le juge de Strasbourg sur le droit communautaire : d'un paradoxe à l'autre' in P Leuprecht and others (eds), *Les Juridictions internationales : complémentarité ou concurrence?* (Bruylant, Bruxelles, 2005) 75 at 82.

[17] The 'substitution' or 'succession' effect has been recognized by the Court when other Treaties were involved. See Joined Cases 21/72 to 24/72 *International Fruit Company* [1972] (n 6), Case 9/73 *Carl Schlüter v Hauptzollamt Lörrach* [1973] ECR 1135 and Case 38/75 *Douaneagent der Nederlandse Spoorwegen v Inspecteur der Invoerrechten en Accijnzen* [1975] ECR 1439. See R Kovar, 'Les accords liant les Communautés européennes et l'ordre juridique communautaire : à propos d'une jurisprudence récente de la Cour de justice' (1975) *Revue du Marché Commun* 345; M Waelbroeck, 'Effect of GATT within the Legal Order of the EEC' (1974) 6 *Journal of World Trade Law* 614 and G White. 'Effects of International Treaties within the Community Order' (1976) 1 *European Law Review* 402.

[18] Joined Cases 21-24/72 *International Fruit Company* [1972] (n 6) para 18. See R Schutze, 'On "Middle Ground". The European Community and Public International Law' (2007) 13 *European University Institute Law Working Papers* at 12–13.

[19] JP Jacqué, 'La Cour de Justice, la Cour européenne des droits de l'homme et la protection des droits fondamentaux. Quelques observations' in M Dony and E Bribosia (eds), *L'avenir du système juridictionnel de l'Union européenne* (Editions de l'Université de Bruxelles, Bruxelles, 2002) 257.

3. THE ISSUE OF ACCESSION TO THE ECHR

12. After the rejection by the ECJ of the thesis of the functional succession, the EC/EU institutions soon realized that the EC/EU would gain access to the ECHR in order to ensure consistency and a more effective protection of fundamental rights.[20]

13. The accession of the Community to the ECHR is one of the classic and recurring issues that comes up from time to time and which does so with increasing force. Often mentioned as a starting point, the Memorandum of the Commission of 1979, in which the Community institution planned its accession to the ECHR, indicated the advantages (almost all of them of a political nature) and disadvantages (of a legal nature) of such accession.[21] This praiseworthy goal was gaining followers until the Court of Justice, in its controversial Opinion 2/94, concluded that there was no legal basis for the Community to accede to the ECHR and that, in order to do so, it was necessary to carry out a revision of the Treaties. Specifically, the Court stated the following:

> Furthermore, it is well settled that fundamental rights form an integral part of the general principles of law whose observance the Court ensures. For that purpose, the Court draws inspiration from the constitutional traditions common to the Member States and from the guidelines supplied by international treaties for the protection of human rights on which the Member States have collaborated or of which they arc signatories. In that regard, the Court has stated that the Convention has special significance (see, in particular, the judgment in Case C-260/89 ERT [1991] ECR I-2925, paragraph 41).
>
> Respect for human rights is therefore a condition of the lawfulness of Community acts. Accession to the Convention would, however, entail a substantial change in the present Community system for the protection of human rights in that it would entail the entry of the Community into a distinct international institutional system as well as integration of all the provisions of the Convention into the Community legal order.
>
> Such a modification of the system for the protection of human rights in the Community, with equally fundamental institutional implications for the Community and for the Member States, would be of constitutional significance and would therefore be such as to go beyond the scope of Article 235. It could be brought about only by way of Treaty amendment.

[20] Memorandum of the Commission *Accession of the Communities to the European Convention on Human Rights* COM (79) 210 final *Bull EC* (Supplement 2/79, 2 May 1979, 12) and the subsequent Resolution of the European Parliament endorsing the Commission Memorandum, OJ C 304/253 (22 November 1982). Equally, the European Economic and Social Committee subscribed the Commission Memorandum by means of its Own-Initiative Opinion of the Economic and Social Committee on the protection of human rights, OJ C 353/1 (31 December 1980).

[21] See Memorandum of the Commission *Accession of the Communities to the European Convention on Human Rights* COM (79) 210 final (n 20) at 11–16.

It must therefore be held that, as Community law now stands, the Community has no competence to accede to the Convention.[22]

14. With the advantage that a deductive scientific methodology implies, that is, knowing the final result (the imminent accession of the EU to the ECHR), it is possible to say that, after the surprising Opinion of the Court, there began a discreet but firm evolution that has been defeating all political reluctance and (almost) all legal objections that have so far prevented formal accession. Perhaps it would be unreasonable to conclude that it has been a process guided and coordinated by the European *establishment*, but the fact is that such a development to which we refer to has been most effective. Indeed, after the decision of the Court, different doctrinal studies followed, criticizing the decision, moreover, submitting arguments in favour of the accession, and even admitting the existence, at the time of the Opinion, of sufficient legal basis in the Treaties.[23] On the other hand, the more reluctant countries, such as Ireland or the United Kingdom, were moderating their positions. The latter were suspicious of the Court's activism and feared that adding a catalogue of rights in the EC/EU system had a centrifugal effect and increased the powers of the EC/EU. Although it is still possible to observe some reluctance (e.g. the Protocols on the interpretation of the Charter in the Constitutional Treaty and the Treaty of Lisbon) today, the fact is that at present all Member States agree on the need for accession.

15. On the other hand, the Court has incorporated the Convention and the jurisprudence of the ECtHR in its legal reasoning; but it has done so through the filter of general principles, which allows control of the process at all times. However, this attitude of the Court, beyond the dialectic of a possible competition with its counterpart in Strasbourg, should be framed in its efforts to preserve the autonomy of EC/EU law, especially when the 'rules of the game'

[22] Opinion 2/94 *Accession by the Community to the ECHR* [1996] ECR I-1759 paras 33–6. The literature about this opinion is huge. See D Simon, 'Chronique, n° 335' (1996) Juin, *Europe* 1; JM Areilza Carvajal, 'El Dictamen 2/1994 del Tribunal de Justicia o cómo no abordar el espinoso asunto de las competencias comunitarias' (1996) 47 *Revista española de derecho constitucional* 333; S O'Leary, 'Accession by the European Community to the European Convention on Human Rights – The Opinion of the ECJ' (1996) 4 *European Human Rights Law Review* 362; P Wachsmann, 'L'avis 2/94 de la Cour de justice relatif à l'adhésion de la Communauté européenne à la Convention de sauvegarde des droits de l'homme et des libertés fondamentales' (1996) 32(3) *Revue Trimestrielle de Droit Européen* 467; G Gaja, 'Opinion 2/94: accession by the Community to the European Convention for the Protection of Human Rights and Fundamental Freedoms' (1996) 33(5) *Common Market Law Review* 973; O de Schutter and Y Lejeune, 'L'adhésion de la Communauté à la Convention européenne des droits de l'homme' (1996) 32(5–6) *Cahiers de droit européen* 555; N Burrows, 'Question of Community Accession to the European Convention Determined' (1997) 22(1) *European Law Review* 58; N Fernández Sola, 'La adhesión de la Comunidad Europea al Convenio Europeo de salvaguarda de los Derechos Humanos y de las Libertades Fundamentales. Comentario al Dictamen 2/94 del Tribunal de Justicia de las Comunidades Europeas' (1997) 144 *Noticias de la Unión Europea* 41; and C Escobar Hernández, 'Comunidad Europea y Convenio Europeo de Derechos Humanos: ¿El fin de una vieja polémica?' (1996) 3 *Revista de Instituciones Europeas* 817.

[23] See the references in the previous note.

remain unstable: Member States agree on the accession but it still seems too far away, the terms on which the Union (after Lisbon) shall take part in the Convention system are still being defined.[24]

Meanwhile, the Strasbourg Court appears to subject the actions of the EU institutions to a *de facto* control, which does not fit very well with the two pillars on which the Luxembourg Court has built the EC/EU legal system: the principles of autonomy and primacy. These episodes of 'competition between courts' over who has the last word in a dispute are not unknown in systems where there is a jurisdiction specializing in fundamental rights.[25]

This possible competitive drift has been smartly offset by the usual informal contacts (that is to say, outside the jurisdiction) between members of both courts, especially between their presidents. This 'judicial diplomacy' has been joined by a high-level 'civil service diplomacy' which, discreetly but gradually, has been developed between the Council of Europe and the European Union.[26]

4. THE LEGAL VALUE OF THE CONVENTION IN EU LAW UNTIL ACCESSION

16. Regarding the legal value of the Convention within the EC/EU legal order, since the Court of Justice in Luxembourg incorporated it into its jurisprudence (*Rutili* case, 1972)[27] and before the Union formally accedes to it, at present, the ECHR has been 'constitutionalized' in Article 6.2 TUE (Article 6 TUE-L) and it constitutes a qualified instrument of interpretation and realization of fundamental rights as general principles. Its relevance is remembered by the Court whenever it has the occasion:

> Fundamental rights form an integral part of the general principles of law the observance of which the Court ensures. For that purpose, the Court draws inspiration from the constitutional traditions common to the Member States and from the guidelines supplied by international instruments for the protection of human rights on which the Member States have collaborated or to which they are signatories. The ECHR has special significance in that respect.[28]

[24] See LI Gordillo, 'Un paso más hacia la estabilización de las relaciones interordinamentales en Europa: la incorporación de la UE al CEDH' (2011) 38 *Revista Española de Derecho Europeo* 173 197–204. See Chapter 6.

[25] As an example, one can see the Spanish case, where similar episodes have arisen between the Constitutional Court and the Supreme Court, often magnified by the media.

[26] One of the most meaningful products of this judicial diplomacy is the *Memorandum of Understanding between the Council of Europe and the European Union*, 10 May 2007, 117th Session of the Committee of Ministers CM(2007)74 (Strasbourg, 10–11 May 2007).

[27] Case 36/75 *Roland Rutili v Ministre de l'intérieur* [1975] ECR 1219.

[28] Case C-540/03 *Parliament v Council* [2006] ECR I-5769 para 35. For a study on the relationship between the two Courts, see S Douglas-Scott, 'A tale of two Courts: Luxembourg, Strasbourg and the growing European Human rights acquis' (2006) 43(3) *Common Market Law Review* 629.

17. That is to say, the Court of Justice considers the ECHR as an element of interpretation of undoubted hermeneutic value, but without direct legal effect. That is, the Court of Justice shall allow its indirect application through the general principles of law, of which it is the supreme guardian and interpreter, thus guaranteeing the autonomy and primacy of EC/EU law. Therefore, the Luxembourg Court is, in principle, the highest interpreter of the ECHR in the EU context. However, for some time now, it appears that the highest court in Luxembourg has relaxed its initial position and is willing to also accept the Strasbourg Court's case law, especially since the entry into force of the Lisbon Treaty.[29] Nevertheless, this incorporation of the Strasbourg case law also operates through the filter of the general principles, allowing the Court of Justice to maintain the autonomy of EC/EU law, although it can also be interpreted as a sign of their willingness to accept the ECtHR as a specialized court (rather than 'higher') in terms of fundamental rights.[30]

18. It has already been mentioned that the obligation to respect the ECHR comes from the Treaties or primary law (Article 6.2 TEU). However, the incorporation operated by the Maastricht Treaty refers to the catalogue of rights, not to the judicial protection mechanism established by the Convention. In order to do so, according to the Luxembourg Court, the Union's accession to the Convention is necessary (as well as the associated amendment of the ECHR itself), and this has not been possible until the entry into force of the Treaty of Lisbon.

Therefore, until then, the Court of Justice shall be the highest interpreter of the Convention at the EU level. This has disturbed the doctrine that has warned of the risk of conflict between the Luxembourg and Strasbourg Courts. Not that these risks are particularly worrying, as it is often the case that national supreme courts give a different interpretation to the Convention from the one they give to the ECtHR. But in these cases, it is possible to obtain a definitive interpretation from Strasbourg, whereas in the case of EU law, no such possibility exists. The risk for the Member States may be that the same right recognized by the Convention could have two different and even contradictory interpretations, one from the ECtHR and another from the ECJ, so that states could be in the position of having to choose between violating the Convention or violating EU law. The responsibility that falls on the Court of Justice is important, because it has to do everything possible to prevent any violation of the

[29] Case C-94/00 *Roquette Frères* [2002] ECR I-9011 para 29; Case C-274/99 P *Connolly v Commission* [2001] ECR I-1611 paras 37–65; and Case C-117/01 *K B v National Health Service Pensions Agency* [2004] ECR I-541 para 33.

[30] Case C-94/00 *Roquette Frères* [2002] (n 29). For a comment, see M Lienemeyer and D Waelbroeck, 'Case C-94/00, Roquette Frères SA v Directeur Général de la Concurrence, de la Consommation et de la Répression des Fraudes. Judgment of the Court of Justice (Full Court) of 22 October 2002' (2003) 40(6) *Common Market Law Review* 1481. The *Memorandum of Understanding between the Council of Europe and the European Union* [2007] (n 26) establishes that 'The European Union regards the Council of Europe as the Europe-wide reference source for human rights'.

Convention, even anticipating what the Strasbourg jurisprudence might be while, at the same time, being loyal to EU law and especially the Treaties.[31]

5. THE LEGAL VALUE OF THE CONVENTION IN THE INTERGOVERNMENTAL PILLARS

19. The so-called intergovernmental pillars created by the Treaty on European Union remained outside the EU institutional and legal structure. The second pillar was related to the Common Foreign and Security Policy and the third one concerned the police and judicial cooperation in criminal matters. From the Treaty of Amsterdam, to these three structures can be added the so-called 'closer cooperation', conceived as a mechanism to progress at different speeds within the process of European construction.[32] In any case, these pillars were not disconnected from the Community as the Community institutions and, particularly, the Council was called to develop them. The resulting structure is, undoubtedly, complex due to the intertwining of legal instruments and decision-making processes in which we could say that the Union has been using the Community to achieve its aims.[33]

20. This is not the time to analyse the pillar structure of the Union, but it is worth recalling the role that the Court of Justice has had in each of them. Thus, speaking in general terms, it can be said that the jurisdiction of the ECJ was complete in the Community pillar and practically nil in the second one. In fact, under Article 46 TEU, the ECJ had no jurisdiction in relation to acts adopted in the framework of CFSP. This article has been repealed by the Treaty of Lisbon. As regards the third pillar, unlike what happens in the CFSP, the ECJ is competent to rule on Cooperation in Criminal Matters. According to the legal regime originated from the last but one amendment of the Treaties (Nice) this competence was subject, however, to a different autonomous system from the one planned for the Community pillar, establishing, in accordance with Article 35 TEU, three new courses of action specific to the third pillar, namely: 1) a limited preliminary action; 2) an action for annulment against framework decisions and the decisions taken by the Council; and 3) an appeal to the courts concerning the application or interpretation of legislative acts or agreements set forth in Article 34 of the TEU, in which either two Member States or a Member State and the Commission can be parties. The Lisbon Treaty has removed those arti-

[31] JP Jacqué (2007) (n 3) at 22–3.

[32] See M Urrea Corres, *La cooperación reforzada en la Unión Europea: concepto, naturaleza y régimen jurídico* (Colex, Madrid, 2002).

[33] On the pillar structure of the EU, see B De Witte, 'The pillar structure and the nature of the European Union: Greek temple or French Gothic cathedral?' in C Gala Durán (tr), T Heukels, N Blokker and M Brus (eds), *The European Union after Amsterdam: a legal analysis* (Europa Institute, Leiden University, Leiden, 1998) 51.

cles (34, 35 and 46, among others), and though formally the pillar structure would disappear, in practice the issue is far from being resolved.[34]

5.1. The ECHR and the Common Foreign and Security Policy

21. The European Union has often been criticized for its apparent attitude of caring more for promoting fundamental rights abroad than at home. The protection of human rights is one of the specific objectives of the Common Foreign and Security Policy, according to Article 11 TEU (Article 24 TEU-L), which incorporates the same language used in the cooperation provisions for development used in Articles 177–181 TEC (Articles 208–211 TFEU) when it states that one of the objectives of the Union is the development and consolidation of democracy and the rule of law, as well as respect for human rights and fundamental freedoms. The instruments used in this sense are related to those normally used in international relations. Thus, since 1995 there are clauses on the protection of human rights in the agreements that deal with trade, development and other cooperation issues.[35]

Likewise, the practice of conditioning the process of access to the precandidates to the Union regarding human rights is also known.[36] Moreover, this practice was encoded in the TEU (Articles 49 and 6) and still remains in the TEU-L:

> Article 49 TEU-L
>
> Any European State which respects the values referred to in Article 2 and is committed to promoting them may apply to become a member of the Union.
>
> Article 2 TEU-L
>
> The Union is founded on the values of respect for human dignity, freedom, democracy, equality, the rule of law and respect for human rights, including the rights of persons belonging to minorities. These values are common to the Member States in a society in which pluralism, non-discrimination, tolerance, justice, solidarity and equality between women and men prevail.

All Member States of the European Union are members of the European Convention on Human Rights and any state interested in joining it has to ratify the ECHR.

[34] González Alonso, LN, '¿Quién dijo que desaparecen los pilares? La configuración jurídica de la acción exterior de la Unión Europea en el Tratado de Lisboa' in Martín y Pérez de Nanclares, J (ed), *El Tratado de Lisboa: la salida de la crisis constitucional* (Iustel, Madrid, 2008).

[35] See E Fierro. 'Legal Basis and Scope of the Human Rights Clauses in EC Bilateral Agreements: Any Room for Positive Interpretation?' (2001) 7(1) *European Law Journal* 41; and B Brandtner and A Rosas, 'Human Rights and the External Relations of the European Community: An Analysis of Doctrine and Practice' (1998) 9(3) *European Journal of International Law* 468.

[36] B de Witte and GN Toggenburg, 'Human Rights and Membership of the European Union' in S Peers and A Ward (eds), *The EU Charter of Fundamental Rights* (Hart Publishing, Oxford, 2004) 59.

22. Another matter of interest in this context is to analyse the impact of the Convention in the acts adopted in the scope of the second pillar. In this sense, it is noteworthy that the system of acts through which the CFSP becomes operational has some peculiarities with respect to those pertaining the classic Community pillar. In short, and without limitation, as a first step the decisions are taken by consensus within the European Council and in the form of 'general guidelines' and 'common strategies', giving this second category (which disappeared with Lisbon) a more concrete dimension (Articles 12 TEU, 25 TEU-L). In order to monitor and adapt to these guidelines and strategies, as well as the possibility of executing international agreements,[37] the Council may adopt actions, positions or any other 'arrangements' (this latest was introduced by Lisbon). However, actions and positions are mandatory for Member States and therefore, in principle, will not have direct effect on individuals.[38]

23. In the European framework, the fight against terrorism has led to the implementation of obligations which have arisen from resolutions of the Security Council of the United Nations (UNSC) relating to so-called 'smart sanctions' (including the drafting of lists of terrorists and related support groups), which are a matter of Common Foreign and Security Policy in which the Council has the main role.[39] Therefore, these resolutions, as well as the preparation of the lists, were developed in the form of common positions. These positions did not, by themselves, impose criminal or economic sanctions on those included in the listings, but would define the policy that Member States would follow. It would then fall to other EU institutions and Member States through their national authorities to take appropriate action against the persons listed.[40] However, instead of incorporating these external decisions as common positions solely set within the second pillar (which would have prevented the CFI and the ECJ from having a legal basis to review them), these common positions were approved using the joint basis of Article 15 (Article 29 TEU-L), for which up to now is known as the second pillar and Article 34 (third pillar) of the TEU.[41] Thus, in response to the resources in which those implied contested their inclusion in these lists contained in the common positions, the ECJ affirmed its com-

[37] The Treaty of Nice already stated the possibility for the Council to sign international agreements (Articles 24 TEU, 37 TEU-L) to comply with Title V 'Provisions on a common foreign and security policy'.

[38] About the legal acts of the second pillar, see K Lenaerts, P Van Nuffel and R Bray, *Constitutional Law of the European Union* 2nd edn (Thompson, London, 2005) 804–11.

[39] The so-called 'targeted sanctions' in the UN's terminology aim to put some pressure on certain people and groups (eg, Government associates) and may consist of impounds, freezing funds or accounts or prohibition of travel. See L Van den Herik, 'The Security Council's Targeted Sanctions Regimes: In Need of Better Protection of the Individual' (2007) 20 *Leiden Journal of International Law* 797.

[40] Council Common Position 2001/931/CFSP on the application of specific measures to combat terrorism (OJ L 344/93, 28 December 2001), Art 4.

[41] Title VI TEU provisions on police and judicial cooperation in criminal matters have been substituted by Part III, Title IV, Chapters 1, 4 and 5 TFEU (ie Arts 67–76 and 82–89 TFEU).

petence to control such acts given the nature of the events relating to the third pillar.[42]

As the EU Courts would note in *Segi* and *Gestoras Pro-Amnistía*, in accordance with Article 34.2(a) TEU, the Council may adopt common positions defining the Union's approach to a particular matter.[43] However, there are no explicit legal proceedings before the EU judge either to conduct a total review of the legality of such acts or to claim compensation for any damage caused.[44] Instead, the jurisdiction of the EU Court is limited to considering to what extent the Council has complied with the established procedure in adopting these acts. Still, according to the Court of First Instance, this does not mean that those included in the lists shall not benefit from an action for damages.

Specifically, the CFI would argue in *Segi*:

> By contrast, the Court of First Instance does have jurisdiction over the present action for damages in so far as the applicants allege failure to observe the powers of the Community. The Community Courts have jurisdiction to review the content of an act adopted in the context of the EU Treaty in order to ascertain whether that act affects the powers of the Community . . .
>
> In so far as the applicants allege misuse of procedure by the Council operating in the field of JHA consisting in an encroachment on the powers of the Community leading to their being completely deprived of judicial protection, the present action comes within the jurisdiction of the Community Courts pursuant to Article 235 EC and the second paragraph of Article 288 EC.[45]

In any case, as later established by the ECJ:

> it is for the Member States and, in particular, their courts and tribunals, to interpret and apply national procedural rules governing the exercise of rights of action in a way that enables natural and legal persons to challenge before the courts the lawfulness of any decision or other national measure relating to the drawing up of an act of the European Union or to its application to them and to seek compensation for any loss suffered.[46]

24. Despite the initial position of the CFI, denoting indifference with regard to its jurisdiction to control the common positions in question, the ECJ valued, in detail, the reasons for the restrictive nature of its powers in relation to such acts given their purpose (defining the Union's approach on a particular matter).

[42] S Peers, 'Salvation outside the Church: Judicial protection in the third Pillar after the Pupino and Segi judgments' (2007) 44(4) *Common Market Law Review* 883.

[43] After the Lisbon Treaty, Title VI TEU provisions on police and judicial cooperation in criminal matters (among them, Art 34) have been substituted by Part III, Title IV, Chapters 1, 4 and 5 TFEU (ie Arts 67–76 and 82–89 TFEU).

[44] See Case T-338/02 *Segi and others v Council* [2004] ECR II-1647 para 46 and Case C-354/04 P *Gestoras Pro Amnistía v Council* [2007] ECR I-1579 para 46, which states that 'Article 35 EU confers no jurisdiction on the Court of Justice to entertain any action for damages whatsoever'.

[45] Case T-338/02 *Segi* [2004] (n 44) paras 41-42.

[46] Case C-354/04 P *Gestoras* [2007] (n 44) para 56 and C-355/04 P *Segi v Council* [2007] ECR I-1657.

According to the ECJ, the restrictions that would result from such positions are called to produce, by themselves, legal effects 'in relation to third parties'.[47] However, as the plaintiffs of these acts argue, those positions could, in fact, deploy these effects. Thus, in the case of *Segi* and *Gestoras*, the ECJ confirmed its jurisdiction to review a common position that, given its content, has a scope that goes beyond the one the EU Treaty gives to this type of act.[48] Therefore, despite the fact that national courts are best qualified to provide legal remedies for this type of listing,

> a national court hearing a dispute which indirectly raises the issue of the validity or interpretation of a common position adopted on the basis of Article 34 EU, as is the case in this instance for part of Common Position 2001/931 and in any event for Article 4 thereof and the Annex thereto, and which has serious doubts whether that common position is really intended to produce legal effects in relation to third parties, would be able, subject to the conditions fixed by Article 35 EU, to ask the Court to give a preliminary ruling. It would then fall to the Court to find, where appropriate, that the common position is intended to produce legal effects in relation to third parties, to accord it its true classification and to give a preliminary ruling.[49]

25. Just as the ECJ was not initially competent to perform a full check of common positions, or to offer compensation to those who suffered damage as a result of their inclusion in the listings, the CFI soon judged itself competent to control its implementing acts in the form of EC legislation such as regulations and decisions to freeze funds.[50] Thus, in its first ruling on the *Organisation des Modjahedines du peuple d'Iran*, the CFI established:

> [T]he contested Common Position requires the adoption of implementing Community and/or national acts in order to be effective. It has not been contended that those implementing acts cannot themselves be the subject-matter of an action for annulment either before the Community Courts or before the national courts.[51]

Moreover,

> It follows from Articles 35 EU and 46 EU that, under Title VI of the EU Treaty, legal remedies seeking a ruling as to validity or annulment are available only as against framework decisions, decisions and the measures implementing conventions provided

[47] Case C-354/04 P *Gestoras* [2007] (n 44) and Case C-355/04 P *Segi* [2007] (n 46) para 52 of both cases.

[48] Case C-354/04 P *Gestoras* [2007] (n 44) and Case C-355/04 P *Segi* [2007] (n 46) para 54 of both cases.

[49] Case C-354/04 P *Gestoras* [2007] (n 44) and Case C-355/04 P *Segi* [2007] (n 46) para 54 of both cases.

[50] The change of opinion of the ECJ would take place in *Kadi/Al Barakaat*: Joined Cases C-402/05 P and C-415/05 P *Kadi* and *Al Barakaat International Foundation v Council* [2008] ECR I-6351. This question will be analysed *in extenso* below.

[51] Case T-228/02 *Organisation des Modjahedines du peuple d'Iran v Council (OMPI)* [2006] ECR II-4665 para 55. See C Eckes, 'Case T-228/02, Organisation des Modjahedines du peuple d'Iran v Council and UK (OMPI), Judgment of the Court of First Instance (Second Chamber) of 12 December 2006' (2007) 44(4) *Common Market Law Review* 1117.

for by Article 34(2)(b), (c) and (d) EU, with the exception of the common positions provided for in Article 34(2)(a) EU.[52]

In this situation, the ICC stated that part of its review power (whose legal basis is Article 230 TEC, Article 263 TFEU) should be to guarantee that the Community rules on the freezing of funds are applied under the legal conditions, in this case, Regulation 2580/2001/EC.[53] This means that,

> the judicial review of the lawfulness of the decision in question extends to the assessment of the facts and circumstances relied on as justifying it, and to the evidence and information on which that assessment is based.[54]

The CFI also affirmed its power to control that

> the right to a fair hearing is observed and that the requirement of a statement of reasons is satisfied and also, where applicable, that the overriding considerations relied on exceptionally by the Council in disregarding those rights are well founded.[55]

However, the CFI recognized a broad discretion to the Council to determine the punitive measures derived from the common position analysed and severely limited its authority to control these events when recognizing that:

> Because the Community Courts may not, in particular, substitute their assessment of the evidence, facts and circumstances justifying the adoption of such measures for that of the Council, the review carried out by the Court of the lawfulness of decisions to freeze funds must be restricted to checking that the rules governing procedure and the statement of reasons have been complied with, that the facts are materially accurate, and that there has been no *manifest error of assessment* of the facts or *misuse of power*. That limited review applies, especially, to the Council's assessment of the factors as to appropriateness on which such decisions are based.[56]

Therefore, the discretion granted to the Council is broad. Only in case of 'manifest error of assessment' would the CFI exercise its control. It is quite revealing that in order to carry out such a difficult task, the CFI shall rely on the jurisprudence of the ECtHR in the complex area of discretion of public authorities.[57]

[52] Case T-228/02 *OMPI* [2006] (n 51) para 52.

[53] Council Regulation (EC) No 2580/2001 on specific restrictive measures directed against certain persons and entities with a view to combating terrorism (OJ L 344/70, 28 December 2001).

[54] Case T-228/02 *OMPI* [2006] (n 51) para 154. Equally, see Case T-47/03 *José María Sison v Council* [2007] ECR II-73 (abstract).

[55] Case T-228/02 *OMPI* [2006] (n 51) para 154.

[56] Case T-228/02 *OMPI* [2006] (n 51) para 159, italics added.

[57] For an explanation of the 'margin of appreciation' concept, widely used by the ECtHR, see JG Merrils, *The development of International Law by the European Court of Human Rights* (Manchester University Press, Manchester, 1988) 136–57; Y Arai-Takahashi, *The Margin of Appreciation Doctrine and the Principle of Proportionality in the Jurisprudence of the ECHR* (Intersentia, Antwerp, 2002) and I De la Rasilla del Moral, 'The Increasingly Marginal Appreciation of the Margin of Appreciation Doctrine' (2006) 7(6) *German Law Journal* 611.

26. Thus, in the *Organisation des Modjahedines du peuple d'Iran* case of 12 December 2006 (*OMPI*), a resolution with many references to the jurisprudence of the ECtHR, the CFI annulled the decision of the Council of Ministers – regarding the above-mentioned organization – that updated the list of persons, groups and entities to which was applied the freezing of funds and other restrictive measures to fight against terrorism, considering that the contested measure infringes the rights of defence, the obligation to state reasons and the right to effective judicial protection. This would be the first of several ocasions where this Court annulled a decision of the Council including this organization on the black list to which is applied Regulation No 2580/2001/EC on specific restrictive measures directed against certain persons and entities aiming to fight against terrorism.[58] After these victories of the *People's Mojahedin Organisation of Iran* (which is the name in English), the Council finally decided, through Common Position 2009/67/CFSP and Council Decision No 2009/62/EC, both of 26 January 2009, to exclude the recurrent organization from the entities' listing to which the law imposes the freezing of funds and other restrictive measures under Regulation No 2580/2001/EC.[59]

27. After its first ruling on the *OMPI* case, the Court of First Instance reiterated, in subsequent cases, its desire to strengthen and develop the line of decisions that began with that case.[60] However, the Court of First Instance clearly distinguished between the *OMPI*, *Al-Aqsa*, *Sison*, *Kongra-Gel* and *PKK* cases on the one hand, and the *Yusuf-Al Barakaat/Kadi* cases of 21 September 2005 and *Ayadi/Hassan* of 12 July 2006, in which it refused to annul the measures imposed by the Council upon the plaintiff.[61] Indeed, the CFI strengthened the

[58] Two other victories of this organization were Case T-256/07 *People's Mojahedin Organization of Iran v Council (PMOI I)* [2008] ECR II-3019 and Case T-284/08 *People's Mojahedin Organization of Iran v Council (PMOI II)* [2008] ECR II-3487 (appealed: C-27/09). Besides, the favourable decision of the British court *Prescribed Organisation Appeal Commission* (POAC) should be taken into account, which is the competent commission to decide on appeals against decisions of the Government that refuse to exclude organizations from its blacklists (list of terrorist groups). See *Lord Alton of Liverpool v Home Secretary* App No PC/02/2006 (POAC Decision, 30 November 2007). This resolution was appealed and subsequently dismissed by the Court of Appeal.

[59] OJ L 23, 27 January 2009. Nonetheless, and although the PMOI is no longer included on the blacklists, France has appealed Case T-284/08 *PMOI II* [2008] (n 58) (C-27/09). See also the report of a group of experts where they criticise the government's determination to keep this organization on the terrorist lists, available at <www.nctb.nl/Images/MKO%20legal%20opinions_tcm91-136094.pdf?cp=91&cs=25485>.

[60] See Case T-47/03 *Sison* [2007] (n 54); Case T-327/03 *Stichting Al-Aqsa v Council* [2007] ECR II-79 (abstract); Case T-253/04 *Kongra-Gel v Council* [2008] ECR II-46; and Case T-229/02 *Osman Ocalan, on behalf of the Kurdistan Workers' Party (PKK)* [2008] ECR II-45 (abstract).

[61] Case T-306/01 *Yusuf and Al Barakaat International Foundation v Council and Commission* [2005] ECR II-3533 (appeal: C-415/05 P), Case T-315/01, *Kadi v Council and Commission* [2005] ECR II-3649 (appeal: C-402/05 P), both of them revoked by Joined Cases C-402/05 P and C-415/05 P *Kadi / Al Barakaat* [2008] (n 50). See also Case T-253/02 *Ayadi v Council* [2006] ECR II-2139 (appeal: C-403/06 P) and Case T-49/04 *Hassan v Council and Commission* [2006] ECR II-52 (abstract) (appeal: C-399/06 P), both of them equally revoked (following the *Kadi* case law) by the ECJ in Joined Cases C-399/06 P and C-403/06 P *Hassan and Ayadi v Council and Commission* [2009] ECR I-11393.

distinction between two types of sanctions, one of the Community, where the EU institutions would have greater leeway and, therefore, the control of the CFI would be more intense (*OMPI*)[62] and another one involving simply the implementation at Community level of specific sanctions established by the Security Council of the UN and in which the EC/EU bodies would not have discretion (*Yusuf-Al Barakaat/Kadi*).

In contrast to the system established by the Security Council to freeze funds of individuals associated with Usama bin Laden, the Al-Qaida network and the Taliban (*Yusuf-Al Barakaat/Kadi*), UNSC Resolution 1373 (2001) leaves to the Member States and the EC/EU the determination of individuals and entities whose funds are to be frozen (*OMPI-PMOI*), which involves the exercise of one's own powers, entailing a discretionary appreciation by the community within the legal framework provided by Resolution 1373. However, even in case of the sanctions against Usama Bin Laden and his associates (in which there is no margin of appreciation) the ECJ in its famous ruling on Joined Cases *Yusuf-Al Barakaat/Kadi* recognized the existence of specific and true limits, beyond the general and uncertain limit derived from the *ius cogens* established by the CFI in its case, which was later overturned.

28. Despite the generous interpretation of the right to refer a preliminary ruling in relation to common positions (*Segi/Gestoras*) and the recognition to those affected of the right to appeal the decisions of the Council concerning the freezing of funds (*OMPI*) before the CFI, the current legal and institutional system is open to criticism to the extent that it does not allow full control over the decisions to freeze funds. The commitment assumed by the Council in combating terrorism and its extensive powers of decision and assessment as regards to the so-called 'smart sanctions' limit the jurisdiction of the CFI to exercise control over a hypothetical 'manifest error of assessment'.[63] Despite the explicit reference to the European Court of Human Rights on the subject, it is difficult to imagine a case that would constitute a 'manifest error' that would lead the CFI to annul a decision of the Council.[64] Furthermore, by using common positions as the instrument for anti-terrorist measures decided at the UNSC, the Council avoids, perhaps deliberately, a full judicial review by the EC/EU Courts. Instead, the conclusion to be derived from this situation is that decisions on placing individuals and organizations on blacklists should be checked at the

[62] This sanction system comes from the UNSC Resolution 1373 (2001). Threats to international peace and security caused by terrorist acts, implemented within the EU by means of Council Common Position 2001/930/CFSP on combating terrorism (OJ L 344/90, 28 December 2001), Council Common Position 2001/931/CFSP on the application of specific measures to combat terrorism and Council Regulation (EC) No 2580/2001. See Council Decision 2001/927/EC establishing the list provided for in Article 2(3) of Council Regulation (EC) No 2580/2001 on specific restrictive measures directed against certain persons and entities with a view to combating terrorism (OJ L 344/83, 28 December 2001).

[63] Case T-228/02 *OMPI* [2006] (n 51) para 159.

[64] J Almqvist, 'A Human Rights Critique of European Judicial Review: Counter-Terrorism Sanction' (2008) 57(2) *International and Comparative Law Quarterly* 303.

national level. Certainly, European states, in part because of the jurisprudence of the ECtHR, have been greatly limiting the assessment powers traditionally enjoyed by the executive.[65]

The CFI and the ECJ have stretched to the limit their powers to protect the fundamental rights of individuals affected by such sanctions, but the reform established in the Lisbon Treaty does not present, in principle, a change that expands the powers of the Court of Justice in this field. Thus, Article 275 TFEU provides that although the ECJ shall not have jurisdiction over the provisions concerning the common foreign and security policy nor with respect to acts adopted on their basis, instead it shall have jurisdiction to monitor compliance with Article 40 TEU-L and to rule on appeals filed under the conditions set forth in Article 263.3 TFEU and regarding the control of the legality of the decisions adopted by the Council by virtue of Chapter 2 of Title V of the Treaty on European Union by which restrictive measures against natural or legal persons are established.[66]

5.2. The ECHR and Police and Judicial Cooperation

29. The implementation of the ECHR by the ECJ in the former third pillar shall be done, as in the case of the old Community pillar already analysed, through the general principles of law. We have already seen how the general principles of law applied by the ECJ in the former first pillar (therefore, called general principles of Community law) had a major impact on the development of EC/EU law. In fact, with this construction of the Luxembourg Court, it has been possible to perform a real control over EC/EU acts while it has served as a filter in order to incorporate into EC/EU law the fundamental rights recognized by the ECHR and specified by the jurisprudence of the ECtHR and by the constitutional traditions common to the Member States. However, the question that arises is whether or not these principles apply to the area of freedom, security and justice (especially to police and judicial cooperation in criminal matters).[67]

30. So far, the ECJ has not expressly stated that all the general principles of law are applicable in this particular field. As for the category of fundamental rights,

[65] See the report of Professor I Cameron, *The European Convention on Human Rights, Due Process and United Nations Security Council Counter-Terrorism Sanctions* (Council of Europe, Strasbourg, 6 February 2006) available at <http://www.coe.int/T/E/Legal_Affairs/Legal_co-operation/Public_international_law>.

[66] See R Van Ooik, 'Cross-Pillar Litigation Before the ECJ: Demarcation of Community and Union Competences' (2008) 4(3) *European Constitutional Law Review* 399; and P Eeckhout, 'Community Terrorism Listings, Fundamental Rights, and UN Security Council Resolutions. In Search of the Right Fit' (2007) 3(2) *European Constitutional Law Review* 183.

[67] See T Tridimas, *The General Principles of EU Law* 2nd edn (Oxford University Press, Oxford, 2006) 36–50.

which is what concerns us here, it is worth remembering that the fundamental precept in the matter is in the TEU. Indeed, in the leading cases in this field, the ECJ has used, in its legal reasoning, Article 6.2 TEU (Article 6 TEU-L).

31. Thus, in its ruling on the *Pupino* case, the ECJ stated:

> [I]n accordance with Article 6(2) EU, the Union must respect fundamental rights, as guaranteed by the European Convention for the Protection of Human Rights and Fundamental Freedoms signed in Rome on 4 November 1950 ('the Convention'), and as they result from the constitutional traditions common to the Member States, as general principles of law.
>
> The Framework Decision must thus be interpreted in such a way that fundamental rights, including in particular the right to a fair trial as set out in Article 6 of the Convention and interpreted by the European Court of Human Rights, are respected.
>
> It is for the national court to ensure that – assuming use of the Special Inquiry and of the special arrangements for the hearing of testimony under Italian law is possible in this case, bearing in mind the obligation to give national law a conforming interpretation – the application of those measures is not likely to make the criminal proceedings against Mrs Pupino, considered as a whole, unfair within the meaning of Article 6 of the Convention, as interpreted by the European Court of Human Rights.'[68]

That is, according to the ECJ, the measures of the third pillar, which in this case was a Framework Decision, had to be interpreted in line with fundamental rights, including the interpretation made by the ECtHR.[69] This statement should also provide that the obligation of national courts to apply the principle of interpretation is limited by general principles of law and, in particular, those of legal certainty and non-retroactivity.[70] One author has observed here an implicit statement that all the principles of Community law should apply to the third pillar, although this claim is risky.[71] In any case, certainly it would confirm that two major principles did apply in this pillar. Besides, another important consequence of the *Pupino* case would be affirming the applicability of the principle of effectiveness in this particular area.[72]

[68] Case C-105/03 *Maria Pupino* [2005] ECR I-5285 paras 58–60.

[69] M Fletcher. 'Extending "indirect effect" to the third pillar: the significance of Pupino?' (2005) 30(6) *European Law Review* 862; D Sarmiento, 'Un paso más en la constitucionalización del Tercer Pilar de la Unión Europea. La Sentencia María Pupino y el efecto directo de las Decisiones marco' (2005) 10 *Revista Electrónica de Estudios Internacionales* 1; A Weyembergh, P De Hert and P Paepe, 'L'effectivité du troisième pilier de l'Union européenne et l'exigence de l'interprétation conforme: la Cour de justice pose ses jalons (note sous l'arrêt Pupino, du 16 juin 2005, de la Cour de justice des Communautés européennes)' (2006) 69 *Revue Trimestrielle des Droits de l'Homme* 269; S Peers, 'Salvation outside the Church: Judicial protection in the third Pillar after the Pupino and Segi judgments' (2007) 44(4) *Common Market Law Review* 883 at 926–8.

[70] Case C-105/2003 *Pupino* [2005] (n 68) para 44. See T Tridimas, *The General Principles of EU Law* 2nd edn (Oxford University Press, Oxford, 2006) 242–97.

[71] S Peers. 'Salvation outside the Church: Judicial protection in the third Pillar after the Pupino and Segi judgments' (2007) 44(4) *Common Market Law Review* 883 at 926–7.

[72] Case C-105/2003 *Pupino* [2005] (n 68) paras 36, 38 and 42. On this principle, called equally 'principle of effectiveness' (Joined Cases C-46/93 and C-48/93 *Brasserie du Pêcheur v Germany* and *The Queen v Secretary of State for Transport, ex parte Factortame Ltd and others* [1996] ECR I-01029 paras 6 and 95) or 'effectiveness of Community law' (Case C-213/89 *The Queen v Secretary*

32. Regarding the *Advocaten voor de Wereld* case, the ECJ confirmed that within the scope of the third pillar, the principles concerning fundamental rights also applied when it came to judging the validity of EU law and the national measures implementing these rules. Notice how the ECJ used the term 'law of the Union' and not 'the law of the Community':

> It must be noted at the outset that, by virtue of Article 6 EU, the Union is founded on the principle of the rule of law and it respects fundamental rights, as guaranteed by the European Convention for the Protection of Human Rights and Fundamental Freedoms, signed in Rome on 4 November 1950, and as they result from the constitutional provisions common to the Member States, as general principles of Community law. It follows that the institutions are subject to review of the conformity of their acts with the Treaties and the general principles of law, just like the Member States when they implement the *law of the Union*.[73]

So, in answer to the question raised by the Belgian Constitutional Court (formerly *Cour d'Arbitrage*) on whether a specific provision of the Framework Decision on the European Arrest Warrant was compatible with Article 6.2 TEU (Article 6 TEU-L), the ECJ established that respect for fundamental rights and, in particular, the principle of equality and non-discrimination applied to the third pillar.[74]

33. Moreover, in the same manner, one could easily argue that the principles relating to fundamental rights can also be applied in relation to national derogations from EC/EU law. Although most of the rulings on this issue refer to the application of general principles concerning fundamental rights of national derogations of single market law,[75] the ECJ has implicitly confirmed that the same rule applies to repeal in other provisions of EC/EU law.[76]

of State for Transport, ex parte Factortame Ltd and others [1990] ECR I-02433 para 20); within the EU legal order, see T Tridimas, *The General Principles of EU Law* 2nd edn (Oxford University Press, Oxford, 2006) 242–97.

[73] See Case C-303/05 *Advocaten voor de Wereld and Leden van de Ministerraad* [2007] ECR I-3633 para 45 (italics added) and Case C-105/2003, *Pupino* [2005] (n 68) para 60. The literature on the *Advocaten* case is huge. See E Herlin-Karnell, 'In the wake of Pupino: Advocaten voor der Wereld and dell'Orto' (2007) 8(12) *German Law Journal* 1147; MA Acosta Sánchez, 'Tribunal de Justicia de las Comunidades Europeas. STJCE 03.05.2007, Advocaten voor de Wereld vzw y Leden Van de Ministerraad – C-303/05 – Cooperación policial y judicial en materia penal – Orden de detención europea' (2007) 28 *Revista de Derecho Comunitario Europeo* 959; C Mapelli Marchena and F Irurzun Montoro, 'La orden europea de detención y entrega a la luz del Tratado de la Unión Europea. Comentario a la Sentencia del JTCE de 3 de mayo de 2007 en el asunto Advocaten voor de Wereld VZW, as. C-303/05' (2007) 24 *Revista española de derecho europeo* 581 and LI Gordillo, 'El juez nacional y el juez europeo ante la Euro-orden' in M Revenga Sánchez (ed), *El poder judicial: VI Congreso de la Asociación de Constitucionalistas de España* (Tirant, Valencia, 2009) 755.

[74] Case C-303/05 *Advocaten voor de Wereld* [2007] (n 73) paras 55–60.

[75] Case C-260/89 *Elliniki Radiophonia Tiléorassi AE (ERT) et al v Dimotiki Etairia Pliroforissis et al* [1991] ECR I-2925 para 24.

[76] Case C-540/03 *Parliament and Council* [2006] (n 28). See S Peers. 'Salvation outside the Church: Judicial protection in the third Pillar after the Pupino and Segi judgments' (2007) 44(4) *Common Market Law Review* 883 at 926.

34. Later, in the *Van Esbroeck* case, the ECJ judged that the provision concerning the prohibition of *bis in idem* was a 'fundamental principle' of Community law.[77] Furthermore, in the *Van Straaten* case, the Court of Luxembourg provided that its interpretation of the rules of *non bis in idem* in Schengen was justified by the 'principles of legal certainty and legitimate expectations'.[78] Thus, although these two sentences do not expressly provide that the *non bis in idem* and the protection of legitimate expectations are general principles of law applicable to the third pillar, it would be difficult to interpret it otherwise.[79]

35. In regard to the principles governing the exercise of the EC/EU competence, that of subsidiarity was expressly mentioned in Article 2 TEU, which in turn makes a reference to Article 5 TEC.[80]

> Article 2 TEU
>
> . . .
>
> The objectives of the Union shall be achieved as provided in this Treaty and in accordance with the conditions and the timetable set out therein while respecting the principle of subsidiarity as defined in Article 5 of the Treaty establishing the European Community.
>
> Article 5 TEC
>
> The Community shall act within the limits of the powers conferred upon it by this Treaty and of the objectives assigned to it therein.
>
> In areas which do not fall within its exclusive competence, the Community shall take action, in accordance with the principle of subsidiarity, only if and in so far as the objectives of the proposed action cannot be sufficiently achieved by the Member States and can therefore, by reason of the scale or effects of the proposed action, be better achieved by the Community.
>
> Any action by the Community shall not go beyond what is necessary to achieve the objectives of this Treaty.

The Lisbon reform has softened the restriction and, although it refers to the beginning, it makes no reference to it in the TFEU. Thus, Article 3 TEU-L provides:

> 6. The Union shall pursue its objectives by appropriate means in accordance with the powers conferred by the Treaties.

36. An Advocate General has assumed that the proportionality principle did also apply in the third pillar as 'a mechanism to facilitate subsidiarity'.[81] Moreover,

[77] Case C-436/04 *Leopold Henri Van Esbroeck* [2006] ECR I-2333 para 40.

[78] Case C-150/05 *Jean Leon Van Straaten v Staat der Nederlanden, Italy* [2006] ECR I-9327 para 59.

[79] In favour, S Peers (2007) *cit* at 927.

[80] On this principle, see the excellent book by M Rodríguez-Izquierdo Serrano, *Primacia y subsidariedad en la Unión Europea* (CEPC, Madrid, 2011).

[81] Case C-303/05 *Advocaten voor de Wereld* [2007] (n 73), Opinion of AG Ruiz-Jarabo, para 61.

there are also frequent references to this principle in the preambles of the third pillar legislation.[82]

37. Meanwhile, the principle of conferred powers was clearly present in the Treaty on European Union, specifically in Articles 5 TEU (Article 5 TEU-L) and Article 43 TEU (Article 20 TEU-L). Moreover, this principle has been referred to in various judgments of the Court of First Instance and in the opinion of Attorney General Mengozzi regarding the *Segi* y *Gestoras* cases.[83]

38. With regard to proportionality, if it governs control of the measures taken by the institutions of the Union, one might conclude, for the sake of consistency, that this principle also did apply in the process of national control measures derived from the law of the third pillar.[84] This statement has already been made by Advocate General Sharpston.[85]

39. Regarding the rights of defence, namely those of a fair trial (that is, including basically the right to be heard, to be assisted by counsel and the right to plead not guilty, all derived from Article 6 ECHR), but which were not considered in the jurisprudence of the third pillar, it would have been surprising if the EC/EU had excluded them from the measures of the third pillar, given material scope (police and judicial cooperation in criminal matters) and its special link with fundamental rights.[86]

40. Thus, the TEU and the ECJ confirmed that many general principles of law recognized in the Community pillar were also applicable to the third pillar. Moreover, both the case law of the CFI and the opinions of several Advocates General have endorsed the application of most of them (although the ECJ seemed reluctant to mention them in this field). Moreover, neither in the jurisprudence of the ECJ nor the CFI (nor in the opinions of the Advocates General) is there any indication that any of the general principles of law must be considered irrelevant in the context of the area once known as the third pillar. There is no reason either to deduce from the Treaties that any of the general principles were or are inapplicable in this area.[87] In fact, the implementation of all general

[82] Case C-303/05 *Advocaten voor de Wereld* [2007] (n 73), Opinion of AG Ruiz-Jarabo, para 62. See T Tridimas, *The General Principles of EU Law* 2nd edn (Oxford University Press, Oxford, 2006) 175–192.

[83] Case T-338/02 *Segi* [2004] (n 44) para 38 and Case T-228/02 *OMPI* [2006] (n 51) para 54. See the Opinion of AG Mengozzi in Case C-354/04 P *Gestoras* [2007] (n 44) and Case C-355/04 P *Segi* [2007] (n 46) para 104.

[84] See T Tridimas *cit* at 234–8.

[85] Case C-367/05 *Norma Kraaijenbrink* [2007] ECR I-6619, Opinion of AG Sharpston, para 60 and Case C-288/05 *Staatsanwaltschaft Augsburg v Jürgen Kretzinger* [2007] ECR I-6441, Opinion of AG Sharpston, paras 64, 65 and 70.

[86] T Tridimas *cit* at 370–417.

[87] This was already stated some time ago by S Peers, 'Who's Judging the Watchmen?: The Judicial System of the "Area of Freedom, Security, and Justice"' (1998) 18 *Yearbook of European Law* 337–78.

principles would be consistent with the rule of law on which the European Union is based (Articles 6.1 TUE, 2 TEU-L), and with the fact that Article 220 TEC (Article 19 TEU-L) dealing with the role of the ECJ to ensure compliance with the law in the interpretation and application of the Treaty applies also to this particular area.[88]

41. Some of the commentators even required that the ECJ, for the sake of legal certainty, should clearly have stated that all general principles of Community law should also apply to the third pillar, thus helping to resolve the tension between the institutional framework scheme provided for in Article 3 TEU and the distinction between the Treaties of the Community and the Union established in Article 5 TEU.[89] In this sense, the reform of the Lisbon Treaty has merged the Community Treaty and Title VI of the TEU, concerning police and judicial cooperation in criminal matters, in the TFEU. As a result, the new Court of Justice of the European Union has acquired full competence in police and judicial cooperation, facilitating the transfer of general principles to what until now was the third pillar.[90]

[88] On the relation between the general principles and Article 220 TEC (19 TEU-L) see Case C-411/05 *Palacios de la Villa* [2007] ECR I-8531, Opinion of AG Mazák, paras 85 and 136 and Case C-442/00 *Rodríguez Caballero v FOGASA* [2002] ECR I-11915 paras 30 and 32.

[89] S Peers. 'Salvation outside the Church: Judicial protection in the third Pillar after the Pupino and Segi judgments' (2007) 44(4) *Common Market Law Review* 883 at 928–9.

[90] Specifically, the provisions dealing with policial and judicial cooperation are now EU policies within Part III TFEU, Title V 'Area of Freedom, Security and Justice' as 'Chapter 4. Judicial cooperation in criminal matters' (Arts 82–6) and 'Chapter 5. Police cooperation' (Arts 87–89). See C Ladenburger, 'Police and Criminal Law in the Treaty of Lisbon. A New Dimension for the Community Method' (2008) 4(1) *European Constitutional Law Review* 20.

5

EC/EU Law According to the European Court of Human Rights

1. PRELIMINARY CONSIDERATIONS

1. The European Convention on Human Rights (ECHR) was adopted on 4 November 1950 and entered into force on 3 September 1953. When the European Coal and Steel Community (ECSC Treaty) was established on 18 April 1951 (this treaty entered into force on 23 July 1952) the ECHR already existed, but had not yet entered into force.[1] All other existing EC/EU treaties were developed once the ECHR was already in force. The drafters of both legal instruments certainly had in mind that they were creating two completely different systems, each one dedicated to an area very different from the other: the protection of certain human rights (ECHR) and the establishment of a European common market for coal and steel (ECSC Treaty).

At first it did not seem that it could produce any kind of influence or correlation between them beyond responding to a new sense of cooperation in the old continent. However, the subsequent evolution of both systems would cause both systems to cross paths in the future. Indeed, the development of the jurisprudence of the European Commission of Human Rights and the European Court of Human Rights (ECtHR) (since 1998 only the latter), mostly through direct appeal to the Court by citizens, has led to what in the European context has been called a true 'European public order' to which the signatories of the ECHR are subject.[2]

On the other hand, the evolution of the primitive European Communities has extended the powers of its institutions and caused its regulatory and enforcement actions to have a real and direct impact on the particular charter of rights and obligations of the citizens of its Member States, even beyond the merely economic or commercial scope. That is why there have been many issues that

[1] It should be noted that in 2002 the European Coal and Steel Community (ECSC) Treaty expired and all the ECSC activities and resources were absorbed by the European Community. See Protocol No 37 'On the financial consequences of the expiry of the ECSC Treaty and on the research fund for coal and steel' to the TFEU (OJ C 83/327, 30 March 2010). On the issues arising from the disappearance of the ESCS, see P Daillier, 'La disparition de la CECA le 23 juillet 2002 – Des problèmes de succession d'organisations internationales?' in JC Gautron (ed), *Les dynamiques du droit européen en début de siècle :* études *en l›honneur de Jean Claude Gautron* (Pedone, Paris, 2004) 19.

[2] J Andriantsimbazovina *et al*, *Les grands arrêts de la Cour européenne des droits de l'homme* 4th edn (PUF, Paris, 2007) 7–17.

have been brought in relation to the functioning of both systems or just the fact that certain states are at the same time signatories and, therefore, subject to meeting the requirements of these two systems.

2. Therefore the question to what extent the communities were legally bound by the ECHR was raised in political, doctrinal and jurisdictional sectors. Once the EC/EU members had committed internationally with third countries, such as Norway and Iceland, to ensure that certain human rights would be respected in their territories, the question arose whether these Member States could still transfer to the EC/EU some of their powers which may affect those rights. Moreover, the question arose whether the Communities were bound by the ECHR since their Member States were bound by it when the Communities were created (the above-mentioned issue of international succession). On the other hand, would the Member States be responsible before third countries (Norway, for example) for a non-fulfilment of the ECHR by the EC/EU?

3. Until 1 November 1998, the date of entry into force of Protocol No 1 to the ECHR, the effective implementation of the Convention was supervised by two bodies: the European Commission of Human Rights and the ECtHR. The Commission was the body on which lay the entire system of guarantees of the Convention. It had multiple tasks: besides being an administrative body in charge of reviewing the applications in order to adopt decisions of a jurisdictional nature, it also exercised other functions. Thus, it was an investigation and conciliation body (trying to provide 'friendly arrangement' between the parties), and even providing legal advice, as their reports helped the Committee of Ministers or even the ECtHR to address the issues in question if necessary. Although formally the Commission operated under the guidance of the Committee of Ministers, it was an independent body. Their members acted individually and had certain privileges and immunities. Under the Convention, all matters brought before the Court would necessarily stem from a lawsuit filed by a state or an individual, NGO or group of individuals before the Commission. The Commission therefore controlled the admissibility of the application. Moreover, in fact, the Commission was designed as a filter against a possible excess of lawsuits brought by individuals against states.[3] If the Commission took the lawsuit into account, it determined the facts and tried to get an amicable settlement. In case this attempt failed, a report was written in which, in addition to stating the facts, it formulated a decision about whether those facts constituted a violation of the obligations linked to the state by virtue of the Convention.[4] From 1 November 1998, the existing control bodies gave way to a

[3] A Queralt Jiménez, *El Tribunal de Estrasburgo: una jurisdicción internacional para la protección de los derechos fundamentales* (Tirant, Valencia, 2003) 139.

[4] For an explanation on the functioning of the ECHR organs before the Protocol No 1 reform, see D López Garrido, 'El Tribunal Europeo de Derechos Humanos. Nota introductoria' in Cortes Generales (ed), *Tribunal Europeo de Derechos Humanos: 25 años de jurisprudencia (1959–1983)* (Cortes Generales, Madrid, 1981) V.

new, permanent European Court of Human Rights which took over the powers of the former Commission and the former Court.[5]

4. It is not among the objectives of this work to carry out an in-depth analysis of the inner functioning or a detailed examination of the conditions of admissibility of the lawsuits submitted before the ECtHR. However, it seems appropriate to clarify, albeit briefly, the meaning of some concepts used in this study. Thus, given that the mechanism of protection established by the ECHR is subsidiary to the domestic courts, one could turn to the Strasbourg Court only after exhausting all the possibilities provided by domestic (national) remedies. The conditions of admissibility of individual claims before the ECtHR are set out in Article 35 of the Convention; moreover, the content coincides with the former Articles 26 and 27 of the ECHR before the amendment of Protocol No 11. Thus, according to Article 35 ECHR, from the formal point of view, having exhausted all domestic legal remedies, the complaint shall be made before the ECtHR within six months from the date of the final domestic decision. It shall not be either anonymous, or essentially the same as an application already examined by the Court, or already submitted to another procedure of international investigation or settlement of disputes and shall not contain new facts. In addition, the ECtHR shall reject those claims that are incompatible with the ECHR on the basis of four criteria on which there is a rich and relevant jurisprudence. Thus, the Governing Body of the Convention may refuse the lawsuit *ratione temporis, ratione loci, ratione personae* or *ratione materiae*.[6]

Therefore, first, the ECtHR shall consider *ratione materiae* inadmissible any individual lawsuit that it may deem incompatible with the provisions of the Convention or its additional ruling Protocols, that is, it concerns a right not included in the catalogue of rights that are known or it refers to lawsuits lacking in foundation or that are abusive. Also those lawsuits that are essentially identical to other claims submitted or already submitted to other entities are declared inadmissible under this criterion. Secondly, the *ratione personae* inadmissibility is closely related to the concept of victim that the Convention uses. Thus, in accordance with Article 34, any person, NGO or group of individuals claiming

[5] For a more detailed explanation after Protocol No 1 see A Queralt Jiménez, *El Tribunal de Estrasburgo: una jurisdicción internacional para la protección de los derechos fundamentales* (Tirant, Valencia, 2003) 259–363. On its functioning after Protocol No 14, see T Laubner, 'Relieving the Court of Its Success? – Protocol No 14 to the European Convention on Human Rights' (2004) 47 *German Yearbook of International Law* 691; S Greer, 'Protocol 14 and the Future of the European Court of Human Rights' (2005) 1 *Public Law* 83; V Starace, 'Modifications Provided by Protocol No 14 concerning Proceedings before the European Court of Human Rights' in A Del Vecchio (ed), *New international tribunals and new international proceedings* (Giuffrè Editore, Roma, 2006) 187; and MI López-Barajas Perea, 'Hacia una mayor eficacia del proceso de amparo internacional. El Protocolo nº 14 a la Convención Europea de Derechos Humanos› (2010) 21 *Revista General de Derecho Europeo*.

[6] For an analysis of admissibility before the ECHR, see P Dijk, GJH Hoof and AW Heringa, *Theory and Practice of the European Convention on Human Rights* (Martinus Nijhoff, The Hague, 1998) 108–26 and J Andriantsimbazovina (2007) (n 2) 722–41.

to be a direct victim of a violation of the Convention or having a personal interest shall file a complaint against a State Party. The concept of victim is independent of the nationality of the person. However, so-called class actions (*actio popularis*), generic allegations or those in the name of an indefinite number of people do not fit here; instead the person who alleges the violation of the Convention must have been directly affected by the violation mentioned. Thirdly, the *ratione loci* inadmissibility is not based on the concept of physical territory of the state but the legal one. That is, Article 1 ECHR provides that the Contracting Parties grant the rights recognized in the Convention to all persons under its jurisdiction. And fourthly, for the ECtHR to hear about a particular case it shall be competent *ratione temporis*, that is, that the facts supporting the claims must have occurred when the Convention for the respondent state was in force. Therefore, it will have to take into account any reservations made by states at the time of the obligation.[7]

2. THE RECOGNITION OF RESPONSIBILITY IN THE CASE LAW OF STRASBOURG

2.1. The Initial Case Law of the Commission

5. The first significant decisions that are relevant to the analysis made here date from the early years of operation of the governing bodies of the Convention, namely, the 1950s and 1960s. In various decisions, the European Commission of Human Rights recognized that under Article 1 ECHR, States Parties were responsible for all acts or omissions of their organs contrary to the Convention, regardless of the fact that they may result from the application of internal law or as a consequence of an international obligation assumed by them. Indeed, the signing of international treaties by Member States of the ECHR did not allow them to escape from the obligations they undertook when adopting it:

> The Commission recalls that if a Member State assume contractual obligations and later on another international agreement that no longer allows him to meet the obligations in the first treaty, it shall be responsible for any breach of the obligations assumed under the first treaty.[8]

6. This responsibility is imposed even more clearly since the Convention is part of the so-called 'European public order', a term set by the Commission in 1961.[9] The effects of the application of these principles will be shown most clearly in

[7] In Spanish, see JA Carrillo Salcedo, *El Convenio Europeo de Derechos Humanos* (Tecnos, Madrid, 2003) 53–9 and A Queralt Jiménez, *El Tribunal de Estrasburgo: una jurisdicción internacional para la protección de los derechos fundamentales* (Tirant, Valencia, 2003) 302–17.

[8] App No 235/56 (Commission Decision, 10 June 1958, 2 DR 257).

[9] Case *Austria v Italy* App No 788/60 (Commission Decision, 11 January 1961, 4 DR 139), which refers to the 'public order of Europe'.

the decision of the European Commission of Human Rights in the *Etienne Tête v France* case (see below).

7. Thus it is hard to deny that, in light of the rules of public international law on successive treaties, the Member States of the current European Union would be exposed to situations of potential responsibility for possible violations of the Convention derived from acts of the EC/EU.[10] On the other hand, even if the responsibility of the Member States is clear in the case of measures implementing an act or an EC/EU provision, the issue is more delicate if in the national implementing measures such state has no discretion and merely complies with the act of the EC/EU.

2.2. From Individual to Collective Responsibility

8. In the 1970s, the issue raised before the European Commission of Human Rights was whether Member States of the Communities could be declared responsible jointly or collectively by an act emanating from the EC institutions and contrary to the ECHR. In this sense, the decision of the Commission *CFDT v The European Communities and subsidiarily against each and all of their Member States* on 10 July 1978 distinguishes several hypotheses.[11] The plaintiffs, *Confédération française démocratique du travail* (CFDT), directly challenged a decision by the Council in which the union representatives part of the Advisory Committee provided for in Article 18 of the ECSC Treaty had been appointed and in which they had excluded the opposing union.[12] This decision considered that the CFDT union violated Articles 11 (freedom of assembly and association), 13 (right to an effective remedy) and 14 (prohibition of discrimination) of the Convention.

> In so far as the application is directed against the European Communities as such the Commission points out that the European Communities are not a Contracting Party to the European Convention on Human Rights (Article 66 of the Convention). To this extent the consideration of the applicant's complaint lies outside the Commission's jurisdiction *ratione personae*.[13]

We shall go back to this point below, since there has been a shift in this regard.

[10] F Tulkens, 'L'Union européenne devant la Cour européenne des droits de l'homme' (2000) 12(1–2) *Revue Universelle des Droits de l'Homme* 50 at 51.

[11] Case *CFDT v European Communities, alternatively: their Member States a) jointly and b) severally (CFDT)* App No 8030/77 (Commission Decision, 10 July 1978, 13 DR 231).

[12] Before going to the Commission, the CFDT Union sought the annulment of the contested Council decision before the ECJ, but it refused to consider the case since ECSC Treaty Articles 33 and 38 did not allow the Union to lodge an appeal (only Member States of the European Commission had that possibility and Article 33 ECSC Treaty allowed only to contest Commission decisions). See Case *CFDT* [1978] (n 11) 305.

[13] Case *CFDT* [1978] (n 11) para 3.

9. The Commission continued:

> In so far as the application is directed against each of the Member States of the European Communities who are at the same time Contracting Parties to the Convention the question might be raised whether the act complained of, which was carried out by an organ of the European Communities, can involve the responsibility of the 9 Member States of the European Communities under the Convention.[14]

In the that case, regardless of the answer to this question, the Commission stated that examination of the action was beyond its competence *ratione personae*, since France had not yet recognized at that time the right to an individual appeal within the meaning established by Article 25 ECHR. As for the other eight Member States of the European Communities, the Commission was of the opinion that consideration of the arguments advanced by the plaintiff (CFDT) were beyond its competence *ratione materiae* because those states, owing to their participation in decisions of the Council of the European Communities, had not, in the case under review, exercised their 'jurisdiction' according to Article 1 of the Convention.

10. This position of the Commission was continued in a subsequent decision of 19 January 1989 in the *Dufay case against the European Communities and subsidiarily all their Member States and each Member State alone* where the appellant challenged his dismissal by the European Parliament and, in particular, the procedure followed before the Court of Justice.[15]

> As long as the action is brought against Member States of the European Communities, which are, at the same time, contracting parties of the Convention, the question that arises is whether the contested measure, issued by a court of the Communities, can compromise each of the twelve Member States of the European Communities within the scope of the Convention.
>
> Even assuming that it could support such an eventuality, it is understood that the jurisdiction of the Commission shall not be established until after exhaustion of specific remedies provided with regard to the control of Community acts. In this scenario, the legal remedies, as established on the Community law, would be assimilated to those remedies generally established by Article 26 of the Convention. Therefore, the remedies provided by Community Law shall constitute internal remedies within the meaning of the aforesaid provision of the Convention.[16]

Under this reasoning, the Commission seems to admit that the ECJ shall be considered domestic jurisdiction for the purpose of the control system established by the ECHR.

[14] Case *CFDT* [1978] (n 11) para 5.

[15] Case *Dufay v les Communautés Européennes, subsidiairement, la collectivité de leurs* États *membres et leurs* États *membres pris individuellement* App No 13539/88 (Commission Decision, 19 January 1989, unpublished).

[16] Case *Dufay* [1989] (n 15) para 2.

As for the merits, formally, the Commission did not rule out an eventual 'joint' responsibility of the Member States of the European Communities. For the *Dufay* case, some other reasons allowed the Commission to reject the appeal and take a position regarding this matter.

2.3. The Consolidation of the Old Principles and the Emergence of New Uncertainties

11. The 1980s and 1990s saw the consolidation of some aspects of the jurisprudence of the Commission but also the emergence of some uncertainties. As for the consolidated aspects, we shall include the decision of the Commission concerning the *Etienne Tête v France* case on 9 December 1987.[17] In this particular case, the appellant contested the conventionality of the law concerning the election of the French representatives to the European Parliament. According to his arguments, the provisions relating to the voting system, the requirements concerning the lists, the assumption by the state of advertising expenditures and the payment of radio ads violated both Article 3 of the Additional Protocol (right to free elections) and Article 14 of the Convention (prohibition of discrimination). It is therefore in this context that the Convention recalls its jurisprudence reinforcing also its previous positions:

> It cannot therefore be accepted that by means of transfers of competence the High Contracting Parties may at the same time exclude matters normally covered by the Convention from the guarantees enshrined therein. What is at stake is respect for fundamental rights, such as those set forth in Article 3 of Protocol No 1 which, in the Convention system, is of vital importance.[18]

12. Another important milestone is the decision of inadmissibility in the *M & Co v Germany* case on 9 February 1990.[19] In this case, the appellant answered the implementation carried out by Germany of a ruling of the ECJ on 7 June 1983 which, in its opinion, had been issued following a procedure that did not fulfil the requirements of Article 6 ECHR.[20] Specifically, it was a procedure to bring his case in alleged violation of competition rules. The relevant company tried to obtain from the German Constitutional Court a resolution prohibiting the Ministry of Justice from carrying out the judgment claiming that the company concerned did not have a fair trial as established by Article 6 of the Convention. This internal appeal was unsuccessful because the German

[17] Case *Etienne Tête v France* App no 11123/84 (Commission Decision, 9 December 1987, 54 DR 62).

[18] Caso *Etienne Tête* (n 17) paras 3, 4.

[19] Case *M & Co v Germany* App No 13258/87 (Commission Decision, 9 February 1990, 64 DR 138).

[20] See Joined Cases 100 to 103/80 *Musique Diffusion française v Commission* [1983] ECR 1825. See A Vandencasteele, 'Affaire 100/80, Arrêt de la Cour du 7 juin 1983' (1984) 20(1) *Revue Trimestrielle de Droit Européen* 203.

Constitutional Court considered that the ECJ guaranteed, in a proper manner, the right to a fair trial and that there was no obligation on the part of the German authorities to verify the lawfulness of a decision of the ECJ prior to its implementation. After this answer, the appellant company went to the European Commission of Human Rights and filed a lawsuit against Germany for violation of Article 6 of the Convention.

13. The Commission rejected the claims of the company concerned, but it is interesting to revisit the arguments and *obiter dicta* used in its decision of inadmissibility.[21]

The Commission began its legal reasoning by recalling the principle of the responsibility of the Member States of the EC derived from the implementation of Community law, relying particularly on the rules of international law on successive treaties. It thus confirmed its previous jurisprudence, namely that according to which States Parties to the Convention are responsible for the implementation of community acts:

> The Commission first recalls that it is in fact not competent ratione personae to examine proceedings before or decisions of organs of the European Communities, the latter not being a Party to the European Convention on Human Rights . . . This does not mean, however, that by granting executory power to a judgment of the European Court of Justice the competent German authorities acted quasi as Community organs and are to that extent beyond the scope of control exercised by the Convention organs. Under Article 1 of the Convention the Member States are responsible for all acts and omissions of their domestic organs allegedly violating the Convention regardless of whether the act or omission in question is a consequence of domestic law or regulations or of the necessity to comply with international obligations . . .
>
> It has next to be observed that the Convention does not prohibit a Member State from transferring powers to international organisations. Nonetheless, the Commission recalls that 'if a State contracts treaty obligations and subsequently concludes another international agreement which disables it from performing its obligations under the first treaty it will be answerable for any resulting breach of its obligations under the earlier treaty'.[22]

14. Notwithstanding the foregoing, the Commission makes an important statement regarding the exercise of its control. Considering that if the transfer of powers does not relieve the states of their responsibility under the Convention by the powers transferred, on the other hand, it would be very difficult to enforce such responsibility since the organization that is going to receive the powers ensures the protection of fundamental rights equivalent to that resulting from the Convention. In fact, the Commission drew inspiration from this point of the German

[21] For a deep analysis of this case see T Giegerich, 'Luxembourg, Karlsruhe, Strassburg – Dreistufiger Grundrechtsschutz in Europa?' (1990) 50 *Zeitschrift für ausländisches öffentliches Recht und Völkerrecht* 836; and F Rigaux, 'L'article 192 du Traité C.E.E. devant la Commission européenne des droits de l'homme' (1991) 7 *Revue Trimestrielle des Droits de l'Homme* 395.

[22] Case *M & Co* [1990] (n 19) 152.

Constitutional Court's jurisprudence under which the Court would not exercise powers over the Community law, 'as long as' (*Solange*) the Communities would ensure effective protection of fundamental rights considered of a level equal to that granted by the German Basic Law.[23] In fact, the Commission stated the following:

> The Commission considers that a transfer of powers does not necessarily exclude a State's responsibility under the Convention with regard to the exercise of the transferred powers. Otherwise the guarantees of the Convention could wantonly be limited or excluded and thus be deprived of their peremptory character. The object and purpose of the Convention as an instrument for the protection of individual human beings requires that its provisions be interpreted and applied so as to make its safeguards practical and effective . . . Therefore the transfer of powers to an international organisation is not incompatible with the Convention provided that within that organisation fundamental rights will receive an equivalent protection.[24]

15. Based on the foregoing, the Commission concluded that the right to a fair trial (Article 6 of the Convention) was secured in an equivalent manner within the scope of Community law and, therefore, declared the application inadmissible since it was '*ratione materiae* incompatible' with the provisions of the Convention:

> The Commission notes that the legal system of the European Communities not only secures fundamental rights but also provides for control of their observance. It is true that the constituent treaties of the European Communities did not contain a catalogue of such rights. However, the Parliament, the Council and the Commission of the European Communities have stressed in a joint declaration of 5 April 1977 that they attach prime importance to the protection of fundamental rights, as derived in particular from the Constitution of the Member States and the European Convention for the Protection of Human Rights and Fundamental Freedoms. They pledged that, in the exercise of their powers and in pursuance of the aims of the European Communities, they would respect and continue to respect these human rights . . . In addition the Court of Justice of the European Communities has developed a case-law according to which it is called upon to control Community acts on the basis of fundamental rights, including those enshrined in the European Convention on Human Rights. In accordance with this reasoning the Court of Justice underlined in the present case that the right to a fair hearing is a fundamental principle of Community law. It stated that Community law contained all criteria which are prerequisites not only to examine but, if necessary, to remedy the applicant company's complaint that its right to a fair hearing was violated . . . However, it came to the conclusion that this complaint was unfounded.
>
> The Commission has also taken into consideration that it would be contrary to the very idea of transferring powers to an international organisation to hold the member States responsible for examining, in each individual case before issuing a writ of

[23] This is the so-called *Solange II* case: 2 BvR 197/83 BVerfGE 73 339 (German Constitutional Court, 22 October 1986).

[24] Case *M & Co* [1990] (n 19) 152–3.

execution for a judgment of the European Court of Justice, whether Article 6 of the Convention was respected in the underlying proceedings.[25]

16. At this point one might wonder about the consequences of that decision of the Commission. If we reduce the matter to the key arguments, we conclude that this decision implies two things. On the one hand, the Commission reaffirms the possibility to engage the responsibility of a state in the case of a failure to comply with the Convention. On the other hand, it seems to limit this possibility by stating that the Community ensures a sufficient guarantee of fundamental rights, both from a procedural point of view as well as from a substantive one, but in any case regarding a fair trial. Indeed, note how the Commission already established in this case that Community law had all the characteristics that made possible not only a review in a procedural context but also, if necessary, the repair of the damage alleged by the appellant company.[26]

17. This decision of the Commission provoked criticism, both for its argument and its final conclusion, among certain members of the ECtHR and some belonging to the ECJ.[27] Thus, while in the *Solange II* decision the German Constitutional Court stated that it would not exercise its powers 'as long as' the Community granted a level of protection 'equivalent' to that which was derived from the Basic Law, it is impossible to find a similar statement in the text of the Decision of the Commission in the *M & Co* case. By declaring the application *ratione materiae* inadmissible, did the European Commission mean that, at least with regard to Article 6 of the Convention and fair trials, it declined to exercise control over any act emanating from an EC organ? It is not clear. The Commission could have declared the action 'manifestly ill-founded'. This formula would clearly leave the door open for further checking, even of the same subject (the right to a fair trial).

18. Some observers believed at the time that this decision should be interpreted narrowly. That is, it would not be necessary to infer general principles that could be subsequently extrapolated beyond the specific case: the enforcement of a judgment of the ECJ and the invocation of the right to a fair trial. In other words, the Commission would have simply decided that the right to a fair trial was adequately secured within the Community legal order, particularly in the field of competition law, so that in this case, Member States were not obliged to verify the compatibility of a decision emanating from the ECJ with the ECHR before agreeing to the implementation of that decision. The issue, these analysts argued, would have been different if it had been about implementing a Regulation or a

[25] Case *M & Co* [1990] (n 19) 153.

[26] See F Tulkens, 'L'Union européenne devant la Cour européenne des droits de l'homme' (2000) 12(1–2) *Revue Universelle des Droits de L'homme* 50 at 53.

[27] An example of this was the speech of M Weitzel, member of the Human Rights Commission, during the visit of a delegation of the ECJ to the ECtHR. This speech was reproduced in *Bulletin des droits de l'homme* (July) 1997 at 279–80.

Directive, or if it had been about implementing a decision of the Court that would have questioned a right other than the provisions of Article 6 of the Convention (right to a fair trial).[28]

19. Indeed, it was difficult to predict the tendency given that two decisions of the Commission, close in time, seemed to prefer each of the possible interpretations. Thus, the decision of the Commission in the *Procola* case of 1 July 1993 opted for a restrictive interpretation.[29] In this case, the European Commission of Human Rights did not hesitate to check whether the legislation of Luxembourg on milk quotas (which did nothing but implement an EC regulation) affected the property rights as guaranteed by Article 1 of the First Protocol of the Convention or not. Moreover, in this case, the Commission adopted a more cautious approach and declared the application inadmissible as it was manifestly ill-founded, rather than declare itself unqualified *ratione materiae*.[30]

20. Soon, another decision of the European Commission of Human Rights, the *Heinz* case, on 10 January 1994, would give the ECtHR the opportunity to revisit its case law. On this occasion, it was a (not jurisdictional) decision of the European Patent Office established by the Munich Convention of 5 October 1973. The person concerned, Mr Heinz, sued collectively all Member States of the Munich Convention that were also part of the ECHR. From his point of view, the decision of the European Patent Office that was adopted in accordance with the Munich Convention violated his right to property as it was guaranteed in Article 1 of the First Protocol of the ECHR.[31] The European Commission mentioned specifically the *M & Co* case law by quoting it widely and declared the appeal inadmissible as it was incompatible *ratione materiae* with the provisions of the Convention. The *M & Co* case was a milestone regarding the interordinal relations between EC law and the ECHR and the principles contained therein were repeated and materialized in subsequent decisions and, especially, judgments of the ECtHR.

21. Thus, through their decisions, the European Commission of Human Rights developed a doctrine on the matter that can be summarized in three points.

[28] F Tulkens (2000) (n 26) at 54.

[29] Case *Procola and others v Luxembourg* App No 14570/89 (Commission Decision, 1 July 1993, 75 DR 5). Subsequently, the ECtHR decided that there was a breach of Art 6 ECHR (ECtHR, 28 September 1995, 326 *Series* A).

[30] See JL Autin and F Sudre, 'La dualité fonctionnelle du Conseil d'État en question devant la Cour européenne des droits de l'homme. À propos de l'arrêt Procola c/ Luxembourg du 28 septembre 1995' (1996) 12(4) *Revue Française de Droit Administratif* 777.

[31] Case *Heinz v the Contracting States party to the European Patent Convention insofar as they are High contracting Parties to the European Convention on Human Rights, i.e. Austria, Belgium, Denmark, France, Germany, Greece, Ireland, Italy, Liechtenstein, Luxembourg, Netherlands, Norway, Portugal, Spain, Sweden, Switzerland and the United Kingdom* App No 21090/92 (Commission Decision, 10 January 1994, 76B DR 125).

First, the applications against the European Community were inadmissible. The Community was not part of the Convention and it never acceded to it. Secondly, it was not possible to make Member States responsible for any breaches of the Convention incurred by the Communities. Community acts stem from different legal personalities than Member States. Although they may have some influence on the adoption of these acts, one cannot make them responsible for the acts.

Finally, the possibility of making Member States responsible for the implementation of Community acts allegedly contrary to the Convention was addressed in a more subtle manner. States are free to transfer powers to supranational organizations. If the ECHR were to limit such transfer, it would have adversely affected international cooperation in general and European integration in particular. The Commission could hardly compel Member States to monitor and eventually review Community acts if EC law did not allow this possibility. In any case, under no circumstances could it be admitted that Communities would take actions contrary to human rights as guaranteed by the Convention.

2.4. Towards a More Rigorous Application of the Principles: The Rejection of the EC/EU Exception

22. The 1990s would mark a consolidation in this case law by carrying out a more rigorous application of the aforementioned principles and, above all, due to the direct intervention of the ECtHR. It would be interesting to see to what extent the ECtHR has assumed the case law of the Commission.

23. The decision of the ECtHR in the *Cantoni v France* case on 15 November 1996 was the beginning of a decisive stage.[32] This was the first case in which the Strasbourg Court had to directly confront the thorny issue concerning the compatibility of an EC/EU act with the ECHR. The ECtHR clearly rejected the immunity of EC/EU law.

24. In regard to the facts, this case was about whether the legal definition of 'medicinal products' that the respondent state (France) had taken from an EC directive was, given its interpretation by the courts (in this case, the *Cour de Cassation*), accurate enough to meet the requirements of the principle of legality of crimes and penalties contained in Article 7 of the Convention. Broadly speaking, this case essentially referred to the criminal conviction of the manager of a large supermarket for the illegal practice of its pharmacy on the basis of Article L.511 of the French Public Health Code, a provision which was

[32] Case *Catoni v France* App No 17862/91 (ECtHR, 15 November 1996, 1996-V 1614).

inspired almost word for word by Article of Directive 65/65/EC.[33] In his defence, Mr Cantoni claimed that the products for which he was incriminated were not 'medicinal' under the meaning of Article L.511 of the Public Health Code and therefore were not the monopoly of chemists. Condemned by the *Tribunal correctionnel*, he appealed for annulment, invoking Article 7 ECHR. He argued that, applied especially to the field of pharmacy, the notion of 'medicinal product' according to the legal texts that had established his conviction had no such clarity that would accurately identify actions that could trigger criminal liability. The *Cour de Cassation* rejected the appeal.[34]

25. In its decision, the European Court of Human Rights strongly rejects the argument of the immunity of EC/EU law:

> The fact, pointed to by the Government, that Article L. 511 of the Public Health Code is based almost word for word on Community Directive 65/65 (see paragraph 12 above) does not remove it from the ambit of Article 7 of the Convention.[35]

Thus, the ECtHR answered the argument that had been suggested by the French Government and which consisted in introducing a sort of 'EC/EU exception' when the action brought to trial had its origin in an obligation under EC/EU law. In other words, according to the argument of the government, to review the national provision due to the lack of precision would be to review the directive.[36] This possible explanation was therefore rejected by the Court in Strasbourg.

26. Even without having found a violation of the Convention in this case, the ECtHR was in a situation of potential conflict between a rule of Community origin and a standard of the ECHR. Indeed, if the Strasbourg Court had found an inconsistency between Article L.511 and Article 7 of the Convention, it would have directly or indirectly reviewed Directive 65/65. That is, access control and predictability that defines the notion of 'medicinal product' may have led, by extension, to a control of conventionality of that directive.[37]

27. Certainly, the decision of the ECtHR does not offer any new arguments. However, it reminds us that, after Opinion 2/94 of the ECJ on EC access to the ECHR, the normative power of the EC/EU institutions does not fully escape the control of the authorities in Strasbourg.[38]

[33] Council Directive 65/65/EEC (OJ L 369, 9 February 1965).

[34] For a deep analysis of the *Cantoni* case, see E Fouassier, *Le Médicament: notion juridique* (Technique & Documentation, Paris, 1999).

[35] Case *Catoni* [1996] (n 32) para 30.

[36] Case *Catoni* [1996] (n 32) para 28.

[37] Case *Catoni* [1996] (n 32) para 26.

[38] Y Petit, 'Médicament, droit français, droit communautaire et Convention européenne des droits de l'homme' (1997) mars, *Europe* 5.

3. CONVENTIONALITY CONTROL OF EC/EU PRIMARY LAW

28. We had to wait until 1999 to face another important advance in the jurisprudence of the Strasbourg Court. In fact, on 18 February 1999 three judgments were made public that addressed the issue of how the ECtHR understands the interordinal relations of the ECHR with other international legal systems. These cases were *Matthews v UK*, *Waite and Kennedy v Germany* and *Beer and Regan v Germany*.[39]

3.1. The ECHR v the Treaties: the *Matthews* Case

29. In the *Matthews v UK* case, the ECtHR ruled on the doctrine that it intended to apply to control the compatibility with the Convention of the national measures taken in implementation of other international laws, even if they were thus 'constitutional'.[40] The highest court in Strasbourg subsequently subordinated the transfer of powers on behalf of international organizations to the fact that fundamental rights continue to be recognized.[41] While it is true that this case decides the question of the relationship between the Convention and EC/EU primary law, beyond the fact that the case was related to the organization of the European Parliament elections in Gibraltar, it is true that the principles outlined above are likely to be extrapolated to other situations that may arise within the European Union, as well as the status of the Convention in relation to the 'constitutional' law of other international organizations.[42]

[39] Case *Matthews v UK* App No 24833/94 (ECtHR 18 February 1999, 1999-I 251); Case *Waite, Kennedy v Germany* App No 26083/94 (ECtHR 18 February 1999, 1999-I 393); and Case *Beer and Regan v Germany* App No 28934/95 (ECtHR 18 February 1999, unpublished).

[40] The Strasbourg Court does not hesitate to award this condition to the EC/EU, for instance in Case *Matthews* [1999] (n 31) paras 26 and 39. See I Canor, 'Primus inter pares. Who is the ultimate guardian of fundamental rights in Europe?' (2000) 25(1) *European Law Review* 3; F Tulkens (2000) (n 26); HG Schermers, 'Matthews v United Kingdom, Judgment of 18 February 1999' (1999) 36(3) *Common Market Law Review* 673; G Cohen-Jonathan and JF Flauss, 'De l'office de la Cour européenne des droits de l'homme dans la protection des droits fondamentaux dans l'Union européenne : l'arrêt Matthews contre Royaume-Uni du 18 février 1999' (1999) 11(7–9) *Revue Universelle des Droits de l'Homme* 253; A Potteau, 'L'article 3 du premier protocole additionnel à la Convention et l'obligation des États membres de l'Union européenne de reconnaître le droit de participer aux élections du Parlement européen' (1999) 40 *Revue Trimestrielle des Droits de l'Homme* 865; and P Ruiz-Jarabo, 'Por una interpretación pacífica de Matthews contra Reino Unido. Colonialismo y derechos fundamentales en Gibraltar' (2002) 18 *Anuario de Derecho Internacional* 229.

[41] Case *Matthews* [1999] (n 39) para 32.

[42] F Tulkens, (2000) (n 26) at 55.

3.1.1. The peculiarities of the Matthews *case*

30. To determine the extent of the sentence on the *Matthews* case it is of interest to note the essential elements of the case. At the beginning of its legal reasoning, the Strasbourg Court clearly raises the question of whether the UK failed to comply with the obligations derived from the Convention by failing to organize elections for the European Parliament.

The legal texts which had to be taken into consideration were instruments that had a 'constitutional' nature. Thus, the Council Decision of 20 September 1976 was signed by the President of the European Council and the Ministers of Foreign Affairs, and the Act regarding the election by direct universal suffrage of the Members of the European Parliament attached to the decision bore the rubric of the Ministers of Foreign Affairs of the Member States.[43] Annex II of that decision stated that the United Kingdom had to apply the provisions of the relevant Act only as regards the United Kingdom. So this was the legal basis that laid the foundations for the refusal to organize elections to the European Parliament in Gibraltar, a fact which led to the court battle initiated by Ms Matthews.

31. In this context, the appellant based her claim on a conflict between the Act concerning the election of the European Parliament by direct universal suffrage and Article 3 of the First Protocol to the Convention.[44] The applicant considered that after the entry into force of the Treaty of Maastricht in 1993, which significantly expanded the powers of the European Parliament, the latter should meet the characteristics of the body of rules referred to in Article 3 of the First Protocol. On the other hand, the British Government considered that 'acts adopted by the Community or consequent to its requirements could not be imputed to the Member States, together or individually, particularly when those acts concerned elections to a constitutional organ of the Community itself'.[45] The United Kingdom also noted that the European Commission of Human Rights had repeatedly refused to submit Community acts to a compatibility control with the Convention. On this last point, the appellant claimed that the rules that had to be taken into account (the Decision of the Council and the Act annexed) constituted an international treaty, rather than an act of an institution whose decisions were not subject to Convention review. Likewise, the applicant argued that, if these agreements involved a transfer of powers to the EC/EU,

[43] Decision 76/787/ECSC, EEC, Euratom of the representatives of the Member States meeting in the Council of 20 September 1976 relating to the Act concerning the election of the representatives of the Assembly by direct universal suffrage (OJ L 278/1, 8 October 1976) amended by Council Decision 2002/772/EC, Euratom amending the Act concerning the election of the representatives of the European Parliament by direct universal suffrage, annexed to Decision 76/787/ECSC, EEC, Euratom (OJ L 283/1, 21 October 2002).

[44] Article 3 of Protocol No 1 (also called the 'Additional Protocol') recognizes the right to free elections: 'The High Contracting Parties undertake to hold free elections at reasonable intervals by secret ballot, under conditions which will ensure the free expression of the opinion of the people in the choice of the legislature.'

[45] Case *Matthews* [1999] (n 39) para 26.

this transfer in favour of an international organization was conditioned by the fundamental rights to receive a protection equivalent to that provided by the Convention, given that the ECJ did not have jurisdiction to prosecute the so-called primary law or EC/EU constitutional law.[46]

3.1.2. The Court's Response

32. These arguments were taken into account by the Court's judgment. First, when analysing Article 1 of the Convention, which provides that states shall secure to everyone within their jurisdiction the rights and freedoms defined in the ECHR, the ECtHR confirms categorically that it 'makes no distinction as to the type of rule or measure concerned, and does not exclude any part of the Member States' "jurisdiction" from scrutiny under the Convention'.[47]

33. Having established this principle, the Court takes up and develops the general doctrine stated by the Commission according to which the ECHR 'does not exclude the transfer of competences to international organisations provided that Convention rights continue to be "secured". Member States' responsibility therefore continues even after such a transfer'.[48]

The process of European integration is no exception to this rule. The ECtHR made clear its competence to verify compliance with fundamental rights even in the legal texts of constitutional nature.

34. Then, the Strasbourg Court emphasized the specific nature of the legal acts challenged. Therefore it concluded that the decision of the Council and the 1976 Act, as well as the Maastricht Treaty amending the EEC Treaty, are all international instruments to which the UK had freely accessed. But owing to their particular nature, none of these rules was likely to be subject to review by the ECJ in order to verify their conformity with fundamental rights.

> . . . the 1976 Act cannot be challenged before the European Court of Justice for the very reason that it is not a 'normal' act of the Community, but is a treaty within the Community legal order. The Maastricht Treaty, too, is not an act of the Community, but a treaty by which a revision of the EEC Treaty was brought about.[49]

That is why the Court concluded that 'the United Kingdom, together with all the other parties to the Maastricht Treaty, is responsible ratione materiae under Article 1 of the Convention and, in particular, under Article 3 of Protocol No 1, for the consequences of that Treaty'.[50]

[46] Case *Matthews* [1999] (n 39) para 27.
[47] Case *Matthews* [1999] (n 39) para 29, quoting another case where a breach of the right to association was recognized. See Case *United Communist Party of Turkey and others v Turkey* App No 19392/92 (ECtHR 30 January 1998, 1998-I) paras 51–61.
[48] Case *Matthews* [1999] (n 39) para 32.
[49] Case *Matthews* [1999] (n 39) para 33.
[50] Case *Matthews* [1999] (n 39) para 33.

35. On the merits of the case, the Court found that the acts resulting from the EC/EU law-making process affect the population of Gibraltar in the same way as those arising solely from the local legislative assembly. Therefore, it considered that there is no reason to believe that the UK is not obliged to recognize the rights guaranteed by Article 3 of the First Protocol (also called the "Additional Protocol"), whether they be purely internal elections or European elections.[51]

3.1.3. The Consequences of the Matthews *Case Law*

36. As to the scope of this ruling, there are some remarks to be made. First, the ECtHR is directly entitled, under Article 1 of the Convention and through its review competence over Member States' action, to assess the compliance with the Convention of internal EC/EU constitutional law.

37. In addition, for national implementation measures of EC/EU law, the Court established a sort of reservation in favour of the EC/EU. Indeed, the ECJ operates a control that can be qualified as 'sufficient', especially when consolidating its tendency to implement directly, as general principles of law, the fundamental rights established in the ECHR. Indeed, at the time of the decision on the *Matthews* case, the ECJ had found for the first time that the excessive length of proceedings before the CFI resulted on a violation of the right to a fair trial according to Article 6 of the Convention.[52] Still, this vote of confidence is already conditioned to the compliance of two requirements. On the one hand, that the rights recognized by the Convention are effectively afforded to any person who should be able also to claim before an independent and impartial body. Furthermore, states have an obligation to ensure that the competences transferred shall be exercised in accordance with the rights recognized by the Convention.[53]

38. On the other hand, it must be stressed that the ECtHR, by stating that the acts submitted to its control could not be subject to judicial review by the ECJ, adopted in this case (even though it recognized itself competent to review EC/EU primary law) an attitude of cooperation rather than of subordination regarding the ECJ.[54] Indeed, the Strasbourg Court implied that the main reason, or at least a very important one, for it to control such acts was that no other judicial body could do it.

39. The contributions of this case law are likely to be applicable also to relations between the Convention and other international organizations (and its

[51] Case *Matthews* [1999] (n 39) paras 34–35.

[52] Case C-185/95 P *Baustahlgewebe v Commission* [1998] ECR I-8417.

[53] See F Tulkens (2000) (n 26) at 56.

[54] M Delmas-Marty, 'Commerce mondial et protection des droits de l'homme' in JF Flauss *et al* (ed), *Commerce mondial et protection des droits de l'homme: les droits de l'homme à l'épreuve de la globalisation des échanges économiques* (Bruylant, Bruxelles, 2001) 1.

constitutional legal instruments). Indeed, the Strasbourg Court established, in separate judgments made on the same day as the *Matthews* case, certain limits on the autonomy of the 'law of the international civil service' and, therefore, to the extension of immunity from jurisdiction from which international organizations benefit in cases of a labour dispute with their employees. These are the above-mentioned cases of *Waite and Kennedy v Germany* and *Beer and Regan v Germany*.

40. The appellants, German and British citizens, were assigned to the European Space Agency (ESA). Owing to the non-renewal of their contracts, they began proceedings against the Agency before the German labour courts, arguing that by virtue of a German law on the transfer of workers, they were considered as agents of that organization. In this national procedure, the ESA pleaded that it enjoyed immunity from jurisdiction before the German court. Finally, the German court dismissed the appeal, so the interested parties filed a complaint before the ECHR pleading a violation of Article 6 ECHR.[55]

41. The ECtHR considered that the absolute immunity from jurisdiction pleaded by the ESA was not in accordance with the right to a court guaranteed by Article 6.1 of the Convention, unless such immunity was due to a legitimate aim and if there was a reasonable relationship of proportionality between the means employed and the aim pursued. In this regard, the ECtHR found that:

> where [ECHR contracting] States establish international organisations in order to pursue or strengthen their cooperation in certain fields of activities, and where they attribute to these organisations certain competences and accord them immunities, there may be implications as to the protection of fundamental rights. It would be incompatible with the purpose and object of the Convention, however, if the Contracting States were thereby absolved from their responsibility under the Convention in relation to the field of activity covered by such attribution.[56]

42. In short, the Strasbourg Court has subordinated the jurisdictional immunity of international organizations to the existence of other 'reasonable alternative means to protect effectively their rights under the Convention'.[57] In this particular case, the channels and possibilities of resources were proved satisfactory and the Court concluded that the German court had not exceeded its margin of appreciation by accepting the immunity from jurisdiction of the ESA.[58]

[55] Case *Beer and Regan* [1999] (n 39) paras 10–18 and Case *Waite and Kennedy* [1999] (n 39) paras 10–28.

[56] Case *Beer and Regan* [1999] (n 39) para 57 and Case *Waite and Kennedy* [1999] (n 39) para 67.

[57] Case *Beer and Regan* [1999] (n 39) para 58 and Case *Waite and Kennedy* [1999] (n 39) para 68.

[58] Caso *Beer and Regan* [1999] (n 39) paras 58–63 and Case *Waite and Kennedy* [1999] (n 39) paras 69–73. See I Brownlie, 'The Responsibility of States for the Acts of International Organizations' in M Ragazzi (ed), *International responsibility today: essays in memory of Oscar Schachter* (Martinus Nijhoff, Leiden, 2005) 355 at 361.

43. These two judgments of the same date as the *Matthews* case (18 February 1999) point out the legal effects of the ECHR beyond the national legislation of states parties and the extent of the international responsibility of the states under the Convention. These decisions emphasize, particularly, the importance of the right to a judge and, in any case, of a fair trial that must be effective in all circumstances.

44. Some scholars have proposed an interpretation of the *Matthews* case and also of the other judgments made public the same day based solely on the rules on succession of public international law treaties.[59] That is, the *Matthews* case, even though it refers to primary EC/EU law, would constitute a practical application of the rule on successive international treaties, under which a state cannot escape the obligations assumed under an international treaty signing another agreement later.[60]

3.2. The Disadvantages of Serving Two Masters: The Continuation of the *Matthews* Case before the ECJ

45. The *Matthews* case was by no means closed with this judgment, but had its sequel before the ECJ, where the difficulties resulting from the absence of a strict hierarchy between the Convention and EC/EU primary law were obvious.[61]

46. Thus, after having been condemned by the ECtHR for having excluded British citizens resident in Gibraltar from the European Parliament elections, in violation of Article 3 of the First Protocol of the Convention, the UK decided to implement the ruling. The problem was that, in order to do so, the Act needed to be modified. In principle, this should not have posed major problems as Annex II was introduced at the specific request of the United Kingdom. But we

[59] O de Schutter and O l'Hoest, 'La Cour européenne des droits de l'homme juge du droit communautaire : Gibraltar, l'Union européenne, et la Convention européenne des droits de l'homme' (2000) 36(1–2) *Cahiers de Droit Européen* 141 at 167–8; and F Krenc, 'La décision Senator Lines ou l'ajournement d'une question délicate' (2005) 16 *Revue Trimestrielle des Droits de l'Homme* 121 at 131.

[60] This very same case law may be observed in ulterior cases, such as Case *Prince Hans-Adam II of Liechtenstein v Germany* App No 42527/98 (ECtHR, 12 July 2001, 2001-VIII) paras 47–48.

[61] Case C-145/04 *Spain v UK* [2006] ECR I-7917. See L Burgorgue-Larsen, 'L'identité de l'Union européenne au coeur d'une controverse territoriale tricentenaire – Quand le statut de Gibraltar réapparaît sur la scène judiciaire européenne (CJCE 12 septembre 2006, aff. C-145/04, Royaume d'Espagne c/ Royaume-Uni de Grande-Bretagne et d'Irlande du Nord)' (2007) 43(1) *Revue trimestrielle de droit européen* 25; JP Jacqué, 'L'affaire Matthews (suite et fin)' (2006) 21 (Mai–Août 2006) *L'Europe des Libertés* 2; J Shaw, 'The Political Representation of Europe's Citizens: Developments' (2008) 4(1) *European Constitutional Law Review* 162; LFM Besselink, 'Case C-145/04 Spain v United Kingdom Case C-300/04' (2008) 45(3) *Common Market Law Review* 787; and I González García, 'Sentencia de 12.09.2006, España / Reino Unido, C-145/04 – PE – Elecciones – Derecho de voto – Ciudadanos de la Commonwealth residentes en Gibraltar y que poseen la ciudadanía de la Unión' (2008) 29 *Revista de Derecho Comunitario Europeo* 215.

also had to take into account the traditional Spanish position regarding Gibraltar, which basically adheres to a strict interpretation of the Treaty of Utrecht and refuses to recognize any changes in the status of the Rock that would one day ground a claim of independence for Gibraltar.[62] Thus, the organization of the European Parliament elections in the area of the colony was contrary to the Spanish position and this led the Spanish Government to reject any amendment to the Act on this point.

47. The United Kingdom was, therefore, in a somewhat paradoxical situation. Either to comply with EC/EU law (as was required), which placed them in a situation of conflict with the ECHR, or to execute the decision of the *Matthews* case (as was also required) and thereby violate EC/EU law. In order to escape this *impasse*, the British authorities negotiated with their Spanish counterparts a statement reflecting a bilateral agreement according to which:

> Recalling Article 6(2) of the Treaty on European Union, which states that the Union shall respect fundamental rights, as guaranteed by the European Convention for the Protection of Human Rights and Fundamental Freedoms, signed in Rome on 4 November 1950 and as they result from the constitutional traditions common to the Member States, as general principles of Community law, the UK will ensure that the necessary changes are made to enable the Gibraltar electorate to vote in elections to the EP as part of and on the same terms as the electorate of an existing UK constituency, in order to ensure the fulfilment of the UK's obligation to implement the judgment of the European Court of Human Rights in the case of *Matthews vs UK*, consistent with the law of the European Union.[63]

48. The Council and the Commission took note of this declaration included in the minutes of the meeting of the Council held on 18 February 2002 which decided the amendment of the Act of 1976 but remained in the same terms as the text of the disputed Annex. The solution was clever because, to meet Spanish demands, Gibraltar would not constitute a constituency, but their voters would participate in elections in a constituency situated in the territory of the United Kingdom.[64] Therefore, the territorial scope of Annex II of the Act of 1976 did not expand (and became Annex I under the new numbering established by Decision 2002/772/EC).

49. In this context, the UK enacted the 2003 law on electoral representation for elections to the European Parliament (European Parliament Representation Act

[62] For more details about the position of Spain vis-à-vis Gibraltar, see the compilation of documents elaborated by the Spanish Ministry of Foreign Affairs available at <http://www.maec.es/es/MenuPpal/Actualidad/PublicacionesDGCE/Publicaciones%20no%20periodicas/Paginas/cuestion-Gibraltar2008.aspx>.

[63] The text of this declaration has been taken from Case C-145/04 *Spain v UK* [2006] (n 61) para 12 where it is stated that it was incorporated to the minutes of the Council Meeting of 18 February 2002.

[64] See JP Jacqué (2006) (n 61) at 2, who writes 'la solution est habile'.

2003 (EPRA 2003)). This law incorporated Gibraltar into one of the existing constituencies in England. The point is that this law not only established a mechanism for British citizens resident in Gibraltar to participate in elections to the European Parliament but also extended the right to vote for the European elections to the so-called 'Qualifying Commonwealth Citizen' (QCC) living in the Rock. The QCC is a specific category of citizens, basically integrated by the citizens of the Member States of the Commonwealth having legal residence and to whom UK law grants certain rights and privileges, to the point of almost equating them to national citizens.[65] All this without considering that, according to the Spanish Government, this 'incorporation' could mean a change in the legal status of the disputed colony.

50. So Spain, which had negotiated the bilateral declaration with the UK, instead challenged its implementation using the barely used procedure of Article 227 TEC (Article 259 TFEU), which allows a Member State to report failure to comply with the Treaties. Usually the Commission, acting as 'guardian of the Treaties', is the body that undertakes the infringement procedure. However, Spain reported the case to the Commission, as required by Article 227 TEC (Article 259 TFEU), but it refused to adopt a reasoned decision, 'given the sensitivity of the underlying bilateral issue'.[66] This position has been severely criticized by the most authorized doctrine.[67] So, finally, Spain sued the UK before the Court of Justice for failure to comply with the obligations derived from the Treaty.

51. The application of the Spanish Government had two main points. On the one hand, it condemned the granting of the right to vote in European Parliament elections conducted by the EPRA 2003 in favour of the QCC which, according to the Kingdom of Spain, would be contrary to EC/EU law (Articles 189 TEC (14 TEU-L), 190 TEC (14 TEU-L and 223 TFEU), 17 TEC (20 TEU-L) and 19 TEC (22 TEU-L)) since these citizens would not have the status of citizens of a Member State of the European Union. The second reason regarding the appeal, the 'underlying bilateral issue', was that British law integrated the territory of Gibraltar into a British constituency, which violated the international agreement adopted at the bilateral declaration because, according to the Spanish Government, British rule should have been limited to incorporating only the

[65] UK law is generous in terms of awarding the right to participate in parliamentary elections to more individuals than just British nationals. See E Giussani, *Constitutional and Administrative Law* (Thomson, London, 2008) 126–9 and 137–8 and L Fransman, *British Nationality Law: Immigration and Nationality Law* 3rd edn (Tottel Publishing, West Sussex, 2009).

[66] Case C-145/04 *Spain v UK* [2006] (n 61) para 32.

[67] See the critics to the European Commission in JP Jacqué (2006) (n 61) at 2: '*Curieuse conception du rôle de la gardienne des traités que de se refuser de se prononcer sur une question en raison des sensibilités politiques sous-jacentes et de passer le mistigri à la Cour de justice*' ('[The Commission] has a curious conception of its own role as the Guardian of the Treaties since it refuses to pronounce itself on the issue arguing the existence of political sensibilities and so decides to pass the buck to the ECJ).'

British voters living in Gibraltar and not in the whole territory.[68] In fact, Spain did nothing but remain faithful to what has been its doctrine regarding Gibraltar, not to recognize any particular status of Gibraltar within the UK that could oppose the Rock vis-à-vis Spain if, one (very unlikely) day, the British Crown renounces its sovereignty over that territory.

52. As regards the first reason (granting voting rights to QCCs), the Court of Justice decided to stick to a favourable interpretation of the right to vote. This was done against the advice of the Advocate General, who had ruled in favour of a restrictive interpretation and, therefore, of the illegality of the contested measure.[69] However, the Court of Justice, given the omissions and the absence of specific prohibitions within the EC/EU legal system, holds the *pro* right to vote interpretation:

> It follows from all of those considerations that, in the current state of Community law, the definition of the persons entitled to vote and to stand as a candidate in elections to the European Parliament falls within the competence of each Member State in compliance with Community law, and that Articles 189 EC, 190 EC, 17 EC and 19 EC do not preclude the Member States from granting that right to vote and to stand as a candidate to certain persons who have close links to them, other than their own nationals or citizens of the Union resident in their territory.
>
> For reasons connected to its constitutional traditions, the United Kingdom chose to grant the right to vote and to stand for election to QCCs who satisfy conditions expressing a specific link with the territory in respect of which the elections are held. In the absence in the Community treaties of provisions stating expressly and precisely which persons have the right to vote and to stand as a candidate in elections to the European Parliament, it does not appear that the United Kingdom's decision to apply to the elections to that Parliament held in Gibraltar the rules governing the franchise and eligibility for election laid down by its national legislation both for national elections in the United Kingdom and for elections to the Gibraltar House of Assembly is contrary to Community law.[70]

The first complaint is relevant to the purpose of determining the scope and limits of 'European citizenship' and the rights attached to it.[71]

53. But the most interesting legal problem arising from the *Matthews* case before the ECtHR is the one set out by the Spanish Government in its second argument within the application. Thus, for the purposes of our analysis, the real problem shall lie in the compatibility of the UK legislation with Annex I of the Act (the former Annex II of 1976).

[68] Case C-145/04 *Spain v UK* [2006] (n 61) para 36.

[69] See Case C-145/04 *Spain v UK* [2006] (n 61), Opinion of AG Tizzano, paras 128–133. AG Tizzano decided to deliver the same Opinion on the very similar Case C-300/04 *MG Eman and OB Sevinger v College van burgemeester en wethouders van Den Haag* [2006] ECR I-8055.

[70] Case C-145/04 *Spain v UK* [2006] (n 61) paras 78–79. The whole justification of the ECJ on this issue is in paras 59–80.

[71] See L Burgorgue-Larsen (2007) (n 61) at 28–39.

54. As clearly stated by Advocate General Tizzano, no one denied that the Annex in question prohibited the United Kingdom from organizing elections for European Parliament in Gibraltar and, to this regard, the situation had not changed, except for the existence of the *Matthews* judgment.[72] Similarly, the Advocate General echoed the consequences for EC/EU law brought about by this case having its origin in a ruling by the ECtHR. Thus, since the obligation to respect fundamental rights comes from primary law (Article 6.2 TEU (6 TEU-L)), the primary law itself (Annex I) shall be applied with respect to that obligation:

> Of course, implementing almost to the letter a clear requirement laid down by case-law, already incorporated in the preamble to the Single European Act, Article F(2) of the Treaty on the European Union (which has become Article 6(2) EU) states that '[t]he Union shall respect fundamental rights, as guaranteed by the European Convention For the Protection of Human Rights and Fundamental Freedoms signed in Rome on 4 November 1950 and as may result from the constitutional traditions common to the Member States, as general principles of Community law.
>
> In the same way, consistent and long-standing Community case-law has made it clear that 'fundamental rights form an integral part of the general principles of law the observance of which the Court ensures' and the Court 'draws inspiration from the constitutional traditions common to the Member States and from the guidelines supplied by international treaties for the protection of human rights on which the Member States have collaborated or to which they are signatories'. In that regard, the ECHR 'has special significance'.[73]

Thus, the Advocate General argued that the fundamental rights as established in Article 6.2 TEU (6 TEU-L) were a part of primary law. It did not establish literally in their conclusions the 'supra-constitutionality' of fundamental rights as recognized and protected by the ECHR, but it opted to emphasize its 'primacy':

> It follows that in the Community legal order 'both the Community and its Member States are required to respect fundamental rights', on a primary basis, (30) and that therefore, in that legal order, 'measures which are incompatible with observance of [those] . . . rights' are not acceptable.[74]

However, this 'primacy' of fundamental rights, read together with the rest of the interpretation of the Advocate General, suggests that it would be equivalent to a kind of 'supra-constitutionality', given that, in the end, in his Opinion, he made them prevail over Annex I.[75]

55. In view of the Advocate General's Opinion, it is understandable that the Court of Justice has carefully avoided issuing a statement on the matter and has, therefore, limited its analysis to the specific issue. Certainly, this approach may cause some shadows, but also sheds some light, though perhaps not yet

[72] Case C-145/04 *Spain v UK* [2006] (n 61), Opinion of AG Tizzano, para 117.
[73] Case C-145/04 *Spain v UK* [2006] (n 61), Opinion of AG Tizzano, paras 119–120.
[74] Case C-145/04 *Spain v UK* [2006] (n 61), Opinion of AG Tizzano, para 121.
[75] See JP Jacqué (2006) (n 61) at 3 and L Burgorgue-Larsen (2007) (n 61) at 42.

definitive, on the implications of a ruling by the ECtHR on a case dealing with the validity of EC/EU law and, in particular with respect to primary law. Indeed, the ECJ found that the UK was obliged to respect the ruling of the ECtHR on the *Matthews* case despite the fact that Annex I has been in force since the 1976 Act and that this obligation was not contested by Spain. It placed its reasoning within the scope of the UK's statement that, according to the Court, reflects an agreement between two states, and examines UK law in relation to this statement.[76] Finally, it isn't difficult to establish that the measures taken by the United Kingdom accounted for necessary adjustments to implement its legislation in Gibraltar and to respect the ruling of the ECtHR.[77]

3.3. The Silence of the ECJ: A Further Step in Strengthening the Convention

56. This evasive attitude of the Court of Justice of the European Communities allows them to go right over two key legal issues. The first one, regarding the relationship between primary law (specified in Annex I of 2002, former Annex II of 1976) and the ECHR. Although the answer appears only implicitly, the final solution adopted by the ECJ can only be explained if the Luxembourg Court supports the primacy of the ECHR (the interpretation of which assures the ECtHR) over primary law. That is, in the particular situation that arose in this case, the UK was confronted by two contradictory requirements: to respect the ruling of the ECtHR on the *Matthews* case as a contracting party of the ECHR and to organize elections to the European Parliament only in its own territory. So, being this the state of things, it seems that the Court of Justice accepts (or maybe imposes?) that on behalf of the obligation to respect the fundamental rights, a state may violate an act of primary law, even if this kind of rule does not admit any exception or derogation in particular and cannot be changed except by unanimous vote of the Council of the European Union. Moreover, it appears that this ruling of the ECJ confirms the 'special significance' not only of the ECHR, but also of the ECtHR, that emerges as a sort of 'superior reference parameter'.[78] In any case, what is already clear in this ruling of the ECJ is that its refusal to condemn the UK is closely linked to the existence of a ruling by the ECtHR.[79]

57. The second question refers to Community law as legal system. Specifically, the question that arises is whether two Member States can, by means of an

[76] Case C-145/04 *Spain v UK* [2006] (n 61) paras 90–93.

[77] Case C-145/04 *Spain v UK* [2006] (n 61) paras 94–97.

[78] L Burgorgue-Larsen (2007) (n 61) at 42. The special significance of the ECHR is totally acknowledged by the ECJ case law. See, for instance, Case C-36/02 *Omega Spielhallen- und Automatenaufstellungs- GmbH v Oberbürgermeisterin der Bundesstadt Bonn* [2004] ECR I-9609 para 33.

[79] Case C-145/04 *Spain v UK* [2006] (n 61) paras 60, 86, 90 and 95.

international agreement, which takes the form of a statement by one accepted by the other, jeopardize the effectiveness of EC/EU law. The answer should be clearly negative, since otherwise the uniform application of EC/EU law, the cornerstone of the whole EC/EU legal system, would be clearly compromised. But the Court conveniently avoids highlighting the incompatibility of the declaration with Annex I. The objective of avoiding any conflict with the ruling in the *Matthews* case pushes it to focus solely on providing a solution to a particular case without stating clearly the underlying legal arguments. It is to be expected that this case has been a very specific solution and that, in the future, the Court of Justice will not allow states to challenge or even question their compliance with the constitutional rules of the EC/EU legal system, not even in such a subtle way as this one.[80]

4. THE CONVENTIONALITY CONTROL OF SECONDARY LAW

4.1. The Approach to the Issue

58. With regard to secondary law, we have seen how the ECtHR faced the issue in the case of directives. Indeed, in the *Cantoni* case it had to deal with some French law which faithfully reproduced the text of an EC directive. This did not prevent the Strasbourg Court from ruling, but it did so based on its analysis of the transposition of French law. That is, the ECtHR could always rely on the leeway theoretically available to the states in order to implement directives. The only thing that was clear in the *Cantoni* case is that the fact that a national law is merely an instrument for transposing an EC directive is not a sufficient argument to prevent the Strasbourg Court from assessing its compatibility with the European Convention. This is what was formerly called the absence of a 'Community exception'.

59. The ultimate test on recognition of the European Court of Human Rights from its own jurisdiction to control Community law would not come until it faced the case regarding a rule pertaining to the so-called secondary law and the issue of direct effect appeared. Indeed, the former European Commission of Human Rights, in the *M & Co* case, had to deal with a case regarding the compatibility of a ruling of the ECJ with the ECHR. However, despite the important considerations that the Commission did that later inspired the doctrine of the ECtHR, by rejecting the admission of the case, the ultimate interpreter of the Convention was unable to make any findings at that time.

60. The opportunity arose again with a very interesting case which included, in addition, a joint lawsuit against the then 15 Member States of the European

[80] See the strong criticism in JP Jacqué (2006) (n 61) at 3–4.

Community: the *Senator Lines* case. But due to the parallel litigation engaged by the lawyers of the German company, finally, the *Senator Lines* company satisfied their claims before the ECJ and the Strasbourg Court had no occasion to rule. Despite the relief that this had for some within the EC/EU institutions, the ECtHR had to face another case in which it did have to establish its position regarding the relationship between the ECHR and the secondary law. The case, which undoubtedly was a milestone regarding the relationship between the ECtHR and the ECJ, was the *Bosphorus v Ireland* case.[81]

4.2. The Expected Response from Strasbourg: The *Bosphorus* Case

4.2.1. *Facts and Pre-litigation*

61. The *Bosphorus* case, a long and complex one, included actions brought before national courts in Ireland and the ECJ before reaching the ECtHR. For a correct understanding of the scope of the ECtHR ruling it is necessary to explain the background of the case.[82] Bosphorus Airways was a Turkish company whose main activity was air transport and travel arrangements. On 17 April 1992 it signed a lease contract with the then Yugoslav national airline

[81] Case *Bosphorus Hava Yolları Turizm ve Ticaret Anonim irketi v Ireland* App No 45036/98 (ECtHR, 30 June 2005, 2005-VI). The literature on this leading case is huge. See JP Jacqué, 'Droit Communautaire et Convention européenne des droits de l'homme, L'arrêt Bosphorus, une jurisprudence "Solange II" de la Cour européenne des droits de l'homme?' (2005) 41(3) *Revue Trimestrielle de Droit Européen* 756; K Kuhnert, 'Bosphorus Double standards in European human rights protection?' (2006) 2(2) *Utrecht Law Review* 177; F Hoffmeister, 'Bosphorus Hava Yollari Turizm ve Ticaret Anonim Sirket v Ireland. App. No. 45036/98' (2006) 100(2) American *Journal of International Law* 442; A Hinarejos Parga, 'Bosphorus v Ireland and the protection of fundamental rights in Europe' (2006) 31(2) *European Law Review* 251; J Andriantsimbazovina, 'La Cour de Strasbourg, gardienne des droits de l'homme dans l'Union européenne. Remarques autour de l'arrêt de Grande Chambre de la Cour européenne des droits de l'homme du 30/06/2005, Bosphorus Hava Yollari ve Ticaret Anonim Sirketi c/ Irlande)' (2006) 2006(3) *Revue Française de Droit Administratif* 566; S Douglas-Scott, 'Bosphorus Hava Yollari Turizm Ve Ticaret Anonim irketi v Ireland' (2006) 41(3) *Common Market Law Review* 243; F Benoît-Rohmer, 'A propos de l'arrêt Bosphorus Air Lines du 30 juin 2005 : l'adhésion contrainte de l'Union à la Convention' (2005) 64 *Revue Trimestrielle des Droits de l'Homme* 827; V Constantinesco, 'C'est comme ci c'était fait ? (Observations à propos de l'arrêt de la Cour européenne des droits de l'homme (grande chambre), Bosphorus airlines, du 30 juin 2005' (2006) 42(3–4) *Cahiers de droit Européen* 363; C Costello, 'The Bosphorus Ruling of the European Court of Human Rights: Fundamental Rights and Blurred Boundaries in Europe' (2006) 6(1) *Human Rights Law Review* 87; C Eckes, 'Does the European Court of Human Rights Provide Protection from the European Community? The Case of Bosphorus Airways' (2007) 13(1) *European Public Law* 47; F Schorkopf, 'The European Court of Human Rights' Judgment in the Case of Bosphorus Hava Yollari Turizm v Ireland' (2005) 6(9) *German Law Journal* 1255; F Kauff-Gazin, 'L'arrêt Bosphorus de la Cour européenne des droits de l'homme : quand le juge de Strasbourg pallie le retard du constituant de l'Union européenne en matière de protection des droits fondamentaux . . .' (2005) 234 *Les Petites Affiches* 9; and G Cano Palomares, 'Un nuevo capítulo en el control del Derecho comunitario por parte del Tribunal de Estrasburgo. (A propósito de la STEDH de 30 de junio de 2005, caso Bosphorus Airways)' (2006) 74 *Revista Vasca de Administración Pública* 317.

[82] The facts are widely explained in the Court decision, see Case *Bosphorus* [2005] (n 81) paras 11–60.

(JAT) by which it leased two commercial aircraft (Boeing model 737-3H9) for a period of four years. On 28 May 1993, when one of those aircraft, having undergone maintenance at the airport in Dublin, was preparing to take off, the Irish authorities ordered its arrest according to Article 8 of Regulation 990/93/ECC,[83] which implemented at the EC/EU level sanctions imposed by the Security Council of the United Nations to the Republics of Serbia and Montenegro on the basis of Chapter VII of the Charter of the United Nations.[84] Article 8 of Regulation 990/93/EEC provided that '[a]ll vessels, freight vehicles, rolling stock and aircraft in which a majority or controlling interest is held by a person or undertaking in or operating from the Federal Republic of Yugoslavia (Serbia and Montenegro) shall be impounded by the competent authorities of the Member States'.

62. Bosphorus said that according to Article 8 of Regulation 990/93/EEC applicable to the circumstances of the case, the seizure of the plane was against its fundamental right to property. It should be noted that, from the beginning, the agreement between Bosphorus and JAT was held in good faith and never intended to circumvent the UN sanctions. The contract was a so-called dry lease, that is, it only had regard to the leasing of the aircraft, so that any cabin crew and pilots would be employed by Bosphorus Airways, which thus had complete daily management of the aircraft during that period. JAT, meanwhile, would remain the owner of the aircraft. Furthermore, in accordance with the sanctions of the Security Council, the income earned by JAT through the leasing was deposited in blocked accounts and neither of the two leased aircraft (that is, the entire fleet that made up the company) were used for flights from or to the former Yugoslavia.

63. Bosphorus appealed the decision of the Irish Minister for Transport to seize the aircraft before the Irish courts, specifically before the High Court of Dublin. In its ruling of 21 June 1994 the High Court quashed the Minister's decision, arguing that the aircraft in question did not meet any of the categories listed in Article 8 of the Regulation.[85] The Minister, in turn, filed an appeal against this decision before the Irish Supreme Court on 8 August 1994. The Irish High Court submitted, in turn, a preliminary ruling before the ECJ in order to

[83] Council Regulation No 990/93/EEC concerning trade between the European Economic Community and the Federal Republic of Yugoslavia (Serbia and Montenegro) (OJ L 102/14, 28 April 1993). This Regulation was repealed by Council Regulation No 2382/96/EC of 9 December 1996 repealing Regulations No 990/93/EEC and No 2471/94/EC concerning the termination of restrictions on economic and financial relations with the Federal Republic of Yugoslavia (Serbia and Montenegro), the United Nations Protected Areas in the Republic of Croatia and those areas of the Republic of Bosnia and Herzegovina under the control of Bosnian Serb forces (OJ L 328/1, 18 December 1996).

[84] See UN Security Council Resolution 820 (Bosnia and Herzegovina) U.N. Doc S/RES/820 (1993) 17 April 1993.

[85] Case *Bosphorus v Minister for Transport* (Dublin High Court, 21 June 1994) 2 *Irish Law Reports Monthly* 1994 at 55.

clarify the scope of Article 8 of Regulation 990/93/EEC. Specifically, the question to the Luxembourg Court was:

> Is Article 8 of Regulation No 990/93/EEC to be construed as applying to an aircraft which is owned by an undertaking the majority or controlling interest in which is held by an undertaking in the Federal Republic of Yugoslavia (Serbia and Montenegro) where such aircraft has been leased by the owner for a term of four years from 22 April 1992 to an undertaking the majority or controlling interest in which is not held by a person or undertaking in or operating from the said Federal Republic of Yugoslavia (Serbia and Montenegro)?[86]

64. Both AG Jacobs and the ECJ responded affirmatively to this question. Unlike the Irish High Court, both established that neither the aims nor the text regarding the resolution of the Security Council of the United Nations provided any reason to depart from the literal meaning of Article 8 of the EC Regulation. Furthermore, the Bosphorus claim supported by its intended fundamental right to property was rejected by the Advocate General and the Court of Justice. The ECJ, which recognized the fact that respect for fundamental rights is a precondition for the legality of EC/EU acts, however, added:

> It is settled case-law that the fundamental rights invoked by Bosphorus Airways are not absolute and their exercise may be subject to restrictions justified by objectives of general interest pursued by the Community.[87]

Following the above reasoning, the ECJ had no difficulty concluding finally that:

> As compared with an objective of general interest so fundamental for the international community, which consists in putting an end to the state of war in the region and to the massive violations of human rights and humanitarian international law in the Republic of Bosnia-Herzegovina, the impounding of the aircraft in question, which is owned by an undertaking based in or operating from the Federal Republic of Yugoslavia, cannot be regarded as inappropriate or disproportionate.[88]

65. In May 1998 the Irish Supreme Court upheld the appeal by the Minister stating that it was bound by the response of the ECJ. The leasing contract of the aircraft seized expired in May 1996 and on 30 July 1997 was returned to JAT, following the withdrawal of the United Nations sanctions.

66. On 25 March 1997, Bosphorus filed an appeal against Ireland in Strasbourg under the ECHR, alleging that the seizure of the aircraft violated its property rights guaranteed by Article 1 of the Additional Protocol. On 13 September 2001 the appeal was granted and on 30 January 2004 the competent court

[86] Case C-84/95 *Bosphorus Hava Yollari Turizm ve Ticaret AS v Minister for Transport, Energy and Communications and others* [1996] ECR I-03953 para 6.
[87] Case C-84/95 *Bosphorus* [1996] (n 86) para 21.
[88] Case C-84/95 *Bosphorus* [1996] (n 86) para 26.

declined its jurisdiction in favour of the Grand Chamber which, after hearing the case on 29 September 2004, finally issued its decision on 20 June 2005. This long process before the Strasbourg Court itself shows that this case was considered important and had a significant impact.

67. The competence of the ECtHR to decide on this case was contested by the Irish Government and by third parties, including the European Commission and governments of the UK and Italy. Although the case involved the application of an EC Regulation and neither the EC nor the EU are members of the Convention, the appellant company alleged that the manner in which Ireland implemented the sanctions regime fell within the definition of 'law' according to Article 1 of the First Protocol and therefore comprised a violation of that provision by Ireland.

4.2.2. The Reasoning of the ECtHR

68. The ECtHR issued a relatively short judgment in which it accepted that the appeal was within the scope of the ECHR. However, it rejected the plaintiff's claims. The Strasbourg Court found that the contested action, the impounding of the aircraft, was implemented by the Irish state in its territory, which was eventually manifest in a decision to seize the aircraft issued by the Minister of Transport. Under these circumstances, the Strasbourg court established that Bosphorus, as addressee of the legal act, was subject to the jurisdiction of Ireland and consequently the application was compatible *ratione loci, personae* and *materiae* with the provisions of the Convention that, according to Article 1, makes contracting states responsible for violations of the rights granted to everyone within their jurisdiction.[89]

69. The ECtHR did not specify anything further about its jurisdiction according to Article 1 of the Convention, and focused on the rest of the Government's objections concerning the scope of responsibility by analysing the application in relation to Article 1 of the Additional Protocol.

4.2.2.1. The Right to Ownership of Bosphorus on the Basis of Ireland's Obligations Arising from EC/EU Law

70. Article 1 of the First Protocol to the European Convention for the Protection of Human Rights and Fundamental Freedoms concerning the protection of the property reads as follows:

> Every natural or legal person is entitled to the peaceful enjoyment of his possessions. No one shall be deprived of his possessions except in the public interest and subject to the conditions provided for by law and by the general principles of international law.

[89] Case *Bosphorus* [2005] (n 81) paras 135–138.

The preceding provisions shall not, however, in any way impair the right of a State to enforce such laws as it deems necessary to control the use of property in accordance with the general interest or to secure the payment of taxes or other contributions or penalties.

71. The ECtHR, after analysing the arguments of the complaint under Article 1 of the First Protocol, decided that the regime of sanctions implied more a 'control of use' than a 'deprivation' of property under Article 1 of the First Protocol.[90]

72. Then, the ECtHR came to consider whether the seizure of the aircraft was justified or not. The Court indicated that under Article 1 of the First Protocol it is necessary to find a balance between the needs arising from the general interest and those from the private person concerned. However, the state has a wide discretion as to the means that may be employed.[91]

73. The Irish Government's actions had to be examined in the light of the obligations enforced by EC/EU law. The ECtHR noted that the interference in the property right contested was not the result of an exercise of discretion by the Irish authorities adopted under Irish law itself or EC/EU law. Instead, it was an Irish state action by which it did nothing but fulfil its obligations under EC/EU law and, particularly, of Article 8 of Regulation 990/93/EEC. The Regulation is binding in its entirety and directly applicable in all Member States, without being able to except its provisions or to escape the obligations imposed by the Regulation.[92] Thus, in accordance with the reasoning of the ECtHR, the general interest pursued by the challenged action was in compliance by Ireland with its obligations derived from EC/EU law. This, the Court concluded, constituted a legitimate interest of considerable importance, given the international law principle of *pacta sunt servanda*, and the growing importance of international cooperation.[93] The question then was whether, and to what extent, the general interest in fulfilling the obligations derived from EC/EU law could justify the interference of Ireland in the right to enjoyment of property of the company concerned.

[90] Case *Bosphorus* [2005] (n 81) paras 141–143.

[91] Case *Bosphorus* [2005] (n 81) para 149. On the margin of appreciation doctrine, see Y Arai-Takahashi, *The Margin of Appreciation Doctrine and the Principle of Proportionality in the Jurisprudence of the ECHR* (Intersentia, Antwerp, 2002) and I De la Rasilla del Moral, 'The Increasingly Marginal Appreciation of the Margin of Appreciation Doctrine' (2006) 7(6) *German Law Journal* 611.

[92] See Art 249 TEC (Art 288 TFEU). On the direct applicability of the Regulation, see Case 34/73 *Fratelli Variola Spa v Amministrazione delle finanze dello Stato* [1973] ECR 981 paras 10–11. On the legal nature and effects of the EU Regulations see K Lenaerts, P Van Nuffel and R Bray, *Constitutional Law of the European Union* 2nd edn (Thompson, London, 2005) at 763–6.

[93] Case *Bosphorus* [2005] (n 81) paras 140–150.

4.2.2.2. The 'Equivalent Protection' Doctrine

74. The ECtHR in its consideration reiterated the doctrine that had previously established the Commission on Human Rights according to which the Convention does not prohibit the contracting parties to transfer sovereign powers to international or supranational organizations.[94] On the other hand, it established that each contracting party is responsible under Article 1 ECHR for all acts and omissions of its organs, regardless of whether such acts are the result of the law of the state in question or if they are required to comply with international legal obligations.[95]

75. In order to reconcile these two positions, the ECtHR recognized that to completely absolve the contracting parties of their responsibilities and obligations on matters which were the subject of a transfer of powers to international organizations would be inconsistent with the object and purpose of the ECHR. In any case, the Strasbourg Court added that:

> In the Court's view, State action taken in compliance with such legal obligations is justified as long as the relevant organisation is considered to protect fundamental rights, as regards both the substantive guarantees offered and the mechanisms controlling their observance, in a manner which can be considered at least equivalent to that for which the Convention provides.[96]

The European Commission of Human Rights already used this formula, which also distinguished the procedural ('mechanisms') and substantive aspects of fundamental rights, in the *M & Co* case.

The Strasbourg Court continued, specifying the meaning of 'equivalent':

> By 'equivalent' the Court means 'comparable'; any requirement that the organisation's protection be 'identical' could run counter to the interest of international cooperation pursued . . . However, any such finding of equivalence could not be final and would be susceptible to review in the light of any relevant change in fundamental rights protection.[97]

76. The ECtHR also made clear that this consideration of 'equivalent protection' should not have to be definitive and could be subject to revision in light of any fundamental change in the system of protection of fundamental rights.[98]

77. Moreover, the Court held that if it was considered that, indeed, the organization in question granted the above-mentioned equivalent protection, it would be assumed that a state would never fail in its obligations to the Convention if it was merely fulfilling (that is, implementing) the obligations arising from its

[94] Case *Bosphorus* [2005] (n 81) para 152.
[95] Case *Bosphorus* [2005] (n 81) para 153.
[96] Case *Bosphorus* [2005] (n 81) para 155.
[97] Case *Bosphorus* [2005] (n 81) para 155.
[98] Case *Bosphorus* [2005] (n 81) para 155.

membership of this organization. However, the ECtHR argued that this presumption may be rebutted if 'in the circumstances of a particular case, it is considered that the protection of Convention rights was manifestly deficient'. In such a case, the interest of international cooperation 'would be outweighed by the Convention's role as a "constitutional instrument of European public order" in the field of human rights'.[99] Instead, the states will be fully and strictly responsible under the Convention by all their actions that are not strictly derived from their international legal obligations.[100]

78. The Court, then, examined whether in this particular case there was a presumption of conformity with the Convention. Since Ireland adopting the contested act did nothing but comply with legal obligations derived from its membership of the EC/EU, the Court then focused on analysing whether the protection of fundamental rights in Community law was adequate, from the point of view of the substantial guarantees offered as well as from the mechanisms for monitoring their compliance.[101]

79. Thus, in terms of 'substantive guarantees', the ECtHR began its argument by bringing up the declaration of AG Jacobs in the *Bosphorus* case before the Luxembourg Court, according to which the respect for fundamental rights had become a condition of the legality of EC/EU acts.[102] Likewise, by establishing such control of respect for fundamental rights by EC/EU acts, the ECJ has referred extensively to the ECHR as well as to the jurisprudence of the ECtHR itself. The Strasbourg Court also emphasized the incorporation of the ECJ case law into the text of the EC/EU Treaties and in the adoption of the European Charter of Fundamental Rights.

80. As to the second element, the Strasbourg Court also found that the mechanisms offered by EC/EU law to ensure respect for fundamental rights was adequate despite exposing explicitly the limitations of the *locus standi* of individuals under Article 230 ECJ (Article 263 TFEU). Nonetheless, it stressed the importance of national courts when providing individuals with procedural remedies and the existence of the preliminary ruling required by Article 234 TEC (Article 267 TFEU).[103]

[99] Case *Bosphorus* [2005] (n 81) para 156. This expression was already used by the ECtHR in Case *Loizidou* [1995] (preliminary objection) para 75. The 'European public order' concept was already sanctioned by the Commission in Case *Austria v Italy* [1961] (n 9). See J Andriantsimbazovina *et al*, *Les grands arrêts de la Cour européenne des droits de l'homme* 4th edn (PUF, Paris, 2007) 7–17.

[100] Case *Bosphorus* [2005] (n 81) para 157.

[101] Case *Bosphorus* [2005] (n 81) para 158.

[102] Case *Bosphorus* [2005] (n 81) para 159. This statement of the AG Jacobs may be found in his Opinion before the ECJ. See Case C-84/95 *Bosphorus* [1996] (n 86), Opinion of AG Jacobs, paras 45–50.

[103] Case *Bosphorus* [2005] (n 81) paras 160–164.

81. The Strasbourg Court concluded that under these circumstances, we may consider that the protection of fundamental rights is, and so was at the time of the events at issue, 'equivalent' to the one guaranteed by the Convention system, so it can be assumed that Ireland did not depart from its obligations under the Convention. Given the nature of the interference, the general interest represented by the sanctions regime and the ruling of the ECJ (in light of the Advocate General's Opinion) the ECtHR ruled that there was no dysfunction of the mechanism for monitoring compliance of the rights guaranteed by the Convention and so, therefore, it could not be argued that the protection of the conventional rights of the appellant was 'manifestly deficient'. Thus, the presumption of respect for the Convention by the respondent state was not destroyed and the rights guaranteed by the ECHR to *Bosphorus* were not violated. That was the end of the case that kept the Turkish company busy with court proceedings for more than 10 years.[104]

4.2.3. *The Scope of the ECtHR Judgment*

4.2.3.1. The Nature of the Relationship between the EU and the ECtHR

82. The *Bosphorus* case was the latest in a series of appeals to the ECtHR that challenged the compatibility of EC/EU law with the ECHR.[105] The importance of this issue is illustrated by the fact that *Bosphorus* has been one of the few cases that have reached the Grand Chamber of the ECtHR. Since neither the Union nor the Community are parties to the ECHR, they cannot be sued before the Court. However, in the interests of good administration of justice Article 36.2 of the ECHR enables the President of the Court of Human Rights to invite a third party to submit comments or even to take part in the hearing. However, in the present case, although the EC/EU Commission was allowed to act as a third party, it is not its role to lead the defence, a role that is assigned to the contracting state, in this case Ireland.

83. It should be recalled that the case law of the control bodies of the Convention rests on two fundamental principles.

The first is that neither the EC nor the EU may be sued before the ECtHR. Neither of the two organizations are parties to the Convention and, therefore, in principle, their activities cannot be directly controlled by the Court. On the other hand, some authors have suggested the possibility that the ECtHR should follow the case law of the WTO and, therefore, it could be considered that, in the EC/EU system, as Member States are responsible for the implementation of

[104] Case *Bosphorus* [2005] (n 81) paras 165–167.

[105] See Case *Senator Lines v the 15 Member States of the EU* App No 56672/00 (ECtHR, 10 March 2004, unpublished), Case *Guérin Automobiles v the 15 Member States of the EU* App No 51717/99 (ECtHR, 4 July 2000, unpublished) and Case *Emesa Sugar v The Netherlands* App No 62023/00 (ECtHR, 13 January 2005, unpublished). All these cases (declared inadmissible by the ECtHR) will be analysed below.

EC/EU law, they actually act as organs of the EC/EU, and therefore it would be responsible under the rules of the WTO and general international law.[106] But such a solution would have led either to a recognition that the EC/EU had succeeded the Member States (thesis of functional succession, see above), which would be difficult, taking into account that the Convention was reserved to the states (until Protocol No 14), or to grant immunity (by succeeding the states without being a member of the ECHR, it is not bound by it), which would be contrary to the second principle.

In fact, according to the second thesis, which is based on Strasbourg case law, the Member States are parties to the Convention and cannot transfer powers to the Community or the Union in order to escape the obligations arising, for them, from the Convention. Indeed, according to Article 1 of the Convention, the High Contracting Parties shall secure to everyone within their jurisdiction the rights and freedoms defined in Section I of the present Convention. Therefore, the existence of the Community (or Union) cannot, under any circumstances, relieve the High Contracting Parties from this obligation.[107] Indeed, in this regard, the provisions of the ECtHR in the *Bosphorus* case are quite interesting:

> In reconciling both these positions and thereby establishing the extent to which a State's action can be justified by its compliance with obligations flowing from its membership of an international organisation to which it has transferred part of its sovereignty, the Court has recognised that absolving Contracting States completely from their Convention responsibility in the areas covered by such a transfer would be incompatible with the purpose and object of the Convention; the guarantees of the Convention could be limited or excluded at will, thereby depriving it of its peremptory character and undermining the practical and effective nature of its safeguards . . . The State is considered to retain Convention liability in respect of treaty commitments subsequent to the entry into force of the Convention.[108]

84. The ECtHR affirmed in this case, once again, its willingness to leave no gap in the application of the Convention. In this sense, the *Bosphorus* case falls in line with the *Ilaşcu* case law:

> It follows from Article 1 that member States must answer for any infringement of the rights and freedoms protected by the Convention committed against individuals placed under their 'jurisdiction'.
>
> The exercise of jurisdiction is a necessary condition for a Contracting State to be able to be held responsible for acts or omissions imputable to it which give rise to an allegation of the infringement of rights and freedoms set forth in the Convention.[109]

[106] See *Report of the Panel. Protection of Trademarks and Geographical Indications for Agricultural Products and Foodstuffs* (WTO, Doc. WT/DS174/R, 15 March 2005) para 7.725.

[107] JP Jacqué, 'Droit constitutionnel national, Droit communautaire, CEDH, Charte des Nations Unies. L'instabilité des rapports de système entre ordres juridiques' (2007) 60 *Revue Française de Droit Constitutionnel* 3 at 23–4.

[108] Case *Bosphorus* [2005] (n 81) para 154.

[109] Case *Ilaşcu and others v Moldova and Russia* App No 48787/99 (ECtHR, 8 July 2004, 2004-VII) para 311.

85. That is, if there exist an act or omission carried out by a contracting party in its territory in violation of the fundamental rights of an individual, the appellant shall have the right to an action and the European Court of Human Rights shall have jurisdiction under Article 1 ECHR, even if the relevant Member State was fulfilling its international obligations. However, in this situation, various possibilities may arise depending on the nature of the EC act. If a Member State has discretion on how to implement its obligations under EC/EU law, the ECtHR will address the issue by examining the act as if it were an ordinary act of the contracting state (*Cantoni* case).[110] Another situation, which will be discussed below, would refer to cases of an act of a EC/EU institution that does not require any domestic implementing measure (see the *Senator Lines* case, below). The last situation that may occur would be one in which a Member State has no discretion, as in the *Bosphorus* case, and just enforces the necessary actions to comply with its obligations derived from EC/EU law. In this case, the ECtHR shall consider whether there is an 'equivalent protection' situation within EC/EU law. As long as the so-called equivalent protection shall exist (sentence taken from the *Solange* decisions of the German Constitutional Court) it shall be considered that the Member State's action is consistent with its obligations under the Convention. In cases where there is no 'equivalent protection', as in the *Matthews* case, the ECtHR shall review the act and check whether it is compatible with the Convention so as to avoid any gap in the protection of fundamental rights guaranteed by the ECHR.[111]

86. In addition, this position entails a clear threat to the primacy of EC/EU law. That is, if the Member States know that their responsibility may be brought up before Strasbourg regarding EC/EU rules the application of which have no leeway or discretion, the primacy of EC/EU law could be jeopardized. In effect, these states could be addressees, at one point, of two contradictory requirements, one under EC/EU law and the other derived from respect for the Convention. Therefore, in order to avoid this potential risk, the states could be tempted to subordinate the application of EC/EU law to the verification of their compatibility with the Convention on the national level. However, the recognition of the primacy under the reservation resulting from this practice is not at all in accordance with the case law of the ECtHR, as established in the *Internationale Handelgesellschaft* case:

> The validity of a Community measure or its effect within a member state cannot be affected by allegations that it runs counter to either fundamental rights as formulated by the Constitution of that State or the principles of a national constitutional structure.[112]

[110] Case *Catoni v France* cit (ECtHR, 15 November 1996, 1996-V 1614), dealing with the implementation of an EC Directive in France.

[111] S Douglas-Scott (2006) (n 81) at 249.

[112] Case 11/70 *Internationale Handelsgesellschaft mbH v Einfuhr- und Vorratsstelle für Getreide und Futtermittel* [1970] ECR-1125 para 3.

87. The ECJ ruling excludes any reserves for alleged unconstitutionality. In effect, the Member State always has the possibility of asking the ECJ to verify the conformity of a EC/EU act with fundamental rights. But this test is carried out in relation to fundamental rights recognized in the context of the then Community (now 'Union'). But there is no guarantee that the Luxembourg Court will adopt the same position as the Strasbourg Court. In this sense, the solution adopted by the ECtHR regarding *Bosphorus* places the Member States in a situation similar to that in which the German authorities found themselves after the German Constitutional Court's decision in *Solange I* authorizing the German judge to verify the compliance of Community law with the rights guaranteed by the national Constitution while there was no Community protection of fundamental rights.[113] If the *Solange I* decision provoked a delicate situation, to the extent that the German Constitutional Court was forced to change its case law a few years later in what is known as *Solange II*, the solution in *Bosphorus* could also introduce an element of uncertainty for Member States in respect of obligations arising for them from EC/EU-legislation and the Convention. Even if we think that cases of conflict would be quite marginal, we must take into account the difficulty of assessing the possibility of future conflict and we must not underestimate the expertise of some lawyers to lodge overlapping appeals before the various courts.[114]

88. The *Bosphorus* judgment of the ECtHR shows greater deference towards EC/EU law and its system of protection than *Matthews* which seems, even, to hide the desire to maintain a relationship of mutual respect or even cooperation between the courts. Moreover, this relatively recent case law of the ECtHR might be willing to indicate that *Matthews* should be interpreted narrowly and confined to those cases in which there is no possibility of appeal before the ECJ (remember that the 1976 Act could not be appealed to the Court of Luxembourg).[115] Therefore, except in those exceptional cases, the ECtHR would avoid at all costs 'piercing the veil' of the EC/EU and hold their Member States for a possible violation of the obligations derived from the Convention. In this sense, *Bosphorus* would be a very prudent and cautious decision.[116]

4.2.3.2. The Problems of the 'Equivalent Protection' Doctrine

89. Another point to be made regarding the *Bosphorus* case is that the judgment seems at some points barely justified. This 'scarcity' would be illustrated by the concept of 'manifestly deficient' that the Strasbourg Court develops in its

[113] See Case *Solange I* 2 BvL 52/71 BVerfGE 37 271 (German Constitutional Court, 29 May 1974).
[114] JP Jacqué (2005) (n 81) at 761.
[115] This interpretation of *Matthews* is advocated by K Lenaerts, P Van Nuffel and R Bray (2005) (n 92) 575–600. Others think that *Matthews* is an example of a hierarchical relationship between the ECtHR and the ECJ. See I Canor. '*Primus inter pares*. Who is the ultimate guardian of fundamental rights in Europe?' (2000) 25(1) *European Law Review* 3 at 2–21.
[116] S Douglas-Scott (2005) (n 92) at 250.

decision. That is, the protection of fundamental rights shall be considered 'equivalent' to that given by the Convention and, therefore, immune to the control exercised by the ECtHR unless the guarantee of these rights within the Community can be described as 'manifestly deficient', in which case the Strasbourg Court shall intervene using the European Convention as an instrument of guarantee of the 'European public order'. The challenge is therefore to specify what is meant by 'manifestly deficient' and how this concept shall be interpreted. The Strasbourg Court, despite its thoroughness in other aspects of its legal reasoning, decided on two pages of its judgment this question, using very general arguments, and emphasizing positive developments in ECJ case law regarding fundamental rights rather than in the circumstances in which the *Bosphorus* case took place.

90. Moreover, the considerations on the general situation of human rights within the EU identified by this judgment do not seem very accurate. That is, given the intention of the Court to approve the EC/EU system for the protection of rights in the ECHR, the judgment passes over the question of application or *locus standi* of individuals before the Court of Justice according to Article 230 TEC (Article 263 TFEU). In fact, in one of the separate opinions of the sentence, allegedly concurrent, this level of protection is indirectly censured, more in agreement with the position taken by AG Jacobs in the *Unión de Pequeños Agricultores* (UPA) case before the ECJ.[117] Indeed, the author of the vote, Judge Ress, stressed that no one should infer from paragraph 162 of the *Bosphorus* decision (which refers to the *locus standi* of individuals before the ECJ) that the Court accepts that Article 6.1 ECHR does not appeal to a higher level of protection.[118]

91. The approval of the EC/EU system by the Strasbourg Court, that is, the word 'equivalent' given by the ECtHR, concluded after an analysis of the protection of fundamental rights in the EC/EU and not having reviewed the particular circumstances of the *Bosphorus* case. The Strasbourg Court seemed satisfied to determine that there were no malfunctions either in the EC/EU control mechanisms or in the substantive guarantees. However, the implementation of the EC Regulation in this case was perhaps too strict and had very negative consequences for the company. Bosphorus suffered great difficulties, which prevented it from continuing its operations, and also lost three years out of the four for which it had leased one of the aircraft to JAT. Moreover, as stated at the hearing, it was the only plane that was seized under this regulation, and ironically, it could not

[117] Case C-50/00 P *Unión de Pequeños Agricultores v Council* [2002] ECR I-6677, Opinion of AG Jacobs, where he advocated a more protecting interpretation of Art 230 TEC (Art 263 TFEU). See JA Usher, 'Direct and individual concern – an effective remedy or a conventional solution?' (2003) 28(5) *European Law Review* 575; and P Gilliaux, 'L'arrêt Unión de Pequeños Agricultores: entre subsidiairité juridicitonnelle et effectivité' (2003) 39(1–2) *Cahiers de Droit Européen* 177.

[118] See Case *Bosphorus* [2005] (n 81), concurrent Opinion of Judge Ress, para 2.

use the aircraft even when the sanctions against the former Yugoslavia were removed and JAT resumed business operations. Nor was there any benefit to the Turkish company from the fact that successive courts recognized that the lease between Bosphorus and the Balkan airline was made in good faith. None of these aspects were taken into consideration in the decision of ECtHR.[119]

92. Finally, as highlighted by a group of judges in a particular joint and concurrent Opinion, the concept 'manifestly deficient' would require a rather low standard of protection of the fundamental rights, 'which is in marked contrast to the supervision generally carried out under the European Convention on Human Rights'.[120] Moreover, in their particular and concurrent aforementioned Opinion, Judge Ress warned that the concept of 'conformity' with the Convention by the international organizations should not be seen as a step towards creating a double standard of protection: the one required to Member States (more rigorous) and the one required to international organizations (less demanding). In the already mentioned concurrent Opinion, it was also rejected that the presumption of conformity was absolute and, therefore, the possibility of a review on a case-by-case basis was dismissed. In fact, in each case, the Court should be appointed to examine the level of protection afforded by EC/EU law before ruling on the application. And in the case of finding it 'manifestly deficient' the Court must remove the immunity granted to EC/EU law. Indeed, such immunity is not absolute and the Opinion of the Strasbourg Court in this case contains an implicit statement that it shall closely monitor the developments in EC/EU case law regarding fundamental rights.[121]

93. One issue that the ECtHR avoids completely is the role of the United Nations in this whole affair. Indeed, by approving the controversial regulation in the *Bosphorus* case, the EC/EU would have done nothing but implement a sanction of the UNSC at the EC/EU level. So, just as Ireland had no leeway in the implementation of the Regulation, the EC/EU could declare, if appropriate, that it has no leeway to put the sanctions of the Security Council into practice either. The *Bosphorus* judgment did not go so far as to establish an ECHR review of the acts issued by the bodies of the United Nations, but the issue was, undoubtedly, discussed during the Court's discussions.[122]

[119] See the critics in S Douglas-Scott (2006) (n 81) at 251.

[120] Case *Bosphorus* [2005] (n 81), Joint concurrent Opinion of Judges Rozakis, Tulkens, Traja, Botoucharova, Zagrebelsky and Garlicki, para 4.

[121] See JP Jacqué (2007) (n 107) at 26.

[122] See below.

5. THE CONVENTIONALITY OF THE ACTS APPLICABLE WITHOUT STATE INTERVENTION

5.1. The Lawsuits against the Communities, the Union and its Member States

94. Some acts of EC/EU law do not require any implementation measures by the Member States. This is the case of internal measures adopted by the EC/EU institutions as well as the regulations that do not require the intervention of national authorities.[123] In this case, there is no action that can be attributed to the state, so, in principle, it seems that it is not possible to file a complaint before the Strasbourg Court.

95. Neither the EU nor the Community can be sued before the ECtHR since neither of the two organizations are members of the Convention. This is derived from the principle of relative effect of treaties, under general international law. That is, an international agreement only binds those that have agreed to respect its provisions. This principle was recognized by the Permanent Court of International Justice on its decision regarding about the case of German Interests in Upper Silesia:

> A treaty only creates law as between the States which are parties to it.[124]

This principle was later codified in the Vienna Convention on the Law of Treaties:

> Article 34. General rule regarding third States.
>
> A treaty does not create either obligations or rights for a third State without its consent.[125]

Moreover, the ECHR states that the ECtHR only hears appeals arising against any of the contracting parties.

> Article 33. Inter-State cases
>
> Any High Contracting Party may refer to the Court any alleged breach of the provisions of the Convention and the protocols thereto by another High Contracting Party.
>
> Article 34. Individual applications
>
> The Court may receive applications from any person, non-governmental organisation or group of individuals claiming to be the victim of a violation by one of the High

[123] As an example of internal legal acts adopted by the EU institutions one can take the measures adopted in the framework of the EU civil service. See J Pipkorn, 'La Communauté Européenne et la Convention Européenne des Droits de l'Homme' (1993) 14 *Revue Trimestrielle des Droits de l'Homme* 221.

[124] See Case *German Interests in Polish Upper Silesia* Judgment No 6 (Permanent Court of International Justice 25 August 1925, Series A 6, 3–83).

[125] Vienna Convention on the Law of Treaties (1969).

> Contracting Parties of the rights set forth in the Convention or the protocols thereto. The High Contracting Parties undertake not to hinder in any way the effective exercise of this right.

Furthermore, Article 19 ECHR provides that the ECtHR has been established '[t]o ensure the observance of the engagements undertaken by the High Contracting Parties in the Convention and the Protocols thereto'. And only the signatories of the Convention have agreed to the terms of Article 1 to guarantee to 'everyone within their jurisdiction' the enjoyment of fundamental rights and freedoms set forth therein. Moreover, the ECJ considered in 1996 that the Community did not have 'as Community law now stands' jurisdiction to accede to the Convention.[126]

96. Therefore, in principle, we should not be surprised by the decision in the *CFDT* (the French Democratic Confederation of Labour) case on 10 July 1978 in which the former European Commission of Human Rights declared inadmissible *ratione personae* the appeal submitted by the French union against the European Communities.[127] In the absence of formal accession by the EC/EU, it would enjoy full jurisdictional immunity and only their Member States, all of which had ratified the Convention, could be brought up before the ECtHR.[128]

97. Twenty years after the *CFDT* decision, an Italian citizen decided to appeal before the Strasbourg Court, within the framework of a public examination in order to cover a few administrative positions, the refusal of the Court of First Instance to provide legal aid. The peculiarity is that the lawsuit was against the Member States of the European Union. The Commission did not accept the lawsuit as being incompatible with the scope of the Convention, but before that it implicitly recognized the importance of the issue:

> First of all, the Commission thinks that it would be interesting to know whether the litigious decisions, adopted by a Community body, could compromise the collective responsibility of the member countries of the European Community as contracting parties of the Convention. However, the Commission does not need to go into this issue in the present case, since even assuming that it had the power to control the respect for the rights guaranteed by the Convention regarding the acts that, as in this particular case, does not pose any effect on the law of the Member States, the application must be rejected in any case.[129]

[126] Opinion 2/94 *Accession by the Community to the ECHR* [1996] ECR I-1759 para 36. See, inter alia, O de Schutter and Y Lejeune, 'L'adhésion de la Communauté à la Convention européenne des droits de l'homme' (1996) 32(5–6) *Cahiers de droit européen* 555 and MI Rofes i Pujol, 'Crónica de la Jurisprudencia del Tribunal de Justicia de las Comunidades Europeas' (1996) 15 *Cuadernos Europeos de Deusto* 148.

[127] See Case *CFDT* [1978] (n 11).

[128] The case law established in *CFDT* would be confirmed in subsequent decisions of the Commission. See, for instance, Case *Asociazione Spirituale per l'Unificazione del Mondo Cristiano v Italy* App No 11574/85 (Commission Decision, 5 October 1985) and Case *Dufay* [1989] (n 15).

[129] Case *Garzilli v The Member States of the European Union* App No 32384/96 (Commission Decision, 22 October 1998, unpublished).

98. A few years later, the appeal filed by the company *Guérin Automobiles* 'against the fifteen States of the European Union' was rejected in the same way but this time by the European Court of Human Rights.[130] Noting that the arguments of the appellant company were beyond the scope of the Convention, the Court found from the outset that the action was unfounded *ratione materiae*.[131] This reason alone:

> Exempts the Court of the need to examine the issue of their compatibility *ratione personae* with the Convention, an issue that, under other circumstances, it would be put forward, since the appeal is intended, not against the not against the European Union (which, not is a party of the Convention), but against the 15 contracting States, which are, at the same time, members of the European Union.[132]

There are many authorized voices who argue that the thesis of collective responsibility of Member States for violations of the Convention originated by acts of EC/EU law (already outlined in the decision in the *Matthews* case) despite not being able to brought up in the *Guérin* case by reasons other than competence *ratione personae*, was in fact not rejected by the ECtHR.[133] Thus, as Tulkens wrote, 'in the current state of the jurisprudence of the Tribunal, the possibility of a responsibility of each Member States derived from their international obligations is theoretically possible'.[134]

99. In its decision in the *Segi* and *Gestoras Pro-Amnistía* cases, the ECtHR again declared inadmissible two actions addressed against Member States of the European Union, this time because the petitioners were not considered victims under the ECHR.[135] In this case, the claimants argued that the common positions adopted by the Council of the European Union in the field of Common Foreign and Security Policy (CFSP) following the attacks of 11 September 2001 went against their rights guaranteed by the Convention. The applicants complained of being treated as a terrorist organization by the Member States of the European Union and demanded that the ECtHR confirm that their EC/EU treaty rights were being violated. In this case, as one author has noticed, there was a very thorough examination of the CFSP, and the ECtHR showed that it was responsible for ensuring compliance with the Convention within the EC/

[130] Case *Guérin* [2000] (n 105).

[131] The legal arguments of this case are based on principles of national legal orders. See D Spielmann, 'Un autre regard : la Cour de Strasbourg et le droit de la Communauté européenne' in G Cohen-Jonathan (ed), *Libertés, justice, tolérance. Mélanges en hommage au Doyen Gérard Cohen-Jonathan* (Bruylant, Bruxelles, 2004) 1447 at 1455.

[132] Case *Guérin* [2000] (n 105).

[133] F Krenc (2005) (n 59) at 133.

[134] F Tulkens (2000) (n 26) at 56.

[135] Case *Segi and others v 15 member States of the EU* App No 6422/02 and Case *Gestoras Pro-Amnistía and others v 15 member States of the EU* App No 9916/02 (ECtHR, 23 May 2002, 2002-V).

EU.[136] By taking into account that the applications were 'in any event inadmissible', the Strasbourg Court has made a new use of the explicit omission of its institutional competence. The Court considered that it did not have:

> to rule on the question whether the applicants exhausted the remedies which the European Union could offer them, such as a compensation claim or even an application for annulment, in the light of the judgment of 3 May 2002 given by the Court of First Instance of the European Communities in Jégo-Quéré et Cie S.A. v. Commission of the European Communities (Case T-177/01).
>
> That is because the applications are in any event inadmissible for the following reasons.[137]

Leaving aside the fact that such common positions are not directly applicable in Member States and that its legality can not be controlled by the EC/EU judge, the considerations made by the ECtHR related to the 'facts' of its decision are especially interesting.[138] Indeed, the Strasbourg Court, interpreting Community law, concludes that:

> CFSP decisions are therefore intergovernmental in nature. By taking part in their preparation and adoption each State engages its responsibility. That responsibility is assumed jointly by the States when they adopt a CFSP decision.[139]

100. Once more, the ECtHR passed over the question of jurisdiction *ratione personae*. However, the Court's considerations would show that it does not disagree that the Member States of the Union can be jointly responsible under the Convention for the effects derived from the acts belonging to the formerly named second pillar of the Union. The same considerations would apply to acts pertaining to primary law (*Matthews* case). Following this reasoning, *mutatis mutandis*, the same could be said of those cases in which the Council decides by unanimous vote, where all states take part directly in the preparation of such acts (with the vote of their representatives), also taking into account that the opposition of one of them is sufficient to prevent the adoption of such decisions.[140]

101. The Strasbourg Court adopted a similar approach in its decision in the case *Emesa Sugar v Netherlands*.[141] In this case, the appellant argued that the Netherlands would be liable for violation of the Convention, but in reality what was at issue was the role of the Advocate General in the proceedings before the ECJ. Indeed, the company *Emesa Sugar* complained that the ECJ had violated the right to a fair trial because it had not authorized the company to make comments concerning the Advocate General's Opinion during the judicial proceedings. The ECtHR case law has criticized the role played by the so-called

136 D Spielmann (2004) (n 131) at 1458.
137 Case *Segi* and Case *Gestoras Pro-Amnistía* [2002] (n 135).
138 D Spielmann (2004) (n 131) at 1456.
139 Case *Segi* and Case *Gestoras Pro-Amnistía* [2002] (n 135).
140 F Krenc (2005) (n 59) at 133–4.
141 Case *Emesa Sugar* [2005] (n 105).

'government commissioner' (*commissaire du gouvernement*) in the Council of State, the model underlying the Advocate General of the ECJ, which is virtually identical.[142]

Unlike what the Dutch Government claimed, annoyed at having to answer for a supranational situation, about which nothing could be done, the ECtHR did not reject the claim due to the lack of jurisdiction. In contrast, the ECtHR did not find it necessary to consider its own jurisdiction and entered into the substance of the matter.[143] After a long analysis of the EC/EU system, the Strasbourg judges concluded that there was no violation of Article 6, as claimed by the appellant.

102. As can be noted, the ECtHR always avoided carrying out deep analysis about its jurisdiction *ratione personae* to hear complaints against the EU and, quite naturally, undertook a detailed analysis of the facts relating to acts of the EC/EU institutions. The jurisprudence of the Commission and the Court of Human Rights is, as one can see, very significant. A formal accession of the Union to the Convention system would prevent governments from being placed in the position of the supranational institutions which thereby unleash their responsibility onto the Member States. While EU Member States have not found the moment or the means to operate the expected accession to the Convention, the ECtHR emerges as the gatekeeper of EU fundamental rights through case law.[144]

5.2. The Expansive Effect of the Obligations of the Convention

103. Leaving aside for the moment the case of the EU and its law, the ECtHR has recognized that the obligations derived from the ECHR may have legal consequences beyond the dispositions and territorial borders of the Member States. In order to achieve this effect, the Court usually makes a broad interpretation of the term 'case law' from Article 1 of the Convention. However, it is still reluctant to pierce the veil of the legal personality of international organizations and shows a particular deference towards them when it is impossible to assign the act involving the violation of a conventional right of a Member State.

104. This is the case, for example, with the judgment that settled a collective complaint against the Member States of the Convention who were also mem-

[142] See F Benoît-Rohmer, 'Le commissaire du gouvernement auprès du Conseil d'État, l'avocat général auprès de la Cour de justice des Communautés européennes et le droit d'un procès équitable' (2001) 37(4) *Revue Trimestrielle de Droit Européen* 727 and F Krenc (2005) (n 59).

[143] Case *Emesa Sugar* [2005] (n 105).

[144] See below.

bers of the North Atlantic Treaty Organization (NATO).[145] In this case the appellants argued that the bombings carried out by NATO forces against Serbian broadcasting buildings were attributable to the Member States. The large differences with the EU regarding the protection of rights (which has its own judicial system through which some control is operated in the scope of fundamental rights) could have based a condemnation if those concerned did not have any other judicial remedy, as clearly shown in the *Matthews* (see above) case law. The ECtHR could have used this case to definitively answer the question whether the acts of an international organization with legal personality can be attributed to their Member States and, therefore, compromise their responsibility under the terms of the Convention. However, the ECtHR continued to put the issue off and, giving preference, in this case, to a territorial concept of the term 'jurisdiction' exercised by a state, did not admit the appeal *ratione loci*.[146]

105. In the *Pellegrini v Italy* case, a 'very important' one, it was established that a state party to the Convention can not grant the *exequatur* to a decision adopted by a court in a country that is not a member of the Convention, without having previously verified that this decision has been taken in compliance with the obligations derived from the Convention, specifically those guarantees regarding a fair trial.[147] From this statement it is derived that Contracting States may jeopardize their conventional responsibility if they are not able to exercise a rigorous control when they have to implement acts from the institutions outside their domestic legal systems. In other words, it is no longer enough to be a High Contracting Party to be released from the obligations derived from the Convention.[148]

106. Indeed, from the moment in which an act from a state (or entity) that is not party to the Convention enters into the legal system of a state which is party to the Convention by deploying the legal effects that can affect individuals under its jurisdiction, the state party's obligation is to ensure these individuals the benefit of the rights and freedoms established by the Convention. Otherwise, it would become responsible by virtue of the ECHR.[149]

[145] Case *Banković and others v Belgium, the Czech Republic, Denmark, France, Germany, Greece, Hungary, Iceland, Italy, Luxembourg, the Netherlands, Norway, Poland, Portugal, Spain, Turkey and the United Kingdom* App No 52207/99 (ECtHR 12 December 2001, 2001-XII).

[146] See G Cohen-Jonathan, 'La territorialisation de la juridiction de la Cour européenne des droits de l'Homme' (2002) 52 *Revue Trimestrielle des Droits de l'Homme* 1055.

[147] Caso *Pellegrini v Italia*, recurso núm. 30882/96, Sentencia del TEDH de 20 julio 2001 (versión definitiva de 20 octubre 2001), *Recueil des arrêts et décisions* 2001-VIII.

[148] JP Costa, 'Le Tribunal de la Rote et l'article 6 de la Convention européenne des droits de l'homme' (2002) 50 *Revue Trimestrielle des Droits de l'Homme* 463 at 475.

[149] F Krenc (2005) (n 59) at 135.

107. A case of great interest in establishing the outline of the term 'jurisdiction' is the *Ilaşcu and others v Moldova and Russia* case.[150] In this case, the ECtHR established:

> [E]ven in the absence of effective control over the Transdniestrian region, Moldova still has a positive obligation under Article 1 of the Convention to take the diplomatic, economic, judicial or other measures that it is in its power to take and are in accordance with international law to secure to the applicants the rights guaranteed by the Convention.[151]

Thus, this statement would bring a strong argument to those who defend, even in the absence of an explicit accession, an extension of the conventional control to the whole EC/EU activity. Indeed, the ECtHR, through its Grand Chamber, stated that:

> [W]here a Contracting State is prevented from exercising its authority over the whole of its territory by a *constraining de facto situation*, such as obtains when a separatist regime is set up, whether or not this is accompanied by military occupation by another State, it does not thereby cease to have jurisdiction within the meaning of Article 1 of the Convention over that part of its territory temporarily subject to a local authority sustained by rebel forces or by another State.
>
> Nevertheless, such a factual situation reduces the scope of that jurisdiction in that the undertaking given by the State under Article 1 must be considered by the Court only in the light of the Contracting State's positive obligations towards persons within its territory. The State in question must endeavour, with all the legal and diplomatic means available to it vis-à-vis foreign States and international organisations, to continue to guarantee the enjoyment of the rights and freedoms defined in the Convention.[152]

That is, even facing a situation described as 'coercive'; states continue to be required to ensure compliance with the Convention. In this regard, the ECHR did not hesitate to check whether or not states had fulfilled the obligations derived from the ECHR.

108. The case law established in the *Ilaş cu* case could be extrapolated to the situation in which the responsibility of the EU Member States would be challenged before the ECtHR as a consequence of an EC/EU act, even if those states had not participated directly in the development of that act. In this case, however, the situation of the Member States would not be as described in the *Ilaşcu* case. Indeed, in this other case, the Member States are the ones that, by establishing the EC/EU, providing them with institutions and granting them powers, have come to a situation that could eventually justify an appeal before the ECtHR. Thus, establishing an analogy with criminal law, if in certain cases Member States could not formally be accused of being the authors of a hypo-

[150] Case *Ilaşcu* [2004] (n 109).

[151] Case *Ilaşcu* [2004] (n 109) para 331.

[152] Case *Ilaşcu* [2004] (n 109) para 333. Italics added. The French version of the judgment uses the expression '*une situation de fait contraignante*'.

thetical crime, it does meet all the conditions required to be branded as collaborators. Moreover, to the extent that they have created the European Union and control its destiny, the Member States would also have the power to remedy the situation at issue by amending, if appropriate, the treaties.[153]

5.3. The *Senator Lines* Case or the Lost Opportunity

5.3.1. The Facts that Provoked the Lawsuit

109. The appellant was a German shipping company, Senator Lines GmbH, incorporated under the form of a limited liability company. This company, along with 15 other companies in the industry, were fined by the European Commission on 16 September 1998, for violation of competition rules, in particular, for abuse of a dominant position.[154] The fine for Senator Lines was €13,750,000, payable within three months from the date of notification of the decision. A few days later, the Commission informed of the possibility of suspending the execution of the fine, provided that an appeal was brought against it and that the corresponding bank guarantee for covering both the main amount and interest was paid.[155]

110. On 7 December 1998, Senator Lines, along with the other companies involved, brought an action for annulment of the fine to the Court of First Instance of the European Communities (CFI). Since it could not provide the required guarantee, the appellant company first requested the Commission itself to exempt it from providing a bank guarantee. This petition was dismissed on 10 February 1999 on the basis of two arguments. The first concerned the predictability of the imposition of the fine. The second argument was economic. Thus, the required bank guarantee was only a small percentage of the yearly billings of the company, which also could be provided by any of the shareholders.

111. Since the Commission refused to grant the exemption of providing the guarantee, the appellant, supported by the German Government, requested the CFI to suspend the fine on 26 February 1999 by virtue of the provisions referring to the adoption of provisional measures by the Court whenever the two conditions common in these cases take place: *periculum in mora* and *fumus boni*

[153] F Krenc (2005) (n 59) at 136.

[154] Commission Decision 1999/243/EC relating to a proceeding pursuant to Articles 85 and 86 of the EC Treaty (Case No IV/35.134 – Trans-Atlantic Conference Agreement) (OJ L 95/1, 9 April 1999).

[155] For a detailed exposition of the facts of the Case, see D Marinas Suárez, '"Senator Lines" contra los quince Estados miembros de la Unión Europea' (2004) 11 *Revista Española de Derecho Europeo* 475 at 479–94.

iuris.[156] The President of the Court of First Instance rejected the suspension requested, considering the non-concurrence of *periculum in mora*. Thus, although accepting as proved the inability of Senator Lines to submit the guarantee as an independent company, he understood that the subsidiary companies themselves were in a position to provide that guarantee, even though the mere refusal of the majority shareholder to provide the assistance requested is not sufficient for the purpose of justifying the *periculum*.[157]

112. In its appeal (against the CFI's refusal to be exempted from providing the guarantee) before the ECJ, Senator Lines stated, among other arguments, that the refusal to defer the collection of the fine prior to consideration of its merits was a violation of its right to be presumed of innocence. It also alleged the risk of being declared bankrupt even before a court could have ruled on the legality and proportionality of the fine. It also argued that the fine imposed was of a criminal nature, and therefore would require a full judicial review.[158] Finally it recalled that it was impossible to force the shareholders to offer their support, despite repeated demands to do so. The action before the ECJ was rejected by an order given on 14 December 1999.[159]

113. Thus, while it seemed that the Commission would rush to proceed with the implementation of its decision, on 30 March 2000 Senator Lines filed an appeal before the ECtHR against the then 15 Member States of the Union.[160] This lawsuit claimed that those 15 states violated 'both individually and collec-

[156] See E Varona Navarro and H González Durantez, 'Interim Measures in Competition Cases Before the European Commission and Courts – The recent NDSIMS Health case has raised certain questions in regard' (2002) 23(10) *European Competition Law Review* 512; M Bacigalupo Sagesse and JA Fuentetaja Pastor, 'Fumus boni iuris, periculum in mora y equilibrio de intereses como presupuestos de la tutela cautelar comunitaria (a propósito del Auto del TJCE de 12 de julio de 1996 y del Auto del Presidente del TPI de 13 de julio de 1996, recaídos en sede cautelar en el asunto de la "enfermedad de las vacas locas")' (1997) 94 *Revista Española de Derecho Administrativo* 287; and B Marina Jalvo, *Medidas provisionales en la actividad administrativa* (Lex Nova, 2007).

[157] Case T-191/98 R *DSR-Senator Lines v Commission* [1999] ECR II-2531 (CFI President's Order).

[158] The Company was a German one, and German Law recognized some time ago the existence of sanctions which have to respect the inherent principles of criminal Law since Case Öztürk v Germany App No 8544/79 (ECtHR, 21 February 1984, 73 Serie A) para 49. See M Delmas-Marty and C Teitgen-Colly, *Punir sans juger? De la répression administrative au droit administratif pénal* (Economica, Paris, 1992) 165–70; M Delmas-Marty, *Pour un droit commun* (Seuil, Paris, 1994) 146; MG Rubio de Casas, 'Potestad sancionatoria de la Administración y garantías del administrado: comentario a la Sentencia del Tribunal Europeo de Derechos Humanos de 21-11-1984: el caso OZTURK' (1984) 104 *Revista de Administración Pública* 375; LE Pettiti, 'Les principes généraux de droit pénal dans la Convention européenne des droits de l'homme' (1987) 1987(1) *Revue de Science Criminelle et de Droit Pénal Comparé* 167 at 174; J Andriantsimbazovina et al (2007) (n 2) 248–50; and MP Canedo Arrillaga, *El procedimiento en derecho comunitario de defensa de la competencia: análisis del principio de proporcionalidad y otros afines* (ProQuest, Cambridge, 1999).

[159] Case C-364/99 P(R) *DSR-Senator Lines v Commission* [1999] ECR I-8733 (ECJ President's Order).

[160] Case *Senator Lines* [2004] (n 105). The full text of the application was published in 12 *Revue Universelle des Droits de l'Homme* (3-5) 2000 at 191–208.

tively' Article 6 ECHR while the Commission of the European Communities did not agree – under the circumstances of the case – the effect of suspending the appeal of the appellant before the Court of First Instance.[161]

The appellant believed that it had been deprived of its fundamental right of access to a court (Article 6 ECHR) as it was legally required to pay the fine even though no court had yet been able to examine the legality of the contested decision. The company also claimed that, 'while it is shown that it is not possible to provide a bank guarantee, as is the case, the requirement of such a guarantee is disproportionate and deprives de facto the appellant of any access to justice'.[162]

The German company said in its application that the EC/EU courts, by rejecting the suspension of the Commission decision, allowed the latter, a 'merely administrative authority', to provoke its bankruptcy without waiting for the decision of the CFI.[163] The failure to access this Court prevented the appellant company to call on the violation of its right to a fair trial, its right to an appeal before a court and the presumption of innocence itself at the domestic Court (in that case, the CFI).

At the same time, Senator Lines made a request to the ECtHR for interim measures designed to force the defendant governments to prevent the Commission from charging the fine before the Community judge had ruled. This request was rejected on 20 April 2000.[164]

114. In March 2001 the Commission obtained an *exequatur* from the German authorities allowing it to charge the fine. However, the Commission reported later that it would not proceed to the enforcement of the penalty as long as the case remained unsolved before the ECtHR (so that the *periculum in mora* derived from the execution was relieved).

Moreover, on 12 December 2002, the Chamber of the ECtHR, towards which the case was initially directed, relinquished jurisdiction in favour of the Grand Chamber under Article 30 of the Convention, which reads:

> Where a case pending before a Chamber raises a serious question affecting the interpretation of the Convention or the protocols thereto, or where the resolution of a question before the Chamber might have a result inconsistent with a judgment previously delivered by the Court, the Chamber may, at any time before it has rendered its judgment, relinquish jurisdiction in favour of the Grand Chamber, unless one of the parties to the case objects.

115. The vicissitudes of the case were over when on 30 September 2003 the CFI annulled the fine imposed on the appellant.[165] As a matter of coincidence, this

[161] See Senators Application (n 160) para 35 .
[162] See Senators Application (n 160) para 103.
[163] See Senators Application (n 160) para 62.
[164] Case *Senator Lines* [2004] (n 160) recital 2 of the heading.
[165] Joined Cases T-191/98 and T-212/98 to T-214/98 *Atlantic Container Line and others v Commission* [2003] ECR II-3275.

decision came a few days before the hearing had finally been set before the ECHR. In view of the CFI ruling, the president of the ECtHR was quick to cancel the originally scheduled hearing.

116. Two procedural issues that occurred in this case should be mentioned. First, a technical difficulty arose from the application of the ad hoc judges (rule 29 of Court's Rules). Given the difficulties in enforcing this rule due to the large number of defendant parties (and the attending Chamber requirements), a judge of common interest is appointed (the British judge Sir Nicolas Bratza).[166] Moreover, it should be also stressed that the European Commission intervened in the proceedings before the Court when it was, in fact, a defendant party.[167] Similarly, as well as the Commission, the CCBE, the European Company Lawyers Association, the FIDH and the International Commission of Jurists also took part. The participation of the Commission and all these organizations shows, if proof were needed, the interest and importance of the issue raised in this case, which was made possible by a provision that is already in the ECHR:

> Article 36. Third Party Intervention.
>
> . . .
>
> 2. The President of the Court may, in the interest of the proper administration of justice, invite any High Contracting Party which is not a party to the proceedings or any person concerned who is not the applicant to submit written comments or take part in hearings.

5.3.2. *The Specifics of the Senator Lines Case*

117. In view of the above and considering the objective of this work, we shall highlight a number of features that enhance the interest of the analysis of the *Senator Lines* case.

118. First, it should be noted that the action is not directed against the Union or the European Community, but specifically refers to the 15 member states of the European Union at that time. These states were all bound individually by the ECHR.

119. This case differs from *Matthews* case since it does not deal with rules of primary law of which the Member States are the authors, but challenges certain

[166] The provision about the common-interest judge was included in rule 30 of the Rules of the Court, then in force (January 2009). The current Rules of the Court (April 2011) still recognizes this possibility in rule 30.

[167] This particular case is an example of the issues which arose from the lack of accession of the EU to the ECHR, where the European Commission could participate in the process, but from a subordinated position, and could not lead the defence. See below.

acts issued directly by the institutions of the EC which, it should be stressed, has been expressly attributed legal personality.[168]

120. Moreover, in this case, the appellant company could address the EC/EU judge to request both the extension of the execution of the decision of the Commission and the annulment of the fine itself.

121. The European Court of Human Rights had a claim that directly challenged the validity of Community acts, unlike the *M & Co*, *Procola* or *Cantoni* cases (see above) in which they discussed the compatibility between the Convention and certain national measures implementing EC/EU law.

122. The institutions from which the acts challenged by the Senator Lines Company derived – the Commission, the Court of First Instance and the Court of Justice of the European Communities – are legally separate from the states. Thus, Article 213.2 TEU (245 TFEU) provides:

> The Members of the Commission shall, in the general interest of the Community, be completely independent in the performance of their duties
>
> In the performance of these duties, they shall neither seek nor take instructions from any government or from any other body.

Moreover, Articles 223 and 224 TEC (Articles 253 and 254 TFEU) state that the judges of the ECJ and CFI shall be chosen from among persons offering every guarantee of independence.

The situation could have been different if the act at issue had been dictated by the Council, given that in this institution the states are represented by their ministers and take part in the decisions through vote. In fact, Article 203 of the TEU (Article 16 TEU L) states that the Council 'shall consist of a representative of each Member State at ministerial level, authorised to commit the government of that Member State'.

In another vein, in this case, the EU Member States did not have any means to prevent the alleged violation of the Convention.

123. Finally, it is worth highlighting the case of Germany in this matter. While German authorities, in compliance with Article 256 TEC (Article 299 TFEU), issued the national enforcing act necessary to enable the Commission to perform the forced payment of the fine, they supported the arguments of the Senator Lines company, which became even more apparent in the proceedings before the CFI. It is paradoxical, at least from a strictly procedural point of view, that Germany encouraged at all times the appellant party (Senator Lines), whereas, before the ECtHR, Germany was, together with the other Member States, the defendant party.

[168] Art 281 TEC states: 'The Community shall have legal personality'. After the Lisbon Treaty, Art 47 TEU-L reads: 'The Union shall have legal personality.'

5.3.3. On the Condition of Victim under the ECHR

124. If the question of admissibility *ratione personae* is, without a doubt, the main point of the appeal, there is another question that the ECtHR should also answer, and this is if Senator Lines could be considered a victim of a violation of the Convention if the fine imposed by the Commission was not collected before the beginning of the judicial process and, in the end, was annulled in another concurrent jurisdictional procedure.[169]

Any natural or legal person turning to the ECtHR must prove their status as victims under Article 34 of the Convention.[170] According to the ECtHR a victim is that person directly affected by the relevant act or omission of the state, regardless of the existence of injury. Unlike what is required by EC/EU law, the appellant is not bound to be perfectly individualized regarding any other person, but he must only establish that he is directly affected by the contested measure.[171]

125. In principle, an appeal lodged before the ECtHR cannot be aimed at preventing a possible violation of the Convention, as the Strasbourg Court can only confirm a violation later, when it has already taken place. Only under 'exceptional circumstances' may the risk of a future violation turn the appellant into a victim of a violation of the Convention.[172]

The ECtHR has admitted the existence of these circumstances in the case *D v UK*, referring to the expulsion of a drug dealer in the terminal phase of AIDS to a Caribbean island where he could not have received any kind of treatment.[173] This exception is not interpreted by the Strasbourg Court in a broad sense, as evidenced by the decision in *Bensaïd v UK*, where the ECtHR held that the expulsion from British territory of an Algerian under treatment for schizophrenia was not a violation of Articles 3 and 8 of the Convention.[174]

Likewise, the risk that a German citizen might be placed on 'death row' led the ECtHR in the well-known case *Soering v UK* to unanimously conclude that:

[169] See the considerations of a member of the Court in a doctrinal paper JP Costa, 'La Convention européenne des droits de l'homme, la Charte des droits fondamentaux de l'Union européenne et la problématique de l'adhésion de l'Union européenne à la Convention' 2004(5) *European University Institute Working Paper Law* 11 at 11.

[170] P Lambert, 'Les bénéficiaires du droit de recours' in VV.AA. (ed), *La procédure devant la nouvelle Cour européenne des droits de l'homme après le Protocole n°11, Actes du séminaire organisé à Bruxelles le l9 octobre 1998, par les instituts de droits de l'homme des barreaux de Paris et de Bruxelles* (Nemesis-Bruylant, Bruxelles, 1999) 7.

[171] Case *Marckx v Belgium* App No 6833/74 (ECtHR, 13 June 1979, 31 Series A) para 27 and Case *Johnston and others v Ireland* App No 9697/82 (ECtHR, 18 December 1986, 112 Series A) para 42.

[172] Case *Noël Narvii Tauira and others v France* App No 28204/95 (Commission Decision, 4 December 1995, 83-A DR 130) paras 2, 2–24 and Cases *Segi* and *Gestoras* (n 135).

[173] Case *D v Reino Unido*, recurso núm. 30240/96, Sentencia del TEDH de 2 mayo 1997, *Recueil des arrêts et décisions* 1997-III.

[174] Case *Bensaïd v UK* App No 44599/98 (ECtHR , 6 February 2001, 2001-I) (final version 6 May 2001).

> if, for example, a Convention State deports or extradites a person to a country where it is certain or where there is a serious risk that the person will be subjected to torture or inhuman treatment the deportation or extradition would, in itself, under such circumstances constitute inhuman treatment for which the deporting or extraditing State would be directly responsible under Article 3 of the Convention.[175]

Notice how in this case it is the 'simple' risk of occurrence of an act constituting a violation which causes the applicant to be considered a 'victim', which represented a significant expansion of that concept.[176]

In previous cases, the appellants had not yet suffered an effective violation of any of the rights guaranteed by the Convention. These were potential victims, individuals who 'cry before feeling any pain'.[177] The restraining orders from which the appellants were the unfortunate recipients contained a violation germ. However, there was a high risk of breaching the rules of the Convention, and so the appellants argued that if the decision they contested in each case was executed, their fundamental rights would be neglected. Far from being merely hypothetical, the threat was real and imminent.[178]

To be considered a victim of a future violation of the Convention, as recently pointed out by the ECtHR, the appellant must provide 'reasonable and convincing evidence of the likelihood that a violation affecting him personally will occur; mere suspicion or conjecture is insufficient in this respect'.[179]

126. The situation would be different if the person had already suffered a violation of their rights, but the status of victim would be liable to be changed by the arrival of later events. In fact, the situation envisaged in this case would be the loss of that status by the appellant.

According to well-established case law and opened up by the *Eckle v Germany* case a favourable decision or action for the appellant is not enough, in principle, to remove the status of 'victim' if the national authorities have recognized, explicitly or substantially, and have repaired, the violation of the Convention.[180] Thus, for instance, in the *Ammur v France* case, when the ECtHR knew of the appeal lodged by some Somali asylum seekers who had been held for several days in the transit zone of Paris-Orly airport, the Strasbourg Court found that

[175] Case *Soering v UK* App No 14038/88 (ECtHR, 7 July 1989, 161 Series A) para 96.

[176] See W Ganshof Van der Meersch, 'L'extradition et la Convention européenne des droits de l'homme. L'affaire Soering' (1990) 1 *Revue Trimestrielle des Droits de l'Homme* 5; RB Lillich, 'The Soering case' (1991) 85 *American Journal of International Law* 128; and F Sudre, 'Extradition et peine de mort : arrêt Soering de la Cour européenne des droits de l'homme, du 7 juillet 1989' (1990) 94(1) *Revue General de Droit International Public* 103.

[177] J Andriantsimbazovina (2007) (n 2) 726.

[178] Applications before the ECtHR do not imply per se the suspension of the contested acts. However, applicants may request for interim measures relying on rule 39 of the Rules of Court (April 2011). In the *Soering* case, the British authorities accepted the subsequent petitions of Strasbourg in order to stop the extradition procedure before a final ruling of the ECtHR.

[179] Cases *Segi* and *Gestoras* [2002] (n 135) restates what was already established in Case *Noël Narvii Tauira* [1995] (n 172).

[180] Case *Eckle v Germany* App No 8130/78 (ECtHR, 15 July 1982, 51 Series A) para 66.

the national judge's decision which declared the existence of an arbitrary deprivation of liberty and which subsequently ordered the release of the appellants was issued after they had been deported to Syria.[181] Likewise, in the *Ekin v France* case, the ECtHR considered that the annulment, with retroactive effect, made by the French *Conseil d'État* of the ministerial decision banning the publication of a book published by the appellant was not, regarding the circumstances of the case, a sufficient remedy for the violation suffered, especially considering the fact that the annulment of the government act came more than nine years after the ban.[182] In the same way, in the *Dalban v Romania* case, the ECtHR considered that the annulment by the Romanian Supreme Court of the defamation convictions upon the appellant, which happened after lodging the appeal before the ECtHR, could not stop her from taking advantage of the guarantees inherent to the freedom of expression, even when the necessary conditions for recognition and compensation for the violation of which had allegedly been subjected were not met.[183]

The *Senator Lines* case differs from previous cases since in *Dalban* it was the public prosecutor's office, not the applicant, who lodged an appeal before the Supreme Court. In addition, this national appeal was introduced years after the submission of the complaint to Strasbourg, while in the *Senator Lines* case, the appeal for annulment preceded chronologically the corresponding one before the ECtHR. Finally, the Romanian Government, unlike the defendant governments in the *Senator Lines* case, recognized that the late Mr Dalban was victim of a violation of a right guaranteed by the Convention.[184]

5.3.4. The Court's Decision: The Status of Victim in Senator Lines and the Passive Legitimation of the EC/EU

127. The final decision of the judges of the ECtHR, highly expected by the doctrine, adopted an unusual look.[185] Indeed, the authors, commentators and other legal experts were eager to know if, finally, the Strasbourg Court would exercise direct control over secondary EC/EU law and, specifically, over an act that derived directly from EC/EU institutions. The reason for being anxious was that the issue was not at all simple, either from the technical point of view or the strategic. The question was, no less, 'whether it was possible to attack an act adopted by the institutions and not by a Member State'.[186]

[181] Case *Amuur v France* App No 19776/92 (ECtHR, 25 June 1996, 1996-III).

[182] Case *Asociación Ekin v France* App No 39288/98 (ECtHR, 17 July 2001, 2001-VIII).

[183] Case *Dalban v Romania* App No 28114/95 (ECtHR 28 September 1999, 1999-VI).

[184] Case *Dalban* [1999] (n 183) para 34.

[185] F Krenc (2005) (n 59), starts his comment with the phrase: 'We were expecting it with great impatience'.

[186] L Burgorgue-Larsen, 'Senator Lines c. les 15 États de l'Union européenne, DR, du 10 mars 2004' (2004) 35 (7 de octubre de 2004) *Chronique de la Cour européenne des droits de l'Homme*, Recueil Dalloz 2533.

128. However, neither this issue nor the other (no less important) that also arose in this case, the EC/EU system of interim and precautionary measures, would be finally resolved by the ECtHR.[187] The Strasbourg Court 'took voluntarily a long time' to give an answer.[188] Thus, on 30 September 2003, the Court of First Instance, before which the question on the validity of the fines imposed by the Commission in the field of maritime restrictive practices was still pending, adopted a surprisingly long sentence (1,648 paragraphs) considering that such fines were not justified.[189] Since neither the Commission nor the other parties appealed the decision of the CFI, it became final.

129. This judgment had direct and immediate impact on the parallel process carried out in Strasbourg. In fact, in a press release of 16 October 2003, the ECtHR announced 'in light of the CFI's judgment' the cancellation of the hearing on the *Senator Lines* case.[190] It was an unprecedented event. A certain parallel could be drawn between this and the *Dalban* case (above) in which the Romanian Supreme Court annulled some decisions before the ECtHR ruled. For this reason, the ECtHR considered in its decision rejecting the appeal that the requirements of Article 34 of the Convention were not met, that is to say, that the applicant did not satisfy the condition of 'victim'. Thus, the Court stated:

> As events transpired, the fine imposed on the applicant company was neither paid nor enforced, and the applicant company's challenge to the fine (along with the related challenge by other companies) was not merely heard, but ended with the final quashing of the fine.[191]

Therefore, the Court concluded:

> Accordingly, the facts of the present case were never such as to permit the applicant company to claim to be a victim of a violation of its Convention rights. By the time of the 'final decision' in the case – the CFI's judgment of 30 September 2003 – it was clear that the applicant company could not produce 'reasonable and convincing' evidence of the likelihood that a violation affecting it would occur, because on that date it was certain that there was no justification for the applicant company's fear of the fine being enforced before the CFI hearing.[192]

[187] On the interim measures, see S de la Sierra, 'El sistema comunitario de tutela cautelar y su control por el tribunal europeo de derechos humanos a la luz del art. 6 del convenio. una oportunidad perdida (La resolución del TEDH de 10 de marzo de 2004 en el asunto Senator Lines GmbH c. los quince Estados Miembros de la Unión Europea, n.º 56672/00)' (2004) 6 *Revista General de Derecho Administrativo* at 11–17.

[188] G Cohen-Jonathan, 'L'adhésion de l'Union européenne à la Convention européenne des droits de l'homme' in VV. AA. (ed), *Quelle justice pour l'Europe? La Charte européenne des droits fondamentaux et la Convention pour l'avenir de l'Europe* (Bruylant, Bruxelles, 2004) 59 at 68.

[189] Joined Cases T-191/98 and T-212/98 to T-214/98 *Atlantic Container* [2003] (n 165).

[190] See the ECtHR Press release issued by the Registrar *Cancellation of hearing in the case Senator Lines GmbH v the 15 Member States of the European Union Press* (16 October 2003).

[191] Case *Senator Lines* [2004] (n 105). Section D. The Court's assessment.

[192] *Ibid.*

130. The violation had not yet happened, but one might wonder whether the conditions existed to consider the appellant company as a potential victim and, therefore, likely to be protected by the Convention system. According to a highly skilled commentator, it 'is far from clear that in the *Senator Lines* case there is a violation of the Convention'.[193] Others argue that 'reliable data exist turning the appellant into potential victim and, therefore, likely to be protected by the Convention system'.[194] The question is not clear.

In the *Soering* case (above), as well as in the *Senator Lines* case, the appellant was unable to prove the existence of a real and effective violation of their fundamental rights. His arguments within the application were all written in the conditional tense. However, this did not prevent the ECtHR from accepting the claim and finding, *in fine*, a breach of Article 3 of the Convention in case the person concerned was extradited. But, unlike the *Senator Lines* case, the measure was not cancelled, but suspended, and could be implemented at all times to the detriment of Mr Soering.

The situation of *Senator Lines* also differs from the cases of *Amuur*, *Ekin* and *Dalban* (above) in that in those cases the violation had already taken place. In those cases they wanted the ECtHR to examine whether the advent of new facts provoked the loss of the victim condition of those appellants, which at the moment of lodging the appeal in Strasbourg met the requirements needed. What was important, then, was whether with the loss of victim status there was also a satisfaction. The ECtHR considers that the position of *Senator Lines* is quite different, because it could not have lost its victim status since it never had this status.

This being so, one might wonder whether the appellant company failed to provide 'reasonable and convincing evidence' of the probable circumstance of a violation of the Convention, in the sense of the *Segi* and *Gestoras* case law. In principle, it should be noted that the fears of the company were not in vain. It is true that the European Commission has always maintained that it would not execute a decision like this one (to collect a fine) until the trial ended. But, in order to do so, it has always been necessary that the company or the individual concerned provide the necessary guarantees, which did not occur in this case. In fact, after lodging the appeal before the ECtHR, the Commission obtained from the German authorities the domestic enforcement act necessary to collect the fine. It was not until April 2002, two years after lodging the appeal before the ECtHR, that the Commission stated that it would not take any enforcement of judgment action while the process was alive in Strasbourg. Moreover, once the Commission decision was overturned by the CFI, the fears of the appellant company were no longer justified.

[193] F Benoît-Rohmer. 'Chronique d'une décision annoncée : l'affaire Senator Lines devant la Cour européenne des droits de l'homme' (2001) 4 *L'Europe des libertés* 2 at 2.

[194] S De la Sierra, 'El sistema comunitario de tutela cautelar y su control por el tribunal europeo de derechos humanos a la luz del art. 6 del convenio. una oportunidad perdida (La resolución del TEDH de 10 de marzo de 2004 en el asunto Senator Lines GmbH c. los quince Estados Miembros de la Unión Europea, n.° 56672/00)' (2004) 6 *Revista General de Derecho Administrativo* at 7–8.

However, we should not confuse the 'probability of the existence of an act that one may see as contrary to the Convention', with the 'probability of a violation of a provision of the Convention'.[195] These are two separate issues and should be analysed sequentially. The review of the first issue does not involve any assessment of the conventionality or not of an act. Thus, in the *Soering* case, the threat was imminent; the extradition was only suspended by interim measures. Taking the above-mentioned into account, the ECtHR would move its position towards the Convention, to finally indicate that the argument according to which the extradition of Mr Soering would violate Article 3 was justified. However, in the *Senator Lines* case, the ECtHR did not rule on the grounds of the appeal, since it was clear that the probability for the fine to be charged was non-existent because it had been annulled by the CFI. The Strasbourg Court merely responded negatively to the first question and, therefore, ruled out considering both the merits of the case and the delicate question of the compatibility *ratione personae* of the appeal with the Convention.

131. Given that the appeal was dismissed because it did not meet the condition of victim, that is, since there was no *locus standi*, the question regarding the passive legitimacy of the EU in the protection system of the ECHR was not analysed by the Court. However, one might wonder if the ECtHR would be prepared to forget about the legal personality of the European Community (now EU), which, not being a member of the Convention, would represent a powerful protection against these sorts of claim, and indirectly condemned it by making its Member States responsible for the EC/EU actions.

Some argue that if it had been accepted that Senator Lines met the necessary conditions to be considered a victim for Convention purposes, the admission of the *ratione personae* should not have been problematic. Besides the existence of small signs that can be scrutinized in the text of the decision (such as the fact that there is a specific reference to the respondent states as a whole) it could be understood that, in fact, the Court does not depart from its previous position. Another point of interest is the fact that the presence of the European Commission as third party in the proceedings was admitted and that, consequently, it was allowed to submit written comments. In addition, there is already a well-qualified precedent in which the ECtHR controlled an act directly derived from the Community institutions and, moreover, made a Member State responsible: *Matthews v UK*.

It is true that there are differences between the *Senator Lines* and *Matthews* cases which, in turn, might justify different treatment. Thus, in *Matthews*, the suspected acts of violating the rights recognized in the Convention – Annex II of the Electoral Act 1975 – had been produced by the Governments of the Member States represented in the Council and, in fact, were of a conventional nature, so that the relationship between the states and the origin of the

[195] See F Krenc (2005) (n 59) at 146–7.

infringement action was evident.[196] Moreover, according to the ECtHR's established case law, the acts that are committed in the territory of a state party fall under its jurisdiction. And this would also be the case of the applicable acts without state intervention. In addition, allowing a total immunity from such action would imply an admission that a transfer of powers (to a supranational body) could suppress the guarantees offered by the Convention, which categorically rejects the Strasbourg Court's line. If the Court remained faithful to the logic underlying the subsequent *Bosphorus* case, it could admit the states' responsibility for an act like the one questioned in the *Senator Lines* case.

However, in the *Senator Lines* case, the act originating the appeal – the Decision imposing the fine – comes from an institution that does not represent the interests of the states, and which in any case is not intergovernmental: the European Commission. For this reason, the link between the state and the violation of human rights is indirect and could pose problems in terms of passive standing of the relevant Member States of the EU.

132. However, although it would be very strange if the ECtHR analysed the *ad intra* decision-making process to determine the responsibility of a state, the Strasbourg Court seems unwilling to leave gaps in the protection of rights derived from the Convention. Thus, at the EC/EU level, we could face situations in which any state party to the Convention could be held responsible for acts that had been adopted without its taking part in the decision (as in the *Senator Lines* case) or that, having done so, it has been the result of a majority decision (to which it has been opposed). However, in the cases in which it was impossible to hold responsible any state, under the doctrine of strict responsibility used by the Strasbourg case law, it would be more than likely for the ECtHR to forget about the legal personality of the EC/EU in order to analyse the EC/EU decision-making process and eventually admit the collective responsibility of Member States.[197] This situation would be close to that depicted by some authors who describe a situation similar to a de facto membership of the EC/EU to the Convention.[198]

133. The *Senator Lines* case prompted the courts in Strasbourg and Luxembourg to face each other. Not all the Strasbourg judges agreed with the 'forced

[196] See A Clapham, 'The European Union before the European Court of Human Rights' in Boisson de Chazournes, C Romano and R Mackenzie (eds), *International Organizations and International Dispute Settlement: Trends and Prospects* (Transnational Publishers, New York, 2002) 73 at 78–9.

[197] See JP Jacqué (2007) (n 107) at 27.

[198] See F Benoît-Rohmer, 'A propos de l'arrêt Bosphorus Air Lines du 30 juin 2005 : l'adhésion contrainte de l'Union à la Convention' (2005) 64 *Revue Trimestrielle des Droits de l'Homme* 827; and V Constantinesco, 'C'est comme ci c'était fait ? (Observations à propos de l'arrêt de la Cour européenne des droits de l'homme (grande chambre), Bosphorus airlines, du 30 juin 2005' (2006) 42(3–4) *Cahiers de droit Européen* 363.

dismissal' of the lawsuit.[199] For some, this was a missed opportunity to make clear that the activity of the EC/EU institutions did not escape the control organs of Strasbourg. For others, however, it was too politicized a case that put too much strain on the relations between the two courts. However, the matter would be put forward, although in different terms, with the already analysed *Bosphorus* case.

6. THE POSSIBLE CONVENTIONALITY CONTROL OF THE ACTS FROM THE OLD SECOND AND THIRD PILLARS

134. The possibility of establishing control of the law of the intergovernmental pillars by the ECtHR was moved forward with the issue of the inclusion of certain persons, groups and legal and natural entities in the list of terrorist organizations founded in the framework of Common Position 2001/931/CFSP, which could affect the effective judicial protection guaranteed by the ECHR. As seen above, the Council of Ministers of the European Union stated that it was necessary to adopt the common position in order to implement UNSC Resolution 1373 (2001) through additional measures. While some of the names included had appeared previously identified by the Security Council, others were made on the basis of information provided by Member States. The common position in question, as already analysed, is a legal act based on Article 15 (Article 20 TEU-L) and Article 34 of the TEU (mainly Articles 82–89 TFEU), by including measures defined both in the Common Foreign and Security Policy and the former third pillar.[200]

135. The dispute between *Segi* and *Gestoras Pro-Amnistía* and the Council regarding their inclusion in that common position has gone through three supranational courts, the ECtHR, the CFI and finally the ECJ. The procedures before the two courts of the EU have already been mentioned above. This section will return to the case before the ECtHR, which also is mentioned above, concerning the status of 'victim' in the Strasbourg case law.[201]

What is relevant here is that, in the cases *Segi* and *Gestoras Pro-Amnistía*, these organizations were only included (as part of the terrorist group ETA) in the Annex of the Common Position in relation to Article 4, which provides that

[199] See L Scheeck, 'Les cours européennes et l'intégration par les droits de l'homme› (Instituto de Estudios Políticos 2006) at 363–4 where the author goes through the testimonies that he collected from the judges, lawyers and Court clerks in Strasbourg and Luxembourg involved in the *Senator* case.

[200] After the Lisbon Treaty, Title VI TEU provisions on police and judicial cooperation in criminal matters (among them, Art 34) have been substituted by Part III, Title IV, Chapters 1, 4 and 5 TFEU (ie Arts 67–76 and 82–89 TFEU).

[201] For a study analysing the journey through the different Courts of the *Segi* and *Gestoras* cases see S Davies. 'Segi and the Future of Judicial Rights Protection in the Third Pillar of the EU' (2008) 14(3) *European Public Law* 311.

Member States shall help each other in preventing and combating terrorism regarding persons, groups or entities appearing on the list. Specifically, Article 4 of Common Position 2001/931/CFSP provides:

> Member States shall, through police and judicial cooperation in criminal matters within the framework of Title VI of the Treaty on European Union, afford each other the widest possible assistance in preventing and combating terrorist acts. To that end they shall, with respect to enquiries and proceedings conducted by their authorities in respect of any of the persons, groups and entities listed in the Annex, fully exploit, upon request, their existing powers in accordance with acts of the European Union and other international agreements, arrangements and conventions which are binding upon Member States.

136. In 2002, *Segi* and *Gestoras Pro-Amnistía* brought an action against the then 15 EU Member States before the ECtHR, alleging violation, inter alia, of the rights to freedom of expression, the presumption of innocence and the right to an effective legal remedy.[202] The ECtHR carried out an unusually thorough review of EU law in general and, specifically, of the provisions of the Common Position that affected the plaintiffs, and after finding out that the appellants had not produced any evidence that would allow the Court to establish that the plaintiffs had been indeed the object of measures against them as a result of the implementation of the common position, it concluded that:

> The mere fact that the names of two of the applicants (Segi and Gestoras Pro-Amnistía) appear in the list referred to in that provision as 'groups or entities involved in terrorist acts' may be embarrassing, but the link is much too tenuous to justify application of the Convention.[203]

That is, the situation of the appellants included in the list of terrorist groups or organizations may be uncomfortable, but since their inclusion on the list was not equivalent to determine their criminal liability, the ECtHR did not intervene. This form of argument would leave the door open for a possible intervention of the Strasbourg Court on the assumption of having criminal consequences for the appellants directly from the common position. Indeed, one might ask whether the conclusion of the ECtHR would have been the same in the event that concrete measures had been taken against individuals on the list, in particular the freezing of their property and financial assets. It seems unlikely that the ECtHR applies the presumption of equivalence in the protection of fundamental rights established between the ECHR and EC/EU law in the *Bosphorus* case to the legal acts adopted within the framework of the intergovernmental pillars, but it constitutes a warning to the EU institutions regarding human rights.[204]

[202] Cases *Segi* and *Gestoras* [2002] (n 135).

[203] Cases *Segi* and *Gestoras* [2002] (n 135). The French version uses the word '*gênant*' whereas the English one says '*embarrassing*'.

[204] J Santos Vara, 'El control judicial de la ejecución de las sanciones antiterroristas del Consejo de Seguridad en la Unión Europea' (2008) 15 *Revista Electrónica de Estudios Internacionales* at 4–5.

Judging by subsequent case law developments in Luxembourg, particularly in relation to the *OMPI-PMOI* and *Yusuf-Al Barakaat/Kadi/Ayadi* cases, it could be argued that the CFI and the ECJ do not remain, at least, indifferent.[205]

[205] See Case T-306/01 *Yusuf and Al Barakaat International Foundation v Council and Commission* [2005] ECR II-3533 and Case T-315/01 *Kadi v Council and Commission* [2005] ECR II-3649; and the final decision of the ECJ on both in Joined Cases C-402/05 P and C-415/05 P *Kadi* and *Al Barakaat International Foundation v Council* [2008] ECR I-6351. See also Case T-253/02 *Ayadi v Council* [2006] ECR II-2139 and Case T-49/04 *Hassan v Council and Commission* [2006] ECR II-52, both of them equally revoked (following the *Kadi* case law) by the ECJ in Joined Cases C-399/06 P and C-403/06 P *Hassan and Ayadi v Council and Commission* [2009] ECR I-11393. See also the *OMPI-PMOI* saga, Case T-228/02 *Organisation des Modjahedines du peuple d'Iran v Council (OMPI)* [2006] ECR II-4665, Case T-256/07 *People's Mojahedin Organization of Iran v Council (PMOI I)* [2008] ECR II-3019 and Case T-284/08 *People's Mojahedin Organization of Iran v Council (PMOI II)* [2008] ECR II-3487.

6

The Dialogue between Strasbourg and Luxembourg: Current Situation and Prospects

1. THE CURRENT SITUATION

1. The answers given by the judges in Strasbourg and Luxembourg to the issues raised by the relationship between EC/EU law and the Convention seem, at first glance, successful as they allow the peaceful coexistence of both systems. However, a closer examination of the issue would reveal a number of difficulties that have major implications for the law of the Union rather than for the system derived from the Convention.

2. The Strasbourg case law involves, first, the de facto surrender of EC/EU law to its control through the statement of responsibility of a Member State. And this is a somewhat paradoxical situation: as we know, Member States have agreed that the Union shall be part of the Convention.[1] This situation puts the EU in a clearly disadvantaged position and almost defenceless. Indeed, the Union, not being a party to the dispute, cannot intervene directly, but only along with a state, a situation where it does not direct the defence.[2] Moreover, since the Union is not party to the Convention, it cannot appoint a judge to the Court. The stock of the situation would be that from a procedural standpoint, it has the drawbacks without enjoying the benefits. Indeed, one might think that lawsuits like *Matthews*, *Bosphorus*, even, against acts applicable without state intervention, would be exceptional, but we must take into account the economic power of the companies concerned – turned into victims before the ECtHR –

[1] That is why some scholars have suggested that *Bosphorus* has operated a de facto accession of the EU into the ECHR system. See F Benoît-Rohmer, 'A propos de l'arrêt Bosphorus Air Lines du 30 juin 2005 : l'adhésion contrainte de l'Union à la Convention' (2005) 64 *Revue Trimestrielle des Droits de l'Homme* 827 and V Constantinesco, 'C'est comme ci c'était fait ? (Observations à propos de l'arrêt de la Cour européenne des droits de l'homme (grande chambre), Bosphorus airlines, du 30 juin 2005' (2006) 42(3–4) *Cahiers de droit Européen* 363.

[2] Following the Rules of Court (2009 and 2011 versions), this possibility is subject to the approval of the President of the Court/Chamber (Rule 36). Nontheless, this possibility would usually be awarded by the President, pursuing proper administration of justice, as part of the fair trial guarantees enshrined in Art 6 ECHR.

that have large resources to mobilize governments and legal experts in their own interests.[3]

3. Despite the stated desire to preserve the phenomenon of European integration, the case law of the Court of Human Rights operates an 'intergovernmentalization' of the EC/EU making the Member States defend community interests, a role that should be played by their own institutions and, especially, by the Commission. This denial of the personality of the EC/EU (or, rather, the restraint of the procedural standing) significantly weakens and sets back the integration process. Therefore, the situation is, at least, an invitation for accession to the Convention, the only truly effective solution which is capable of returning to the EU the role that truly belongs to it.[4]

4. The current case law of the ECtHR contains a threat, at least a latent threat, to the primacy of EC/EU law. This would occur in the event of finding a violation of the Convention, in which case the Member States might be in the difficult position of having to choose between violating EC/EU law or violating the European Convention.[5] In this context, which recalls that suffered by the UK as a result of the *Matthews* case (see Chapter 5), the Member State would be required to remedy a situation that does not depend on itself, but on the EC/EU legislator or the Court of Justice or the European Commission. If, finally, it decides to implement the ruling of the Strasbourg Court, it will breach EC/EU law. Even in the unlikely event that the Court accepted that respect for fundamental rights could constitute a justification for this breach, the uniform application of EC/EU law would no longer be assured.[6] On the other hand, individuals could apply to the Court of Justice demanding that the state take responsibility for failure to comply. But also, given that the ECtHR has reserved the right to determine on a case by case basis if the system's protection level is comparable to that of the EC/EU, legal certainty does not appear to be fully guaranteed. In this situation, and to protect themselves against claims before the Strasbourg Court, Member States might be tempted to refrain from applying EC/EU law in certain cases.[7]

[3] The ECtHR has always several cases similar to those commented on where applicants sue collectively EU Member States. See S Douglas-Scott, 'A tale of two Courts: Luxembourg, Strasbourg and the growing European Human rights acquis' (2006) 43(3) *Common Market Law Review* 629 at 638 note 41.

[4] On the duality between the EC and the EU, see JR Canedo Arrillaga and LI Gordillo, 'La nueva Unión Europea: de la doble personalidad a la crisis de personalidad' (2010) 78 *Revista de Derecho Político* 337. This question will be also analysed below.

[5] A similar situation (though focused on the issues of EC law and national constitutional law) is analysed in DR Phelan, *Revolt or Revolution: The Constitutional Boundaries of the European Community* (Sweet & Maxwell, Dublin, 1997).

[6] Case C-145/04 *Spain v UK* [2006] ECR I-7917, Opinion of AG Tizzano, paras 128–31.

[7] For instance, that would be the case for the refusal by a Member State to implement EU sanctions that do not respect fundamental rights to its companies in the area of antitrust law.

5. To return to the EC/EU institutions in place, to preserve primacy and completely restore legal certainty (prerequisite for the existence of any rule of law) there are two ways, both subject to the adoption of a policy decision. So on the one hand, Member States could collectively denounce the ECHR, a solution that seems politically very unlikely. On the other hand, the more affordable solution would be the accession to the European Convention by the Union, which would establish a clear hierarchy between the two legal systems.[8]

2. OUTLOOK: ACCESSION TO THE EUROPEAN CONVENTION ON HUMAN RIGHTS

6. For its part, as previously seen in the *Bosphorus* case, currently the Strasbourg Court exercises indirect control over EC/EU law by means of reviewing national implementation measures, but, in any case, it has given a general presumption of conformity of the Convention to EC/EU law. Even though this attitude enables cohabitation between the two highest instances, for most commentators it looks like a temporary solution, while waiting for the desired accession.[9] For the moment, the Lisbon Treaty assumes the rights included within the ECHR as general principles of law (Article 6.3 TUE-L). The difference from a true accession is clear; in the meantime, the highest interpreter of the ECHR within the EU legal system would be the very same ECJ.

7. ECJ Opinion 2/94, 28 March 1996, concluded that, at that time, there was no legal basis that would enable the Community to accede to the Convention. The doctrine and the political class concluded that it was necessary to have an express provision providing this accession in the Treaties. On the other hand, the Juncker report, drafted after the failure of the 'Constitution for Europe' for the Council of Europe, proposed to accelerate the incorporation of the Union to the Convention, without a comprehensive reform of the Treaties, by an ad hoc protocol annex to the existing Treaties to allow accession to the Union.[10]

8. The persuasive efforts exercised by the European establishment described above, together with the jurisprudential developments of both courts, pushed political leaders to make a decision on accession to the ECHR. From the above, it could be easily deduced that policy makers accepted the accomplished facts.

[8] This was the solution adopted by the Constitutional Treaty, Art I-9(2) and by the Treaty of Lisbon, Art 6 TFEU: 'The Union shall accede to the European Convention for the Protection of Human Rights and Fundamental Freedoms'.

[9] See JP Jacqué, *Droit institutionnel de l'Union Européenne* 4th edn (Dalloz, Paris, 2006) 72–3; JP Jacqué, 'Droit constitutionnel national, Droit communautaire, CEDH, Charte des Nations Unies. L'instabilité des rapports de système entre ordres juridiques' (2007) 60 *Revue Française de Droit Constitutionnel* 3; and LI Gordillo, 'Un paso más hacia la estabilización de las relaciones interordinamentales en Europa: la incorporación de la UE al CEDH' (2011) 38 *Revista Española de Derecho Europeo* 173.

[10] J-C Juncker, 'European Union: A sole ambition for the European Continent', Council of Europe, Parliamentary Assembly (Strasbourg, 11 April 2006) Doc 10897 at 5.

In any case, it is clear that, as the doctrine states, accession to the ECHR will bring coherence to the Community legal system, will increase legal certainty and will strengthen the legitimacy of the Union. In this regard, Article I-9 of the unsuccessful 'Constitution for Europe', a product of the all-time unanimity regarding the issue, anticipated the accession of the Union (specifically endowed with legal personality) to the European Convention. Finally, there was enough legal basis to undertake an act of constitutional significance.[11]

Moreover, the procedure for concluding the agreement on the accession was the regular one for concluding international agreements according to Article III-325, which required that the decision concluding the agreement shall be adopted by qualified majority (paragraph 8) and established the need for approval by the European Parliament (paragraph 6(a)ii). Protocol No 32 annexed to the Constitutional Treaty stated that the accession agreement was to preserve the specific characteristics of the Union and its law, which refers to two issues that the doctrine and some documents had stated earlier: the issue on the participation of the Union in the control organs of the Convention (Court, Committee of Ministers) and the establishment of a system that would (re-)direct any lawsuit to be submitted against the Union and/or Member States and thus prevent the Strasbourg Court from becoming a judge in the distribution of responsibilities between Member States and the European Union.[12]

9. Despite the failure of the ratification process of the 'Constitution for Europe', in this matter, as in many others, the consensus reached in the past was recovered, and the Lisbon Treaty also foresaw the incorporation of the Union to the Convention. Indeed, the new wording of Article 6.2 TEU-L establishes that the Union 'shall accede' to the ECHR and such accession shall not affect the Union's competences as defined in the Treaties. The Treaty of Lisbon restates the agreements and improvements of the Constitution and includes a specific Protocol on accession to the ECHR where, as in Protocol No 32 of the Constitutional Treaty, it establishes a mandate to the negotiators intended to preserve the specific characteristics of the EU and its law. Thus, the agreement on the accession of the Union must involve specific provisions regarding the participation of the Union – which is not a state – in the Convention organs themselves, and also establish the necessary mechanisms to ensure that the actions brought by third states and individual appeals are correctly submitted against Member States, the Union, or both. Furthermore, it must be taken into account that a possible accession shall not affect the powers of the Union or the legal status of the Member States in the Convention system.[13]

[11] See Opinion 2/94 *Accession to the ECHR* [1996] ECR I-1759 para 35, stating that 'such a modification of the system for the protection of human rights . . . would be of constitutional significance'.

[12] F Sudre, 'Article I-9' in L Burgorgue-Larsen, A Levade and F Picod (eds), *Traité établissant une Constitution pour l'Europe : commentaire article par article* (Bruylant, Bruxelles, 2007) 141.

[13] See Protocol relating to Article 6(2) of the Treaty on European Union on the accession of the Union to the European Convention on the Protection of Human Rights and Fundamental Freedoms, Treaty of Lisbon (OJ C 306/155, 17 December 2007).

10. Moreover, the accession process is not exactly a bed of roses. First, there is the possibility of a double institutional veto. In fact, according to Article 218.8 TFEU, the agreement allowing accession has to be unanimously adopted by the Council (in the case of the 'Constitution' only a qualified majority was needed). As in the Constitutional Treaty, a prior approval from the European Parliament (Article 218.6(a)ii TFEU) is still required by a majority of votes issued. From there, the entry into force of the accession agreement is subject to approval by all Member States in accordance with their respective constitutional rules. In this sense, there is a backwards movement regarding the Constitutional Treaty confirming the constitutionality of the accession to the Treaty, which Opinion 2/94 already pointed out.

It is interesting to stress that even the Parliamentary Assembly of the Council of Europe, in Resolution 1610 (2008) adopted at their meeting held on 17 April, talked about the opportunity to introduce such changes in the approval process of the accession decision. The doctrine says that, if just a qualified majority required integrating the Union to the ECHR, it would have meant a transfer of power that would have forced some Member States to hold a referendum to ratify the Lisbon Treaty.[14] This strengthening of the procedural requirements of accession conducted by the governments of the Member States does not go well with the approach of the Heads of State and Governments of the Council of Europe (among which were all the members of the EU) during the summit in Warsaw on May 2005 to accelerate the work necessary for the accession so that it would take place as soon as possible. It is even quite shocking regarding the accession imposition that Article 6.2 TEU-L contains.

11. Furthermore, until very recently accession to the European Convention was limited to the Member States. It was necessary to make some adjustments in the Council of Europe to give access to an international organization as well as participation in its organs.[15] After the ratification of Protocol No 14 by Russia, a new paragraph has been added to Article 59 ECHR, according to which the EU shall accede to the Convention. However, this reform has not made all the technical changes necessary to allow accession.[16] Besides, some doubts will be

[14] See F Benoît-Rohmer, 'Contribution. Accession of the EC/EU to the ECHR', Parliamentary Assembly, Council of Europe (Strasbourg, 18 March 2008) Doc 11533 at 20.

[15] See E Myjer, 'Can the EU join the ECHR? General conditions and practical arrangements' in I Pernice, J Kokott and C Saunders (eds), *The Future of the European Judicial System in a Comparative Perspective* (Nomos, Baden-Baden, 2006) 297 and the report by the Comité directeur pour les Droits de l'Homme, *Étude des questions juridiques et techniques d'une eventuelle adhésion des CE/de l'UE à la Convention européenne des Droits de l'Homme* DG-II(2002)006, [CDDH(2002)010 Addendum 2] (Council of Europe, 28 June 2002).

[16] In fact, this aspect of the amendments is rather symbolic since it only adds a new paragraph to Art 59 stating that 'The European Union may accede to this Convention'. See the *Explanatory report to the Protocol No. 14 to the Convention for the Protection of Human Rights and Fundamental Freedoms, amending the control system of the Convention* CETS No 194 (Council of Europe, 13 May 2004) para 101. The document where the technical changes necessary to implement such accession have been explained better is the Étude des questions juridiques et techniques d'une eventuelle adhésion des CE/de l'UE à la Convention européenne des Droits de l'Homme (2002) (n 15).

cleared only when put into practice. To what extent will the Court of Justice consider the Court of Strasbourg as a specialized jurisdiction or as a hierarchically superior court? What hierarchical rank will the European Convention have concerning Union law?[17] Will the accession agreement prevent the Strasbourg Court from becoming the judge who distributes competences between the Union and the Member States?[18]

After the entry into force of the Treaty of Lisbon, and taking advantage of the willingness to proceed with the accession both in Brussels and Strasbourg, the European establishment started negotiations in July 2010.[19] Among the technical issues that arose during the negotiations was the question of the appointment of an EU judge to the ECtHR, the establishment of a mechanism that avoids that as a consequence of an applicant's choice the ECtHR could become the judge of the division of powers and competences within the EU or the preservation of the monopoly or interpretation of EU law by the ECJ.[20]

12. Another issue worth mentioning concerns the future of the *Bosphorus* case law in the event that accession of the Union to the Convention takes finally place. We should remember that such a resolution granted a presumption of conformity with the Convention in favour of EC/EU legal acts. We should wonder if this would still be the position of the Strasbourg Court if the Union acceded to the Convention.

As already mentioned, the basis of the presumption established by the Court considers the fact that states are free to take part in international organizations and that such participation is even possible when that organization keeps a standard of protection of human rights equivalent to that offered by the

[17] Note that the ECJ has given reassurance that the Treaties should prevail over any other international agreements carried out by the EC/EU. See Opinion 1/75 *Opinion given pursuant to Article 228 (1) of the EEC Treaty (Local Costs)* [1975] ECR 1355.

[18] See F Sudre (2007) (n 12).

[19] See the press release *European Commission and Council of Europe kick off joint talks on EU's accession to the Convention on Human Rights*, Press release – 545(2010), 7 July 2010 and the Steering Committee on Human Rights *Report, 70th meeting* (15–18 June 2010, CCDH(2010)010. Previously, the Council awarded the Commission a mandate to carry out the negotiations with the Council of Europe. The text of the mandate (with the Council's instructions to the Commission) is still a restricted document. See T Lock, 'EU accession to the ECHR: Implications for judicial review in Strasbourg' (2010) 35(6) *European Law Review* 777 at 778, note 11. See also the *Discussion document of the Court of Justice of the European Union on certain aspects of the accession of the European Union to the European Convention for the Protection of Human Rights and Fundamental Freedoms* (ECJ, 5 May 2010) and the *Joint communication from the Presidents of the European Court of Human Rights and the Court of Justice of the European Union*, further to the meeting between the two courts in January 2011 (ECJ, 24 January 2011), both available at <http://curia.europa.eu/jcms/jcms/P_64268/>.

[20] For a deeper analysis of these issues, see LI Gordillo, 'Un paso más hacia la estabilización de las relaciones interordinamentales en Europa: la incorporación de la UE al CEDH' (2011) 38 *Revista Española de Derecho Europeo* 173, the report issued from the 6th meeting of the Steering Committee on Human Rights (*6e* réunion du Groupe informel sur l'adhésion de l'UE à la Convention (CDDH-UE) 15–18 mars 2011, Strasbourg) and the papers delivered by Jacqué and de Schutter before the Constitutional Affairs Committee of the European Parliament (Strasbourg/Brussels, 18 March 2010).

Strasbourg system. The result of this approach is that EU Member States are not accountable to the ECtHR for the actions carried out in pursuance of acts of the Union in those fields where all their area of responsibility has been transferred to it, and, at the same time, the Union let their potential responsibility go due to the presumption of conformity. However, such a presumption, which has been widely criticized even by some of the trial court judges in their dissenting opinions, would be very difficult to sustain in the case of the accession of the European Union.

What arguments would justify that legal acts from an institution which has not yet acceded to the Convention enjoy a presumption of conformity with the ECHR when measures implemented by other partners (such as Norway), all of them states, do not enjoy the same status? Let us not forget that, as long as the issues regarding what we have known until very recently as the second pillar are very unlikely to be fully controlled by the ECJ, the system could suffer from a lack of conformity with the Strasbourg standard.

13. From a substantial point of view the accession of the EU to the ECtHR will entail, at least, three important consequences for the interordinal relations between EU law and the ECtHR. First of all, the scope of the judicial review taking into account fundamental rights will be wider. Although Article 275 TFEU excludes the judicial review of CFSC, except for specific measures against individuals, the ECHR, on the other hand, would be fully applicable. Secondly, the ECtHR will extend its control to the whole EU law as well as to the national acts implementing EU law. Member States would only be responsible if EU law awarded them a margin of appreciation when implementing supranational law, but its responsibility would only be within these limits. It would be up to the ECJ to declare the existence and scope of this margin of appreciation. Finally, accession will entail the abandonment of the *Bosphorus* case law. As has been said, this jurisprudence established a sort of double standard, so the EC/EU did not need to accomplish exactly the same level of protection as the contracting parties of the ECHR. With a formal accession, this situation (a sort of deference to the EU) should disappear in order not to create differences between members of the Convention.

III

The United Nations Charter, European Union Law and the European Convention on Human Rights

PRELIMINARY CONSIDERATIONS

1. In September 2008, the European Court of Justice issued the most important case to date regarding the interordinal relations between the EU and international law. The case that will remain in the annals of international case law under the name of *Kadi* referred to a lawsuit filed by a citizen against an implementing measure of a decision by the UNSC declaring that he was involved in terrorist activities and therefore requested the freezing of their funds. This ruling has been hailed by human rights activists, has comforted those worried by the responsibility of the Security Council and has been extensively analysed by some of the doctrine writers, especially those who support the strengthening of the legal autonomy of the EU's legal order.

2. By adopting a dualistic approach to the international legal order and towards the relationship between EC/EU law and international law, the European Court of Justice would be close enough to the position adopted by the United States Supreme Court in its recent law case.

The term 'dualism', as well as the term 'monism', is used by the doctrine in different ways.[1] In this case, it has been used to refer to a concept that understands national and international law as distinct and different legal systems in which national law would establish the conditions under which international law would

[1] On the concept of 'dualism', see H Triepel, *Völkerrecht und Landesrecht* (JCB Mohr (Paul Siebeck), Tübingen, 1907); H Triepel. 'Les rapports entre le Droit interne et le Droit international' (1925) 1(1923) *Recueil des Cours de l'Académie de Droit International de La Haye* 73; and D Anzilotti, *Corso di diritto internazionale* (Athenaeum, Roma, 1912). On the 'monist theory', see JL Kunz, 'La primauté du droit des gens' (1925) VI *Revue de Droit International et de Legislation Comparé* 556. However, the 'must read' work in this field is H Kelsen, 'Les rapports de système entre le droit interne et le droit international public' (1926) 14(1926) *Recueil des Cours de l'Académie de Droit International de La Haye* 227, especially at 263–320. See also A Verdross, 'Le fondement du droit international' (1927) 16 *Recueil des Cours de l'Académie de Droit International de La Haye* 247. For a summary on the dualism, monism and their respective limitations, see B Mirkine-Guetzévitch, 'Droit international et droit constitutionnel' (1931) 38(1931-IV) *Recueil des Cours de l'Académie de Droit International de La Haye* 307; and B Mirkine-Guetzévitch, *Derecho constitucional internacional* (L Legaz y Lecambra, tr) (Revista de Derecho Privado, Madrid, 1936) at 29–61.

enter into the national scope and the legal consequences of such action.[2] However, a more specialized and technical concept uses the term 'dualistic' to make reference to that legal order in which international law would require a transposition (or domestic implementing act) in order to be part of the national legal order.[3]

Thus, in the *Medellín* case, the US Supreme Court declared the separation of international law regarding national constitutional law and the lack of competence from the national courts to establish the relationship between the two of them.[4] This case did not make reference to the Security Council resolutions, but to a decision of the International Court of Justice which the Supreme Court did not consider executable in the US without a prior act of Congress.[5]

These two resolutions – *Kadi* and *Medellín* – refer, of course, to different kinds of international obligations. On the one hand, the *Medellín* case concerns an international decision that recognizes certain procedural rights to the defendants. In *Kadi*, on the other hand, it was a decision of an international organization that had ignored due process rights of the person concerned and therefore the reasons to reject the implementation of that resolution were different. However, the decision in *Kadi* goes further: while in *Medellín* an act of the Congress could cause international opinion to have legal effects in the national legal order, in *Kadi*, the ECJ made clear that the EU Council could not implement the Security Council resolution as it was, since, by doing so, it would violate certain fundamental rights that the ECJ has recognized as general principles of law. Nevertheless, the Council has already shown its rejection towards that kind of resolution in the cases brought before the CFI and its practice in a case already analysed, *OMPI*, consisted in passing another Decision with the same content but adding that it had complied with the requirements established by the opinion that overturned its earlier act.[6]

[2] This is the concept of the German public law legal scholarship. See Case *Görgülü*, 2 BvR 1481/04 (German Constitutional Court, 14 October 2004) para 34 on the legal effects of the ECHR system within German law. For a comment, see M Hartwig, 'Much Ado About Human Rights: The Federal Constitutional Court Confronts the European Court of Human Rights' (2005) 6(5) *German Law Journal* 869; and F Hoffmeister, 'Germany: Status of European Convention on Human Rights in domestic law' (2006) 4(4) *International Journal of Constitutional Law* 722.

[3] See JG Starke, 'Monism and Dualism in the Theory of International Law' (1936) XVII *British Yearbook of International Law* 66; J Turley, 'Dualistic Values in the Age of International Legisprudence' (1993) 44 *Hastings Law Journal* 185; CA Bradley and JL Goldsmith, 'Federal Courts and the Incorporation of International Law' (1998) 111 *Harvard Law Review* 2260; G de Búrca and O Gerstenberg, 'The Denationalization of Constitutional Law' (2005) 47(1) *Harvard International Law Journal* 243 at 244–54.

[4] Case *Medellín v Texas*, 552 US 491 (2008). For a comment of this case, see ME Wojcik, 'United States Supreme Court: Medellin v Texas: Introductory Note' (2008) 3 *International Legal Materials* 281; and ME McGuinness, 'Medellín v Texas – US Supreme Court opinion on state courts' obligation to respect an International Court of Justice judgment and on the president's power to enforce it' (2008) 102(3) *American Journal of International Law* 622.

[5] A similar case was *Sanchez Llamas v Oregon* 548 US 331 (2006). See S Koh, '"Respectful Consideration" After Sanchez-Llamas v Oregon: Why the Supreme Court Owes More to the International Court of Justice' (2007) 93 *Cornell Law Review* 243; and A Aleinikoff, 'Transnational Spaces: Norms and Legitimacy' (2008) 33(2) *Yale Journal of International Law* 479.

[6] See the *OMPI-PMOI* saga, Case T-228/02 *Organisation des Modjahedines du peuple d'Iran v Council (OMPI)* [2006] ECR II-4665, Case T-256/07 *People's Mojahedin Organization of Iran v*

Despite the differences between the two cases (*Kadi* and *Medellín*), it is the similarity between the approach that *Kadi* makes to the core question on the relationship between international law and the national legal order and the one carried out by the US Supreme Court in *Medellín*, and the fact that by doing so, the ECJ moves away from its previous jurisprudence, that constitutes one of its most important features.[7] Thus, despite the praise that the decision in the *Kadi* case has received from various authorities, the core of the decision would go against the image that the EU projects of itself as an organization that respects the international legal order, the exceptionalism practised by the US, and their political ambitions to emerge on the international scene as a 'normative power' committed to multilateralism and friendly with international law.[8]

Moreover, this judgment is also quite interesting, since it establishes the relationship of EC/EU law regarding international law and decides at certain points of its ruling to use a 'chauvinist' language and a self-sufficient spirit, and was dictated not by a court of a powerful state but by an organization that comes from international law.[9]

3. The *Kadi* case is one of the many recent examples of situations that relate to actions initiated and/or under the auspices of the United Nations Organization, which caused damages to the individuals concerned who, in turn, have brought their cases before major European courts. The legal, common and, of course, human dilemmas that these situations demonstrate are examples of more general and deeper problems such as the increasing complexity and political and legal density of international legality, as well as the multiplicity of public authorities that have an effect on the welfare of human beings in different aspects.

So on the one hand, *Kadi* would be just another example of an increasingly common phenomenon, a specific conflict between rules that belong to different legal orders (or sub-legal orders) in the international legal scene. But then again, it would be a very particular and specific case as it refers to some of the most important and fundamental rules of international law, specifically Article 103

Council (PMOI I) [2008] ECR II-3019 and Case T-284/08 *People's Mojahedin Organization of Iran v Council (PMOI II)* [2008] ECR II-3487.

[7] The same concept is entrusted in the legal reasoning of Case *Munaf v Geren*, 553 US 674 (2008). See SI Vladeck, 'United States Supreme Court: Munaf v Geren – Introductory Note' (2008) 5 *International Legal Materials* 705 and HG Cohen, 'Munaf v Geren – US Supreme Court opinion on extraterritorial application of the writ of habeas corpus' (2008) 102(4) *American Journal of International Law* 854.

[8] The concept of 'normative power' applied to the EU would refer to the current practice for the EU to extend certain basic identity principles such as human rights, democracy, the rule of law and protection of the environment. See I Manners, 'Normative Power Europe: A Contradiction in Terms?' (2002) 40(2) *Journal of Common Market Studies* 235 and I Manners, 'The normative ethics of the European Union' (2008) 84(1) *International Affairs* 45.

[9] I basically follow Professor de Búrca's understanding of the relationship between EU and international law. See her outstanding paper G de Búrca, 'The European Court of Justice and the International Legal Order after Kadi' (2009) 01/09 *Jean Monnet Working Papers* April 2009 and the subsequent article published as G de Búrca, 'The European Court of Justice and the International Legal Order After Kadi' (2010) 51 *Harvard International Law Journal* 1.

of the UN Charter, Chapter VII of the Charter on the Security Council resolutions and the peremptory or *ius cogens* rules.[10]

Article 103 of the UN Charter provides that:

> In the event of a conflict between the obligations of the Members of the United Nations under the present Charter and their obligations under any other international agreement, their obligations under the present Charter shall prevail.

Under Chapter VII of the Charter, the UNSC 'shall determine the existence of any threat to the peace, breach of the peace, or act of aggression and shall make recommendations, or decide what measures shall be taken . . . to maintain or restore international peace and security', including measures that do not involve the use of force such as economic sanctions.[11]

In the *Kadi* case there was a direct conflict between the law of the United Nations, established to ensure international security and with their aspirations to general applicability and universal normative force and the EU dispositions, whose nature lies between an international organization and a political entity of a constitutional nature, all within the context of a lawsuit in which the person concerned put forward a violation of their fundamental rights as a result of the interaction of these two legal orders.

Some might consider this case basically as a reaction to growing concerns on the regime of the so-called 'smart sanctions' of the UN Security Council and on the strong influence exerted by the United States on the listing and de-listing process within this body. Further analysis, however, suggests that it goes beyond the scope of those sanctions. The language used and the type of argument of this awaited opinion of the ECJ would suggest that the High Court of Luxembourg wanted to send a clear message about how he perceives the relationship between EC/EU law and international law and on the autonomy of the EU legal order.[12]

4. This third part will analyse the interordinal relations and interactions established in the law of the United Nations Organization, particularly regarding the sanctions approved by the UNS and EU law, so a new chapter will be devoted to the Security Council, its forms of action and the difficulties requiring responsibility to international organizations. Then, particular attention will be paid to

[10] On this concept, see A Orakhelashvili, *Peremptory Norms in International Law* (Oxford University Press, Oxford, 2006); and L Hannikainen, *Peremptory norms (jus cogens) in international law: historical development, criteria, present status* (Lakimiesliiton Kustannus, Helsinki, 1988). For a critical study, see A d'Amato, 'It's a Bird, It's a Plane, It's Jus Cogens' (1990) 6(1) *Connecticut Journal of International Law* 1.

[11] See Arts 39 to 51 of the UN Charter, especially Arts 39 and 41. On the other hand, Art 24 states: 'Por su parte, el artículo 25 estipula: "The Members of the United Nations agree to accept and carry out the decisions of the Security Council in accordance with the present Charter".' The Charter of the United Nations was signed on 26 June 1945, in San Francisco, at the conclusion of the United Nations Conference on International Organization, and came into force on 24 October 1945.

[12] G de Búrca (2009) (n 9) at 5.

the resolutions of the Security Council and the ECHR, mainly the possibility that the UN shall be bound by the ECHR in the light of the recent case law of the ECtHR on the matter. The last chapter will discuss the different possibilities for the articulation of the relationship between supranational legal systems, especially from the point of view of the EU order, taking into account the consequences derived from the choice of either approach.

7

The UN Security Council as a 'Global Law Enforcement Power'

1. RESPONSIBILITY OF INTERNATIONAL ORGANIZATIONS

1. There is an increasing number of international organizations, from those based on functional or regional philosophies created to face specific transnational needs or to achieve specific objectives, up to those large multilateral organizations created to address more general or fundamental common tasks (political economic, cultural, military, technical, etc), each with many variations.[1] In fact, given the diversity of profiles, the internationalist doctrine has faced difficulties in building a general theory or even a specific definition of the international organization.[2]

Thus, a classical definition of international organization would be that of a voluntary association of subjects of international law, established by international acts and illustrated in relations between parties by rules of international law, specified in a stable entity, endowed with organs and institutions, through which it carries out common goals of the fellow members through the development of special functions and the exercise of powers conferred for that purpose.[3]

Similarly, in the traditional sense, the term international organization means a union of several subjects of international law, established on an equal basis, equipped with their own rules and with entities and institutions, which aims to achieve, according to its constitutive act, a goal shared by its members.[4]

Thus, in principle, international organizations would not be higher political institutions, but organizations based on the principle of cooperation and respect for the sovereignty of the state. However, scholars have theorized about a new kind of organization – the integration or supranational organization – which

[1] JA Pastor Ridruejo, *Curso de Derecho internacional Público y Organizaciones internacionales* 13th edn (Tecnos, Madrid, 2010) 657–67.

[2] See, in extenso, HG Schermers, 'Les organisations internationales' in M Bedjaoui (ed), *Droit international. Bilan et perspectives* (Pedone, Paris, 1991) 69.

[3] A Piero Sereni, *Diritto internazionale* (Giuffrè, Milano, 1960) 804.

[4] R Monaco, *Lezioni di organizzazione internazionale i diritto delle istituzioni internazionali* (Giappichelli, Torino, 1965) 12.

would detract from the above theories.[5] Such organizations would go beyond the imperative of cooperation of any international organization to 'capture the alienation of certain sovereign powers in pursuit of a larger unit within which the boundaries become more flexible and permeable'.[6] In contrast to the characteristics of the organizations for cooperation, the integration ones would be distinguished by the transfer of sovereign powers by Member States, initially in specific subjects, in their favour, which are exercised through legitimated bodies entitled to act directly on citizens.[7] Moreover, these organizations would reduce or limit the sovereignty of their Member States, as they were intended to create an entity with their own powers to achieve common goals, usually economic or political ones.[8]

2. Together with these developments at the institutional level, there is a large amount of literature and great doctrinal interest towards what has been called 'legal pluralism' but also the well-known 'international fragmentation' (or 'fragmentation of international law'), both derived from the increased density of the international legal environment.[9] Thus, whereas before the debate was focused on local and infra-state orders that coexisted in the same spatial area

[5] Colliard and Dubois, for instance, establish the distinction between cooperation and integration international organizations depending on the intensity of the cooperation. In order to measure it, they take into account facts such as the extent of the powers transferred, the more or less binding powers and the degree of independence vis-à-vis the Member States. See C Colliard and L Dubois, *Institutions internationales* (Dalloz, Paris, 1995) 171.

[6] E Pérez Vera, 'Reflexiones sobre los procesos de integración regional' (1977) 4(3) *Revista de Instituciones Europeas* 669 at 670.

[7] P Braillard and MR Djalili, *Les relations internationales* (PUF, Paris, 1992) 113.

[8] The literature is huge. For a general overview, see HG Schermers and NM Blokker, *International Institutional Law: Unity Within Diversity* 4th edn (Martinus Nijhoff, The Hague, 2004) 21–39. A political analysis may be found at N Mariscal Berástegui, *Teorías políticas de la integración europea* (Tecnos, Madrid, 2003).

[9] Among the numerous works on legal pluralism, see PS Berman, 'Global Legal Pluralism' (2007) 80(6) *Southern California Review* 1155; PS Berman, 'A pluralist approach to international law' (2007) 32(2) *The Yale Journal of International Law* 301; N Krisch, 'The Pluralism of Global Administrative Law' (2006) 17(1) *European Journal of International Law* 247; N Walker, 'The Idea of Constitutional Pluralism' (2002) 65(3) *The Modern Law Review* 317; D Halberstam, 'Constitutionalism and Pluralism in Marbury and Van Gend' in MP Maduro and L Azoulai (eds), *The Past and Future of EU Law: The Classics of EU Law Revisited on the 50th Anniversary of the Rome Treaty* (Hart Publishing, Oxford, 2010) 26; BZ Tamanaha, 'Understanding Legal Pluralism: Past to Present, Local to Global' (2008) 30 *Sydney Law Review* 375. On the 'international fragmentation', see M Koskenniemi and P Leino, 'Fragmentation of International Law? Postmodern Anxieties' (2002) 15(3) *Leiden Journal of International Law* 553, G Teubner and A Fischer-Lescano, 'Regime-Collisions: the Vain Search for Legal Unity in the Fragmentation of Global Law' (2004) 25(4) *Michigan Journal of International Law* 999; I Buffard and others, *International Law between universalism and fragmentation: Festschrift in honour of Gerhard Hafner* (Martinus Nijhoff, Leiden, 2008). The International Law Commission (ILC) set up a Working Group in 2002 under the name of 'Fragmentation of International Law: Difficulties arising from the Diversification and Expansion of International Law' to study this issue. The Group delivered a report to the UN General Assembly in 2006. See the report *Conclusions of the Work of the Study Group on the Fragmentation of International Law: Difficulties arising from the Diversification and Expansion of International Law* (U.N. Doc.A/CN.4/L.702, 18 July 2006, ref. GE.06-62863 [E] 200706). For more information, see the site of this Working Group at <http://untreaty.un.org/ilc/guide/1_9.htm>.

of national character, now the interest is directed towards the state, to the global legal orders that coexist in the world with the existing state and infra-state systems.[10]

Given the lack of a homogeneous international legal order to define responsibilities and assign jurisdictions, the relationship between these different types of entities with each other, as well as the relationship between the states, international organizations and other international actors, is complicated and some of the problems generated are still without a final solution. There are significant overlaps in the jurisdiction that these different subjects are trying to exercise, and their powers and responsibilities are generally neither defined nor concretized in such a way as to avoid conflicts with others or either how such conflicts should be addressed.[11]

This can be understood in two different ways. On the one hand, the interest in these overlaps and other complications derived from the increasing fragmentation of international legal order would be the formalist view, derived from the Kelsenian desire to establish a global legal order perfectly hierarchized as a result of the transposition of the governing principles of the state legal order to the international level.[12] Another point of view, however, would argue that in the situation described above there is an interest that goes beyond the mere desire of establishing some specific orderly principles or the defence of the hegemony expectations of international legal liberalism.[13]

Many of these international organizations have been enlarging their powers from their very inception, increasingly exerting the functions of a government and increasing their autonomy and authority and, at the same time, usually showing two complementary trends. First, they tend to focus and strengthen their executive and administrative powers. In order to do so, they grant powers to the national executive bodies purporting to represent the state interests in the international forum and the new bureaucratic structures that constitute the secretariats and institutional frameworks of these organizations.[14] Secondly, these organizations tend not to provide mechanisms or require responsibility to control their activity, although they are features that do appear at the state level. Thus, this model of international governance is particularly distant from the citizen and generates

[10] M Sousa Santos, *Toward a New Legal Common Sense* 2nd edn (Cambridge University Press, Cambridge, 2003) 92.

[11] For a summary of the mechanisms of international law in general and the Vienna Convention on the Law of Treaties in particular in order to solve these issues, see the report *Conclusions of the Work of the Study Group on the Fragmentation of International Law* [2006] (n 9) para 14.

[12] See the classic, H Kelsen, *Principles of International Law* (Rinehart, New York, 1952) 401–50. See also D Kennedy, 'One, Two, Three, Many Legal Orders: Legal Pluralism and the Cosmopolitan Dream' (2007) 31(3) *New York University Review of Law and Social Change* 641.

[13] G de Búrca, 'The European Court of Justice and the International Legal Order after Kadi' (2009) 01/09 *Jean Monnet Working Papers* April 2009 at 8.

[14] KL Scheppele, 'The Migration of Anti-Constitutional Ideas: The Post-9/11 Globalization of Public Law and the International State of Emergency' in S Choudhry (ed), *The Migration of Constitutional Ideas* (Oxford University Press, Oxford, 2006) 347 and KL Scheppele, 'The International State of Emergency: Challenges to Constitutionalism after September 11' (2009) Paper 49 *Digital Commons UM Law* April 2009.

important problems regarding responsibility in the increasingly complex transnational scenario.[15]

3. When undue harm is caused by policies or acts of international organizations, generally there is no adequate way of ensuring that individuals concerned can have redress. The draft articles of the International Law Commission on 'Responsibility of International Organizations' are based on the work of the Commission devoted to state responsibility (*Draft Articles on State Responsibility*), one detail of which is that the recipient of the redress would be the state and not the individual.[16]

Even when national courts are at first receptive to hearing actions against international organizations, there are usually rules on immunity and other procedural barriers that limit, sometimes even invalidate, the ability of the courts to legally hold responsible these organizations for their actions.[17]

4. A possible explanation for the lack of legal mechanisms for demanding responsibility of international organizations would consist in suggesting that, in practice, such a mechanism is not necessary for individuals, given the structure and nature of international organizations. In other words, the logic of the

[15] The literature is huge. Among others, see PB Stephan, 'Accountability and International Lawmaking: Rules, Rents and Legitimacy' (1997) 17(2) *Northwestern Journal of International Law and Business* 681; RO Keohane, 'Global Governance and Democratic Accountability' in D Held and M Koenig-Archibugi (eds), *Taming Globalization: Frontiers of Governance* (Polity Press, London, 2003) 130; RO Keohane and JS Nye, 'Redefining Accountability for Global Governance' in M Kahler and DA Lake (eds), *Governance in a Global Economy: Political Authority in Transition* (Princeton University Press, Princeton, 2003) 386; RW Grant and RO Keohane, 'Accountability and Abuses of Power in World Politics' (2005) 99(1) *American Political Science Review* 29; TN Hale, 'Transparency, Accountability and Global Governance' (2008) 14(1) *Global Governance* 73; AM Slaughter, 'Globalization, Accountability, and the Future of Administrative Law: The Accountability of Government Networks' (2001) 8(2) *Indiana Journal of Global Legal Studies* 347.

[16] The work of the ILC entitled Draft Articles on Responsibility of States for Internationally Wrongful Acts was endorsed by the UN General Assembly in its 85 Session (Resolution, A/RES/56/83, 12 December 2001). See J Crawford, *The International Law Commission's Articles on State Responsibility: Introduction, Text and Commentaries* (Cambridge University Press, Cambridge, 2002) 1–60.

[17] A Reinisch, *International Organizations Before National Courts* (Cambridge University Press, Cambridge, 2000) 317–90; A Reinisch, 'Developing Human Rights and Humanitarian Law Accountability of the Security Council for the Imposition of Economic Sanctions' (2001) 95(4) *American Journal of International Law* 851 at 866–7, where the author disserts on the possibility of bringing the UN before national Courts. See also K Wellens, *Remedies Against International Organizations* (Cambridge University Press, Cambridge, 2002); K Wellens, 'Fragmentation of International Law and Establishing an Accountability Regime for International Organizations: The Role of the Judiciary in Closing the Gap' (2004) 25(4) *Michigan Journal of International Law* 1159; and M Singer, 'Jurisdictional Immunity of International Organizations: Human Rights and Functional Necessity Concerns' (1995) 36(1) *Virginia Journal of International Law* 53. On the issues of the accountability of international organizations vis-à-vis UN sanctions, see M Bothe, 'Security Council's Targeted Sanctions against Presumed Terrorists: The Need to Comply with Human Rights Standards' (2008) 6(3) *Journal of International Criminal Justice* 541; and J Reich, 'Due Process and Sanctions Targeted Against Individuals Pursuant to Resolution 1267 (1999)' (2008) 33(2) *Yale Journal of International Law* 505 available at SSRN: http://ssrn.com/abstract=1268163.

institutional design of most of them assumes that such organizations cannot affect individuals directly. As long as these organizations are established between states, they will not exercise their powers directly on individuals, either from a legal point of view or from an institutional one.[18] Instead, there will be agents or intermediaries, that is, different levels of national and sub-national authority, who would implement and apply the rules or policies established at the intergovernmental level and would work at these national and subnational levels where they would exercise the mechanisms requiring responsibility. From this point of view, it should cause no surprise that the UN, or even the EU, when it acts as an intergovernmental organization under the former second pillar (Common Foreign and Security Policy), had to answer for damages caused to individuals for acts derived from their organs. While states could respond against each other within international organizations, and executive bodies that represent the states within these organizations had to render accounts before their governments and parliaments, or demand accountability to the civil servants incardinated in the bureaucratic structures of the organization before other institutions of the said organization, it would not be necessary to create a legal framework stating the direct liability of those organizations vis-à-vis those affected by their actions.[19]

However, this argument would simplify the issue and would be too tenuous. This traditional characterization of the sphere of influence and the impact of international organizations would ignore how they have evolved and the fact that many of these organizations have been steadily acquiring relevant administrative powers, and even passing important regulations. Even if the eventual impact of their actions were conditioned through a chain of acts and intermediate measures, it would be unusual for such intermediate acts to be appealable because it is considered that the national authorities would, if necessary, be required to implement the rules of the supranational organization. The court that dealt with the case would be reluctant to control such measures directly fearing, among other things, that it might cause the state concerned to incur international responsibility. Thus, the ultimate responsibility derived from the act of the organization would fall to the organization itself.

Thus, to introduce the case that I shall discuss below, an example of this would be that led by the UNSC. This UN body exercises some legislative functions under Chapter VII of the Charter when, for example, it adopts resolutions which require states to freeze funds and assets of individuals suspected or

[18] An important exception would be the European Communities, whose founding treaties guaranteed them certain powers that in fact implied direct effect of their decisions upon individuals. Those treaties also established a limited accountability before the ECJ. A few ECtHR judges still doubt that the accountability mechanisms within the EU could be enough to fulfil the ECHR standards. Case *Bosphorus Hava Yolları Turizm ve Ticaret Anonim irketi v Ireland* App No 45036/98 (ECtHR, 30 June 2005, 2005-VI), Joint concurrent Opinion of Judges Rozakis, Tulkens, Traja, Botoucharova, Zagrebelsky and Garlicki.

[19] See A Reinisch (2000) (n 17) 233–51.

involved in terrorist activities.[20] Likewise, another example of the exercise of legislative powers would be the establishment of the Counter-Terrorism and Sanctions Committees.[21] Those decisions, obviously, require the appropriate implementation by states or by regional organizations such as, for instance, the EU, in order to effectively (beyond issues of reputation or public image) restrict the property rights of individuals. Notwithstanding the foregoing, it would be inaccurate to conclude that the primary responsibility for damage caused as a result of the freezing of funds of persons wrongly included in a list lies with the state that has just enforced a binding resolution of the Security Council before the same UNSC that mistakenly included the name of a person on a list of terrorists whose assets had to be seized. In the event of concluding that the state is legally liable for the damage, Article 103 of the UN Charter would provide the state concerned a defence mechanism based on the top hierarchy of the United Nations legal order, subordinating the protection of the individual and the possible liability of the state concerned by the damage caused to the obligations derived from the Charter that would be superior and would invalidate any other commitment of the state.

Another example of direct impact, and even potentially harmful measures, authorized by the United Nations refers to acts of territorial administration of the said organization. Like the evolution of the regulatory powers of the Security Council, lately the emergence of other government duties by the said UN body has been observed, that is, the administration of territories in specific situations of conflict or subsequent to it.[22] This type of territorial administration of the United Nations has been seen in East Timor, Bosnia and Kosovo and it is clear that the power of management and governance entails the possibility of specific damage. Even in this situation the potential for damage caused directly by the United Nations is much more evident; the question regarding accountability mechanisms and the legal responsibility for such regional authorities has no easy answer.[23]

[20] M Fremuth and J Griebel, 'On the Security Council as a Legislator: A Blessing or a Curse for the International Community?' (2007) 76(4) *Nordic Journal of International Law* 339; LM Hinojosa Martínez, 'The Legislative Role of the Security Council in its fight against Terrorism: Legal, Political and Practical Limits' (2008) 57(2) *International and Comparative Law Quarterly* 333 and JL Cohen, 'A Global State of Emergency or the Further Constitutionalization of International Law: A Pluralist Approach' (2008) 15(4) *Constellations* 456.

[21] An updated list with all the UN Security Council Sanctions Committees is available at <http://www.un.org/Docs/sc/unsc_structure.html>.

[22] The administration of territories under the auspices of the UN is not new. See the UN Charter, Chapter XII entitled 'International Trusteeship System'. However, it should be pointed out that under this system, former colonies in transition to newly independent states were generally administered on a provisional basis by the ancient colonial power, and not by the UN itself, as has been recently the case. See R Wide, *International Territorial Administration: How trusteeship and the civilizing mission never went away* (Oxford University Press, Oxford, 2008) 47–98.

[23] See Opinion 280/2004 on *Human Rights in Kosovo: Possible establishment of review mechanisms* (Venice Commission, 11 October 2004, CDL-AD(2004)033) and the UN Secretary General *Report on the interpretation of the Resolution 1244* (12 July 2009, S/1999/779, 99-20410 (E) 120799) where it was established that when exercising its powers, the UN Administration in Kosovo had to respect internationally recognized human rights.

Moreover, the actions taken to establish internal mechanisms of responsibility have not produced the expected results.[24]

5. A second possible explanation for the lack of legal mechanisms to demand responsibility to the international organizations will focus on arguing that the direct responsibility of these organizations in favour of individuals would undermine the functioning of the organization. This thesis is based not on the argument that organizations are unable to cause such damage to warrant the establishment of responsibility, but on the argument that insists that this liability would interfere with the functioning of the organization.[25] This obviously functional explanation varies depending on the objectives and purposes of the organization, but in general it means that international cooperation is in itself a value that must be promoted and protected and that the collateral damage resulting from such cooperation should not lead to the imposition of the legal obligation to take responsibility for damages. As we shall recall, this is the thesis that supports the argument of the ECtHR. According to the ECtHR:

> The Court has also long recognised the growing importance of international cooperation and of the consequent need to secure the proper functioning of international organisations.[26]

Otherwise, this argument goes on, there is a risk that the organization itself will be inhibited too, which would prevent the achievement of certain policies, afraid of being held responsible and having to face the consequences. This type of functional argument is the basis for most of the rules of immunity.[27] But this reasoning to exclude responsibility is overstated. While it is clear that the routine imposition of legal responsibility for any damage caused is a deterrent for an organization that seeks objectives that necessarily involve risks for the interests and rights of others, a rule prescribing absolute immunity or freedom from any kind of liability would entail the opposite risk, that is, it would guarantee the impunity against possible arbitrariness and abuse by the immune organization.

Furthermore, their arguments supporting the idea that the mere existence of legal liability would make the functioning of the organization difficult seem exaggerated. So while it seems reasonable to suggest that the imposition of an

[24] B Knoll, 'Too Little, Too Late: The Human Rights Advisory Panel in Kosovo' (2007) 7(5) *European Human Rights Law Review* 534. See also the Venice Commission Opinion 280/2004 (n 23) and the report *Consideration of reports submitted by states parties under Art 40 of the Covenant. Concluding observations of the Human Rights Committee* (14 August 2006, CCPR/C/UNK/CO/1, GE.06-43691 (E) 080906).

[25] G de Búrca (2009) (n 13) at 12.

[26] Case *Bosphorus* [2005] (n 18). On the International cooperation and the cooperation in the Framework of the UN, see Case *Behrami v France* App No 71412/01 and Case *Saramati v France, Germany and Norway* App No 78166/01 (ECtHR, 2 May 2007, unpublished) paras 145–52.

[27] A Reinisch (2000) (n 17) 233–9, JF Lalive, 'L'immunité de juridiction des Etats et des organisations internationales' (1954) 84(1953-III) *Recueil des cours de l'Académie de Droit International de la Haye* 210; and F Morgenstern, *Legal Problems of International Organizations* (Cambridge University Press, Cambridge, 1986).

unreasonably high standard of responsibility would undermine the regular work of an international organization, there is a wide range of possibilities between this option and the simple rule of immunity.[28] So, there would not be compelling reasons to exclude a set of carefully established principles on responsibility from being set somewhere between the risk of defensive practices derived from too high a standard of responsibility and the risk of abuse arising from impunity.

Finally, another similar argument, though of a more institutional and functional nature, to exclude national or regional authorities from requiring the legal responsibility of international organizations supports the idea that this would mean an abuse of the legal powers of those authorities.[29]

6. Moreover, several characterizations of the international legal environment also emphasize the existence of overlapping, multiple connections and intersections of different levels of authority. This would give the impression that the main problem would be how to manage a variety of jurisdictional claims that may arise, how to deal with potential conflict of authority and how to foster dialogue and mutual courtesy going from a responsibility scenario to a more appropriate one through deference or complementary principles.[30]

However, the problem may also involve the proliferation of international organizations and institutions. Rather than multiplying the potential bodies and mechanisms of accountability and jurisdictional control, in fact they leave a gap in responsibility where the international organization does not provide any kind of control mechanism, and national public or intermediate authorities consider that they are not responsible for those and that they have no power to question the responsibility of another national or international authority.[31]

7. In fact, these dilemmas relating to accountability and international responsibility emerged in the *Kadi/Al Barakaat* case before the ECJ and the *Behrami/Saramati* case before the ECtHR, where the complex nature of the international organizations concerned sharpened the dilemma regarding responsibility

[28] RO Keohane and JS Nye, 'Redefining Accountability for Global Governance' in M Kahler and DA Lake (eds), *Governance in a Global Economy: Political Authority in Transition* (Princeton University Press, Princeton, 2003) 386; and RW Grant and RO Keohane, 'Accountability and Abuses of Power in World Politics' (2005) 99(1) *American Politcal Science Review* 29.

[29] A similar argument was brought up by the UK in the *Kadi* case and it was subsequently dismissed by the Advocate General. See Joined Cases C-402/05 P and C-415/05 P *Kadi* and *Al Barakaat International Foundation v Council* [2008] ECR I-6351, Opinion of AG Poiares Maduro. See below.

[30] PS Berman, 'Global Legal Pluralism' (2007) 80(6) *Southern California Review* 1155. In a nutshell, the idea would be to recover the *comitas gentium* already theorized by the classic Dutch School. See EM Meijers, 'L'histoire des principes fondamentaux du droit international privé à partir du Moyen Age, spécialement dans l'Europe occidentale' (1970) 49(1934-III) *Recueil des cours de l'Académie de Droit International de la Haye* 543.

[31] American scholarship has also produced its own new-fashioned concept, the 'jurisdictional redundancy'. See R Cover, 'The Uses of Jurisdictional Redundancy: Interests, Ideology and Innovation' (1981) 22(4) *William & Mary Law Review* 639.

brought about in the aforementioned European regional courts.[32] As for the UNSC, it has not only expanded its role and powers beyond what was originally envisaged in the Charter to include a type of legislative measure used in the context of the fight against or significant government powers exercised in Kosovo and elsewhere, but their anomalous and complex composition, the deep ideological divisions and political struggles that have burdened their operation have also weakened its legitimacy as the main world government body responsible for peace and security.[33] Nevertheless, if the UN in general and its Security Council in particular suffer from a legitimacy deficit, the state of the EU, although substantially better, is not idyllic. Thus, while from one point of view the EU is the most successful contemporary example as far as regional integration is concerned, having built a strong economic union from the six original members to today's 27 (with candidates waiting to join it), from another point of view it is internally divided and externally it constitutes a weak actor on the international scene whose ultimate failure consists in not being able to have a single Constitution (but a set of rules enshrined in different international instruments, such as the Charter, TEU-L, TFEU, EURATOM Treaty), which has blasted the long-standing desire to improve their political and democratic legitimacy.[34]

2. DIRECT, SELECTIVE OR 'SMART' SANCTIONS

8. In accordance with Article 24.1 of the UN Charter, the Security Council has as its primary responsibility maintaining international peace and security.[35] Thus, after determining, as provided in Article 39, that a situation constitutes a threat or breach of the peace, the Security Council may call upon states to adopt provisional measures (Article 40), measures not involving the use of force, which are usually called sanctions (Article 41) and, finally, military actions against the perpetrators of the threat or breach (Article 42).[36] The Security Council rarely

[32] Joined Cases C-402/05 P and C-415/05 P *Kadi* and *Al Barakaat* [2008] (n 29) and Cases *Behrami* and *Saramati* [2007] (n 26). This case law will be analysed below.

[33] For a critical analysis on the accountability of the UN Security Council, see M Koskenniemi, 'The Police in the Temple Order, Justice and the UN: A Dialectical View' (1995) 6(1) *European Journal of International Law* 325.

[34] The literature is huge on this issue. See E Odvar and JE Fossum, 'Europe in Search of Legitimacy: Strategies of Legitimation Assessed' (2004) 25 *International Political Science Review* 435; L Hansen and M Williams, 'The Myths of Europe: Legitimacy, Community and the "Crisis" of the EU' (2002) 37(2) *Journal of Common Market Studies* 233; and M Horeth, 'No way out for the Beast? The Unsolved Legitimacy Problem of European Governance' (1999) 6(2) *Journal of European Public Policy* 249.

[35] For a general work, see G Abi-Saab, 'The Concept of Sanction in International Law' in V Gowlland-Debbas (ed), *United Nations Sanctions and International Law* (Kluwer Law International, The Hague, 2001) 29.

[36] See I Österdahl, *Threat to the Peace: The Interpretation by the Security Council of Article 39 of the UN Charter* (Iustus, Uppsala, 1998) and JA Frowein and N Krisch, 'Introduction to Chapter VII, Articles 39–43' in B Simma (ed), *The Charter of the United Nations: A Commentary* 2nd edn (Oxford University Press, Oxford, 2002) 701.

explicitly establishes what item constitutes the legal basis of their resolutions, instead it just states that is acting 'according to Chapter VII of the Charter'.[37]

The types of measure not involving the use of armed force varies a lot, but it is possible to distinguish between economic and trade embargoes aimed directly and specifically against a particular entity and a range of less direct measures. There is no generally accepted definition of these 'targeted' or 'selective' (*ciblées*, in French) sanctions imposed by the Security Council, however, it is obvious that the concept includes the freezing of financial deposits, the suspension of loans and financial aid, denial and restriction of access to foreign financial markets, trade embargoes on weapons and luxury goods, flight bans and the refusal of international displacements, visas and studies abroad.[38] These 'targeted' or 'selective' sanctions are also known as 'smart', drawing a grim parallel with the 'smart bombs' that are aimed at specific targets.[39]

Not all the Security Council sanctions regimes involve punishing particular individuals. The main sanction systems that do punish particular individuals are those of Angola, Liberia, Sierra Leone and Afghanistan. Thus, when sanctions are aimed against individuals, they are executed through so-called 'blacklists'. The Security Council adopts a resolution, and entrusts to a sanctions committee, consisting of representatives of all members of the Security Council itself, the task of finalizing the list of people affected by the sanctions regime.[40]

9. The issue of 'smart' sanctions has attracted the interest of the doctrine. There is a lot of literature on the subject, specifically on the role of the UN Secretary-General in the coordination, monitoring and control of the effectiveness of the measures, but there is no unanimous opinion on the effectiveness of

[37] See the Security Council Resolution 1160 (1998) on the letters from the United Kingdom (S/1998/223) and the United States (S/1998/272). For an analysis of the Security Council powers in the fight against terrorism, see C Denis, *Le pouvoir normatif du Conseil de Sécurité des Nations Unies: portée et limites* (Bruylant, Bruxelles, 2004) 133–61; M Hilaire, *United Nations Law and the Security Council* (Ashgate, Surrey, 2005) 253–90; and JM Farrall, *United Nations Sanctions and the Rule of Law* (University Press, Cambridge, 2007) 79–181.

[38] A few examples are included in *Report of the Secretary-General To The Security Council On The Protection of Civilians in Armed Conflict* (8 September 1999, S/1999/957) para 54 and *The Adverse Consequences of Economic Sanctions on the Enjoyment of Human Rights. Review of Further Developments in Fields with Which the Subcommission Has Been or May Be Concerned* (UN Economic and Social Council, 21 June 2000, E/CN.4/Sub.2/2000/33) (known as the Bossuyt Report) paras 11–17. See also V Gowlland-Debbas, 'UN Sanctions and International Law: An Overview' in V Gowlland-Debbas (ed), *United Nations Sanctions and International Law* (Kluwer Law International, The Hague, 2001) 1; and L Picchio Forlati and LA Sicilianos, *Economic Sanctions in International Law/Les sanctions* économiques *en droit International* (Martinus Nijhoff Publishers, Leiden, 2004).

[39] D Cortright and GA López, *The Sanctions Decade: Assessing UN Strategies in the 1990s* in (Lynne Rienner, Boulder, 2000) 240.

[40] An updated list of the UN Security Council Sanctions Committees is available at <http://www.un.org/sc/committees/>.

these sanctions.[41] Moreover, the 'smart' sanctions have been studied and discussed further at numerous diplomatic and academic forums, and in conferences sponsored by non-governmental organizations, including the Interlaken, Bonn–Berlin and Stockholm processes, where the sanctions implementation systems were discussed and, in particular, improvement proposals.[42] General economic sanctions affect the lives of a greater number of people than the targeted sanctions which, nevertheless, have a clear target. However, the question whether certain legal guarantees, including those on human rights, should or should not apply to the 'smart' sanctions of the UN has only been raised quite recently.[43]

Moreover, the Security Council is not the only body applying sanction regimes. In addition to the sanctioning activity of the EU already seen (see above, the *PMOI-OMPI* cases), the United States, for example, has set up different unilateral sanction regimes and, among others, has been using the 'blacklists' techniques even before the Security Council.[44] These unilateral sanctions regimes (United States) and regional (EU) can be problematic from the point of view of the legal guarantees and, thus, would share some characteristics with the United Nations system itself. Anyway, as we shall see more specifically in the case of the EU, the sanction regulations have a number of distinctive features derived from the attribution of competences between the EC/EU and the states, the structure (formerly based on pillars and now with different decision-making processes) of the Union that prepare its implementation within the UN

[41] See M Doxey, *International Sanctions in Contemporary Perspective* 2nd edn (St Martin's Press, New York, 1996); P Wallensteen and C Staibano, *International Sanctions: Between Words and Wars in the Global System* (Routledge/Frank Cass, London, 2005); RA Pape, 'Why Economic Sanctions Do Not Work' (1997) 22(2) *International Security* 90; RA Pape, 'Why Economic Sanctions Still Do Not Work' (1998) 23(1) *International Security* 66; Elliott, KA, 'The Sanctions Glass: Half Full or Completely Empty?' (1998) 23(1) *International Security* 50; DA Baldwin, 'The Sanctions Debate and the Logic of Choice' (1999) 24(3) *International Security* 80; and D Cortright and GA López, *Sanctions and the Search for Security: Challenges to UN Action* (Lynne Rienner, London, 2002).

[42] All these forums have produced their respective final reports. See T Biersteker, *Targeted Financial Sanctions. A Manual for Design and Implementation. Contribution from the Interlaken Process* (Brown University, Providence, 2001); M Brzoska, *Design and Implementation of Arms Embargoes and Travel and Aviation Related Sanctions: Results of the 'Bonn–Berlin Process'* (International Center for Conversion, Bonn, 2001); and P Wallensteen and C Staibano, *Making targeted sanctions effective: guidelines for the implementation of UN policy options* (Elanders Gotab, Stockholm, 2003).

[43] See, for instance, Professor Cameron's report to the Swedish Government at the time of the Stockholm Process, *Report to the Swedish Foreign Office on Legal Safeguards and Targeted Sanctions* (October 2002) at <http://www.smartsanctions.se/Litterature.htm>. The main conclusions are also included in I Cameron, 'UN Targeted Sanctions, Legal Safeguards, and the ECHR' (2003) 72 *Nordic Journal of International Law* 159. See also Cameron's report *The European Convention on Human Rights, Due Process and United Nations Security Council Counter-Terrorism Sanctions* [2006] (Council of Europe, Strasbourg, 6 February 2006) available at <http://www.coe.int/T/E/Legal_Affairs/Legal_co-operation/Public_international_law>.

[44] See, inter alia, PL Fitzgerald, 'If Property Rights Were Treated Like Human Rights, They Could Never Get away with This: Blacklisting and Due Process in US Economic Sanctions Programs' (1999) 51(1) *Hastings Law Journal* 73; and PL Fitzgerald, 'Managing "Smart Sanctions" Against Terrorism Wisely' (2002) 36(4) *New England Law Review* 957.

sanctions and, even, compatibility problems with the regime of the World Trade Organization.[45]

3. THE LIMITS OF THE SECURITY COUNCIL'S POWER

10. The Security Council began to use targeted sanctions with the sanctions regime established against the organization *União Nacional para a Independência Total de Angola*, UNITA (National Union for the Total Independence of Angola) in 1997 and 1998.[46] This regime has already finished, but at that time 157 people were subject to seizure of funds and displacement bans.[47] The last blacklist regarding Sierra Leone has about 30 people who are banned from travelling.[48] As for Liberia, travel bans affect 47 people.[49] The sanctions regime regarding Sierra Leone and Liberia has led to complaints and discussions in the corresponding sanctions committees regarding the reasons for adding names to the blacklist.[50] However, since the purpose of these sanctions was to punish government and rebel leaders, the discussions focused on how to identify for certain the government/rebel circles and what relations or links with those circles could justify inclusion in the listings.

11. The above cases illustrate the problems posed by the sanctioning process in relation to the rights of those concerned. The information regarding inclusion of those sanctioned in the blacklists comes from governments through their intelligence services and other sources whose identity is rarely aired. The

[45] This issue will be analysed below. For a general overview, see B Brandtner and A Rosas, 'Human Rights and the External Relations of the European Community: An Analysis of Doctrine and Practice' (1998) 9(3) *European Journal of International Law* 468; I Canor, '"Can two walk together, except they be agreed?" The relationship between international law and European law: The incorporation of United Nations sanctions against Yugoslavia into European Community law through the perspective of the European Court of Justice' (1998) 35(1) *Common Market Law Review* 137; T Andersson, I Cameron and K Nordback, 'EU blacklisting: the renaissance of imperial power, but on a global scale' (2003) 14(2) *European Business Law Review* 111.

[46] UN Security Council Resolution 1127 (1997) established some movement and travel restrictions to UNITA leaders and their relatives (28 August 1997, S/RES/1127). UN Security Council Resolutions 1173 (1998) (12 June 2998, S/RES/1173) and 1176 (1998) (24 June 1998, S/RES/1176) established financial sanctions to UNIITA members.

[47] See the UN Security Council Press release SC/7162 (4 October 2001) at <http://www.un.org/News/Press/docs/2001/sc7162.doc.htm>. Through the Resolution 1448 (2002) (9 December 2002, S/RES/1448) the UN Security Council decided to cease the effects of all these sanctions (the dissolution of this sanctions committee was effective on 12 December).

[48] See the Press release SC/8192 (20 September 2004) available at <http://www.un.org/News/Press/docs/2004/sc8192.doc.htm>.

[49] The travel ban list established by Resolution 1521 (2003) on the situation in Liberia, para 4, was updated for the last time on 16 December 2009. The list is available at <http://www.un.org/sc/committees/1521/1521_list.htm>.

[50] See the answer of the UN Sanctions Committee on Liberia to the questions asked by Gambia and Lebanon (S/AC.39/2002/Note. 8) and the Yearly Report of the Sanctions Committee on Sierra Leone (S/2002/470) at 35, both quoted by I Cameron, 'UN Targeted Sanctions, Legal Safeguards, and the ECHR' (2003) 72 *Nordic Journal of International Law* 159 at 163 note 17.

process of blacklisting is quite obscure; otherwise, secrets and information flows, perfectly controlled by governments, have a bilateral rather than multilateral nature. That is, no evidence is presented publicly, but only in rare cases when a state is particularly interested or pushes hard to receive it. Individuals concerned are in a particularly vulnerable situation because they are subject to targeted sanctions, but in order to face them they have to resort to their respective governments or to their home countries so that they intercede on their behalf before the Security Council.[51]

In this context, there is a clear tension between these sanctions, or the process by which they are established, and the national and international protection standards of fundamental rights. Thus, it would be possible to argue that the Security Council would be limited by the provisions of the UN Charter in particular and by international law in general.

3.1. The Limitations According to the Charter

12. The most important source of obligations of the Security Council derives from the UN Charter itself. The preamble of the Charter describes the special commitment of their signatories to 'reaffirm faith in fundamental human rights, in the dignity and value of the human being' and to 'create conditions under which justice can be maintained'. These general obligations recognized by the signatories are then summarized over the articles of the Charter through purposes, principles and rules governing both the UN itself and the conduct to be observed by their members.

Article 1 states that one of the purposes of the UN is to '*promote* and *encourage* respect for human rights and for fundamental freedoms for all without distinction as to race, sex, language, or religion'. Thus, under this provision, also when it comes to 'take effective collective measures for the prevention and removal of threats to the peace' actions shall be taken 'in conformity with the principles of justice and international law'. Article 2 then provides seven general principles to guide the operation of the organization and their members, including to fulfil 'in good faith the obligations assumed by them in accordance with the present Charter' and to provide the UN 'every assistance in any action it takes in accordance with the present Charter'.[52]

[51] I Cameron, 'UN Targeted Sanctions, Legal Safeguards, and the ECHR' (2003) 72 *Nordic Journal of International Law* 159 at 165–6.

[52] NJ Schrijver, 'Interpreting the Principles and Purposes of the United Nations' in PJ Van Krieken (ed), *Refugee Law in Context. The Exclusion Clause* (TMC Asser Institute, The Hague, 1999) 237; R Wolfrum, 'Article 1' in B Simma (ed), *The Charter of the United Nations: A Commentary* 2nd edn (Oxford University Press, Oxford, 2002) 40; A Randelzhofer, 'Article 2' in B Simma (ed), *The Charter of the United Nations: A Commentary* 2nd edn (Oxford University Press, Oxford, 2002) 64; and JP Müller and R Kolb, 'Article 2.2' in B Simma (ed), *The Charter of the United Nations: A Commentary* 2nd edn (Oxford University Press, Oxford, 2002) 91.

These principles and purposes of Articles 1 and 2 materialize again later in other specific obligations of the members and the Organization itself. Thus, for example, Article 55 specifically states that the UN:

> Shall promote . . . universal respect for, and observance of, human rights and fundamental freedoms for all without distinction as to race, sex, language, or religion.

On the other hand, Article 56 establishes the corresponding obligation according to which:

> All Members pledge themselves to take joint and separate action in co-operation with the Organization for the achievement of the purposes set forth in Article 55.

In addition, the Security Council, in particular, is subject to the same general restrictions established by the Charter. Thus, in accordance with Article 24.2, 'the Security Council shall act in accordance with the Purposes and Principles of the United Nations'. On the other hand, Article 25 establishes the following:

> The Members of the United Nations agree to accept and carry out the decisions of the Security Council *in accordance with* the present Charter.[53]

13. In any case, the Security Council has a considerable margin of *manoeuvre* when acting under Chapter VII of the Charter, which can lead to a compromise of certain rights or interests generally protected by international law. Thus, when intervening to stop hostilities that have already begun, the Security Council does not need to take into consideration the general principles of international law relating to respect for the legal positions of the contentious parties.[54] Likewise, according to Article 2.7 of the Charter, the ban on the United Nations from 'tak[ing] part in matters essentially within the domestic jurisdiction of States', which, also, is an established general principle of international law, 'is not contrary to the application of coercive measures' that the Security Council shall establish under Chapter VII. Furthermore, when acting in accordance with the purposes and principles of the Charter, the Security Council has considerable discretion because the purposes and principles tend to 'establish guidelines rather than specific limits on the actions of the Council'.[55]

Despite the wide leeway that the Security Council has, both the letter and spirit of the Charter indicate an obligation on the part of the UN in general and the Security Council in particular to hold its action to the constitutional limits

[53] Italics added. There are disputes on the interpretation of this final expression of Art 25. For some, it could indicate that Member States are only bound by Security Council decisions that effectively respect substantive and procedural rules of the Charter. Others just think that this article expressly states the obligation to respect, implement and fulfil the decisions of the Security Council. See J Delbrück, 'Article 24' in B Simma (ed), *The Charter of the United Nations: A Commentary* 2nd edn (Oxford University Press, Oxford, 2002) 455.

[54] R Wolfrum, 'Article 1' in B Simma (ed), *The Charter of the United Nations: A Commentary* 2nd edn (University Press, Oxford, 2002) 40 at 40–43 adds that this situation allows the Security Council to act within a wider margin to manoeuvre, especially during the first moments of a conflict.

[55] JA Frowein and N Krisch (2002) (n 36) at 710.

established by the Charter itself, which would also include the general respect for human rights recognized by international law.[56] Therefore, the provisions of the Charter would determine the obligation of the Member States to cooperate with the UN just as long as the organization adjusts its performance to the limits imposed by its foundational text, including the respect for human rights. The principles and purposes of the Charter, including adherence to human rights, are general and consequently written in a not very specific language. But this feature only reflects the situation of the state of development of human rights at the international level at the time of adoption of the Charter. This legal instrument, designed as a starting point towards the establishment and strengthening of international legal regimes, including the protection of human rights, shall be interpreted in the light of the developments produced regarding the protection of human rights.[57]

14. Arguments in favour of this thesis can be found in the international doctrine and case law interpreting the legal concepts contained in the Charter, and the principles and purposes, in the light of modern international law of human rights, most of whose legal instruments have been sponsored by the UN itself. Thus, there are some who support the binding effect of the United Nations, besides the binding nature of the Declaration of Human Rights, to the International Covenant on Civil and Political Rights and the International Covenant on Economic, Social and Cultural rights since, although the UN is not a member of these treaties through ratification, these instruments represent the subsequent realization of the vision that human rights were in the original purposes of the Charter.[58] On the other hand, the International Court of Justice has established that racial discrimination constitutes 'a flagrant violation of the purposes and principles of the Charter'.[59] The Court also concluded that:

> Wrongfully to deprive human beings of their freedom and to subject them to physical constraint in conditions of hardship is in itself manifestly incompatible with the principles of the Charter of the United Nations, as well as with the fundamental principles enunciated in the Universal Declaration of Human Rights.[60]

[56] On the constitutional nature of the Charter, see E de Wet, *The Chapter VII Powers of the United Nations Security Council* (Hart, Oxford, 2004) 92–116.

[57] D Halberstam and E Stein, 'The United Nations, the European Union, and the King of Sweden: Economic sanctions and individual rights in a plural world order' (2009) 46(1) *Common Market Law Review* 13 at 18.

[58] See E de Wet, 'Human Rights Limitations to Economic Enforcement Measures Under Article 41 of the United Nations Charter and the Iraqi Sanctions Regime' (2001) 14 *Leiden Journal of International Law* 277 at 284.

[59] Case *Legal Consequences for States of the Continued Presence of South Africa in Namibia (South West Africa) notwithstanding Security Council Resolution 276 (1970)* Advisory Opinion (ICJ, 21 June 1971, *Reports* 16-66) para 131.

[60] Case *United States Diplomatic and Consular Staff in Tehran (United States of America v Iran) Judgment* (ICJ, 24 May 1980, *Reports* 3–47) para 91.

This would mean that even if there were any truth in the idea that according to the Charter 'peace is above justice', the measures taken under Chapter VII cannot legally ignore the concerns and interests reflected in the basic legal instruments regarding human rights and humanitarian law.[61] The rules on human rights and humanitarian law, rather than establishing precise limits to the powers exercised by the Security Council under Chapter VII, would constitute the guidelines in the exercise of such powers. That is, a total ignorance of those rules, given they are part of the purposes of the Organization, according to Article 1.3, would imply a direct violation of the Charter. In any case, the Security Council has to keep the balance in each case between human rights and humanitarian law on the one hand, and the fundamental objective of maintaining peace.[62] Moreover, the international rules on human rights recognize this obligation to maintain the equilibrium between peace and human rights.[63]

15. International courts seem to confirm this point of view. The International Court of Justice recognized 30 years ago that the Security Council was bound by the purposes and principles established in Articles 1 and 2 of the Charter.[64] More recently, the Appeals Chamber of the ICC for the former Yugoslavia concluded that even when acting under Chapter VII, the Security Council exercises considerable discretion.

> But this does not mean that its powers are unlimited. The Security Council is an organ of an international organization, established by a treaty which serves as a constitutional framework for that organization. The Security Council is thus subjected to certain constitutional limitations, however broad its powers under the constitution may be. Those powers cannot, in any case, go beyond the limits of the jurisdiction of the Organization at large, not to mention other specific limitations or those which may derive from the internal division of power within the Organization. In any case, neither the text nor the spirit of the Charter conceives of the Security Council as *legibus solutus* (unbound by law).[65]

[61] Some scholars argue that the UN Charter establishes a system where peace is above justice or even international law. For a critical comment, see N Elaraby, 'Some Reflections on The Role of the Security Council and the Prohibition of the Use of Force in International Relations: Article 2(4) Revisited in Light of Recent Developments' in Frowein, JA *et al* (ed), *Verhandeln für den Frieden / Negotiating for peace. Liber amicorum Tono Eitel* (Springer, Berlin, 2003) 41 at 62–7.

[62] See JA Frowein and N Krisch, 'Introduction to Chapter VII, Articles 39-43' in B Simma (ed), *The Charter of the United Nations: A Commentary* 2nd edn (Oxford University Press, Oxford, 2002) 701 at 711 and E de Wet, *The Chapter VII Powers of the United Nations Security Council* (Hart, Oxford, 2004) 133–77.

[63] For instance, states of emergency and the principles that must inform state action in those cases are established in Art 4 International Covenant on Civil and Political Rights (UN Doc. A/6316 1966). On this question, see J Oraá Oraá, *Human Rights in States of Emergency in International Law* (Clarendon, Oxford, 1992).

[64] See the Case *Legal Consequences for States of the Continued Presence of South Africa in Namibia (. . .)* [1971] (n 59) para 110. Moreover, in para 115 the ICJ states that UN Security Council Resolutions were in accordance with the principles and purposes of the Charter and were 'consequently binding on all States Members of the United Nations, which are thus under obligation to accept and carry them out'.

[65] Case IT-94-1 *Prosecutor v Tadić* (ICTY, 2 October 1995) para 28, available at <http://www.icty.org/x/cases/tadic/acdec/en/51002.htm>.

This limitation derived from the United Nations Charter was already recognized by the International Court of Justice:

> The political character of an organ cannot release it from the observance of the treaty provisions established by the Charter when they constitute limitations on its powers or criteria for its judgment.[66]

The aforementioned suggests that even when acting under Chapter VII, the Security Council should adopt only those measures that are appropriate to end a threat or to suppress a breach of international security.[67] Moreover, human rights 'are now part of the concept of international public order'.[68]

3.2. The Limits Imposed by International Law

16. It can be understood that the Security Council is bound by international law in two different ways. On the one hand, as a body of the United Nations, with personality recognized in the international legal order, the Security Council is obliged to respect international law.[69] To be exact, in principle, the UN would not be bound to respect international treaties on human rights since it is not a signatory of those instruments. However, the Organization itself is bound by customary international law and by general principles of international law, at least insofar as the Charter does not provide otherwise.[70] Hence, the UN Security Council shall be exempted from respecting the general prohibition to the use of force and non-intervention apart from not being subject to general principles of international law in their intervention to stop the hostilities that may have begun. However, from the standpoint of customary international law of human rights, the Charter seems only to reaffirm the importance of such rights in such operations and the legitimacy of UN actions. Therefore, while many rules derived from international customary law and general principles of international law have traditionally been applied only to the actions of states,

[66] Case *Conditions of Admission of a State to Membership in the United Nations (Article 4 of the Charter)* Advisory Opinion (ICJ, 28 May 1948, *Reports* 57–119) at 64.

[67] A Reinisch (2001) (n 17) at 858–9.

[68] I Brownlie, 'The decisions of political organs of the United Nations and the rule of law' in RSJ Macdonald (ed), *Essays in honour of Wang Tieya* (Martinus Nijhoff, Dordrecht, 1994) 91 at 93.

[69] On the legal personality of the UN, see Case *Reparation for Injuries Suffered in the Service of the United Nations* Advisory Opinion (ICJ, 11 April 1949, *Reports* 174–220) 179. This Decision is also known as the '*Bernadotte* case'. See P Gautier, 'The Reparation for Injuries Case Revisited: The Personality of the European Union' (2000) 4 *Max Planck Yearbook of United Nations Law* 331 at 337–41. On the binding effect of international law over the Security Council, see the Case *Interpretation of the Agreement of 25 March 1951 between the WHO and Egypt* Advisory Opinion (ICJ, 20 December 1980, *Reports* 73–98) at 89–90. A Bianchi, 'Assessing the Effectiveness of the UN Security Council's Anti-terrorism Measures: The Quest for Legitimacy and Cohesion' (2006) 17(5) *European Journal of International Law* 881 at 886.

[70] HG Schermers and NM Blokker, *International Institutional Law: Unity Within Diversity* 4th edn (Martinus Nijhoff, The Hague, 2004) 834 and 994.

the UN has increasingly limited those rules, as their actions are getting closer to the schemes of actions of the state powers.[71] The specific configuration of international standards on human rights should take into account the specific context in which the UN activity takes place, but the general principle about the applicability of these rules in the UN as an international actor vested with legal personality remains.[72]

17. Secondly, as analysed above in the case of the EC/EU, states cannot simply avoid the application of international law on human rights through the creation of an organization to which they commission activities and tasks that would violate human rights if they were directly carried out by Member States. Again, the implementation of standards should take into account the specific international context in which they shall be applied. But members cannot avoid the standards of human rights by transferring the commission of the abuses to the UN. From this statement, which some writers have dubbed the 'principle of non-circumvention', two consequences would result.[73]

18. Thus, on one hand, the principle of non-circumvention would mean that states remain strictly liable for the abuses they incur regarding the human rights of an international organization that they govern and control or to which they could have transferred powers to act on its behalf.[74] The draft articles on responsibility of international organizations prepared by the International Law Commission establish the following provision:

> **Article 60.** Responsibility of a member State seeking to avoid compliance
>
> 1. A State member of an international organization incurs international responsibility if it seeks to avoid complying with one of its own international obligations by taking advantage of the fact that the organization has competence in relation to the subject matter of that obligation, thereby prompting the organization to commit an act that, if committed by the State, would have constituted a breach of the obligation.

[71] On the application of the International Humanitarian Law to the UN Territorial Administrations, see SR Ratner, 'Foreign Occupation and International Territorial Administration: The Challenges of Convergence' (2005) 16(4) *European Journal of International Law* 695.

[72] See JE Álvarez, *International Organizations as Law-makers* (Oxford University Press, Oxford, 2005) 180, where the author argues that certain human rights provisions should be modified in order to fully bind the UN. See Case IT-94-1 *Prosecutor v Tadić* [1995] (n 65) paras 43–48, where it is argued that the traditional system of separation of powers within the national arena cannot be applied to the international one as such, but in any case, human rights principle should be preserved.

[73] D Halberstam and E Stein (2009) (n 57) at 21. The authors theorize on the 'principle of non-circumvention'.

[74] See the *Report of the International Law Commission*, Sixty-first session (4 May to 5 June and 6 July to 7 August 2009, UN Doc A/64/10 2009) at 19–39, which includes the *Draft articles on International organizations' responsibility*. See also the previous reports of the ILC, *Report of the International Law Commission*, Fifty-eighth session (1 May to 9 June and 3 July to 11 August 2006, UN Doc A/61/10 2006); and the Special Report of Mr Roberto Ago: R Ago, 'Second report on State responsibility. The origin of international responsibility' (1970) II *Yearbook of the International Law Commission* 177.

2. Paragraph 1 applies whether or not the act in question is internationally wrongful for the international organization.[75]

This draft article refers to cases in which a State avoids one of their international obligations when using the different legal capacity of the international organization it belongs to. Even when the State no longer controls the decisions of the international organization it may, however, incur international responsibility by virtue of having voluntarily agreed to be bound by the decisions of the international organization in question through an internal act of law.[76]

As seen above, the ECtHR case law provides some examples of states that may be responsible when conferring powers to an international organization and have failed to ensure compliance with the obligations under the Convention. In the *Waite and Kennedy v Germany* and *Beer and Regan v Germany* cases, already mentioned, the ECtHR considered the question of whether the right of access to the jurisdiction had been unduly undermined by a state which granted immunity to the European Space Agency, of which it was a member, in relation to labour demands. Although the Strasbourg Court concluded, in this case, that the essence of the right to access to a court of the applicant under the Convention had not been undermined, the ECtHR noted that it was not possible when transferring powers to international organizations for contracting states to be exempted from all responsibility under the Convention in the area of activity subject to the attribution.[77]

Furthermore, if, in addition, the state directly takes part in the implementation of decisions and policies of the international organization concerned and, therefore, takes part in the enforcement of acts that would have been illegal if adopted by the state individually, it shall be possible to find new arguments in favour of the state's responsibility.[78] The draft articles on international responsibility of international organizations provides in this regard:

Article 13. Aid or assistance in the commission of an internationally wrongful act

An international organization which aids or assists a State or another international organization in the commission of an internationally wrongful act by the State or the latter organization is internationally responsible for doing so if:

a. That organization does so with knowledge of the circumstances of the internationally wrongful act; and

[75] See the *Report of the International Law Commission*, Sixty-first session (2009) (n 74), p 38. The comment on this provision is at 167–70.

[76] See *Matthews v UK* App No 24833/94 (ECtHR 18 February 1999, 1999-I 251) para 32, when the ECtHR dismisses the argument of the UK following which acts adopted by the EC (to which the UK had transferred certain powers) could not be attributed to the UK. See D Sarooshi, 'International Organizations and Their Exercise of Sovereign Powers' (Oxford University Press, Oxford, 2007) 101–7.

[77] See Case *Beer and Regan v Germany* App No 28934/95 (ECtHR 18 February 1999, unpublished) para 57; and Case *Waite, Kennedy v Germany* App No 26083/94 (ECtHR 18 February 1999, 1999-I 393) para 67. A similar approach was advocated long before in A di Blasé, 'Sulla responsabilità internazionale per attività dell'ONU' (1974) 57 *Rivista di Diritto Internazionale* 250 at 275–6.

[78] See the *Report of the International Law Commission*, Sixty-first session (2009) (n 74) 23. The comment on this provision is at 84–6.

b. The act would be internationally wrongful if committed by that organization.

In the *Bosphorus* case, the ECtHR, echoing an earlier doctrine of the Commission (*M & Co v Germany*, see above) said that a state could not be freed from the obligations under the ECHR by transferring functions to an international organization because, otherwise, the guarantees provided in the Convention could be limited or excluded at the discretion of the states.[79] As seen above, the ECtHR finally resolved that the respondent state had not incurred responsibility because the relevant fundamental rights were protected within the EC/EU in a way that can be considered at least equivalent to that required by the Convention, but for the first time it fully analysed an act emanating from an international organization whose validity was saved by setting the controversial equal protection doctrine, concluding that if the controversial act had been approved and executed directly by Ireland without any EC/EU connection, the state concerned might have been condemned by the ECtHR.[80]

The development of this principle of state responsibility should occupy an important place in the implementation of Security Council decisions to freeze financial assets of individuals or in the international administration of territories.[81]

19. Moreover, the 'principle of non-circumvention' would also mean that international organizations can, sometimes, consider themselves bound by the obligations to which their Member States are subject. The main argument in favour of this thesis would come from the already analysed theory of functional succession.[82] That is, the theory of functional succession essentially means that when an international organization exercises the powers that previously belonged to a state or group of states in the context of a specific international legal regime, then the said international organization succeeds that state (or group of states) not only in the rights but also in the obligations derived from that particular international legal regime.[83]

Apart from its application to the EC/EU in order to justify its links to certain commercial and customs agreements, this theory had its interest in the context

[79] Case *Bosphorus* [2005] (n 18) para 154.

[80] See Case *Bosphorus* [2005] (n 18) para 155 and the Joint concurrent Opinion of Judges Rozakis, Tulkens, Traja, Botoucharova, Zagrebelsky and Garlicki para 4.

[81] This is the opinion of D Halberstam and E Stein (2009) (n 57) at 22, but they point out the negative precedent of the Case *Behrami* [2007] (n 26).

[82] See P Pescatore, 'La Cour de Justice des Communautés Européennes et la Convention Européenne des Droits de l'Homme' in GJ Wiarda, F Matscher and H Petzold (eds), *Protecting human rights, the European dimension: studies in honour of / Protection des droits de l'homme, la dimension européenne. Mélanges en l'honneur de Gérard J Wiarda* 2nd edn (C Heymann, Köln, 1990) 441.

[83] G Thallinger. 'Sense and sensibility of the human rights obligations of the United Nations Security Council' (2007) 67(4) *Zeitschrift für ausländisches* öffentliches *Recht und Völkerrecht* 1015 at 1026 and A Reinisch (2001) (n 17) at 858.

of the succession of the League of Nations by the United Nations Organization.[84] A partial and limited application of this principle of succession can also be found in the context of the UN regional authorities.[85]

3.3. In Search of Legitimacy: The Gradual Assimilation of Constitutional Principles

20. Another possible way to limit the power of the Security Council and determine its action regarding respect for human rights depends largely on a development that has barely begun. The thesis is that in the extent to which the powers of the United Nations increase – and especially in the sense of assuming powers hitherto exercised by the states – the Organization will assimilate certain principles concerning the protection of human rights and how to exercise the power taken from the constitutional traditions of their Member States and other international instruments that do not directly bind it in order to strengthen its own legitimacy and that of its acts.[86] That is, the UN would 'freely' choose the path of self-limitation of its power through principles of a constitutional nature to – just as other international organizations (for example, the EC/EU) did at the time – legitimize their power and, incidentally, provide arguments in favour of the validity of their actions in the jurisdictions that will eventually control their actions.[87]

But it should be noted that this process of assimilation of constitutional principles is not an obstacle to the implementation of international human rights standards to the United Nations by virtue of another kind of legal relationship (see above). That is, the binding nature of international law of human rights is not rejected. However, as an additional and independent source of fundamental rights, the gradual assimilation of constitutional principles would differ from the traditional sources of international law. The legal nature of this process would, therefore, be different from the accession to international treaties, the obligation of customary international law or the general principles of international law. It would be a different case from the one resulting from the implementation of international succession or the delegation of powers subject to compliance with predetermined principles. On the other hand, the process described here would involve the incorporation of fundamental rights protection

[84] Case *International Status of South West Africa* Advisory Opinion (ICJ, 11 July 1950, *Reports* 128–219) at 132–38, where it was established that the UN kept certain rights and competences once attributed to the League of Nations in the context of the South-West Africa Mandate (17 December 1920) by virtue of succession.

[85] C Stahn, *The Law and Practice of International Territorial Administration Versailles to Iraq and Beyond* (Cambridge University Press, Cambridge, 2008) 492–6.

[86] D Halberstam and E Stein (2009) (n 57) at 24. Authors call this concept 'Constitutional absorption'.

[87] On the unilateral obligation to respect certain principles by the UN Territorial Administrations, see C Stahn (2008) (n 85) 481–4.

principles derived from international legal instruments on the subject and, following the expression already used in EU circles, the common constitutional traditions of their Member States. Thus, these principles, once assumed by the Organization, would have a different development in the context of the United Nations. That is, the UN, after carrying out a comparative analysis of the constitutional systems of its Member States and the international treaties on the subject, would draw out some principles that will subsequently be assumed by the bodies integrating the UN institutional structure and would constitute an independent source to legitimate their acts.

21. The recent practice of United Nations might suggest that, indeed, the assimilation of certain principles is under way. This source is, however, limited to international law. For example, in response to the request of the UN Security Council that the UN Interim Administration Mission in Kosovo (UNMIK) protect human rights in Kosovo – Resolution 1244 (1999) – the Secretary-General stated in his report:

> In assuming its responsibilities, UNMIK will be guided by internationally recognized standards of human rights as the basis for the exercise of its authority in Kosovo. UNMIK will embed a culture of human rights in all areas of activity, and will adopt human rights policies in respect of its administrative functions.[88]

Shortly thereafter, the first regulation adopted by the UNMIK established in its articles:

> Section 2. Observance of internationally recognized standards
>
> In exercising their functions, all persons undertaking public duties or holding public office in Kosovo shall observe internationally recognized human rights standards and shall not discriminate against any person on any ground such as sex, race, color, language religion, political or other opinion, national, ethnic or social origin, association with a national community, property, birth or other status.[89]

The first rule was quickly followed by a more general regulation on the law applicable in Kosovo, which incorporated the law of the territory under UN administration to a battery of international conventions on protection of human rights that abolished the death penalty.[90] Likewise, the United Nations

[88] See the R*eport of the Secretary-General on the United Nations Interim Administration Mission in Kosovo* (12 July 1999, UN Doc S/1999/779) para 42.

[89] Regulation UNMIK/REG/1999/1 on the Authority of the Interim Administration in Kosovo (25 July 1999), text available at <http://www.unmikonline.org/regulations/1999/reg01-99.htm>.

[90] Regulation UNMIK/REG/1999/24 on the Law Applicable in Kosovo (12 December 1999), text available at <http://www.unmikonline.org/regulations/1999/reg24-99.htm>. This regulation was amended by Regulation UNMIK/REG/2000/59 amending UNMIK Regulation No 1999/24 on the Law Applicable in Kosovo (27 October 2000), text available at <http://www.unmikonline.org/regulations/2000/reg59-00.htm>. One should also take into account Regulation UNMIK/REG/2001/9 on a Constitutional Framework for provisional self-government in Kosovo (15 May 2001), text available at <http://www.unmikonline.org/regulations/2001/reg09-01.htm> and Regulation UNMIK/REG/2002/9 on an amendment to the Constitutional Framework for provisional self-government (3 May 2002), text available at < http://www.unmikonline.org/regulations/2002/RE2002_09.pdf>.

Transitional Administration in East Timor (UNTAET) issued virtually identical rules on how public officials and civil servants should carry out their work.[91] Similarly, on 6 August 1999, the then Secretary-General issued a bulletin 'for the purpose of setting out fundamental principles and rules of international humanitarian law applicable to United Nations forces conducting operations under United Nations command and control'.[92] Without specifically establishing whether or not the United Nations is directly bound by international humanitarian law, the document establishes rules that reaffirm the essential part of the law of international humanitarian law set forth in the four Geneva Conventions of 1949 and the two additional Protocols of 1977, which are the principal instruments of humanitarian law.[93] The General Assembly has also been active in this area, for example, with its cross-cutting strategies to promote gender equality in all areas of work and supervising and even censoring the Security Council regarding the impact of its sanctions programmes in human rights.[94]

22. While some see these actions as a confirmation that the UN is subject to compliance with internationally recognized guarantees regarding human rights, others remain sceptical about whether it is a matter of an allegedly legal obligation or a gracious and voluntary acceptance of responsibility, and so therefore, it would be would be reversible and far from being jurisdictional or legally enforceable.[95] Although many of these documents incorporate rights that certainly exceed traditional norms on human rights (for example, UNMIK and UNTAET regulations prohibit the death penalty), these statements seem to represent the first steps in a long and complex assimilation process of constitutional principles that have only just begun. If these first steps are followed by further statements (which, ultimately, could be enacted with full legal effect) and specific references to international standards, step by step, it could give form to an *acquis* capable of penetrating the rules governing the United Nations and ultimately become fully binding.[96]

[91] Regulation UNTAET/REG/1991/1 on the Authority of the Transitional Administration in East Timor (27 November 1999), text available at <http://www.un.org/peace/etimor/untaetR/etreg1.htm>.

[92] See the Preamble of the *Secretary-General's Bulletin Observance by United Nations forces of international humanitarian law* (6 August 1999, UN Doc ST/SGB/1999/13).

[93] SR Ratner. 'Foreign Occupation and International Territorial Administration: The Challenges of Convergence' (2005) 16(4) *European Journal of International Law* 695 at 705.

[94] JE Álvarez (2005) (n 72) 169.

[95] Among those who see a confirmation of the binding effects of human rights vis-à-vis the UN, see E de Wet (2004) (n 56) 320. For a more sceptical opinion, see JE Álvarez (2005) (n 72) 171 and 179.

[96] SR Ratner, 'Foreign Occupation and International Territorial Administration: The Challenges of Convergence' (2005) 16(4) *European Journal of International Law* 695 at 705–6; and JE Álvarez (2005) (n 72) 88–9.

23. This idea of the gradual assimilation of constitutional principles by the United Nations, is, of course, directly inspired in the development of the protection of fundamental rights in the EU.[97] The European Community, through its Court of Justice, developed guarantees regarding fundamental rights before the adoption of the Maastricht Treaty, when the protection of these rights was finally incorporated into the articles of the founding treaty of the EU (Article 6 TEU and TEU-L). The European Community developed rights whose scope was beyond the traditional international customary norms or general principles of international law. It did so by developing fundamental rights in an independent way and, thus, imposing upon itself limits to the exercise of its own power. Finally, the European Community developed these principles and adopted them by means of extracting them from the different legal systems of its Member States and by resorting to the ECJ, which, as mentioned above, interpreted and built the category of the common constitutional traditions which, together with the ECHR, would be integrated into the constitutional order of the EU through the general principles of law.[98]

24. This is not to suggest that the United Nations shall ever become a political entity with a comparable level of integration to the EU or that the UN Member States shall give up renewal processes of the Organization through traditional procedures (for instance, reform the Charter) to increase and strengthen their legitimacy. This is just to stress that as the powers of the United Nations are rising steadily and gradually, and because the UN is beginning to exercise powers previously reserved to the states (see sanctions aimed at individuals), it would be desirable that the expansion of UN power shall be matched by a proportional increase in the levels of assurance and protection of human rights by their bodies, to strengthen the legitimacy of the exercise of their power in particular and the authority of the Organization in the international field in general.[99]

Some seem to deplore the acts of restraint because it would blur the necessary recognition of the binding nature of customary international law regarding human rights.[100] However, this process of assimilation of constitutional principles would allow an international organization like the United Nations to develop a specific list of rights adapted to the nature of their objectives and competences that could strengthen both the organization and its legitimacy as the human rights defence. This process would be likely to move along the path already initiated by customary international law of human rights and the rather limited constitutional traditions that may be common among a wide variety of

[97] For a deep study on the evolution of human rights protection within the EC, specially during the first period, see JHH Weiler, 'The Transformation of Europe' (1991) 100(8) *The Yale Law Journal* 2403.

[98] D Halberstam, 'The Bride of Messina: Constitutionalism and Democracy in Europe' (2005) 30(6) *European Law Review* 775 at 800–1.

[99] D Halberstam and E Stein (2009) (n 57) at 27.

[100] C Stahn (2008) (n 85) 483–4.

members of the Organization. This process would also provide the autonomy and flexibility necessary to adapt the traditional schemes of protection of fundamental rights of the states to the new sanctions regimes established by the Security Council, to the judicial processes of the courts and organs established *ad hoc* by the Council and territorial administrations led by the UN.[101]

This process should not be used to dissolve or empty of its content the fundamental rights according to traditional conceptions. Take the case of the right to private property, for example. Even without reaching a level of protection given by the general rules of customary international law or the constitutional traditions common to the many and various members of the UN, it should be incorporated into the law of the United Nations as a principle of constitutional nature. Thus, as a basic principle that must be respected by the UN and its organs, this principle would enjoy a flexibility that would allow it to be implemented by the territorial administration of the UN in areas of instability and transition and at the same time would base more protection from the point of view of both substantive and procedural guarantees, in the context of 'smart' economic sanctions.[102]

4. THE PRACTICE OF THE SECURITY COUNCIL IN ECONOMIC SANCTIONS AGAINST INDIVIDUALS

25. Counter-terrorism measures have become a major ongoing effort of the Security Council, especially since the late 1990s.[103] In particular, as we have seen, the executive organ of the United Nations has developed the concept of so-called targeted or smart sanctions, directed against certain persons, groups or sectors, thus avoiding the broad and ineffective general embargoes on states which affected more civilians than the leaders at which they were aimed.[104] As will be seen later, in the case of European citizens and European residents (including those with funds in Europe) these smart sanctions unify the state, the EU and the UN against the individual who is suspected of financing terrorism.

[101] J E Álvarez, *International Organizations As Law-makers* (Oxford University Press, Oxford, 2005) 180.

[102] D Halberstam and E Stein, (2009) (n 57) at 27.

[103] See *Fourth report of the Analytical Support and Sanctions Monitoring Team appointed pursuant to Security Council resolutions 1526 (2004) and 1617 (2005) concerning Al-Qaida and the Taliban and associated individuals and entities* (16 March 2006, UN Doc S/2006/154) 5–19. For a general overview on the history of the UN sanctions regimes, see V Gowlland-Debbas, 'Sanctions Regimes under Article 41 of the Charter' in V Gowlland-Debbas (ed), *National implementation of United Nations sanctions: a comparative study* (Martinus Nijhoff, Leiden, 2004) 3, especially at 7–17.

[104] On the different treaties to fight terrorism sponsored by the UN, see P Kovács, 'The United Nations in the Fight Against International Terrorism' in V Nanda (ed), *Law in the War on International Terrorism* (Transnational Publishers, Ardsley, 2005) 41.

4.1. The Sanctions Regime

26. Through a series of resolutions, starting with Resolution 1267 (1999), the UNSC established a series of sanctions against the Taliban, Usama bin Laden and, finally, Al-Qaida and those who supported them.[105] The reasons given in the beginning were the increased production of opium and the Taliban's refusal to extradite bin Laden, who was then accused of being responsible for the bombings of US embassies in Nairobi and Dar-es-Salaam, to the US. All states were called to freeze funds and other financial assets or economic resources of persons and entities designated in the resolutions, to prevent them from entering their territory or the transit through their territories of individuals appointed and to prevent the supply, sale and transfer, directly or indirectly, to persons and entities appointed, from their territories out of their territory or by means of vessels or aircraft showing their flags, of weapons and any kind of materials. The Committee 1267 (Sanctions Committee), composed of members of the Security Council, was established to set and periodically review a list of names and to monitor the compliance with sanctions by the states.[106] In subsequent resolutions, the Security Council expanded the sanctions, specified the requirements for their implementation by the states and established a monitoring team.[107] In the version of 29 July 2011, the consolidated list of individuals and entities to which the sanctions must be applied included 341 names: 250 people associated with the Taliban, 255 individuals associated with Al-Qaida and 91

[105] Security Council Resolution 1267 (1999) on the situation in Afghanistan (15 October 1999, UN Doc S/RES/1267). See the Resolutions of the Security Council concerning Al-Qaida and associated individuals and entities 1267 (1999), 1333 (2000), 1390 (2002), 1455 (2003), 1526 (2004), 1617 (2005), 1735 (2006), 1822 (2008), 1904 (2009) and 1989 (2011), all of them available through the site of the Security Council Committee pursuant to Resolutions 1267 (1999) and 1989 (2011) at <http://www.un.org/sc/committees/1267/aq_sanctions_list.shtml>. See also JA Frowein, 'The UN Anti-Terrorism Administration and the Rule of Law' in PM Dupuy and others (eds), *Völkerrecht als Wertordnung, Common Values in International Law. Festschrift für Christian Tomuschat* (NP Engel Verlag, Kehl, 2006) 785; JM Farrall, *United Nations Sanctions and the Rule of Law* (Cambridge University Press, Cambridge, 2007) 497–509.

[106] See, in particular, the 'Guidelines' of the Security Council Committee pursuant to Resolution 1267 (1999) concerning Al-Qaida and the Taliban and associated individuals and entities (Adopted on 7 November 2002, as amended on 10 April 2003, 21 December 2005, 29 November 2006, 12 February 2007, 9 December 2008, 22 July 20101, and 26 January 2011) available at <http://www.un.org/sc/committees/1267/pdf/1267_guidelines.pdf>.

[107] See Resolutions 1333 (2000), 1373 (2001), 1390 (2002), 1526 (2004), 1617 (2005), 1617 (2005), 1730 (2006), 1732 (2006), 1735 (2006), 1822 (2008), 1904 (2009) and 1989 (2011). All the relevant resolutions are available (with a brief explanation of their content) at <http://www.un.org/sc/committees/1267/resolutions.shtml>. See also the *Eleventh report of the Analytical Support and Sanctions Implementation Monitoring Team established pursuant to Security Council resolution 1526 (2004) and extended by resolution 1904 (2009) concerning Al-Qaida and the Taliban and associated individuals and entities* (13 April 2011, UN Doc S/2011/245) 13–18. For a comment, see E Rosand, 'The Security Council's Efforts to Monitor the Implementation of Al-Qaida/Taliban Sanctions' (2004) 98(4) *American Journal of International Law* 745.

entities and other groups or companies associated with Al-Qaida.[108] According to data from the last report of the monitoring team that included an update on that matter, at the end of 2007 the frozen assets were approximately $85 million in 36 different states.[109] Opinions on the degree of effectiveness of sanctions are not unanimous, and also require a large commitment in terms of resources by national authorities in order to be executed.[110]

In accordance with the guidelines of the Committee of sanctions against Al-Qaida and the Taliban, an individual can submit to his government or country of residence a revision request (delisting) and that government must report to the government of the proposing state (which requested the inclusion of that person on the list). If, following consultations, the two governments fail to reach an agreement, the matter will be submitted to the Sanctions Committee, which will meet privately and decide by consensus. The case may also be submitted to the Security Council.[111] The Committee is required to update the list when it receives new information. As an exception, states may authorize the partial lifting of the freeze of funds to pay basic expenses, including food, rent, mortgage, medicines, medical treatment, legal fees and more, but the Committee shall be notified in advance and may oppose it within 48 hours.[112]

Until 2006 it was not possible for an individual to have direct contact with the United Nations. The individual was totally dependent on the (good) will of his/her state government to defend its case in the exercise of diplomatic protection. However, within the scope of EU law an individual could sue the government before a national court if it refuses to protect him.[113] Thus, in response to criticism about the foreclosure proceedings of the blacklist, the Security Council urged the Secretary-General to establish a 'focal point' in the Secretariat to receive for the first time requests from individuals or groups.[114] However, the

[108] See the consolidated *List established and maintained by the Committee pursuant to resolutions 1267 (1999) and 1989 (2011) with respect to individuals, groups, undertakings and other entities associated with Al-Qaida* available at <http://www.un.org/sc/committees/1267/AQList.htm>.

[109] *Eighth Report of the Analytical Support and Sanctions Monitoring Team pursuant to Resolution 1735 (2006) concerning Al-Qaida and the Taliban and associated individuals and entities* (14 May 2008, UN Doc S/2008/324) 21.

[110] A Bianchi, 'Assessing the Effectiveness of the UN Security Council's Anti-terrorism Measures: The Quest for Legitimacy and Cohesion' (2006) 17(5) *European Journal of International Law* 881 at 892–900. For a critical study of the UN sanctions regime, see J Herbst, *Rechtskontrolle des UN-Sicherheitsrates* (Peter Lang-Verlag, Frankfurt am Main, 1999) 24–7.

[111] See the 'Guidelines' of the Security Council Committee pursuant to Resolution 1267 (1999) (n 106); E Miller, 'The Use of Targeted Sanctions in the Fight against International Terrorism: What about Human Rights?' (2003) 97 *American Society of International Law Proceedings* 46 at 49–50; and E Hey, 'The High-level Summit, International Institutional Reform and International Law' (2005) 2(1) *Journal of International Law & International Relations* 5.

[112] See UN Security Council Resolution 1452 (2002).

[113] Case T-315/01 *Kadi* [2005] para 270, where a suggestion of the UK in that sense was accepted. See D Halberstam and E Stein (2009) (n 57) at 27.

[114] See UN Security Council Resolution 1730 (2006) (n 107). The focal point allowed listed individuals and entities to put forward a case for delisting without having to rely on the support of their state of residence or nationality. It was operative from 30 March 2007 until 3 June 2010 (date of the appointment of the first Ombudsperson by letter of the Secretary-General, 4 June 2010, S/2010/282). See the report concerning the review of the Consolidated List conducted from 30 June 2008 to

proceedings before the focal point did not allow individuals to take part either personally or through a representative or legal counsel in the review process, or for the UN or any of the governments to provide the applicant with any information beyond the situation in which their foreclosure request was placed on the list. Thus, following the process described in the guidelines text that was made public, the resolution of any request of an individual remained an essentially diplomatic process in which the individual had a minor role.[115] This process did not imply any warranty regarding the rights of defence for the person concerned.[116]

27. Owing to the criticism of the lack of transparency and low standards of human rights protection within the sanctions procedures as well as the issues which arose before the European courts (mainly the ECJ, such as in *Kadi*), the Security Council adopted Resolution 1904 (2009), which created the Office of the Ombudsperson of the Security Council's 1267 Committee.[117] Therefore, since 4 June 2010 (date of the appointment of the Ombudsperson) individuals, groups, undertakings or entities seeking to be removed from the Security Council's Al-Qaida Sanctions Committee List may submit their request for delisting to this 'independent and impartial' authority instead of using the focal point, which no longer receives delisting requests. As is written in its founding resolution, the aim of this figure is to 'assist' the 1267 Sanctions Committee when considering delisting requests.[118] In order to accomplish this mission, Resolution 1904 describes in its Annex II the tasks of this Ombudsperson during the delisting process, which basically is split into four separate procedures: Information Gathering (two months), Dialogue (two months, with possible extension of two more months), Committee Discussion and Decision (two months). The Dialogue phase is the critical one, since for the first time 'it gives the Petitioner an opportunity to be heard, to address issues and answer questions with the goal of ensuring that his or her position is fully explained and understood'.[119] This dialogue implies the participation of the petitioner, relevant states, the Committee and the Monitoring Team, but it cannot be sub-

31 July 2010 by the Committee, *Report of the Analytical Support and Sanctions Monitoring Team on the outcome of the review described in paragraph 25 of Resolution 1822 (2008) submitted pursuant to paragraph 30 of Resolution 1904 (2009)* (29 September 2010, S/2010/497).

[115] As of 29 June 2011, from the 25 requests for delisting relating to the focal point process dealing with the Al-Qaida sanctions Committee, three individuals (from a total of 18) and 17 entities (from 22) were successfully delisted.

[116] From 30 June 2008 to 31 July 2010, the Committee examined 488 names of individuals, groups and entities subject to the Al-Qaida and Taliban sanctions regime and subsequently removed 45 names from the List as a result. See the *Report of the Analytical Support and Sanctions Monitoring Team on the outcome of the review (. . .)* (2010) (n 114) at 4.

[117] For a comment on this newly created office, see GL Willis, 'Security Council Targeted Sanctions, Due Process And The 1267 Ombudsperson' (2011) 42(3) 673 especially at 737–45.

[118] Resolution 1904 (17 December 2009) para 20.

[119] See the notes on the *Procedure for requests for delisting submitted to the office of the Ombudsperson,* available at <http://www.un.org/en/sc/ombudsperson/procedure.shtml>.

stituted by a real procedure, where the parties have to produce public evidence and the parties (especially the petitioner) are assisted by lawyers, nor are procedural guarantees of a constitutional nature applicable.[120] It does not imply a real guarantee for the petitioner.[121]

The European General Court (formerly the CFI) has recently stated that the creation of the UN Ombudsperson does not solve the due process concerns within the UN listings regime. The EU Court has stressed that 'the Security Council has still not deemed it appropriate to establish an independent and impartial body responsible for hearing and determining, as regards matters of law and fact, actions against individual decisions taken by the Sanctions Committee'. That is why, continues the Court, 'the focal point . . . *nor* the Office of the Ombudsperson cannot be equated with the provision of an effective judicial procedure for review of decisions of the Sanctions Committee'.[122]

To sum up, one can say that this new delisting procedure has considerable improvements, such as this enhanced assistance to the petitioners, which no longer need to rely on the grey area of diplomatic protection or the impersonal methods of the 'focal point'. But this kind of institutionalized mediation (or even an assisted negotiation) may in no way be 'equivalent' nor 'comparable' to a real and fair trial, as prescribed by the Universal Declaration of Human Rights, the ECHR, EU law or the constitutional law of the democratic countries.[123]

28. Unlike the list elaborated by the Committee on sanctions against Al-Qaida and the Taliban established by virtue of Resolution 1267 just analysed, Resolution 1373 does not provide a centralized list, but instead delegates in independent lists that the states or the EU have set themselves.[124] The particular responsibility

[120] For instance, as stated in its first Report, even the Ombudsperson had problems with access to classified or confidential information. See *the Report of the Office of the Ombudsperson pursuant to Security Council Resolution 1904 (2009)* (24 January 2011, S/2011/29) paras 33–5. Other problems encountered by this office were, for instance, that the petitioner is not provided with the factual reasons for delisting, also the petitioner's inability to know the identity of the country that initially placed him or her on the sanctions list (which can lead to a disadvantage for the petitioner in answering a case) and the lack of resources to translate materials.

[121] It is too early to assess the effectiveness of this procedure. However, in 29 July 2011, from the 14 cases brought before the Office of the Ombudsperson, two people (case 2 and case 5) have been delisted. See <http://www.un.org/en/sc/ombudsperson/status.shtml>.

[122] See Case T-85/09 *Kadi v Commission (Kadi II)* [2010] unpublished para 128 (Appeal: C-584/10 P, C-593/10 P and C-595/10 P). See also *Her Majesty's Treasury v Mohammed Jabar Ahmed and others* [2010] UKSC 2 & 5 (UK Supreme Court, 27 January 2010) paras 77, 78, 149, 181, 182, 218 and 239 and *Ninth report of the Analytical Support and Sanctions Monitoring Team, submitted pursuant to Resolution 1822 (2008) concerning Al-Qaida and the Taliban and associated individuals and entities* (13 May 2009, S/2009/245) at 9–15.

[123] I intentionally play with the words used by the ECtHR in *Bosphorus* [2005] (n 18) para 150.

[124] See UN Security Council Resolutions 1373 (2001) and 1624 (2005) establishing the Security Council Counter Terrorism Committee. For an overview of the work of this Committee, see the *Global Survey on the Implementation of Security Council Resolution 1373 (2001)* (Counter-Terrorism Committee Executive Directorate, 2010) and the *Technical Guide to the Implementation of Security Council Resolution 1373 (2001)* (Counter-Terrorism Committee Executive Directorate, 2009), both available at <http://www.un.org/en/sc/ctc/>. After the last update on 18 July 2011, the EU maintains 11 persons and 25 groups and entities on its current black list. See Council Decision

of states in the creation and maintenance of the latter lists arguably alters its legal scope. In fact, these lists created and maintained by the states do not provoke the same issues regarding the conflict between the guarantees derived from human rights and the respect for UN law, as the Security Council does not provide, in these cases, the freezing of assets of individuals and certain specific entities. Indeed, in its latest decision of the *OMPI-PMOI* (see Chapter 5) the CFI again recalled that the fundamental rights recognized in the EU are fully applicable to the autonomous decision of the EU to include and keep their blacklists to certain individuals and entities who are subject to a freezing of funds regime.[125]

4.2. Judicial Control of the Sanctions Regime

29. The International Court of Justice (ICJ) has not established any kind of direct control over the validity of the Security Council acts because, so far, it has successfully managed to avoid giving a clear answer to the question of whether it has jurisdiction to decide on the legality of the Security Council acts.[126] However, the Court has incidentally analysed the legality of these acts and those of other entities of the UN when solving a dispute brought up by one or more states or at the time of issuing an advisory opinion.[127]

Thus, in the *Lockerbie* case, for instance, the ICJ implicitly recognized the power to control the ultra vires of a decision of the Security Council, though in the end it considered that in that case the Security Council's action in question was valid by virtue of a supremacy clause in Article 103 of the Charter,

2011/430/CFSP updating the list of persons, groups and entities subject to Articles 2, 3 and 4 of Common Position 2001/931/CFSP on the application of specific measures to combat terrorism (OJ L 188/47, 19 July 2011). For a doctrinal study of the question, see E Guild, 'The Uses and Abuses of Counter-Terrorism Policies in Europe: The Case of the 'Terrorist Lists'' (2008) 46(1) *Journal of Common Market Studies* 173.

[125] Case T-284/08 *People's Mojahedin Organization of Iran v Council (PMOI II)* [2008] ECR II-3487 para 75, which copies literally para 155 of Case T-228/02 *Organisation des Modjahedines du peuple d'Iran v Council (OMPI)* [2006] ECR II-4665. This organization was delisted by Council Common Position 2009/67/CFSP (OJ L 23/37, 27 January 2009) due to the CFI decision on Case T-284/08 *People's Mojahedin Organization of Iran v Council (PMOI II)* [2008] ECR II-3487.

[126] A Reinisch (2001) (n 17) at 865. In general, on the possibility of ICJ control over the Security Council, see JE Álvarez, ‹Judging the Security Council› (1996) 90(1) *American Journal of International Law* 1; L Caflisch, 'Is the International Court Entitled to Review Security Council Resolutions Adopted under Chapter VII of the United Nations Charter?' in N Al-Nauimi and R Meese (eds), *International Legal Issues Arising under the United Nations Decade of International Law* (Kluwer, The Hague, 1995) 633; D Akande, 'The International Court of Justice and the Security Council: Is there Room for Judicial Control of Decisions of the Political Organs of the United Nations?' (1997) 46(2) ICLQ 309; E de Wet, 'Judicial Review as an Emerging General Principle of Law and its Implications for the International Court of Justice' (2000) 47(2) *Netherlands International Law Review* 181; and GL Willis. 'Security Council Targeted Sanctions, Due Process And The 1267 Ombudsperson' (2011) 42(3) 673.

[127] See E de Wet (2004) (n 56) 83–91.

which thus prevailed over the rights that Libya may have had under another treaty.[128]

But the processes before the ICJ referred to are usually beyond the reach of an individual, because only the states have access to the ICJ and requests for advisory opinions are reserved for the UN bodies. Also falling outside the scope of the recipients of smart sanctions is the indirect control of an international court in the course of proceedings against an individual, as in the case against *Duško Tadić*.[129] Thus, the doctrine does not expect much from the control systems dominated by the states, in which the individual appears as a mere extra, even when the organization concerned shares the principles derived from the rule of law. Because, even if there is some kind of judicial control, it will arrive too late and will be fully mediated by the political pressure exercised by different governments.[130] Moreover, given that individuals do not have *ius standi* it seems that this is the ideal forum to try to get some kind of compensation in cases involving 'smart sanctions'.[131]

Once the international remedies route is closed, it could be interesting to control the actions of the Security Council, even partially, before the national courts. In this context, it should be noted that the control exercised by the courts varies widely from system to system. In the German case, for example, in principle it is not possible for any act of public authority to be exempted from judicial control.[132] However, as a general rule, any attempt to sue the United Nations for the Security Council acts before a national court would be dismissed based on the principle of immunity from jurisdiction.[133] Although there is no general and omni-comprehensive database on the subject, some individual cases show that, in general terms, the appeals submitted before national courts have failed to provide comfort to particular plaintiffs.[134] For example, the House of Lords (the UK's highest court prior to the new Supreme Court) dismissed a lawsuit against the British Government in which a failure to guarantee the right to freedom under Article 5.1 ECHR was alleged due to an arrest made by the

[128] Case *Questions of Interpretation and Application of the 1971 Montreal Convention arising from the Aerial Incident at Lockerbie (Libyan Arab Jamahiriya v United Kingdom)* Provisional Measures Order (ICJ, 14 April 1992, *Reports* 3–16) para 39.

[129] Case IT-94-1 *Prosecutor v Tadić* [1995] (n 65).

[130] See B Simma, 'From bilateralism to community interest in International Law' (1994) 250(VI) *Recueil des Cours de l'Académie de Droit International de La Haye* 217, Section 'Community interest and the constitution of international society' at 283.

[131] In fact some scholars have already pointed out the possibility of an indirect control of Security Council decisions before other organs (such an arbitration panel or the WTO panel): see JE Álvarez (1996) (n 126) at 11–13.

[132] W Rüfner, 'Basic Elements of German Law on State Liability' in J Bell and AW Bradley (eds), *Governmental Liability: A Comparative Study* (British Institute for International & Comparative Law, London, 1992) 249.

[133] A Reinisch (2001) (n 17) at 866.

[134] There are currently around 10 cases before national courts and the ECtHR dealing with the UN sanctions. See *Eleventh report of the Analytical Support and Sanctions Implementation Monitoring Team established pursuant to Security Council Resolution 1526 (2004)* [2011] (n 107) at 28–30. See also T Andersson, I Cameron and K Nordback, 'EU blacklisting: the renaissance of imperial power, but on a global scale' (2003) 14(2) *European Business Law Review* 111 at 119.

British armed forces in Iraq. The ruling recognized that the detention without trial of people in Iraq by armed forces acting under Resolution 1546 (2004) was attributable to the UK rather than the United Nations. However, by virtue of Articles 25 (obligation to accept and carry out Security Council decisions) and 103 of the UN Charter (prevalence of obligations derived from the Charter over any other international agreement) the acts in question were fully valid and did not violate the international commitments made by the UK regarding human rights.[135] However, in another case, another court overturned some government decisions freezing certain funds for being unconstitutional, but only because those orders had not been ratified by Parliament.[136] In the courts of other national member countries (Germany, Ireland and Switzerland) they haven't achieved much better results.[137] However, as an exception, a Belgian court threatened the government with imposing high daily compulsory fines until the release of funds of the applicant, who was unfairly accused of collaborating with terrorists.[138]

The human rights commitment of the Member States should be reinforced at the European regional level, in a broad sense, where the plaintiffs could sue the state that would undertake or implement those actions to the detriment of individual rights before the ECtHR.[139] Thus, the appellants could argue that, by freezing their funds pursuant to a Security Council resolution, the state in question would have violated rights guaranteed by the ECHR. Following its earlier case law in the case of the European Community (see above), the ECtHR, in principle, refused to have the power to prosecute claims against the United Nations or against acts directly attributable to the United Nations or against decisions adopted by the states within the UN bodies. Thus, as discussed below, the ECtHR has declined to be able to hear claims against a state exercising delegated powers by the Security Council of the United Nations and which is providing troops to a UN subsidiary body.[140] But if the decision to freeze assets belonging to an individual can be attributed to a state – even if it is executed under the obligation to implement Security Council decisions – the individual may file an appeal before the ECtHR, after having exhausted previous remedies

[135] Case *Regina (Al-Jedstda) v Secretary of State for Defence* [2007] UKHL 58 (House of Lords, 12 December 2007) paras 32–9.

[136] Case *A, K, M, Q & G v HM Treasury* [2008] EWHC 869 (Admin) (Court of Appeal – Administrative Court, 24 April 2008) paras 24–32.

[137] S Schmahl, 'Effektiver Rechtsschutz gegen "targeted sanctions" des UN-Sicherheitsrats?' (2006) 41(4) *Europarecht* 566 at 570. For some information about the pending cases, see *Eleventh report of the Analytical Support and Sanctions Implementation Monitoring Team established pursuant to Security Council Resolution 1526* (2004) [2011] (n 107) at 28–30.

[138] As a result of this judicial decision, the Belgian Government started a delisting request before the Security Council. See *Third report of the Analytical Support and Sanctions Monitoring Team appointed pursuant to resolution 1526 (2004) concerning Al-Qaida and the Taliban and associated individuals and entities* (9 September 2005, S/2005/572) 48–9 (paras 3–4). See V Gowlland-Debbas, 'UN Sanctions and International Law: An Overview' in V Gowlland-Debbas (ed), *United Nations Sanctions and International Law* (Kluwer Law International, The Hague, 2001) 1 at 22–28.

[139] D Halberstam and E Stein (2009) (n 57) at 33.

[140] Case *Behrami* [2007] (n 26) para 122.

(including the possible preliminary ruling before the ECJ). This was the solution adopted in *Bosphorus* (see Chapter 5), where the ECtHR accepted control of a state measure that enforced at state level a regulation of the EC/EU which, moreover, although the ECtHR did not make any comment on it, was adopted to implement a Security Council resolution.[141]

Having thus described the situation, it is necessary to analyse the regime of sanctions within the EU, an entity that appears interposed between the state level and the level of the UN and whose Member States are also members of the United Nations. Thus, from the procedural point of view, the individual could resort to an EC/EU measure that would implement a Security Council resolution. If the measure affects it directly and individually, as is the case when the name of the person concerned is on a list of individuals and entities whose assets are frozen in the EU, the person concerned can lodge an appeal before the Court of First Instance to annul the EC/EU regulation of execution to the extent of its concern, as highlighted in the *Kadi* case.[142] However, the situation is much more complex from the point of view of the internal relationships.

By transforming the Security Council resolutions into EC/EU law, Member States are subject not only to the obligations derived from international law, but also to the obligation of implementing that EC/EU law derived from the membership of the EC/EU itself. There is the remote possibility that states move away from the traditional deference shown towards the EC/EU and which could ultimately resort to their primitive competence to protect fundamental rights.[143] However, in light of the general obligation of the Member States to comply with EC/EU law, states could instead put aside their control ability in respect of the protection of fundamental rights conferred by the EC/EU.[144] As will be discussed below, it was perhaps the fear of the ECJ that Member States would thereby intervene (if they found the EC/EU failing to grant adequate protection to their citizens) violating their obligation to comply with EC/EU law and jeopardizing the uniform application of EC/EU law, that might have inspired the *Kadi/Al Barakaat* case law.[145]

[141] Case *Bosphorus* [2005] (n 18) paras 43–47.

[142] Joined Cases C-402/05 P and C-415/05 P *Kadi* and *Al Barakaat International Foundation v Council* [2008] ECR I-6351. Another possibility would be a damages claim as a compensation for the frozen assets. See Case C-354/04 P *Gestoras* [2007] para 48 and Case T-184/95 *Dorsch Consult Ingenieurgesellschaft mbH v Council and Commission* [1998] ECR II-00667 para 73, where, by the way, it was established that the UN and not the EC would be responsible for the damages arising from a Regulation implementing a UN sanction. This case was appealed and the subsequently dismissed (Case C-237/98 P *Dorsch Consult v Council and Commission* [2000] ECR I-4549). See G Zagel, 'Article 301 TEC on Economic Sanctions' in H Smit and P Herzog (eds), *The Law of the European Community. A Commentary on the EC Treaty* (Matthew Bender, New York, 2005) 402.1.

[143] Some authors have advocated for this possibility in case the EC/EU could not control the abuses of fundamental rights within its area of competence. See S Schmahl (2006) (n 137) at 574–6.

[144] See, for instance, *Bosphorus* [2005] (n 18).

[145] This issue will be widely analysed below.

8

European Union Law and Security Council Resolutions: Participation of the European Union in the United Nations Sanctions Regime

1. THE TRADITIONAL RELATIONSHIP BETWEEN EC/EU LAW AND INTERNATIONAL LAW

1. The European Community had its international legal personality recognized from the beginning and, consequently, its attachment to international responsibility did not cause too many problems.[1] In the case of the EU, much has been discussed about its international personality.[2] The Lisbon Treaty recovers the consensus reached in the drafting of the Constitutional Treaty on the need for the EU to have a specific and unique legal personality. In fact, Article 47 TEU-L provides:

> The Union has legal personality.[3]

[1] Arts 281 TEC and 184 Treaty establishing the European Atomic Energy Community expressly recognized that both the EC and the EAEC had international legal personality. See K Lenaerts, P Van Nuffel and R Bray, *Constitutional Law of the European Union* 2nd edn (Thompson, London, 2005) 815–18.

[2] The literature on this matter is huge. See, among others, N Fernández Sola, 'La subjetividad internacional de la Unión Europea' (2002) 11 *Revista de Derecho Comunitario Europeo* 85; P Lachmann, 'International Legal Personality of the EC: Capacity and Competence' (1984) 10 *Legal Issues of European Integration* 3; E Bribosia and A Weyembergh, 'La personnalité juridique de l'Union européenne' in M Dony (ed), *L'Union Européenne et le monde après Amsterdam* (Éditions de l'Université, Bruxelles, 1999) 37; JC Gautron, 'Article I-7 – Personnalité juridique' in L Burgorgue-Larsen, A Levade and F Picod (eds), *Traité établissant une Constitution pour l'Europe: commentaire article par article* (Bruylant, Bruxelles, 2007) 117; and JR Canedo Arrillaga and LI Gordillo, 'La nueva Unión Europea: de la doble personalidad a la crisis de personalidad' (2010) 78 *Revista de Derecho Político* 337. See the document *Presidency introductory note: legal personality of the Union* (EC/IGC/CONF.3871/96, 16 July 1996), the report of the Council legal service *Comments on the draft amendments to Article 24 TEU* (SN 5332/1/00 REV 1, 24 November 2000) – where the implicit legal personality of the EU is recognized – and the *Final report of Working Group III on Legal Personality* (CONV 305/02, 1 October 2002), which inspired the last reform operated by the Lisbon Treaty.

[3] Consolidated versions of the Treaty on European Union and the Treaty on the Functioning of the European Union, including the Charter of Fundamental Rights of the European Union (OJ C 83, 30 March 2010).

Thus, the Lisbon Treaty extinguishes the European Community, which is succeeded by the EU itself. In this sense, the last clause of the last paragraph of Article 1 TEU-L amended by Lisbon provides:

> The Union shall replace and succeed the European Community.[4]

Thus, the powers and functions previously exercised by the Union and the Community would be consolidated in a European Union with international legal personality. In the case of both the binomial EC/EU prior to Lisbon (the Community, either directly or by giving international legal coverage to the activities of the institutions under the former second or third pillars) and the EU that will emerge after the entry into force of the most recent reform, we find ourselves before an international legal actor whose external behaviour is subject to and governed by international law.[5] Thus, the functions and duties previously exercised by the EU and the EC are consolidated in a single EU with international legal personality, and interesting perspectives can be foreseen regarding its representation before international organizations such as the possibility of accession by the EU to other international organizations or to reinforce its perception in the international scene.[6] From the standpoint of the formulation of European foreign policy, the decision on the legal personality of the EU has resulted in an improvement, at least formally, in the pillar structure, which will lead to greater unity and coherence of that policy. However, the disappearance of the pillars does not mean that all areas of foreign policy are going to be brought under the same procedures of decision making and under the same management pattern. Instead, they will keep their own separate procedures.[7]

1.1. The Founding Principles of the Relationship

2. In its crucial ruling in *Costa v ENEL*, the Luxembourg Court laid the groundwork for the autonomy of Community legal order:

[4] As is well known, the TEC came to be known as the Treaty on the Functioning of the European Union (TFEU). The Lisbon Treaty establishes that there is no hierarchical relationship between the TUE-L and the TFEU since '[t]hose two Treaties shall have the same legal value' (see Art 1 TEU-L).

[5] C Tomuschat, 'The International Responsibility of the European Union' in E Cannizzaro (ed), *The European Union as an Actor in International Relations* (Kluwer, The Hague, 2002) 177.

[6] F Aldecoa Luzárraga, 'La política exterior común en el Tratado de Lisboa: instrumentos para hacer de la Unión un actor de la globalización' in CR Fernández Liesa and CM Díaz Barrado (eds), *El Tratado de Lisboa. Análisis y perspectivas* (Instituto Universitario de Estudios Internacionales y Europeos 'Francisco de Vitoria', Dykinson, Madrid, 2008) 231.

[7] Some scholars argue that despite the unification operated by the attempted Constitutional Treaty (first) and the Lisbon Treaty (finally) the basics of the classic pillar structure division still prevail within the internal order. See W Wessels, 'A "saut constitutionnel" out of an intergovernmental trap? The Provisions of the Constitutional Treaty for the Common Foreign, Security and Defence Policy' (2004) 5/04 *Jean Monnet Working Papers* May 2009 at 10 and LN González Alonso, '¿Quién dijo que desaparecen los pilares? La configuración jurídica de la acción exterior de la Unión Europea en el Tratado de Lisboa' in Martín y Pérez de Nanclares, J (ed), *El Tratado de Lisboa: la salida de la crisis constitucional* (Iustel, Madrid, 2008) 393.

> By contrast with ordinary international treaties, the EEC Treaty has created its own legal system.[8]

However, this assertion must be clarified to some extent due to the implications of international law. First, the Vienna Convention on the Law of Treaties refers only to treaties in general and makes no distinction between ordinary and extraordinary treaties.[9] Secondly, the fact that the EC/EU is based on its own (and even self-integrated) legal order cannot affect the international obligations of the EC/EU or other international organization because, in this sense, EC/EU law would be similar to a national law regarding its relationship with international law.[10] Moreover, the fact that the Union is based on a constitutional charter does not alter the legal regime by which it is subject to international law. Let's not forget that, according to a fundamental principle of international law, 'in the relations between Powers who are contracting Parties to a treaty, the provisions of municipal law cannot prevail over those of the treaty'.[11] In addition, the primacy of international law over national law would also be applied to national constitutional provisions. In this regard, the Permanent Court of International Justice already stated that 'a State cannot rely, as against another State, on the provisions of the latter's Constitution'.[12]

3. It is deduced from Article 307 TEU, now Article 351 TFEU, that the EU is trying to fit into the international legal order. Indeed, the provision states that:

> The rights and obligations arising from agreements concluded before 1 January 1958 or, for acceding States, before the date of their accession, between one or more Member States on the one hand, and one or more third countries on the other, shall not be affected by the provisions of the Treaties.
>
> To the extent that such agreements are not compatible with the Treaties, the Member State or States concerned shall take all appropriate steps to eliminate the incompatibilities established. Member States shall, where necessary, assist each other to this end and shall, where appropriate, adopt a common attitude.
>
> In applying the agreements referred to in the first paragraph, Member States shall take into account the fact that the advantages accorded under the Treaties by each Member State form an integral part of the establishment of the Union and are thereby inseparably linked with the creation of common institutions, the conferring of powers upon them and the granting of the same advantages by all the other Member States.

[8] Case 6/64 *Costa v ENEL* [1964] ECR-1141, at 593.

[9] A Pellet, 'Les fondements juridiques internationaux du droit communautaire' (1997) V(2) *Collected Courses of the Academy of European Law* 193 at 243.

[10] C Leben, 'À propos de la nature juridique des Communautés européennes' (1991) 14 *Droits. Revue française de théorie juridique* 61 at 64; T Schilling, 'The Autonomy of the Community Legal Order: An Analysis of Possible Foundations' (1996) 37(2) *Harvard International Law Journal* 389 at 403–9; and P Daillier and A Pellet, *Droit international public* 7th edn (LGDJ, Paris, 2002) 281.

[11] Case *The Greco-Bulgarian 'Communities'* [1930] at 32.

[12] Case *Treatment of Polish Nationals and Other Persons of Polish Origin or Speech in the Danzig Territory* Advisory Opinion No 23 (Permanent Court of International Justice 4 February 1932, Series A/B 44 1933, 3–46) 24.

Likewise, the ECJ has ensured that the external behaviour of the EC/EU fully respects its obligations derived from international law.[13] The Court even determines the validity of secondary EC/EU legislation to the extent that

> the European Community must respect international law in the exercise of its powers and . . . consequently, [the contested legislative provision] must be interpreted, and its scope limited, in the light of the relevant rules of the international law of the sea.[14]

Gradually, the ECJ has been progressively using references to customary international law so that it is recognized as an autonomous source of law in that autonomous legal order that the community is.[15] It is also worth recalling the Advisory Opinion of the International Court of Justice in which this court established that international organizations are limited in their actions under international law in the same way as any other subject of international law. As stated by the ICJ:

> International organizations are subjects of international law and, as such, are bound by any obligations incumbent upon them under general rules of international law, under their constitutions or under international agreements to which they are parties.[16]

So the reason that the ECJ determines the validity of EC/EU law regarding international obligations is far from being a mere gesture of deference by the Luxembourg Court. It is rather a legal obligation that must be respected so as not to incur international responsibility.[17]

4. Nonetheless, to ensure the autonomy of the EC/EU legal order in the complex interplay required between international law, EC/EU law itself and the national laws of Member States, the Court has developed an extensive and elaborate construction regarding its competence of legality control.[18] In its main decision on the matter, Opinion 1/75 of the ECJ, established that its jurisdiction allows it to declare void the EC act by which an international agreement was concluded:

> The question whether the conclusion of a given agreement is within the power of the Community and whether, in a given case, such power has been exercised in conformity with the provisions of the Treaty is, in principle, a question which may be submitted to the Court of Justice, either directly, under article 169 or article 173 of the Treaty, or in accordance with the preliminary procedure.[19]

[13] See Joined Cases 21/72 and 24/72 *International Fruit Company and others v Produktschap voor Groenten en Fruit* [1972] ECR 1219 para 6.

[14] Case C-286/90 *Anklagemindigheden v Poulsen and Diva Navigation* [1992] ECR I-06019 para 9.

[15] C Timmermans, 'The EU and Public International Law' (1999) 4 *European Foreign Affairs Review* 181.

[16] Case *Interpretation of the Agreement of 25 March 1951 between the WHO and Egypt* [1980] para 37.

[17] Case C-327/91 *France v Commission* [1994] ECR I-03641 para 25.

[18] See J Díez-Hochtleitner Rodríguez, *La posición del Derecho internacional en el ordenamiento comunitario* (McGraw-Hill, Madrid, 1998) 97–146.

[19] Opinion 1/75, *Opinion given purusant to Article 228 (1) of the EEC Treaty (Local Costs)* [1975] ECR 1355.

It is interesting to compare this case law with the statement, 20 years later, of the Advocate General, Mr Tesauro, according to whom the ECJ does not exclude the possibility of directly challenging the validity of an agreement.[20] Thus, some authors support this view and have stressed that the special nature of the EC/EU legal order confers on the Union some unique institutional powers that would result in the general rule of international law not being applied as set out in Article 27 of the Vienna Convention on the Law of Treaties held between States and International Organizations or between International Organizations, carried out in Vienna on 21 March 1986.[21] That provision states that a party 'may not invoke the provisions of its internal law as a justification for its failure to perform a treaty'.

However, the ECJ's conception of the role of international law in the legal community order has been criticized by the international doctrine that has characterized this Court's perception of 'solipsistic' and even 'imperialist', derived from a Eurocentric attitude.[22] So according to this opinion, the ECJ would understand the EC/EU legal order not only as an autonomous and independent order but also as a self-enclosed and sealed order in which the international obligations that the Union had to meet are conditioned to comply with EC/EU primary law.

5. Despite these criticisms, we must not forget that the ECJ is the ultimate guardian of the Treaties, whose interpretation it must ensure. As explained above, the ECJ introduced through its jurisprudence the fundamental rights within the EC/EU order by referring to the general principles of law and suggesting that as a hierarchically superior source of law they imposed and prevailed over legislation. At the same time, the fundamental principle of primacy of EC/EU law, whose importance cannot be dismissed, is based on the premise that the exercise of powers of the institutions must be consistent with the founding Treaties. It is interesting to note that the principle of primacy is also a creation of the Luxembourg Court case law that has not yet been included in the existing Treaties.[23] Therefore, the ECJ shall ensure the compliance with

[20] See Case C-327/91 *France v Commission* [1994] (n 17), Opinion of AG Tesauro, para 9.

[21] See the Vienna Convention on the Law of Treaties [1969] and D Simon, 'Les fondements de l'autonomie du droit communautaire' in VV AA (ed), *Droit international et droit communautaire: perspectives actuelles* (Pedone, Paris, 2000) 207.

[22] M Koskenniemi, 'International Law: Constitutionalism, Managerialism and the Ethos of Legal Education' (2007) 1(1) *European Journal of Legal Studies* 1 at 2, where he uses those Kelsenian adjectives; and A Pellet, 'Les fondements juridiques internationaux du droit communautaire' (1997) V(2) *Collected Courses of the Academy of European Law* 193.

[23] Article I-6 of the Constitutional Treaty recognized this principle in a positive legal text for the first time, although the Declaration on Article I-6 established that this article just 'reflects existing case-law of the Court of Justice of the European Communities and of the Court of First Instance' (OJ C 310/420, 16 December 2004). The Lisbon Treaty only mentions this principle within Declaration No 17 concerning primacy (OJ C 306/256, 17 December 2007).

the Treaty, a task that extends to the Union's external action because otherwise it could affect the autonomy of the Community legal order.[24]

1.2. The Control Exercised by the ECJ through EC/EU Law

6. The TEC corresponds to a monistic model. In this sense, in an earlier ruling, the Court established that international agreements to which the Community is party bind it from the time of their completion. The ECJ established that:

> The provisions of the agreement [between Greece and the EEC], from the coming into force thereof, form an integral part of Community law.[25]

Thus, the conclusion of an agreement is a unilateral act of the relevant EC/EU institution and, therefore, is required to stick to its assigned competence framework (Article 7 TEU, Article 13 TEU-L) and, in case of abuse, Article 220 (Article 19 TEU-L) shall be applied, according to which the CFI and the ECJ shall ensure compliance with the law in the interpretation and application of the Treaty.

7. According to a well-established principle of international law the conclusion of an agreement, from the moment that the agreement is binding on the contracting parties, is a matter of international law and not of national law.[26] However, the ECJ has reconsidered its previous case law regarding the entry into force of international obligations that may bind the Community (or the EU after Lisbon) analysing international agreements that had been concluded breaching Community provisions of a constitutional nature. If the agreement has been concluded without following the procedure established by the Treaties, the ECJ shall deprive it of effects within the EC/EU's scope by accepting control of the legality of the EC/EU measure under which the completion of the agreement was authorized, although the suspension of an agreement should be performed according to the Law of Treaties.[27] That is, the Court had established a distinction between legal assumptions underlying the conclusion of a treaty and its entry into force in the EC/EU legal order.[28] In the 'Legal context and back-

[24] B Kunoy and A Dawes, 'Plate tectonics in Luxembourg: The ménage à trois between EC law, international law and the European Convention on Human Rights following the UN sanctions cases' (2009) 46(1) *Common Market Law Review* 73 at 86.

[25] Case 181/73 *Haegemann v Belgian State* [1974] ECR 449 para 5. Opinion 1/91 *Draft agreement between the Community, on the one hand, and the countries of the European Free Trade Association, on the other, relating to the creation of the European Economic Area* [1991] ECR I-06079, paras 3 and 37.

[26] See P Daillier and A Pellet, *Droit international public* 7th edn (LGDJ, Paris, 2002) 181.

[27] B Kunoy, 'The Jurisdiction of the ECJ to Review the Legality of the Transposition of an International Act in the EC Legal Order' (2007) 76(1) *Nordic Journal of International Law* 19. See also the *Case Gabčíkovo-Nagymaros Project (Hungary/Slovakia) Judgment* (ICJ, 25 September 1997, Report 7-84) para 47.2.

[28] PJG Kapteyn, 'Quelques réflexions sur le contrôle de la constitutionnalité des accords conclus par la Communauté avec des pays tiers' in GC Rodríguez Iglesias and others (eds), *Mélanges en hommage à Fernand Schockweiler* (Nomos, Baden-Baden, 1999) 275 at 276.

ground to the dispute' part of the decision in a case decided in 1994 the ECJ wrote:

> By application lodged at the Court Registry on 16 December 1991, the French Republic brought an action under the first paragraph of Article 173 of the EEC Treaty and Article 33 of the ECSC Treaty for a declaration that the Agreement signed on 23 September 1991 by the Commission of the European Communities and the Government of the United States of America regarding the application of their competition laws (hereinafter 'the Agreement') is void.[29]

That is, the French Government sought the annulment of the act of the Commission by which it was decided to conclude the agreement, but not the agreement itself.[30] On the other hand, Article 46 of the Vienna Convention regarding competence to conclude treaties provides that:

> 1. A State may not invoke the fact that its consent to be bound by a treaty has been expressed in violation of a provision of its internal law regarding competence to conclude treaties as invalidating its consent unless that violation was manifest and concerned a rule of its internal law of fundamental importance.
>
> 2. A violation is manifest if it would be objectively evident to any State conducting itself in the matter in accordance with normal practice and in good faith.

In this sense, the strict conditions set by the international law of treaties were not fulfilled when the ECJ declared the agreement void *ab initio*.[31] The Court's position was not comfortable because, first, 'in case of breach of contract by the Commission, it could give raise to the liability of the Community at the international level'[32] but the contrary 'would affect the system itself'.[33] The exercise of the powers of EU institutions on international issues cannot, therefore, escape the judicial control of the Court of Justice or, where appropriate, the Court of First Instance.[34] However, the ECJ seems to forget the fact that the entry into force and termination of the Treaties, except as otherwise provided therein, are governed by international law (Article 27.2 Vienna Convention 1969) and to deprive an agreement of its original purposes is even worse than cancelling it.[35]

[29] Case C-327/91 *France v Commission* [1994] (n 17), para 1 (in the section 'Legal context and background').

[30] This was because 'in order for an action to be admissible . . . [before the ECJ], the contested act must be an act of an institution which produces legal effects'; see Case C-327/91 *France v Commission* [1994] (n 17), para 14.

[31] K Lenaerts and E de Smijter, 'The European Union as an Actor under International Law' (2000) 19(1) *Yearbook of European Law* 95 at 99.

[32] Case C-327/91 *France v Commission* [1994] (n 17), para 25 *in fine*.

[33] Case C-327/91 *France v Commission* [1994] (n 17), Opinion of AG Tesauro, para 12.

[34] Case C-327/91 *France v Commission* [1994] (n 17), para 16. This position has been reiterated by the ECJ in the Case C-122/95 *Germany v Council* [1998] ECR I-00973 para 42.

[35] See C, Kaddous, 'L'ârret France c. Commission de 1994 (accord concurrence) et le contrôle de la légalité des accords externes en vertu de l'article 173 CE : la difficile réconciliation de l'orthodoxie communautaire avec l'orthodoxie internationale' (1996) 32(5–6) *Cahiers de Droit Européen* 613 at 630; and J Charpentier, 'Le contrôle par la Cour de justice de la conformité au Traité des accords en vigueur conclus par la Communauté' (1997) 409 *Revue du marché commun et de l'Union européenne* 413 at 413.

8. However, in a statement of 30 May 2006, the Court of Justice seems to have departed from the approach described above.[36] Thus, although the ECJ annulled the Council decision approving the conclusion of an agreement with the United States due to the incorrect choice of the legal basis (in this case Article 95 TEU, Article 114 TFEU), it limited the effects of this annulment stating that 'the Community cannot rely on its own law as justification for not fulfilling the Agreement'.[37] This latest response is clearly contrary to the position held in *France v Commission*, where the ECJ declared void 'the act whereby the Commission sought to conclude the Agreement' in question and did not limit the effect of such annulment.[38]

At the same time, in the ruling of May 2006, Case *PNR*, the Court also seems to base its decision to limit the effects of the annulment on the fact that in light of

> the close link that exists between the Agreement and the decision on adequacy, it appears justified, for reasons of legal certainty and in order to protect the persons concerned, to preserve the effect of the decision on adequacy during that same period.[39]

Thus, in this latter case the ECJ decision to limit the effects of the annulment of the Council's decision was not solely based on the fact that the EC/EU cannot invoke its own domestic law in order not to comply with its international obligations, but also in an additional argument. Consequently, it is possible that in the absence of that additional argument, the Court had put forward its former case law and, therefore, had deprived the agreement in question of its effects within the EC/EU.[40]

2. THE COURT OF FIRST INSTANCE AS GUARDIAN OF THE *IUS COGENS*

2.1. The Origin of the Matter: The Decision of the CFI in the *Kadi* and *Yusuf and Al Barakaat* Cases

9. The origin of the *Kadi* and *Yusuf/Al Barakaat* cases, decided by the CFI and later annulled by the ECJ, will be a kind of leitmotif of the following considerations. and is found, as briefly mentioned above, in the UN Security Council resolutions adopted in the fight against international terrorism frameworks

[36] Joined Cases C-317/04 and C-318/04 *Parliament v Council* [2006] ECR I-4721 (also known as the *PNR* Case (*Passenger Name Records*)) paras 54–61 and 67–70. On this case, see G Gilmore and J Rijpma, 'Joined Cases C-317/04 and C-318/04, European Parliament v Council and Commission, Judgment of the Grand Chamber of 30 May 2006, [2006] ECR I-4721' (2007) 44(4) *Common Market Law Review* 1081; and M Mendez, 'Passenger Name Record Agreement – European Court of Justice' (2007) 3(1) *European Constitutional Law Review* 127.

[37] Joined Cases C-317/04 and C-318/04 *PNR* [2006] (n 36), para 73.

[38] Case C-327/91 *France v Commission* [1994] (n 17), para 15.

[39] Joined Cases C-317/04 and C-318/04 *PNR* [2006] (n 36), para 73.

[40] B Kunoy and A Dawes (2009) (n 24) at 88.

and, in particular, against the regime of the Taliban, Usama bin Laden and the terrorist network Al-Qaida.[41]

In this context, and considering the need for EC/EU action for the proper implementation of these resolutions, the Council of the European Union adopted a number of Common Positions in the CFSP field that transposed into the EC/EU order the obligations imposed on Member States by the Security Council.[42] In turn, while developing these Common Positions, a set of regulations were established to be used as the legal basis of Articles 60 TEU (75 TFEU), 301 TEU (215 TFEU) and 308 TEU (352 TFEU) through which certain specific economic sanctions were established that Member States had to adopt.[43]

Specifically, in the *Kadi* and *Al Barakaat* cases the rule at issue was Council Regulation 881/2002/EC of 27 May 2002 implementing the resolutions that in that year amended the regime of sanctions. Unlike the previous ones, the Council adopted this Regulation using the legal basis of Articles 60 TEU (75 TFEU), 301 TEU (215 TFEU) and 308 TEU (352 TFEU). Article 1 of the Regulation defines what is meant by 'funds', 'freezing of funds', 'economic resources' and Article 2 specifies the measures to be adopted.

In the list of natural and legal persons concerned included in Annex I, there were, among others, the names of Mr Yasin Al-Qadi, alias Kadi, a resident of Saudi Arabia, and of the entity Al Barakaat or Barakaat International Foundation, based in Sweden. Their inclusion on the Regulation 881/2002/EC

[41] See the resolutions of the Security Council concerning Al-Qaida and associated individuals and entities 1267 (1999), 1333 (2000), 1390 (2002), 1455 (2003), 1526 (2004), 1617 (2005), 1735 (2006), 1822 (2008), 1904 (2009) and 1989 (2011), all of them available through the site of the Security Council Committee pursuant to resolutions 1267 (1999) and 1989 (2011) at <http://www.un.org/sc/committees/1267/aq_sanctions_list.shtml>. For a comment, see E Sanfrutos Cano, 'Unión Europea: Comentario a la STJCE de 3 de septiembre de 2008 en los asuntos acumulados C-402/2005 P y C-415/2005 P, Yassin Abdullah Kadi y Al Barakaat International Foundation c. Consejo y Comisión' (2009) 7 *Gaceta jurídica de la Unión Europea y de la competencia* 69 at 71–3.

[42] See Council Common Position 1999/727/CFSP concerning restrictive measures against the Taliban (OJ L 294/1, 16 November 1999), Council Common Position 96/746/CFSP concerning additional restrictive measures against the Taliban and amending Common Position (OJ L 57/1, 27 February 2001), Council Common Position 2002/402/CFSP concerning restrictive measures against Usama bin Laden, members of the Al-Qaida organisation and the Taliban and other individuals, groups, undertakings and entities associated with them and repealing Common Positions 96/746/CFSP, 1999/727/CFSP, 2001/154/CFSP and 2001/771/CFSP (OJ L 139/4, 29 May 2002) and Council Decision 2011/487/CFSP amending Common Position 2002/402/CFSP concerning restrictive measures against Usama bin Laden, members of the Al-Qaida organisation and the Taliban and other individuals, groups, undertakings and entities associated with them (OJ L 199/73, 2 August 2011).

[43] See Council Regulation 337/2000/EC concerning a flight ban and a freeze of funds and other financial resources in respect of the Taliban of Afghanistan (OJ L 43/1, 16 February 2000), Council Regulation 467/2001/EC prohibiting the export of certain goods and services to Afghanistan, strengthening the flight ban and extending the freeze of funds and other financial resources in respect of the Taliban of Afghanistan, and repealing Regulation 337/2000/EC (OJ L 67/1, 9 March 2001), Council Regulation 881/2002/EC imposing certain specific restrictive measures directed against certain persons and entities associated with Usama bin Laden, the Al-Qaida network and the Taliban, and repealing Council Regulation 467/2001/EC (OJ L 139/9, 29 May 2002), Commission Implementing Regulation 748/2011/EU amending for the 153rd time Council Regulation 881/2002/EC (OJ L 198/1, 30 July 2011) and Council Regulation 754/2011/EU amending Regulation 881/2002/EC (OJ L 199/23, 2 August 2011).

list was a direct consequence of the publication by the relevant Sanctions Committee of the United Nations of two new additions to its consolidated list of entities and individuals who must be subjected to the freezing of funds by virtue of the Security Council resolutions mentioned above.[44]

In December 2001, Mr Kadi and Al Barakaat both lodged an appeal for annulment against the controversial regulation before the Court of First Instance. Mr Kadi claimed three reasons for annulment: violation of the right to be heard, violation of the right to respect for property and of the principle of proportionality and, third, violation of the right to effective judicial protection. Al Barakaat completed these substantive grounds based on the violation of fundamental rights with other arguments so that, according to the applicant, it would prove the lack of competence of the Council to adopt the contested Regulation and another regarding the infringement of Article 249 TEU (Article 288 TFEU).

10. The Court of First Instance delivered two similar opinions that solved the *Kadi* and *Yusuf* and *Al Barakaat* cases on 21 September 2005 which, despite the considerations to be discussed later on, dismissed both appeals in their entirety.[45] First, the CFI discussed the alleged lack of competence of the Council to adopt the regulation object of the appeal.[46] Then, it delivered a judgment on the question regarding fundamental rights.[47]

So, first, the CFI discussed the issue concerning the competence of the Council to adopt the controversial regulation on the legal basis of Articles 60 TEU (75 TFEU), 301 TEU (215 TFEU) and 308 TEU (352 TFEU). On this issue, the CFI considered that Articles 60 (75 TFEU) and 301 TEU (215 TFEU) do not alone constitute sufficient legal basis. On the other hand, Article 308 TEU (352 TFEU) alone does not justify the action of the EC/EU. However, the CFI considered that the Council was competent to adopt the controversial Regulation on the joint basis of Articles 60 TEU (75 TFEU), 301 TEU (215 TFEU) and 308 TEU (352 TFEU).[48] Specifically, the CFI bases its conclusion on the 'bridging' clauses nature of Articles 60 (75 TFEU) and 301 TEU (215 TFEU), which together with Article 308 TCE (352 TFEU) allowed the EC/EU action to achieve the objectives of the Union in the CFSP scope, to which it adds the requirement

[44] The relevant UN Sanctions Committee was established by Resolution 1267 (1999), also known as Al-Qaida and Taliban sanctions committee (n 41). The site of the Committee with updated information is available at <http://www.un.org/sc/committees/1267/index.shtml>.

[45] Case T-306/01 *Yusuf and Al Barakaat International Foundation v Council and Commission* [2005] ECR II-3533 and Case T-315/01 *Kadi v Council and Commission* [2005] ECR II-3649; both of them appealed and subsequently revoked by Joined Cases C-402/05 P and C-415/05 P *Kadi* and *Al Barakaat International Foundation v Council* [2008] ECR I-6351.

[46] Case T-306/01 *Yusuf and Al Barakaat* [2005] (n 45), paras 79–189 and Case T-315/01 *Kadi* [2005] (n 45), paras 64–135.

[47] Case T-306/01 *Yusuf and Al Barakaat* [2005] (n 45), paras 190-347 and Case T-315/01 *Kadi* [2005] (n 45), paras 136–292.

[48] Case T-306/01 *Yusuf and Al Barakaat* [2005] (n 45), para 170 and Case T-315/01 *Kadi* [2005] (n 45), para 135.

of consistency derived from Article 3 TEU (13 TEU-L) establishing a single, common institutional framework for the Community and the Union.[49] Thus, the CFI states that:

> Under Articles 60 EC and 301 EC, action by the Community is therefore in actual fact action by the Union, the implementation of which finds its footing on the Community pillar after the Council has adopted a common position or a joint action under the CFSP.[50]

Secondly, the CFI discussed the issue of the violation of the plaintiffs' fundamental rights, forcing it to consider the question of the relationship between the UN legal order and the national and community legal orders. As a result of this analysis, the Court of First Instance rejected control of the legality of EC/EU implementing measures in relation to the UNSEC resolutions adopted under Chapter VII of the Charter notwithstanding that such acts could violate certain fundamental rights guaranteed by the EC/EU legal order. The CFI, however, considered that the EU courts had the ability to control the legality of those EC/EU measures (implementing Security Council sanctions) from the point of view of certain peremptory norms of international law, in other words, the *ius cogens*.[51] On this concept, the Vienna Convention on the Law of Treaties 1969 provides:

> Article 53. Treaties conflicting with a peremptory norm of general international law ('jus cogens').
>
> A treaty is void if, at the time of its conclusion, it conflicts with a peremptory norm of general international law. For the purposes of the present Convention, a peremptory norm of general international law is a norm accepted and recognized by the international community of States as a whole as a norm from which no derogation is permitted and which can be modified only by a subsequent norm of general international law having the same character.

Thus, the opinion of the Court of First Instance considered that the resolutions of the Security Council would enjoy such a primacy that it would be virtually impossible for the community courts to carry out direct or incidental control.[52]

[49] The question of the legal bases to adopt the Regulation will be seen below.

[50] Case T-306/01 *Yusuf and Al Barakaat* [2005] (n 45), para 161 and Case T-315/01 *Kadi* [2005] (n 45), para 125.

[51] Case T-306/01 *Yusuf and Al Barakaat* [2005] (n 45), paras 272–277 and Case T-315/01 *Kadi* [2005] (n 45), paras 226–231.

[52] See Case *A, K, M, Q & G v HM Treasury* [2008] EWCA Civ 1187 (Supreme Court of judicature – Court of Appeal – Civil Division, 30 October 2008) para 18 and the subsequent appeal Case *Her Majesty's Treasury v Mohammed Jabar Ahmed and others* [2010] UKSC 2 & 5 (UK Supreme Court, 27 January 2010).

2.2. The Structural Limits of the EU Jurisdiction

11. From a very early stage, the ECJ established a teleological and normative approach to its mission of ensuring that law is respected in the interpretation and application of the Treaties. Thus, in its famous opinion *Les Verts* of 1986 it established that the founding Treaties constitute the constitutional charter of the then community legal order.[53] Years later, the Court of First Instance recalled that

> The access to the courts is one of the constituent elements of a community of law and is guaranteed in the legal order based in the EC Treaty since it has established a complete system of remedies and procedures designed to let the Court of Justice control the legality of the acts of the institutions.[54]

In the same way, nowadays it is firmly established that the validity of any EC/EU measure intended to produce legal effects may be subject to the control of EU courts, that is, they would have jurisdiction to control 'any measure which produces binding legal effects capable of affecting the interests of the appellant, modifying their legal status'.[55] The fact that the act in question is regulated by international law before the opinions of the CFI in *Yusuf* and *Kadi* was for the community court an irrelevant question because 'the exercise of the powers conferred to the institutions of the Community at international level can not escape the judicial control of the law laid down by the . . . Treaty'.[56]

12. The CFI considered in *Yusuf* and *Kadi*, and did the same in successive appeals that involved UN sanctions, that EU courts only have a limited jurisdiction to control the validity of EC/EU measures when such measures are the implementation of obligations derived from the UN law where EU institutions have 'no autonomous discretion' enabling them to establish something else.[57] If EU courts had full jurisdiction, they would be performing an indirect control of the legality of Security Council resolutions that are being implemented, something that the CFI flatly rejected:

> [T]he claim that the Court of First Instance has jurisdiction to review indirectly the lawfulness of such a decision according to the standard of protection of fundamental rights as recognised by the Community legal order, cannot be justified either on the basis of international law or on the basis of Community law.[58]

[53] Case 294/83 *Les Verts v Parliament* [1986] ECR 1339 para 23.

[54] Joined Cases T-377/00, T-379/00, T-380/00, T-260/01 and T-272/01 *Philip Morris International v Commission* [2003] ECR II-1 para 121. The appeal was subsequently dismissed in Case C-131/03 P *Reynolds Tobacco and others v Commission* [2006] ECR I-7795.

[55] Case 60/81 *IBM v Commission* [1981] ECR 2639 para 9.

[56] Case C-327/91 *France v Commission* [1994] (n 17), para 16.

[57] Case T-306/01 *Yusuf and Al Barakaat* [2005] (n 45), paras 264–265 and Case T-315/01 *Kadi* [2005] (n 45), paras 213–214.

[58] Case T-306/01 *Yusuf and Al Barakaat* [2005] (n 45), para 272 and Case T-315/01 *Kadi* [2005] (n 45), para 221.

According to the CFI, there were structural limits to the control that had to exercise the supervisory authority imposed by general international law or by the CFI itself.[59] These arguments were repeated by the CFI in successive cases in which individuals challenge the legality of EC/EU measures that implemented at the community level Security Council resolutions and decisions of the relevant Sanctions Committee.[60]

Therefore, one can state that the case law of the CFI reflects its conception of the role of United Nations law in the legal community order. Specifically, in the opinions of the *Yusuf* and *Kadi* cases, the EC/EU Court affirmed that:

> It has to be added that, with particular regard to Article 307 EC and to Article 103 of the Charter of the United Nations, reference to infringements either of fundamental rights as protected by the Community legal order or of the principles of that legal order cannot affect the validity of a Security Council measure or its effect in the territory of the Community.[61]

Therefore, it is clear that in these opinions, the CFI sets itself apart from the position taken by the ECJ, which had established its jurisdiction to control EC/EU measures that will implement international acts in the EC/EU order and, thus, it regarded itself competent to indirectly control the legality of international obligations assumed by the EC/EU.[62] The new conception expressed by the CFI in the cases of the UN sanctions limited the scope of jurisdiction of EU courts only in cases of certain 'structural limits'.[63]

13. The CFI stated in the *Yusuf* and *Kadi* cases that Article 103 of the UN Charter provides that the Charter prevails over any other treaty, including, in accordance with Article 25 thereof, the decisions adopted by the Security Council.[64] However, the Court did not take into account whether the actions of the Security Council, when implementing the regime of sanctions established in Resolution 1267, did so in accordance with the purposes and principles set out

[59] Case T-306/01 *Yusuf and Al Barakaat* [2005] (n 45), para 263 and Case T-315/01 *Kadi* [2005] (n 45), para 212.

[60] See Case T-253/02 *Ayadi v Council* [2006] ECR II-2139, paras 116–117, Case T-49/04 *Hassan Council and Commission* [2006] ECR II-52 (abstract), paras 92–93 (both of them revoked by Joined Cases C-399/06 P and C-403/06 P *Hassan and Ayadi v Council and Commission* [2009] ECR I-11393 and Case T-362/04 *Minin v Commission* [2007] ECR II-2003 para 101.

[61] Case T-306/01 *Yusuf and Al Barakaat* [2005] (n 45), para 275 and Case T-315/01 *Kadi* [2005] (n 45), para 224.

[62] See C Kaddous, 'L'ârret France c. Commission de 1994 (accord concurrence) et le contrôle de la légalité des accords externes en vertu de l'article 173 CE : la difficile réconciliation de l'orthodoxie communautaire avec l'orthodoxie internationale' (1996) 32(5–6) *Cahiers de Droit Européen* 613 at 621–32; and B Kunoy, 'The Jurisdiction of the ECJ to Review the Legality of the Transposition of an International Act in the EC Legal Order' (2007) 76(1) *Nordic Journal of International Law* 19 at 29–35.

[63] Case T-306/01 *Yusuf and Al Barakaat* [2005] (n 45), para 263 and Case T-315/01 *Kadi* [2005] (n 45), para 212.

[64] Case T-306/01 *Yusuf and Al Barakaat* [2005] (n 45), para 234 and Case T-315/01 *Kadi* [2005] (n 45), para 184.

in Article 24.2 of the Charter. Thus, if the Security Council resolutions do not comply with the provision referred to, they are ultra vires.[65]

Moreover, the CFI considered that

> the applicant's arguments based on the view that the Community legal order is a legal order independent of the United Nations, governed by its own rules of law, must be rejected.[66]

The Court of First Instance also ignored its prior case law according to which access to the courts is one of the founding principles of EC/EU law as well as the provisions of Resolution 1624 of the Security Council itself, which reads:

> States must ensure that any measures taken to implement [the sanctions regime established] . . . of this resolution comply with all of their obligations under international law, in particular international human rights law, refugee law, and humanitarian law.[67]

In this regard, the Security Council is bound by general international law and by those rights which are considered to be derived from the obligations under the UN Charter on Human Rights, especially the principles established in the Universal Declaration of Human Rights, the International Covenant on Civil and Political Rights and the International Covenant on Economic, Social and Cultural Rights.[68]

14. The CFI's argument in the cases of UN sanctions is the antithesis of the famous ruling of the ECJ in *Costa v ENEL*, in which it was established that 'by contrast with ordinary international treaties, the EEC Treaty has created its own legal system' and paved the way for the establishment of an autonomous legal order.[69] It is, therefore, difficult to understand how the reasoning of the CFI, which denies its jurisdiction in *Kadi* and in the following cases on the Security Council sanctions, can fit with the established jurisprudence of the ECJ according to which the Treaty of the European Community set forth a complete system of remedies and procedures designed to enable the Court of Justice to control the legality of the measures adopted by the institutions.[70] Moreover, whereas the *Internationale Handelsgesellschaft* case established that the validity of an act could only be judged in the light of Community law, in the *Yusuf* and *Kadi* cases the CFI expressly disclaims its jurisdiction alleging 'structural limits'.[71]

[65] E de Wet, *The Chapter VII Powers of the United Nations Security Council* (Hart, Oxford, 2004) 344.

[66] Case T-315/01 *Kadi* [2005] (n 45), para 208.

[67] UN Security Council Resolution 1624 (2005) 14 September, para 4.

[68] The Universal and customary nature of the Universal Declaration of Human Rights was confirmed by the Vienna Declaration and Programme of Action, adopted by the World Conference on Human Rights, held at Vienna from 14 to 25 June 1993, and subsequently endorsed by the UN General Assembly Resolution A/RES/48/121 (85th plenary meeting, 20 December 1993).

[69] Case 6/64 *Costa v ENEL* [1964] (n 8) 593.

[70] Case 294/83 *Les Verts* [1986] (n 53), para 23.

[71] See Case 11/70 *Internationale Handelsgesellschaft mbH v Einfuhr- und Vorratsstelle für Getreide und Futtermittel* [1970] ECR-1125, para 3, Case T-306/01 *Yusuf and Al Barakaat* [2005] (n 45), para 263 and Case T-315/01 *Kadi* [2005] (n 45), para 212

Thus, the 'structural limits' that the CFI claimed led it to embrace a position that rather than initiate proceedings before the EU courts, the individuals concerned had to apply to the competent authorities of Member States to protect their interests in the international scope, thus departing from the fundamental principle which establishes that

> an action for annulment must therefore be available in the case of all measures adopted by the institutions, whatever their nature or form, which are intended to have legal effects.[72]

2.3. The Introduction of Diplomatic Protection into the EC/EU Legal Order

15. The CFI, in order to remedy the lack of protection of fundamental rights at the EU level in the absence of an action for annulment against an EC/EU act based on the law of the United Nations, surprisingly, turned to general international law even when the EC/EU Treaties created their own legal order that directly affects not only governments and institutions, but also citizens of the Member States.[73]

The *Ayadi* and *Minin* cases represent, however, a significant jurisprudential development in comparison with the reasoning expressed by the CFI in *Yusuf* and *Kadi*. Thus, the CFI imposed the introduction of diplomatic protection in the EC/EU legal order as a substitute for the judicial remedies' deficiencies. The reason for the CFI to delegate the obligation to exercise diplomatic protection in the Member States is due to the legal reality that such protection can only be activated if there is a link to state nationality. Needless to say, European citizenship cannot be compared to a classic nationality and nor does it meet the requirements of nationality for the purposes of diplomatic protection claims that the EU could not exercise in favour of these citizens. Moreover, according to the special *rapporteur* of the UN International Law Commission on diplomatic protection:

> The European Union treaty provisions purporting to confer the right to diplomatic protection on all European Union citizens by all member States of the European Union is therefore flawed – unless it is interpreted as applicable to consular assistance only. It is submitted that this is indeed its intention.[74]

Thus, the CFI established in the *Ayadi* case that Member States 'are obliged to act promptly to ensure that the case concerned is submitted', through diplomatic protection, 'without delay and in a fairly and impartially way'.[75] But in

[72] Case 22/70 *Commission v Council – European Agreement on Road Transport* (*EART*) [1971] ECR 263 para 42.

[73] Case 26/62 *Van Gend en Loos v Nederlandse Administratie der Belastingen* [1963] ECR 3.

[74] See the *Seventh report on diplomatic protection* by John Dugard, Special Rapporteur (ILC Fifty-eighth session Geneva, 1 May to 9 June and 3 July to 11 August 2006, A/CN.4/567) para 19.

[75] Case T-253/02 *Ayadi* [2006] (n 60), para 149.

addition, the CFI stated in the *Hassan* case that if the individuals concerned believe that the competent national authority has violated their right to request the removal of their names from the blacklist, those citizens shall take advantage of all judicial remedies existing at national level.[76] Thus, the Court of First Instance imposed the obligation on Member States to exercise diplomatic protection on behalf of those affected if the inclusion of one of their nationals in the United Nations lists was contrary to the fundamental rights of citizenship recognized by the law of the state concerned. Therefore, in regard to diplomatic protection, the CFI went beyond what is established in general international law, which considers that diplomatic protection on behalf of citizens is not an obligation of the state.[77] On the other hand, although, as pointed out by the International Court of Justice, international law does not impose a positive obligation on states to exercise diplomatic protection in respect of their nationals, this court itself has established that:

> within the limits prescribed by international law, a State may exercise diplomatic protection by whatever means and to whatever extent it thinks fit, for it is its own right that the State is asserting.[78]

Consequently, one could argue that the Court of First Instance considers this right to diplomatic protection to be a 'functional equivalent' to a Court of Justice.[79] However, the success of the exercise of diplomatic protection depends largely on the relationships that the state of the citizen concerned has with the United States, as practically all natural and legal persons included in the lists of the Security Council have been included at the request of that government.[80] Therefore, it is clear that the process to come out of the lists does not necessarily follow legal principles but is rather subject to an arbitrary decision, since it requires reaching a consensus in which it is also necessary to be on good terms with the US Government. Moreover, let us not forget that while the obligation of the EU courts to protect fundamental rights is extended to all individuals under its jurisdiction, the exercise of diplomatic protection depends on the nationality of the victim. This dichotomy emphasizes the erroneous reasoning of the CFI, which suggested replacing the set of legal and procedural resources that exist in the EC/EU order by a requirement that the Member States exercise

[76] Case T-49/04 *Hassan* [2006] (n 60), paras 122–123.

[77] *Seventh report on diplomatic protection* by John Dugard, Special Rapporteur (n 74), para 22. Nonetheless the Special Rapporteur thinks that despite the exercise of diplomatic protection being a matter of the relationship between a state and its nationals, 'however, it should be ensured that the injured individual in whose interest the claim was raised will benefit from the exercise of diplomatic protection' (para 93).

[78] Case *Barcelona Traction, Light and Power Company, Limited (Second Phase)* Judgment (ICJ, 5 February 1970, *Reports* 3–53) para 78.

[79] I Ley, 'Legal Protection Against the UN-Security Council Between European and International Law: A Kafkaesque Situation?' (2007) 8(3) *German Law Journal* 279 at 283.

[80] *Ibid* 283–4.

diplomatic protection on their own nationals.[81] Mr Kadi, for example, was a national of Saudi Arabia and, therefore, the EC/EU courts can neither compel Member States to exercise diplomatic protection in favour of non-EU citizens nor require third states to do it with their own nationals.

16. In the *Ayadi* case the CFI did not hide the fact that the exercise of diplomatic protection is not a subjective right of EU citizens that can be directly enforceable.[82] In fact, as the CFI stated:

> Admittedly, [the De-listing procedure before the UN sanctions committee] . . . confers no right directly on the persons concerned themselves to be heard by the Committee, the only authority competent to give a decision, on a State's petition, on the re-examination of their case, with the result that they are dependent, essentially, on the diplomatic protection afforded by the States to their nationals.[83]

It should be recalled that according to a recognized principle of international law, confirmed by the International Court of Justice:

> The State must be viewed as the sole judge to decide whether its protection will be granted, to what extent it is granted, and when it will cease. It retains in this respect a discretionary power the exercise of which may be determined by considerations of a political or other nature, unrelated to the particular case.[84]

As mentioned above, the CFI was aware of the discretion with which the Member States exercise diplomatic protection in international law. To remedy the lack of judicial control regarding the legality of the sanctions, the Court considered that the exercise of diplomatic protection should be mandatory for Member States. However, in addition to the political weakness of the reasoning expressed in *Ayadi* and *Menin*, that does not take into account the possible lack of effectiveness of Member States in the decision process of the UN. There are significant gaps in the Court's reasoning, since it compromises the citizens' *status* as individuals to whom the EC/EU law is directly applied because, by exercising diplomatic protection, the state is exercising its own prerogatives and is not acting under any particular substantive law either derived from the national or the EU legal order.[85]

[81] Criticism of this case law is large. See, inter alia, B Kunoy and A Dawes (2009) (n 24). Nonetheless, for a comment that welcomes this 'courageous' and 'well-balanced construction', see C Tomuschat. 'Case T-306/01, Ahmed Ali Yusuf and Al Barakaat International Foundation v Council and Commission, judgment of the Court of First Instance of 21 September 2005; Case T-315/01, Yassin Abdullah Kadi v Council and Commission, judgment of the Court of First Instance of 21 September 2005' (2006) 43(2) *Common Market Law Review* 537 at 551.

[82] See J Heliskoski, 'Case T-253/02, Chafiq Ayadi v Council, judgment of the Court of First Instance of 12 July 2006; Case T-49/04, Faraj Hassan v Council and Commission' (2007) 44(4) *Common Market Law Review* 1143.

[83] Case T-253/02 *Ayadi* [2006] (n 60), para 141.

[84] Case *Barcelona Traction, Light and Power Company, Limited (Second Phase)* [1970] (n 78), para 79.

[85] B Kunoy and A Dawes (2009) (n 24) at 95.

This principle, known as 'Vattel's theory' since the eighteenth century and which is the essence of diplomatic protection,[86] was formulated more carefully by the Permanent Court of International Justice in the *Mavrommatis Palestine Concessions* case when it stated that:

> By taking up the case of one of its subjects and by resorting to diplomatic action or international judicial proceedings on his behalf, a State is in reality asserting its own rights – its right to ensure, in the person of its subjects, respect for the rules of international law.[87]

It is also interesting to remember that in 1972 the ICJ established in an obiter dictum that the instruments of protection of regional organizations are better prepared to protect an individual against refusal of access to the courts than the exercise of diplomatic protection. Thus,

> [w]ith regard more particularly to human rights . . . it should be noted that these also include protection against denial of justice. However, on the universal level, the instruments which embody human rights do not confer on States the capacity to protect the victims of infringements of such rights irrespective of their nationality. It is therefore still on the regional level that a solution to this problem has had to be sought; thus, within the Council of Europe, of which Spain is not a member, the problem of admissibility encountered by the claim in the present case has been resolved by the European Convention on Human Rights, which entitles each State which is a party to the Convention to lodge a complaint against any other contracting State for violation of the Convention, irrespective of the nationality of the victim.[88]

17. It is therefore strange that the Court of First Instance accepted that the exercise of diplomatic protection in international law by Member States could be enough to defend the rights of nationals affected by UN sanctions especially when the ICJ, 35 years ago, had expressly provided that wherever the regional protection instruments were, they were more appropriate to protect the rights of individuals than the exercise of diplomatic protection. Although legal or natural persons are not conferred a civil right to ensure the effectiveness of these fundamental rights of citizens at the community level, the CFI said that the exercise of diplomatic protection 'is not, however, to be deemed improper in the light of the mandatory prescriptions of the public international order'.[89]

In any case, this reasoning of the CFI is contrary to the very essence of constitutional principles found at the basis of EC/EU law, especially the fact that such order affects both Member States and their citizens.[90]

[86] See E Vattel, *El derecho de gentes o principios de la ley natural aplicados a la conducta, y a los negocios de las naciones y de los soberanos* (MM Pascual Hernández (tr)) (Imprenta León Amarita, Madrid, 1834) 333 (para 71.2).

[87] Case *Mavrommatis Palestine Concessions* Judgment No 2 (Permanent Court of International Justice 30 August 1924, *Series* A02, 5-37) 12.

[88] Case *Barcelona Traction, Light and Power Company, Limited (Second Phase)* [1970] (n 70), para 91.

[89] Case T-253/02 *Ayadi* [2006] (n 60), para 141.

[90] Case 26/62 *Van Gend en Loos* [1963] (n 73).

3. THE ECJ AS CONSTITUTIONAL GUARDIAN

3.1. The Action before the ECJ: The Decision of the Court of Justice in the *Kadi* and *Al Barakaat* cases

18. Regarding the dismissal of their claims by the CFI, Mr Kadi and Al Barakaat filed actions before the ECJ for annulment of the judgments of the CFI and the recognition of their original claims.[91] The reasons alleged by the appellants repeated, in essence, the arguments submitted before the CFI and can be grouped around two main issues, the first regarding the legal basis of the controversial regulation and the second relating to the control of possible violations of fundamental rights. Through its now famous decision of 3 September 2008, the ECJ took partially into consideration the claims of the appellants and reversed the judgments of the CFI and of the regulation concerned, but their effects remained for three months, the time necessary to ensure that the Council issue a new regulation to relist the appellants, though apparently, now, protecting their fundamental rights (see below).

The fundamental differences between the ECJ and the CFI are evident. Where the CFI did not hesitate to venture into the field of international law (which earned it major criticism, especially from the French doctrine), the ECJ stuck voluntary and exclusively to the scope of EC/EU law.[92] That is, the ECJ's opinion underlies the adage that EC/EU law has adequate legal remedies to ensure respect for fundamental rights and, in the words of the most critical authors, it does not have to 'play' at being an 'International Law professor'.[93]

19. The ECJ's opinion on *Kadi*, which had significant media exposure, dealt with three important issues of varying complexity. In order of increasing difficulty, it examined the legal basis for adopting the controversial regulation, then addressed the problem of fully reviewing the contested measure and, finally, considered the competence of the EU jurisdiction in order to control the legality of implementing a decision of the Security Council of the United Nations.[94]

[91] Because of their inner connection, the ECJ decided by Art 43 of its Rules to join both cases (C-402/05 P and C-415/05 P). They will be subsequently known by the name of the first appellant, Mr Kadi.

[92] For a few critical comments to the CFI decision, see G Guillaume, 'Jus cogens et souveraineté' in JP Puissochet *et al* (ed), *L'État souverain dans le monde d'aujourd'hui – Melanges en l'honneur de Jean-Pierre Puissochet* (Pedone, Paris, 2008) 127; D Simon and F Mariatte, 'Le Tribunal de première instance des Communautés : Professeur de droit international?' (2005) Décembre *Europe* 6 especially at 9–10, JP Jacqué, 'Le Tribunal de première instance face aux résolutions du Conseil de sécurité des Nations Unies. "Merci Monsieur le Professeur"' (2006) 19 *L'Europe des libertés* 2, especially at 5–6.

[93] This expression was used in one of the earliest and most quoted comments on the CFI decision: D Simon and F Mariatte (2005) (n 92).

[94] The literature is huge and still increasing. See, inter alia, M Tzanou, 'Case-note on Joined Cases C-402/05 P & C-415/05 P Yassin Abdullah Kadi & Al Barakaat International Foundation v Council of European Union & Commission of European Communities' (2009) 10(2) *German Law*

As regards the first issue, the one of the legal basis, let us say here, so as not to return to the same issue in the subsequent analysis, that the ECJ 'did what it could'.[95] The judgment structured its reasoning on this procedural question in three points. First, it pointed out that Articles 60 TEU (75 TFEU) and 301 TEC (215 TFEU) cannot by themselves constitute a sufficient legal basis for the restrictive measure as long as those provisions relate substantially to the movement of capital or to the economic relations regarding third countries, which are neither Usama bin Laden nor the Al-Qaida network.[96] Secondly, the opinion states that Article 308 TEC (352 TFEU), which allows the Council to adopt the necessary provisions when an EC action is necessary to achieve, within the internal market, one of the objectives of the EC/EU, and this Treaty has not provided the necessary powers for this purpose, cannot justify the adoption of EC/EU acts regarding the Common Foreign and Security Policy (CFSP), which is an objective of the EU and not of the EC.[97] Nevertheless, thirdly and finally, the legal basis of the Regulation could be found in the combination of Articles 60 TEU (75 TFEU), 301 TEC (215 TFEU) and 308 TEC (352 TFEU). For the ECJ, the implementation of restrictive measures of an economic nature decided within the framework of the CFSP through the use of an EC/EU instrument has a connection with the functioning of the internal market that is one of the objectives of the EC/EU within the sense of Article 308 TEC (352 TFEU). Moreover, this Article would permit the limits of the scope of application *ratione personae* of Articles 60 TEU (75 TFEU) and 301 TEC (215 TFEU) to be exceeded to enable the imposition of restrictive measures on individuals who have no link with the leaders of a third state.[98]

Then, the ECJ examined the other issues regarding, on the one hand, the competence of the EU courts to review the legality of a regulation implementing a

Journal 123, D Halberstam and E Stein, 'The United Nations, the European Union, and the King of Sweden: Economic sanctions and individual rights in a plural world order' (2009) 46(1) *Common Market Law Review* 13; P Cassia and F Donnat, 'Terrorisme international et droits fondamentaux : les leçons du droit communautaire Commentaire sous Cour de justice des Communautés européennes, 3 septembre 2008, Kadi et Al Barakaat International Foundation, aff. C-402/05 P et C-415/05 P' (2008) 24(6) *Revue Française de Droit Administratif* 1204; T Tridimas, 'Terrorism and the ECJ: Empowerment and democracy in the EC legal order' (2009) 34(1) *European Law Review* 103; E Sanfrutos Cano, 'Unión Europea: Comentario a la STJCE de 3 de septiembre de 2008 en los asuntos acumulados C-402/2005 P y C-415/2005 P, Yassin Abdullah Kadi y Al Barakaat International Foundation c. Consejo y Comisión' (2009) 7 *Gaceta jurídica de la Unión Europea y de la competencia* 69; and G de Búrca, 'The European Court of Justice and the International Legal Order After Kadi' (2010) 51 *Harvard International Law Journal* 1.

[95] See P Cassia and F Donnat, 'Terrorisme international et droits fondamentaux : les leçons du droit communautaire Commentaire sous Cour de justice des Communautés européennes, 3 septembre 2008, Kadi et Al Barakaat International Foundation, aff. C-402/05 P et C-415/05 P' (2008) 24(6) *Revue Française de Droit Administratif* 1204 at 1205.

[96] Joined Cases C-402/05 P and C-415/05 P *Kadi* and *Al Barakaat International Foundation v Council* [2008] ECR I-6351 paras 163–193.

[97] Joined Cases C-402/05 P and C-415/05 P *Kadi* and *Al Barakaat* [2008] (n 96), paras 194–211, specially para 198.

[98] Joined Cases C-402/05 P and C-415/05 P *Kadi* and *Al Barakaat* [2008] (n 96), paras 212–236, specially paras 227 and 229–230.

decision of the Security Council of the United Nations and, on the other hand, to the compliance of specific restrictive measures (called 'smart' in the UN's language) with fundamental rights.[99] In this sense, the Grand Chamber, in line with the provisions of their conclusions by Advocate General Poiares Maduro, determined that the CFI was wrong to conclude that EC/EU courts have no jurisdiction to fully review the legality of EC/EU measures, even when these measures are the implementation of legal obligations derived from United Nations law which does not grant the EC/EU any 'independent discretion' to act otherwise.[100] Thus, the ECJ reaffirmed the autonomy of the EC/EU legal order in relation to all the categories of international law and established EC/EU courts as the ultimate judges of the compatibility of EC/EU legislation with fundamental rights.

3.2. The Establishment of the Autonomy of EC/EU Law in Relation to All Norms of International Law

20. It is important to understand the reasons for the decision of the ECJ to annul the judgments of the CFI. In fact, none of the courts agreed, albeit for different reasons, that international law shall bind the United Nations Charter to prevail over EC/EU law or to set structural limits to the control power that EU courts bear. Meanwhile, the CFI based its argument on the fact that the EC/EU is either a UN member or an addressee of the resolutions of the Security Council, or the successor of the rights and obligations of Member States under international public law.[101] On the other hand, the ECJ justified its position by stating that:

> the Charter of the United Nations does not impose the choice of a particular model for the implementation of resolutions adopted by the Security Council under Chapter VII of the Charter, since they are to be given effect in accordance with the procedure applicable in that respect in the domestic legal order of each Member of the United Nations. The Charter of the United Nations leaves the Members of the United Nations a free choice among the various possible models for transposition of those resolutions into their domestic legal order.[102]

21. Instead, the disagreement between the ECJ and the CFI was limited to their differing interpretations of the relationship between different key regulations of the TEU. For the CFI, the EC/EU legal order allowed the United Nations law to set limits on the fundamental rights guaranteed by EC/EU law. This conclusion, which in the words of the Advocate General 'essentially amounts to a rule of

[99] Note how the ECJ prefers the expression 'restrictive measures' and avoids the term 'sanction'.
[100] Joined Cases C-402/05 P and C-415/05 P *Kadi* and *Al Barakaat* [2008] (n 96), para 84.
[101] Case T-306/01 *Yusuf and Al-Barakaat* [2005] (n 45), para 242 and Case T-315/01 *Kadi* [2005] (n 45), para 192.
[102] Joined Cases C-402/05 P and C-415/05 P *Kadi* and *Al Barakaat* [2008] (n 96), para 298.

primacy, flowing from the EC Treaty, essentially equivalent to a primacy rule derived from the EC Treaty',[103] is based on two arguments.

First of all, the CFI considered that in light of the succession theory developed by the ECJ in the *International Fruit Company* case (see above) and given that in the areas covered by the TEU the EC/EU had assumed the powers previously exercised by Member States in the field governed by the Charter, the provisions of the UN Charter governing these same areas had a binding effect for the EC/EU. That is, in the words of the CFI:

> It therefore appears that, in so far as under the EC Treaty the Community has assumed powers previously exercised by Member States in the area governed by the Charter of the United Nations, the provisions of that Charter have the effect of binding the Community (see, by analogy, on the question whether the Community is bound by the General Agreement on Tariffs and Trade (GATT) of 1947, International Fruit, paragraph 18; see also, in that it recognises that the Community exercises circumscribed powers when giving effect to a trade embargo imposed by a resolution of the Security Council, Dorsch Consult v Council and Commission . . .).
>
> Following that reasoning, it must be held, first, that the Community may not infringe the obligations imposed on its Member States by the Charter of the United Nations or impede their performance and, second, that in the exercise of its powers it is bound, by the very Treaty by which it was established, to adopt all the measures necessary to enable its Member States to fulfill those obligations.[104]

Secondly, the CFI considered that the claim that the EU courts could have jurisdiction to control the legality of EC/EU measures to constitute the implementation of the obligations derived from the United Nations that do not grant the EC/EU any autonomous discretion is contrary to several provisions of the TEU (particularly Articles 5 (5 TEU-L), 10 (4 TEU-L), 297 (347 TFEU) and 307.1 (351 TFEU)),[105] contrary to the EU Treaty (specifically, Article 5 TEU, 13 TEU-L)[106] and to the general principle of EC/EU law which states that EC/EU powers shall be exercised in accordance with international law.[107] Moreover, the CFI adopted a

[103] Joined Cases C-402/05 P and C-415/05 P *Kadi* and *Al Barakaat* [2008] (n 96), Opinion of AG Poiares Maduro, para 18.

[104] Case T-306/01 *Yusuf* and *Al Barakaat* [2005] (n 45), paras 253–254 and Case T-315/01 *Kadi* [2005] (n 45), paras 203–204. The same reasoning, with other wording, appears in Case T-253/02 *Ayadi* [2006] (n 60), para 116, Case T-49/04 *Hassan* [2006] (n 60), para 92 and Case T-362/04 *Minin* [2007] (n 60), paras 67 and 101.

[105] Briefly, Art 5 TEC (5 TEU-L) establishes the principles of subsidiarity, Art 10 TEC (4 TEU-L) the principle of cooperation, Art 297 TEC (347 TFEU) allows certain restrictions within the internal market when Member States have to carry out obligations for the purpose of maintaining peace and international security and Art 307.1 TEC (351 TFEU) says that the rights and obligations arising from international agreements concluded before the establishment of the Communities (or the accession of the relevant state) shall not be affected by the provisions of the Treaties.

[106] Art 5 TEU (13 TEU-L) establishes that EU institutions shall act within the limits of the powers conferred by Treaties, and in conformity with the procedures, conditions and objectives set out in them.

[107] Case T-306/01 *Yusuf* and *Al Barakaat* [2005] (n 45), para 273, Case T-315/01 *Kadi* [2005] (n 45), para 222, Case T-253/02 *Ayadi* [2006] (n 60), para 116, Case T-49/04 *Hassan* [2006] (n 60), para 92 and Case T-362/04 *Minin* [2007] (n 60), para 101. See also Case C-286/90 *Anklagemindigheden v Poulsen* [1992] (n 14), para 9 and Case C-162/96 *Racke v Hauptzollamt Mainz* [1998] ECR I-03655

very ambitious internationalist approach considering the EC/EU legal order as any other kind of domestic order to the effects of its relationship regarding the legal order derived from the UN, all of them being subordinate to the UN Charter, which would be at the top of the normative pyramid.[108]

22. On the other hand, the ECJ dismissed the argument according to which its control over the contested regulation would actually lead to the indirect control of the Security Council resolution behind it. By doing so, the ECJ reaffirmed the distinction that has traditionally been established (not without criticism) between the control of the legality of an international agreement, that the EU courts cannot carry out, and the review of the EC/EU measures used to give effect to the international agreement concerned, action that the EU courts themselves can undertake, since the annulment of an EC/EU measure intended to give effect to an international rule is not a threat to the primacy of the said rule in the international legal order.[109] Indeed, in the words of the ECJ in the *Kadi* case:

> In this regard it must be emphasized that, in circumstances such as those of these cases, the review of lawfulness thus to be ensured by the Community judicature applies to the Community act intended to give effect to the international agreement at issue, and not to the latter as such.
>
> With more particular regard to a Community act which, like the contested regulation, is intended to give effect to a resolution adopted by the Security Council under Chapter VII of the Charter of the United Nations, it is not, therefore, for the Community judicature, under the exclusive jurisdiction provided for by Article 220 EC, to review the lawfulness of such a resolution adopted by an international body, even if that review were to be limited to examination of the compatibility of that resolution with jus cogens.
>
> However, any judgment given by the Community judicature deciding that a Community measure intended to give effect to such a resolution is contrary to a higher rule of law in the Community legal order would not entail any challenge to the primacy of that resolution in international law.[110]

paras 45–46. However, these two last cases dealt only with the relationship between secondary law and international law (and not primary law (treaties) and international law).

[108] One of the first comments in fact welcomed this 'courageous' case law. See C Tomuschat, 'Case T-306/01, Ahmed Ali Yusuf and Al Barakaat International Foundation v Council and Commission, judgment of the Court of First Instance of 21 September 2005; Case T-315/01, Yassin Abdullah Kadi v Council and Commission, judgment of the Court of First Instance of 21 September 2005' (2006) 43(2) *Common Market Law Review* 537 at 551. For a critique of the then CFI-established subordination of EC/EU law to UN law, see P Eeckhout. 'Community Terrorism Listings, Fundamental Rights, and UN Security Council Resolutions. In Search of the Right Fit' (2007) 3(2) *European Constitutional Law Review* 183 and J Almqvist, 'A Human Rights Critique of European Judicial Review: Counter-Terrorism Sanction' (2008) 57(2) *International and Comparative Law Quarterly* 303.

[109] On the distinction between the control of the agreements as such and the control of the implementing measures of the agreements, see Case C-327/91 *France v Commission* [1994] (n 17), paras 21 and 24–25 and ID Hendry, S Hyett and I Macleod, *The External Relations of the European Communities: A Manual of Law and Practice* (Clarendon, Oxford, 1999) 129–32.

[110] Joined Cases C-402/05 P and C-415/05 P *Kadi* and *Al Barakaat* [2008] (n 96), paras 286–288.

If the EC Treaty has established a complete system of legal remedies and procedures that ensure that all acts of the institutions are subject to judicial control, then all EC/EU measures should be subject to the same degree of control, regardless of the legal nature of the measure (for example, a Security Council resolution) in its origin.[111]

23. The ECJ also considered that while the EC/EU must respect international law and, in particular, the law derived from the United Nations, in the exercise of its powers, there is no legal basis in the TEU to justify the argument according to which the measures adopted in development of the Security Council resolutions of the UN enjoy immunity from jurisdiction, that is, they are not subject to judicial review by the EC/EU courts.[112] In addition, although Articles 297 TEU (347 TFEU) and 307 TEU (351 TFEU) may justify certain derogations of primary law (see above),

> [t]hose provisions cannot, however, be understood to authorise any derogation from the principles of liberty, democracy and respect for human rights and fundamental freedoms enshrined in Article 6(1) EU as a foundation of the Union.[113]

The control exercised by EU courts, in the field of the domestic and autonomous legal order of the EC/EU, on the validity of an EC/EU measure in the light of fundamental rights is a constitutional guarantee derived from the Treaties and cannot be jeopardized by the provisions of an international agreement, or even by those derived from the UN Charter.[114] In that sense, the fact that the ECJ deals with the UN Charter, at least in regard to its relationship with EC/EU law, in the same way as any other international treaty, is in fact due to its conventional position according to which EC/EU and international legal orders do operate on separate levels and, for the ECJ, their relations are regulated only by the EC/EU law itself.[115] Therefore, there is no reason to argue that the UN Charter, as well as national constitutional rules, is in a position to challenge or affect the nature, meaning, or primacy of the fundamental rights guaranteed by the EC/EU legal order.[116]

[111] See Editorial, 'The rule of law as the backbone of the EU' (2007) 44(4) *Common Market Law Review* 875.

[112] The obligation of the EC/EU to exercise its competences in accordance with international law is also pointed out in the Joined Cases C-402/05 P and C-415/05 P *Kadi* and *Al Barakaat* [2008] (n 96), para 291.

[113] Joined Cases C-402/05 P and C-415/05 P *Kadi* and *Al Barakaat* [2008] (n 96), para 303.

[114] Joined Cases C-402/05 P and C-415/05 P *Kadi* and *Al Barakaat* [2008] (n 96), paras 316–317.

[115] Thus, as can be seen above, the ECJ has denied effects within the EC/EU to international agreements adopted in accordance with the wrong legal basis (Case C-317/04 and C-318/04 *PNR* [2006] (n 36)), agreements adopted in disregarding the principle of cooperation (C-25/94 *Commission v Council* [1996] ECR I-1469 paras 40–51) or simply contrary to the general principles of Community law (Case C-122/95 *Germany v Council* [1998] (n 34)).

[116] On the application of this principle to national constitutional law, see inter alia Case 11/70 *Internationale Handelsgesellschaft* [1970] (n 71), para 3, Case 234/85 *Keller* [1986] ECR 2897 para 7 and Joined Cases 97–99/87 *Dow Chemical Ibérica and others v Commission* [1989] ECR 3165 para 38.

24. Finally, even if the EC/EU legal order could grant the Security Council resolutions some primacy effect over EC/EU law, such primacy would reach only to acts of secondary EC/EU law and not to primary law nor to the general principles of law among which are included fundamental rights. In fact, as clearly established by the Luxembourg Court:

> Nor can an immunity from jurisdiction for the contested regulation with regard to the review of its compatibility with fundamental rights, arising from the alleged absolute primacy of the resolutions of the Security Council to which that measure is designed to give effect, find any basis in the place that obligations under the Charter of the United Nations would occupy in the hierarchy of norms within the Community legal order if those obligations were to be classified in that hierarchy.
>
> Article 300(7) EC provides that agreements concluded under the conditions set out in that article are to be binding on the institutions of the Community and on Member States.
>
> Thus, by virtue of that provision, supposing it to be applicable to the Charter of the United Nations, the latter would have primacy over acts of secondary Community law . . .
>
> That primacy at the level of Community law would not, however, extend to primary law, in particular to the general principles of which fundamental rights form part.[117]

Thus, let us conclude that the ECJ re-established the traditional hierarchy of norms within the EC/EU legal order that the CFI had wrongly modified.[118]

3.3. The ECJ as the Final Guardian of Fundamental Rights

25. For different reasons, the opinion of the ECJ in *Kadi* re-establishes EU courts (the ECJ, the CFI (now the General Court) and also the Civil Service Tribunal) as the last guardians of the compatibility of EC/EU legislation with fundamental rights.

26. First, the opinion establishes that the level of control by the community courts of the measures that implement obligations derived from international law in the EC/EU legal order will no longer depend on whether the EC/EU institutions had discretion or not.[119] Following the Court of First Instance case law

[117] Joined Cases C-402/05 P and C-415/05 P *Kadi* and *Al Barakaat* [2008] (n 96), paras 305–308. See Case C-308/06 *Intertanko and others* [2008] ECR I-4057 para 42, where the Court stressed that '[i]t is clear from Article 300(7) EC that the Community institutions are bound by agreements concluded by the Community and, consequently, that those agreements have primacy over secondary Community legislation'. See also Case C-61/94 *Commission v Germany* [1996] ECR I-3989 para 52 and Case C-311/04 *Algemene Scheeps Agentuur Dordrecht* [2006] ECR I-609 para 25.

[118] See NG Vitzthum, 'Les compétences législatives et juridictionnelles de la Communauté européenne dans la lutte contre le terrorisme – l'affaire "Kadi"' (2008) 11(3) *Zeitschrift für Europarechtliche Studien* 375 at 420–26, where the author doubts on the primacy of UN Security Council Resolutions over EC/EU law.

[119] C Eckes, 'Case T-228/02, Organisation des Modjahedines du peuple d'Iran v Council and UK (OMPI), Judgment of the Court of First Instance (Second Chamber) of 12 December 2006' (2007) 44(4) *Common Market Law Review* 1117 at 1119.

in *Kadi*, *Yusuf* and *Al Barakaat*, *Ayadi*, *Hassan*, *Minin*, *OMPI*, *Kongra-Gel*, *PKK*, *Al-Aqsa* and *Sison* (see above), the scope of the jurisdiction of community courts to control the EC/EU measures to impose sanctions on individuals suspected of being associated with terrorism was artificially conditioned by whether EC/EU measures that imposed those sanctions simply reproduced the lists passed in the UN Security Council or if, on the contrary, they were independently adopted by the EC/EU.[120] Thus, while the legality of the sanctions on individuals imposed by EC/EU acts based on lists of the UN sanctions committees was only subjected to a most unlikely indirect control in the light of *ius cogens*, individuals who were subject to autonomous sanctions adopted by the Community could, however, require a greater degree of protection of their rights from a procedural point of view, and even substantive.[121] On the other hand, the ruling of the ECJ on *Kadi* will ensure that all economic sanctions imposed on individuals by the EC/EU shall be subject to the same level of control by the EU courts, regardless of whether or not the EC/EU has exercised a certain degree of discretion.

27. Secondly, the ECJ rejects the notion that there are 'political questions' on which the EC/EU courts have no jurisdiction.[122]

The term 'political question', better known in the European public law doctrine as 'political or government act', refers to that area of government activity exempt from jurisdictional control. It is commonly accepted by the doctrine that the United States Supreme Court was the authority that first recognized the courts' inability to control or decide on the whole 'political question' in its opinion on the *Luther v Borden* case of 1849.[123] However, the original French Council of State had already dealt with a similar question in its famous opinion

[120] See Case T-306/01 *Yusuf* and *Al Barakaat* [2005] (n 45), Case T-315/01 *Kadi* [2005] (n 45), Case T-253/02 *Ayadi* [2006] (n 60), Case T-49/04 *Hassan* [2006] (n 60), Case T-362/04 *Minin* [2007] (n 60), Case T-47/03 *José María Sison v Council* [2007] ECR II-73 (abstract), Case T-327/03 *Stichting Al-Aqsa v Council* [2007] ECR II-79 (abstract), Case T-253/04 *Kongra-Gel v Council* [2008] ECR II-46, Case T-229/02 *Osman Ocalan, on behalf of the Kurdistan Workers' Party (PKK)* [2008] ECR II-45, Case T-85/09 *Kadi v Commission (Kadi II)* [2010] unpublished, and the *OMPI-PMOI* saga, Case T-228/02 *OMPI* [2006] ECR II-4665, Case T-256/07 *PMOI I* [2008] ECR II-3019, and Case T-284/08 *PMOI II* [2008] ECR II-3487.

[121] On the other hand, one can also argue that, for instance, in the Cases *OMPI-PMOI* saga, *Kongra-Gel*, *PKK*, *Al-Aqsa* and *Sison* since the CFI stuck to the procedural aspects, the Court was excessively deferential vis-à-vis the Council and its listing and de-listing decisions and therefore disregarded a substantive protection of the fundamental rights. See C Eckes (2007) *cit* 1129 and T Tridimas and JA Gutiérrez Fons, 'EU law, international law, and economic sanctions against terrorism: the judiciary in distress?' (2009) 32(2) *Fordham International Law Journal* 660 at 697–702.

[122] Joined Cases C-402/05 P and C-415/05 P *Kadi* and *Al Barakaat* [2008] (n 96), Opinion of AG Poiares Maduro, paras 33–34 and notes 39–40.

[123] Case *Luther v Borden*, 48 US 1 (1849). However, some argue that one can find the principles of this doctrine in the famous Case *Marbury v Madison*, 5 US (Cranch 1) 137 (1803). On the 'political question' doctrine in the US, see E Chemerinsky, *Constitutional Law. Principles and Policies* 3rd edn (Aspen, New York, 2006) 129–49 and 284–6. See also GR Stone *et al*, *Constitutional Law* 5th edn (Aspen, New York, 2005) 119–58.

on the *Laffitte* case of 1822.[124] Whoever has the honour of having inaugurated this theory, the main thing is that it says that a sector of government activity shall not be controlled by the courts. Obviously, the lack of control is an issue that conflicts with the basic principles of the rule of law, so the trend in the modern constitutional rule of law is to accept a decreasing margin of autonomy to the government and, in any case, it shall always be liable to the control process by which the 'political' or 'government' decision is adopted.[125]

One argument in favour of using the theory of the 'political question' in the *Kadi* case was brought up by the European Commission itself, by the Council and by the United Kingdom, who said that matters relating to the maintenance of international peace and security were not likely to be submitted to judicial control. The opinion of the CFI in the *OMPI* case already suggested that restrictions in EU courts' competences to control the validity of the EC/EU measures establishing the implementation of the UN Security Council resolutions were only based on the fact that said control could not lead, in any way, the institution to review its position and that the proper scope of the sanctions should not be subject to judicial control.[126]

Although the opinion of the ECJ does not completely fall on this issue, it did implicitly reject it by stating that:

> the Community judicature must, in accordance with the powers conferred on it by the EC Treaty, ensure the review, in principle the full review, of the lawfulness of all Community acts in the light of the fundamental rights forming an integral part of the general principles of Community law, including review of Community measures which, like the contested regulation, are designed to give effect to the resolutions adopted by the Security Council under Chapter VII of the Charter of the United Nations.[127]

[124] Case *Laffitte* (French *Conseil d'État*, 1 May 1822, 1821–1825 *Lebon* 2002). See also Case *d'Aumale et Michel Lévy* (French *Conseil d'État*, 9 May 1867, 1867 *Lebon* 472) and the case law reversal in favour of a higher judicial control in Case *Prince Napoléon* (French *Conseil d'État*, 19 February 1875, 1875 *Lebon* 155). On these cases, see M Long *et al*, *Les grands arrêts de la jurisprudence administrative* 15th edn (Dalloz, Paris, 2005) 16–26; JF Lachaume and H Pauliat, *Droit administratif. Les grandes décisions de la jurisprudence* (PUF, Paris, 2007) 665–78; and P Duez, *Les actes de gouvernement* (Dalloz, Paris, 2006 (reprint of the original of 1935)) 30–7.

[125] Spanish scholarship has studied the theory of the 'political question' and its implications deeply. See E García de Enterría, 'La lucha contra las inmunidades del poder en el derecho administrativo (poderes discrecionales, poderes de gobierno, poderes normativos)' (1962) 38(159) *Revista de Administración Pública* 205; A Sáiz Arnáiz, 'Los actos políticos del Gobierno en la jurisprudencia del Tribunal Supremo' (1994) 134 *Revista de administración pública* 225; A Embid Irujo, F Carreras Serra and E Gómez-Reino y Carnota, 'Funciones constitucionales y actos del gobierno' in LJ Parejo Alfonso (ed), *Estudios sobre el gobierno: Seminario sobre el Proyecto de Ley Reguladora del Gobierno* (Universidad Carlos III, Madrid, 1996) 243; J Jordano Fraga, '¿Jaque mate al acto político?' (1997) 95 *Revista Española de Derecho Administrativo* 417; F Navas Castillo, 'Veinticinco años de actos de Gobierno' (2003–2004) 58–59 *Revista de Derecho Político* 621; and D Cuadrado Zuloaga, 'Los llamados actos políticos' (2007) 22 *Actualidad administrativa* 2745.

[126] Case T-228/02 *OMPI* [2006] (n 120), paras 100 and 112–13.

[127] Joined Cases C-402/05 P and C-415/05 P *Kadi* and *Al Barakaat* [2008] (n 96), para 326.

Thus all EC/EU acts, regardless of their purpose and content, are subject to the same standard of control regarding fundamental rights by the EU courts.

The ECJ also correctly rejected the claims of the Commission and the United Kingdom according to which the control by the Court of Justice of the UN sanction measures shall be limited to establish whether the violation of human rights is particularly flagrant and obvious or, as stated by the Advocate General collecting the claims of the United Kingdom, simply 'of the most marginal kind'.[128] Moreover, when an EC/EU measure imposes severe restrictions on fundamental rights of individuals alleging an extraordinary danger to public safety, the use of this enabling budget increases, and does not decrease, the need for EU courts to exercise a complete and detailed legality control on those measures.

In fact, it is worth recalling here a legitimate argument, because there has been much discussion about the traditional indifference of EU citizens towards the EU institutions.[129] Perhaps this feeling would have only increased if the legal protection conferred by EC/EU law before the UN sanctions exceeding the limits of fundamental rights had been the one initially set with so many limitations and exceptions by the Court of First Instance. Thus it would seem that the ECJ deliberately sought not to deepen the constructive *international* dialogue that has been generally presented as one of the strengths of the EU as a global actor; however, it preferred to strengthen the *internal* constitutional dialogue with its own citizens.[130] And the step given by the ECJ in its search for legitimacy maybe should not be criticized but applauded.

28. Finally, by annulling the opinions of the CFI in the *Kadi*, *Yusuf* and *Al Barakaat* cases, the ECJ has ensured that the uniformity of EC/EU law shall not be compromised. Some authors have expressed their concern about the fact that if the ECJ had supported the positions of the CFI and, consequently, had granted jurisdictional immunity to EC/EU measures in order to implement the sanctions of the UN Security Council, national courts would have been tempted to intervene and ultimately provide adequate judicial control themselves, instead of the EU courts.[131] In this sense, we should remember the famous case law of the German Constitutional Court (*Bundesverfassungsgericht*) in the *Solange*

[128] Joined Cases C-402/05 P and C-415/05 P *Kadi* and *Al Barakaat* [2008] (n 96), para 272 and the Opinion of AG Poiares Maduro, para 35.

[129] A Peters. 'European democracy after the 2003 Convention' (2004) 41(1) *Common Market Law Review* 37 at 84–5; AJ Menéndez, 'Between Laeken and the Deep Blue Sea – An Assessment of the Draft Constitutional Treaty from a Deliberative-Democratic Standpoint' (2005) 11(1) *European Public Law* 105 and J Snell, '"European constitutional settlement", an ever-closer union, and the Treaty of Lisbon: democracy or relevance?' (2008) 33(5) *European Law Review* 619.

[130] See B Kunoy and A Dawes (2009) (n 24) at 102; and G de Búrca, 'The European Court of Justice and the International Legal Order after Kadi' (2009) 01/09 *Jean Monnet Working Papers* April 2009 at 45–55. On the question of pluralism v constitutionalism, see below.

[131] B Kunoy (2007) (n 27) at 36–7; MT Karayigit, 'The Yusuf and Kadi Judgments: The Scope of the EC Competences in Respect of Restrictive Measures' (2006) 33(4) *Legal Issues of Economic Integration* 379; and N Lavranos, 'Judicial Review of UN Sanctions by the Court of First Instance' (2006) 11(4) *European Foreign Affairs Review* 471.

and *Bananenmarktordnung* cases, where the Karlsruhe highest court reserved the right to control the legality of Community acts in relation to the Basic Law if the protection level of the fundamental rights guaranteed by the EC legal order falls below a minimum standard threshold of protection issued by the German Constitution.[132] This concern would also be justified by the fact that since the ECHR rejected, in its opinion on the *Bosphorus* case, control of the conventionality of EC/EU law unless the protection afforded to the rights protected in the ECHR by the Community was 'manifestly deficient', there would not be an effective judicial control of EC/EU acts implementing UN sanctions either in the EC/EU nor within the scope of the Convention. In fact, this issue would be aggravated by the opinion of some very senior voices that support, with good arguments, that the Sanctions Committee established under Resolution 1267 (1999) of the UN Security Council is contrary to the Convention because it does not grant enough protection against arbitrary decisions and because there is no mechanism for the accuracy of the claims submitted before the said Committee.[133]

By establishing again the EU courts as the ultimate guardians of fundamental rights guaranteed by the EC/EU legal order, the ECJ achieves in its decision in the *Kadi* case avoidance of any temptation on the part of national courts to unilaterally control the legality of EC/EU measures and acts in the light of their national constitutional legal orders. In this sense, there was every hope that in the cases relating to the implementation of sanctions established by the United Nations and waiting for an appeal before the ECJ the Luxembourg Court should keep and confirm its case law regarding *Kadi*, in order to avoid any hint of doubt about its commitment to the protection of fundamental rights and, therefore, prevent national courts from being tempted to intervene in the future, since in these cases the issue whether the review system of the UN Sanctions Committee, after some minor innovations (like the focal point or the Ombudsperson), could provide a level of protection of fundamental rights similar to that afforded by the Community legal order. Following the latest ECJ case law, it seems that the Court is willing to honour its *Kadi* case law.[134]

29. Therefore, in light of the considerations of the ECJ in the *Kadi* and *Al Barakaat* cases it is highly unlikely that the Luxembourg Court will approve, at

[132] Case *Solange I* 2 BvL 52/71 BVerfGE 37 271 (German Constitutional Court, 29 May 1974); Case *Solange II* 2 BvR 197/83 BVerfGE 73 339 (German Constitutional Court, 22 October 1986); and Case *Bananenmarktordnung* 2 BvL 1/97 BVerfGE 102 147 (German Constitutional Court, 7 June 2000). For a comment, see M Kumm, 'Who is the final arbiter of constitutionality in Europe? Three conceptions of the relationship between the German Federal Constitutional Court and the European Court of Justice' (1999) 36(3) *Common Market Law Review* 351; and F Hoffmeister, 'German Bundesverfassungsgericht: Alcan, Decision of 17 February 2000; Constitutional review of EC Regulation on bananas' (2001) 38 *Common Market Law Review* 791.

[133] See Cameron, *The European Convention on Human Rights, Due Process and United Nations Security Council Counter-Terrorism Sanctions* (Council of Europe, Strasbourg, 6 February 2006) available at http://www.coe.int/T/E/Legal_Affairs/Legal_co-operation/Public_international_law at 2.

[134] See, eg, Joined Cases C-399/06 P and C-403/06 P *Hassan and Ayadi* [2009] (n 60).

least for a while, the system of the UN Sanctions Committees since they seem to be well below the minimum level of protection required by the Community legal order.[135] Indeed, in a recent case, the General Court (formerly the CFI) has stated that neither the focal point nor the Office of the Ombudsperson (two major improvements within the UN sanctions review process) 'cannot be equated with the provision of an effective judicial procedure for review of decisions of the Sanctions Committee'.[136]

[135] See R Geiss, 'Humanitarian Safeguards in Economic Sanctions Regimes: A Call for Automatic Suspension Clauses, Periodic Monitoring, and Follow-Up Assessment of Long-Term Effects' (2005) 18 (Spring) *Harvard Human Rights Journal* 167; LG Radicati di Brozolo and M Megliani, 'Freezing the Assets of International Terrorist Organisations' in A Bianchi (ed), *Enforcing International Law Norms Against Terrorism* (Hart, Oxford, 2004) 377.

[136] Case T-85/09 *Kadi v Commission (Kadi II)* [2010] (n 120), para 128.

9

European Convention on Human Rights and Security Council Resolutions: The Contribution of the European Court of Human Rights

1. PRELIMINARY CONSIDERATIONS: THE NEED TO ESTABLISH A STANDARD OF ADEQUATE PROTECTION IN THE TERRITORIES ADMINISTERED BY THE UN

1.1. '*Quis Custodiet Ipsos Custodes?*'*

1. As seen before, since the end of the Cold War the Security Council of the United Nations has become an important guardian of human rights. According to the Council's international practice, international peace and security require the avoidance of situations of human suffering, especially when they are on a large scale.[1] The Security Council has had to face a number of humanitarian crises caused by the flagrant violation of the most basic human rights and has taken action under Chapter VII of the UN Charter. In some post-conflict scenarios the Council has established some international administrations in order to guide the communities concerned to establish their own government structures based on the rule of law, democracy and human rights protection. Member States of the United Nations traditionally support the Council in these activities, particularly the EU Member States, which consider the proliferation of the defence of human rights a main objective of their foreign and security policy (Article 11 TEU, Article 24 TEU-L).

Likewise, according to a document approved by the European Council in 2003 under the auspices of the High Representative for Common Foreign and Security Policy:

* This is a Latin phrase traditionally attributed to Juvenal from his Satires (Satire VI, lines 347–8 in DJ Juvenal, *Sátiras (Satirae)* (Espasa, Madrid, 1965)), which usually translate as 'Who will guard the guards themselves?', 'Who watches the watchmen?' and similar.

[1] See the document *50 Years of UN Peacekeeping Operations* (UN Department of Public Information, October 1998) available at <http://www.un.org/Depts/DPKO/pk50_w.htm> and I Österdahl, *Threat to the Peace: The Interpretation by the Security Council of Article 39 of the UN Charter* (Iustus, Uppsala, 1998) 85–91.

> The quality of international society depends on the quality of the governments that are its foundation. The best protection for our security is a world of well-governed democratic states. Spreading good governance, supporting social and political reform, dealing with corruption and abuse of power, establishing the rule of law and protecting human rights are the best means of strengthening the international order.[2]

2. However, despite these impeccable purposes, one might ask, following on from the title of this section, what happens if the guardian of human rights itself violates them? This question has been raised recently regarding two cases brought before the ECtHR pointing out the weakness of the international administration of territories, in this case of Kosovo.[3] On the basis of Resolution 1244 (1999), the UN Security Council established a civil administration, known as UNMIK, as a subsidiary organ of the United Nations and an international security force, the Kosovo Force (KFOR), commanded by NATO (North Atlantic Treaty Organization) and made up of contingents brought in by the UN Member States. In this context, one might ask who would be responsible if a child died because the international administration had not been able to defuse some unexploded cluster bombs and, likewise, who would take up responsibility for the arrest of a Kosovar suspected of murder and illegal possession of arms who was denied access to court for six months.

According to UNMIK regulations, the international presence in Kosovo agreed to respect the highest standards, including the most important international general and regional treaties on human rights protection.[4] Similarly, the states that contributed with troops are bound by international treaties on human rights. The national Constitutions, the ECHR and the International Covenant on Civil and Political Rights make up, in effect, a substantive corpus of fundamental rights. However, in Kosovo there are only some very basic mechanisms to control legality.[5] At the UN level, there is no institution to control the actions of the UN Security Council or of the bodies established by the latter regarding human rights.[6] In accordance with the provisions of Regulation

[2] See *A Secure Europe in a better world. European Security Strategy* (European Union Institute for Security Studies, Paris, 2003) 16. This document was drafted by the then EU High Representative for the CFSP and subsequently adopted by the European Council meeting of 12 December 2003.

[3] UN Security Council Resolution 1244 (1999), 10 June 1999.

[4] See Regulation UNMIK/REG/1999/24 on the Law Applicable in Kosovo (12 December 1999), text available at http://www.unmikonline.org/regulations/1999/reg24-99.htm, amended by Regulation UNMIK/REG/2000/59 amending UNMIK Regulation No 1999/24 on the Law Applicable in Kosovo (27 October 2000), text available at <http://www.unmikonline.org/regulations/2000/reg59-00.htm>. See also Regulation UNMIK/REG/2001/9 on a Constitutional Framework for provisional self-government in Kosovo (15 May 2001), text available at <http://www.unmikonline.org/regulations/2001/reg09-01.htm> and Regulation UNMIK/REG/2002/9 on an amendment to the Constitutional Framework for provisional self-government (3 May 2002), text available at < http://www.unmikonline.org/regulations/2002/RE2002_09.pdf>.

[5] C Stahn, *The Law and Practice of International Territorial Administration Versailles to Iraq and Beyond* (Cambridge University Press, Cambridge, 2008) 308–32.

[6] See, inter alia, A Reinisch, 'Developing Human Rights and Humanitarian Law Accountability of the Security Council for the Imposition of Economic Sanctions' (2001) 95(4) *American Journal of International Law* 851.

2000/47 of the UNMIK administration, KFOR, its personnel, UNMIK itself and its personnel all enjoy immunity in Kosovo.[7] At the request of the Council of Europe, the Venice Commission proposed the establishment of a court of human rights in Kosovo, a move that did not elicit much enthusiasm or significant support.[8] However, at least an advisory commission on human rights was established in 2006 to consider complaints from individuals alleging to be victims of human rights violations by UNMIK, but not by KFOR.[9] The aim is to enhance the protection that was previously guaranteed by the Ombudsperson, whose competence to monitor the actions of the UNMIK administration was transferred to that committee.[10] In any case, none of these mechanisms provide, either individually or as a whole, the same effective protection that the Member States of the Council of Europe guarantee to all persons under its jurisdiction covered by the ECHR.

3. In this context, some inconsistencies came to light between the obligations to respect human rights incumbent on the Member States of the Council of Europe, which derive from their own Constitutions, and the international treaties to which they belong. The same thing applies for the Security Council of the United Nations. It would affect the credibility and success of a mission to build peace if the international community compelled the parties concerned to respect certain international standards regarding human rights protection, while the peacekeeping forces of the peacemaker states enjoyed immunity through the Security Council of the United Nations. With the *Behrami* and *Saramati* cases, the ECtHR had an opportunity to intervene and stop this credibility gap regarding the protection of human rights. However, the ECtHR declared both cases inadmissible because it was not competent *ratione personae*. The actions pleaded could not be attributed to France or Norway. Liability before the ECtHR of the states that contributed troops was denied, and the UN, which, as we already know, has no control mechanism regarding human rights in its

[7] See Regulation UNMIK/REG/2000/47, on the status, privileges and immunities of KFOR and UNMIK and their personnel in Kosovo (18 August 2000), available at <http://www.unmikonline.org/regulations/2000/reg47-00.htm>.

[8] See Opinion 280/2004 on *Human Rights in Kosovo: Possible establishment of review mechanisms* (Venice Commission, 11 October 2004, CDL-AD(2004)033) para 111 and the report *Consideration of reports submitted by states parties under Art 40 of the Covenant. Concluding observations of the Human Rights Committee* (14 August 2006, CCPR/C/UNK/CO/1, GE.06-43691 (E) 080906).

[9] Regulation UNMIK/REG/2006/12 On the Establishment of the Human Rights Advisory Panel (23 March 2006), amended by Regulation UNMIK/REG/2007/3 Amending UNMIK Regulation No 2006/12 on the Establishment of the Human Rights Advisory Panel (12 January 2007), both available at <http://www.unmikonline.org/regulations/unmikgazette/02english/E2006regs/E2006regs.htm>.

[10] Kosovo's Ombudsperson institution was established by Regulation UNMIK/REG/2000/38 on the Ombudsperson Institution in Kosovo (16 February 2006), amended by Regulation UNMIK/REG/2006/6 amending UNMIK Regulation No 2006/6 on the Ombudsperson Institution in Kosovo (19 March 2007). The text of these Regulations are available at <http://www.unmikonline.org/regulations/unmikgazette/02english/E2006regs/E2006regs.htm>. See CPM Waters, 'Nationalising Kosovo's Ombudsperson' (2007) 12(1) *Journal of Conflict and Security Law* 139.

Security Council, was liable for the possible international responsibility. But we should bear in mind that the alternative would have required indirect control of the actions of the Security Council, that is, to submit the UN to the ECHR. Maybe that was too much for the ECtHR, which after *Bosphorus* already had enough with carrying out indirect control over the EC/EU.[11]

1.2. The *Behrami* and *Saramati* Lawsuits before the ECtHR

4. The *Behrami* and *Saramati* cases must be understood in the presence of the Kosovo international security force (KFOR) and the UN Interim Administration Mission in Kosovo (UNMIK), both established by Resolution 1244 (1999) of the Security Council. The two lawsuits were joined by the Grand Chamber of the ECtHR by virtue of the option offered in this sense by Article 42.1 of its Rules.[12]

The first case, *Behrami and Behrami v France*, are rooted in the NATO air strikes during the spring of 1999 which left the territory of Kosovo full of unexploded mines. Thus, in March 2000, a group of children who were playing in a field with such abandoned explosives, ignoring the danger, handled one of the bombs, which exploded, killing one of the sons of Mrs Behrami and seriously injuring the other brother. The appellants, Ms Behrami on behalf of his deceased son Gadaf and the survivor Bekir Behrami, who suffered severe injuries, after unsuccessfully appealing to the territorial administration of the UN in Kosovo, filed a complaint before the ECtHR. The plaintiffs considered that since the French KFOR troops did not properly clear the minefield where children played, France did not comply with its obligations under the ECHR. Specifically, the Behrami family relied on Article 2 of the ECHR, the right to life.[13]

[11] Comments on *Behrami* and *Saramati* are numerous. See, inter alia, H Krieger, 'A Credibility Gap: The Behrami and Saramati Decision of the European Court of Human Rights' (2009) 13(1–2) *Journal of International Peacekeeping* 159; M Milanovic and T Papic, 'As Bad as it Gets: The European Court of Human Rights' Behrami and Saramati Decision and General International Law' (2008) 58(2) *International and Comparative Law Quarterly* 267; A Sari, 'Jurisdiction and International Responsibility in Peace Support Operations: The Behrami and Saramati Cases' (2008) 8(1) *Human Rights Law Review* 151; A Rey Aneiros, 'Tribunal Europeo de Derechos Humanos – TEDH – Resolución de admisibilidad de 02.05.2007, Behrami y Behrami c. Francia, 71412/01, y Saramati c. Francia, Alemania y Noruega, 78166/01 – Seguridad colectiva y derechos humanos – Responsabilidad por violaciones de derechos humanos por fuerzas de mantenimiento de la paz' (2008) 30 *Revista de Derecho Comunitario Europeo* 511; P Lagrange, 'Responsabilité des Etats pour actes accomplis en application du Chapitre VII de la Charte des Nations Unies. Observations à propos de la décision de la Cour européenne des Droits de l'Homme (Grande Chambre) sur la recevabilité des requêtes Behrami et Behrami c. France et Saramati c. Allemagne, France et Norvège, 31 mai 2007' (2008) 112(1) *Revue Générale de Droit International Public* 85; and KM Larsen, 'Attribution of Conduct in Peace Operations: The "Ultimate Authority and Control" Test' (2008) 19(3) *European Journal of International Law* 509.

[12] Case *Behrami v France* App No 71412/01 and Case *Saramati v France, Germany and Norway* App No 78166/01 (ECtHR, 2 May 2007, unpublished), paras 2–4, where the ECtHR sums up the background of the cases.

[13] Cases *Behrami* and *Saramati* [2007] (n 12), paras 5–7.

The second case, *Saramati v Germany, France and Norway*, refers to the lawsuit filed by an individual who, having been previously arrested by the UNMIK police, was again detained by order of KFOR from July 2001 to January 2002, under suspicion of belonging to armed groups operating along the border with the Former Yugoslav Republic of Macedonia and because of the need to establish a secure environment for the operations of KFOR forces. Charged with attempted murder and illegal possession of weapons and explosives, Mr Saramati was found guilty of the first of those charges by a trial court, but finally the Supreme Court of Kosovo quashed the conviction and ordered his release and returned the case to the court of first instance to rule on the fundamentals.[14] In his appeal, Mr Saramati invoked Article 5 (right to liberty and security) both by itself and in conjunction with Article 13 (right to an effective remedy) of the Convention to complain about the extrajudicial detention by KFOR from 13 July 2001 up to 26 January 2002. Likewise, he declared under Article 6.1 (right to a fair trial) that he did not have access to a court and reported the failure of the respondent states (Germany, France and Norway) to comply with the positive obligation derived from Article 1 to acknowledge to people living in Kosovo the rights guaranteed under the ECHR.[15]

5. Given these claims, the ECtHR developed an argument layout that can be structured in three stages. First, it established which entity – KFOR or MINUK – was in charge in cases of arrests and clearing and de-mining. Secondly, it analysed whether the contested action of KFOR (the detention in the *Saramati* case) and the omission of UNMIK (the failure to comply with proper clearing and de-mining in *Behrami*) could be attributed to the UN. Thirdly, the Court questioned the issue of whether, despite everything, it had jurisdiction *ratione personae* to control the acts or omissions of the respondent states committed in the name of the UN.

In its analysis, the Court first became interested in the responsibility right of international organizations, devoting the 'effective control' criterion assumed by the International Law Commission to hold an international organization responsible for a harmful act due to the behaviour of an organ of a Member State. Then, it focused on its own European human rights protection right, excluding in this case (and for the benefit of the UN) the idea of 'equal protection' that had already used in the *Bosphorus* case.[16]

[14] A Rey Aneiros (2008) (n 11) at 513.

[15] Cases *Behrami* and *Saramati* [2007] (n 12), paras 8–17.

[16] See Case *Bosphorus Hava Yolları Turizm ve Ticaret Anonim irketi v Ireland* App No 45036/98 (ECtHR, 30 June 2004, 2005-VI).

2. THE IDEA OF 'EFFECTIVE CONTROL' IN THE ATTRIBUTION OF STATES' ACTS TO THE UN

6. To determine its jurisdiction *ratione personae* and the admissibility of both lawsuits, the ECtHR had to examine the role of the respondent states within the civilian and military devices that exercised, at the time of the facts, the relevant control over Kosovo. The purpose of this review was to determine whether the facts alleged by the appellants had to be charged to the states parties of the ECHR or to the international organization on whose behalf they acted.

Thus, the ECtHR had to determine whether the failure to clear the minefields that had caused damage to the Behrami brothers was attributable to France, which was responsible for the command of KFOR in the Mitrovica sector, or to UNMIK, a subsidiary organ of the UN. Then, the Strasbourg Court had to determine whether the extrajudicial arrest of Mr Saramati was attributable to France, Germany and Norway, as some of their military commanders had, as members of the COMKFOR (the high military command of KFOR), contributed to this situation, or whether this arrest was attributable to the UN and, therefore, the organization should assume responsibility, as this organization would control KFOR through the Security Council, which is one of its organs. The analysis of this latter issue was more than adequate, given that KFOR does not answer the traditional layout of the UN peacekeeping operation; instead it would rather be an ad hoc operation, comparable to the multinational forces authorized by the Security Council to use all necessary means by virtue of Chapter VII of the UN Charter, those forces for which the control exercised by the body that had created them had not always been the most satisfactory.[17]

2.1. The Attribution of the Omission at Issue to a Subsidiary Organ of the United Nations (UNMIK)

7. To establish its jurisdiction, the ECtHR analysed in detail which of the two entities, UNMIK or KFOR, was responsible for clearing and de-mining and, therefore, for the damage caused to the Behrami brothers.

After the air strikes against the Federal Republic of Yugoslavia (FRY) and the agreement by the latter to withdraw its troops from Kosovo, the future KFOR (actually, the military authorities of NATO) and the FRY and Republic of Serbia Governments signed a Military Technical Agreement (MTA) on 9 June 1999 by which the parties agreed to withdraw the FRY troops and accepted the presence of a security force in Kosovo once the Security Council passed a resolution to

[17] See R Christakis and K Bannelier, 'Acteur vigilant ou spectateur impuissant ? Le contrôle exercé par le Conseil de sécurité sur les Etats autorisés à recourir à la force' (2004) 37(2) *Revue belge de droit international/Belgian Review of international Law/Belgisch tijdschrift voor internationaal recht* 498.

this effect.[18] So, the next day, 10 June, the Security Council adopted Resolution 1244 (1999), which provided that an 'Agreement should be reached on the following principles to move towards a resolution of the Kosovo crisis':

> Deployment in Kosovo under United Nations auspices of effective international civil and security presences, acting as may be decided under Chapter VII of the Charter, capable of guaranteeing the achievement of common objectives.
>
> The international security presence with substantial North Atlantic Treaty Organization participation must be deployed under unified command and control and authorized to establish a safe environment for all people in Kosovo and to facilitate the safe return to their homes of all displaced persons and refugees.[19]

The KFOR troops were to be grouped into four multinational brigades each with responsibility for a particular area of operation, each under the authority of the leading state.[20] Resolution 1244 also provided the deployment, under the UN, of an interim administration in Kosovo (UNMIK) and invited the Secretary General to establish this administration with the help of international organizations and to appoint a special representative to oversee its implementation in the field. Thus, UNMIK was commissioned by the Security Council to manage the territory and population of Kosovo and, to that purpose, it was granted with all powers (legislative, executive and judicial). To this end, it should also work in close cooperation with KFOR. However, UNMIK differs from KFOR in both its nature and its objectives.

Thus, although, according to the respondent state and third parties involved, it did not really matter which of the two operations was responsible for the matters of clearing and de-mining, as both were international structures established by the Security Council before which they had to answer for their actions, on the other hand, for the appellants the distinction was crucial.[21] In fact, they argued, that the issue of clearing and de-mining was the responsibility of KFOR, by virtue of its mandate, and that the nature and structure of this force differed widely from those of UNMIK to the point of making the personal liability of the respondent state possible.

Relying on the Military Technical Agreement (MTA) in Resolution 1244 (1999), in reports from the UN Secretary-General and a report of the International Committee of the Red Cross, the appellants stated that it was indeed KFOR (and not the UN or UNMIK) that, at the time of the events, was

[18] As stated in the ECtHR decision on the Cases *Behrami* and *Saramati* [2007] (n 12), para 40: 'The letter of 10 June 1999 from NATO submitting the MTA to the SG of the UN and the latter's letter onwards to the UNSC, described the MTA as having been signed by the "NATO military authorities"'.

[19] See UN Security Council Resolution 1244 (4011th meeting, 10 June 1999) Annex II paras 3–4.

[20] In August 2005 the North Atlantic Council (NAC) decided to restructure the KFOR and to substitute the four existing multinational brigades for five Battalions. See P Lagrange (2008) (n 11) at 89 note 8.

[21] The third parties intervening in these Cases under Rule 44 of the ECtHR were Denmark, Estonia, Greece, Poland, Portugal, the United Kingdom, Germany and the United Nations; see the headnote of the Cases *Behrami* and *Saramati* [2007] (n 12).

responsible for clearing and de-mining. Therefore, the responsibility of this organization should be compromised and, since it has no international legal personality distinct from that of the states that compose it, finally France should be the one taking on the responsibility since this country had control of the KFOR task force that was responsible for the Mitrovica sector (where the incident occurred).[22]

In fact, still according to the appellants, neither the actions nor the omissions of KFOR soldiers are attributable to the UN or NATO.[23] KFOR would be a multinational force led by NATO and consisting of troops from Member States but also outside the organization. KFOR had not been established as an organ or force of the UN, contrary to other forces in peacekeeping, such as UNMIK, which would be deployed under the UN command. That is,

> If KFOR had been such a UN force (with the prefix 'UN'), it would have had a UN Commander in Chief, troops would not have accepted instructions from TCNs and all personnel would have had UN immunities.[24]

So, in this case, given that there wasn't a unified chain of command under the authority of the Security Council, the applicants pleaded that 'neither the acts nor omissions of KFOR soldiers were attributable to the UN or NATO'.[25]

Only recognition of the responsibility of KFOR could have allowed the appellants to establish the responsibility of France and, from there, the jurisdiction of the ECtHR *ratione personae*. The existence of a sufficient jurisdictional link (within the meaning of Article 1 of the ECHR) between the plaintiffs and France – in which case it would be under the extraterritorial jurisdiction of such country – could not be accepted by the Court except in the event that the facts of the case at issue could actually be attributed to France and not to the UN, an organization with a legal personality distinct from the Member States and not being a party to the Convention. All this would be comprehensible in case of recognition of some responsibility from the KFOR *sui generis* structure but hardly possible under the hypothesis of attributing the facts of the case at issue to UNMIK, the peacekeeping operation, in the traditional sense, of the United Nations. However, the ECtHR rejected this reasoning considering, after a certainly reprehensible analysis of the texts in its possession, that the inaction causing the damage did not come from KFOR but from UNMIK, whose actions, as a subsidiary organ of the UN, should be charged to the UN.[26]

8. The ECtHR begins its analysis by establishing that Resolution 1244 (1999) of the Security Council envisaged that KFOR would be responsible for monitoring the process of clearing and de-mining until UNMIK could replace it. The latter

[22] See Cases *Behrami* and *Saramati* [2007] (n 12), para 73.
[23] See Cases *Behrami* and *Saramati* [2007] (n 12), para 77.
[24] See Cases *Behrami* and *Saramati* [2007] (n 12), para 77.
[25] See Cases *Behrami* and *Saramati* [2007] (n 12), para 77.
[26] For a critique to this conclusion of the ECtHR, see P Lagrange (2008) (n 11) at 91.

should, in fact, be in charge of the clearing and de-mining operations by virtue of the humanitarian pillar of its competence, especially through the creation of a mine action centre, the United Nations Mine Action Coordination Centre in Kosovo (UNMACC or UNMIK MACC), established by the authority of the deputy of the special envoy of the UN Secretary General. The ECtHR assessed that:

> The UN submissions to this Court, the . . . Evaluation Report, the Concept Plan, FRAGO 300 and the letters of the Deputy SRSG of August and October 1999 to KFOR . . . confirm, in the first place, that the mandate for supervising de-mining was *de facto* and *de jure* taken over by UNMACC, created by UNMIK, at the very latest, by October 1999 and therefore prior to the detonation date in the *Behrami* case and, secondly, that KFOR remained involved in de-mining as a service provider whose personnel therefore acted on UNMIK's behalf.[27]

Consequently, the ECtHR considered that the supervision of the clearing and de-mining tasks fell within the competence established under the mandate of UNMIK and that the disputed omission should be attributed to this organ.

However, the arguments presented by the UN led to the opposite solution. Indeed, for this organization:

> UNMIK's responsibility for de-mining was dependent on accurate information being available on locations and, since UNMACC was unaware of the location of the unmarked CBUs relevant to the present case, it took no action to de-mine.
>
> In sum, while the de-mining operation would have fallen within UNMACCs mandate, in the absence of the necessary location information from KFOR, the impugned inaction could not be attributed to UNMIK.[28]

To rely on this reasoning used by the UN itself, and therefore, on mere partial responsibility from KFOR, beyond its consistency, would not have automatically implied the acknowledgement of the competence of the ECtHR. As stated below, regarding the *Saramati* case, admission of responsibility by KFOR did not make the ECtHR establish its jurisdiction *ratione personae*, contrary to what the appellants expected.

9. Once the responsibility of UNMIK was admitted, they had to determine whether the acts should be attributed to the UN or could be attributed to certain Member States. The ECtHR began by recalling that when acting under Chapter VII of the UN Charter, and although no specific article of the document can be invoked, the Security Council has usually been able to delegate its civil administration powers to a subsidiary body, UNMIK, established by the Secretary-General. This quality of subsidiary body is here determined since, relying on the work of the International Law Commission; the Strasbourg Court shall consider that:

[27] See Cases *Behrami* and *Saramati* [2007] (n 12), para 125.

[28] See Cases *Behrami* and *Saramati* [2007] (n 12), paras 119–120.

whether the delegation of power by the UNSC to the SG and/or UNMIK also respected the role of the UNSC for which Article 24 of the Charter provided, UNMIK was a subsidiary organ of the UN institutionally directly and fully answerable to the UNSC.[29]

In its 2004 report, on the occasion of the comments on the then draft Article 5 (now 6) on the international responsibility of international organizations, the International Law Commission stated that:

> The United Nations assumes that in principle it has exclusive control of the deployment of national contingents in a peacekeeping force.[30]

This premise led the UN legal counsel to conclude that:

> As a subsidiary organ of the United Nations, an act of a peacekeeping force is, in principle, imputable to the Organization, and if committed in violation of an international obligation entails the international responsibility of the Organization and its liability in compensation.[31]

According to the Commission itself, that statement from the legal counsel sums up the UN practice in respect of the United Nations operations in the Congo (Operation of the United Nations in Congo, ONUC), the United Nations Peacekeeping Force in Cyprus (UNFICYP) and other subsequent peacekeeping forces.[32]

In view of this reasoning, the Strasbourg Court deemed that the omission at issue is, in principle, attributable to the UN, within the meaning given to this term by the International Law Commission in its Article 3 (2004 version) of its draft of articles on responsibility of international organizations. Indeed, this draft article reads as follows:

> Article 3. General principles
>
> 1. Every internationally wrongful act of an international organization entails the international responsibility of the international organization.
> 2. There is an internationally wrongful act of an international organization when conduct consisting of an action or omission:
>
>   (a) Is attributable to the international organization under international law; and
>   (b) Constitutes a breach of an international obligation of that organization.

[29] Cases *Behrami* and *Saramati* [2007] (n 12), para 142.

[30] See *Report of the International Law Commission*, Fifty-sixth session (3 May to 4 June and 5 July to 6 August 2004, UN Doc A/59/10 2004) at 111. The same quote can be found five years later in the *Report of the International Law Commission*, Sixty-first session (2009) (4 May to 5 June and 6 July to 7 August 2009, UN Doc A/64/10 2009) 66 (commenting the same draft article that, with the new numbering, is Art 6).

[31] See the Letter by the United Nations Legal Counsel to the Director of the Codification Division (3 February 2004, UN Doc A/CN.4/545, sect. II.G).

[32] *Report of the International Law Commission*, Fifty-sixth session (2004) (n 30) 112.

In this sense, the attribution of responsibility was not, however, so evident in the case of the action at issue attributed to KFOR.[33]

2.2. Attribution of the Contested Acts to KFOR

10. Mr Saramati also wanted the ECtHR to recognize the responsibility of KFOR in his extrajudicial detention. Only in this way, following the reasoning of the Behrami family, would he be able to establish the responsibility of France and Norway, since the authorities incorporated into the headquarters of KFOR (COMKFOR) of French and Norwegian nationality were the ones that issued the arrest orders the object of the appeal.[34] Still pending, to get the Court to acknowledge that the responsibility for the acts of KFOR could be attributed to these two states and not to the UN, the international organization that was at the origin of the creation of that international force (a 'presence' according to the UN resolution), or to NATO, an international organization that was the *de facto* head of the unified command.

The ECtHR quickly established the responsibility of KFOR in the arrest of Mr Saramati. In fact:

> Having regard to the MTA (notably paragraph 2 of Article 1), UNSC Resolution 1244 (paragraph 9 as well as paragraph 4 of Annex 2 to the Resolution) as confirmed by FRAGO997 and later COMKFOR Detention Directive 42 (see paragraph 51 above), the Court considers it evident that KFOR's security mandate included issuing detention orders.[35]

However, after a long analysis carried out on the basis of the concept of 'effective control', the Strasbourg Court further considered that the acts of KFOR should be attributed to the UN and not to the states in command.

The KFOR multinational force placed under the unified command of the integrating Member States and authorized to use force by virtue of Chapter VII of the UN Charter would be a 'joint operation', according to the terminology frequently used by UN agencies, actually assimilated (despite some peculiarities) to the different multinational forces or *ad hoc* coalitions, authorized by the Security Council, that is, authorized by this entity to use all necessary means to ensure respect for their resolutions.[36] Then, it could not, unlike UNMIK, be

[33] In the 2009 version of the Draft articles, former Art 3 was split into Arts 3 (Responsibility of an international organization for its internationally wrongful acts) and 4 (Elements of an internationally wrongful act of an international organization). For the ILC comments of these provisions, see *Report of the International Law Commission*, Sixty-first session (2009) (n 30) 52–6

[34] The ECtHR decided to withdraw the *Saramati* case against Germany; see Cases *Behrami* and *Saramati* [2007] (n 12), paras 64–65 and the final decision.

[35] Cases *Behrami* and *Saramati* [2007] (n 12), para 124.

[36] For a legal analysis of these multinational coalitions, see D Sarooshi, *The United Nations and the Development of Collective Security: The Delegation by the UN Security Council of Its Chapter VII Powers* (Oxford University Press, Oxford, 2000); ND White and O Ülgen, 'The Security Council and the Decentralized Military Option: Constitutionality and Function' (1997) 44(3) *Netherlands*

considered as a subsidiary organ of the UN, capable in principle of engaging the responsibility of this organization for its actions. As regards the military actions, in particular, and according to the Secretary-General:

> The international responsibility of the United Nations for combat-related activities of United Nations forces is premised on the assumption that the operation in question is under the exclusive command and control of the United Nations. Where a Chapter VII-authorized operation is conducted under national command and control, international responsibility for the activities of the force is vested in the State or States conducting the operation. The determination of responsibility becomes particularly difficult, however, in cases where a State or States provide the United Nations with forces in support of a United Nations operation but not necessarily as an integral part thereof, and where operational command and control is unified or coordinated . . .
>
> In joint operations, international responsibility for the conduct of the troops lies where operational command and control is vested according to the arrangements establishing the modalities of cooperation between the State or States providing the troops and the United Nations. In the absence of formal arrangements between the United Nations and the State or States providing troops, responsibility would be determined in each and every case according to the degree of effective control exercised by either party in the conduct of the operation.[37]

This notion of effective control has been confirmed by the International Law Commission in its draft Article 5 on responsibility of international organizations (2004 version), both for joint operations and for peacekeeping whenever it shall be possible to distinguish areas of 'effective control' that correspond to the UN and to the state contributing troops.[38] An issue that, otherwise, the Strasbourg Court would not have taken into consideration in relation to UNMIK.

11. In any case, adopting in their consideration the notion of effective control to determine if the contested acts of KFOR could be attributed to the UN or not, the ECtHR redefined a number of issues which disturbed the doctrine since there are ad hoc coalitions authorized by the Security Council to use all necessary means under Chapter VII of the Charter.[39]

International Law Review 378; N Blokker, 'Is the authorization authorized? Powers and practice of the UN Security Council to authorize the use of force by "coalitions of the able and willing"' (2000) 11(3) *European Journal of International Law* 541; and LA Sicilianos, 'L'autorisation par le conseil de sécurité de recourir à la force: Une tentative d'évaluation' (2002) 106(1) *Revue générale de droit international public* 5.

[37] *Report of the Secretary-General to the General Assembly in its Fifty-first session*. 'Agenda item 129 Financing of the United Nations Protection Force, the United Nations Confidence Restoration Operation in Croatia, the United Nations Preventive Deployment Force and the United Nations Peace Forces headquarters' and 'Agenda item 140 (a) Administrative and budgetary aspects of the financing of the United Nations peacekeeping operations: financing of the United Nations peacekeeping operations' (20 September 1996, UN Doc A/51/389) paras 17–18.

[38] *Report of the International Law Commission*, Fifty-sixth session (2004) (n 32) 113. As stated before, this provision corresponds to Art 6 of the Draft articles within the 2009 version. See *Report of the International Law Commission*, Sixty-first session (2009) (n 30) 67.

[39] See N Blokker 'Is the authorization authorized? Powers and practice of the UN Security Council to authorize the use of force by 'coalitions of the able and willing" (2000) 11(3) *European Journal of International Law* 541.

The Strasbourg Court started from Resolution 1244 (1999) and the fact that the Security Council had delegated to the organizations and Member States that offered to intervene the power to establish an international security presence in Kosovo and to ensure the operational command. The ECtHR specified the meaning of 'delegation', as opposed to the term 'authorization', indifferently used in Resolution 1244 (1999). Thus, according to the Court:

> [The] use of the term 'delegation' in the present decision refers to the empowering by the UNSC of another entity to exercise its function as opposed to 'authorising' an entity to carry out functions which it could not itself perform.[40]

But this distinction is only apparent. First, because the notion of authorization would seem the most appropriate in the case of the Council's practice by which it enables Member States to use force: by definition, to authorize is to grant the power to do something, that is, leave the choice to those who are granted the authorization. But to authorize is also to allow, to make possible, and to grant the right to do something that otherwise could not be done. Secondly, because delegating – in the sense that the ECtHR gives to this term – to the organizations and Member States willing to it the power to establish an international security presence in Kosovo, the Security Council has certainly conferred on another entity the power to exercise some of its functions – peacekeeping by force, if necessary – but above all, it has also authorized another entity to carry out tasks that the Council cannot *de facto* do on its own, since it has not been able to conclude the agreements referred to in Article 43 of the Charter.[41] This provision states:

> 1. All Members of the United Nations, in order to contribute to the maintenance of international peace and security, undertake to make available to the Security Council, on its call and in accordance with a special agreement or agreements, armed forces, assistance, and facilities, including rights of passage, necessary for the purpose of maintaining international peace and security.
>
> 2. Such agreement or agreements shall govern the numbers and types of forces, their degree of readiness and general location, and the nature of the facilities and assistance to be provided.
>
> 3. The agreement or agreements shall be negotiated as soon as possible on the initiative of the Security Council. They shall be concluded between the Security Council and Members or between the Security Council and groups of Members and shall be subject to ratification by the signatory states in accordance with their respective constitutional processes.

Then, the ECtHR analysed the legal basis of such delegation:

> While the Resolution referred to Chapter VII of the Charter, it did not identify the precise Articles of that Chapter under which the UNSC was acting and the Court

[40] Cases *Behrami* and *Saramati* [2007] (n 12), para 43.
[41] P Lagrange (2008) (n 11) at 95.

notes that there are a number of possible bases in Chapter VII for this delegation by the UNSC.[42]

The Court establishes that although the resolution does not mention on the basis of which articles the Security Council acts, given that 'there are a number of possible bases in Chapter VII for this delegation [it mentions Articles 41, 42 and 48]' it considers that that chapter of the Charter 'provided a [sufficient] framework for the above-described delegation of the UNSC's security powers to KFOR and of its civil administration powers to UNMIK'.[43] Thus, the ECtHR, citing plenty of doctrine, upheld the usual practice of the Security Council, which hardly ever explicitly establishes which specific article provides the legal basis of its resolutions, but merely confirms that it acts 'according to Chapter VII of the Charter'.[44] Indeed, formally, any literal provisions of the Charter would allow it to support the practice of the authorization, but many other loose provisions would provide the legal fragmentary basis that would establish the legality of the enabling technique.[45] Thus, since it is not possible to establish it in a specific article of the Charter, the Security Council should be brought under a purposive interpretation of the provisions of the text to claim the right to delegate some of their powers under specific circumstances and objectives. The lawfulness of the authorization to use all necessary means could, thus, be inferred from the implied powers held by the Security Council by virtue of certain general provisions of the Charter and, above all, of its Chapter VII. This is, indeed, the conclusion reached by the ECtHR.

12. Having clarified the above, the Court had to determine if the action at issue, the alleged extrajudicial detention carried out by KFOR, could be attributed to the UN. However,

> While Chapter VII constituted the foundation for the above-described delegation of UNSC security powers, that delegation must be sufficiently limited so as to remain compatible with the degree of centralisation of UNSC collective security constitutionally necessary under the Charter and, more specifically, for the acts of the delegate entity to be attributable to the UN.[46]

The ECtHR considered, then, that the key issue to be addressed was whether the Security Council had kept 'the authority and control and if only the

[42] Cases *Behrami* and *Saramati* [2007] (n 12), para 130.

[43] Cases *Behrami* and *Saramati* [2007] (n 12), para 130.

[44] See Security Council Resolution 1244 (1999) on the situation relating Kosovo (10 June 1999, UN Doc S/RES/1244).

[45] S Chesterman, *Just War or Just Peace? Humanitarian Intervention and International Law* (Oxford University Press, Oxford, 2002) 167–9; E de Wet, *The Chapter VII Powers of the United Nations Security Council* (Hart, Oxford, 2004) 260–5; J Friedrich. 'UNMIK in Kosovo: Struggling with Uncertainty' (2005) 9(1) *Max Planck Yearbook of United Nations Law* 225 at 233–5; and R Wolfrum, 'International Administration in Post-Conflict Situations by the United Nations and Other International Actors' 9(1) *Max Planck Yearbook of United Nations Law* 649 at 667–72.

[46] Cases *Behrami* and *Saramati* [2007] (n 12), para 132.

operational command had been delegated', which was proved through different arguments.[47]

So, first, the Court finds out that the resolution has set limits on the delegation sufficiently defined determining the mandate with the required accuracy, given that the objectives are defined, the roles and responsibilities assigned, as well as the means to be used.[48] Then, it makes certain that 'the leaders of the military presence should under resolution report to the Security Council so as to enable it to exercise its authority and general control' through the reports sent to the Secretary General and submitted before the Council, which is an additional guarantee since the Secretary General has to 'represent the general interests of the United Nations'.[49]

The existence of a clear mandate and the establishment of *a posteriori* control operated on the grounds of reports allow the minimum conditions of adequate control, turning the Security Council into a 'watchful actor' and not a 'powerless spectator' of the states' action authorized by him to use force.[50] So far, and with the exception of the authorization granted by Resolution 678 (1990), the surveillance operated by the Security Council on empowered states has always been conducted almost exclusively using written reports which allow them to have an idea of the situation or to justify a decision on the matter. These reports are in principle sent directly by empowered Member States or by the state commanding the operation or they are sent indirectly through the intermediary of the Secretary-General.[51] The frequency of these reports depends on the circumstances, although the Council almost always attaches a certain frequency to this obligation. Regarding the importance of the reports, this is a matter left, in principle, to the discretion of the Member States and the Secretary-General, depending on the magnitude of the events and, more debatably, the goodwill of the states empowered by the Council. Whatever the form of control, it is only exercised *a posteriori*. Its effectiveness depends on the breadth of its scope of application and thus the prior definition made on that control by the Security Council. However, there is one constant: the more clearly defined the mandate in the resolution and the more assistance given to that con-

[47] Cases *Behrami* and *Saramati* [2007] (n 12), para 133.

[48] Cases *Behrami* and *Saramati* [2007] (n 12), para 134.

[49] Cases *Behrami* and *Saramati* [2007] (n 12), para 134.

[50] See the suggestive title of the article R Christakis and K Bannelier, 'Acteur vigilant ou spectateur impuissant ? Le contrôle exercé par le Conseil de sécurité sur les Etats autorisés à recourir à la force' (2004) 37(2) *Revue belge de droit international/Belgian Review of international Law/Belgisch tijdschrift voor internationaal recht* 498.

[51] For an example of the obligation to send the reports directly from the relevant states to the Security Council, see UNSC Resolution 787 (1992) 16 November on Bosnia and Herzegovina, para 15. On the other hand, see UNSC Resolution 84 (1950) 7 July on assistance to South Korea, determing North Korea broke the peace para 6. In this last case, only the US could send the reports to the Security Council. Cases of indirect sending of reports through the Secretary-General are more common. See UNSC Resolution 1080 (1996) 15 November establishing a multinational humanitarian intervention force in the African Great Lakes region, para 11; or UNSC Resolution 1529 (2004) 29 February deploying an international force to Haiti following a rebellion, para 9.

trol carried out by the Security Council, the more effective and accurate that control shall be.

Unfortunately, the result of the practice carried out by the Council is that the tasks entrusted to the Member States are generally ill-defined and often too broad to enable effective monitoring.[52] Only the duration of the operation is subject to real control power since, in order to limit the risk of a 'reverse veto', the Council usually accompanies its empowerment by a time limit, so that any extension requires a new decision from this point.[53]

This elementary precaution was not introduced in Resolution 1244 (1999). In fact, paragraph 19 states that

> the international civil and security presences are established for an initial period of 12 months, to continue thereafter unless the Security Council decides otherwise.

Under this formulation, any permanent member of the Security Council could, indeed, use its right to veto in order to oppose an end to the empowerment. The risk is certainly limited, but the ECtHR has focused on this issue, although it eventually did 'not consider this factor alone sufficient to conclude that the UNSC did not retain ultimate authority and control'.[54]

On the other hand, for the European Court of Human Rights, by virtue of Resolution 1244 (1999), the Security Council 'was to retain ultimate authority and control over the security mission and it delegated to NATO (in consultation with non-NATO member states) the power to establish, as well as the operational command of, the international presence, KFOR'.[55] As the appellant mentioned, it did not really matter in this case that the degree of control of the states providing troops sometimes removed those troops from the international mandate compromising the operational command unit, making the unified command purely formal.

Thus, according to the European Commission for Democracy through Law (Venice Commission), the term 'unified command and control' is of military origin and means only a limited form of authority transfer over the troops. States contributing to KFOR have not transferred the 'full command' of their soldiers. As a general rule, in fact, states participating in a NATO-led operation only transfer the skills inherent to 'operational control' and/or 'operational command'. These competencies enable the NATO commanders to give operational orders to

[52] P Lagrange, 'Sécurité collective et exercice par le Conseil de sécurité du système d'autorisation de la coercition' in SFDI (Société française pour le droit international) (ed), *Les métamorphoses de la sécurité collective : droit, pratique et enjeux stratégiques* (Pedone, Paris, 2005) 55 at 75–8.

[53] The situation would be that in which a permanent member of the Security Council already compromised with an operation authorised by the UNSC decided to oppose (eg for strategic reasons) a new resolution willing to end the operation. See DD Caron, 'The legitimacy of the collective authority of the Security Council' (1993) 87(4) *American Journal of International Law* 552; and G Cottereau, 'Rebondissement d'octobre en Iraq : la résolution 949 du Conseil de Sécurité (15 octobre 1994)' (1999) 40 *Annuaire français de droit international* 175.

[54] Cases *Behrami* and *Saramati* [2007] (n 12), para 134.

[55] Cases *Behrami* and *Saramati* [2007] (n 12), para 135.

the respective commanders of national contingents. The latter are thus obliged to execute those orders on the basis of their own national authority.[56]

Thus, for the ECtHR, it is essential that 'KFOR was exercising lawfully delegated Chapter VII powers of the UNSC' and that this body holds the authority and ultimate control of the operation as a whole, even when the effective command over the operational issues concerned belongs to NATO. For these reasons, the ECtHR considered that the action at issue is, in principle, 'attributable' to the UN, within the meaning given to this term by the International Law Commission.[57]

The reasoning is not the purest, and other solutions could have been reached, as states providing contingents are quite free regarding the assessment of their mission and the operational management of their troops. It was particularly unnecessary to examine at what point the chain of command escaped from single command in order to then move to UN responsibility for the sole reason that the Security Council had the authority and ultimate control over the security mission. However, the ECtHR was right to distinguish between UNMIK and KFOR and to apply a different and more rigorous reasoning regarding the latter. There is, indeed, a difference in nature between the forces authorized to use all necessary means in joint operations, to which KFOR may conform, and the forces deployed directly by the UN, in the framework of a peacekeeping operation in the strict sense, even more while limited to ensuring a civilian presence, as in the case of UNMIK.

13. The main difference (and the appellants saw it clearly) lay in the forces command and in the control exercised over them by the organization that is the source of its constitution. The forces that have intervened so far, authorized by the Security Council, on the model of the KFOR, have always been multinational forces deployed only by states that have decided to intervene keeping their national symbols, with no other distinctive sign – blue helmet, symbol or flag – which could be linked to the UN.[58] On the contrary, the forces deployed in the case of peacekeeping in the strict sense are genuine international forces, also integrated by different national contingents, but raising the colours of the UN and certain distinctive signs: the blue helmet and the UN acronym painted in white on their vehicles. No doubt UNMIK constitutes a particular peacekeeping operation, the management of a territory where civilians have replaced the traditional blue helmets. However, it could be compared to more classic peacekeeping forces due to the conditions of its creation and the fact that administrators and police within it are under the direct command of the organization, through the Secretary-General and his representative.

[56] See the Venice Commission Opinion 280/2004 (n 8), para 14.

[57] Cases *Behrami* and *Saramati* [2007] (n 12), para 141.

[58] In this sense, the forces deployed in Korea in 1950 would be an exception. See UNSC Resolution 84 (1950).

Moreover, the main difference between the qualified forces and the peacekeeping forces is of course the responsibility of their respective commanders. The control and responsibility for peacekeeping troops, in fact, belongs solely to the United Nations. National contingents are thus under UN command. They execute orders from their superiors, who, in turn, obey the Secretary-General and his delegates and not, at least in principle, their respective governments. It is mainly this latter aspect, linked to the nature of the command, that gives the UN police forces their international and non-multinational character. Likewise, it ensures a strong legitimacy. Thus, these forces, being led by the United Nations, are displayed under the direct intervention of the organization itself. Therefore, they are the responsibility of the UN: any action of any of its agents is attributable to the organization that would be so liable, and each of its agents benefits during their service in the colours of the UN from the privileges and immunities traditionally recognized for its agents.[59] This situation is in no way comparable to that given in the case of an authorized operation, where the unified command is not at international level, but all the more integrated, 'unified' under the responsibility of a state leader or, as in the case of KFOR, a local organization.

On the other hand, the command has consequences for control: the direction of the peacekeeping forces by the Secretary-General guarantees, in fact, effective control, both a priori and a posteriori. But this is no longer the case since they are authorized multinational forces and the scope of control can only be assessed case by case, certainly in the light of the formal requirements imposed by the Security Council – which has been verified by the ECtHR – but also taking into account the effectiveness of the response to these demands, which the Court could only do partially and imperfectly.[60] In this area, it is a long way from theory to practice, as already shown, for example, by the situation in Somalia, where in the absence of formal control of the most rigorous kind, the UN very soon lost control of the situation.[61]

14. Let us not forget that there is a significant difference in the financing of these two types of operation, even though, in Resolution 1244 (1999), the Security Council did not bother to specify the nature of the financing of KFOR. The funding for authorized operations is always state-operated, that is, all costs are borne by the states involved and assisted, where appropriate, by the voluntary contributions of some Member States who have failed or have not wanted to participate more specifically in the intervention.[62] Conversely, a principle of

[59] Cases *Behrami* and *Saramati* [2007] (n 12), para 46. See Regulation UNMIK/REG/2000/47, on the status, privileges and immunities of KFOR and UNMIK and their personnel in Kosovo (n 7).

[60] See P Lagrange (2008) (n 11) at 100.

[61] See the *Report of the Commission of inquiry established pursuant to Security Council Resolution 885 (1993) to investigate armed attacks on UNOSOM II personnel which led to casualties among them* (24 February 1994, UN Doc S/1994/653) paras 176–248.

[62] Cases *Behrami* and *Saramati* [2007] (n 12), para 77. In Somalia, for instance, Operation Restore Hope was exclusively funded by the participating states, without further compensation from the

collective responsibility has been gradually developed in order to finance peacekeeping. It is a truly characteristic system of the UN in the sense that, formally, it is this organization, through its members, which funds their peacekeeping operations. Member States are those that provide resources, but they do not appoint troops to an operation in a discretionary way. On the contrary, that decision belongs to the organization. If funding for a military intervention is guaranteed only by the states participating in it, is no longer in a position to conclude categorically that we are facing an international operation, especially a UN operation. Indeed, from the moment at which the states fund their actions themselves, the states involved will no longer be considered completely disinterested. If they accept a financial commitment of that type, it is necessarily because they expect some sort of economic, political or strategic benefit.[63]

Therefore, with structures such as KFOR, it seems that there are all sorts of circumstances in which a difference may be made in relation to peacekeeping operations carried out by subsidiary bodies of the UN, mainly because the former have a coercive vocation and involve a possible recourse to armed force beyond self-defence, a skill over which Member States wish to maintain complete control. Likely, if the acts of UNMIK could and should in principle be attributed to the UN, who should assume this responsibility, it was not like that for KFOR, and the ECtHR could deservedly verify that the UN had, in fact, effective control over this structure. In the present case, however, the Court did not consider this criterion insufficient, implicitly deciding to add an additional argument drawn from the public nature of the operation carried out.

3. THE REFUSAL OF THE APPLICATION OF THE THEORY OF 'EQUAL PROTECTION' TO THE UN

15. After establishing that the action and the omission in issue were, in principle, attributable to the UN, and considering that this organization, which is not part of the ECHR, has a different legal status from its Member States, the ECtHR must, third and finally, consider the question regarding its *ratione personae* competence to examine the acts of the defendant states carried out on behalf of the UN but also, more generally, consider the relationship between the Convention and actions carried out by the UN by virtue of Chapter VII of its Charter.

In the absence of a recognized express conventional *ratione materiae* competence regarding the UN, the ECtHR could be tempted to apply its jurisprudence developed under the EU. However, in this case it deemed it inappropriate to

UN. The US, which sent its own troops, assumed around 85% of the cost of the operation, which was around $600 million. UNSC Resolution 794 (1992) creating a Unified Task Force in Somalia foresaw, however, the establishment of 'a fund through which the contributions . . . could be channelled to the States or operations concerned'. See MK Cusimano, *Operation Restore Hope: the Bush administration's decision to intervene in Somalia* (Institute for the Study of Diplomacy Publications, School of Foreign Service, Georgetown University, Washington DC, 1995).

[63] P Lagrange (2008) (n 11) at 101.

apply the concept of 'equivalent protection' established by the *Bosphorus* case, taking into account the nature of public order and the imperative nature of the collective security mission assigned to the UN.

3.1. The Impossibility of Using the Theory of Equal Protection: UN Immunity Regarding the ECHR

16. The case could have been resolved by recognizing the UN's responsibility for the acts of the claimant states in the field of operations carried out by KFOR and UNMIK. However, the reasoning of the ECtHR followed a different path.

Let us not forget how, through its opinion in the *Bosphorus* case (see above), the Court considered that although the ECHR does not prohibit Member States from transferring sovereign powers to an international organization for cooperation in certain sectors of its activity, states are still responsible under Article 1 of this Treaty for all acts and omissions of its organs, even if they do nothing but comply with their international legal obligations.[64] Indeed, the ECHR makes no distinction as to the type of standards or measures that states may adopt and does not exempt any part of the jurisdiction of the Member States from the obligation to comply with the Convention.[65] The ECtHR also stated that, while the act of a state is justified by respect for the obligations arising from its membership to an international organization and as long as such organization granted fundamental rights 'in a manner which can be considered at least equivalent to that for which the Convention provides', it could be presumed that the requirements of the ECHR were respected by the state.[66]

This assumption is not, however, irrefutable and could in fact be destroyed in a particular case if the ECtHR considered that the level of protection of the rights guaranteed by the Convention is 'manifestly deficient'. In this case, the role of the Convention as a 'constitutional instrument of European public order' in the field of human rights would prevail over the interests of international cooperation.[67]

17. In the present case, the appellants referred to this case law in order to argue that the protection of fundamental rights provided by KFOR, both at the procedural and substantial level, was not 'equivalent' to the one guaranteed by the Convention, in the sense given to that term by the ECtHR in its opinion on the *Bosphorus* case, which destroyed, according to them, the presumption of compliance with the Convention by the respondent states. This argument did

[64] Case *Bosphorus* [2005] (n 16), para 152.

[65] Case *Bosphorus* [2005] (n 16), para 153.

[66] Case *Bosphorus* [2005] (n 16), para 155.

[67] See Case *Bosphorus* [2005] (n 16), para 156 and Case *Loizidou v Turkey* App no 15318/89 (ECtHR, 23 March 1995, Series A vol 310), para 75. This question has been analysed in previous chapters.

not lack foundation, especially in the case of Mr Saramati, who suffered a long-term extrajudicial detention in conditions that certainly would not have happened if the same case had occurred in France, Norway or Germany. The ECtHR, however, will not accept this reasoning, arguing fundamental differences in the circumstances that surrounded the two cases.

Thus, in the *Bosphorus* case, the appellants responded to a national measure of Ireland which applied an EC/EU regulation after having just a preliminary ruling by the ECJ. In application of the coercive measures adopted by the Security Council under Chapter VII of the Charter and implemented by an EU regulation, as seen at the time, Ireland seized an aircraft belonging to the Yugoslav national company but which was on hire to the Turkish charter flight company Bosphorus. In this case the ECtHR considered that in this situation in which Ireland was limited to implementing certain restrictive measures derived from EC/EU regulations, it was comprehensible that the aircraft in question was under the jurisdiction of the Irish authorities, within the meaning of Article 1 of the Convention. As recalled by the Court in the *Saramati* case, the Strasbourg Court recognized, in the *Bosphorus* case, its competence, especially, *ratione personae,* in relation to the respondent state (Ireland), even when the dispute was prompted by an EU regulation adopted in turn, pursuant to a Security Council resolution, and this is an aspect that the ECtHR did not clarify.[68]

18. However, in the *Behrami* and *Saramati* cases, for the Strasbourg Court, the acts and omissions in litigation of the KFOR and UNMIK could not be imputed to the respondent states and, besides, they have neither taken place in their territory nor are derived from decisions taken by the authorities.[69] In the cases before us, the respondent states did not adopt national measures implementing UN decisions, with or without discretion, but, in the opinion of the Court, they did nothing but take part in the implementation of a decision of the UN Security Council. Therefore, the ECtHR is not focused on finding out if the respondent states exercised extra-territorial jurisdiction in Kosovo, but to determine if the ECtHR itself was competent to examine under the Convention the role played by those states within the civil and security presences whose actions should be attributed to the United Nations Organization:

> [These] cases are therefore clearly distinguishable from the *Bosphorus* case in terms both of the responsibility of the respondent States under Article 1 and of the Court's competence *ratione personae*.[70]

If the notion of equal protection as it was conceived in the *Bosphorus* opinion is not applicable in this situation, this is because in both cases (*Bosphorus*,

[68] Cases *Behrami* and *Saramati* [2007] (n 12), para 151.
[69] Cases *Behrami* and *Saramati* [2007] (n 12), para 151.
[70] Cases *Behrami* and *Saramati* [2007] (n 12), para 151.

on the one hand, and *Behrami* and *Saramati*, on the other) the situations were very different, but also due to a second aspect which was most decisive: the particular nature of the UN, an international organization of universal scope, invested with a public mission of collective security.

3.2. The Particular Character of the UN and the Imperative Nature of its Mission

19. In the above-mentioned ECtHR decision, the Strasbourg Court characterized the particular nature of the UN establishing that:

> There exists, in any event, a fundamental distinction between the nature of the international organisation and of the international cooperation with which the Court was there concerned and those in the present cases. As the Court has found above, UNMIK was a subsidiary organ of the UN created under Chapter VII and KFOR was exercising powers lawfully delegated under Chapter VII of the Charter by the UNSC. As such, their actions were directly attributable to the UN, an organisation of universal jurisdiction fulfilling its imperative collective security objective.[71]

By confirming that the actions and omissions at issue were directly applicable to the UN and voluntarily dismissing the position taken in relation to the EU, the Court finally declared itself incompetent *ratione personae*, thus agreeing to grant immunity from total jurisdiction to the acts adopted on behalf of the UN under Chapter VII of the Charter.

20. Then, one might wonder what reasons led the ECtHR to establish a difference in treatment between the EU and the UNO, particularly in so far as according to the main arguments of the *Bosphorus* case where the distinction was not predictable at all. The response of the ECtHR is based on a collective security mission of the UN, a mission considered as mandatory or one of public order by the Court.

In a more doctrinal view, to which the ECtHR seems to be used, it will first invoke the temporary aspect. Indeed, the UN and its Charter precede the ECHR, which reminds the Court also that the vast majority of states party to the Convention were previously part of the UN and, in addition, all states party to the Convention are members of the UN.[72] Then, it shall remember the particularly close ties between the two institutions (the UN and the Council of Europe) and that one of the objectives of the ECHR is to ensure the collective enforcement of certain rights set forth in the Universal Declaration of Human Rights, proclaimed by the UN General Assembly in 1948.

[71] Cases *Behrami* and *Saramati* [2007] (n 12), para 151.

[72] On the academic or doctrinal approach that the ECtHR likes to use, see G Cohen-Jonathan and F Flauss, 'Cour européenne des droits de l'homme et droit international général' (2006) 52 *Annuaire Français de Droit International* 660 at 665.

From a strictly legal point of view, the ECtHR then proclaimed its 'fidelity' to the UN, quoting Article 103 of the Charter, as understood in the light of the interpretation that the International Court of Justice, according to which the obligations concerning UN Member States under the Charter prevail over any other obligation arising from another international agreement, whether it has been concluded before or after the Charter or whether it has or has not a purely regional scope.[73]

Likewise, the ECtHR invoked Article 25 of the Charter, also in light of the interpretation made by the International Court of Justice, according to which the obligations of Member States derived from a Security Council resolution prevail over those derived from any other international instrument.[74]

21. For the Strasbourg Court, this subordination is especially based on the imperative character derived from the primary objective of the UN and, consequently, from the powers granted to the Security Council under Chapter VII to address this objective. Under the Charter, the first and main objective of the UN is peacekeeping and international security. The protection of human rights certainly contributes significantly to the establishment of this international peace. And it is equally true that the drafters of the Charter sought above all to ensure that peace through a mechanism that would allow an effective guarantee, if necessary through the adoption of coercive measures. These exceptional means, exorbitant powers in light of common law and provided in Chapter VII of the Charter, were made available to an exceptional body: the Security Council, whose responsibility, essential as regards the objective of peacekeeping, 'in this respect is unique and has evolved as a counterpart to the prohibition, now customary international law, on the unilateral use of force'.[75]

This responsibility was exercised by the Security Council through operations initiated under Chapter VII, which are 'fundamental to the mission of the UN to secure international peace and security'.[76] However, in the absence of a conclusion of special agreements under Article 43, the effectiveness and efficiency of these operations relies on voluntary and specific participation in each case of the Member States. Let us not forget that Articles 43 to 45 of the Charter provide the conclusion of agreements between Member States and the Security Council under which the former are committed to provide the latter with the ground and air forces necessary for peacekeeping and security. Given that any such agreement has not been concluded, the UN has no legal instrument to

[73] Cases *Behrami* and *Saramati* [2007] (n 12), para 147 which refers to 27, where the ECtHR quotes several cases of the ICJ. See *Case Military and Paramilitary Activities in and against Nicaragua (Nicaragua v United States of America)* Judgment (ICJ, 26 November 1984, *Reports*, 392–443) para 107.

[74] Cases *Behrami* and *Saramati* [2007] (n 12), para 27, quoting Case *Libyan Arab Jamahiriya v United Kingdom* Provisional measures (1992) (n 12), para 42.

[75] Cases *Behrami* and *Saramati* [2007] (n 12), para 148.

[76] Cases *Behrami* and *Saramati* [2007] (n 12), para 149.

force Member States to use their means and resources for the missions established under Chapter VII.[77]

Consequently, the ECtHR concluded, the Convention could not be interpreted in such a sense as to control the actions and omissions of the contracting parties covered by the Security Council resolutions and which occurred before or during such missions. However, it is interesting to underline the reason(s) which led the Court to dismiss control in this case while it did not hesitate to keep it in the case of national acts applying EC/EU law (the *Bosphorus* case). In this sense, the ECtHR said that submitting acts executed under Security Council resolutions to conventional control could be seen as interference in the performance of an essential mission of the UN in this field, even in the effective conduct of such operations. This would be like imposing conditions on the execution of a Security Council resolution that were not envisaged by the wording of the resolution itself, especially with regard to the procedural requirements, difficult to observe in a situation of potential conflict.[78] Thus, the ECtHR shall consider that given that this is an action within the collective security system, the system of protection of human rights of the Council of Europe cannot interfere in this imperative mandate. Therefore, it shall conclude that the complaints submitted are inadmissible from the *ratione personae* point of view. However, this reasoning is based on a contradiction. That is, if the ECtHR considers that the respondent states have no jurisdiction according to Article 1 of the Convention because they act on behalf of the UN, it is difficult to understand why it is then put forward if it has *ratione personae* competence or why it ends up justifying the non-implementation of the Convention in the mission consisting of peacekeeping international security and in the fact that the operation was carried out in virtue of Chapter VII of the Charter.[79]

22. However, the Court shall go even further by stating that it would no longer consider its competence either to control other voluntary acts of the defendant states, such as the vote of a permanent member of the UNSC in favour of the relevant Chapter VII Resolution, or the contribution of troops to the security mission, since 'such acts may not have amounted to obligations flowing from membership of the UN but they remained crucial to the effective fulfilment by the UNSC of its Chapter VII mandate and, consequently, by the UN of its imperative peace and security aim'.[80]

Thus, the ECtHR would be aligned to the broad deference thesis towards the UN legal order that, a few months before the Strasbourg hearing, used the Court

[77] Cases *Behrami* and *Saramati* [2007] (n 12), para 24. On this question, see DW Bowett, GP Barton and R Higgins, *United Nations Forces: A Legal Study* (Praeger, New York, 1964 (reprinted 2008)) 313–60.

[78] Cases *Behrami* and *Saramati* [2007] (n 12), para 149.

[79] See A Rey Aneiros (2008) (n 11) at 523. Also critical is the comment of A Sari, 'Jurisdiction and International Responsibility in Peace Support Operations: The Behrami and Saramati Cases' (2008) 8(1) *Human Rights Law Review* 151 at 159–63.

[80] Cases *Behrami* and *Saramati* [2007] (n 12), para 149.

of First Instance before being widely criticized by the doctrine and censured by the ECJ itself, which, as seen above, would invalidate its decision.[81]

4. THE ECHR AND THE REAFFIRMATION OF THE IDENTITY OF THE CONVENTION: A 'EUROPEAN' AND NOT A 'UNIVERSAL' PUBLIC ORDER INSTRUMENT

23. As already mentioned in the *Bosphorus* case, the ECtHR clearly rejected analysis of the question of compatibility between Resolution 820 (1993) of the Security Council and the respect for fundamental rights as guaranteed by the ECHR, hiding in a voluntary and rather forced manner behind the EU regulation.[82] Thus, the Strasbourg Court rejected control if the United Nations ensured protection of fundamental rights equivalent to that guaranteed by the Convention leaving the question in the *Bosphorus* case unanswered. However, the lawsuits of the *Behrami* and *Saramati* families would force the ECtHR to rule expressly on the issue. Nevertheless, the Court also neglected to consider whether the level of protection guaranteed by the UN, this time, under the particular nature and mission of this international organization of public order and general interest was in accordance with the ECHR.

Some may see in the Court's attitude a way to establish a 'dual function'.[83] As defined by Georges Scelle, according to this theory, national governments and their agents carry out a 'dual' role: acting as state organs when they operate in the exclusive context of national law, but acting as international players when they operate in the international law field. In this sense, when one or more national officers carry out executive actions, such as an armed intervention, they would act as organs or executive international agents. For the French author, in the interstate order, where there are no governments or specific international agents, the agents and state governments fulfilling their functions would be vested with this dual role. These agents and governments are *national* when acting within the framework of their legal order, but are *international* when acting in relation to the international order. This is what the author calls the 'basic rule of the dual function'.[84]

[81] For instance, see the Case T-315/01 *Kadi* [2005] and D Simon and F Mariatte, 'Le Tribunal de première instance des Communautés: Professeur de droit international?' (2005) Décembre *Europe* 6.

[82] This aspect was not disregarded by the scholarship. See, inter alia, S Douglas-Scott, 'Bosphorus Hava Yollari Turizm Ve Ticaret Anonim irketi v Ireland' (2006) 41(3) *Common Market Law Review* 243 at 252–3 and F Kauff-Gazin, 'L'arrêt Bosphorus de la Cour européenne des droits de l'homme : quand le juge de Strasbourg pallie le retard du constituant de l'Union européenne en matière de protection des droits fondamentaux . . .' (2005) 234 *Les Petites Affiches* 9 at 13.

[83] P Lagrange (2008) (n 11) 107.

[84] See the classic G Scelle, 'Théorie et pratique de la fonction exécutive en droit international' (1937) 55((1936-I)) *Recueil des cours de l'Académie de Droit International de la Haye* 87 and G Scelle, 'Règles générales du droit de la paix' (1934) 46((1933-IV)) *Recueil des cours de l'Académie de Droit International de La Haye* 327. For an analysis of Scelle's work, see A Cassese, 'Remarks on Scelle's Theory of "Role Splitting" (dédoublement fonctionnel) in International Law' (1990) 1(1) *European Journal of International Law* 210 and P de Sena and MC Vitucci, 'The European Courts

Thus, applying this theory to the case at hand, when a state executes a decision of an international organization, it would be possible to consider that, by doing so, it carries out one of the objectives of the organization.[85] The ECtHR considers that the state would act on its own account when the goal of the organization is in line with the particular and related interests of the Member States; however, it shall be considered that it is acting on behalf of the international organization when carrying out objectives of general interest, different (or overlapping) from the coinciding individual interests of members of the organization. This would, in effect, be the meaning that the ECtHR has given to the 'imperative' nature of the goal that the operations at issue in these cases want to achieve, if compared to the different solution reached in the *Bosphorus* case.[86] Therefore, it seems plausible that the ECtHR has established the theory of 'dual function' with this case law.

However, the ultimate reasons that led the Strasbourg Court to rule in this sense seem to be more pragmatic. Even if the Court had agreed to grant the UN the 'label' of 'equal protection', given that this concept can be considered case by case, according to the ECtHR's will, to admit its competence would have left the door open to a proliferation of individual lawsuits. Although the decision in the *Behrami* and *Saramati* cases may be interpreted in the sense that it weakens or attenuates the *Bosphorus* case law, it is true that having recognized its jurisdiction the Court could face a difficult situation from a pragmatic point of view. That is, someone at the end of the world might have a chance of success before the ECtHR alleging non-observance of the Convention by a part of the United Nations force consisting of a small part of the personnel provided by some Member State of the ECHR.[87]

In the short term, this would be the situation for the respondent states on the action of the United Nations and international security. Thus, the defendants and third parties appealed to the serious consequences of extending Article 1, which requires states to guarantee the rights derived from the ECHR to anyone under its jurisdiction to the peacekeeping operations and, especially, the ability to discourage states to participate in these missions and to make these already complex peacekeeping operations inoperative because of the overlapping and also regarding the differences in standards of regional and national protection.[88] Finally, the Court recalled the difficulties that post-conflict situations give rise to, especially the fact that total protection of fundamental rights was not possible in the reconstruction context in which the facts are carried out. If the states contributing troops feared for their joint responsibility if the protection

and the Security Council: Between Dédoublement Fonctionnel and Balancing of Values' (2009) 20 *European Journal of International Law* 193.

[85] G Scelle, 'Règles générales du droit de la paix' (1934) 46((1933-IV)) *Recueil des cours de l'Académie de Droit International de La Haye* 327 at 358.

[86] See R Rivier and P Lagrange, 'Travaux de la Commission du droit international et de la sixième commission' (2005) 51 *Annuaire français de droit international* 340 at 341.

[87] P Lagrange (2008) (n 11) at 108.

[88] Cases *Behrami* and *Saramati* [2007] (n 12), para 90.

standards fall below the Convention threshold, this could discourage their participation in such missions which would go against the spirit of the Convention and its jurisprudence that has supported international cooperation and the proper functioning of international organizations.[89]

However, even admitting the merits of the above argument put forward by the respondent states, an extreme interpretation of the argument could lead to justifying that everything is permitted in an international operation carried out on behalf of the UN or, perhaps, that there would be a double standard and that, therefore, the states party to the Convention could be released from the obligations they voluntarily accepted at the time. Certainly, this does not seem to be the intention of the ECtHR, but instead, it sided with the arguments of some of the state governments sued, according to which the particular circumstances require specific responses.[90] In favour of this view, one might propose the text of the Convention itself, whose Article 15 allows repeal of some provisions in case of war or public emergency threatening the life of a state.

As regards the argument that, by accepting its competence, the ECtHR would face a multitude of claims from all corners of the world where the UN had deployed a mission, one may say that individuals who suffer damage caused by these peace operations usually are very limited in order to claim compensation, given the jurisdictional immunities enjoyed by such missions.[91] Therefore, an interpretation, even though exceptional, of its competence may have contributed to reaffirming the general principle of access to justice, albeit in specific cases.

24. Those who praise the decision of the ECtHR appeal, in effect, to the fact that any other position could have run the risk of depriving the UN of the few troops that some European states still accept to entrust, in general without much enthusiasm, to carry out its international peace mission.[92]

Those who censured it emphasize that the authorization of the Security Council to organize the security forces in third states should not carry an implicit authorization to violate the conventional commitments undertaken by states participating in the purposes and principles of the Charter that, besides, are not inconsistent with the mandate to act within that framework.[93]

[89] Cases *Behrami* and *Saramati* [2007] (n 12), para 108. See also Case *Banković and others v Belgium, the Czech Republic, Denmark, France, Germany, Greece, Hungary, Iceland, Italy, Luxembourg, the Netherlands, Norway, Poland, Portugal, Spain, Turkey and the United Kingdom* App No 52207/99 (ECtHR 12 December 2001, 2001-XII) para 62, Case *Ilaşcu and others v Moldova and Russia* App No 48787/99 (ECtHR, 8 July 2004, 2004-VII) para 332 and Case *Bosphorus* [2005] (n 16), para 150.

[90] See the arguments of the Danish and German governments in Cases *Behrami* and *Saramati* [2007] (n 12), paras 99 and 108.

[91] A Sari, 'Jurisdiction and International Responsibility in Peace Support Operations: The Behrami and Saramati Cases' (2008) 8(1) *Human Rights Law Review* 151 at 168.

[92] P Lagrange (2008) (n 11) at 109.

[93] See A Rey Aneiros (2008) (n 11) at 523. Also critical are H Krieger, 'A Credibility Gap: The Behrami and Saramati Decision of the European Court of Human Rights' (2009) 13(1–2) *Journal*

In any case, if the ratio decidendi of this decision – that the ECtHR has no jurisdiction over actions that are ultimately attributable to the Security Council and would be inappropriate to expand the *Bosphorus* case law to the acts of an international organization that occurred outside the territorial scope of the Convention – is in itself questionable, then even more so is the way in which the application of the *Bosphorus* doctrine was discarded in this case. Indeed, the argument derived from the extraterritorial nature of the facts in litigation against the application of the *Bosphorus* case law is weak, since the issue was not argued or discussed in the decision which, however, is particularly detailed in other less important aspects.[94]

Although, on the other hand, asking the ECtHR, as a last resort, to become the controlling body of the UN, was perhaps asking too much. This would imply a qualitative change in the nature of the ECHR itself, that would turn from an instrument of European public order to another of international public order.[95] However, if the abuses by these troops get worse, falling below the conventional standard of protection, and the lawsuits increase, it would not be completely preposterous for the ECtHR to reconsider its position if, in addition, there is some other element of connection with the European environment (regarding the abuses over nationals of Member States of the Convention) making it difficult to avoid its jurisdiction as the body responsible for the validity of the Convention as a 'constitutional instrument of European public order'.[96]

However, let us not build our hopes up in this regard. This situation is a fair way from the case of the EU in which, in the end, the ECJ intervened in *Kadi* annulling the CFI decision (which is very similar to this one) to ensure the unity of EC/EU law before running the risk of national courts deciding to 'take the law into their own hands' and intervening in cases where the protection of fundamental rights of their nationals fall below the standards of their national Constitutions, thus breaking the unity and supremacy of EC/EU law which the ECJ is obliged to guarantee.

of International Peacekeeping 159; M Milanovic and T Papic, 'As Bad as it Gets: The European Court of Human Rights' Behrami and Saramati Decision and General International Law' (2008) 58(2) *International and Comparative Law Quarterly* 267; and A Sari, 'Jurisdiction and International Responsibility in Peace Support Operations: The Behrami and Saramati Cases' (2008) 8(1) *Human Rights Law Review* 151.

[94] See G de Búrca 'The European Court of Justice and the International Legal Order after Kadi' (2009) 01/09 *Jean Monnet Working Papers* April 2009 at 21.

[95] On the ECHR as an instrument of European public order, see J Andriantsimbazovina *et al*, *Les grands arrêts de la Cour européenne des droits de l'homme* in 4th edn (PUF, Paris, 2007) 7–17.

[96] See Case *Loizidou* [1995] (n 67), para 75.

IV

Interlocking Supranational Orders of a Constitutional Nature

1. In previous Parts, we have gone through cases and situations where the instability of interordinal relations implied a problem of constitutional significance (*Solange*, *Bosphorus*, *Behrami-Saramati* . . .). As already noted, apart from its academic interest, this issue ends up having an impact on the legal security (in terms of predictability) and fundamental rights of individuals, compromising the very existence of a rule of law. In this Part, we shall discuss how to address the constitutional problem that arises when the minimum standard considered by some orders as indispensable is not respected, such as where the application of an EC/EU regulation (being a direct development of a UN sanction) does not comply with one or more of the fundamental rights recognized as such in the national Constitution and in the very same 'EU Constitution'.

2. The problem arose within the EU legal order in the now famous *Kadi* case, where the application of the right to a fair trial (also called due process guarantees) was contested within the EU legal order. When the CFI and subsequently the ECJ were confronted with this issue, the European jurisdiction had to analyse the legal value of international law in general and UN law in particular within the EU system. As other constitutional courts of Member States were once asked, the EU courts had to deal with the real constitutional nature (or not) of the EU legal system itself, that is, whether or not international (or UN) law was able to prevail over EU constitutional guarantees. Adopting one or the other option means more than the solution to the specific case. It was for the EU courts to pronounce themselves for a pluralistic or constitutional approach within the issue of the relationship between UN and EU law and even the role that the EU was able to play in the global (legal and non-legal) governance.

3. In this Part, we will use the *Kadi* case to illustrate the different approaches towards UN law in particular (and international law in general) that the EU could (and in fact did) adopt and the various possibilities for coordinating the relationships among all the legal orders of constitutional nature analysed (state, ECHR, EU, UN), especially from the standpoint of the EU order, taking into account the consequences derived from the option for either approach. Besides describing the complex situation, a new approach called interordinal constitutionalism, a form of soft constitutionalism, will be proposed. In the concluding section, the main ideas derived from the theories, cases and situations discussed throughout this book will be outlined.

10

International Law According to the European Supranational Courts

1. THE DIFFERENT APPROACHES THAT FOUNDED THE DECISIONS OF THE CFI, ECJ AND THE ECTHR

1. The reactions of CFI and ECJ regarding *Kadi*, on the one hand, and the reaction of the ECtHR in the *Behrami* and *Saramati* cases, on the other hand, giving rise to a similar question on the responsibility of an international organization, show three different views within a spectrum of possible answers to some of the key issues of constitutional law, international law and global governance. It should be noted that the issues in question referred not to any international organization but to the primary organization of almost universal membership that was created to achieve key objectives in the peace and security fields, secured by clear legal rules (especially Chapter VII and Article 103 of the Charter) that indicate the priority that must be given to its decisions. These cases were faced with key issues regarding the authority and effectiveness of international law and its institutions, and the proper relationship between international obligations (also derived from regional organizations) of different origin and nature.

In each of the instances examined, appeal was made to a regional court to rule over the legality of an act of the Security Council, and in each case the various courts gave different answers to the question of whether they had jurisdiction for it and, if so, what would be the control parameter – that is, in relation to what legal order or which values would these UNSC decisions be reviewed. And in each case, the answer was based on a different set of assumptions about the nature, source and structure of the legal authority that the Security Council of the UN enjoyed.

2. First, the ECtHR concluded that because the challenged acts before it were attributable to the Security Council more than to the participating states and given the scope and importance of the UN mission, the ECtHR had jurisdiction to hear about the claim regarding the violation of human rights brought before it.[1]

[1] Case *Behrami v France* App no 71412/01 and Case *Saramati v France, Germany and Norway* App No 78166/01 (ECtHR, 2 May 2007, unpublished), para 149.

Secondly, the CFI adopted the position according to which even though the EU was directly bound by the resolutions of the Security Council, and although the court had no jurisdiction to directly control the actions of the Security Council, it did have the jurisdiction to indirectly control the actions of the Security Council for possible violation of the minimum international standards of the *ius cogens*.[2]

In the appeal for annulment before the ECJ, the Advocate General stated that the EC/EU was not internally bound by Security Council resolutions and that the ECJ did have jurisdiction to control the compatibility of an EC/EU regulation implementing a Security Council resolution with the standards on fundamental rights protected by EC/EU law.[3] The ECJ, referring in general terms to the respect that the EC/EU has towards international treaties, including the UN Charter and the Security Council resolutions, stressed the fact that any international treaty could affect the autonomy of the EC/EU legal order, and even though the United Nations Charter could be understood as an integrating part of the EC/EU order, it would be placed below the normative level of treaties and under the general principles of law.[4]

To sum up, the ECtHR showed strong and considerable deference towards the Security Council of the UN, the CFI showed modest deference, and the ECJ (and the Advocate General) showed little or no deference at all.[5]

3. Moreover, in relation to the premises that underlie the various courts, it is clear that this response is explicitly or implicitly conditioned by a different conception of the role the court in question is attributed in the international order.[6] Thus, the conception of their particular role is based on a different understanding of the nature, origin and structure of the regulatory authority within the international legal order.

As for the ECtHR, it adopted a more cautious stance, defining itself as a specialized regional court established and bound by international law. That is, the ECtHR characterized itself as a component in the international view in which the UN is the last global forum for transnational cooperation in the pursuit of collective security, whose authority should not be questioned by a regional human rights court, and whose acts should not be subject to the conditions set by the ECHR. This concept is derived not so much from formal legal texts examined by the ECtHR that could limit its jurisdiction to what has been

[2] Case T-306/01 *Yusuf and Al Barakaat International Foundation v Council and Commission* [2005] ECR II-3533 para 277 and Case T-315/01 *Kadi v Council and Commission* [2005] ECR II-3649, para 226.

[3] Joined Cases C-402/05 P and C-415/05 P *Kadi* and *Al Barakaat International Foundation v Council* [2008] ECR I-6351, Opinion of AG Poiares Maduro, paras 24 and 31.

[4] Joined Cases C-402/05 P and C-415/05 P *Kadi* and *Al Barakaat* [2008] (n 3), paras 305–8.

[5] See G de Búrca, 'The European Court of Justice and the International Legal Order after Kadi' (2009) 01/09 *Jean Monnet Working Papers* April 2009 at 38.

[6] This complex situation has been defined as a 'disorder of orders'. See N Walker, 'Beyond boundary disputes and basic grids: Mapping the global disorder of normative orders' (2008) 6(3–4) *International Journal of Constitutional Law* 373.

strictly and exclusively established in the ECHR, but rather from a teleological interpretation that rejects the dynamic conception of replacing the protection gaps adopted by the ECtHR in other contexts to extend its jurisdiction, as this concept would be inappropriate in the context of United Nations action. Indeed, in the *Issa v Turkey* case, the ECtHR did not rule out that the military forces of a state party to the Convention (Turkey) that performed an operation on the territory of a third country (Iraq) could compromise the responsibility of the state party under the Convention as such forces 'exercised, temporarily, an effective global control over a part of the territory' of the third country.[7]

This approach to the issue, so deferential in the *Behrami* and *Saramati* cases is certainly extreme, given that the ECtHR did not suggest, even implicitly, any kind of exception, regardless of the nature of the violation of human rights in question or was either possible to contemplate the possibility that some actions may not be authorized by the Security Council resolution. The ECtHR considered that its own authority emanated from the same original source that the UN institutions, that is, international law, although in the case of the Strasbourg Court an instrument of international law was confined to one specific area (human rights) and territory (that of its Member States, primarily Europe).[8] From this point of view, the decisions of the UN Security Council adopted under Chapter VII constitute a particular binding authority and hierarchically superior source that would have priority over the ECHR and would prevent the ECtHR from exercising indirect control over the effects of such decisions.

4. Meanwhile, the CFI adopted a much more complex approach. It concluded that the Member States of the EU were bound, both by virtue of international law and EC/EU law, by the prevailing obligations established under the UN Charter, including those derived from the resolutions of the Security Council. Likewise it established that the EC/EU itself was indirectly linked through the obligations of its Member States derived from the Charter, though, since the EC/EU is either a member of the UN or an addressee of the resolutions of the Security Council, such indirect linkage of the EC/EU was due to the EU Treaties rather than to general international law.[9] On this specific point, the conclusion of the CFI did not differ much from the ECtHR. In fact, it took the position according to which customary and conventional international law determines that international obligations established under the UN Charter are binding on

[7] Case *Issa and others v Turkey* App No 31821/96 (ECtHR 16 November 2004, unpublished) para 74. For an explanation of the extraterritorial jurisdiction of the ECtHR, see J Andriantsimbazovina *et al*, *Les grands arrêts de la Cour européenne des droits de l'homme* 4th edn (PUF, Paris, 2007) 705–8.

[8] A similar case that dealt with the question of whether Art 103 UN Charter applied to a UNSC Resolution acting under Chapter VII would imply the primacy of the latter resolution over the essential content of the ECHR: see Case *Regina (Al-Jedstda)* [2007] UKHL, paras 35–37. For a comment of this decision, see A Orakhelashvili, *Peremptory Norms in International Law* (Oxford University Press, Oxford, 2006), especially at 342.

[9] Case T-306/01 *Yusuf and Al Barakaat* [2005] (n 2), para 243 and Case T-315/01 *Kadi* [2005] (n 2), para 193.

the EC/EU and prevail over any other contrary obligations. However, the CFI case law in *Yusuf/Al Barakaat* and *Kadi* was significantly separated from that of the ECtHR in two aspects.

First, the CFI concluded the compulsory and prevalence nature of Security Council resolutions through a reasoning based on the text of the Vienna Convention on the Law of Treaties, the provisions of the UN Charter, customary international law and the text of the EC Treaty.[10] The purposes and objectives of the UN were not taken into account, nor were they placed on a level above the particular objectives of the EU. Thus, the reasoning of the CFI was essentially formalistic and was confined to the strict limits of its own jurisdiction, according to a hierarchy of norms adopted on the basis of a set of general international and regional treaties where the EU Treaties are included.

A second difference between the reasoning of the CFI and the ECtHR would be that the first reaffirmed its own competence (and even its obligation by virtue of the interpretation made of the *ius cogens*), despite the binding and precedence nature over any other obligation of the Security Council resolutions, to exercise a minimum and residual control regarding the legality of such decisions. To some extent, the CFI seemed to be following the logic and even the conclusion finally taken by the ECtHR when it stated that:

> the claim that the Court of First Instance has jurisdiction to review indirectly the lawfulness of such a decision according to the standard of protection of fundamental rights as recognised by the Community legal order, cannot be justified either on the basis of international law or on the basis of Community law.[11]

However, the CFI continued justifying its jurisdiction by virtue of international law, in the sense that *ius cogens* norms recognized by customary international law and the Vienna Convention on the Law of Treaties, and the purposes and principles of the UN itself, impose limits on the powers of the Security Council that should be monitored.[12] Moreover, even though its decision characterized the EC/EU legal order as formally subordinate to that established by the UN Charter, the CFI did not show any institutional reluctance (as happened to the ECtHR in *Behrami* and *Saramati*) on the question of assuming the task of controlling, certainly out of the ordinary, the Security Council of the United Nations.

5. The ECJ, broadly following the conclusions of the Advocate General, Mr Poiares Maduro, took a very different approach from the ECtHR in *Behrami* and *Saramati* or to that from the CFI in *Yusuf/Al Barakaat* and *Kadi*. While the Advocate General addressed the issue of the EC/EU obligations under inter-

[10] Case T-306/01 *Yusuf and Al Barakaat* [2005] (n 2), paras 273–274 and Case T-315/01 *Kadi* [2005] (n 2), paras 222–223.

[11] Case T-306/01 *Yusuf and Al Barakaat* [2005] (n 2), para 272 and Case T-315/01 *Kadi* [2005] (n 2), para 221.

[12] Case T-306/01 *Yusuf and Al Barakaat* [2005] (n 2), paras 277-282 and Case T-315/01 *Kadi* [2005] (n 2), paras 226–231.

national law, or the status of international law within the EU legal order as a marginal element of the case, the ECJ went fully into it and made it clear that if they were to adopt a unified position (that is, define a single universal standardized pyramid), which it did since it concluded that the EC/EU order was a separate legal order and even, domestic regarding international law, it would place international treaties, including the UN Charter and the Security Council resolutions, below the EC/EU Treaties.[13] Both the Luxembourg Court and the Advocate General concluded that the ECJ's primary obligation is to protect the values of the 'internal' constitutional order of the EU, including the fundamental rights protected therein, regardless of whether this leads to undermining the actions of the UN Security Council.

Given these assumptions, which are based on a dualistic conception of international law in the EC/EU legal order, neither the Advocate General nor the ECJ saw a problem in the applicability of Article 103 of the Charter. In addition, the Advocate General added that his conclusion about the primacy of EU rules on the Security Council resolutions had to be understood without prejudice to the rule laid down in Article 103 of the Charter.[14] On the other hand, the ECJ established that the annulment of a regulation to implement a Security Council resolution for violation of EC/EU legal principles would not jeopardize the primacy of that resolution in the field of international law.[15] Thus, the ECJ should take its decisions under the EC/EU legal order (and especially its constitutional rules, which some call 'the EU constitutional law') and not public international law, even if this means that the EC/EU or its Member States may be held responsible from the point of view of international law due to the violation of obligations derived from the UN Charter. Moreover, both the Advocate General and the ECJ put forward two different and separate sources of law – internal (or domestic) EC/EU law, on the one hand, and international law on the other – and as to the effects of Mr Kadi's lawsuit against the validity of EC/EU regulations implemented by a Security Council resolution, the first would interest the Court. In other words, the decision in *Kadi* by the ECJ is based on the theory that there are distinct and different sources of legal authority and regardless of whether the EC/EU could be exposed to international sanctions for breaching the Security Council resolutions, this would not affect the obligation of the ECJ to control the implementation of Security Council decision using for that purpose the European standards on fundamental rights as a benchmark.[16]

[13] Joined Cases C-402/05 P and C-415/05 P *Kadi and Al Barakaat* [2008] (n 4), para 308.

[14] Joined Cases C-402/05 P and C-415/05 P *Kadi and Al Barakaat* [2008] (n 4), Opinion of the AG Poiares Maduro, para 39.

[15] Joined Cases C-402/05 P and C-415/05 P *Kadi and Al Barakaat* [2008] (n 4), para 288.

[16] See G de Búrca (2009) (n 5) at 41.

2. THE LACK OF UNANIMITY: DIFFERENT SOLUTIONS TO THE SAME PROBLEM

6. None of the three European Courts (ECJ, CFI and ECtHR) that considered the cases above could successfully claim jurisdiction to control the actions of the UNSC. Yet, when they had to face the challenge of changing the methods of global governance, given the increase in the exercise of *quasi*-legislative powers by the Security Council in particular – and more specifically, given the attempts of the individuals concerned to force a certain degree of responsibility through appeals before regional international courts – the three courts chose to take different positions regarding the problem.

The approach adopted by the CFI is a sort of compromise of deference, in the sense of rejecting the idea of binding the Security Council to an absolute respect for EC/EU protection standards, but insisting, on the other hand, on control of the legality of its action at least in relation to unavailable minimum standards of international law. These *ius cogens* rules would be at best limited and more controversial kinds of rule that would not be open to a more dynamic and fluid sort of development as the 'general principles' are or even customary international law is. The CFI's vision of international legal context would, therefore, follow a vertical design, hierarchical and integrated, in which the EU would be below the UN, but in which lower courts such as the CFI are nevertheless entitled or even obliged by the international order itself to review the actions of the UN bodies under peremptory norms of international law.

The position adopted by the ECtHR is of total and complete deference towards the UN Security Council, denying its own jurisdiction both with form and with substantial arguments. As in the case of the CFI, the ECtHR's position suggests a vertical, hierarchical and integrated view of the international legal order but, unlike the CFI, this vertical order does not allow the exercise of judicial control of a universal body of global security by any specialized international regional court.

On the other hand, the ECJ did not pretend in any way to compromise either the Security Council or the global governance that the UN exercises (or tries to exercise), but, on the contrary, it refers to the general respect that the EC/EU must show regarding the rules of general international law, and insists that in its jurisdiction to control the implementation of the Security Council resolutions, ensuring compliance with security standards established within the EC/EU does not imply any control of the resolution as such.[17] Thus, for the ECJ, the international order would be horizontal, not integrated, which together with the EU would exist in parallel with other constitutional systems that would, in turn, constitute independent and separate legal orders, in whose context the Court would not have any role or competence assigned to coordinate the relationship

[17] Joined Cases C-402/05 P and C-415/05 P *Kadi and Al Barakaat* [2008] (n 4), paras 286–288.

and the development of common principles among international legal systems (including the resolutions of the Security Council of the UN) and the EC/EU legal order.[18]

The apparently opposing views of the CFI and the ECtHR have, in turn, more in common with each other, at a fundamental level, than with the approach made by the ECJ, in the sense that they presupposed and are based on the existence of a common international legal system and an international community of which they, as different regional courts, are part, and in which they have a task to carry out by coordinating the relationship between their respective sub-orders (the EC/EU legal order and the ECHR, respectively) and other parts of the international legal order.

7. Each of the three legal concepts analysed so far have suffered criticisms and remarks. Some have criticized the unexpected move of the CFI under which it granted itself the power to control – even though only indirectly – the supreme political body of the United Nations,[19] especially insofar as it is not clear that the ICJ itself is willing to subject the Security Council to a similar control.[20] Meanwhile, another doctrinal sector has criticized the CFI for giving up a more ambitious role as a supervisor body and to subordinate the EC/EU order to the UN Security Council resolutions.[21] There are also those who have criticized the ECtHR, due to its refusal of jurisdiction in *Behrami* and *Saramati*, for abandoning its dynamic and progressive conception of human rights protection under the ECHR and for tolerating a significant gap regarding legal responsibility derived from human rights violations which have occurred in Europe.[22] Others have interpreted the Opinion of the Advocate General, Mr Poiares Maduro, in *Kadi* in the sense that EC/EU law itself would exempt the EC/EU from the obligation to comply with UN resolutions adopted under Article 103 of the Charter and would allow supervision of EU rules implemented by Security Council resolutions with the standards on fundamental rights established by the EU itself.[23]

[18] See G de Búrca (2009) (n 5) at 42.

[19] M Winkler, 'When Legal Systems Collide: Judicial Review of Freezing Measures in the Context of International Terrorism' Paper 40 *Yale Law Student Scholarship Series* May 2009; and A Aust, 'The Role of Human Rights in Limiting the Enforcement Powers of the Security Council: A Practitioner's View' in E de Wet, A Nollkaemper and P Dijkstra (eds), *Review of the Security Council by Member States* (Metro-Intersentia, Amsterdam, 2003) 31, especially at 35–8.

[20] This issue has been analysed in previous chapters. For a brief exposition of the question see J Álvarez, 'Judging the Security Council' (1996) 90(1) *American Journal of International Law* 1.

[21] See P Eeckhout. 'Community Terrorism Listings, Fundamental Rights, and UN Security Council Resolutions. In Search of the Right Fit' (2007) 3(2) *European Constitutional Law Review* 183; and J Almqvist, 'A Human Rights Critique of European Judicial Review: Counter-Terrorism Sanction' (2008) 57(2) *International and Comparative Law Quarterly* 303.

[22] KM Larsen, 'Attribution of Conduct in Peace Operations: The 'Ultimate Authority and Control' Test' (2008) 19(3) *European Journal of International Law* 509; and M Milanovic and T Papic, 'As Bad as it Gets: The European Court of Human Rights' Behrami and Saramati Decision and General International Law' (2008) 58(2) *International and Comparative Law Quarterly* 267.

[23] N Lavranos, 'The Interface between European and National Procedural Law: UN Sanctions and Judicial Review' in D Obradovic and N Lavranos (eds), *Interface between EU Law and National Law* (Europa Law Publishing, Groningen, 2007) 347; and N Lavranos, 'UN sanctions and Judicial Review'

However, initial responses to the ECJ decision in *Kadi* are, in general, positive.[24]

If one were to describe the different legal concepts analysed according to the level of protection and strengthening of European standards of protection of fundamental rights, the ECJ would be outstanding. Clearly, the Court of Justice does not directly challenge the authority of the Security Council as the supreme political body with great expertise in counter-terrorism, but indirectly it does contest this absolute authority by overriding the implementation carried out by the EC/EU regarding the Security Council resolutions in question. In the same vein, the approach made by the ECtHR, which, paradoxically, is the Court from which we would have expected a more favourable attitude towards human rights protection, is somewhat disappointing. Indeed, using arguments pertaining to a sort of judicial *Realpolitik*, the Strasbourg Court resigned from a more active role in monitoring compliance with the standards of protection of the ECHR and, instead, even seemed to place the protection afforded to human rights below the obligation to promote international peace and security, in a new kind of global hierarchy of values.

in J Wouters, PA Nollkaemper and E de Wet (eds), *The Europeanisation of International law. The Status of International Law in the EU and its member States* (TMC Asser Press, The Hague, 2008) 185 at 191–200.

[24] See, inter alia, D Halberstam and E Stein. 'The United Nations, the European Union, and the King of Sweden: Economic sanctions and individual rights in a plural world order' (2009) 46(1) *Common Market Law Review* 13, although they regret that the ECJ did not adopt a more aggressive position (at 72); B Kunoy and A Dawes, 'Plate tectonics in Luxembourg: The ménage à trois between EC law, international law and the European Convention on Human Rights following the UN sanctions cases' (2009) 46(1) *Common Market Law Review* 73; and P Cassia and F Donnat, 'Terrorisme international et droits fondamentaux : les leçons du droit communautaire Commentaire sous Cour de justice des Communautés européennes, 3 septembre 2008, Kadi et Al Barakaat International Foundation, aff. C-402/05 P et C-415/05 P' (2008) 24(6) *Revue Française de Droit Administratif* 1204.

11

The Pluralistic Conception versus the Constitutional Conception of the International Legal Order

1. PRELIMINARY CONSIDERATIONS

1. The different responses of various European courts to the problem of UN decisions review merely reflect the current debate between the authors who support a constitutional approach of the international system and those who support a pluralistic one. Specifically, the different views of the ECtHR and the CFI, on the one hand, and the ECJ on the other hand, reflect these two prevalent and distinct doctrines, as to the problem of multiplication, overlapping and conflict between legal orders on the international scene.

The ECJ, essentially following the Opinion of the Advocate General, Mr Poiares Maduro, adopted a clearly pluralistic position towards the problem of the relationship between EC/EU law and the international order, whereas the CFI and the ECtHR in their respective resolutions and with their differences clearly went for, as one might imagine, a constitutional position. Pluralistic conceptions share with dualism the emphasis given to the existence of distinct and separate legal orders, but while pluralism stresses the plurality of different regulatory systems, the traditional dualistic approach has focused on the relationship between national (or domestic) law and international law. Likewise, the traditional constitutionalist approaches to the international legal order coincide significantly with the monistic ones on their assumptions of the existence of a single and integrated legal order, but the category that vindicates a constitutionalist approach of the international legal order is extensive and includes some positions that do not necessarily assume that inherent integration and could not easily be equated with the traditional monistic theory.

2. Contrary to what one might usually think, the main difference between constitutional and pluralist approaches is not that one has a normative orientation and the other a descriptive one, although many of the pluralistic approach supporters have the advantage that their descriptive explanations seem more plausible and some variants of the constitutional approach may seem unrealistic and unattractive given the deep and wide diversity of orders. However, both contemporary constitutional approaches to international legal order and the pluralistic share descriptive and normative arguments, as discussed below.

2. PLURALIST CONCEPTIONS OF INTERNATIONAL LAW AND GLOBAL GOVERNANCE

3. There is a growing and active doctrine that intercedes for a pluralistic conception of international law and global governance.[1] Although some of the early literature on legal pluralism was of a more sociological than legal nature, the latest doctrine on international and global legal pluralism is notable for its support for the normative advantages of the conception.[2] Its supporters state that it emphasizes the value of diversity and the difference among the different normative and governance systems, either national or international, and criticize the approaches for being undesirable and implausible as they seek to achieve coherence among the different levels of legal orders and government. There are, however, other threads within the growing doctrine on global legal pluralism, some of which support a more orthodox position and others of which are in favour of a milder variant. In this sense, one of the authors who defend this thesis pleads for the existence of a softer legal pluralism within the European context, resulting from the interaction between the EU and the ECHR system, than that proposed for the global context. Thus, Europe emphasizes the importance of mutual persuasion and at the same time the autonomy and authority of each of the legal orders is emphasized.[3]

[1] See, inter alia, PS Berman, 'Global Legal Pluralism' (2007) 80(6) *Southern California Review* 1155; PS Berman, 'A pluralist approach to international law' (2007) 32(2) *Yale Journal of International Law* 301; N Krisch, 'The Pluralism of Global Administrative Law' (2006) 17(1) *European Journal of International Law* 247; N Walker, 'The Idea of Constitutional Pluralism' (2002) 65(3) *Modern Law Review* 317; D Halberstam, 'Constitutionalism and Pluralism in Marbury and Van Gend' in MP Maduro and L Azoulai (eds), *The Past and Future of EU Law: The Classics of EU Law Revisited on the 50th Anniversary of the Rome Treaty* (Hart Publishing, Oxford, 2010) 26; BZ Tamanaha, 'Understanding Legal Pluralism: Past to Present, Local to Global' (2008) 30 *Sydney Law Review* 375; and N MacCormick, 'Juridical Pluralism and the Risk of Constitutional Conflict' in N MacCormick (ed), *Questioning Sovereignty. Law State and Nation in the European Commonwealth* (OUP, Oxford, 1999) 97 at 120 (where he characterizes pluralism as the relationship model of the EU). See also the trilogy M Delmas-Marty, *Les Forces imaginantes du droit I. Le relatif et l'universel* (Seuil, Paris, 2004); M Delmas-Marty, *Les Forces imaginantes du droit II. Le pluralisme ordonné* (Seuil, Paris, 2006); and M Delmas-Marty, *Les Forces imaginantes du droit III. La Refondation des pouvoirs* (Seuil, Paris, 2007).

[2] As examples of the sociological inclination of the first legal pluralism, see M Galanter, 'Justice in Many Rooms: Courts, Private Ordering and Indigenous Law' (1981) 19 *Journal of Legal Pluralism and Unofficial Law* 1; J Griffiths, 'What is Legal Pluralism?' (1986) 24 *Journal of Legal Pluralism and Unofficial Law* 1; SE Merry, 'Legal Pluralism' (1988) 22(5) *Law & Society Review* 869; and N MacCormick, 'Juridical Pluralism and the Risk of Constitutional Conflict' in N MacCormick (ed), *Questioning Sovereignty. Law State and Nation in the European Commonwealth* (OUP, Oxford, 1999) 97.

[3] N Krisch, 'The Open Architecture of European Human Rights Law' (2008) 71(2) *Modern Law Review* 183.

4. The literature on international legal pluralism runs with that on the ways of coordinating global governance. In fact, the most interesting developments in this field concern the problem of responsibility and accountability of international actors such as the UN Security Council and its position in the global governance, especially through the direct imposition of economic sanctions on individuals, as has been already analysed in this work. Thus, the representatives of legal pluralism state that the pragmatic type settings that this pluralism supports are preferable to approaches based on ideals of coherence and unity. Thus, they argue that the pluralist approach, compared with the constitutionalist approach, would lead to a higher level of transnational responsibility. In general, they support the 'messy' (and disconnected) global view of international responsibility and accountability at the administrative level stating that it allows mutual influence and a gradual approach, while avoiding the various levels or legal or governmental plans to exercise a control over each other.[4] Thus, pluralistic conceptions would surpass the constitutional one, which takes the unity as a sort of legal idealism and pushes the legal and political order towards a unified framework minimizing the importance of the extent of the legitimate diversity of the global community. Understanding the international legal order from the pluralist conception leads to the assumption that interordinal relations would be governed by politics rather than law, with different actors and rules competing in a race to reach the authority through politics rather than legal arguments.[5] The mutual adjustment carried out on a case-by-case basis among the different legal orders that pluralism preaches would thus be preferable to the imposition of new conceptions of sovereignty or universal harmonization structures.[6]

5. Pluralistic approaches to international law support the preservation of a space for discussion, resistance and innovation, promoting, likewise, tolerance and mutual readjustments among legal orders.[7] In addition, there are those who, pleading for a legal order to take up legal pluralism, deny the very existence of the concept of 'international community'.[8] Even with the growing interest in the doctrine of so-called 'constitutional pluralism', which explains the global legal order as a plurality not only of legal systems but also of national constitutional systems, transnational and networking-based, the proliferation

[4] N Krisch (2006) (n 1). See also N MacCormick (1999) (n 1), esp at 121 where he stresses that this concept would diminish the risk of normative conflicts.

[5] This is, indeed, the main argument that sustains the concepts of professor Delmas-Marty in her trilogy. See, especially, the conclusion of her third book, M Delmas-Marty (2007) (n 1) 253–79. See also N Krisch (2008) (n 3).

[6] PS Berman (2007) (n 1) at 1163.

[7] PS Berman (2007) (n 1) at 1237. See also JL Cohen, 'A Global State of Emergency or the Further Constitutionalization of International Law: A Pluralist Approach' (2008) 15(4) *Constellations* 456.

[8] See D Kennedy, 'One, Two, Three, Many Legal Orders: Legal Pluralism and the Cosmopolitan Dream' (2007) 31(3) *New York University Review of Law and Social Change* 641 and O Kennedy, 'The Mystery of Global Governance' (2008) 34(3) *Ohio Northern University Law Review* 827 at 839 and 853.

of separate systems relating primarily through an '"agonistic" process of negotiation' is emphasized.[9] And despite the regulatory emphasis placed on tolerance, accommodation and deference and mutual learning, there is some agreement that the proliferation of self-integrated constitutional systems that seek to establish their own authority may instead emphasize the conflict and constrain communication or, even, 'encourage a strident fundamentalism, a refusal of dialogue with other sites and processes or with internal challenges to their authority'.[10]

6. In short, what links pluralist approaches of the international legal order is the common emphasis (and its interpretation) of the meaning of the existence of a multitude of different and distinct legal systems, and the probability of collisions and claims of authority and legitimacy and the struggle for primacy in certain contexts. From the point of view of its supporters, the many and varied points of friction in the global legal pluralism and the constant threat of mutual rejection of claims of authority from various regional and functional areas is an ideal breeding ground for the promotion of sensitive and responsible global governance, contrary to constitutional or cosmopolitan models that emphasize coherence or unity. Supporters of an orthodox pluralism deny the possibility of a common system of values of universal orientation and question the usefulness of the idea of an international community. They do not seek to develop a common communications framework to redress the various claims of authority of different political entities or different legal orders. Rather than support the coordination between legal systems, more orthodox pluralism would promote interaction processes ad hoc, pragmatic and with a heavy political look.[11]

Pluralistic approaches embrace diversity, competition and lack of coordination among orders for being, in its opinion, the most appropriate way to reach an optimal level of responsibility and international accountability. And mostly, pluralistic conceptions of the international scene have been consciously defended as a means of correcting the constitutional monism or sovereigntist positions, which would be presented as naive, misleading and even dangerously overturned in the ideas of unity, universalism and consensus.[12] On the other hand, constitutional approaches are characterized by the pluralist doctrine as misunderstood or even dangerous attempts that seek to extrapolate the model of the national government, their political solutions and political structures and political models of the international scene.

[9] N Walker (2002) (n 1) at 359.

[10] N Walker (2002) (n 1) at 358.

[11] G de Búrca 'The European Court of Justice and the International Legal Order after Kadi' (2009) 01/09 *Jean Monnet Working Papers* April 2009 at 48.

[12] N Krisch (2006) (n 1); PS Berman, 'Global Legal Pluralism' (2007) (n 1); D Kennedy (2007) (n 8); O Kennedy (2008) (n 8); and JL Cohen (2008) (n 7).

3. THE CONSTITUTIONAL CONCEPTION OF INTERNATIONAL LAW AND GLOBAL GOVERNANCE

7. Unlike the doctrine in the field of legal pluralism which, although increasing, is quite recent and not excessive, there is an abundant literature on the constitutional conceptions of international law.[13] An important part is the German doctrine from the last century whose origins are usually placed in the Kantian cosmopolitanism.[14] And as was to be expected from such a broad literature regarding a concept so suggestive and complex to define as constitutionalism, there is a wide variety of arguments and conceptions in this field.[15] A risk inherent to the concept of 'constitutionalism' consists in the extension and excessive use that has been made of it, to the point that it does not overclarify the description of a particular approach to international law and global governance as 'constitutionalist'.[16] Thus, there are some who have severely criticized the

[13] See, inter alia, the collective books RSJ Macdonald and DM Johnston (eds), *Towards World Constitutionalism: Issues in the Legal Ordering of the World Community* (Martinus Nijhoff, Leiden 2005); C Joerges and EU Petersmann (eds), *Constitutionalism, Multilevel Trade Governance and Social Regulation* (Hart, Oxford, 2006) and JL Dunoff and JP Trachtman (eds), *Ruling the World? Constitutionalism, International Law, and Global Governance* (Cambridge University Press, Cambridge, 2009). See also R Bustos Gisbert, *La Constitución Red: Un estudio sobre supraestatalidad y Constitución* (IVAP, Oñate, 2005) 177–205; B Simma, 'From bilateralism to community interest in International Law' (1994) 250(VI) *Recueil des Cours de l'Académie de Droit International de La Haye* 217; C Tomuschat, 'Obligations arising for states without or against their will' (1993) 241(IV) *Recueil des Cours de l'Académie de Droit International de La Haye* 195; B Fassbender, 'The United Nations Charter as Constitution of the International Community' (1998) 36(3) *Columbia Journal of Transnational Law* 529 and its update B Fassbender, *The United Nations Charter as the Constitution of the International Community* (Martinus Nijhoff, Leiden, 2009); A Peters, 'Compensatory Constitutionalism: The Function and Potential of Fundamental International Norms and Structures' (2006) 19(3) *Leiden Journal of International Law* 579; and P Carrozza, 'Constitutionalism's Post Modern Opening' in M Loughlin and N Walker (eds), *The Paradox of Constitutionalism. Constituent Power and Constitutional Form* (OUP, Oxford, 2008) 169. For a summary of the most relevant German doctrine, see A Von Bogdandy, 'Constitutionalism in International Law: Comment on a Proposal from Germany' (2006) 47(1) *Harvard International Law Journal* 223 and A Von Bogdandy, 'El constitucionalismo en el derecho internacional: comentario sobre una propuesta alemana' (2007) 5 *Puente@Europa* 34. For the issues arising from International trade, see EU Petersmann, 'Constitutionalism and the Regulation of International Markets: How to Define the "Development Objectives" of the World Trading System?' (2007) 23 *European University Institute Law Working Papers*; DA Cass, *The Constitutionalization of the World Trade Organization. Legitimacy, Democracy, and Community in the International Trading System* (Oxford University Press, Oxford, 2005); and M Krajewski, 'Democratic Legitimacy and Constitutional Perspectives of the WTO' (2001) 35(1) *Journal of World Trade* 167.

[14] Specifically, cosmopolitanism has its origin in the thesis of the philosopher from Königsberg published for the first time in 1795. See I Kant, *Zum ewigen Frieden: ein philosophischer Entwurf* (Meiner Verlag, Hamburg, 1992 (first published in 1795)). See also O Höffe (ed), *Immanuel Kant: Zum ewigen Frieden* (2nd edn Akademie, Berlin 2004); and N Arriola Etxaniz, 'El cosmopolitismo como teoría defensora del gobierno mundial' (2008) 56(2) *Estudios de Deusto* 11.

[15] An explanation of three possible approaches to constitutionalism and international legal order is available at B Fassbender, *The United Nations Charter as the Constitution of the International Community* (Martinus Nijhoff, Leiden, 2009) 585–93.

[16] On the complex concept of 'Constitution', see R Bustos Gisbert (2006) (n 13) 19–24 and 75–87. On the dangers of applying concepts inherent to national constitutionalism into the international legal order, see N Walker, 'Making a World of Difference? Habermas, Cosmopolitanism and the

inflationist use of the term 'Constitution', comparing it with an increase in regulation or with the evolution of a hierarchical legal system.[17]

8. However, there are many variants of the international-constitutionalists concepts that could be considered as such in the sense of the terms 'international' and 'constitutionalists'. Among them we should highlight the influential German school represented by Verdross, Simma and Tomuschat, stressing the idea of an international legal order based on an international community and international solidarity as opposed to the concept based on separate and distinct interests of national states individually considered.[18] In this latter sense there are those who categorically conclude that the essential object of international constitutionalism has been to force states to comply with the constitutional principles of the international community.[19]

9. Another option would be Hayek's thesis about the role of the economy in global governance, which would be a version of international constitutionalism proposing the limitation of political power and which puts forward the need for a global law of integration protecting human rights and economic freedoms, with direct effect and legally enforceable.[20]

Constitutionalization of International Law' in OA Payrow Shabani (ed), *Multiculturalism and Law: A Critical Debate* (University of Wales Press, Cardiff, 2007) 219.

[17] See B Fassbender, 'The Meaning of International Constitutional Law' in RSJ Macdonald and DM Johnston (eds), *Towards World Constitutionalism: Issues in the Legal Ordering of the World Community* (Martinus Nijhoff, Leiden, 2005) 837. Nonetheless this author has also advocated for the UN Charter to be considered as the Constitution of the international legal order. See B Fassbender, 'The United Nations Charter as Constitution of the International Community' (1998) 36(3) *Columbia Journal of Transnational Law* 529.

[18] A Verdross, *Die Einheit des rechtlichen Weltbildes auf der Grundlage der Völkerrechtsverfassung* (Mohr, Tübingen, 1923); A Verdross, *Die Verfassung der Völkerrechtsgemeinschaft* (Springer, Wien-Berlin, 1926); B Simma, 'From bilateralism to community interest in International Law' (1994) 250(VI) *Recueil des Cours de l'Académie de Droit International de La Haye* 217; C Tomuschat, 'Obligations arising for states without or against their will' (1993) 241(IV) *Recueil des Cours de l'Académie de Droit International de La Haye* 195; C Tomuschat, 'International Law: ensuring the survival of mankind on the eve of a new century. General Course on Public International Law' (1999) 281 *Recueil des cours de l'Académie de Droit International de La Haye* 9 at 72–90, where he advocates the existence of an international community (although he refuses that his international community could be a super-state in which states would be like provinces or regions) and even a 'Constitution of Mankind'. This thesis was already exposed in his previous work, C Tomuschat, 'International Law as the Constitution of Mankind' in United Nations (ed), *International Law on the Eve of the Twenty-first Century. Views from the International Law Commission / Le droit international à l'aube du XXIe siècle: réflexions de codificateurs* (United Nations, New York, 1997) 37.

[19] BO Bryde, 'International Democratic Constitutionalism' in RSJ Macdonald and DM Johnston (eds), *Towards World Constitutionalism: Issues in the Legal Ordering of the World Community* (Martinus Nijhoff, Leiden, 2005) 103 at 115.

[20] The main representative would be Professor Petersmann. See EU Petersmann, 'Constitutionalism and the Regulation of International Markets: How to Define the "Development Objectives" of the World Trading System?' (2007) 23 *European University Institute Law Working Papers*; EU Petersmann, 'Why Rational Choice Theory Requires a Multilevel Constitutional Approach to International Economic Law – A Response to the Case for Reforming the WTO's Enforcement Mechanism' (2008) 2008(1) *University of Illinois Law Review* 359; EU Petersmann, 'Justice in International Economic Law? From the "International Law among States" to "International Integration Law" and

10. Another view of international constitutionalism is the *law of lawmaking*, which puts forward the need for a law through which the processes of transnational decision making can be structured so as to ensure their legitimacy and the *rule of law*.[21] Underlying these approaches is the desire that the various forms of transnational governance that would otherwise escape the national constitutional review should, however, be governed by the law. Specifically, these concepts have shown the need to transfer, to the transnational context, a set of constitutional principles similar to those that have developed in the national constitutional context such as the rule of law, separation of powers – and mutual control between them – the protection of fundamental rights, and democracy.[22] Many supporters of the constitutional approach of the international order wanted to see in the development of the EU with its extremely dense legal order and positive argument that a constitutional approach beyond the state is possible and plausible.[23] What the orthodox conceptions of international constitutionalism have in common is their defence for a sort of systemic unity that would imply the existence of a set of basic rules and principles previously agreed upon to coordinate the global governance. On the other hand, the most orthodox thinking proposes to establish a previously agreed hierarchy among these basic rules and principles to solve conflicts of authority between the different levels and spheres of the government.[24]

11. Constitutional approaches to the order and international order have drawn criticism and debates, even from the internationalist doctrine.[25] Indeed, one of the most active exponents of the German school has stated that international constitutionalism, as a legal project, could simply be too ambitious and could lead to excessive over-regulation.[26] Other objections would say that the objective

"International Constitutional Law"' (2007) 2006(I) *The Global Community Yearbook of International Law and Jurisprudence* 105; and EU Petersmann, 'State Sovereignty, Popular Sovereignty and Individual Sovereignty: From Constitutional Nationalism to Multilevel Constitutionalism in International Economic Law?' in W Shan, P Simons and D Singh (eds), *Redefining Sovereignty in International Economic Law. Studies in International Trade Law* (Hart, Oxford, 2008) 27.

[21] C Joerges, 'Constitutionalism in Postnational Constellations: Contrasting. Social Regulation in the EU and in the WTO' in C Joerges and EU Petersmann (eds), *Constitutionalism, Multilevel Trade Governance and Social Regulation* (Hart, Oxford, 2006) 491.

[22] A Peters, 'Compensatory Constitutionalism: The Function and Potential of Fundamental International Norms and Structures' (2006) 19(3) *Leiden Journal of International Law* 579.

[23] See, inter alia, E de Wet, 'The International Constitutional Order' (2006) 55(1) *International and Comparative Law Quarterly* 51 at 52–3.

[24] The most developed theory in this aspect would be the one from Professor Christian Tomuschat. See C Tomuschat (1999) (n 18) especially at 305–434. See N Walker (2002) (n 1) at 353–4; and R Bustos Gisbert (2006) (n 13) 189–205.

[25] See JL Dunoff, 'Constitutional Conceits: The WTO's "Constitution" and the Discipline of International Law' (2006) 17(3) *European Journal of International Law* 647.

[26] A Von Bogdandy, 'Constitutionalism in International Law: Comment on a Proposal from Germany' (2006) 47(1) *Harvard International Law Journal* 223 at 242, where the author seems to argue that an excessive legal density would be difficult to accept by the international community. See R Howse and K Nicolaïdis, 'Legitimacy and Global Governance: Why a Constitution for the WTO is a step too far?' in R Porter *et al* (eds), *Equity, Efficiency and Legitimacy: The Multilateral System at the Millennium* (Brookings Institution, Washington DC, 2001) 227.

of international (or global) constitutionalism can be perceived as a threat due to jurisprudential, ethical, cultural, social and political reasons. In this sense, Johnston stresses that the jurisprudential objections come from the supporters of legal realism who fear that too much constitutional ideology in international law would strengthen the current strict interpretation of the law in the professional community and are reinforced by ethical reserves on the improper situation in which international judges would find themselves as they would be forced to decide disputes over the interpretation of constitutional texts. Thus, those who criticize global constitutionalism with cultural and ethical arguments would be very likely to find allies in the related fields of social activities that support the cause of local communities considered vulnerable to exploitation or insensitive practices of the central authority of state and power of large corporations.[27]

As long as the EU is used as the original model, there would be obvious problems in extrapolating the categories and structures from this example, since even the meaning of the idea of constitutionalism in the EU context has been put into question.[28]

12. However, despite the criticisms, some former sceptics are joining the club of the constitutional approach supporters and, based on certain Kantian assumptions, they have lauded the benefits of a constitutional and cosmopolitan vision of international law.[29]

Thus, for Habermas, the main attraction of the universal philosopher's cosmopolitan project would be the cognitive process of globalization and mutual adoption of perspectives that Kant associated with practical reason.[30] According to an authorized interpreter, for Habermas, constitutionalism of international law seems to be equally in the substantive quality of the general rules, in its institutional effectiveness and its capacity for globalization.[31] Habermas pursued the reaffirmation of Kantian cosmopolitanism as the basis of international legal order, rather than the Schmitt's hegemonic unilateralism.[32] However, despite embracing the peace ideals of Kant or the objectives ensuring freedom

[27] DM Johnston, 'World Constitutionalism in the Theory of International Law' in RSJ Macdonald and DM Johnston (eds), *Towards World Constitutionalism: Issues in the Legal Ordering of the World Community* (Martinus Nijhoff, Leiden, 2005) 3 at 19.

[28] Though this vision seems to be in a minority. See D Grimm, 'The Constitution in the process of Denationalization' (2005) 12(4) *Constellations* 447 at 458–9; and D Grimm, 'Integration by Constitution' (2005) 3(2–3) *International Journal of Constitutional Law* 193.

[29] Note the differences between M Koskenniemi, 'Global Legal Pluralism: Multiple Legal Regimes and Multiple Modes of Thought' in (2005) and M Koskenniemi, 'Constitutionalism as Mindset: Reflections on Kantian Themes About International Law and Globalization' (2007) 8(1) *Theoretical Inquiries in Law* 9, especially at 31–6.

[30] J Habermas, *El Occidente escindido: pequeños escritos políticos X* (JL López de Lizaga (tr)) (Trotta, Madrid, 2006) (original title: *Der gespaltene Westen: Kleine Politische Schriften X*, 2004) 113–87.

[31] N Walker (2007) (n 16) at 228.

[32] In that sense, he opens the last chapter of his recent book asking himself 'Does the Constitutionalization of International Law still have any chance?' (Habermas (2006) (n 13) 113), vis-à-vis the prevalence of the use of brute force (at 114).

and security of constitutionalism, it rejects the idea of a world republic and believes in a different way of constitutionalizing international law.[33] Describing the constitutional process in the development of modern nation states as the one that is no longer a mere instrument of power trying to assert the dominant interests in a hegemonic manner, it claims that great powers are more likely to meet justice and cooperation expectations if they are used to seeing themselves on the supranational level as members of a global community, and even more when they are perceived in this role from the perspective of their own national public spheres, before which they have to be legitimated.[34]

Other new converts, revisiting Kantian thinking, have supported a sort of 'constitutional idiosyncrasy' in relation to the international legal order.[35] Thus, apart from criticizing the use of the terminology of institutional hierarchies by the internationalist doctrine, it claims that the constitutionalism that would inspire Kant's thinking would not be so much an institutional or structural project, but rather a 'program of moral and political regeneration'.[36] In this way, the philosopher of Königsberg had tried to institutionalize a kind of thought or, more specifically, of constitutional idiosyncrasy from which to apprehend the world in ways that tend towards universality and impartiality.[37] Following this line of argument, to sum up, given that constitutional terminology is not only a structure of politicians' internal thinking, but also informs political debates and is used by the technical bureaucracy, categories such as fundamental rights, the division of powers and responsibility of public authorities, with all their historical importance would fill the structural gaps in current institutions and would lead what would otherwise be mere administrative routines to political debate.[38]

4. SOFT CONSTITUTIONALIST APPROACHES TO ACHIEVE INTERORDINAL CONSTITUTIONALISM

13. In this context, and inspired by these neo-Kantian principles, there emerged a third way, which Professor de Búrca has called the 'soft constitutionalist approach' and which took elements from the less orthodox versions of constitutional pluralism. The interesting thing is that the latter position could offer the ECJ an attractive alternative to more orthodox pluralist and constitutionalist approaches.[39] The theories of this 'soft constitutionalist approach' could be summed up in three ways. First, to assume the existence of an international

[33] Habermas (2006) (n 30) at 121 (where he revisits the Kantian proposal for a World republic) and 133 (where he finally refuses this possibility).
[34] Habermas (2006) (n 30) at 138–9.
[35] M Koskenniemi (2007) (n 29).
[36] M Koskenniemi (2007) (n 29) at 18.
[37] M Koskenniemi (2007) (n 29) at 33.
[38] M Koskenniemi (2007) (n 29) at 34.
[39] G de Búrca, (2009) (n 11) at 53–5.

community of some kind. Second, and derived from the Kantian moral and categorical imperative, this model would emphasize the possibility of universal principles inspiring the different legal orders which coexist in this community.[40] Third, there need to exist common rules or principles of communication between these orders that allow to re-address the real conflicts that may arise. These three characteristics clearly distinguish soft constitutionalism from pluralistic approaches, since these assume the existence of a different plurality and separated from entities rejecting the idea of a global community, they emphasize the autonomous decision-making processes based on their own authority and in the native values of each of the entities, while channelling communication and conflict resolution through 'agonizing' political processes, ad hoc negotiations and specific and pragmatic adjustments. The soft constitutional approach also differs from more orthodox constitutionalist conceptions because it would not insist on a clear hierarchy of rules, but rather in a series of commonly traded and shared principles to redirect conflicts.

14. The authors who share, to a greater or lesser extent, this soft approach would differ from the strictly monistic doctrine or that based on a clearly hierarchical conception of the international order because it is identified with pluralist thinking (nothing else) on the assumption of diversity and mechanisms for negotiation and dialogue to manage conflict. Thus, the 'soft' constitutional doctrine claims the use of universalized standards, mutual deference, general coherence and commitment to a common international order.[41]

15. That is, the ideal model to assure a peaceful interordinal constitutionalism will be a soft constitutional approach like the one described that assumes the existence of an international or global emerging society, in which the principles underlying the different legal orders (nationals and international) shall be universalized and, finally, in which there are common rules or principles to re-address the inevitable conflicts that may occur, while the whole system slowly

[40] See I Kant, *Crítica de la razón práctica* (E Miñana y Villagrasa and M García Morente (trs)) (Espasa-Calpe, Madrid, 1975) (original title: *Kritik der praktischen Vernunft*, first published in 1788) 39–55. For a brief comment on this work, see E Colomer, *El pensamiento alemán de Kant a Heidegger. Vol. I. La Filosofía Trascendental: Kant* (Herder, Barcelona, 1986) 203–50.

[41] Some elements of a 'soft version' may be found in N Walker (2002) (n 1) at 355–6; A Von Bogdandy, 'Pluralism, direct effect, and the ultimate say: On the relationship between international and domestic constitutional law' (2008) 6(3–4) *International Journal of Constitutional Law* 397; WW Burke-White, 'International Legal Pluralism' (2004) 25(4) *Michigan Journal of International Law* 963; AM Slaughter, *A New World Order* (Princeton University Press, Princeton, 2004) 65–103 (where the author deals with the role of the judges) and 216–71 (where she presents her recipe for a righteous World order). See also M Kumm, 'Constitutional Democracy Encounters International Law: Terms of Engagement' in S Choudhry (ed), *The Migration of Constitutional Ideas* (Oxford University Press, Oxford, 2006) 256; D Halberstam, 'Constitutionalism and Pluralism in Marbury and Van Gend' in MP Maduro and L Azoulai (eds), *The Past and Future of EU Law: The Classics of EU Law Revisited on the 50th Anniversary of the Rome Treaty* (Hart Publishing, Oxford, 2010) 26; and JL Cohen, 'A Global State of Emergency or the Further Constitutionalization of International Law: A Pluralist Approach' (2008) 15(4) *Constellations* 456.

navigates to a kind of synchronization of the standards of protection of fundamental rights. In fact, the greater this synchronization in fundamental rights protection standards is, the greater chance of coming to an ever closer worldwide union through law.

16. However, as previously mentioned, both the CFI in the *Yusuf and Al Barakaat* and *Kadi* cases and the ECtHR in the *Behrami* and *Saramati* cases adopted a strict and orthodox constitutionalist approach based on the systemic unit of international legal order and the European regional order, as well as on the existence of a hierarchy of normative authority within this integrated system. Moreover, the Opinion of Advocate General Poiares Maduro and the final decision of the ECJ opted instead for a strictly pluralistic approach introducing the EC/EU as a separate and self-integrated system which determines its relationship with the international legal order from its own internal principles and values and their priorities and goals rather than according to any of the common principles or rules of international law.

As we will see below in more detail, the soft constitutionalist approach towards international legal order described here would have given the ECJ a better framework to deal with the dilemma of the *Kadi and Al Barakaat* case than the orthodox constitutionalist approach used by the CFI or the strictly pluralist one used by the Advocate General in his conclusions. In fact, a soft constitutionalist approach would have fit better with the aspirations of the EU as a relevant international actor and its commitment to respect the international order, not allowing it to ignore the aspects of international responsibility and the protection of fundamental rights, concerns that inspired the conclusions of the Advocate General. Indeed, if the ECJ, the Supreme Court of the regional international organization par excellence, had relied on rules of international law instead of sticking only to EU standards when it comes to censoring the implementation of the resolution of the Security Council for lacking the most basic procedural guarantees, would not only have provided an excellent example for other states and organizations that have implemented the UN sanctions, or are in the process of so doing, but also would have added some substance to the rhetoric of Europe as a regulatory, civil or ethical power.[42]

[42] See I Manners, 'Normative Power Europe: A Contradiction in Terms?' (2002) 40(2) *Journal of Common Market Studies* 235; and I Manners, 'The normative ethics of the European Union' (2008) 84(1) *International Affairs* 45.

12

The Position of the European Union on the International Scene after the *Kadi* Case

1. IS THE PLURALISTIC APPROACH GAINING SUPPORT WITHIN THE ECJ?

1. The ECJ opinion regarding *Kadi and Al Barakaat* seems, at first glance, a triumph of the principles of a pluralist conception of international legal order. Not only did the ECJ adopt a pluralistic view of the question of interordinal relations between EC/EU law and international law but also, in doing so, it annulled the EC Regulation implementing the resolutions of the UN Security Council because they did not comply with the minimum procedural guarantees. Thus, the argument according to which a strict and orthodox pluralist approach is more propitious to strengthen international responsibility would seem to be supported by this opinion and its result. In this respect Resolution 1822 of the Security Council of 30 June 2008 introduced some reforms, however small, in response to the type of claims brought by the appellants, such as Mr Kadi, regarding the UN resolutions. Thus, the Security Council:

> *Demands* that Member States receiving notification as in paragraph 15 above take, in accordance with their domestic laws and practices, all possible measures to notify or inform in a timely manner the listed individual or entity of the designation and to include with this notification a copy of the publicly releasable portion of the statement of case.[1]

So, basically, this is an obligation to inform the concerned party that it is to be included on the (black) list and to include together with the notification a copy of the 'publicly releasable portion of the statement of case'. However, it was not envisaged that a real review or control body would be established, despite being well aware of the meaning of Advocate General Poiares Maduro's

[1] See UNSC Resolution 1822 (2008) 30 June on threats to international peace and security caused by terrorist acts, para 17.

conclusions, and of the existence of some proposals of certain governments in this regard.[2]

As expected, the ECJ totally ignored the provisions of Resolution 1822 (2008) of the Security Council in its opinion. Instead, the Court focused only on the question of whether the EC/EU enforcement measure violated the principles of the EC/EU domestic constitutional order, without referring to any principles of international law and making no reference to the UN or any other entity.

2. Moreover, from a short-term view , the final result in the *Kadi and Al Barakaat* case may be admirable, given the insistence on a minimum of procedural and judicial guarantees for those whose assets are frozen indefinitely in virtue of the implementation of the UN resolution. However, the highly pluralistic approach underlying the ECJ opinion contrasts with the traditional image of itself that the EU presents, as a body with a particular attitude of respect for international law and its institutions. At the same time this position entails some risk and cost for the Union. Indeed, the legal reasoning of the ECJ regarding *Kadi and Al Barakaat* is focused exclusively on the EC/EU itself and its order, and the Court declined to enter into a dynamic of international dialogue.

2. THE USE OF ARGUMENTS OF INTERNATIONAL LAW

3. The ECJ could have adopted a different approach in order to base its decision.[3] Specifically, the ECJ decided, at one point, to follow the soft constitutionalism approach that Professor de Búrca supported but, in the end, it decided not to follow that path. Specifically, the ECJ said:

> It must however be noted that the Charter of the United Nations does not impose the choice of a particular model for the implementation of resolutions adopted by the Security Council under Chapter VII of the Charter, since they are to be given effect in accordance with the procedure applicable in that respect in the domestic legal order of each Member of the United Nations. The Charter of the United Nations leaves the Members of the United Nations a free choice among the various possible models for transposition of those resolutions into their domestic legal order.[4]

[2] At that time there were already some proposals dealing, for instance, with the creation of a panel of experts sitting at the focal points. See *Eighth Report of the Analytical Support and Sanctions Monitoring Team pursuant to Resolution 1735 (2006) concerning Al-Qaida and the Taliban* (2008), UN Doc S/2008/324 paras 39–41 and the document *Security Council Report, Monthly Forecast,* January 2007, 22 December 2006, 20–1, available at <www.securitycouncilreport.org>. On the latest improvements of the review process before the sanctions committee (ie the Office of the Ombudsperson), see specifically Part III Chapter I.

[3] Some say that the ECJ had no choice. See J Reich. 'Due Process and Sanctions Targeted Against Individuals Pursuant to Resolution 1267 (1999)' (2008) 33(2) *Yale Journal of International Law* 505.

[4] Joined Cases C-402/05 P and C-415/05 P *Kadi* and *Al Barakaat International Foundation v Council* [2008] ECR I-6351, para 298.

That is, the ECJ found that the UN Charter allowed Member States to decide how to implement the resolutions of the Security Council under their legal order. This would have provided an argument by which the ECJ could have reached a result materially identical (controlling or reversing the implementation of Community Regulations), giving the chance to adopt a more committed position with the international order as if it had as its reference the principles of international law instead of focusing so much on the particularism of fundamental rights within the EU. In other words, the ECJ could have insisted on the respect for basic principles of fair trial and protection of human rights to which international law requires, even when those principles were looked down upon in the framework of the preparation and exclusion of the lists of the Security Council.[5] By doing this, the ECJ missed a good opportunity to contribute to international dialogue on fair trial as part of customary international law, which would have been of great interest not only to the EU but also the entire international community. The ECJ could have used international customary law-based arguments as a basis for upholding the right to trial with all guarantees, or even the United Nations Charter itself, as well as general principles of international law and *ius cogens* principles put forward at the time by the CFI. That is, the ECJ could have concluded that the Security Council resolutions could not be implemented like that, without inclusion by the EU, within the margin of appreciation to implement, as the resolutions granted, of procedural guarantees to protect the rights and interests of those concerned. This would have involved using the EU's implementation of Security Council resolutions as an opportunity to correct these deficiencies.[6]

By focusing solely on internal guarantees for the protection of fundamental rights granted by the EU and ignoring international law, the ECJ not only lost the opportunity to influence a major international debate on an issue that affects all Member States of the UN, but also lost the chance to develop a way to facilitate the mutual influence between the legal orders of the EU and those of the UN. The fact that the ECJ chose a pluralistic language and reasoning sent a clear message to other international actors on the autonomy of the EC/EU legal system and the importance and prevalence that shall be given to certain principles and values internally. If there are courts outside the EU that might have a tendency to start a sort of transnational dialogue or to introduce in their decisions categories and concepts developed by other courts, the decision of the

[5] See A Bianchi, 'Assessing the Effectiveness of the UN Security Council's Anti-terrorism Measures: The Quest for Legitimacy and Cohesion' (2006) 17(5) *European Journal of International Law* 881. For a proposal in order to conciliate UNSC sanctions with the ECHR standards, see I Cameron, 'UN Targeted Sanctions, Legal Safeguards, and the ECHR' (2003) 72 *Nordic Journal of International Law* 159 at 208–11.

[6] Others share this view but instead of defending that it was up to the EU to compensate the lack of protection in the exercise of its margin of appreciation within the implementation process, this should have been a task of the member States. See M Nettesheim, 'UN sanctions against individuals – A challenge to the architecture of European Union governance' (2007) 44(3) *Common Market Law Review* 567 at 590 and 592.

ECJ may discourage them by focusing on the categories and local conceptions of fundamental rights, especially regarding the Security Council resolutions adopted under Chapter VII of the Charter or even the other rules of international law, which could lead them, if the worst came to the worst, to interpret downward their constitutional opening clauses (for example, Article 10.2 of the Spanish Constitution, if appropriate).[7]

3. THE *SOLANGE* DOCTRINE

4. Another possibility that the ECJ could have used in order to deal with the conflict in the *Kadi and Al Barakaat* case is the approach adopted at the time by the German Constitutional Court in its famous *Solange* saga.[8] However, the ECJ refused to continue along the path of the judicial dialogue initiated at the time by the highest court in Karlsruhe with an international order of a regional nature that could threaten the fundamental rights protected by the Basic Law of Bonn.[9] Instead, the ECJ decided in *Kadi and Al Barakaat* on an introspective approach and a type of argument that emphasized the specific conditions imposed by the general principles of EC/EU law and the important autonomy of the EC /EU legal order.

Returning to the *Solange* case law of the German Constitutional Court, which for many authors provided a model based on argumentative persuasion that would have allowed the type of conflict in *Kadi and Al Barakaat* to be readdressed, it's possible to see that the German court's decision – especially in *Solange II* – is built from the perspective of mutual dialogue and looking beyond their own internal order, which reflects, in general terms, the essence of the above-mentioned soft constitutionalist approach.[10] The conflict that arose in the German case was between a provision of the Basic Law and a Community regulation, but in the end, it was also a conflict between internal constitutional rules of a political entity and the legal obligations imposed by an international (or supranational) system to which it belonged. Therefore, in the opinion of the *Solange I* case, the German Constitutional Court declared that:

[7] See G de Búrca, 'The European Court of Justice and the International Legal Order after Kadi' (2009) 01/09 *Jean Monnet Working Papers* April 2009 at 58.

[8] See Case *Solange I* 2 BvL 52/71 BVerfGE 37 271 (German Constitutional Court, 29 May 1974); Case *Solange II* 2 BvR 197/83 BVerfGE 73 339 (German Constitutional Court, 22 October 1986).

[9] For an analysis of the 'dialogue' technique and its utility, see A Stone Sweet, 'Constitucional Dialogues in the European Community' in AM Slaughter, A Stone Sweet and JHH Weiler (eds), *The European Courts & National Courts. Doctrine and Jurisprudence. Legal change in its social context* (Hart, Oxford, 1998) 305.

[10] On the use of the *Solange* doctrine to solve *Kadi*, see S Griller 'International Law, Human Rights and the Community's Autonomous Legal Order. Notes on the European Court of Justice Decision in Kadi' (2008) 4(3) *European Constitutional Law Review* 528 at 549. See also Joined Cases C-402/05 P and C-415/05 P *Kadi and Al Barakaat* [2008] (n 4), Opinion of AG Poiares Maduro, paras 38 and 54.

from the special partnership established with the creation of the Community between the community itself arose . . . for the competent bodies, especially for courts called upon to exercise the legal control – the European Court and the Federal Constitutional Court – the obligation to be concerned in their case law about the agreement of both legal orders.[11]

The relationship between the then European Community and Germany was presented by the Highest Court in Karlsruhe in terms of hierarchy, but it was neither described in strictly pluralist terms nor seeking confrontation. Instead, the decision of the German Court emphasized the mutual relationship of corrective nature that existed between the two legal orders:

The link of the Federal Republic of Germany (and all Member States) through the Treaty is not unilateral regarding the meaning and spirit of the treaties, but instead it also links the Community, established to solve the conflict hereby detailed and to seek, therefore, a regulation that is consistent with a binding mandate of constitutional law of the Federal Republic of Germany. The invocation of a conflict of this nature is not a violation of the Treaty itself, but rather to set in motion the mechanism of the Treaty within the European institutions to solve the conflict in a political sphere.[12]

Stressing, then, the dynamic nature of this mutual relationship, the German Constitutional Court established specifically what it considered to be a poor protection of fundamental rights standards at the EC level and declared that its control over the implementation of Community measures regarding fundamental rights was not only in favour of the Constitutional Court itself, but 'also in favour of the Community and Community law'.[13] Later, in the opinion known as *Solange II* of 1986, the German Constitutional Court adopted a much more respectful attitude (which certainly could have inspired the ECtHR in *Bosphorus*, see above) providing that, given the improvements in the level of protection of fundamental rights carried out by the European Community since the first opinion in *Solange* of 1974, the *Bundesverfassungsgericht* would not examine the compatibility of community legislation with the fundamental rights established

[11] See Case *Solange I* (German Constitutional Court, 1974) (n 8), para 278. Literally, the decision states: '*Deshalb erwächst aus dem besonderen Verhältnis, das zwischen der Gemeinschaft und ihren Mitgliedern durch die Gründung der Gemeinschaft entstanden ist, für die zuständigen Organe, insbesondere für die beiden zur Rechtskontrolle berufenen Gerichte – den Europäischen Gerichtshof und das Bundesverfassungsgericht – zunächst die Pflicht, sich um die Konkordanz beider Rechtsordnungen in ihrer Rechtsprechung zu bemühen*'.

[12] See Case *Solange I* (German Constitutional Court, 1974) (n 8), para 278, where the German Court wrote: '*Die Bindung der Bundesrepublik Deutschland (und aller Mitgliedstaaten) durch den Vertrag ist nach Sinn und Geist der Verträge nicht einseitig, sondern bindet auch die durch sie geschaffene Gemeinschaft, das ihre zu tun, um den hier unterstellten Konflikt zu lösen, also nach einer Regelung zu suchen, die sich mit einem zwingenden Gebot des Verfassungsrechts der Bundesrepublik Deutschland verträgt. Die Berufung auf einen solchen Konflikt ist also nicht schon eine Vertragsverletzung, sondern setzt den Vertragsmechanismus innerhalb der europäischen Organe in Gang, der den Konflikt politisch löst*'.

[13] See Case *Solange I* (German Constitutional Court, 1974) (n 8), para 284: '*Die Konzentrierung dieser Entscheidung beim Bundesverfassungsgericht ist nicht nur verfassungsrechtlich aus demselben Grund geboten, der zum sog. Verwerfungsmonopol des Gerichts geführt hat, sondern liegt auch im Interesse der Gemeinschaft und ihres Rechts*'.

in the Basic Law as long as the ECJ continued to protect those fundamental rights in a proper manner.[14]

4. THE SOLUTION CHOSEN BY THE ECJ AND THE EU AS INTERNATIONAL ACTORS

5. The option followed by the ECJ in *Kadi and Al Barakaat* not to adopt an approach like *Solange* and, instead, to reject any kind of judicial intervention in the process of defining interordinal relations and avoid any dialogue concerning the possible rules of international law that the Security Council would be obliged to comply with, seems to have been carefully calculated. In fact, it seems that it was deliberately designed by the ECJ as an opportunity to reaffirm the autonomy, authority and separation of the EC/EU law regarding the international legal order. More than a decision that could be circumscribed to the particular context of the powers and limitations of the Security Council in combating terrorism, the decision in the *Kadi and Al Barakaat* case seems to have been chosen by the ECJ to reaffirm the autonomy of European constitutionalism, already stated in its famous *Van Gend en Loos* opinion in 1964. This would, therefore, be the most striking feature of this opinion, and one that should surprise those who argue that the difference between the EU and US approaches towards International Law lies in the more sensitive and open attitude of the EU (including the ECJ), in contrast with the more close minded and reluctant position of the US and its Supreme Court.[15]

6. In the US there has been a heated debate not only about the status of customary international law and the obligation of national courts to apply it but also, and despite the literality supremacy clause included within the US Constitution, on the position of international treaties in domestic law.[16] The changing nature of the doctrinal debate in the US during recent years on the fundamental issue

[14] See Case *Solange II* (German Constitutional Court, 1986) (n 8), subsequently confirmed by Case *Bananenmarktordnung* (German Constitutional Court, 2000) (n 8), also known for some as '*Solange III*'. W Zimmer, 'De nouvelles bases pour la coopération entre la Cour Constitutionnelle Fédérale et la Cour de Justice de Luxembourg? (à propos de BVerfGE, 7 juin 2000, Solange III)' (2001) Mai *Europe* 3. See also Case *Bosphorus Hava Yolları Turizm ve Ticaret Anonim irketi v Ireland* App No 45036/98 (ECtHR, 30 June 2004, 2005-VI) [2005], para 155.

[15] See G de Búrca (2009) (n 7) at 60–1.

[16] This discussion has been recently revisited due to the Case *Medellín v Texas*, 552 US 491 (2008). For an overview of the different positions, see CA Bradley, J Goldsmith and DH Moore, 'Sosa, Customary International Law, and the Continuing Relevance of Erie' (2007) 120(4) *Harvard Law Review* 869; JL Goldsmith and EA Posner, *The Limits of International Law* (Oxford University Press, Oxford, 2005) 23–78 and 83–162. On the status of the international treaties and the supremacy clause (Art VI, s 2 US Constitution), see CM Vázquez, 'Treaties As Law of the Land: The Supremacy Clause and the Judicial Enforcement of Treaties' (2008) 122(2) *Harvard Law Review* 599. On the *Medellín* case, see ME Wojcik, 'United States Supreme Court: Medellin v Texas : Introductory Note' (2008) 3 *International Legal Materials* 281; and ME McGuinness, 'Medellín v Texas – US Supreme Court opinion on state courts' obligation to respect an International Court of Justice judgment and on the President's power to enforce it' (2008) 102(3) *American Journal of International Law* 622.

of the legal status and position of international law reflects, to some extent, the approaches within the American political system towards international law, which are also changing, and the commitments arising from it. This conception could be described as the reflection of an attitude of exceptionalism, unilateralism and a widespread distrust towards international law and its institutions.[17] The power of the US on the international scene, along with the conviction of many Americans about the benefits of the governance system and the functioning of democracy in this country, partially explains the sceptical and cautious way in which they understand international law and its institutions, given that this law and its institutions would be perceived as not very democratic and even likely to harm US interests.

On the contrary, as already mentioned, Europe in general and the EU in particular have traditionally been associated with an attitude of respect for and fidelity to international law and its institutions.[18] In fact, that circumstance has become an explicit feature of the image that the EU has of itself and wants to keep regarding the other international actors.[19] In fact, Article 3 TEU-L provides:

> 5. In its relations with the wider world, the Union shall uphold and promote its values and interests and contribute to the protection of its citizens. It shall contribute to peace, security, the sustainable development of the Earth, solidarity and mutual respect among peoples, free and fair trade, eradication of poverty and the protection of human rights, in particular the rights of the child, as well as to the strict observance and the development of international law, including respect for the principles of the United Nations Charter.

In addition to these obligations established in its constitutional texts and to its great and eloquent statements the ECJ, in turn, has professed a great respect for international law, at least in the few cases concerning foreign affairs. As seen above, Article 300.7 TEU provided that international agreements held by the

[17] The literature on this issue is huge. See, inter alia, HH Koh, 'On American Exceptionalism' (2003) 55(5) *Stanford Law Review* 1479; PJ Spiro, 'The New Sovereigntists: American Exceptionalism and Its False Prophets' (2000) 79(6) *Foreign Affairs* 9; PM Dupuy, 'The Place and Role of Unilateralism in Contemporary International Law' (2000) 11(1) *European Journal of International Law* 19; C Chinkin, 'The state that acts alone: bully, good Samaritan or iconoclast?' (2000) 11(1) *European Journal of International Law* 31; P Sands, '"Unilateralism", values, and International Law' 11(2) *European Journal of International Law* 291; B Jansen, 'The limits of unilateralism from a European perspective' 11(1)*European Journal of International Law* 309; G Simpson, 'The situation on the international legal theory front: the power of rules and the rule of power' 11(1)*European Journal of International Law* 439; and M Ignatieff (ed), *American Exceptionalism and Human Rights* (Princeton University Press, Princeton, 2005).

[18] For a critical vision of this traditional conception of Europe, see S Safrin, 'The unexceptionalism of US exceptionalism' (2008) 41(5) *Vanderbilt Journal of Transnational Law* 1307 or the more nuanced approach in M Licková, 'European Exceptionalism in International Law' (2008) 19(3) *European Journal of International Law* 463.

[19] See the speech of Patrícia Galvão Teles, from the Legal Affairs Department of the Foreign Affairs Ministry of Portugal on behalf of the EU Presidency at the Sixty-second session of the UN General Assembly, '*Agenda Item 86. Rule of law at the national and international levels*', 25 October 2007 available at <http://www.europa-eu-un.org/articles/es/article_7569_es.htm>. See also I Manners and R Whitman, 'The "difference engine": constructing and representing the international identity of the European Union' (2003) 10(3) *Journal of European Public Policy* 380.

European Community were binding for the EC and for the Member States (a provision which, obviously, disappears in the new Article 218 TFEU). The ECJ completed the terms of this provision by providing that once an international treaty is concluded by the Community and enters into force, its provisions are an 'integral part' of EC/EU law.[20] Regarding the implications to these international agreements for being an 'integral part' of the EC/EU legal order, the ECJ has almost always stated, except in the case of the GATT agreements, that international treaties held by the EC have direct effect and particulars may rely on their provisions before the national courts.[21] In relation to the international treaties of which the EC is not a party, but of which all states are at the same time members of the EC/EU, as seen above, the ECJ concluded that in the particular case of the GATT agreements of 1947 the Community was bound by the obligations previously incurred by its Member States.[22] As in the GATT agreements, neither the Community nor the Union are parties to the UN Charter, but the Court of First Instance in the *Yusuf and Al Barakaat* and *Kadi* cases followed a similar argument to the ECJ case law on the GATT agreements establishing that the Community was, however, bound by the UN Charter.[23]

As regards the particular case of customary international law, the ECJ has had the opportunity to establish on several occasions that the EC/EU must respect the rules of customary international law in the exercise of its powers and that those rules are binding on the Community and are part of its internal legal order.[24]

In previous cases in which the question of the control of EU measures that implemented Security Council resolutions was raised, the ECJ, without questioning its own authority to undertake such control, nonetheless ended up expressing itself in very different terms from those used in the *Kadi and Al Barakaat* case. Indeed, in the *Bosphorus* case (before the ECJ), for example, the language used by the ECJ was considerably more internationalist than in the case of *Kadi*, referring to the objectives of the international community and its

[20] See Case 181/73 *Haegemann v Belgian State* [1974] ECR 449 para 5. Opinion 1/91 *Draft agreement between the Community, on the one hand, and the countries of the European Free Trade Association, on the other, relating to the creation of the European Economic Area* [1991] ECR I-06079 paras 3 and 37.

[21] On the GATT Agreements, see G Zonnekeyn, *Direct Effect of WTO Law* (Cameron & May, London, 2008). On the direct effect of international treaties within EU legal system, see K Lenaerts, P Van Nuffel and R Bray, *Constitutional Law of the European Union* 2nd edn (Thompson, London, 2005) 739–49 and P Craig and G de Búrca, *EU Law. Text, Cases and Materials* 4th edn (Oxford University Press, London, 2008) 206–13.

[22] As one may remember, this very same argument, called the 'functional succession' theory, was not enough to convince the ECJ that the EC could already have acceded to the ECHR. See P Pescatore, 'La Cour de Justice des Communautés Europées et la Convention Européenne des Droits de l'Homme' in GJ Wiarda, F Matscher and H Petzold (eds), *Protecting human rights, the European dimension: studies in honour of / Protection des droits de l'homme, la dimension européenne. Mélanges en l'honneur de Gérard J. Wiarda* 2nd edn (C Heymann, Köln, 1990) 441.

[23] Case T-306/01 *Yusuf and Al Barakaat International Foundation v Council and Commission* [2005] ECR II-3533, paras 233–238 and Case T-315/01 *Kadi v Council and Commission* [2005] ECR II-3649 paras 183–188.

[24] See Case C-286/90 *Anklagemindigheden v Poulsen and Diva Navigation* [1992] ECR I-06019, para 9 and Case C-162/96 *Racke v Hauptzollamt Mainz* [1998] ECR I-03655, paras 45–46.

fundamental interests, rather than focusing on the autonomy of the EC/EU legal system. Thus, regarding the preliminary ruling solved in its decision on the *Bosphorus* case, the ECJ concluded that:

> As compared with an objective of general interest so fundamental for the international community, which consists in putting an end to the state of war in the region and to the massive violations of human rights and humanitarian international law in the Republic of Bosnia-Herzegovina, the impounding of the aircraft in question, which is owned by an undertaking based in or operating from the Federal Republic of Yugoslavia, cannot be regarded as inappropriate or disproportionate.[25]

Similarly, in the *Ebony Maritime* case, the ECJ held that:

> In making that determination, the national court must take account, in particular, of the fact that the objective pursued by the Regulation, which is to bring to an end the state of war in the region concerned and the massive violations of human rights and humanitarian international law in the Republic of Bosnia-Herzegovina, is one of fundamental general interest for the international community.[26]

7. Moreover, the general perception, based on normative texts and fuelled by political speeches and judicial decisions, of the EU as an organization that keeps a special fidelity to international law has been backed up by the citizens and the doctrine itself. Some of these comments have focused on the phenomenon of Europe as a *normative power* or a *soft power* which, without the military power of the US, believes it can influence the international scene through persuasion, negotiation, international agreement and certain incentives, as well as proving to be a reliable partner that respects international law.[27] Others have focused on trying to make a comparison between the EU and the US, praising the approach and attitude of the EU, precisely to provide an alternative, in the field of international relations, to the unilateralist approach practised especially lately by the US.[28] Even the American authors who sometimes make critical comments about the EU recognize, however, that both the Union and the European powers are, at least, prepared to trust and respect international law and its institutions.[29]

[25] Case C-84/95 *Bosphorus* [1996] (n 14), para 26.

[26] Case C-177/95 *Ebony Maritime and Loten Navigation v Prefetto della Provincia di Brindisi* [1997] ECR I-1111 para 38.

[27] On the EU as a 'normative power', see I Manners, 'Normative Power Europe: A Contradiction in Terms?' (2002) 40(2) *Journal of Common Market Studies* 235 and I Manners, 'The normative ethics of the European Union' (2008) 84(1) *International Affairs* 45. For an overview of the EU as 'soft power', see J Nye, *Soft Power: The Means to Success in World Politics* (Public Affairs, New York, 2008) and J McCormick, *The European Superpower* (Palgrave Macmillan, New York, 2006), who points out how the EU has succeeded in the international arena using 'soft' methods differently from the US, which uses 'hard' ones. See also R Howse and K Nicolaïdis, 'This is My EUtopia: Narrative as Power' (2002) 40(4) *Journal of Common Market Studies* 767 and T Dunne, 'Good citizen Europe' (2008) 84(1) *International Affairs* 13.

[28] See J Habermas, *El Occidente escindido: pequeños escritos políticos* X (JL López de Lizaga (tr)) (Trotta, Madrid, 2006) 55–61 (transcript of an interview with the philosopher).

[29] R Kagan, *Of Paradise and Power: America and Europe in the New World Order* (Knopf, New York, 2003) and J Rubenfeld, 'Unilateralism and Constitutionalism' (2004) 79(6) *New York University Law Review* 1971.

8. For all the above, one cannot exclude the possibility that the ECJ might back off back off a little in its approaches and takes up some of those described in the first two alternatives. So, possibly affected by the long period of uncertainty about the final ratification and entry into force of the Treaty of Lisbon after the 'No' to the Constitutional Treaty (uncertainty that was only answered at the end of 2009), the progressive intergovernmentalization showed by the EU (the Commission is relegated to the role of a mere qualified Secretariat) and the signs that come from Strasbourg (*Bosphorus* decision) and from the UN (through the 'smart sanctions'), the ECJ has 'pounded the table' and has emerged as the only institution capable of defending the European project, in this case through a vigorous defence of the autonomy of its constitutional order. But it is not clear that the ECJ is in this position, and in other cases it might start to reintroduce international law arguments in its legal reasoning, assuming a soft constitutionalist approach and fully recovering its credibility as the model of 'good international citizen' that it has always wanted to be.[30]

[30] The EU as a good citizen is characterized in T Dunne, 'Good citizen Europe' (2008) 84(1) *International Affairs* 13.

Conclusions

I. The establishment of a 'soft constitutionalist' based model that guarantees legal certainty, that is viable in the long term and that, in short, both provides a response to the conflicts between different legal regulatory systems that may arise and establishes the relationships between the various legal systems of a constitutional nature within Europe, requires the exercise of political will, at least with respect to two points: on the one hand, there is a need to clarify interordinal relations between the EU and the ECHR; and, on the other, the establishment of a jurisdictional control system for the sanctions imposed by the UN Security Council.

1. Far from being a more or less remote theoretical possibility, the conflicts arising from the relationships, interaction and overlapping of different legal systems constitute a tangible reality that has obliged the highest guardians of each of them to state their positions in this regard. Experience has demonstrated that, fortunately, pragmatism and prudence have prevailed up to now, thanks to the flexible and conciliatory attitude shown by superior courts to date. The solutions that have been found have all been grounded on the same principle, which appears, with greater or lesser reservations, to be globally accepted. This precept consists in the recognition of other legal systems by the superior court in question, while at the same refusing to accept complete subordination to the other, given that this would challenge the very essence of the legal system concerned. Thus, at the end of the day, each system implicitly proclaims its ultimate supremacy over the others. Because the identity of each legal system is based upon its founding values, it is not surprising that fundamental rights have acted as vectors in the evolution of interordinal relations and that the safeguarding of human rights has been the 'topic of conversation' in the 'dialogue' between the highest interpreters and guardians of the various different legal systems involved.

2. The model proposed in this book for the European area, which, in sum, is capable of being universal in nature, based on the 'soft constitutionalist' approaches, would be a kind of interordinal constitutionalism. That is, a model that assumes the existence of an international or global emerging society, in which the principles underlying the different legal orders (nationals and international) shall be universalized and, finally, in which there are common rules or principles to re-address the inevitable conflicts that may occur, while the whole system slowly navigates to a kind of synchronization of the standards of protection of fundamental rights. In fact, the greater this synchronization in fundamental rights protection standards is, the greater chance of coming to an ever closer worldwide union through law.

3. It may be argued that, in the course of the dialogue that has taken place among these highest courts, which are ultimately responsible for their respective legal systems, the foregoing principles have been followed more or less openly. Thus, as a general rule, the courts have tended to admit the existence of their counterparts as keepers of the other legal systems. They have tried to construct their judgments on the basis of potentiating those principles that are common to both legal systems, so as to facilitate acceptance of their decisions by the other tribunal. The situation might therefore be compared to a sort of 'cold war' among these superior courts. In other words, the courts' decisions are based on a game of reciprocal dissuasion founded on a kind of mutually assured destruction, for crossing the Rubicon of the 'boundaries' established in a given legal system might give rise to a conflict whereby the opposing judge would be led to criticize the legitimacy of the other legal system and explicitly deny its presumption of supremacy. Nevertheless, in the situation we have described, the lack of certain rules that might help to resolve disputes or conflicts which are, in the end, probably inevitable, is apparent.

In this context, the political authorities may be tempted not to intervene, so as not to upset the delicate checks and balances the courts have been constructing over time, though rather more by way of silence than by affirmation. However, as well as compromising their responsibilities, such evasive conduct forces judges to assume justiciability over matters that are not within their incumbency and which they would be unlikely to exercise to their full extent. In fact, although jurisprudential solutions in this field are indispensable, they can only be provisional. For expecting the courts to provide a definitive answer would lead to their own legitimacy being undermined and would render them vulnerable to the facile criticism that they were drifting towards the politicization of justice or 'governance by judges'. Unfortunately, this failure to define the boundaries clearly, which the superior courts have deliberately sought in order to facilitate acceptance by their counterparts who are responsible for protecting other legal systems, has the disadvantage of calling into question the value of legal certainty as perceived on the European continent, which in turn challenges the very foundations of the rule of law and the organisation of society.

4. So, it is up to the politicians to define simpler and clearer rules to regulate the relationships between legal regulatory systems, in the best case (and most unlikely) scenario, or (as seems more probable) to at least lay down some minimum guidelines to permit conflicts arising between legal systems in the European context to be effectively channelled. This would not only tend to clarify jurisdictional functions but would also guarantee juridical certainty. The foregoing proposal does not mean to say that the courts would cease to perform an essential role since, given the complexity of the transnational world in the global era, the codification of certain rules will not be sufficient (nor should it be so) to respond to all the possible situations that might arise. But the courts' scope of action would be demarcated by political power, which is the responsible authority vis-à-vis citizens. Thus, the work of the judges and their operational limits would find themselves supported in the democratic debate and, furthermore, their judgments would consequently enjoy greater legitimacy.

5. Among the minimum, most basic and most urgent measures needed to resolve conflicts between legal systems, to which we have referred above, would be the accession of the EU to the ECHR and the setting up of a true system of jurisdictional control of the sanctions imposed by the United Nations Security Council that directly affect individuals ('blacklists' and 'targeted sanctions').

If the EU were to sign up to the ECHR, this would enable the interordinal relations between European law and the Convention to be clarified. Specifically, in the procedural ambit, light would be shed on the relations between the ECJ and the ECtHR. In this way, the ECtHR would become a 'specialized' (instead of the rather non-diplomatic 'superior') authority in the field of fundamental rights. In other words, in the event that the ECJ failed to uphold or were to misapply any of the rights included in the Convention, the person affected thereby could appeal in the last resort to the ECtHR, just as all citizens of states that are signatories to the ECHR may now do.

In addition, it will be necessary to set up a system of control of the sanctions imposed by the UN Security Council that is eminently jurisdictional. It would be enough to create a separate organ of the Council that was protected by sufficient guarantees of independence (that is, rights of 'immunity'), to which those affected by UN sanctions could appeal directly, without the need for any intervention on the part of their governments, on the grounds both of form and on the merits. The basic documents in the ambit of human rights to be used by such a body, that is to say the parameters of reference for the standard of protection to be applied, would be the traditional international texts (the Universal Declaration, the ECHR, etc) that the UN has already established as fundamental precepts in this field, for instance, in its territorial administrative authorities (such as MINUK). These rules must be observed both by UN officials and by the local population concerned. In this sense, the recent creation of the Office of the Ombudsperson within the Al-Qaida sanctions committee, as discussed in this book, is a step forward, but it does not constitute a guarantee equivalent to most basic due process rights.

Although these two measures are necessary, and perhaps even essential, they alone cannot ensure an interlock of legal orders that is both viable and successful in the long term. What is also required is that the highest authorities of the various legal regimes comply with the other two premises of what we have called 'interordinal constitutionalism' (based on the soft constitutionalist approaches), namely to accept the existence of an international global society and to promote the universalization of the principles that foster the different legal systems that live together in this community.

II. The European Court of Justice will reinforce its doctrine in the field of human rights when it considers there is a need to guarantee, shore up or legitimise the existence of the legal system for which it is ultimately responsible.

6. The development of EU law inspired by the ECJ has not been entirely innocent. Although it cannot be denied that the ECJ was inclined to remain faithful to a culture of human rights protection that permeated the whole of Europe, particularly after the Second World War, it must not be forgotten that the Luxembourg Court had other interests too. By taking on the concerns raised with respect to fundamental rights by, among others, the Constitutional Court of Germany, the ECJ sought to earn legitimacy and authority so as to preserve the primacy of EU law and its uniform application throughout EU territory. This approach by the Luxembourg Court might be deemed 'interested concern' for fundamental rights. Its reappearance tends to coincide with those occasions when the Court feels its authority threatened and sees the need to reinforce its own legitimacy and that of the laws it has the duty to uphold. This may be observed recently in the Court's judgment in the 2008 case of *Kadi and Al Barakaat*, which was decided after the admonition intimated by the ECtHR in the *Bosphorus* case in 2005.

7. Indeed, the ECJ has been under threats coming from two new fronts. On the one hand, the ECtHR has assumed the authority to oversee, at least indirectly and in the last resort, compliance by EU law with Strasbourg standards. And on the other, UN law and the resolutions of its Security Council have obliged European institutions to implement various economic sanctions against individuals who are subject to their jurisdiction, but with the difficulty that such penalties fail to respect the most basic standards of protection of fundamental rights, such as the right to a fair trial or the right to appeal. In this context, national courts and, at the end of the day, the ECtHR, will be tempted to intervene to safeguard people's individual rights. However, it may be argued against this view that the ECtHR refused to step in in a case where the UN itself had failed to abide by these minimum standards. This may be true, but the Court's attitude was due rather to the nature of the United Nations, an organization dedicated to pursuing world peace, and not an institution originally founded on the basis of an internal common market.

8. Thus, in view of the danger that the laws it has a duty to protect might be displaced either by a national court or by the ECtHR wielding the argument that citizens require at least minimum safeguarding, the ECJ has taken the initiative and flourished the protection of fundamental rights as grounds sufficient to compromise its own international responsibility, so long as the application of

EU law is thus guaranteed. The Court has no doubt considered the fact that it is more difficult to question a desire to safeguard human rights than to ensure the supremacy of EU law a persuasive argument.

9. Furthermore, the hardening of the EU's commitment to fundamental rights by submitting UN sanctions to strong judicial supervision would tend to reinforce European citizens' feelings of adherence to the European project. In other words, if the citizens perceive that the EU is protecting their fundamental rights to the point of jeopardizing its own international reputation (as states' national constitutional courts did in the past), they will have the sensation that the EU is not merely a bureaucratic artefact without a proper identity but is rather a real union, based upon the rule of law, that is capable of stepping in, if necessary, to safeguard the rights of its citizens.

III. The ECtHR ensures that the Convention represents the minimum standard in the field of fundamental rights and with respect to EU law and consolidates its position as the tribunal specialized in human rights in relation to the ECJ.

10. Rather than a relationship of hierarchy between the ECtHR and the ECJ, their dealings have given rise more to an association of cooperation and, lately, of specialization, to the extent that the Human Rights Court is, with the acquiescence of the ECJ, becoming the specialized court in guaranteeing fundamental rights, as a last resort, in Europe.

11. The justification that the ECtHR has found to subject legal acts emanating from the EU to indirect monitoring is fairly similar to the premise of functional succession, which nevertheless was rejected in the past by the ECJ. Although neither the EC was, nor the EU (still) is, party to the ECHR, their Member States are signatories to the Convention, and they cannot therefore wield the argument that powers have been transferred to the Community or the Union so as to evade the obligations incumbent upon them under the ECHR. Consequently, although it is not possible to bring a claim directly against the EU before the Luxembourg Court, the ECtHR will admit suits against acts of Member States to which European law is applicable, although they do not enjoy any margin of appreciation in situations of a 'manifestly deficient' level of protection. The situation in practice, therefore, is not unlike that described by the defenders of functional succession.

12. For its part, the ECJ rejects the concept of hierarchical superiority, or at least it does in these terms. On the other hand, it appears to be coming round to accepting the specialized jurisdiction (or 'superior judicial authority') exercised by the ECtHR in relation to human rights, if as a result it receives the acknowledgment of its counterpart in Strasbourg. In this way, by subjecting itself to the standards of the ECtHR, it reduces or dilutes the risk that the national superior courts of Member States might be attracted to the idea of assuming supervision of European law, thus challenging the supremacy and uniform application of the law that the ECJ is bound to enforce. The sword of Damocles hanging over the Court of Justice means that it is obliged to incorporate the jurisprudence of the ECtHR into its decisions and, what is more, make an additional effort (in terms of both quality and quantity of legal arguments) to ensure that the legal acts enacted by the EU institutions respect the European-wide public order established by the guardian of the ECHR.

IV. The delay in the accession of the EU to the ECHR will intensify the 'intergovernmentalization' of the organization.

13. The case law now emanating from Strasbourg entails the *de facto* submission of EU law to the ECHR by means of a declaration of responsibility of a Member State by the ECtHR. Strangely enough, this occurs when Member States have not yet agreed that the EU should form part of the Convention. While it is true that accession is envisaged in the reforms introduced by the Lisbon Treaty, it is always dependent on the Member States' will. Negotiations are required, first within the EU and then later with the organs of the Council. So, the current situation in which the EU finds itself places it in a position of evident disadvantage, which might even be considered as a defenceless position. For, in effect, as the Union cannot be party to litigation, it is unable to intervene directly, but can only do so together with a Member State, which means that it cannot in any way direct its own defence. Furthermore, because the Union is not party to the Convention, it is not entitled to appoint a judge to the Court. Thus, from a procedural point of view, the balance of the situation is that the EU suffers all the disadvantages and enjoys none of the benefits.

14. Despite its stated wish to protect the phenomenon of EU integration, the judgments handed down by the Court of Human Rights have given rise to an 'intergovernmentalization' of the EU, by leading the Member States to defend the interests of the Union. This function should of course be performed by the Union's institutions, particularly the Commission. Moreover, in the event that judgment is issued against them, Member States may be inclined to pass on any compensation payments to be met by the Union itself, either directly or by more subtle means. This negation of personality on the part of the EU (or, rather, the limitation of its procedural *ius standi*) clearly weakens it and entails a step back in the integration process. This situation therefore supposes, at the very least, a stimulus for the Union to sign up to the Convention, which is really the only effective and appropriate solution to give back to the EU the role that truly belongs to it. Indeed, for the sake of the European project, let's hope that the long-awaited accession happens sooner rather than later.

V. The ECJ will approve a constitutionalist approach to the interordinal relations and will accept with less reservation the supremacy of the laws emanating from the United Nations Organization to the extent that the UN legal order assumes the minimum standards of protection of fundamental rights that are applicable in the EU.

15. First, it has always been the nature of the EU (and, before it, of the EC) to be especially committed to respecting international law and institutions. After all, it owes its existence to international law. Nevertheless, in recent judgments the ECJ has indicated that this subjection to international law does not represent a blank cheque. Emulating the jurisprudence of the ECtHR, it has on certain occasions reserved to itself the possibility of indirectly supervising the ECtHR by way of acts of application, in the event that certain minimum standards of fundamental rights protection are not respected. Questioning the applicability of international law within itself is not a pleasant task for such an organization committed to European integration, whose internationalist vocation entails compliance with UN laws.

In the second place, the regulation of relations between or among various legal orders may be inspired by different models or conceptions of interordinal relations and of world governance itself. Such concepts may range from the most orthodox and hierarchical constitutionalist approach to essentially pluralist models, including all the intermediate structures that have been elaborated with greater or lesser variations in the attempt to reach a point of encounter.

Thirdly, the European legal regulatory regime has traditionally been founded on a clearly constitutionalist conception of international law. The ECJ has always defended the doctrine of the hierarchical supremacy of EU law over national laws, even with respect to precepts included in state Constitutions. Consequently, it does seem that the ideal approach, and the one that more closely reflects the legal tradition on the continent that inspired the Community of Law (what is now the EU), is not so much the pluralist concept but rather the constitutionalist view. Furthermore, it may be argued that, when the ECJ has opted to follow a pluralist approach, that decision has been due to some exceptional reason or circumstances outside the normal or ideal state of things.

Accordingly, insofar as regulation of the association between EU law and the law issued by UN bodies is concerned, the definitive model will become more constitutionalist (or hierarchical) as the UN's acceptance of the standards of protection of fundamental rights that are guaranteed in Europe becomes stronger. The inverse will also apply, of course, namely that the model will be more pluralist if the level of harmonization weakens.

VI. The United Nations Organization will have to improve its standards of protection of fundamental rights to guarantee the efficacy of the laws emanating from its institutions in general, and of Security Council sanctions in particular.

16. No organization will ever admit that it does not respect the most basic human rights. The UN in general and the Security Council in particular are peculiar in this respect because there is no supervisory organ above them from which individual persons who are affected by their decisions may seek redress. One may wonder as to the possibility of the General Assembly one day requesting a consultative Opinion from the ICJ on the duty of the Security Council to respect human rights. However, if it were to do so, the response it received, which would undoubtedly be positive, would have very limited effects in practice. The Security Council will never admit that it violates fundamental rights. When it acts, we can be practically 100 per cent sure that the question of whether the measures it adopts infringe such rights is not even considered. On the contrary, the Council's view is no doubt that in the long term its actions will tend to guarantee everyone's rights in a safer world.

17. The real problem and the true threat to the effectiveness of the sanctions imposed by the Security Council is, paradoxically, the lack of a qualified monitoring body. Member States of the UN and, through them, other supranational organizations, such as the EU, are under the obligation to comply with the Council's resolutions and implement the sanctions it imposes. Individuals, however, do not have at their disposal any specialized body before which they can challenge the admissibility of such penalties, which leads them, in the end, to have recourse to national state courts and tribunals. Alternatively, they may turn towards the EU courts, as happened in the case of Mr Kadi, due to the Community-wide ramifications of the matter. In the long run, if unjustifiable abuse has occurred, domestic courts (in this case, a supranational court) will end up intervening to protect individuals, thus undermining the effectiveness of sanctions adopted in the UN and calling into question the very legitimacy of the sanctioning system.

18. Consequently, if the system really wants to be viable and the Security Council wishes to be sure that its sanctions will finally be applied, it will have to assume a minimum standard of rights protection, not just from a formal perspective (for which the use of the expression 'Considering that . . .' in penalizing resolutions would suffice), but also in substantive terms. In this case this would entail setting up a procedure for review that met the minimum guarantees of due process and right of appeal that are recognized inter alia by the ECHR. Otherwise, Security Council sanctions will run the risk of either not being applied or of having their effects annulled by national or regional courts to which affected individuals may appeal. The creation of the Ombudsperson does constitute an improvement of the system, but it is still not enough.

19. The ECtHR has not yet declared its position on this question. However, in the hypothetical case of an individual whose assets are placed in a state that is not a member of the EU but is a signatory to the Convention, it is more than likely that the Human Rights Court would withhold the deference it has shown towards UN territorial authorities in cases such as *Behrami* and *Saramati* and would intervene. In fact, it is very possible that, following the lead of the ECJ in the *Kadi and Al Barakaat* case, the ECtHR will, in similar circumstances, end up finding against a state that enforces UN sanctions on the grounds that it failed to abide by the minimum guarantees of a fair trial when freezing the assets of the person affected thereby.

VII. Instead of deepening the fragmentation of law, the admonitions sent by the highest courts of some legal systems to their counterparts in others, the drawing of demarcation lines and the warnings of possible indirect review in the future permit coexistence, preventing the break up of the mosaic formed by the legal regimes that are condemned to coexist on the international scene and which ensure worldwide legal governance.

20. The greater density of the international legal arena now adds further complexity to the already complicated legal panorama of the post-war era. For, while the period prior to the creation of international organizations dedicated to securing peace and harmony saw the scholarship concentrating on questions concerning the relationship between local and infranational legal systems that coexisted simultaneously within the same national ambit, today, in the era of economic (and also juridical) globalization, the focus is more on supranational, global legal regulatory systems that coexist across the world along with pre-existing state and infranational systems. In any country of the EU, at least, cohabitation may be found between the legal system of that country and those of the EU, the protective regime of the ECHR and UN law, without prejudice, moreover, to the other international obligations assumed by states (such as those arising from membership of the WTO) and to the particular circumstances of federal states.

Owing to the inexistence of a structured international (super-) legal system that determines jurisdictions and powers, the interordinal relations among these various different entities and among countries, international organizations and other global bodies are complex. The problems that are created in such a context tend to be resolved by the courts on a case-by-case basis, while the political powers-that-be lack the will to establish even a minimum level of principles that might lead to a coherently definitive solution. Not only is there significant overlap in jurisdictional competence among these different bodies, but their powers are not normally delimited or specified so as to avoid conflicts between them and, furthermore, there is no definition either of the manner in which such disputes should be dealt with.

21. In this ambit of evident concurrence in jurisdiction, with increasing fragmentation of the international law, the role played by the courts and other review organs has acquired great significance. This is the case not so much because of a desire on the part of magistrates to set up a 'governance of judges' but is rather due to the lack of complete mechanisms for resolving conflicts. Thus, there is a general fear that in this state of things certain decisions by the courts which in fact exercise indirect supervision over the acts emanating from other legal systems, or given unilateral acts on the part of the Security Council, tend to cause the 'fragmentation' that commentators speak of to descend into the total destruction and disintegration of the international legal structure, leaving only small independent islets or domains as 'legal Taifa Kingdoms'. This scenario would make it impossible to establish a world governance of a more legal nature, subject to provisions derived from the rule of law, which might complement global economic governance.

Nevertheless, it may be concluded from the contents of this book that the courts and other organs of control, which have shown considerable common sense and sound judgement, are making moves and reacting in kind to their counterparts, responsible for other legal systems, in cases of potential conflict. To put it another way, instead of emphasising differences and reinforcing the boundaries separating the various legal orders, their 'admonitions' in the form of obiter dicta that warn of impassable frontiers, or certain declarations or actions of intergovernmental bodies, or other more subtle forms of indirect control, have to date produced very positive results. On the one hand, they have allowed the governing bodies of the other legal systems concerned to show some flexibility when interpreting and applying the law for which they are responsible, while on the other, they have enabled the corresponding legislative organs at least to come round to the view that measures must be taken. Though it is not easy to find examples of the latter, one instance might be the provision in the Treaty of Lisbon for the long-awaited accession by the EU to the ECtHR.

In this respect, it seems necessary for certain demarcation lines to be drawn and sometimes strong (legal) words to be uttered in the dialogue between jurisdictions and legal systems in order to keep fragmentation within tolerable limits and maintain interconnecting links that avoid total rupture or an irreparable frontal collision but instead facilitate the possibility of world governance or, at least, of living together in peace. Therefore, between what is possible (that is, pluralist or constitutionalist models and all the concepts in between) and what is desirable (perhaps a pure constitutionalist structure based on an ordered, hierarchy-based common legal system), in the end the organs of control will opt for what is viable (an intermediate approach, somewhere between constitutionalism and pluralism, and closer to the model we have put forward here – an interordinal constitutionalism – involving a certain amount of controlled fragmentation).

Bibliography

Abi-Saab, G, 'The Concept of Sanction in International Law' in Gowlland-Debbas, V (ed), *United Nations Sanctions and International Law* (Kluwer Law International, The Hague, 2001).

Ackermann, T, 'Case C-36/02, Omega Spielhallen- und Automatenaufstellungs- GmbH v Oberburgermeisterin der Bundesstadt Bonn' (2005) 42(4) *Common Market Law Review* 1107.

Acosta Sánchez, MA, 'Tribunal de Justicia de las Comunidades Europeas. STJCE 03.05.2007, Advocaten voor de Wereld vzw y Leden Van de Ministerraad – C-303/05 – Cooperación policial y judicial en materia penal – Orden de detención europea' (2007) 28 *Revista de Derecho Comunitario Europeo* 959.

Ago, R, 'Second report on State responsibility. The origin international responsibility' (1970) II *Yearbook of the International Law Commission* 177.

Aguiar de Luque, L, 'La Carta europea de derechos y las constituciones nacionales' in Pizzorusso, A (ed), *Riflessi della Carta europea dei diritti sulla giustizia e la giurisprudenza costituzionale: Italia e Spagna a confronto. Dottorato di ricerca in 'giustizia costituzionale e diritti fondamentali': giornata italo-spagnola di giustizia costituzionale* (Giuffrè, Milano, 2003).

——, 'Los derechos fundamentales en el proceso de integración europea' (2003) 18 *Cuadernos de Derecho Público* 173.

Akande, D, 'The International Court of Justice and the Security Council: Is there Room for Judicial Control of Decisions of the Political Organs of the United Nations?' (1997) 46(2) *International and Comparative Law Quarterly* 309.

Aláez Corral, B and Álvarez Álvarez, L, *Las decisiones básicas del Tribunal Constitucional Federal alemán en las encrucijadas del cambio de milenio* (BOE-CEPC, Madrid, 2008).

Aldecoa Luzárraga, F, 'La política exterior común en el Tratado de Lisboa: instrumentos para hacer de la Unión un actor de la globalización' in Fernández Liesa, CR and Díaz Barrado CM (eds), *El Tratado de Lisboa. Análisis y perspectivas* (Instituto Universitario de Estudios Internacionales y Europeos 'Francisco de Vitoria', Dykinson, Madrid, 2008).

Aleinikoff, A, 'Transnational Spaces: Norms and Legitimacy' (2008) 33(2) *Yale Journal of International Law* 479.

Alemanno, A, 'À la recherche d'un juste équilibre entre libertés fondamentales et droits fondamentaux dans le cadre du marché intérieur' (2004) 2004(4) *Revue du Droit de l'Union Européenne* 709.

Alì, A, 'La tutela dei diritti fondamentali della persona umana nell'Unione europea' in de Cesari, P (ed), *Trattato di diritto privato dell'Unione europea, II. Persona e famiglia* (Giappichelli, Torino, 2008).

Almqvist, J, 'A Human Rights Critique of European Judicial Review: Counter-Terrorism Sanction' (2008) 57(2) *International and Comparative Law Quarterly* 303.

Alonso García, R, *Sistema Jurídico de la Unión Europea* 1st edn (Thompson-Civitas, Madrid, 2007).

Alonso García, R, 'Constitución Española y Constitución Europea: Guión para una colisión virtual y otros matices sobre el principio de primacía' (2005) 73 *Revista Española de Derecho Constitucional* 339.

——, 'Los tribunales constitucionales y el control del Derecho interno conectado con el comunitario' (2005) 2 Foro: *Revista de ciencias jurídicas y sociales* 153.

——, 'The Spanish Constitution and the European Constitution: the script for a virtual collision and other observations on the principle of primacy' (2005) 6(6) *German Law Journal* 1001.

Alston, P and Weiler, J, 'An "Ever Closer Union" in Need of a Human Rights Policy' (1998) 9(4) *European Journal of International Law* 658.

Alter, KJ, *Establishing the supremacy of European Law: the making of an International Rule of Law in Europe* (Oxford University Press, Oxford, 2002).

Álvarez, J, 'Judging the Security Council' (1996) 90(1) *American Journal of International Law* 1.

Álvarez, JE, *International Organizations as Law-makers* (Oxford University Press, Oxford, 2005).

Andersson, T, Cameron, I and Nordback, K, 'EU blacklisting: the renaissance of imperial power, but on a global scale' (2003) 14(2) *European Business Law Review* 111.

Andrés Sáez de Santamaría, MP, *El informe del Consejo de Estado sobre la inserción del Derecho europeo en el ordenamiento español: texto del informe, estudios y ponencias* (Consejo de Estado-CEPC, 2008).

Andriantsimbazovina, J *et al*, *Les grands arrêts de la Cour européenne des droits de l'homme* 4th edn (PUF, Paris, 2007).

Andriantsimbazovina, J, 'La Cour de Strasbourg, gardienne des droits de l'homme dans l'Union européenne. Remarques autour de l'arrêt de Grande Chambre de la Cour européenne des droits de l'homme du 30/06/2005, Bosphorus Hava Yollari ve Ticaret Anonim Sirketi c/ Irlande)' (2006) 2006(3) *Revue Française de Droit Administratif* 566.

Anzilotti, D, *Corso di diritto internazionale* (Athenaeum, Roma, 1912).

Arai-Takahashi, Y, *The Margin of Appreciation Doctrine and the Principle of Proportionality in the Jurisprudence of the ECHR* (Intersentia, Antwerp, 2002).

Areilza Carvajal, JM, 'La inserción de España en la nueva Unión Europea: la relación entre la Constitución española y el Tratado constitucional. Comentario a la DTC 1/2004, de 13 de diciembre de 2004' (2005) 73 *Revista Española de Derecho Constitucional* 365.

——, 'El Dictamen 2/1994 del Tribunal de Justicia o cómo no abordar el espinoso asunto de las competencias comunitarias' (1996) 47 *Revista española de derecho constitucional* 333.

Arriola Etxaniz, N, 'El cosmopolitismo como teoría defensora del gobierno mundial' (2008) 56(2) *Estudios de Deusto* 11.

Aust, A, 'The Role of Human Rights in Limiting the Enforcement Powers of the Security Council: A Practitioner's View' in de Wet, E, Nollkaemper, A and Dijkstra, P (eds), *Review of the Security Council by Member States* (Metro-Intersentia, Amsterdam, 2003).

Autin, JL and Sudre, F, 'La dualité fonctionnelle du Conseil d'État en question devant la Cour européenne des droits de l'homme. À propos de l'arrêt Procola c/ Luxembourg du 28 septembre 1995' (1996) 12(4) *Revue Française de Droit Administratif* 777.

Baardman, B, 'Cour de Justice, 13 juillet 1966, affaires jointes 56 et 58–64, Consten S.à.R.L. et Grundig-Verkaufs-GmbH contre Commission' (1966) 2 *Cahiers de Droit Européen* 669.

Bacigalupo Sagesse, M and Fuentetaja Pastor, JA, 'Fumus boni iuris, periculum in mora y equilibrio de intereses como presupuestos de la tutela cautelar comunitaria (a propósito del Auto del TJCE de 12 de julio de 1996 y del Auto del Presidente del TPI de 13 de julio de 1996, recaídos en sede cautelar en el asunto de la "enfermedad de las vacas locas")' (1997) 94 *Revista Española de Derecho Administrativo* 287.
Baldwin, DA, 'The Sanctions Debate and the Logic of Choice' (1999) 24(3) *International Security* 80.
Bamforth, N, 'Sexual Orientation Discrimination after Grant v South-West Trains' (2000) 63(5) *Modern Law Review* 694.
Baño León, JM, 'Los derechos fundamentales en la Comunidad Europea y la competencia del juez nacional' (1987) 54 *Revista Española de Derecho Administrativo* 277.
Barav, A, 'Cour Constitutionnelle italienne et droit communautaire: le fantôme de Simmenthal' (1985) 21(2) *Revue Trimestrielle de Droit Européen* 313.
——, 'Les effets du droit communautaire directement applicable' (1978) 14 *Cahiers de Droit Européen* 265.
Benda, E, 'Dignidad humana y derechos de la personalidad' in López Pina, A (tr), Hesse, C *et al* (eds), *Manual de Derecho Constitucional* 2nd edn (Marcial Pons-IVAP, Madrid, 2001).
Benoît-Rohmer, F, 'Coup d'arrêt à la réforme indispensable de la Cour européenne des droits de l'homme' (2007) *L'Europe des Libertés* June 2009.
——, 'Contribution. Accession of the EC/EU to the ECHR' (Parliamentary Assembly, Council of Europe, Strasbourg, 18 March 2008) Doc 11533.
——, 'A propos de l'arrêt Bosphorus Air Lines du 30 juin 2005 : l'adhésion contrainte de l'Union à la Convention' (2005) 64 *Revue Trimestrielle des Droits de l'Homme* 827.
——, 'L'affaire Emesa Sugar: L'institution de l'avocat général de la Cour de justice des Communautés européennes à l'épreuve de la jurisprudence Vermeulen de la Cour européenne des droits de l'homme' (2001) 37(3–4) *Cahiers de Droit Européen* 403.
——, 'Chronique d'une décision annoncée: l'affaire Senator Lines devant la Cour européenne des droits de l'homme' (2001) 4 *L'Europe des libertés* 2.
——, 'Le commissaire du gouvernement auprès du Conseil d'État, l'avocat général auprès de la Cour de justice des Communautés européennes et le droit d'un procès équitable' (2001) 37(4) *Revue Trimestrielle de Droit Européen* 727.
Berman, PS, 'A pluralist approach to international law' (2007) 32(2) *The Yale Journal of International Law* 301.
——, 'Global Legal Pluralism' (2007) 80(6) *Southern California Review* 1155.
Berramdane, A, 'Le traité de Lisbonne et le retour des États' (2008) 9–10 *La Semaine Juridique* 23.
Besselink, L, 'Entrapped by the maximum standard: On Fundamental Rights, Pluralism and Subsidiarity in the European Union' (1998) 35(3) *Common Market Law Review* 629.
Besselink, LFM, 'Case C-145/04 Spain v United Kingdom Case C-300/04' (2008) 45(3) *Common Market Law Review* 787.
Bianchi, A, 'Assessing the Effectiveness of the UN Security Council's Anti-terrorism Measures: The Quest for Legitimacy and Cohesion' (2006) 17(5) *European Journal of International Law* 881.

Biersteker, T, *Targeted Financial Sanctions. A Manual for Design and Implementation. Contribution from the Interlaken Process* (Brown University, Providence, 2001).

Blanquet, M, 'Article I-5 – Relations entre l'Union et les Etats membres' in Burgorgue-Larsen, L, Levade, A and Picod, F (eds), *Traité établissant une Constitution pour l'Europe: commentaire article par article* (Bruylant, Bruxelles, 2007).

Bleckmann, A, *Die Bindung der Europäischen Gemeinschaft an die Europäische Menschenrechtskonvention* (C Heymanns, Köln, 1986).

——, 'Die Grundrechte im Europäischen Gemeinschaftsrecht, ein Beitrag zu den Methoden des EG-Rechts' (1981) *Europäische Grundrechte Zeitschrift* 257.

Blokker, N, 'Is the authorization authorized? Powers and practice of the UN Security Council to authorize the use of force by "coalitions of the able and willing"' (2000) 11(3) *European Journal of International Law* 541.

Bothe, M, 'Security Council's Targeted Sanctions against Presumed Terrorists: The Need to Comply with Human Rights Standards' (2008) 6(3) *Journal of International Criminal Justice* 541.

Bowett, DW, GP Barton and R Higgins, *United Nations Forces: A Legal Study* (Praeger, New York, 1964 (reprinted 2008)).

Bradley, CA and Goldsmith, JL, 'Federal Courts and the Incorporation of International Law' (1998) 111 *Harvard Law Review* 2260.

Bradley, CA, Goldsmith, J and Moore, DH, 'Sosa, Customary International Law, and the Continuing Relevance of Erie' (2007) 120(4) *Harvard Law Review* 869.

Bradley, K, 'Sense and Sensibility: Parliament v Council Continued' (1991) 16(3) *European Law Review* 245.

Braillard, P and Djalili, MR, *Les relations internationales* (PUF, Paris, 1992).

Brandtner, B and Rosas, A, 'Human Rights and the External Relations of the European Community: An Analysis of Doctrine and Practice' (1998) 9(3) *European Journal of International Law* 468.

Bravo-Ferrer Delgado, M and La Casta Muñoa, N, 'Joined Cases C-297/88 and C-197/89, Massam Dzodzi v Belgian State; Case C-231/89, Krystyna Gmurzynska- Bscher v Oberfinanzdirektion Köln' (1992) 29(1) *Common Market Law Review* 152.

Bribosia, E and Weyembergh, A, 'La personnalité juridique de l'Union européenne' in Dony, M (ed), *L'Union Européenne et le monde après Amsterdam* (Éditions de l'Université, Bruxelles, 1999).

Brinkhorst, LJ and Schermers, HG, *Judicial remedies in the European Communities: a case book* 2nd edn (Kluwer, Deventer, 1977).

Brown, C, 'Case C-112/00, Eugen Schmidberger, Internationale Transporte und Planzuge v Austria' (2003) 40(6) *Common Market Law Review* 1499.

Brownlie, I, 'The Responsibility of States for the Acts of International Organizations' in Ragazzi, M (ed), *International responsibility today: essays in memory of Oscar Schachter* (Martinus Nijhoff, Leiden, 2005).

——, *Principles of Public International Law* 6th edn (Oxford University Press, Oxford, 2003).

——, 'The decisions of political organs of the United Nations and the rule of law' in Macdonald, RSJ (ed), *Essays in honour of Wang Tieya* (Martinus Nijhoff, Dordrecht, 1994).

Bruce, E, 'La primauté du droit communautaire. Retour sur la portée de l'article 88-1 de la Constitution dans la jurisprudence récente du Conseil constitutionnel' (2005) 192 *Les Petites Affiches* 3.

Bryde, BO, 'International Democratic Constitutionalism' in Macdonald, RSJ and Johnston DM (eds), *Towards World Constitutionalism: Issues in the Legal Ordering of the World Community* (Martinus Nijhoff, Leiden, 2005).

Brzoska, M, *Design and Implementation of Arms Embargoes and Travel and Aviation Related Sanctions: Results of the 'Bonn-Berlin Process'* (International Center for Conversion, Bonn, 2001).

Bucher, A, 'L'Ordre public et le But social des Lois en Droit international privé' (1994) 239 (1993-II) *Recueil des Cours de l'Académie de Droit International de La Haye* 9.

Buffard, I *et al*, *International Law between universalism and fragmentation: Festschrift in honour of Gerhard Hafner* (Martinus Nijhoff, Leiden, 2008).

Bulterman, M and Kranenborg, HR, 'What if rules on free movement and human rights collide? About laser games and human dignity: the Omega case' (2006) 31(1) *European Law Review* 93.

Burgorgue-Larsen, L, 'L'identité de l'Union européenne au coeur d'une controverse territoriale tricentenaire – Quand le statut de Gibraltar réapparaît sur la scène judiciaire européenne (CJCE 12 septembre 2006, aff. C-145/04, Royaume d'Espagne c/ Royaume-Uni de Grande-Bretagne et d'Irlande du Nord)' (2007) 43(1) *Revue trimestrielle de droit européen* 25.

——, 'La déclaration du 13 décembre 2004 (DTC nº /2004): "Un Solange II à l'espagnole"' (2005) 18 *Cahiers du Conseil Constitutionnel* 154.

——, 'Senator Lines c. les 15 États de l'Union européenne, DR, du 10 mars 2004' (2004) 35 (7 octobre 2004) *Chronique de la Cour européenne des droits de l'Homme*, Recueil Dalloz 2533.

——, 'La protection du domicile des personnes morales : (arrêt "Stés Colas est et autres" du 16 avril 2002)' in Tavernier, P (ed), *La France et la Cour européenne des droits de l'homme : la jurisprudence en 2002 : présentation, commentaires et débats* (Bruylant, Bruxelles, 2003).

Burke-White, WW, 'International Legal Pluralism' (2004) 25(4) *Michigan Journal of International Law* 963.

Burrows, N, 'Development Cooperation Defined' (1997) 22(6) *European Law Review* 594.

——, 'Question of Community Accession to the European Convention Determined' (1997) 22(1) *European Law Review* 58.

——, 'The Risks of Widening without Deepening' (1992) 17(4) *European Law Review* 352.

Bustos Gisbert, R, *La Constitución Red: Un estudio sobre supraestatalidad y Constitución* (IVAP, Oñate, 2005).

Caflisch, L, 'Is the International Court Entitled to Review Security Council Resolutions Adopted under Chapter VII of the United Nations Charter?' in Al-Nauimi, N and Meese, R (eds), *International Legal Issues Arising under the United Nations Decade of International Law* (Kluwer, The Hague, 1995).

Calhoun, JC and Lence, RM, *Union and Liberty: The Political Philosophy of John C Calhoun* (Liberty Fund, Indianapolis, 1992).

Callewaert, J, 'Les droits fondamentaux entre cours nationales et européennes' (2001) 48 *Revue Trimestrielle des Droits de l'Homme* 1183.

Calvo Caravaca, AL and Canedo Arrillaga, MP, 'Non bis in idem en Derecho antitrust' (2006) 54(1) *Estudios de Deusto* 11.

Calvo Caravaca, AL and Carrascosa González, J, *Derecho Internacional Privado* (Comares, Granada, 2008).

Camby, JP, 'Le droit communautaire est-il soluble dans la Constitution?' (2004) 4 *Revue du droit public et de la science politique en France et à l'étranger* 878.

Cameron, I, 'UN Targeted Sanctions, Legal Safeguards, and the ECHR' (2003) 72 *Nordic Journal of International Law* 159.

Canedo Arrillaga, JR and Gordillo Pérez, LI, 'La nueva Unión Europea: de la doble personalidad a la crisis de personalidad' (2010) 78 *Revista de Derecho Político* 337.

——, 'Los derechos fundamentales en la Unión Europea a la espera de Lisboa' (2008) 39 *Cuadernos Europeos de Deusto* 27.

Canedo Arrillaga, MP, *El procedimiento en derecho comunitario de defensa de la competencia: análisis del principio de proporcionalidad y otros afines* (ProQuest, Cambridge, 1999).

Cano Palomares, G, 'Un nuevo capítulo en el control del Derecho comunitario por parte del Tribunal de Estrasburgo (A propósito de la STEDH de 30 de junio de 2005, caso Bosphorus Airways)' (2006) 74 *Revista Vasca de Administración Pública* 317.

Canor I, 'Primus inter pares. Who is the ultimate guardian of fundamental rights in Europe?' (2000) 25(1) *European Law Review* 3.

——, '"Can two walk together, except they be agreed?" The relationship between international law and European law: The incorporation of United Nations sanctions against Yugoslavia into European Community law through the perspective of the European Court of Justice' (1998) 35(1) *Common Market Law Review* 137.

Caron, DD, 'The legitimacy of the collective authority of the Security Council' (1993) 87(4) *American Journal of International Law* 552.

Carreau, D, 'Droit communautaire et droits nationaux: concurrence ou primauté? La contribution de l'arrêt Simmenthal' (1978) 14 *Revue Trimestrielle de Droit Européen* 381.

Carrillo Salcedo, JA, *El Convenio Europeo de Derechos Humanos* (Tecnos, Madrid, 2003).

Carrozza, P, 'Constitutionalism's Post-Modern Opening' in Loughlin, M and Walker, N (eds), *The Paradox of Constitutionalism. Constituent Power and Constitutional Form* (Oxford University Press, Oxford, 2008).

Cartabia, M, 'Europe and Rights: Taking Dialogue Seriously' (2009) 5(1) *European Constitutional Law Review* 5.

——, *Principi inviolabili e integrazione europea* (Giuffrè, Milano, 1995).

—— *et al* (eds), *Constitución europea y constituciones nacionales* (Tirant, Valencia, 2005).

Cascajo Castro, JL, 'Constitución y Derecho constitucional en la Unión Europea' (2005) 15 *Teoría y realidad constitucional* 89.

——, 'Integración europea y constituciones nacionales' (2005) 1 *Revista d'estudis autonòmics i federals* 61.

——, 'Notas para un breve ensayo sobre "Constitución e interpretación constitucional"' (2003) 51(1) *Estudios de Deusto* 81.

Cass, DA, *The Constitutionalization of the World Trade Organization. Legitimacy, Democracy, and Community in the International Trading System* (Oxford University Press, Oxford, 2005).

Cassese, A, 'Remarks on Scelle's Theory of "Role Splitting" (dedoublement fonctionnel) in International Law' (1990) 1(1) *European Journal of International Law* 210.

Cassia, P and Donnat, F, 'Terrorisme international et droits fondamentaux : les leçons du droit communautaire Commentaire sous Cour de justice des Communautés européénnes, 3 septembre 2008, Kadi et Al Barakaat International Foundation, aff. C-402/05 P et C-415/05 P' (2008) 24(6) *Revue Française de Droit Administratif* 1204.

Castillo de la Torre, F, 'Case C-141/02 P, Commission v T-Mobile Austria GmbH, formerly max.mobil, judgment of the Court of Justice (Grand Chamber) of 22 February 2005' (2005) 42(6) *Common Market Law Review* 1751.

Celotto, A, 'Derecho UE y derecho nacional: primauté vs contralímites' in Cartabia, M and others (eds), *Constitución europea y constituciones nacionales* (Tirant, Valencia, 2005).

Chalmers, D, 'Competition and Industrial Property. Television and the European Court of Justice, Libertarianism Run Rife' (1992) 17(3) *European Law Review* 248.

Chaltiel, F, 'Nouvelle précision sur les rapports entre le droit constitutionnel et le droit communautaire La décision du Conseil constitutionnel du 27 juillet 2006 sur la loi relative aux droits d'auteurs' (2006) 68 *Revue Française de Droit Constitutionnel* 837.

Chamussy, D, 'Le Conseil constitutionnel face à la primauté du droit communautaire. Cons. const. 19 novembre 2004, Traité établissant une constitution pour l'Europe' (2005) 61(4) *Actualité Juridique – Droit Administratif* 219.

Charpentier, J, 'Le contrôle par la Cour de justice de la conformité au Traité des accords en vigueur conclus par la Communauté' (1997) 409 *Revue du marché commun et de l'Union européenne* 413.

Charpy, C, 'The Status of (Secondary) Community Law in the French Internal Order. The Recent Case-Law of the Conseil Constitutionnel and the Conseil d'Etat' (2007) 3(3) *European Constitutional Law Review* 436.

Chemerinsky, E, *Constitutional Law. Principles and Policies* 3rd edn (Aspen, New York, 2006).

Chesterman, S, *Just War or Just Peace? Humanitarian Intervention and International Law* (Oxford University Press, Oxford, 2002).

Chinkin, C, 'The state that acts alone: bully, good samaritan or iconoclast?' (2000) 11(1) *European Journal of International Law* 31.

Christakis, R and Bannelier, K, 'Acteur vigilant ou spectateur impuissant ? Le contrôle exercé par le Conseil de sécurité sur les Etats autorisés à recourir à la force' (2004) 37(2) *Revue belge de droit international/Belgian Review of international Law/Belgisch tijdschrift voor internationaal recht* 498.

Chueca Sancho, AG, *Los derechos fundamentales en la Unión Europea* 2nd edn (Bosch, Barcelona, 1999).

Churchill, RR and Foster, NG, 'European Community Law and Prior Treaty Obligations of Member States: The Spanish Fishermen's Cases' (1987) 36(3) *International and Comparative Law Quarterly* 504.

Claes, M, *The National Courts' Mandate in the European Constitution* (Hart, Oxford, 2006).

——, 'Constitucionalizando Europa desde su fuente: las "cláusulas europeas" en las Constituciones nacionales: evolución y tipología' in Cartabia, M *et al* (eds), *Constitución europea y constituciones nacionales* (Tirant, Valencia, 2005).

Clapham, A, 'The European Union before the European Court of Human Rights' in Boisson de Chazournes, L, Romano, C and Mackenzie, R (eds), *International Organizations and International Dispute Settlement: Trends and Prospects* (Transnational Publishers, New York, 2002).

——, *Human Rights in Private Sphere* (Clarendon Press, Oxford, 1993).

Clapham, A, Cassese, A and Weiler, JHH, *European Union – The Human Rights Challenge Vol III, Human Rights and the European Community: The Substantive Law* (Nomos, Baden-Baden, 1991).

Cohen-Jonathan, G, 'L'adhésion de l'Union européenne à la Convention européenne des droits de l'homme' in VV. AA. (ed), *Quelle justice pour l'Europe? La Charte européenne des droits fondamentaux et la Convention pour l'avenir de l'Europe* (Bruylant, Bruxelles, 2004).

——, 'La territorialisation de la juridiction de la Cour européenne des droits de l'Homme' (2002) 52 *Revue Trimestrielle des Droits de l'Homme* 1055.

—— and Flauss, F, 'Cour européenne des droits de l'homme et droit international général' (2006) 52 *Annuaire Français de Droit International* 660.

——, 'De l'office de la Cour européenne des droits de l'homme dans la protection des droits fondamentaux dans l'Union européenne : l'arrêt Matthews contre Royaume-Uni du 18 février 1999' (1999) 11(7–9) *Revue Universelle des Droits de l'Homme* 253.

Cohen, HG, 'Munaf v Geren – US Supreme Court opinion on extraterritorial application of the writ of habeas corpus' (2008) 102(4) *American Journal of International Law* 854.

Cohen, JL, 'A Global State of Emergency or the Further Constitutionalization of International Law: A Pluralist Approach' (2008) 15(4) *Constellations* 456.

Colinet, C, 'La protection du droit de propriété dans la Communauté européenne au travers de l'arrêt "Hauer" de la Cour de justice des Communautés européennes, du 13/12/1979' in Bieber, R *et al* (eds), *Das Europa der zweiten Generation – Gedächtnisschrift für Christoph Sasse* (Nomos, Baden-Baden, 1981).

Colliard, C and Dubois, L, *Institutions internationales* (Dalloz, Paris, 1995).

Colneric, N *et al* (eds), *Une communauté de droit: Festschrift für Gil Carlos Rodríguez Iglesias* (BWV Berliner Wissenshafts, Berlin, 2003).

Colomer, E, *El pensamiento alemán de Kant a Heidegger. Vol. I. La Filosofía Trascendental: Kant* (Herder, Barcelona, 1986).

Connor, T, 'Community Discrimination Law: No Right to Equal Treatment in Employment in Respect of Same Sex Partner' (1998) 23(4) *European Law Review* 378.

Constantinesco, V, 'C'est comme ci c'était fait? (Observations à propos de l'arrêt de la Cour européenne des droits de l'homme (grande chambre), Bosphorus airlines, du 30 juin 2005' (2006) 42(3–4) *Cahiers de droit Européen* 363.

——, 'La primauté du droit communautaire, mythe ou réalité?' in Constantinesco, LJ *et al* (eds), *Rechtsvergleichung, Europarecht und Staatenintegration: Gedächtnisschrift für Léontin-Jean Constantinesco* (Carl Heymans, Köln, 1983).

—— and Simon, D, 'Chronique de jurisprudence de la Cour de justice des Communautés européennes. Institutions et ordre juridique communautaire' (1989) *Journal du droit international* 395.

Corcuera Atienza, J *et al*, *La protección de los derechos fundamentales en la Unión Europea* (Dykinson, Madrid, 2002).

Cortright, D and López, GA, *Sanctions and the Search for Security: Challenges to UN Action* (Lynne Rienner, London, 2002).

——, *The Sanctions Decade: Assessing UN Strategies in the 1990s* (Lynne Rienner, Boulder, 2000).

Costa, JP, 'La Convention européenne des droits de l'homme, la Charte des droits fondamentaux de l'Union européenne et la problématique de l'adhésion de l'Union européenne à la Convention' 2004(5) *European University Institute Working Paper Law* 11.

——, 'Le Tribunal de la Rote et l'article 6 de la Convention européenne des droits de l'homme' (2002) 50 *Revue Trimestrielle des Droits de l'Homme* 463.

Costato, L, 'Potere d'iniziativa dell'affittuario e destino delle quote latte a fine rapporto' (1989) II *Rivista di diritto agrario* 265.

Costello, C, 'The Bosphorus Ruling of the European Court of Human Rights: Fundamental Rights and Blurred Boundaries in Europe' (2006) 6(1) *Human Rights Law Review* 87.

Cottereau, G, 'Rebondissement d'octobre en Iraq : la résolution 949 du Conseil de Sécurité (15 octobre 1994)' (1999) 40 *Annuaire français de droit international* 175.

Cover, R, 'The Uses of Jurisdictional Redundancy: Interests, Ideology and Innovation' (1981) 22(4) *William & Mary Law Review* 639.

Craig, P, 'The Lisbon Treaty, Process, Architecture and Substance' (2008) 33(2) *European Law Review* 137

—— and de Búrca, G, *EC Law – Text, Cases and Materials* (Oxford University Press, London, 1995).

——, *EU Law – Text, Cases and Materials* 2nd edn (Oxford University Press, London, 1998).

——, *EU Law – Text, Cases and Materials* 3rd edn (Oxford University Press, London, 2003).

——, *EU Law. Text, Cases and Materials* 4th edn (Oxford University Press, London, 2008).

Crawford, J, *The International Law Commission's Articles on State Responsibility: Introduction, Text and Commentaries* (Cambridge University Press, Cambridge 2002).

Cruz Villalón, P, 'El Tratado según la constitución: tres planteamientos' in Carrillo López, M and López Bofill, H (eds), *La Constitución Europea : actas del III Congreso Nacional de Constitucionalistas de España* (Tirant, Valencia, 2006).

Cuadrado Zuloaga, D, 'Los llamados actos políticos' (2007) 22 *Actualidad administrativa* 2745.

Cusimano, MK, *Operation Restore Hope: the Bush administration's decision to intervene in Somalia* (Institute for the Study of Diplomacy Publications, School of Foreign Service, Georgetown University, Washington DC, 1995).

d'Amato, A, 'It's a Bird, It's a Plane, It's Jus Cogens' (1990) 6(1) *Connecticut Journal of International Law* 1.

Daillier, P, 'La disparition de la CECA le 23 juillet 2002 – Des problèmes de succession d'organisations internationales?' in Gautron, JC (ed), *Les dynamiques du droit européen en début de siècle : études en l'honneur de Jean Claude Gautron* (Pedone, Paris, 2004).

Daillier, P and Pellet, A, *Droit international public* 7th edn (LGDJ, Paris, 2002).

Dauses, MA, 'The protection of fundamental rights in the Community legal order' (1985) 10(6) *European Law Review* 398.

Davies, S, 'Segi and the Future of Judicial Rights Protection in the Third Pillar of the EU' (2008) 14(3) *European Public Law* 311.

de Búrca, G, 'The European Court of Justice and the International Legal Order After Kadi' (2010) 51 *Harvard International Law Journal* 1.

——, 'The European Court of Justice and the International Legal Order after Kadi' (2009) 01/09 *Jean Monnet Working Papers* April 2009.

—— and Gerstenberg, O, 'The Denationalization of Constitutional Law' (2005) 47(1) *Harvard International Law Journal* 243.

de la Rasilla del Moral, I, 'The Increasingly Marginal Appreciation of the Margin of Appreciation Doctrine' (2006) 7(6) *German Law Journal* 611.

de la Sierra, S, 'El sistema comunitario de tutela cautelar y su control por el tribunal europeo de derechos humanos a la luz del art. 6 del convenio. una oportunidad perdida (La resolución del TEDH de 10 de marzo de 2004 en el asunto Senator Lines GmbH c. los quince Estados Miembros de la Unión Europea, n.º 56672/00)' (2004) 6 *Revista General de Derecho Administrativo*.

de Montalvo Jääskeläinen, F, 'Constitución de Estonia' (2005) 65 *Revista de las Cortes Generales* 219.

de Schutter, O, 'Promoting and Protecting Fundamental Rights in the European Union: The relations between the European Convention of Human Rights, the European Charter and the EU Member States' constitutions. Briefing Paper' (European Parliament, Directorate General Internal Policies of the Union, Brussels).

—— and l'Hoest, O, 'La Cour européenne des droits de l'homme juge du droit communautaire : Gibraltar, l'Union européenne, et la Convention européenne des droits de l'homme' (2000) 36(1–2) *Cahiers de Droit Européen* 141.

—— and Lejeune, Y, 'L'adhésion de la Communauté à la Convention européenne des droits de l'homme' (1996) 32(5–6) *Cahiers de droit européen* 555.

de Sena, P and Vitucci, MC, 'The European Courts and the Security Council: Between Dédoublement Fonctionnel and Balancing of Values' (2009) 20(1) *European Journal of International Law* 193.

de Vergottini, G, *Diritto costituzionale* 6th edn (CEDAM, Padova, 2008).

de Wet, E, 'The International Constitutional Order' (2006) 55(1) *International and Comparative Law Quarterly* 51.

——, *The Chapter VII Powers of the United Nations Security Council* (Hart, Oxford, 2004).

——, 'Human Rights Limitations to Economic Enforcement Measures Under Article 41 of the United Nations Charter and the Iraqi Sanctions Regime' (2001) 14 *Leiden Journal of International Law* 277.

——, 'Judicial Review as an Emerging General Principle of Law and its Implications for the International Court of Justice' (2000) 47(2) *Netherlands International Law Review* 181.

de Witte, B and Toggenburg, GN, 'Human Rights and Membership of the European Union' in Peers, S and Ward, A (eds), *The EU Charter of Fundamental Rights* (Hart Publishing, Oxford, 2004).

de Witte, B, 'Article I-6 – Le droit de l'Union' in Burgorgue-Larsen, L, Levade, A and Picod, F (eds), *Traité établissant une Constitution pour l'Europe : commentaire article par article* (Bruylant, Bruxelles, 2007).

——, 'Direct Effect, Supremacy, and the Nature of the Legal Order' in Craig, P and de Búrca, G (eds), *The Evolution of EU Law* (Oxford University Press, Oxford, 1999).

——, 'The pillar structure and the nature of the European Union: Greek temple or French Gothic cathedral?' in Gala Durán, C (tr), Heukels, T, Blokker, N and Brus, M (eds), *The European Union after Amsterdam: a legal analysis* (Europa Institute, Leiden University, Leiden, 1998).

del Valle Gálvez, JA, 'Constitution espagnole et Traité constitutionnel européen – La Déclaration du Tribunal Constitucional du 13 décembre 2004' (2005) 41(5–6) *Cahiers de Droit Européen* 705.

Delbrück, J, 'Article 24' in Simma, B (ed), *The Charter of the United Nations: A Commentary* 2nd edn (Oxford University Press, Oxford. 2002).

Delmas-Marty, M, *Les Forces imaginantes du droit III. La Refondation des pouvoirs* (Seuil, Paris, 2007).

——, *Les Forces imaginantes du droit II. Le pluralisme ordonné* (Seuil, Paris, 2006).

——, *Les Forces imaginantes du droit I. Le relatif et l'universel* (Seuil, Paris, 2004).

——, 'Commerce mondial et protection des droits de l'homme' in Flauss, JF *et al* (ed), *Commerce mondial et protection des droits de l'homme: les droits de l'homme à l'épreuve de la globalisation des échanges économiques* (Bruylant, Bruxelles, 2001).

——, *Pour un droit commun* (Seuil, Paris, 1994).

—— and Teitgen-Colly, C, *Punir sans juger? De la répression administrative au droit administratif pénal* (Economica, Paris, 1992).

Denis, C, *Le pouvoir normatif du Conseil de Sécurité des Nations Unies: portée et limites* (Bruylant, Bruxelles, 2004).

di Blase, A, 'Sulla responsabilità internazionale per attività dell'ONU' (1974) 57 *Rivista di Diritto Internazionale* 250.

Díaz, E, *Estado de Derecho y sociedad democrática* 1966 edn (Taurus, Madrid, 1998).

Díez-Hochtleitner Rodríguez, J, *La posición del Derecho internacional en el ordenamiento comunitario* (McGraw-Hill, Madrid, 1998).

Dijk, P., Hoof, GJH and Heringa, AW, *Theory and Practice of the European Convention on Human Rights* (Martinus Nijhoff, The Hague, 1998).

Dougan, M, 'The Treaty of Lisbon 2007: Winning minds, not hearts' (2008) 45(3) *Common Market Law Review* 617.

Douglas-Scott, S, 'A tale of two Courts: Luxembourg, Strasbourg and the growing European Human rights acquis' (2006) 43(3) *Common Market Law Review* 629.

——, 'Bosphorus Hava Yollari Turizm Ve Ticaret Anonim Şirketi v Ireland' (2006) 41(3) *Common Market Law Review* 243.

Doukas, D, 'The verdict of the German Federal Constitutional Court on the Lisbon Treaty: Not guilty, but don't do it again!' (2009) 34(6) *European Law Review* 866.

Doxey, M, *International Sanctions in Contemporary Perspective* 2nd edn (St Martin's Press, New York, 1996).

Dubois, L, *Droit Communautaire et protection des droits fondamentaux dans les États membres* (Economica, Paris, 1995).

Duez, P, *Les actes de gouvernement* (Dalloz, Paris, 2006 (reprint of the 1935 original)).

Dugard, J, 'Judicial Review of Sanctions' in Gowlland-Debbas, V (ed), *United Nations Sanctions and International Law* (Kluwer Law International, The Hague, 2001).

Dunne, T, 'Good citizen Europe' (2008) 84(1) *International Affairs* 13.

Dunoff, JL, 'Constitutional Conceits: The WTO's 'Constitution' and the Discipline of International Law' (2006) 17(3) *European Journal of International Law* 647.

—— and Trachtman, JP (eds), *Ruling the World? Constitutionalism, International Law, and Global Governance* (Cambridge University Press, Cambridge, 2009).

Dupuy, PM, 'The Place and Role of Unilateralism in Contemporary International Law' (2000) 11(1) *European Journal of International Law* 19.

Dutheil de la Rochere, J, 'Conseil constitutionnel (French Constitutional Court), Decision No 2004–496 of 10 June 2004, Loi pour la confiance dans l'économie numérique (e-commerce)' (2005) 42(3) *Common Market Law Review* 859.

Eckes, C, 'Case T-228/02, Organisation des Modjahedines du peuple d'Iran v Council and UK (OMPI), Judgment of the Court of First Instance (Second Chamber) of 12 December 2006' (2007) 44(4) *Common Market Law Review* 1117.

——, 'Does the European Court of Human Rights Provide Protection from the European Community? – The Case of Bosphorus Airways' (2007) 13(1) *European Public Law* 47.

Editorial, 'The CFSP under the EU Constitutional Treaty – Issues of depillarization' (2005) 42(2) *Common Market Law Review* 325.

Editorial, 'The rule of law as the backbone of the EU' (2007) 44(4) *Common Market Law Review* 875.

Eeckhout, P, 'Community Terrorism Listings, Fundamental Rights, and UN Security Council Resolutions. In Search of the Right Fit' (2007) 3(2) *European Constitutional Law Review* 183.

Ehlermann, CD, 'Anmerkung zu EuGH, Urteil v. 12.11.1969, Rs. 29/69' (1970) *Europarecht* 41.

Ehlers, D and Becker, U, *European fundamental rights and freedoms* (Walter de Gruyter, Berlin, 2007).

Elaraby, N, 'Some Reflections on The Role of the Security Council and the Prohibition of the Use of Force in International Relations: Article 2(4) Revisited in Light of Recent Developments' in Frowein, JA *et al* (ed), *Verhandeln für den Frieden/ Negotiating for peace. Liber amicorum Tono Eitel* (Springer, Berlin, 2003).

Elliott, KA, 'The Sanctions Glass: Half Full or Completely Empty?' (1998) 23(1) *International Security* 50.

Embid Irujo, A, Carreras Serra, F and Gómez-Reino y Carnota, E, 'Funciones constitucionales y actos del gobierno' in Parejo Alfonso, LJ (ed), *Estudios sobre el gobierno: Seminario sobre el Proyecto de Ley Reguladora del Gobierno* (Universidad Carlos III, Madrid, 1996).

Emeri, C and Gautron, JC, 'La réforme du régime financier des Communautés et la décision du Conseil constitutionnel français du 21 juin 1970' (1971) 1 *Revue du droit public et de la science politique* 157.

Emiliou, N, 'State Liability under Community Law: Shedding more light on the Francovich Principle?' (1996) 21(5) *European Law Review* 399.

Escobar Hernández, C, 'Comunidad Europea y Convenio Europeo de Derechos Humanos: ¿El fin de una vieja polémica?' (1996) 3 *Revista de Instituciones Europeas* 817.

Everling, U, 'Will Europe Slip on Bananas? The Bananas Judgment of the Court of Justice and National Courts' (1996) 33(3) *Common Market Law Review* 401.

——, 'The Maastricht Judgment of the German Federal Constitutional Court and its Significance for the Development of the European Union' (1994) 14 *Yearbook of European Law* 1.

Farrall, JM, *United Nations Sanctions and the Rule of Law* (Cambridge University Press, Cambridge, 2007).

Fassbender, B, *The United Nations Charter as the Constitution of the International Community* (Martinus Nijhoff, Leiden, 2009).

——, 'The Meaning of International Constitutional Law' in Macdonald, RSJ and Johnston, DM (eds), *Towards World Constitutionalism: Issues in the Legal Ordering of the World Community* (Martinus Nijhoff, Leiden, 2005).

——, 'The United Nations Charter as Constitution of the International Community' (1998) 36(3) *Columbia Journal of Transnational Law* 529.

Favoreu, L, 'El bloque de la constitucionalidad' (1990) 5 *Revista del Centro de Estudios Constitucionales* 45.

——, 'La décision du conseil constitutionnel du 22 Mai 1985 rélative au Protocole no. 6 additionnel à la Convention européenne des droits de l'homme' (1986) 31 *Annuaire Français de Droit International* 868.
——, 'Le contrôle de constitutionnalité du Traité de Maastricht et le développement du droit constitutionnel international' XCVII(1-2) *Revue Générale de Droit International Public* 39.
—— and Gaia, P *et al*, *Droit constitutionnel* 10th edn (Dalloz, Paris, 2007).
—— and Philip, L, 'Maastricht I, II, III' in Favoreu, L *et al* (ed), *Les grandes décisions du Conseil Constitutionnel* 12th edn (Dalloz, Paris, 2003).
Feldman, JP, *La bataille américaine du fédéralisme: John C Calhoun et l'annulation (1828–1833)* (PUF, Paris, 2004).
Fernández Sola, N, 'La subjetividad internacional de la Unión Europea' (2002) 11 *Revista de Derecho Comunitario Europeo* 85.
——, 'La adhesión de la Comunidad Europea al Convenio Europeo de salvaguarda de los Derechos Humanos y de las Libertades Fundamentales. Comentario al Dictamen 2/94 del Tribunal de Justicia de las Comunidades Europeas' (1997) 144 *Noticias de la Unión Europea* 41.
Fierro, E, 'Legal Basis and Scope of the Human Rights Clauses in EC Bilateral Agreements: Any Room for Positive Interpretation?' (2001) 7(1) *European Law Journal* 41.
Fitzgerald, PL, 'Managing "Smart Sanctions" Against Terrorism Wisely' (2002) 36(4) *New England Law Review* 957.
——, 'If Property Rights Were Treated Like Human Rights, They Could Never Get away with This: Blacklisting and Due Process in US Economic Sanctions Programs' (1999) 51(1) *Hastings Law Journal* 73.
Fletcher, M, 'Extending "indirect effect" to the third pillar: the significance of Pupino?' (2005) 30(6) *European Law Review* 862.
Forrester, IS, 'Legal Professional Privilege: Limitations on the Commission's Powers of Inspection following the AM & S Judgment' (1983) 20(1) *Common Market Law Review* 75.
Foster, N, 'General Issues in the Kent Kirk Case' (1985) 10(5) *European Law Review* 276.
Fouassier, E, *Le Médicament: notion juridique* (Technique & Documentation, Paris, 1999).
Fox, GH and Roth, BR, *Democratic Governance and International Law* (Cambridge University Press, Cambridge, 2000).
Fransman, L, *British Nationality Law: Immigration and Nationality Law* 3rd edn (Tottel Publishing, West Sussex, 2009).
Fremuth, M and Griebel, J, 'On the Security Council as a Legislator: A Blessing or a Curse for the International Community?' (2007) 76(4) *Nordic Journal of International Law* 339.
Friedrich, J, 'UNMIK in Kosovo: Struggling with Uncertainty' (2005) 9(1) *Max Planck Yearbook of United Nations Law* 225.
Frowein, JA, 'The UN Anti-Terrorism Administration and the Rule of Law' in Dupuy, PM *et al* (eds), *Völkerrecht als Wertordnung, Common Values in International Law. Festschrift für Christian Tomuschat* (NP Engel Verlag, Kehl, 2006).
—— Krisch, N, 'Introduction to Chapter VII, Articles 39–43' in Simma, B (ed), *The Charter of the United Nations: A Commentary* 2nd edn (Oxford University Press, Oxford, 2002).
Gaïa, P, 'Commentaire de la décision du Conseil constitutionnel no. 91-294 du 25 juillet 1991 : loi autorisant l'approbation de la Convention d'application de l'Accord de Schengen, du 14 juin 1985' (1992) 17(1) *Revue de la recherche juridique* 25.

Gaja, G, 'Opinion 2/94: accession by the Community to the European Convention for the Protection of Human Rights and fundamental Freedoms' (1996) 33(5) *Common Market Law Review* 973.

——, 'New Developments in a Continuing Story: the Relationship Between EEC Law and Italian Law' (1990) 27(1) *Common Market Law Review* 83.

Galanter, M, 'Justice in Many Rooms: Courts, Private Ordering and Indigenous Law' (1981) 19 *Journal of Legal Pluralism and Unofficial Law* 1.

Ganshof Van der Meersch, W, 'L'extradition et la Convention européenne des droits de l'homme. L'affaire Soering' (1990) 1 *Revue Trimestrielle des Droits de l'Homme* 5.

García de Enterría, E, 'La lucha contra las inmunidades del poder en el derecho administrativo (poderes discrecionales, poderes de gobierno, poderes normativos)' (1962) 38(159) *Revista de Administración Pública* 205.

Gautier, P, 'The Reparation for Injuries Case Revisited: The Personality of the European Union' (2000) 4 *Max Planck Yearbook of United Nations Law* 331.

Gautron, JC, 'Article I-11 – Principes fondamentaux' in Burgorgue-Larsen, L, Levade, A and Picod, F (eds), *Traité établissant une Constitution pour l'Europe : commentaire article par article* (Bruylant, Bruxelles, 2007).

——, 'Article I-7 – Personnalité juridique' in Burgorgue-Larsen, L, Levade, A and Picod, F (eds), *Traité établissant une Constitution pour l'Europe : commentaire article par article* (Bruylant, Bruxelles, 2007).

Gayet, MF and Simon, D, 'Constatation de manquement et effet direct du droit communautaire' (1973) 9 *Cahiers de Droit Européen* 301.

Geiss, R, 'Humanitarian Safeguards in Economic Sanctions Regimes: A Call for Automatic Suspension Clauses, Periodic Monitoring, and Follow-Up Assessment of Long-Term Effects' (2005) 18(Spring) *Harvard Human Rights Journal* 167.

Genevois, B, 'Le Conseil constitutionnel et la primauté du droit communautaire' (2005) 2005(2) *Revue Française de Droit Administratif* 239.

——, 'Le Conseil constitutionnel et le droit communautaire dérivé' (2004) 2004(4) *Revue Française de Droit Administratif* 651.

——, 'Le Traité sur l'Union Européenne et la Constitution révisée, à propos de la décision du Conseil constitutionnel n° 92-312 DC du 2 septembre 1992' (1992) 8(6) *Revue Française de Droit Administratif* 937.

——, 'Le Traité sur l'Union Européenne et la Constitution, à propos de la décision du Conseil constitutionnel n° 92-308 DC du 9 avril 1992' (1992) 8(3) *Revue Française de Droit Administratif* 373.

Gerkrath, J, 'Le principe de l'égalité de traitement et l'accès des femmes aux emplois dans les unités armées dans la Bundeswehr' (2000) Décembre *Europe* 5.

Gianfrancesco, E, 'I limiti alla costituzione di gruppi politici all'interno del Parlamento europeo' (2002) *I Diritto pubblico comparato ed europeo* 278.

Giegerich, T, 'Luxembourg, Karlsruhe, Strassbourg – Dreistufiger Grundrechsschutz in Europa?' (1990) 50 *Zeitschrift für ausländisches öffentliches Recht und Völkerrecht* 836.

Gilliaux, P, 'L'arrêt Unión de Pequeños Agricultores: entre subsidiairité juridicitonnelle et effectivité' (2003) 39(1–2) *Cahiers de Droit Européen* 177.

Gilmore, G and Rijpma, J, 'Joined Cases C-317/04 and C-318/04, European Parliament v Council and Commission, Judgment of the Grand Chamber of 30 May 2006, [2006] ECR I-4721' (2007) 44(4) *Common Market Law Review* 1081.

Gimeno Verdejo, C, 'La sentencia "protección penal del medio ambiente a través del Derecho Penal". Clarificación del reparto de competencias entre el primer y el tercer pilar del Tratado de la Unión Europea' (2006) 34 *Cuadernos Europeos de Deusto* 189.

Giussani, E, *Constitutional and Administrative Law* (Thomson, London, 2008).

Goldsmith, JL and Posner, EA, *The Limits of International Law* (Oxford University Press, Oxford, 2005).

Gómez Fernández, I, 'La Constitución Española "frente" al Tratado por el que se establece una Constitución para Europa: entre la necesidad y la conveniencia de una reforma constitucional' (2005) 14 *Revista Española de Derecho Europeo* 297.

——, *Conflicto y Cooperación entre la Constitución y el Derecho Internacional* (Tirant, Valencia, 2005).

González Alonso, LN, '¿Quién dijo que desaparecen los pilares? La configuración jurídica de la acción exterior de la Unión Europea en el Tratado de Lisboa' in Martín y Pérez de Nanclares, J (ed), *El Tratado de Lisboa: la salida de la crisis constitucional* (Iustel, Madrid, 2008).

González García, I, 'Sentencia de 12.09.2006, España / Reino Unido, C-145/04 – PE – Elecciones – Derecho de voto – Ciudadanos de la Commonwealth residentes en Gibraltar y que poseen la ciudadanía de la Unión' (2008) 29 *Revista de Derecho Comunitario Europeo* 215.

González Vaqué, L, 'La sentencia "Comisión/Consejo" de 13 de septiembre de 2005: la Comunidad es competente para exigir que los Estados miembros impongan sanciones penales' (2005) 239 *Gaceta Jurídica de la CE y de la Competencia* 47.

——, 'El difícil equilibrio entre la libre circulación de mercancías y los derechos fundamentales en materia de libertad de expresión y de reunión: la sentencia "Schmidberger"' (2003) 227 *Gaceta Jurídica de la Unión Europea y de la Competencia* 61.

Gordillo, LI, 'Un paso más hacia la estabilización de las relaciones interordinamentales en Europa: la incorporación de la UE al CEDH' (2011) 38 *Revista Española de Derecho Europeo* 173.

——, 'El juez nacional y el juez europeo ante la Euro-orden' in Revenga Sánchez, M (ed), *El poder judicial: VI Congreso de la Asociación de Constitucionalistas de España* (Tirant, Valencia, 2009).

——, 'Constitución, constitucionalización y constitucionalismo de la Unión' (2005) 53(2) *Estudios de Deusto* 253.

Gowlland-Debbas, V, 'Sanctions Regimes under Article 41 of the Charter' in Gowlland-Debbas, V (ed), *National implementation of United Nations sanctions: a comparative study* (Martinus Nijhoff, Leiden, 2004).

——, 'UN Sanctions and International Law: An Overview' in Gowlland-Debbas, V (ed), *United Nations Sanctions and International Law* (Kluwer Law International, The Hague, 2001).

Grant, RW and Keohane, RO, 'Accountability and Abuses of Power in World Politics' (2005) 99(1) *American Politcal Science Review* 29.

Greer, S, 'Protocol 14 and the Future of the European Court of Human Rights' (2005) 1 *Public Law* 83.

Grewe, C, 'Le "traité de paix" avec la Cour de Luxembourg: l'arrêt de la Cour constitutionnelle allemande du 7 juin 2000 relatif au règlement du marché de la banane' (2001) 37(1) *Revue Trimestrielle de Droit Européen* 1.

Griffiths, J, 'What is Legal Pluralism?' (1986) 24 *Journal of Legal Pluralism and Unofficial Law* 1.

Griller, S, 'International Law, Human Rights and the Community's Autonomous Legal Order. Notes on the European Court of Justice Decision in Kadi' (2008) 4(3) *European Constitutional Law Review* 528.

——, 'Is this a Constitution? Remarks on a Contested Concept' in Griller, S and Ziller, J (eds), *The Lisbon Treaty: EU Constitutionalism Without a Constitutional Treaty?* (Springer, Vienna, 2008).

——, 'Primacy of Community Law: A hidden Agenda of the Charter of Fundamental Rights' in Melissas, D and Pernice, I (eds), *Perspectives of the Nice Treaty and the Intergovernmental Conference in 2004* (Nomos, Baden-Baden, 2002).

Grimm, D, 'Integration by Constitution' (2005) 3(2–3) *International Journal of Constitutional Law* 193.

——, 'The Constitution in the process of Denationalization' (2005) 12(4) *Constellations* 447.

Groussot, X, *General principles of Community Law* (Europa Law, Groningen, 2006).

Guild, E, 'The Uses and Abuses of Counter-Terrorism Policies in Europe: The Case of the "Terrorist Lists"' (2008) 46(1) *Journal of Common Market Studies* 173.

Guillaume, G, 'Jus cogens et souveraineté' in Puissochet, JP *et al* (eds), *L'État souverain dans le monde d'aujourd'hui – Melanges en l'honneur de Jean-Pierre Puissochet* (Pedone, Paris, 2008).

Häberle, P, *El Estado constitucional* (Fix-Fierro, H (tr)) (UNAM, México, 2001).

Habermas, J, *El Occidente escindido: pequeños escritos políticos X* (López de Lizaga, JL (tr)) (Trotta, Madrid, 2006).

Hailbronner, K, 'The European Union from the Perspective of the German Constitutional Court' (1995) 37 *German Yearbook of International Law* 93.

Halberstam, D, 'Constitutionalism and Pluralism in Marbury and Van Gend' in Maduro, MP and Azoulai, L (eds), *The Past and Future of EU Law: The Classics of EU Law Revisited on the 50th Anniversary of the Rome Treaty* (Hart Publishing, Oxford, 2010).

——, 'The Bride of Messina: Constitutionalism and Democracy in Europe' (2005) 30(6) *European Law Review* 775.

—— and Stein, E, 'The United Nations, the European Union, and the King of Sweden: Economic sanctions and individual rights in a plural world order' (2009) 46(1) *Common Market Law Review* 13.

Hale, TN, 'Transparency, Accountability and Global Governance' (2008) 14(1) *Global Governance* 73.

Hanf, D, 'Talking with the "pouvoir constituant" in Times of Constitutional Reform: The European Court of Justice on Private Applicants' Access to Justice' (2003) 10 *Maastricht Journal of European and Comparative Law* 265.

Hannikainen, L, *Peremptory norms (jus cogens) in international law: historical development, criteria, present status* (Lakimiesliiton Kustannus, Helsinki, 1988).

Hänsch, K, 'The Spirit of the Time: A Reply to Roman Herzog and Lüder Gerken' (2007) 3(2) *European Constitutional Law Review* 219.

Hansen, L and Williams, M, 'The Myths of Europe: Legitimacy, Community and the "Crisis" of the EU' (2002) 37(2) *Journal of Common Market Studies* 233.

Hardy, M, 'Opinion 1/76 of the Court of Justice: The Rhine Case and the Treaty-making Powers of the Community' (1977) 14 *Common Market Law Review* 561.

Hartley, TC, *The Foundations of European Community Law* 7th edn (Oxford University Press, Oxford 2007).

——, 'International Competence of the Community' (1977) 2 *European Law Review* 275.
——, 'Fundamental Rights in Community Law' (1975) *European Law Review* 54.
Hartwig, M, 'Much Ado About Human Rights: The Federal Constitutional Court Confronts the European Court of Human Rights' (2005) 6(5) *German Law Journal* 869.
Hebel, HAM, Lammers, JG and Schukking, J (eds), *Reflections on the International Criminal Court. Essays in Honour of Adriaan Bos* (Cambridge University Press, Cambridge, 1999).
Heliskoski, J, 'Case T-253/02, Chafiq Ayadi v Council, Judgment of the Court of First Instance of 12 July 2006; Case T-49/04, Faraj Hassan v Council and Commission' (2007) 44(4) *Common Market Law Review* 1143.
Hendry, ID, Hyett, S and Macleod, I, *The External Relations of the European Communities: A Manual of Law and Practice* (Clarendon, Oxford, 1999).
Herbst, J, *Rechtskontrolle des UN-Sicherheitsrates* (Peter Lang-Verlag, Frankfurt am Main, 1999).
Herdegen, M, 'Maastricht and the German Constitutional Court: Constitutional Restraints for "an ever closer Union"' (1994) 31(2) *Common Market Law Review* 235.
Herlin-Karnell, E, 'In the wake of Pupino: Advocaten voor der Wereld and dell'Orto' (2007) 8(12) *German Law Journal* 1147.
Herzog, R and Gerken, L, 'The Spirit of the Time: Revise the European Constitution to Protect National Parliamentary Democracy' (2007) 3(2) *European Constitutional Law Review* 209.
——, *Stop the European Court of Justice* (Centrum für Europäische Politik, 2008).
Heuschling, L, État de droit, Rechtsstaat, Rule of Law (Dalloz, Paris, 2002).
Hey, E, 'The High-level Summit, International Institutional Reform and International Law' (2005) 2(1) *Journal of International Law & International Relations* 5.
Hierro, LL, Laporta, FJ and Ruiz Miguel A (eds), *Revisión de Elías Díaz. Sus libros y sus críticos* (CEPC, Madrid, 2007).
Hilaire, M, *United Nations Law and the Security Council* (Ashgate, Surrey, 2005).
Hinarejos Parga, A, 'Recent Human Rights Developments in the EU Courts: The Charter of Fundamental Rights, the European Arrest Warrant and Terror Lists' (2007) 7(4) *Human Rights Law Review* 793.
——, 'Bosphorus v Ireland and the protection of fundamental rights in Europe' (2006) 31(2) *European Law Review* 251.
Hinojosa Martínez, LM, 'The Legislative Role of the Security Council in its fight against Terrorism: Legal, Political and Practical Limits' (2008) 57(2) *International and Comparative Law Quarterly* 333.
Höffe, O (ed), *Immanuel Kant: Zum ewigen Frieden* 2nd edn (Akademie, Berlin, 2004).
Hoffmeister, F, 'Bosphorus Hava Yollari Turizm ve Ticaret Anonim Sirket v Ireland. App. No. 45036/98' (2006) 100(2) *American Journal of International Law* 442.
——, 'Germany: Status of European Convention on Human Rights in domestic law' (2006) 4(4) *International Journal of Constitutional Law* 722.
——, 'German Bundesverfassungsgericht: Alcan, Decision of 17 February 2000; Constitutional review of EC Regulation on bananas' (2001) 38(3) *Common Market Law Review* 791.
Horeth, M, 'No way out for the Beast? The Unsolved Legitimacy Problem of European Governance' (1999) 6(2) *Journal of European Public Policy* 249.

Hornsby, SB, 'Public and private resale price maintenance systems in the publishing sector: the need for equal treatment in European Law' (1985) 10(6) *European Law Review* 381.

Howse, R and Nicolaïdis, K, 'This is My EUtopia: Narrative as Power' (2002) 40(4) *Journal of Common Market Studies* 767.

——, 'Legitimacy and Global Governance: Why a Constitution for the WTO is a step too far?' in Porter, R *et al* (eds), *Equity, Efficiency and Legitimacy: The Multilateral System at the Millenium* (Brookings Institution, Washington DC, 2001).

Ignatieff, M (ed), *American Exceptionalism and Human Rights* (Princeton University Press, Princeton, 2005).

Imbrechts, L, 'L'égalité de rémunération entre hommes et femmes' (1986) 22(2) *Revue Trimestrielle de Droit Européen* 231.

Jacobs, FG, White RC and Ovey, C, Jacobs and White: the European Convention on Human Rights (Oxford University Press, Oxford, 2006).

Jacqué, JP, 'Droit constitutionnel national, Droit communautaire, CEDH, Charte des Nations Unies. L'instabilité des rapports de système entre ordres juridiques' (2007) 60 *Revue Française de Droit Constitutionnel* 3.

——, 'L'affaire Matthews (suite et fin)' (2006) 21(Mai–Août 2006) *L'Europe des Libertés* 2.

——, 'Le Tribunal de première instance face aux résolutions du Conseil de sécurité des Nations Unies. "Merci Monsieur le Professeur"' (2006) 19 *L'Europe des Libertés* 2.

——, *Droit institutionnel de l'Union Européenne* 4th edn (Dalloz, Paris, 2006).

——, 'Droit Communautaire et Convention européenne des droits de l'homme, l'arrêt Bosphorus, une jurisprudence "Solange II" de la Cour européenne des droits de l'homme?' (2005) 41(3) *Revue Trimestrielle de Droit Européen* 756.

——, 'Droits fondamentaux et compétences internes de la Communauté européenne' in Cohen-Jonathan, G (ed), *Libertés, justice, tolérance. Mélanges en hommage au Doyen Gérard Cohen-Jonathan* (Bruylant, Bruxelles, 2004).

——, 'Les principes constitutionnels fondamentaux dans le Projet de Traité établissant la Constitution Européenne' in Rossi, LS (ed), *Vers une nouvelle architecture de l'Union européenne: le projet de Traité Constitution* (Bruylant, Bruxelles, 2004).

——, 'The principle of institutional balance' (2004) 41(2) *Common Market Law Review* 383.

——, 'Back to Philadelphia' (2002) 463 *Revue du Marché Commun et de l'Union Européenne* 661.

——, 'La Cour de Justice, la Cour européenne des droits de l'homme et la protection des droits fondamentaux. Quelques observations' in Dony, M and Bribosia, E (eds), *L'avenir du système juridictionnel de l'Union européenne* (Editions de l'Université de Bruxelles, Bruxelles, 2002).

——, 'La légitimation active du Parlement européen ou il n'était pas nécessaire d'espérer pour entreprendre' (1990) 26(4) *Revue Trimestrielle de Droit Européen* 620.

——, 'A propos de la guerre des juges: accords et désaccords entre le juge français et la Cour de justice des Communautés européennes' (1981) 1981(4) 5.

——, 'Recours en annulation, campagne d'information pour l'élection du Parlement européen' (1986) 22(3) *Revue Trimestrielle de Droit Européen* 500.

Jansen, B, 'The limits of unilateralism from a European perspective' (2000) 11(2) *European Journal of International Law* 309.

Jimenez-Blanco Carrillo de Albornoz, A, 'Notas a la Sentencia 64/1991, de 22 de marzo (Asunto APESCO)' (1994) 118 *Noticias de la Unión Europea* 63.

Joerges, C, 'Constitutionalism in Postnational Constellations: Contrasting. Social Regulation in the EU and in the WTO' in Joerges, C and Petersmann EU (eds), *Constitutionalism, Multilevel Trade Governance and Social Regulation* (Hart, Oxford, 2006).

—— and Petersmann, EU (eds), *Constitutionalism, Multilevel Trade Governance and Social Regulation* (Hart, Oxford, 2006).

Johnston, DM, 'World Constitutionalism in the Theory of International Law' in Macdonald, RSJ and Johnston DM (eds), *Towards World Constitutionalism: Issues in the Legal Ordering of the World Community* (Martinus Nijhoff, Leiden, 2005).

Jordano Fraga, J, '¿Jaque mate al acto político?' (1997) 95 *Revista Española de Derecho Administrativo* 417.

Jover Gómez-Ferrer, JM, *Constitución y Derecho comunitario* (Universidad Carlos III-Boletín Oficial del Estado, Madrid, 2004).

Juncker, J-C, 'European Union: A sole ambition for the European Continent' (Council of Europe Parliamentary Assembly, Strasbourg, 11 April 2006) Doc 10897.

Juvenal, DJ, *Sátiras (Satirae)* (Espasa, Madrid, 1965).

Kaddous, C, 'L'ârret France c. Commission de 1994 (accord concurrence) et le contrôle de la légalité des accords externes en vertu de l'article 173 CE : la difficile réconciliation de l'orthodoxie communautaire avec l'orthodoxie internationale' (1996) 32(5-6) *Cahiers de Droit Européen* 613.

Kadelbach, S, 'Union Citizenship' in Von Bogdandy, A and Bast, J (eds), *Principles of European Constitutional Law* (Hart, Oxford, 2006).

Kagan, R, *Of Paradise and Power: America and Europe in the New World Order* (Knopf, New York, 2003).

Kämmerer, JA, 'Gleichberechtigung am Gewehr' (2000) 2000(1) *Europarecht* 102.

Kant, I, *Sobre la paz perpetua* 7th edn (Tecnos, Madrid, 2005).

——, *Zum ewigen Frieden: ein philosophischer Entwurf* (Meiner Verlag, Hamburg, 1992 (first published in 1795)).

——, *Crítica de la razón práctica* (Miñana y Villagrasa, E and García Morente, M (trs)) (Espasa-Calpe, Madrid, 1975).

Kapteyn, PJG, 'Quelques réflexions sur le contrôle de la constitutionnalité des accords conclus par la Communauté avec des pays tiers' in Rodríguez Iglesias, GC et al (eds), *Mélanges en hommage à Fernand Schockweiler* (Nomos, Baden-Baden, 1999).

Karamaoun, N, 'Le contrôle effectué par le juge de Strasbourg sur le droit communautaire: d'un paradoxe à l'autre' in Leuprecht, P et al (eds), *Les Juridictions internationales : complémentarité ou concurrence?* (Bruylant, Bruxelles, 2005).

Karayigit, MT, 'The Yusuf and Kadi Judgments: The Scope of the EC Competences in Respect of Restrictive Measures' (2006) 33(4) *Legal Issues of Economic Integration* 379.

Kauff-Gazin, F, 'L'arrêt Bosphorus de la Cour européenne des droits de l'homme: quand le juge de Strasbourg pallie le retard du constituant de l'Union européenne en matière de protection des droits fondamentaux . . .' (2005) 234 *Les Petites Affiches* 9.

Kelsen, H, *Principios de Derecho Internacional Público* (Caminos, H and Hermida EC (trs)) (El Ateneo, Buenos Aires, 1965).

——, *Principles of International Law* (Rinehart, New York, 1952).

——, 'Les rapports de système entre le droit interne et le droit international public' (1926) 14(1926) *Recueil des Cours de l'Académie de Droit International de La Haye* 227.

Kennedy, D, 'One, Two, Three, Many Legal Orders: Legal Pluralism and the Cosmopolitan Dream' (2007) 31(3) *New York University Review of Law and Social Change* 641.

Kennedy, O, 'The Mystery of Global Governance' (2008) 34(3) *Ohio Northern University Law Review* 827.

Keohane, RO, 'Global Governance and Democratic Accountability' in Held, D and Koenig-Archibugi M (eds), *Taming Globalization: Frontiers of Governance* (Polity Press, London, 2003).

—— and Nye, JS, 'Redefining Accountability for Global Governance' in Kahler, M and Lake DA (eds), *Governance in a Global Economy: Political Authority in Transition* (Princeton University Press, Princeton, 2003).

Kinder-Gest, P, 'Primauté du droit communautaire et droit anglais ou comment concilier l'inconciliable?' (1991) 4 *Revue des affaires européennes* 19.

Kingreen, T, 'Basic Rights of Equality and Social Rights' in Ehlers, E (ed), *European Fundamental Rights and Freedoms* (De Gruyter Recht, Berlin, 2007).

Knoll, B, 'Too Little, Too Late: The Human Rights Advisory Panel in Kosovo' (2007) 7(5) *European Human Rights Law Review* 534.

Koh, HH, 'On American Exceptionalism' (2003) 55(5) *Stanford Law Review* 1479.

Koh, S, '"Respectful Consideration" After Sanchez-Llamas v Oregon: Why the Supreme Court Owes More to the International Court of Justice' (2007) 93 *Cornell Law Review* 243.

Koskenniemi, M, 'Constitutionalism as Mindset: Reflections on Kantian Themes about International Law and Globalization' (2007) 8(1) *Theoretical Inquiries in Law* 9.

——, 'International Law: Constitutionalism, Managerialism and the Ethos of Legal Education' (2007) 1(1) *European Journal of Legal Studies* 1.

——, 'Global Legal Pluralism: Multiple Legal Regimes and Multiple Modes of Thought' (Lecture delivered at Helsinki University on 18 November 2005), available at <http://www.helsinki.fi/eci/Publications/MKPluralism-Harvard-05d%5B1%5D.pdf>.

——, 'The Police in the Temple Order, Justice and the UN: A Dialectical View' (1995) 6(1) *European Journal of International Law* 325.

—— and Leino, P, 'Fragmentation of International Law? Postmodern Anxieties' (2002) 15(3) *Leiden Journal of International Law* 553.

Kovács, P, 'The United Nations in the Fight Against International Terrorism' in Nanda, V (ed), *Law in the War on International Terrorism* (Transnational Publishers, Ardsley, 2005).

Kovar, R, 'Cour de Justice, 23 avril 1986, affaire C-294/83, Parti écologiste "Les Verts" contre Parlement européen' (1987) 23(3–4) *Cahiers de Droit Européen* 314.

——, 'Les accords liant les Communautés européennes et l'ordre juridique communautaire: à propos d'une jurisprudence récente de la Cour de justice' (1975) *Revue du Marché Commun* 345.

—— and Simon, D, 'A propos de la Décision du Conseil constitutionnel français du 30 décembre 1976 relative à l'élection de l'assemblée parlamentaire européenne au suffrage universel direct' (1977) 13(4) *Revue Trimestrielle de Droit Européen* 665.

Kowalik-Bánczyk, K, 'Should We Polish It Up? The Polish Constitutional Tribunal and the Idea of Supremacy of EU Law' (2005) 6(10) *German Law Journal* 1356.

Krajewski, M, 'Democratic Legitimacy and Constitutional Perspectives of the WTO' (2001) 35(1) *Journal of World Trade* 167.

Krenc, F, 'La décision Senator Lines ou L'ajournement d'une question délicate' (2005) 16 *Revue Trimestrielle des Droits de l'Homme* 121.

Krieger, H, 'A Credibility Gap: The Behrami and Saramati Decision of the European Court of Human Rights' (2009) 13(1–2) *Journal of International Peacekeeping* 159.

Krisch, N, 'The Open Architecture of European Human Rights Law' (2008) 71(2) *The Modern Law Review* 183.

Krisch, N, 'The Pluralism of Global Administrative Law' (2006) 17(1) *European Journal of International Law* 247.

Kuhnert, K, 'Bosphorus – Double standards in European human rights protection?' (2006) 2(2) *Utrecht Law Review* 177.

Kuijper, PJ, 'The evolution of the Third Pillar from Maastricht to the European constitution: Institutional aspects' (2004) 41(2) *Common Market Law Review* 609.

Kumm, M, 'Constitutional Democracy Encounters International Law: Terms of Engagement' in Choudhry, S (ed), *The Migration of Constitutional Ideas* (Oxford University Press, Oxford, 2006).

——, 'The Jurisprudence of Constitutional Conflict: Constitutional Supremacy in Europe before and after the Constitutional Treaty' (2005) 11(3) *European Law Journal* 262.

——, 'Who is the final arbiter of constitutionality in Europe? Three conceptions of the relationship between the German Federal Constitutional Court and the European Court of Justice' (1999) 36(3) *Common Market Law Review* 351.

Kunoy, B, 'The Jurisdiction of the ECJ to Review the Legality of the Transposition of an International Act in the EC Legal Order' (2007) 76(1) *Nordic Journal of International Law* 19.

—— and Dawes, A, 'Plate tectonics in Luxembourg: The ménage à trois between EC law, international law and the European Convention on Human Rights following the UN sanctions cases' (2009) 46(1) *Common Market Law Review* 73.

Kunz, JL, 'La primauté du droit des gens' (1925) VI *Revue de Droit International et de Legislation Comparé* 556.

La Pérgola, A, *Constitución del Estado y normas internacionales* (Cascajo Castro, JL and Rodríguez-Zapata Pérez, J (trs)) (UNAM, México 1985).

La Pérgola, A, *Costituzione e adattamento dell'ordinamento interno al diritto internazionale* (Giuffrè, Milano, 1961).

—— and del Duca, P, 'Community Law, International Law and the Italian Constitution' (1985) 79(3) *American Journal of International Law* 598.

Lachaume, JF and Pauliat, H, *Droit administratif. Les grandes décisions de la jurisprudence* (PUF, Paris, 2007).

Lachmann, P, 'International Legal Personality of the EC: Capacity and Competence' (1984) 10 *Legal Issues of European Integration* 3.

Ladenburger, C, 'Police and Criminal Law in the Treaty of Lisbon. A New Dimension for the Community Method' (2008) 4(1) *European Constitutional Law Review* 20.

Lagrange, P, 'Responsabilité des Etats pour actes accomplis en application du Chapitre VII de la Charte des Nations Unies. Observations à propos de la décision de la Cour européenne des Droits de l'Homme (Grande Chambre) sur la recevabilité des requêtes Behrami et Behrami c. France et Saramati c. Allemagne, France et Norvège, 31 mai 2007' (2008) 112(1) *Revue Générale de Droit International Public* 85.

Lagrange, P, 'Sécurité collective et exercice par le Conseil de sécurité du système d'autorisation de la coercition' in SFDI (Société française pour le droit international) (ed), *Les métamorphoses de la sécurité collective: droit, pratique et enjeux stratégiques* (Pedone, Paris, 2005).

Lalive, JF, 'L'immunité de juridiction des Etats et des organisations internationales' (1954) 84(1953-III) *Recueil des cours de l'Académie de Droit International de la Haye* 210.

Lambert, P, 'Les bénéficiaires du droit de recours' in VV AA (ed), *La procédure devant la nouvelle Cour européenne des droits de l'homme après le Protocole n° 11, Actes du séminaire organisé à Bruxelles le 19 octobre 1998, par les instituts de droits de l'homme des barreaux de Paris et de Bruxelles* (Nemesis-Bruylant, Bruxelles, 1999).

Langer, J, 'Case C-273/97, Angela Maria Sirdar v The Army Board, Secretary of State for Defence. Case C-285/98, Tanja Kreil v Germany' (2000) 37(6) *Common Market Law Review* 1433.

Larsen, KM, 'Attribution of Conduct in Peace Operations: The "Ultimate Authority and Control" Test' (2008) 19(3) *European Journal of International Law* 509.

Laubinger, HW and Repkewitz, U, 'Freiwilliger Waffendienst von Frauen in der Bundeswehr' (2000) 91 *Verwaltungsarchiv* 297.

Laubner, T, 'Relieving the Court of Its Success? Protocol No 14 to the European Convention on Human Rights' (2004) 47 *German Yearbook of International Law*, 691.

Laursen, F, Vanhoonacker, S, *The Intergovernmental Conference on Political Union – Institutional Reforms, New Policies and International Identity of the European Community* (EIPA-IEAP, Martinus Nijhoff, Maastricht, 1992).

Lauwaars, RK, 'Joined Cases 46/87 and 227/88, Hoechst AG v Commission; Case 85/87, Dow Benelux NV v Comisión' (1990) 27(2) *Common Market Law Review* 355.

Lavranos, N, 'Judicial Review of UN Sanctions by the Court of First Instance' (2006) 11(4) *European Foreign Affairs Review* 471.

Lavranos, N, 'UN Sanctions and Judicial Review' in Wouters, J, Nollkaemper, PA and de Wet, E (eds), *The Europeanisation of International Law. The Status of International Law in the EU and its Member States* (TMC Asser Press, The Hague, 2008).

——, 'The Interface between European and National Procedural Law: UN Sanctions and Judicial Review' in Obradovic, D and Lavranos, N (eds), *Interface between EU Law and National Law* (Europa Law Publishing, Groningen, 2007).

Lazowski, A, 'Accession Treaty – Polish Constitutional Tribunal' (2007) 3(1) *European Constitutional Law Review* 148.

Leben, C, 'À propos de la nature juridique des Communautés européennes' (1991) 14 *Droits. Revue française de théorie juridique* 61.

Legaz y Lacambra, L, 'La primacía del Derecho de gentes sobre el Derecho interno como problema jurídico y político' (1977) 152 *Revista de Política Internacional* 7.

Leisner, W, *Grundrechte und Privatrecht* in (CH Beck, München, 1960).

Lenaerts, K, 'Fundamental Rights in the European Union' (2000) 25(6) *European Law Review* 575.

——, 'Interlocking Legal Orders in the European Union and Comparative Law' (2003) 52(4) *International and Comparative Law Quarterly* 873.

——, 'Le respect des Droits fondamentaux en tant que principe constitucionnel de l'Union Européenne' in Dony, M, de Walsche, A and Waelbroeck, M (eds), *Mélanges en hommage à Michel Waelbroeck* (Bruylant, Bruxelles, 1999).

——, Van Nuffel, P and Bray, R, *Constitutional Law of the European Union* 2nd edn (Thompson, London, 2005).

—— and de Smijter, E, 'The European Union as an Actor under International Law' (2000) 19(1) *Yearbook of European Law* 95.

——, 'The United Nations and the European Union: Living Apart Together' in Wellens, K (ed), *International Law: Theory and Practice: Essays in honour of Eric Suy* (Kluwer Law International, Deventer, 1998).

Lenoir, N, 'Les rapports entre le droit constitutionnel français et le droit international à travers le filtre de l'article 54 de la Constitution de 1958' in Dupuy, PM (ed), *Droit international et droit interne dans la jurisprudence comparée du Conseil constitutionnel et du Conseil d'État* (Panthéon-Assas, Paris, 2001).

Levade, A, 'Le Conseil constitutionnel aux prises avec le droit communautaire derive' (2004) 4 *Revue du droit public et de la science politique en France et à l'étranger* 889.

Ley, I, 'Legal Protection Against the UN Security Council Between European and International Law: A Kafkaesque Situation?' (2007) 8(3) *German Law Journal* 279.

Lickovà, M, 'European Exceptionalism in International Law' (2008) 19(3) *European Journal of International Law* 463.

Lienemeyer, M and Waelbroeck, D, 'Case C-94/00, Roquette Frères SA v Directeur Général de la Concurrence, de la Consommation et de la Répression des Fraudes. Judgment of the Court of Justice (Full Court) of 22 October 2002' (2003) 40(6) *Common Market Law Review* 1481.

Lillich, RB, 'The Soering case' (1991) 85 *American Journal of International Law* 128.

Liñán Nogueras, DJ and Mangas Martín, A, *Instituciones y Derecho de la Unión Europea* 4th edn (Tecnos, Madrid, 2004).

Lock, T, 'EU accession to the ECHR: Implications for judicial review in Strasbourg' (2010) 35(6) *European Law Review* 777.

Loewenstein, K, 'The Government and Politics of Germany' in Shotwell, JT (ed), *Governments of Continental Europe* (Macmillan, New York, 1940).

Long, M *et al*, *Les grands arrêts de la jurisprudence administrative* 15th edn (Dalloz, Paris, 2005).

López Castillo, A, 'La Unión Europea "en constitución" y la Constitución estatal en espera de reformas: a propósito de la DTC 1/2004, de 13 de diciembre de 2004' (2005) 15 *Teoría y realidad constitucional* 427.

——, 'La Unión Europea en "constitución" y la Constitución estatal en (espera) de reformas: A propósito de la DTC1/2004 de 13 de diciembre' in López Castillo, A, Sáiz Arnáiz., A and Ferreres Comella, V (eds), *Constitución Española y Constitución Europea. Análisis de la Declaración del Tribunal Constitucional (DTC 1/2004, de 13 de diciembre)* (CEPC, Madrid, 2005).

——, 'Un nuevo paso en la andadura iuscomunitaria del Tribunal Constitucional Federal de Alemania. El Auto (Sala Segunda) de 7 de junio de 2000' (2001) 61 *Revista Española de Derecho Constitucional* 349.

——, *Constitución e integración: el fundamento constitucional de la integración supranacional europea en España y en la RFA* (CEC, Madrid, 1996).

— and Menéndez, AJ, Sentencia Lisboa del Tribunal Constitucional Federal Alemán (CEPC, Madrid, 2011).

——, A, Sáiz Arnáiz, A and Ferreres Comella, V, *Constitución Española y Constitución Europea. Análisis de la Declaración del Tribunal Constitucional (DTC 1/2004, de 13 de diciembre)* (CEPC, Madrid, 2005).

López Garrido, D, 'El Tribunal Europeo de Derechos Humanos. Nota introductoria' in Cortes Generales (ed), *Tribunal Europeo de Derechos Humanos: 25 años de jurisprudencia (1959–1983)* (Cortes Generales, Madrid, 1981).

López Guerra, L, 'Hacia un concepto europeo de derechos fundamentales' (2003) 65(2) *Revista Vasca de Administración Pública* 191.

López-Barajas Perea, MI, 'Hacia una mayor eficacia del proceso de amparo internacional. El Protocolo nº 14 a la Convención Europea de Derechos Humanos' (2010) 21 *Revista General de Derecho Europeo*.

Louis, JV and Ronse, T, *L'ordre juridique de l'Union européenne* (Bruylant, Bruxelles, 2005).

Maccormick, N, 'Juridicial Pluralism and the Risk of Constitutional Conflict' in Maccormick, N (ed), *Questioning Sovereignty. Law State and Nation in the European Commonwealth* (Oxford University Press, Oxford, 1999).

Macdonald, RSJ and Johnston, DM (eds), *Towards World Constitutionalism: Issues in the Legal Ordering of the World Community* (Martinus Nijhoff, Leiden, 2005).

Magnette, P, *Le régime politique de l'Union européenne* (Presses de Sciences-politiques, Paris, 2003).

Magnon, X *et al*, *QPC – La question prioritaire de constitutionnalité. Pratique et contentieux* (Litec, Paris, 2011).

Magnon, X, 'La QPC face au droit de l'Union : la brute, les bons et le truand' (2010) 84(4) *Revue Française de Droit Constitutionnel* 761.

——, 'Le chemin communautaire du Conseil constitutionnel : entre ombre et lumière, principe et conséquence de la spécificité constitutionnelle du droit communautaire (Commentaire du volet communautaire des décisions du Conseil constitutionnel n° 2004-496 DC du 10 juin 2004, Loi pour la confiance dans l'économie numérique, et n° 2004-497 DC du 1er juillet 2004, Loi relative aux communications électroniques et aux services de communication audiovisuelle)' (2004) 8–9 *Europe* 6.

Mangas Martín, A, 'Artículo 52. Alcance e interpretación de los derechos y principios' in Mangas Martín, A (ed), *Carta de los Derechos Fundamentales de la Unión Europea* (Fundación BBVA, Bilbao, 2008).

——, 'La Declaración del Tribunal Constitucional sobre el artículo 13.2 de la Constitución: una reforma constitucional innecesaria o insuficiente' (1992) 44(2) *Revista Española de Derecho Internacional* 381.

——, 'La Constitución y la ley ante el Derecho comunitario (Comentario a la sentencia del Tribunal Constitucional español 28/1991, de 14 de febrero, sobre la Ley Orgánica del Régimen Electoral General y el Acta relativa a las elecciones al Parlamento Europeo)' (1987) 14(2) *Revista de Instituciones Europeas* 587.

Mangas Martín, A, *La Constitución Europea* (Iustel, Madrid, 2005).

Manners, I, 'The normative ethics of the European Union' (2008) 84(1) *International Affairs* 45.

——, 'Normative Power Europe: A Contradiction in Terms?' (2002) 40(2) *Journal of Common Market Studies* 235.

—— and Whitman, R, 'The "difference engine": constructing and representing the international identity of the European Union' (2003) 10(3) *Journal of European Public Policy* 380.

Mapelli Marchena, C and Irurzun Montoro, F, 'La orden europea de detención y entrega a la luz del Tratado de la Unión Europea. Comentario a la Sentencia del JTCE de 3 de mayo de 2007 en el asunto Advocaten voor de Wereld VZW, as. C-303/05' (2007) 24 *Revista española de derecho europeo* 581.

Marina Jalvo, B, *Medidas provisionales en la actividad administrativa* (Lex Nova, 2007).

Marinas Suárez, D, '"Senator Lines" contra los quince Estados miembros de la Unión Europea' (2004) 11 *Revista Española de Derecho Europeo* 475.

Mariscal Berástegui, N, *Teorías políticas de la integración europea* (Tecnos, Madrid, 2003).

Martín Vida, MA, 'La reforma del artículo 12a de la Ley Fundamental de Bonn a raíz de la Sentencia "Kreil" del Tribunal de Justicia' (2004) 1 *Revista de Derecho Constitucional Europeo* 357.

Martín y Pérez de Nanclares, J, 'La declaración 1/2004 del Tribunal Constitucional: un giro jurisprudencial en la concepción del artículo 93 de la Constitución española' (2005) 6 *Revista General de Derecho Europeo*.

Masson, B, 'L'harmonisation des conditions du regroupement familial : la Cour fait la leçon sur le titre IV CE (CJCE, 27 juin 2006, Parlement européen c/Conseil de l'Union européenne)' (2006) 42(4) *Revue Trimestrielle de Droit Européen* 673.

Mathieu, B, 'Constitution européenne et constitutions nationales : l'habile convergence des juges constitutionnels français et espagnol. À propos des décisions n° 2004-505 DC du Conseil constitutionnel français et 1/2004 DTC du Tribunal constitutionnel espagnol' 18 *Cahiers du Conseil Constitutionnel* 141.

Matía Portilla, FJ, 'La eficacia de la Carta de Niza' in Matía Portilla, FJ (ed), *La protección de los Derechos fundamentales en la Unión Europea* (Civitas, Madrid, 2002).

—— *et al* (ed), *La protección de los derechos fundamentales en la Unión Europea* (Civitas, Madrid, 2002).

Maubernard, C, 'Le "droit fondamental à la dignité humaine" en droit communautaire : la brevetabilité du vivant à l'épreuve de la jurisprudence de la Cour dejustice des Communautés européennes' (2003) 14(54) *Revue Trimestrielle des Droits de l'Homme* 483.

Mccormick, J, *The European Superpower* (Palgrave Macmillan, New York, 2006).

McGuinness, ME, 'Medellín v Texas – US Supreme Court opinion on state courts' obligation to respect an International Court of Justice judgment and on the president's power to enforce it' (2008) 102(3) *American Journal of International Law* 622.

McKendrick, E, Kronke, H and Goode, R, *Transnational Commercial Law: Text, Cases, and Materials* (Oxford University Press, Oxford, 2007).

Mclaughlin, AC, *A Constitutional History of the United States* (Appleton-Century-Crofts, New York, 1935).

Mehdi, R, 'French supreme courts and European Union law: Between historical compromise and accepted loyalty' (2011) 48(2) *Common Market Law Review* 439.

Meijers, EM, 'L'histoire des principes fondamentaux du droit international privé à partir du Moyen Age, spécialement dans l'Europe occidentale' (1970) 49(1934-III) *Recueil des cours de l'Académie de Droit International de la Haye* 543.

Mendelson, MM, 'The European Court of Justice and human rights' (1981) 1 *Yearbook of European Law* 125.

Mendez, M, 'Passenger Name Record Agreement – European Court of Justice' (2007) 3(1) *European Constitutional Law Review* 127.

Menéndez, AJ, 'Between Laeken and the Deep Blue Sea – An Assessment of the Draft Constitutional Treaty from a Deliberative-Democratic Standpoint' (2005) 11(1) *European Public Law* 105.

Meron, T, *The Humanization of International Law* (Brill Academic Publishers, Leiden, 2006).

Merrils, JG, *The development of International Law by the European Court of Human Rights* (Manchester University Press, Manchester, 1988).

Merry, SE, 'Legal Pluralism' (1988) 22(5) *Law & Society Review* 869.

Michael, L, 'El Estado federal experimental' (2006) 6 *Revista de Derecho Constitucional Europeo* 11.

Milanovic, M and Papic, T, 'As Bad as it Gets: The European Court of Human Rights' Behrami and Saramati Decision and General International Law' (2008) 58(2) *International and Comparative Law Quarterly* 267.

Miller, E, 'The Use of Targeted Sanctions in the Fight against International Terrorism: What about Human Rights?' (2003) 97 *American Society of International Law Proceedings* 46.

Mirkine-Guetzévitch, B, *Derecho constitucional internacional* (Legaz y Lecambra, L (tr)) (Revista de Derecho Privado, Madrid, 1936).

——, 'Droit international et droit constitutionnel' (1931) 38(1931-IV) *Recueil des Cours de l'Académie de Droit International de La Haye* 307.

Mischo, J, 'Hoechst, Colas, Roquette: illustration d'une convergence' in Colneric, N, Puissochet, JP and Ruiz-Jarabo y Colomer, DV (eds), *Une communauté de droit: Festschrift für Gil Carlos Rodríguez Iglesias* (Berliner Wissenshafts, Berlin, 2003).

Monaco, R, *Lezioni di organizzazione internazionale i diritto delle istituzioni internazionali* (Giappichelli, Torino, 1965).

Morgenstern, F, *Legal Problems of International Organizations* (Cambridge University Press, Cambridge, 1986).

Müller, JP and Kolb, R, 'Article 2.2' in Simma, B (ed), *The Charter of the United Nations: A Commentary* 2nd edn (Oxford University Press, Oxford, 2002).

Myjer, E, 'Can The EU join the ECHR – General conditions and practical arrangements' in Pernice, I, Kokott, J and Saunders, C (eds), *The Future of the European Judicial System in a Comparative Perspective* (Nomos, Baden-Baden, 2006).

Navas Castillo, F, 'Veinticinco años de actos de Gobierno' (2003–2004) 58–59 *Revista de Derecho Político* 621.

Nettesheim, M, 'UN sanctions against individuals – A challenge to the architecture of European Union governance' (2007) 44(3) *Common Market Law Review* 567.

Nußberger, A, 'Poland: The Constitutional Tribunal on the implementation of the European Arrest Warrant' (2008) 6(1) *International Journal of Constitutional Law* 162.

Nye, J, *Soft Power: The Means to Success in World Politics* (Public Affairs, New York, 2008).

O'Leary, S, 'Accession by the European Community to the European Convention on Human Rights – The Opinion of the ECJ' (1996) 4 *European Human Rights Law Review* 362.

O'Neill, A and Coppel, J, 'The European Court of Justice: taking rights seriously?' (1992) 29(4) *Common Market Law Review* 669.

Odvar, E and Fossum, JE, 'Europe in Search of Legitimacy: Strategies of Legitimation Assessed' (2004) 25 *International Political Science Review* 435.

Öhlinger, T, 'Die Ratifikation des Verfassungsvertrages in Österreich – Anmerkungen zum konstitutionellen Gehalt des Verfassungsvertrages' in Hummer, W and Obwexer, W (eds), *Der Vertrag über eine Verfassung für Europa* (Nomos, Baden-Baden, 2007).

Oliver, P, 'Case C-46/93 and C-48/93, Brasserie du Pêcheur v Germany, and The Queen v Secretary of State for Transport ex parte Factortame *et al*' (1997) 34(3) *Common Market Law Review* 635.

Oraá Oraá, J, *Human Rights in States of Emergency in International Law* (Clarendon, Oxford, 1992).

Orakhekashvili, A, 'R (on the application of Al-Jedda) (FC) v Secretary of State for Defence – UK House of Lords judgment on relationship between UN Security Council resolution authorizing detention in Iraq and European Convention on Human Rights' (2008) 102(2) *American Journal of International Law* 337.

——, *Peremptory Norms in International Law* (Oxford University Press, Oxford, 2006).

Ortúzar Andechaga, L, 'Efecto directo de las directivas respecto de la Administracion. (Sentencia de 22 de junio de 1989, asunto 103/88, Constanzo)' (1990) 13 *Revista de Estudios e Investigación de las Comunidades Europeas* 29.

Ost, F and Van de Kerchove, M, *De la pyramide au réseau? Pour une théorie dialectique du droit* (Publications des facultés universitaires Saint-Louis, Bruxelles, 2002).

Österdahl, I, *Threat to the Peace: The Interpretation by the Security Council of Article 39 of the UN Charter* (Iustus, Uppsala, 1998).

Pagone, GT, 'Legal Professional Privilege in the European Communities: The AM & S Case and Australian Law' (1984) 33(3) *International & Comparative Law Quarterly* 663.

Pape, RA, 'Why Economic Sanctions Still Do Not Work' (1998) 23(1) *International Security* 66.

——, 'Why Economic Sanctions Do Not Work' (1997) 22(2) *International Security* 90.

Pastor Ridruejo, JA, *Curso de Derecho internacional Público y Organizaciones internacionales* 13th edn (Tecnos, Madrid, 2010).

Peers, S, 'The European Community's criminal law competence: The plot thickens' (2008) 33(3) *Common Market Law Review* 399.

——, 'Salvation outside the Church: Judicial protection in the third Pillar after the Pupino and Segi judgments' (2007) 44(4) *Common Market Law Review* 883.

——, 'Bosphorus – European Court of Human Rights. Limited responsibility of European Union member states for actions within the scope of Community law. Judgment of 30 June 2005, Bosphorus Airways v Ireland, Application No 45036/98' (2006) 2(3) *European Constitutional Law Review* 443.

——, 'Case C-268/94, Portugal v Council' (1998) 35(2) *Common Market Law Review* 539.

——, 'Who's Judging the Watchmen? The Judicial System of the "Area of Freedom, Security, and Justice"' (1998) 18 *Yearbook of European Law* 337.

—— and Ward, A (eds), *The European Union Charter of Fundamental Rights. Politics, Law and Policy* (Hart, Oxford, 2004).

Pellet, A, 'Les fondements juridiques internationaux du droit communautaire' (1997) V(2) *Collected Courses of the Academy of European Law* 193.

Perdikis, N and Read, R (eds), *The WTO and the Regulation of International Trade. Recent Trade Disputes between the European Union and the United States* (Edward Elgar, Northampton, 2005).

Pérez Serrano, N, 'La noble obra política de un gran Juez (Juan Marshall)' (Real Academia de Ciencias Morales y Políticas, Madrid, 1955).

Pérez Tremps, P, 'La jurisdicción constitucional y la integración europea' (2009) 29 *Revista Española de Derecho Europeo* 19.

——, *Constitución Española y Comunidad Europea* (Civitas, Madrid, 1994).

——, 'Justicia comunitaria, justicia constitucional y tribunales ordinarios frente al Derecho Comunitario (Comentario a la Sentencia de la Corte Constitucional italiana número 170/1984, de 8 de junio)' (1985) 13 *Revista Española de Derecho Constitucional* 157.

Pérez Tremps, P, and Sáiz Arnaiz, A, 'Spain's Ratification of the Treaty Establishing a Constitution for Europe: Prior Constitutional Review, Referendum and Parliamentary Approval' in Albi, A and Ziller, J (eds), *The European Constitution and national constitutions: ratification and beyond* (Kluwer, Alphen aan den Rijn, 2007).

Pérez Vera, E, 'Citoyenneté de l'Union européenne, nationalité et condition des étrangers' (1996) 261 *Recueil des Cours de l'Académie de Droit International de La Haye* 243.

——, 'Reflexiones sobre los procesos de integración regional' (1977) 4(3) *Revista de Instituciones Europeas* 669.

Pernice, I, 'Les bananes et les droits fondamentaux: la Cour constitutionnelle allemande fait le point' (2001) 37(3–4) *Cahiers de Droit Européen* 427.

Pescatore, P, 'La coopération entre la Cour communautaire, les juridictions nationales et la Cour européenne des droits de l'Homme dans la protection des droits fondamentaux – Enquête sur un problème virtuel' (2003) 466 *Revue du Marché Commun et de l'Union Européenne* 151.

——, 'La Cour de Justice des Communautés Européenes et la Convention Européenne des Droits de l'Homme' in Wiarda, GJ, Matscher, F and Petzold, H (eds), *Protecting human rights, the European dimension: studies in honour of / Protection des droits de l'homme, la dimension européenne. Mélanges en l'honneur de Gérard J Wiarda* 2nd edn (C Heymann, Köln, 1990).

——, 'The context and significance of fundamental rights in the law of the European Communities' (1981) 2(3–4) *Human Rights Law Journal* 295.

——, 'External relations in the case law of the Court of Justice of the European Communities' (1979) 16(4) *Common Market Law Review* 615.

Peters, A, 'Compensatory Constitutionalism: The Function and Potential of Fundamental International Norms and Structures' (2006) 19(3) *Leiden Journal of International Law* 579.

——, 'European democracy after the 2003 Convention' (2004) 41(1) *Common Market Law Review* 37.

Petersmann, EU, 'State Sovereignty, Popular Sovereignty and Individual Sovereignty: From Constitutional Nationalism to Multilevel Constitutionalism in International Economic Law?' in Shan, W, Simons, P and Singh, D (eds), *Redefining Sovereignty in International Economic Law. Studies in International Trade Law* (Hart, Oxford, 2008).

——, 'Why Rational Choice Theory Requires a Multilevel Constitutional Approach to International Economic Law – A reponse to The Case for Reforming the WTO's Enforcement Mechanism' (2008) 2008(1) *University of Illinois Law Review* 359.

——, 'Constitutionalism and the Regulation of International Markets: How to Define the "Development Objectives" of the World Trading System?' (2007) 23 *European University Institute Law Working Papers*.

——, 'Justice in International Economic Law? From the "International Law among States" to "International Integration Law" and "International Constitutional Law"' (2007) 2006(I) *The Global Community Yearbook of International Law and Jurisprudence* 105.

Petit, Y, 'Médicament, droit français, droit communautaire et Convention européenne des droits de l'homme' (1997) mars 1997 *Europe* 5.

Pettiti, LE, 'Les principes généraux de droit pénal dans la Convention européenne des droits de l'homme' (1987) 1987(1) *Revue de Science Criminelle et de Droit Pénal Comparé* 167.

Phelan, DR, Revolt or Revolution: The Constiutional Boundaries of the European Community (Sweet & Maxwell, Dublin, 1997).
——, 'Right to Life of The Unborn v Promotion of Trade in Services: The European Court of Justice and the Normative Shaping of the European Union' (1992) 55(5) *Modern Law Review* 670.
Picchio Forlati, L and Sicilianos, LA, *Economic Sanctions in International Law/Les sanctions économiques en droit International* (Martinus Nijhoff Publishers, Leiden, 2004).
Picod, F, 'Le contrôle de constitutionnalité des actes de droit dérivé de l'Union européenne' (2005) 18 *Les Cahiers du Conseil Constitutionnel* 144.
Piero Sereni, A, *Diritto internazionale* (Giuffrè, Milano, 1960).
Pipkorn, J, 'La Communauté Européenne et la Convention Européenne des Droits de l'Homme' (1993) 14 *Revue Trimestrielle des Droits de l'Homme* 221.
Plaza, C, 'The Constitution for Europe and the Spanish Constitutional Court' (2006) 12(3) *European Public Law* 253.
Pliakos, A, 'Le contrôle de constitutionnalité et le droit de l'Union européenne: la réaffirmation du principe de primauté' (2010) 46(3–5) *Cahiers de Droit Européen* 487.
Poiares Maduro, M, 'Contrapunctual Law: Europe's Constitutional Pluralism in Action' in Walker, N (ed), *Sovereignty in transition* (Oxford, Hart, 2003 (reprinted 2006)).
Potteau, A, 'L'article 3 du premier protocole additionnel à la Convention et l'obligation des États membres de l'Union européenne de reconnaître le droit de participer aux élections du Parlement européen' (1999) 40 *Revue Trimestrielle des Droits de l'Homme* 865.
Queralt Jiménez, A, *La interpretacion de los derechos: del Tribunal de Estrasburgo al Tribunal Constitucional* (CEPC, Madrid, 2008).
——, 'Los usos del canon europeo en la jurisprudencia del Tribunal Constitucional: una muestra del proceso de armonización europea en materia de derechos fundamentales' (2007) 20 *Teoria y Realidad Constitucional* 435.
——, *El Tribunal de Estrasburgo: una jurisdicción internacional para la protección de los derechos fundamentales* (Tirant, Valencia, 2003).
Radicati di Brozolo, LG and Megliani, M, 'Freezing the Assets of International Terrorist Organisations' in Bianchi, A (ed), *Enforcing International Law Norms Against Terrorism* (Hart, Oxford, 2004).
Randelzhofer, A, 'Article 2' in Simma, B (ed), *The Charter of the United Nations: A Commentary* 2nd edn (Oxford University Press, Oxford, 2002).
Ratner, SR, 'Foreign Occupation and International Territorial Administration: The Challenges of Convergence' (2005) 16(4) *European Journal of International Law* 695.
Reich, J, 'Due Process and Sanctions Targeted Against Individuals Pursuant to Resolution 1267 (1999)' (2008) 33(2) *Yale Journal of International Law* 505.
Reinisch, A, 'Developing Human Rights and Humanitarian Law Accountability of the Security Council for the Imposition of Economic Sanctions' (2001) 95(4) *American Journal of International Law* 851.
——, *International Organizations Before National Courts* (Cambridge University Press, Cambridge, 2000).
Rey Aneiros, A, 'Tribunal Europeo de Derechos Humanos – TEDH – Resolución de admisibilidad de 02.05.2007, Behrami y Behrami c. Francia, 71412/01, y Saramati c. Francia, Alemania y Noruega, 78166/01 – Seguridad colectiva y derechos humanos – Responsabilidad por violaciones de derechos humanos por fuerzas de mantenimiento de la paz' (2008) 30 *Revista de Derecho Comunitario Europeo* 511.

Rideau, J, *De la Communauté de droit à l'Union de droit: continuités et avatars européens* (LGDJ, Paris, 2000).
Riesenfeld, SA and Buxbaum, RM, 'NV Algemene Transport- En Expeditie Onderneming van Gend & Loos c. Administration Fiscale Neerlandaise: A Pioneering Decision of the Court of Justice of the European Communities' (1964) 58(1) *American Journal of International Law* 152.
Rigaux, A and Simon, D, 'Entraves résultant d'actes de particuliers' (2003) Août–Septembre *Europe* 15.
Rigaux, F, 'L'article 192 du Traité CEE devant la Commission européenne des droits de l'homme' (1991) 7 *Revue Trimestrielle des Droits de l'Homme* 395.
Rivier, R and Lagrange, P, 'Travaux de la Commission du droit international et de la sixième commission' (2005) 51 *Annuaire français de droit international* 340.
Rodríguez Iglesias, GC, 'The Protection of Fundamental Rights in the Case Law of the Court of Justice of the European Communities' (1995) 1(2) *Columbia Journal of European Law* 169.
—— and Wölker, U, 'Derecho Comunitario, derechos fundamentales y control de constitucionalidad: la decisión del Tribunal Constitucional Federal Alemán de 22 de octubre de 1986' (1987) 14(3) *Revista de Instituciones Europeas* 667.
Rodríguez-Izquierdo Serrano, M, *Primacia y subsidariedad en la Unión Europea* (CEPC, Madrid, 2011).
Rodríguez, A, '¿Quién debe ser el defensor de la Constitución española? comentario a la DTC 1/2004, de 13 de diciembre' (2005) 5 *Revista de Derecho Constitucional Europeo* 327.
Rofes i Pujol, MI, 'Crónica de la Jurisprudencia del Tribunal de Justicia de las Comunidades Europeas' (1996) 15 *Cuadernos Europeos de Deusto* 148.
Ronkes Agerbeek, F, 'Freedom of expression in the Brenner corridor: the Schmidberger case' (2004) 29(2) *European Law Review* 255.
Rosand, E, 'The Security Council's Efforts to Monitor the Implementation of AlQaida/Taliban Sanctions' (2004) 98(4) *American Journal of International Law* 745.
Rossi, LS, 'Corte costituzionale (Italian Constitutional Court): Decisions 348 and 349/2007 of 22 October 2007, and 102 and 103/2008, of 12 February 2008' (2009) 46(1) *Common Market Law Review* 319.
Rousseau, D, *La question prioritaire de constitutionnalité* (Lextenso éditions, Paris, 2010).
Roux, J, 'Le Conseil constitutionnel, le droit communautaire derive et la Constitution' (2004) 4 *Revue du droit public et de la science politique en France et à l'étranger* 912.
Rubenfeld, J, 'Unilateralism and Constitutionalism' (2004) 79(6) *New York University Law Review* 1971.
Rubio de Casas, MG, 'Potestad sancionatoria de la Administración y garantías del administrado: comentario a la Sentencia del Tribunal Europeo de Derechos Humanos de 21-11-1984: el caso OZTURK' (1984) 104 *Revista de Administración Pública* 375.
Rüfner, W, 'Basic Elements of German Law on State Liability' in Bell, J and Bradley, AW (eds), *Governmental Liability: A Comparative Study* (British Institute for International & Comparative Law, London, 1992).
——, 'Drittwirkung der Grundrechte – Versuch einer Bilanz' in Selmer, P and Von Münch, I (eds), *Gedächtnisschrift für Wolfgang Martens* (De Gruyter, Berlin, 1987).
Ruggeri, A, 'Trattato costituzionale, europeizzazione dei "controlimiti" e tecniche di risoluzione delle antinomie tra diritto comunitario e diritto interno (profili problem-

atici)' in Staiano, S (ed), *Giurisprudenza costituzionale e principi fondamentali: alla ricerca del nucleo duro delle costituzioni: atti del convegno annuale del Gruppo di Pisa, Capri, 3–4 giugno 2005* (G Giappichelli, Torino, 2006).

——, '"Tradizioni costituzionali comuni" e "controlimiti", tra teoria delle fonti e teoria dell'interpretazione' (2003) 2003(1) *Diritto Pubblico Comparato ed Europeo* 102.

Ruiz-Jarabo, P, 'Por una interpretación pacífica de Matthews contra Reino Unido. Colonialismo y derechos fundamentales en Gibraltar' (2002) 18 *Anuario de Derecho Internacional* 229.

Safrin, S, 'The unexceptionalism of US exceptionalism' (2008) 41(5) *Vanderbilt Journal of Transnational Law* 1307.

Sáiz Arnáiz, A, 'De primacía, supremacía y derechos fundamentales en la Europea integrada: la Declaración del Tribunal Constitucional de 13 de diciembre de 2004 y el Tratado por el que se establece una Constitución para Europa' in López Castillo, A, Sáiz Arnáiz, A and Ferreres Comella, V (eds), *Constitución Española y Constitución Europea. Análisis de la Declaración del Tribunal Constitucional (DTC 1/2004, de 13 de diciembre)* (CEPC, Madrid, 2005).

——, *La apertura constitucional al Derecho internacional y europeo de los derechos humanos. El artículo 10.2 de la Constitución española* (CGPJ, Madrid, 1999).

——, 'El Derecho Comunitario, ¿parámetro de la constitucionalidad de las leyes internas? (a propósito de la sentencia nº 384 de 1994, de la Corte Costituzionale italiana)' (1995) 22(2) *Revista de Instituciones Europeas* 571.

——, 'Los actos políticos del Gobierno en la jurisprudencia del Tribunal Supremo' (1994) 134 *Revista de administración pública* 225.

Sales, E, 'La transposition des directives communautaires : une exigence de valeur constitutionnelle sous réserve de constitutionnalité' (2005) 41(3) *Revue Trimestrielle de Droit Européen* 597.

Sands, P, '"Unilateralism", values, and International Law' (2000) 11(2) *European Journal of International Law* 291.

Sanfrutos Cano, E, 'Unión Europea: Comentario a la STJCE de 3 de septiembre de 2008 en los asuntos acumulados C-402/2005 P y C-415/2005 P, Yassin Abdullah Kadi y Al Barakaat International Foundation c. Consejo y Comisión' (2009) 7 *Gaceta jurídica de la Unión Europea y de la competencia* 69.

Santos Vara, J, 'El control judicial de la ejecución de las sanciones antiterroristas del Consejo de Seguridad en la Unión Europea' (2008) 15 *Revista Electrónica de Estudios Internacionales*.

Sari, A, 'Jurisdiction and International Responsibility in Peace Support Operations: The Behrami and Saramati Cases' (2008) 8(1) *Human Rights Law Review* 151.

Sarmiento, D, 'L'arrêt Melki : esquisse d'un dialogue des juges constitutionnels et européens sur toile de fond française' (2010) 46(3) *Revue Trimestrielle de Droit Européen* 588.

——, 'Un paso más en la constitucionalización del Tercer Pilar de la Unión Europea. La Sentencia María Pupino y el efecto directo de las Decisiones marco' (2005) 10 *Revista Electrónica de Estudios Internacionales* 1.

Sarooshi, D, *International Organizations and Their Exercise of Sovereign Powers* (Oxford University Press, Oxford, 2007).

Sarooshi, D, *The United Nations and the Development of Collective Security: The Delegation by the UN Security Council of Its Chapter VII Powers* (Oxford University Press, Oxford, 2000).

Scelle, G, 'Théorie et pratique de la fonction exécutive en droit international' (1937) 55((1936-I)) *Recueil des cours de l'Académie de Droit International de la Haye* 87.

——, 'Règles générales du droit de la paix' (1934) 46((1933-IV)) *Recueil des cours de l'Académie de Droit International de La Haye* 327.

Scheeck, L, *Les cours européennes et l'integration par les droits de l'homme* (Instituto de Estudios Políticos, 2006).

Scheppele, KL, 'The International State of Emergency: Challenges to Constitutionalism after September 11' (2009) Paper 49 *Digital Commons UM Law* April 2009.

——, 'The Migration of Anti-Constitutional Ideas: The Post-9/11 Globalization of Public Law and the International State of Emergency' in Choudhry, S (ed), *The Migration of Constitutional Ideas* (Oxford University Press, Oxford, 2006).

Schermers, HG, 'Matthews v United Kingdom, Judgment of 18 February 1999' (1999) 36(3) *Common Market Law Review* 673.

——, 'Les organisations internationales' in Bedjaoui, M (ed), *Droit international. Bilan et perspectives* (Pedone, Paris, 1991).

——, 'The European Communities Bound by Fundamental Human Rights' (1990) 27(2) *Common Market Law Review* 249.

—— and Blokker, NM, *International Institutional Law: Unity Within Diversity* 4th edn (Martinus Nijhoff, The Hague, 2004).

—— and Waelbroeck, D, *Judicial Protection in the European Union* 6th edn (Kluwer, The Hague, 2001).

Scheuner, U, 'Fundamental Rights in European Community Law and in National Constitutional Law' (1975) 12 *Common Market Law Review* 171.

Schilling, T, 'The Autonomy of the Community Legal Order: An Analysis of Possible Foundations' (1996) 37(2) *Harvard International Law Journal* 389.

Schmahl, S, 'Effektiver Rechtsschutz gegen "targeted sanctions" des UN-Sicherheitsrats?' (2006) 41(4) *Europarecht* 566.

Schorkopf, F, 'The European Court of Human Rights' Judgment in the Case of Bosphorus Hava Yollari Turizm v Ireland' (2005) 6(9) *German Law Journal* 1255.

Schrans, G, 'L'application du droit communautaire des ententes économiques par la Cour de justice des Communautés européennes (affaire Grundig-Consten)' (1967) 20 *Revue Critique de Jurisprudence Belge* 180.

Schrijver, NJ, 'Interpreting the Principles and Purposes of the United Nations' in Van Krieken, PJ (ed), *Refugee Law in Context. The Exclusion Clause* (TMC Asser Institute, The Hague, 1999).

Schroeder, W and Selmayr, M, 'Die EG, das GATT und die Vollzugslehre' (1998) 7 *Juristenzeitung* 344.

Schutze, R, 'On 'Middle Ground'. The European Community and Public International Law' (2007) 13 *European University Institute Law Working Papers*.

Schwarze, J, 'The Administrative Law of the Community and the Protection of Human Rights' (1986) 23(2) *Common Market Law Review* 401.

Scott, C, '"Transnational Law" as proto-concept: Three conceptions' (2009) 10(6-7) *German Law Journal* 859.

Shaw, J, 'The Political Representation of Europe's Citizens: Developments' (2008) 4(1) *European Constitutional Law Review* 162.

——, 'Recent Developments in the Field of Competition Procedure' (1990) 15(4) *European Law Review* 326.

——, 'The AKZO Saga Continues' (1987) 12(4) *European Law Review* 199.

Sicilianos, LA, 'L'autorisation par le conseil de sécurité de recourir à la force: Une tentative d'évaluation' (2002) 106(1) *Revue générale de droit international public* 5.

Simma, B, 'From bilateralism to community interest in International Law' (1994) 250(VI) *Recueil des Cours de l'Académie de Droit International de La Haye* 217.

Simon, D, *Le système juridique communautaire* 3rd edn (PUF, Paris, 2001).

——, 'Les fondements de l'autonomie du droit communautaire' in VV AA (ed), *Droit international et droit communautaire: perspectives actuelles* (Pedone, Paris, 2000).

——, *Le système juridique communautaire* 2nd edn (PUF, Paris, 1998).

——, 'Kremzow contre l'Autriche' (1997) Juillet *Europe* 10.

——, *Le système juridique communautaire* (PUF, Paris, 1997).

——, 'Chronique, n° 335' (1996) Juin *Europe* 1.

—— and Rigaux, A, 'La priorité de la question prioritaire de constitutionnalité : harmonie(s) et dissonances(s) des monologues juridictionnels croisés' (2010) 29 *Cahiers du Conseil Constitutionnel* 63.

—— and Rigaux, A, 'L'avis de la Cour de justice sur le projet d'accord CEE/AELE portant création de l'Espace économique européen (EEE)' (1992) Février *Europe* 1.

—— and Mariatte, F, 'Le Tribunal de première instance des Communautés: Professeur de droit international?' (2005) Décembre *Europe* 6.

Simpson, G, 'The situation on the international legal theory front: the power of rules and the rule of power' (2000) 11(2) *European Journal of International Law* 439.

Singer, M, 'Jurisdictional Immunity of International Organizations: Human Rights and Functional Necessity Concerns' (1995) 36(1) *Virginia Journal of International Law* 53.

Slaughter, AM, *A New World Order* (Princeton University Press, Princeton 2004).

——, 'Globalization, Accountability, and the Future of Administrative Law: The Accountability of Government Networks' (2001) 8(2) *Indiana Journal of Global Legal Studies* 347.

——, Stone Sweet, A and Weiler, JHH, *The European Courts & National Courts. Doctrine and Jurisprudence. Legal change in its social context* (Hart, Oxford, 1998).

Slot, PJ, 'Case C-202/88, France v Commission (Telecom); Case C-41/90, Hofner and Elser v Macroton GmbH; Case C-260/89, Elliniki Radiophonia Tileorassi (ERT) v Dimotiki' (1991) 28(4) *Common Market Law Review* 964.

Snell, J, '"European constitutional settlement", an ever-closer union, and the Treaty of Lisbon: democracy or relevance?' (2008) 33(5) *European Law Review* 619.

Söderman, J, 'The European Ombudsman. Annual Report 2011' Office for Official Publications (Luxembourg).

Sousa Santos, M, *Toward a New Legal Common Sense* 2nd edn (Cambridge University Press, Cambridge, 2003).

Spielmann, D, 'Un autre regard : la Cour de Strasbourg et le droit de la Communauté européenne' in Cohen-Jonathan, G (ed), *Libertés, justice, tolérance. Mélanges en hommage au Doyen Gérard Cohen-Jonathan* (Bruylant, Bruxelles, 2004).

Spiro, PJ, 'The New Sovereigntists: American Exceptionalism and Its False Prophets' (2000) 79(6) *Foreign Affairs* 9.

Spranger, TM, 'Case C-377/98, Kingdom of the Netherlands v European Parliament and Council of the European Union, Judgment of the Full Court of 9 October 2001, [2001] ECR I-7079' (2002) 39(5) *Common Market Law Review* 1147.

Stahn, C, *The Law and Practice of International Territorial Administration Versailles to Iraq and Beyond* (Cambridge University Press, Cambridge, 2008).

Starace, V, 'Modifications Provided by Protocol No 14 concerning Proceedings before the European Court of Human Rights' in del Vecchio, A (ed), *New international tribunals and new international proceedings* (Giuffrè Editore, Roma, 2006).

Starck, C, 'Derechos fundamentales y Derecho Privado' (2002) 66 *Revista Española de Derecho Constitucional* 65.

Starke, JG, 'Monism and Dualism in the Theory of International Law' (1936) XVII *British Yearbook of International Law* 66.

Stephan, PB, 'Accountability and International Lawmaking: Rules, Rents and Legitimacy' (1997) 17(2) *Northwestern Journal of International Law and Business* 681.

Stoll, PT and Schorkop, F, *WTO. World Economic Order, World Trade Law* (Max Planck Institute for International and Comparative Law, Martinus Nijhoff, The Hague, 2006).

Stone Sweet, A, 'Constitutional Dialogues in the European Community' in Slaughter, AM, Stone Sweet, A and Weiler, JHH (eds), *The European Courts & National Courts. Doctrine and Jurisprudence. Legal change in its social context* (Hart, Oxford, 1998).

Stone, GR *et al*, *Constitutional Law* 5th edn (Aspen, New York, 2005).

Su, H, 'Can Constitution-Building Advance European Integration? A Three-Pillared Institutionalist Analysis' (2004) 26(4) *Journal of European Integration* 353.

Sudre, F, 'Article I-9' in Burgorgue-Larsen, L, Levade, A and Picod, F (eds), *Traité établissant une Constitution pour l'Europe: commentaire article par article* (Bruylant, Bruxelles, 2007).

——, 'Extradition et peine de mort : arrêt Soering de la Cour européenne des droits de l'homme, du 7 juillet 1989' (1990) 94(1) *Revue General de Droit International Public* 103.

Tamanaha, BZ, 'Understanding Legal Pluralism: Past to Present, Local to Global' (2008) 30 *Sydney Law Review* 375.

Taylor, SM, 'Article 90 and Telecommunications Monopolies' (1994) 15(6) *European Competition Law Review* 322.

Teubner, G and Fischer-Lescano, A, 'Regime-Collisions : the Vain Search for Legal Unity in the Fragmentation of Global Law' (2004) 25(4) *Michigan Journal of International Law* 999.

Thallinger, G, 'Sense and sensibility of the human rights obligations of the United Nations Security Council' (2007) 67(4) *Zeitschrift für ausländisches öffentliches Recht und Völkerrecht* 1015.

Timmermans, C, 'The EU and Public International Law' (1999) 4 *European Foreign Affairs Review* 181.

Tizzano, A, 'La protection des droits fondamentaux en Europe : la Cour de justice et les juridictions constitutionnelles nationales' (2006) 2006(1) *Revue du Droit de l'Union Européenne* 9.

Tobler, C and Waaldijk, K, 'Case C-267/06, Tadao Maruko v Versorgungsanstalt der deutschen Bühnen, Judgment of the Grand Chamber of the Court of Justice of 1 April 2008' (2009) 46(2) *Common Market Law Review* 723.

Tomuschat, C, 'The Ruling of the German Constitutional Court on the Treaty of Lisbon' (2009) 10(8) *German Law Journal* 1259.

——, 'Case T-306/01, Ahmed Ali Yusuf and Al Barakaat International Foundation v Council and Commission, judgment of the Court of First Instance of 21 September 2005; Case T-315/01, Yassin Abdullah Kadi v Council and Commission, judgment of the Court of First Instance of 21 September 2005' (2006) 43(2) *Common Market Law Review* 537.

——, 'Artikel 281' in Von der Groeben, H and Schwarze, J (eds), *Vertrag über die Europäische Union und Vertrag zur Gründung der Europäischen Gemeinschaft. Kommentar* 6th edn (Nomos, Baden-Baden, 2004).

——, 'The International Responsibility of the European Union' in Cannizzaro, E (ed), *The European Union as an Actor in International Relations* (Kluwer, The Hague, 2002).

——, 'International Law: ensuring the survival of mankind on the eve of a new century. General Course on Public International Law' (1999) 281 *Recueil des cours de l'Académie de Droit International de La Haye* 9.

——, 'International Law as the Constitution of Mankind' in United Nations (ed), *International Law on the Eve of the Twenty-first Century. Views from the International Law Commission / Le droit international à l'aube du XXIe siècle: réflexions de codificateurs* (United Nations, New York, 1997).

——, 'Obligations arising for states without or against their will' (1993) 241(IV) *Recueil des Cours de l'Académie de Droit International de La Haye* 195.

——, 'La libre circulation et le statut politique des ressortissants communautaires. Cour de justice des Communautés européennes, 28.10.1975, affaire 36/75 (Rutili)' (1976) 12 *Cahiers de Droit Européen* 58.

Toner, H, 'Impact assessments and fundamental rights protection in EU law' (2006) 31(3) *European Law Review* 316.

Trebilcock, MJ and Howse, R, *The Regulation of International Trade* 2nd edn (Routledge, London, 1999).

Triantafyllou, D, 'The European Charter of fundamental rights and the "rule of law": restricting fundamental rights by reference' (2002) 39(1) *Common Market Law Review* 53.

Tridimas, T, 'Terrorism and the ECJ: Empowerment and democracy in the EC legal order' (2009) 34(1) *European Law Review* 103.

Tridimas, T, *The General Principles of EU Law* 2nd edn (Oxford University Press, Oxford, 2006).

—— and Gutiérrez Fons, JA, 'EU law, International law, and economic sanctions against terrorism: the judiciary in distress?' (2009) 32(2) *Fordham International Law Journal* 660.

Triepel, H, 'Les rapports entre le Droit interne et le Droit international' (1925) 1(1923) *Recueil des Cours de l'Académie de Droit International de La Haye* 73.

——, *Völkerrecht und Landesrecht* (JCB Mohr (Paul Siebeck), Tübingen, 1907).

Tulkens, F, 'L'Union européenne devant la Cour européenne des droits de l'homme' (2000) 12(1–2) *Revue Universelle des Droits de l'Homme* 50.

Turley, J, 'Dualistic Values in the Age of International Legisprudence' (1993) 44 *Hastings Law Journal* 185.

Tzanou, M, 'Case-note on Joined Cases C-402/05 P & C-415/05 P Yassin Abdullah Kadi & Al Barakaat International Foundation v Council of European Union & Commission of European Communities' (2009) 10(2) *German Law Journal* 123.

Uerpmann-Wittzack, R, 'The Constitutional Role of Multilateral Treaty Systems' in Von Bogdandy, A and Bast, J (eds), *Principles of European Constitutional Law* (Hart, Oxford, 2006).

Ugartemendia Eceizabarrena, JI, 'El "recurso" a la prejudicial (234 TCE) como "cuestión" de amparo. A propósito de la' (2004) 11 *Revista Española de Derecho Europeo* 441.

Urrea Corres, M, *La cooperación reforzada en la Unión Europea: concepto, naturaleza y régimen jurídico* (Colex, Madrid, 2002).

Usher, JA, 'Direct and individual concern – an effective remedy or a conventional solution?' (2003) 28(5) *European Law Review* 575.
——, 'Article 173 EEC: Breach of a General Principle as a Ground for Annulment' (1978) 3 *European Law Review* 383.
——, 'The influence of national concepts on decisions of the European Court – a Case Study: The Transocean Case' (1976) 1 *European Law Review* 359.
Van den Herik, L, 'The Security Council's Targeted Sanctions Regimes: In Need of Better Protection of the Individual' (2007) 20 *Leiden Journal of International Law* 797.
Van Gerven, W, 'Harmonization of Private Law: do we need it?' (2004) 41(2) *Common Market Law Review* 505.
Van Ooik, R, 'Cross-Pillar Litigation Before the ECJ: Demarcation of Community and Union Competences' (2008) 4(3) *European Constitutional Law Review* 399.
Van Rijn, T, 'Joined Cases 209 to 215, 218/78, Heinz van Landewijck Sárl a.o. v Commission of the European Communities (FEDETAB)' (1982) 19(3) *Common Market Law Review* 351.
Vandencasteele, A, 'Affaire 100/80, Arrêt de la Cour du 7 juin 1983' (1984) 20(1) *Revue Trimestrielle de Droit Européen* 203.
Varona Navarro, E and González Durantez, H, 'Interim Measures in Competition Cases Before the European Commission and Courts – The recent NDSIMS Health case has raised certain questions in regard' (2002) 23(10) *European Competition Law Review* 512.
Vattel, E, *El derecho de gentes o principios de la ley natural aplicados a la conducta, y a los negocios de las naciones y de los soberanos* (Pascual Hernández, MM (tr)) (Imprenta León Amarita, Madrid, 1834).
Vázquez, CM, 'Treaties As Law of the Land: The Supremacy Clause and the Judicial Enforcement of Treaties' (2008) 122(2) *Harvard Law Review* 599.
Venegas Grau, M, *Derechos fundamentales y derecho privado: los derechos fundamentales en las relaciones entre particulares y el principio de autonomía privada* (Universidad Carlos III, Madrid, 2004).
Verdross, A, 'Le fondement du droit international' (1927) 16(1927) *Recueil des Cours de l'Académie de Droit International de La Haye* 247.
——, *Die Verfassung der Völkerrechtsgemeinschaft* (Springer, Wien–Berlin, 1926).
——, *Die Einheit des rechtlichen Weltbildes auf der Grundlage der Völkerrechtsverfassung* (Mohr, Tübingen, 1923).
Virally, M, 'Sur un pont aux ânes : les rapports entre droit international et droits internes' in Roling, H *et al* (ed), *Mélanges offerts à Henri Rolin. Problèmes de droit des gens* (Pedone, Paris, 1964).
Vitzthum, NG, 'Les compétences législatives et juridictionnelles de la Communauté européenne dans la lutte contre le terrorisme – l'affaire "Kadi"' (2008) 11(3) *Zeitschrift für Europarechtliche Studien* 375.
Vladeck, SI, 'United States Supreme Court: Munaf v Geren – Introductory Note' (2008) 5 *International Legal Materials* 705.
Von Bogdandy, A, 'Pluralism, direct effect, and the ultimate say: On the relationship between international and domestic constitutional law' (2008) 6(3–4) *International Journal of Constitutional Law* 397.
——, 'El constitucionalismo en el derecho internacional: comentario sobre una propuesta alemana' (2007) 5 *Puente@Europa* 34.
——, 'Constitutionalism in International Law: Comment on a Proposal from Germany' (2006) 47(1) *Harvard International Law Journal* 223.

——, 'The European Union as a Human Rights organization? Human Rights and the core of the European Union' (2000) 37(6) *Common Market Law Review* 1307.

Von Puttkamer, E, 'Föderative Elemente im deutschen Staatsrecht seit 1648' in (Musterschmidt, *Göttingen*, 1955).

Wachsmann, P, 'L'avis 2/94 de la Cour de justice relatif à l'adhésion de la Communauté européenne à la Convention de sauvegarde des droits de l'homme et des libertés fondamentales' (1996) 32(3) *Revue Trimestrielle de Droit Européen* 467.

Waelbroeck, D, 'Fundamental rights in the European Union – possible developments in the years to come' in Dashwood, A *et al* (ed), *The Developing role of the European Court of Justice* (European Policy Forum and Frankfurter Institut, London and Frankfurt am Main, 1995).

Waelbroeck, M, 'Effect of GATT within the Legal Order of the EEC' (1974) 6 *Journal of World Trade Law* 614.

Walker, N, 'Beyond boundary disputes and basic grids: Mapping the global disorder of normative orders' (2008) 6(3–4) *International Journal of Constitutional Law* 373.

——, 'Making a World of Difference? Habermas, Cosmopolitanism and the Constitutionalization of International Law' in Payrow Shabani, OA (ed), *Multiculturalism and Law: A Critical Debate* (University of Wales Press, Cardiff, 2007).

Walker, N, 'The Idea of Constitutional Pluralism' (2002) 65(3) *Modern Law Review* 317.

Wallensteen, P and Staibano, C, *International Sanctions: Between Words and Wars in the Global System* (Routledge/Frank Cass, London, 2005).

——, *Making targeted sanctions effective: guidelines for the implementation of UN policy options* (Elanders Gotab, Stockholm, 2003).

Waters, CPM, 'Nationalising Kosovo's Ombudsperson' (2007) 12(1) *Journal of Conflict and Security Law* 139.

Weiler, J and Lockhart, N, '"Taking Rights Seriously" seriously: the European Court and its Fundamental Rights Jurisprudence – Part I' (1995) 32(1) *Common Market Law Review* 51.

——, '"Taking Rights Seriously" seriously: the European Court and its Fundamental Rights Jurisprudence – Part II' (1995) 32(2) *Common Market Law Review* 579.

Weiler, JHH, 'The European Court at a Crossroads: Community Human Rights and Member State Actino' in Capotorti, F *et al* (ed), *Du droit international au droit de l'intégration – Liber amicorum Pierre Pescatore* (Nomos Verlag, Baden-Baden, 1987).

——, 'The Transformation of Europe' (1991) 100(8) *Yale Law Journal* 2403.

——, *The Constitution of Europe. 'Do the New Clothes Have an Emperor?' and Other Essays on European Integration* (Cambridge University Press, Cambridge, 1999).

Wellens, K, 'Fragmentation of International Law and Establishing an Accountability Regime for International Organizations: The Role of the Judiciary in Closing the Gap' (2004) 25(4) *Michigan Journal of International Law* 1159.

——, *Remedies Against International Organizations* (Cambridge University Press, Cambridge, 2002).

Wessels, W, 'A "saut constitutionnel" out of an intergovernmental trap? The Provisions of the Constitutional Treaty for the Common Foreign, Security and Defence Policy' (2004) 5/04 *Jean Monnet Working Papers* May 2009.

Weyembergh, A, de Hert, P and Paepe, P, 'L'effectivité du troisième pilier de l'Union européenne et l'exigence de l'interprétation conforme : la Cour de justice pose ses jalons (note sous l'arrêt Pupino, du 16 juin 2005, de la Cour de justice des Communautés européennes)' (2006) 69 *Revue Trimestrielle des Droits de l'Homme* 269.

White, G, 'Effects of International Treaties within the Community Order' (1976) 1 *European Law Review* 402.

White, ND and Ülgen, O, 'The Security Council and the Decentralized Military Option: Constitutionality and Function' (1997) 44(3) *Netherlands International Law Review* 378.

Wide, R, *International Territorial Administration: How trusteeship and the civilizing mission never went away* (Oxford University Press, Oxford, 2008).

Wilkinson, B, 'Abortion, the Irish Constitution and the EEC' (1992) *Spring Public Law* 20.

Willis, GL, 'Security Council Targeted Sanctions, Due Process and the 1267 Ombudsperson' (2011) 42(3) *Georgetown Journal of International Law* 673.

Willis, PR, '"You have the right to remain silent . . .", or do you? The privilege against self-incrimination following Mannesmannröhren-Werke and others' (2001) 22(8) *European Competition Law Review* 313.

Winkler, M, 'When Legal Systems Collide: Judicial Review of Freezing Measures in the Context of International Terrorism' Paper 40 *Yale Law Student Scholarship Series* May 2009.

Winter, JA, 'Case 48/71, Second Art Treasures Case. Commission of the EC v Italian Republic' (1973) 10(3) *Common Market Law Review* 318 and 327.

Wojcik, ME, 'United States Supreme Court: Medellin v Texas: Introductory Note' (2008) 3 *International Legal Materials* 281.

Wolfrum, R, 'International Administration in Post-Conflict Situations by the United Nations and Other International Actors' (2005) 9(1) *Max Planck Yearbook of United Nations Law* 649.

——, 'Article 1' in Simma, B (ed), *The Charter of the United Nations: A Commentary* 2nd edn (Oxford University Press, Oxford, 2002).

Zagel, G, 'Article 301 TEC on Economic Sanctions' in Smit, H and Herzog, P (eds), *The Law of the European Community. A Commentary on the EC Treaty* (Matthew Bender, New York, 2005).

Ziller, J, *Il nouvo Trattato europeo* (Il Mulino, Bologna, 2007).

Zimmer, W, 'De nouvelles bases pour la coopération entre la Cour Constitutionnelle Fédérale et la Cour de Justice de Luxembourg? (à propos de BverfGE, 7 juin 2000, Solange III)' (2001) Mai *Europe* 3.

Zonnekeyn, G, *Direct Effect of WTO Law* (Cameron & May, London, 2008).

Zuleeg, M, 'Der Schutz der Menschenrechte im Gemeinschaftsrecht' (1992) *Die Öffentliche Verwaltung* 937.

Zumbansen, P, 'Transnational Law' in Smits, J (ed), *Encyclopedia of Comparative Law* (Edward Elgar, Northampton, 2006).

Index